KB212943

eduwill

독자님의 목소리에 귀 기울입니다

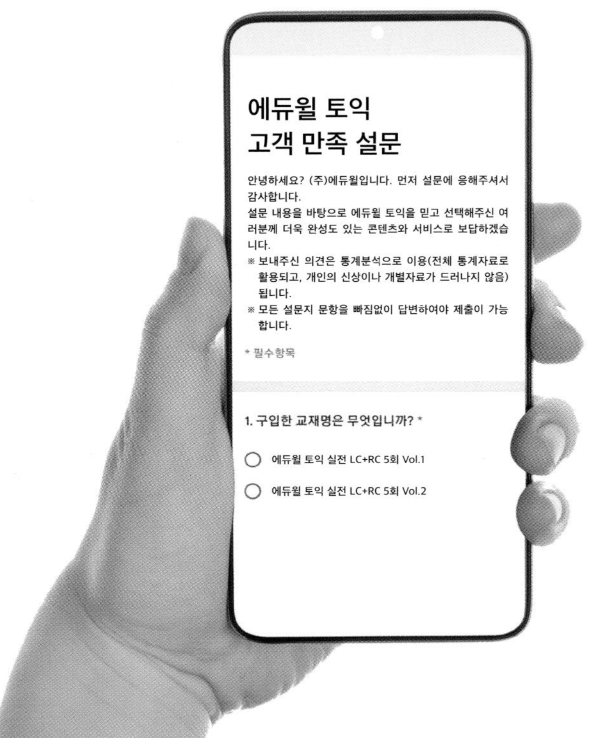

불편한 점이나
더 필요한 서비스가 있다면
말씀해 주세요.

에듀윌 토익을
믿고 선택해 주신 여러분께
더욱 완성도 있는 콘텐츠로
보답하겠습니다.

설문조사 참여 시
스타벅스 아메리카노 지급

참여 방법 QR 코드 스캔 → 설문조사 참여(1분만 투자하세요!)

추첨 방법 매월 적극적으로 의견을 주신 2분을 추첨하여 개별 연락

경　품 스타벅스 아메리카노 Tall

에듀윌 토익 설문조사
바로 가기

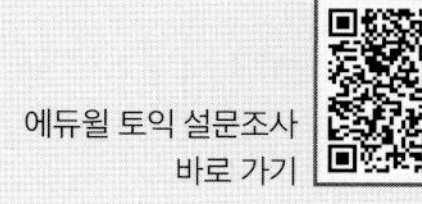

에듀윌 토익

실전 LC+RC

Vol.2

에듀윌이
너를
지지할게

ENERGY

시작하라.

그 자체가 천재성이고,
힘이며, 마력이다.

– 요한 볼프강 폰 괴테(Johann Wolfgang von Goethe)

실전 그대로, LC+RC 5회 모의고사

실전은 기세야, 기세

"시험이라는 게 뭐야? 앞으로 치고 나가는 거야. 그 흐름, 그 리듬을 놓치면 완전 꽝이야."
영화 〈기생충〉에서 4수생 '기우'가 영어 문제를 풀다가 헤매는 '다혜'의 손목을 덥석 잡으며 던지는 말이다. 토익 시험이라고 다를까! 한두 문제에 발목을 잡혀서는 곤란하다. Answer Sheet의 200번째 동그라미에서 연필을 떼기 전까지는 집중력을 놓아서는 안 된다. 시험장에서 실력보다 중요한 것은 "시험 전체를 어떻게 치고 나가는가, 어떻게 장악하는가" 하는 기세며, 깡이다. 리스닝을 망쳤다고 해서 그 기분이 리딩에 이어져도 안 되며, 한두 개 어려운 문제에 사로잡혀 바로 뒷장의 말도 안 되게 쉬운 문제들을 풀어 보지도 못한 채 떠나보내서는 안 된다.
〈에듀윌 토익 실전 LC+RC〉는 실제 토익 시험 그대로 LC와 RC를 합쳐 200문항을 한 회분으로 제작했다. 총 120분의 시험 시간을 정확히 설정해 놓고, 첫 문제를 푸는 순간부터 마킹을 끝내는 순간까지 집중력을 유지해 가며 시험을 장악해 보기 바란다. 그렇게 5회분만 시험을 '치고 나가는' 연습을 해 둔다면 실제 시험장에서도 작은 실수나 함정에 흔들리지 않고 자신의 실력을 십분 발휘할 수 있을 것이다.

빈출과 신유형의 절묘한 블렌딩

매 시험에서 어김없이 등장하는 빈출 유형은 그대로 유지하되 최근 기출 시험에서 등장한 새로운 문제 유형이나 낯선 소재, 어휘, 오답 함정 등을 적극 반영하였다. 따라서 단 5회분의 모의고사로 토익의 전반적인 경향을 파악하는 동시에 다양한 변형 문제들에 적응할 수 있는 충분한 스킬을 연마할 수 있을 것이다.

여섯 가지 버전의 MP3로 확실한 리스닝 훈련

귀로 듣고 푸는 리스닝에 많이 듣는 것보다 더 나은 훈련 방법은 없다. 양질전화, 많이 들으면 잘 듣게 된다. 특히 파트1과 2의 경우는 상당수의 어휘와 표현들이 수차례 기출에서 반복되어 쓰이는 만큼 빈출 표현들만 정확히 들을 수만 있다면 단기간에 큰 폭의 점수 향상을 기대할 수 있다. 파트3 대화와 파트4 담화 역시 유사한 소재와 일정한 스토리라인을 완전히 벗어나기 힘들고, 구어체에서 기본적으로 쓰이는 패턴들과 콜로케이션들이 반복적으로 사용되고 있기에 꾸준한 듣기 훈련만한 비법은 없다. 본서에서는 많이 들으면서도 효과적으로 들을 수 있도록 다양한 음원들을 제공한다. 대사만을 반복해 들을 수 있도록 편집한 반복 듣기용 MP3, 영국/호주 발음만 집중 연습할 수 있도록 파트4를 통째로 영국/호주 발음으로 재녹음한 MP3, 음원을 빠르게 편집한 고속 버전, 그 밖에 시험장 환경에 익숙해질 수 있도록 시험장 소음과 매미 소음 버전을 함께 제공한다.

[테스트별 핵심 어휘]로 완벽한 복습

마지막으로 각 회차에 쓰인 토익 필수 어휘들과 어려운 어휘들을 모아 해설편 끝에 수록해 놓았다. 문제를 다 풀고 철저하게 복습한 다음, 어휘 부록만 따로 떼어 들고 다니며 배운 단어들을 틈틈이 반복 암기해 두도록 하자.

에듀윌 어학연구소 드림

목차

정답 및 해설

책의 구성 및 특징

최신 기출 경향 완전 분석 및 반영

최신 토익 시험 문제를 밀도 있게 분석하여, 출제 경향과 빈출 유형을 파악한 후 최상의 문제들로만 엄선하여 실었습니다.

실전 모의고사 5회분

과도하게 많은 문제로 중도에 포기하기보다는 부담 없이 알찬 분량 5회분으로 성취감도 느끼고, 실전 훈련도 충분하도록 기획하였습니다.

테스트별 핵심 어휘

해설집의 뒷부분에 각 테스트에 나왔던 핵심 어휘 및 표현들을 모아 다시 한번 확실하게 익힐 수 있게 하였습니다.

다양한 버전의 MP3 파일 무료 제공

리스닝 MP3 파일을 테스트별, 파트별, 문항별로 다운로드할 수 있습니다. 테스트별 MP3 파일은 고속, 매미 소리, 고사장 소음 버전으로도 제공하니 필요한 것으로 골라서 들으세요. 또한 복습 시 불필요한 시간 소모를 최소화하기 위해 파트별 대화문과 담화문 스크립트만 반복해서 들을 수 있는 파일도 제공합니다.

맞힌 문제는 다음에 또 맞히기 위해, 틀린 문제는 또 틀리지 않기 위해 다양한 버전의 MP3 파일을 적극적으로 활용해 보세요. 그러다 보면 실제 시험에서 리스닝 내용이 귀에 쏙쏙 박히는 놀라운 경험을 하게 될 겁니다.

TOEIC 소개

토익이란?

TOEIC은 Test of English for International Communication(국제적인 의사소통을 위한 영어 시험)의 약자로, 영어가 모국어가 아닌 사람들이 비즈니스 현장 및 일상생활에서 필요한 실용 영어 능력을 갖추었는가를 평가하는 시험입니다.

시험 구성

구성	파트			문항 수		시간	배점
LISTENING Comprehension	PART 1	사진 묘사		6	100	45분	495점
	PART 2	질의 응답		25			
	PART 3	짧은 대화		39			
	PART 4	짧은 담화		30			
READING Comprehension	PART 5	단문 빈칸 채우기		30	100	75분	495점
	PART 6	장문 빈칸 채우기		16			
	PART 7	독해	단일 지문	29			
			이중 지문	10			
			삼중 지문	15			
합계	**7 PARTS**			**200문항**		**120분**	**990점**

출제 범위 및 주제

업무 및 일상생활에서 쓰이는 실용적인 주제들이 출제됩니다. 특정 문화나 특정 직업 분야에만 해당되는 주제는 출제하지 않으며, 듣기 평가의 경우 미국, 영국, 호주 등 다양한 국가의 발음이 섞여 출제됩니다.

일반 업무	계약, 협상, 영업, 홍보, 마케팅, 사업 계획
재무 회계	예산, 투자, 세금, 청구, 회계
개발	연구, 제품 개발
제조	공장 경영, 생산 조립 라인, 품질 관리
인사	채용, 승진, 퇴직, 직원 교육, 입사 지원
사무실	회의, 메모/전화/팩스/이메일, 사무 장비 및 가구
행사	학회, 연회, 회식, 시상식, 박람회, 제품 시연회
부동산	건축, 부동산 매매/임대, 기업 부지, 전기/수도/가스 설비
여행/여가	교통수단, 공항/역, 여행 일정, 호텔 및 자동차 예약/연기/취소, 영화, 전시, 공연

접수 방법

- 한국 TOEIC 위원회 사이트(www.toeic.co.kr)에서 인터넷 접수 기간을 확인하고 접수합니다.
- 시험 접수 시 최근 6개월 이내에 촬영한 jpg 형식의 사진 파일이 필요하므로 미리 준비합니다.
- 시험 11~13일 전부터는 특별 추가 접수 기간에 해당하여 추가 비용이 발생하므로, 접수 일정을 미리 확인하여 정기 접수 기간 내에 접수하도록 합니다.

시험 당일 준비물

신분증	주민등록증, 운전면허증, 기간 만료 전 여권, 공무원증 등 규정 신분증만 인정 (중 · 고등학생의 경우 학생증, 청소년증도 인정)
필기구	연필, 지우개 (볼펜, 사인펜은 사용 불가)

시험 진행

오전 시험	오후 시험	진행 내용
09:30 - 09:45	02:30 - 02:45	답안지 작성 오리엔테이션
09:45 - 09:50	02:45 - 02:50	쉬는 시간
09:50 - 10:05	02:50 - 03:05	신분증 확인
10:05 - 10:10	03:05 - 03:10	문제지 배부 및 파본 확인
10:10 - 10:55	03:10 - 03:55	듣기 평가 (LC)
10:55 - 12:10	03:55 - 05:10	독해 평가 (RC)

성적 확인

성적 발표	시험일로부터 약 12일 후에 한국 TOEIC 위원회 사이트(www.toeic.co.kr) 및 애플리케이션을 통해 확인 가능합니다.
성적표 수령	온라인 출력 또는 우편 수령 중에서 선택할 수 있고, 온라인 출력과 우편 수령 모두 1회 발급만 무료이며, 그 이후에는 유료로 발급됩니다.

TOEIC 파트별 문제 형태

PART 1 사진 묘사

파트 소개	제시된 사진을 보고, 4개의 문장을 들은 뒤 그중 사진을 가장 잘 묘사한 문장을 고르는 파트
문항 수	6문항
사진 유형	1인 사진, 2인 이상 사진, 사물 및 풍경 사진

문제지 형태

1.

2.

Number 1.

Look at the picture marked number 1 in your test book.

(A) He's staring at a vase.
(B) He's pouring a beverage.
(C) He's spreading out a tablecloth.
(D) He's sipping from a coffee cup.

PART 2 질의 응답

파트 소개	질문과 3개의 응답을 듣고, 질문에 가장 적절한 응답을 고르는 파트
문항 수	25문항
문제 유형	의문사 의문문, 일반 의문문, 부가 의문문, 선택 의문문, 간접 의문문, 제안 · 요청문, 평서문

문제지 형태

PART 2

Directions: You will hear a question or statement and three responses spoken in English. They will not be printed in your test book and will be spoken only one time. Select the best response to the question or statement and mark the letter (A), (B), or (C) on your answer sheet.

7. Mark your answer on your answer sheet.
8. Mark your answer on your answer sheet.
9. Mark your answer on your answer sheet.
10. Mark your answer on your answer sheet.
11. Mark your answer on your answer sheet.
12. Mark your answer on your answer sheet.
13. Mark your answer on your answer sheet.
14. Mark your answer on your answer sheet.
15. Mark your answer on your answer sheet.
16. Mark your answer on your answer sheet.
17. Mark your answer on your answer sheet.
18. Mark your answer on your answer sheet.
19. Mark your answer on your answer sheet.
20. Mark your answer on your answer sheet.
21. Mark your answer on your answer sheet.
22. Mark your answer on your answer sheet.
23. Mark your answer on your answer sheet.
24. Mark your answer on your answer sheet.
25. Mark your answer on your answer sheet.
26. Mark your answer on your answer sheet.
27. Mark your answer on your answer sheet.
28. Mark your answer on your answer sheet.
29. Mark your answer on your answer sheet.
30. Mark your answer on your answer sheet.
31. Mark your answer on your answer sheet.

Number 7.

When will the landlord inspect the property?

(A) No, it failed the inspection.
(B) I'll e-mail him about it.
(C) Do you like the apartment?

TOEIC 파트별 문제 형태

PART 3 짧은 대화

파트 소개	두 명 또는 세 명의 대화를 듣고, 이와 관련된 3개의 문제에 대해 가장 적절한 답을 고르는 파트
문항 수	39문항 (13개 대화문×3문항)
대화 유형	2인 대화 (11개)와 3인 대화 (2개)로 이루어지며, 2인 대화 중 마지막 3세트 (62~70번)는 시각 자료와 함께 제시된다.
문제 유형	주제 · 목적, 장소, 직업 · 신분, 세부사항, 제안 · 요청, 앞으로 일어날 일, 의도 파악, 시각 자료 연계

문제지 형태

PART 3

Directions: You will hear some conversations between two or more people. You will be asked to answer three questions about what the speakers say in each conversation. Select the best response to each question and mark the letter (A), (B), (C), or (D) on your answer sheet. The conversations will not be printed in your test book and will be spoken only one time.

32. Where is the conversation taking place?
(A) At a bookstore
(B) At a dry cleaner's
(C) At a department store
(D) At a post office

33. What does the man check?
(A) The available sizes
(B) The sale price
(C) The delivery fees
(D) The shipment date

34. What does the man recommend doing?
(A) Checking for an item online
(B) Placing a rush order
(C) Visiting another branch
(D) Purchasing a different brand

35. What most likely is the man's job?
(A) Head of marketing
(B) Graphic designer
(C) Repairperson
(D) Personnel manager

36. What has the woman ordered for the man?
(A) A uniform
(B) A desk
(C) A file cabinet
(D) A laptop computer

37. What does the woman remind the man to do?
(A) Sign up for a workshop
(B) Read a user manual
(C) Transport an item carefully
(D) Contact a customer

38. What does the man want his friend's opinion about?
(A) A payment method
(B) A reservation time
(C) A food order
(D) A seating option

39. Why does the man say, "That's more than I expected"?

43. Wh
(B) A new shipment will arrive.
(C) The man will conduct an interview.
(D) Photos will be added to a Web site.

Questions 32-34 refer to the following conversation.

M Welcome to Madison Department Store. Can I help you find anything today?

W I'm wondering if these jeans come in a size fourteen. I didn't see any on the shelf.

M I think twelve is the largest size we carry, but let me look it up on the computer.

W Thanks. I really like this style.

M Hmm... yes, twelve is the largest...

PART 4 짧은 담화

파트 소개	한 사람이 말하는 담화를 듣고, 이와 관련된 3개의 문제에 대해 가장 적절한 답을 고르는 파트
문항 수	30문항(10개 담화문×3문항)
담화 유형	전화 메시지, 공지, 광고, 방송, 소개, 연설, 회의 등으로 이루어지며, 마지막 2세트(95~100번)는 시각 자료와 함께 제시된다.
문제 유형	주제 · 목적, 장소, 직업 · 신분, 세부사항, 제안 · 요청, 앞으로 일어날 일, 의도 파악, 시각 자료 연계

문제지 형태

PART 4

Directions: You will hear some talks given by a single speaker. You will be asked to answer three questions about what the speaker says in each talk. Select the best response to each question and mark the letter (A), (B), (C), or (D) on your answer sheet. The talks will not be printed in your test book and will be spoken only one time.

71. How does each workshop tour end?
(A) An employee answers questions.
(B) An informative video is shown.
(C) A group photo is taken.
(D) A piece of equipment is demonstrated.

72. What does each tour participant receive?
(A) A piece of jewelry
(B) A voucher
(C) A map of the site
(D) A beverage

73. What do the listeners receive a warning about?
(A) Which entrance to use
(B) Where to meet
(C) What clothing to bring
(D) How to book in advance

74. Who most likely is giving the speech?
(A) A factory worker
(B) A driving instructor
(C) A gym manager
(D) A bank employee

75. What have the listeners been given?
(A) A product sample
(B) An employee directory
(C) A daily pass
(D) A list of classes

76. What does the speaker mean when she says, "You won't see anything like it again"?
(A) A membership process can be confusing.
(B) A presentation is worth watching.
(C) The business is expected to succeed.
(D) Listeners should take advantage of an offer.

77. What kind of business do the listeners most likely work for?
(A) A construction company
(B) An international delivery service
(C) A newspaper publisher
(D) A medical facility

78. What does the speaker say he is reassured about?
(A) A worker's attention to detail
(B) An investor's future plan
(C) The responses from a customer survey
(D) T

79. Wha
(A) E
(B) A
(C) A
(D) S

80. Why
(A) It
(B) It
(C) T
(D) T

81. Why
indir
(A) T
(B) T
(C) T
(D) T

82. Wha
(A) Talk to the speaker
(B) Show a ticket
(C) Come back later
(D) Present a receipt

Questions 71-73 refer to the following announcement.

Are you tired of the same old tourist sites? Try something new and tour the Lodgevile Jewelry Workshop. You'll get to see each step of the jewelry-making process. And, at the end, you'll have the chance to get your questions addressed by one of our talented jewelry makers. Each participant is given a beautiful bracelet to identify their tour group, and this gift is yours to keep...

TOEIC 파트별 문제 형태

PART 5 단문 빈칸 채우기

파트 소개	빈칸이 포함된 하나의 문장이 주어지고, 빈칸에 알맞은 단어나 구를 4개의 선택지 중에서 고르는 파트	
문항 수	30문항	
문제 유형	문법	시제(종종 태, 수 일치와 연계), 대명사, 분사, 한정사, 부정사, 동명사, 능동태/수동태, 그리고 품사 관련 문제가 주로 출제된다. 품사는 명사 및 부사와 관련된 문제가 2~3개 정도 출제되며, 빈도는 낮지만 전치사 관련 문제가 출제되기도 한다.
	어휘	같은 품사의 단어들을 제시하고 그중 문맥에 적절한 어휘를 고르는 문제다. 동사, 명사, 형용사, 부사 어휘가 각각 2~3문제씩, 전치사 어휘가 평균 3문제씩 출제된다. 그밖에 접속사나 어구 문제가 출제되기도 한다.

문제지 형태

READING TEST

In the Reading test, you will read a variety of texts and answer several different types of reading comprehension questions. The entire Reading test will last 75 minutes. There are three parts, and directions are given for each part. You are encouraged to answer as many questions as possible within the time allowed.

You must mark your answers on the separate answer sheet. Do not write your answers in your test book.

PART 5

Directions: A word or phrase is missing in each of the sentences below. Four answer choices are given below each sentence. Select the best answer to complete the sentence. Then mark the letter (A), (B), (C), or (D) on your answer sheet.

101. Some officials ------- expressed concerns about the changes to the corporate tax structure.
(A) privacy
(B) privatize
(C) private
(D) privately

102. The new electric car from Baylor Motors is intended for ------- journeys within an urban environment.
(A) shortness
(B) short
(C) shortly
(D) shorten

103. Ames Manufacturing developed a packaging method that ------- much less cardboard.
(A) uses
(B) using
(C) to use
(D) use

104. The building's owner increased the fees ------- parking lot access.
(A) for
(B) about
(C) at
(D) among

105. Few market analysts ------- predicted the industry effects of the factory's closure.
(A) locally
(B) constantly
(C) kindly
(D) correctly

106. Customers who wish to ------- us a review on social media are encouraged to do so.
(A) explain
(B) say
(C) give
(D) have

107. Every weekend ------- the month of August, the hotel's restaurant features live musical performances.
(A) even
(B) during
(C) when
(D) while

108. Portland Insurance's employees should complete a form with ------- desired vacation days.
(A) their
(B) its
(C) themselves
(D) it

PART 6 장문 빈칸 채우기

파트 소개	4개의 빈칸이 포함된 지문이 주어지고, 각각의 빈칸에 들어갈 알맞은 단어나 구, 문장을 고르는 파트
문항 수	16문항(4개 지문×4문항)
문제 유형	4개의 문제 중 문맥에 맞는 문장 고르기 문제가 항상 1개씩 나오며, 평균적으로 어휘 문제가 2개, 품사를 포함한 문법 문제가 1문제씩 출제된다. 지문에 따라서 품사 및 문법 문제가 2개, 어휘 문제가 1개 출제되기도 한다. 문법은 문맥의 흐름을 통해 파악해야 하는 시제 문제가 가장 비중 있게 출제되며, 어휘 문제에서도 문맥을 자연스럽게 연결해 주는 접속부사를 고르는 문제가 자주 등장한다.

문제지 형태

PART 6

Directions: Read the texts that follow. A word, phrase, or sentence is missing in parts of each text. Four answer choices for each question are given below the text. Select the best answer to complete the text. Then mark the letter (A), (B), (C), or (D) on your answer sheet.

Questions 131-134 refer to the following letter.

Georgina Harrison
962 Warner Street
Cape Girardeau, MO 63703

Dear Ms. Harrison,

Thank you for your interest in making a group booking at Westside Hotel. I have attached a comprehensive ------- (**131.**) of our amenities for your convenience. We aim to personalize the guest experience. We are prepared to meet the needs of most guests on short notice. However, if you have ------- (**132.**) requests, we may need advance notice in order to fulfill them. Once your booking is made, you may be charged a fee according to our cancellation policy. ------- (**133.**). Before confirming your booking, please download a copy of the payment details and ------- (**134.**) them carefully.

Warmest regards,

The Westside Hotel Team

131. (A) describe
(B) describes
(C) described
(D) description

132. (A) unusual
(B) absent
(C) plain
(D) flexible

133. (A) The front desk is open twenty-four hours a day.
(B) You should complete the form with honest feedback.
(C) We appreciate your ongoing patronage.
(D) The terms of this are included on our Web site.

134. (A) reviewing
(B) review
(C) to review
(D) reviewed

TOEIC 파트별 문제 형태

PART 7 독해

파트 소개	지문을 읽고, 지문 내용과 관련된 2~5개 문제에 대해 가장 적절한 답을 고르는 파트		
지문 / 문항 수	단일 지문	10개 (지문당 2~4 문항 ; 총 29문항)	총 15개 지문 (54문항)
	이중 지문	2개 (지문당 5문항 ; 총 10문항)	
	삼중 지문	3개 (지문당 5문항 ; 총 15문항)	
지문 유형	이메일 · 편지, 광고, 공지 · 회람, 기사, 양식 (웹페이지, 설문지, 청구서 등), 문자 메시지 대화문 등		
문제 유형	주제 · 목적, 세부사항, 사실 확인, 추론, 문장 넣기, 의도 파악, 동의어 찾기		

문제지 형태 (단일 지문)

PART 7

Directions: In this part, you will read a selection of texts, such as magazine and newspaper articles, e-mails, and instant messages. Each text or set of texts is followed by several questions. Select the best answer for each question and mark the letter (A), (B), (C), or (D) on your answer sheet.

Questions 147-148 refer to the following article.

New Library Program Creates "Buzz"

April 30—This summer, Syracuse Library is launching a program to help local bees. The number of local bees has sharply declined, and the library aims to help these creatures. It will have a special section with books about bees and will host lectures about how they benefit the environment. Anyone who attends a lecture will be given a free pack of seeds for flowers that will attract bees.

147. What is the purpose of the program?
(A) To support the bee population
(B) To teach people a new skill
(C) To attract new library members
(D) To raise money for a charity

148. How can participants get a free gift?
(A) By completing a survey
(B) By attending a talk
(C) By making a donation
(D) By showing a library card

문제지 형태 (삼중 지문)

Questions 186-190 refer to the following article and forms.

Oakdale (April 9)—Preparations are underway for Oakdale's 8th Annual Health and Well-Being Expo, which will take place on Sunday, June 19. The expo will feature businesses offering a variety of health-related goods and services. Additionally, local physicians and nurses will provide free screenings for blood pressure and cholesterol levels as well as a basic eye exam.

After many years at Juniper Hall, the expo has been moved to the Bayridge Convention Center this year. "Due to the growing popularity of the event, Juniper Hall could no longer contain the number of vendors interested in participating in the expo," said Ken Exley, one of the event planners. "Visitors can easily find what they're looking for, with vendors of vitamins and health supplements in the main hall, massage therapists and spa representatives in the east wing, and gym representatives and sports-related

To register, visit www.oakdalehealthe
get a twenty percent discount.

Annual He
Vend

Name: *Anna Pierson*
Business/Company: *Sunrise S*

I was informed about th
Oakdale Business Associat
as a vendor, and I reache
would have liked a larger
spoke to some other vendo
has the same needs, so it
future.

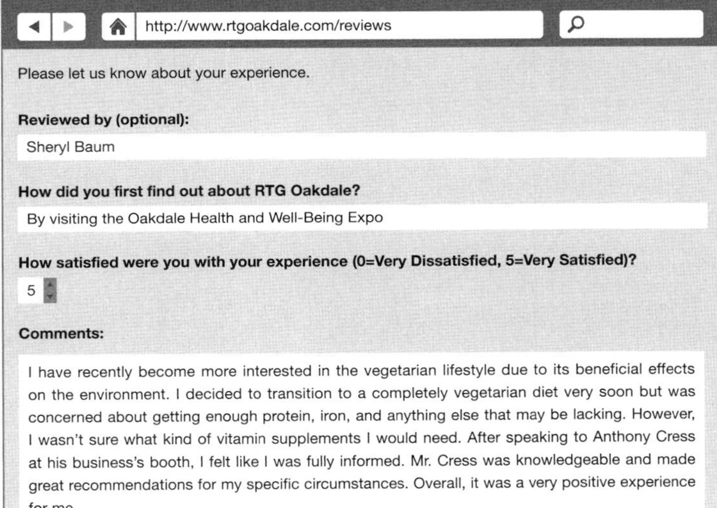
http://www.rtgoakdale.com/reviews

Please let us know about your experience.

Reviewed by (optional):
Sheryl Baum

How did you first find out about RTG Oakdale?
By visiting the Oakdale Health and Well-Being Expo

How satisfied were you with your experience (0=Very Dissatisfied, 5=Very Satisfied)?
5

Comments:
I have recently become more interested in the vegetarian lifestyle due to its beneficial effects on the environment. I decided to transition to a completely vegetarian diet very soon but was concerned about getting enough protein, iron, and anything else that may be lacking. However, I wasn't sure what kind of vitamin supplements I would need. After speaking to Anthony Cress at his business's booth, I felt like I was fully informed. Mr. Cress was knowledgeable and made great recommendations for my specific circumstances. Overall, it was a very positive experience for me.

186. According to the article, why did the event planners use a different site this year?
(A) To ensure more space
(B) To minimize traffic problems
(C) To promote a new building
(D) To reduce travel times

187. What is suggested about Ms. Pierson?
(A) She qualified for early registration.
(B) She recently started her business.
(C) She has participated in past events.
(D) She was eligible for a discount.

188. What does Ms. Pierson recommend for the next expo?
(A) Addressing some noise complaints
(B) Providing more power outlets
(C) Offering booths in various sizes
(D) Advertising the event to more people

189. What is implied about Mr. Cress?
(A) He has lived in Oakdale for a long time.
(B) He worked at a booth in the main hall.
(C) He was an event planner for the expo.
(D) He is considering hiring Ms. Baum.

190. What does Ms. Baum plan to do?
(A) Undertake further research on a topic
(B) Write another online review
(C) Change her daily eating habits
(D) Start a health-related business

점수 환산표

본 점수 환산표는 교재에 수록된 TEST 5회분의 점수 환산을 위해 만든 표입니다.
각 TEST를 마치고 난 후, 본인의 예상 점수대를 가늠해 보세요.

LISTENING RAW SCORE (맞힌 개수)	LISTENING SCALED SCORE (환산 점수)
96-100	475-495
91-95	435-495
86-90	405-475
81-85	370-450
76-80	345-420
71-75	320-390
66-70	290-360
61-65	265-335
56-60	235-310
51-55	210-280
46-50	180-255
41-45	155-230
36-40	125-205
31-35	105-175
26-30	85-145
21-25	60-115
16-20	30-90
11-15	5-70
6-10	5-60
1-5	5-50
0	5

READING RAW SCORE (맞힌 개수)	READING SCALED SCORE (환산 점수)
96-100	460-495
91-95	425-490
86-90	395-465
81-85	370-440
76-80	335-415
71-75	310-390
66-70	280-365
61-65	250-335
56-60	220-305
51-55	195-270
46-50	165-240
41-45	140-215
36-40	115-180
31-35	95-145
26-30	75-120
21-25	60-95
16-20	45-75
11-15	30-55
6-10	10-40
1-5	5-30
0	5

학습 스케줄러

2주 집중 완성 학습

	1일	2일	3일	4일	5일
1주	(월 일)	(월 일)	(월 일)	(월 일)	(월 일)
	TEST 01 풀기	TEST 01 복습	TEST 02 풀기	TEST 02 복습	TEST 03 풀기
	6일	7일	8일	9일	10일
2주	(월 일)	(월 일)	(월 일)	(월 일)	(월 일)
	TEST 03 복습	TEST 04 풀기	TEST 04 복습	TEST 05 풀기	TEST 05 복습

4주 실력 완성 학습

	1일	2일	3일	4일	5일
1주	(월 일)	(월 일)	(월 일)	(월 일)	(월 일)
	TEST 01 LC 풀기	TEST 01 LC 복습	TEST 01 RC 풀기	TEST 01 RC 복습	TEST 02 LC 풀기
	6일	7일	8일	9일	10일
2주	(월 일)	(월 일)	(월 일)	(월 일)	(월 일)
	TEST 02 LC 복습	TEST 02 RC 풀기	TEST 02 RC 복습	TEST 03 LC 풀기	TEST 03 LC 복습
	11일	12일	13일	14일	15일
3주	(월 일)	(월 일)	(월 일)	(월 일)	(월 일)
	TEST 03 RC 풀기	TEST 03 RC 복습	TEST 04 LC 풀기	TEST 04 LC 복습	TEST 04 RC 풀기
	16일	17일	18일	19일	20일
4주	(월 일)	(월 일)	(월 일)	(월 일)	(월 일)
	TEST 04 RC 복습	TEST 05 LC 풀기	TEST 05 LC 복습	TEST 05 RC 풀기	TEST 05 RC 복습

자동 채점 서비스
바로가기

에 듀 윌 토 익 실 전 서

LC+RC

TEST 01

LISTENING TEST

PART 1

PART 2

PART 3

PART 4

READING TEST

PART 5

PART 6

PART 7

LISTENING TEST

In the Listening test, you will be asked to demonstrate how well you understand spoken English. The entire Listening test will last approximately 45 minutes. There are four parts, and directions are given for each part. You must mark your answers on the separate answer sheet. Do not write your answers in your test book.

PART 1

Directions: For each question in this part, you will hear four statements about a picture in your test book. When you hear the statements, you must select the one statement that best describes what you see in the picture. Then find the number of the question on your answer sheet and mark your answer. The statements will not be printed in your test book and will be spoken only one time.

Statement (C), "He's making a phone call," is the best description of the picture, so you should select answer (C) and mark it on your answer sheet.

1.

2.

GO ON TO THE NEXT PAGE

3.

4.

5.

6.

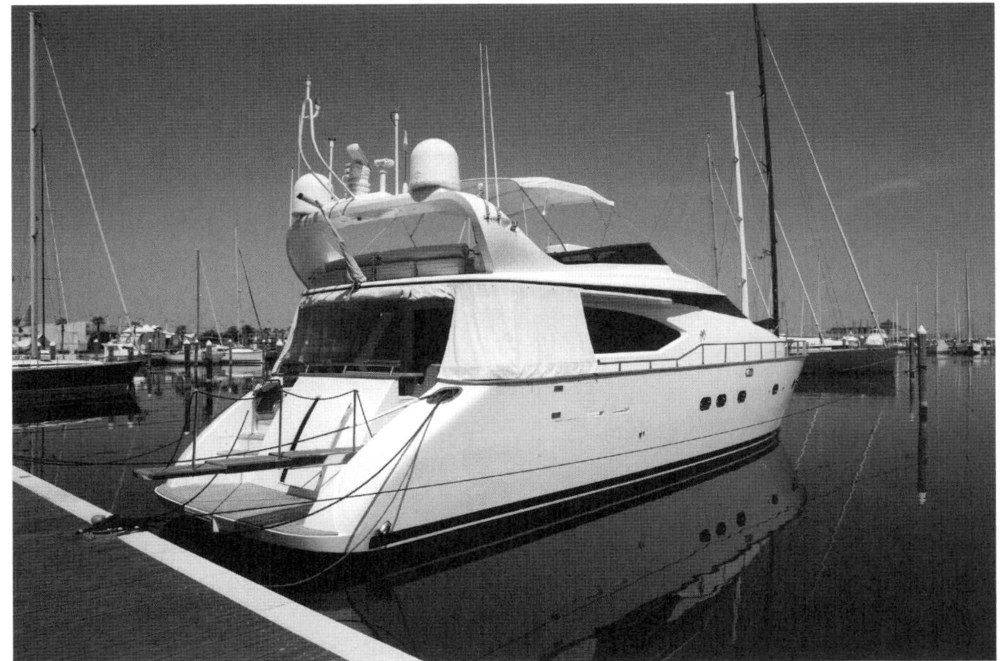

GO ON TO THE NEXT PAGE →

PART 2

Directions: You will hear a question or statement and three responses spoken in English. They will not be printed in your test book and will be spoken only one time. Select the best response to the question or statement and mark the letter (A), (B), or (C) on your answer sheet.

7. Mark your answer on your answer sheet.
8. Mark your answer on your answer sheet.
9. Mark your answer on your answer sheet.
10. Mark your answer on your answer sheet.
11. Mark your answer on your answer sheet.
12. Mark your answer on your answer sheet.
13. Mark your answer on your answer sheet.
14. Mark your answer on your answer sheet.
15. Mark your answer on your answer sheet.
16. Mark your answer on your answer sheet.
17. Mark your answer on your answer sheet.
18. Mark your answer on your answer sheet.
19. Mark your answer on your answer sheet.
20. Mark your answer on your answer sheet.
21. Mark your answer on your answer sheet.
22. Mark your answer on your answer sheet.
23. Mark your answer on your answer sheet.
24. Mark your answer on your answer sheet.
25. Mark your answer on your answer sheet.
26. Mark your answer on your answer sheet.
27. Mark your answer on your answer sheet.
28. Mark your answer on your answer sheet.
29. Mark your answer on your answer sheet.
30. Mark your answer on your answer sheet.
31. Mark your answer on your answer sheet.

PART 3

Directions: You will hear some conversations between two or more people. You will be asked to answer three questions about what the speakers say in each conversation. Select the best response to each question and mark the letter (A), (B), (C), or (D) on your answer sheet. The conversations will not be printed in your test book and will be spoken only one time.

32. What is the conversation mainly about?
(A) A boat ride
(B) A history lecture
(C) A nature hike
(D) A bicycle tour

33. What does the woman ask the man to do?
(A) Select a size
(B) Show a receipt
(C) Provide a phone number
(D) Show an ID card

34. What does the woman suggest purchasing?
(A) A map
(B) A beverage
(C) A gift card
(D) A parking pass

---

35. Where do the speakers most likely work?
(A) At an appliance repair business
(B) At a dental clinic
(C) At a government office
(D) At a dry-cleaning company

36. What does the woman ask the man to do?
(A) Inspect a property
(B) Reschedule a visit
(C) Accompany her on a trip
(D) Print out a list

37. What will the woman most likely do next?
(A) Join a conference call
(B) Sign a form
(C) Look at a catalog
(D) Rearrange some furniture

---

38. Where do the speakers most likely work?
(A) At an event planning agency
(B) At a health food shop
(C) At a dance academy
(D) At a party supply store

39. What does the man ask the woman to confirm?
(A) The location of an event
(B) The number of participants
(C) The updates to a schedule
(D) The topic of a talk

40. What will the man do tomorrow?
(A) Research a company
(B) Contact a city office
(C) Edit some slides
(D) Come to work early

---

41. Why did Mr. Powell call?
(A) To dispute an incorrect bill
(B) To complain about some damaged items
(C) To report an error on a Web site
(D) To inquire about a late delivery

42. Where do the speakers most likely work?
(A) At an electronics store
(B) At a camping supply company
(C) At a clothing outlet
(D) At a ceramics factory

43. What does the woman think caused a problem?
(A) A tight deadline
(B) A computer error
(C) An inexperienced employee
(D) A change in containers

GO ON TO THE NEXT PAGE

44. Who most likely is the woman?
(A) A construction worker
(B) An event planner
(C) A gardener
(D) A real estate agent

45. What is the conversation mainly about?
(A) Changes in a policy
(B) Improvements to a property
(C) An increase in fees
(D) An order of materials

46. What will the woman do next?
(A) Contact a colleague
(B) Review a budget
(C) Print a contract for the man
(D) Show the man some drawings

---

47. Who most likely are the speakers?
(A) Professional photographers
(B) Fashion designers
(C) Maintenance workers
(D) Art instructors

48. What does the man say they need to do?
(A) Hire an assistant
(B) Order some components
(C) Rent a vehicle
(D) Create a presentation

49. What will the woman give to the man?
(A) A discount code
(B) A business card
(C) Driving directions
(D) Extra tickets

---

50. Where most likely are the speakers?
(A) In an airport
(B) In a supermarket
(C) In an office building
(D) In a hotel

51. What type of business does the man work for?
(A) An architecture firm
(B) An employment agency
(C) A marketing firm
(D) A travel agency

52. What is the woman concerned about?
(A) Disruptions from noise
(B) Access to an entrance
(C) Losing power to the site
(D) A lack of storage options

---

53. Why is the man calling?
(A) To introduce a product
(B) To volunteer for a project
(C) To check an item's availability
(D) To promote an event

54. What does the woman mean when she says, "I've hardly touched it"?
(A) A microwave is in excellent condition.
(B) Microwaved food may not be healthy.
(C) She does not know how to operate a device.
(D) She was displeased with a product's design.

55. What does the woman plan to do tomorrow?
(A) Go out of town
(B) Hire a moving company
(C) Work late
(D) Cook a meal

---

56. What industry do the men work in?
(A) Shipping
(B) Energy
(C) Entertainment
(D) Finance

57. What does the woman inquire about?
(A) What the new job responsibilities include
(B) When a position begins
(C) How much a monthly salary is
(D) Whether a training course is needed

58. What benefit of the role is mentioned?
(A) Annual performance bonuses
(B) Use of a company credit card
(C) Flexible work hours
(D) Opportunities for promotion

---

59. What has the man recently done?
(A) He moved to a new home.
(B) He paved a section of his property.
(C) He purchased patio furniture.
(D) He opened a landscaping business.

60. Why does the man say, "I've never worked with outdoor tiles"?
(A) To ask for advice
(B) To request additional time
(C) To reject a job offer
(D) To explain a budget

61. What will the speakers most likely do next?
(A) View a price list
(B) Wait for a manager
(C) Look at some products
(D) Book an installation appointment

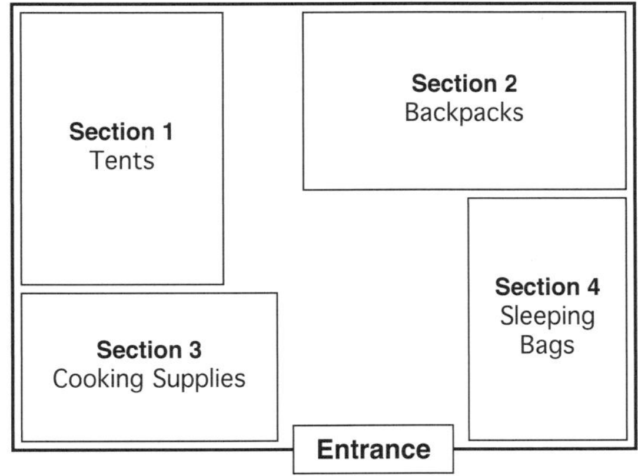

62. Who most likely are the speakers?
(A) Building inspectors
(B) Factory workers
(C) Tour guides
(D) Sales clerks

63. Look at the graphic. Where will a special activity take place today?
(A) In Section 1
(B) In Section 2
(C) In Section 3
(D) In Section 4

64. Why will the woman most likely visit Joanne's office?
(A) To call a repairperson
(B) To order some supplies
(C) To print some signs
(D) To check a manual

GO ON TO THE NEXT PAGE

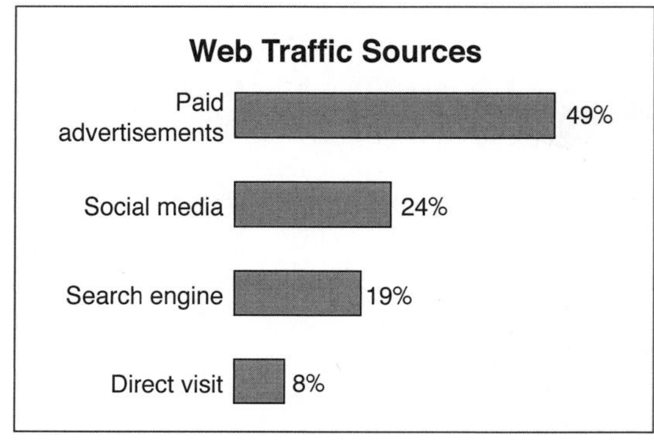

65. Look at the graphic. Which percentage is the woman pleased about?
(A) 49%
(B) 24%
(C) 19%
(D) 8%

66. What is the focus of the speakers' charity?
(A) Protecting animals
(B) Helping the environment
(C) Restoring disaster-impacted areas
(D) Promoting education

67. How has a sign-up process been changed?
(A) It no longer has a charge.
(B) It has a longer deadline.
(C) It is available through different methods.
(D) It is reviewed by a panel of volunteers.

Line 1. Brand: Bravo
Line 2. Color: Dark Brown
Line 3. Price: $95
Line 4. Size: 7

68. What is scheduled to take place tomorrow?
(A) A store inspection
(B) A press conference
(C) A product launch
(D) A branch opening

69. Look at the graphic. Which line does the woman say she will change?
(A) Line 1
(B) Line 2
(C) Line 3
(D) Line 4

70. What does the man plan to do?
(A) Speak to some coworkers
(B) E-mail an updated schedule
(C) Conduct an interview
(D) Call a manufacturer

PART 4

Directions: You will hear some talks given by a single speaker. You will be asked to answer three questions about what the speaker says in each talk. Select the best response to each question and mark the letter (A), (B), (C), or (D) on your answer sheet. The talks will not be printed in your test book and will be spoken only one time.

71. Where is the announcement taking place?
(A) On a ferry
(B) In a taxi
(C) On a train
(D) On an airplane

72. What does the speaker recommend doing?
(A) Looking at the scenery
(B) Listening for more updates
(C) Checking for personal items
(D) Keeping a ticket receipt

73. According to the speaker, why are the listeners lucky?
(A) There are fewer visitors.
(B) The fog has lifted.
(C) The train has arrived early.
(D) Seat upgrades are available.

74. What kind of business does the speaker own?
(A) An interior design company
(B) A bookstore
(C) A technology firm
(D) A catering company

75. How did Lucia Kraus help the speaker?
(A) By recommending a service
(B) By investing in a business
(C) By providing some supplies
(D) By working additional hours

76. What does the speaker want the listener to see?
(A) Some clothing items
(B) A Web site
(C) Some employees' comments
(D) A proposed contract

77. Who most likely is the speaker?
(A) A restaurant worker
(B) A bus driver
(C) A theater owner
(D) A fitness instructor

78. Why does the speaker plan to wait?
(A) Heavy traffic is expected in the area.
(B) A participant is absent.
(C) Some supplies are on the way.
(D) A vehicle is being checked.

79. What are some of the listeners encouraged to do?
(A) Present a form of ID
(B) Pay attention to a screen
(C) Take a group picture
(D) Pick up a schedule

80. What is the podcast series about?
(A) Scientific breakthroughs
(B) Travel destinations
(C) Unique architecture
(D) Wildlife and nature

81. How did the speaker learn about Ken Morgan's work?
(A) From a previous guest
(B) From an online search
(C) From a magazine article
(D) From a podcast listener

82. What will the listeners hear next?
(A) A show topic
(B) A song
(C) An advertisement
(D) A weather report

GO ON TO THE NEXT PAGE →

83. According to the speaker, what will happen in August?
(A) A clearance sale will be held.
(B) A company relocation will take place.
(C) A new manager will be hired.
(D) A corporate merger will be finalized.

84. What is Melissa Collins in charge of?
(A) Ordering equipment
(B) Making repairs
(C) Taking inventory
(D) Screening applicants

85. What does the speaker imply when she says, "we've never had to do this before"?
(A) A process should be reviewed.
(B) A request is considered unfair.
(C) Some questions may not be answered.
(D) Some information was not updated.

---

86. What industry do the listeners most likely work in?
(A) Telecommunications
(B) Hospitality
(C) Manufacturing
(D) Healthcare

87. According to the speaker, what is different about the conference this year?
(A) It can be viewed online.
(B) The lecturers are from different countries.
(C) The participants can give feedback.
(D) Presenters have more time for questions.

88. What are some of the listeners encouraged to do?
(A) Wear their name tags
(B) Purchase some related books
(C) Help themselves to refreshments
(D) Sign up for a training session

---

89. Where do the listeners most likely work?
(A) At a warehouse
(B) At a vehicle factory
(C) At a research facility
(D) At a government office

90. What is the speaker worried about?
(A) Implementing new policies
(B) Damaging equipment
(C) Getting behind schedule
(D) Filling job vacancies

91. Why does the speaker say, "I'll be here with my phone on"?
(A) To propose a solution
(B) To apologize for interruptions
(C) To encourage feedback
(D) To express urgency

---

92. Where does the speaker work?
(A) At a construction company
(B) At an advertising agency
(C) At a print shop
(D) At a museum

93. What has Hartford Enterprises agreed to provide?
(A) A draft of an article
(B) A larger deposit
(C) A current catalog
(D) A list of measurements

94. Why does the speaker say, "they could become a regular client"?
(A) To explain a decision
(B) To justify a discount
(C) To express surprise
(D) To correct an error

Price per Dozen	
Sunflower $32	Lily $30
Rose $25	Tulip $18

95. Why does the speaker thank some of the listeners?
(A) For noticing an error
(B) For staying late
(C) For recommending a supplier
(D) For working an extra shift

96. Look at the graphic. How much will the Towson Art Gallery pay per dozen for the order?
(A) $32
(B) $30
(C) $25
(D) $18

97. What will the speaker do at noon?
(A) Set up a display
(B) Label some containers
(C) Provide a meal
(D) Order some furniture

Special Guests	
Author	Fabiano Baresi
Editor	Wei Chang
Literary Agent	Madri Kamal
Cover Artist	Ines Faust

98. What type of book is being promoted?
(A) Poetry
(B) Science fiction
(C) Romance
(D) Mystery

99. According to the speaker, what will happen next week?
(A) A writing contest will begin.
(B) A book price will increase.
(C) An award winner will be announced.
(D) A class will be offered.

100. Look at the graphic. Who could not attend the event?
(A) Fabiano Baresi
(B) Wei Change
(C) Madri Kamal
(D) Ines Faust

This is the end of the Listening test. Turn to Part 5 in your test book.

READING TEST

In the Reading test, you will read a variety of texts and answer several different types of reading comprehension questions. The entire Reading test will last 75 minutes. There are three parts, and directions are given for each part. You are encouraged to answer as many questions as possible within the time allowed.

You must mark your answers on the separate answer sheet. Do not write your answers in your test book.

PART 5

Directions: A word or phrase is missing in each of the sentences below. Four answer choices are given below each sentence. Select the best answer to complete the sentence. Then mark the letter (A), (B), (C), or (D) on your answer sheet.

101. If the parade goes ------- as planned, the planning committee members will be pleased.

(A) preciseness
(B) precisely
(C) precise
(D) precision

102. The gallery's VIP guests are invited to take a tour with the artists ------- 7 P.M.

(A) of
(B) at
(C) for
(D) in

103. Mr. Latham was recognized at the annual meeting for ------- efforts in securing the merger deal.

(A) he
(B) him
(C) himself
(D) his

104. Felosa Media announced that it will raise the monthly fee ------- its video streaming service.

(A) for
(B) along
(C) nearby
(D) as

105. ------- the tourist season begins, repairs will be made to the pier at Bremond Bay.

(A) Before
(B) Whereas
(C) As if
(D) So that

106. Ms. Revilla's order of printer paper from Office World is scheduled for ------- Friday afternoon.

(A) status
(B) delivery
(C) warranty
(D) account

107. Most consumers rated ------- models as being more efficient than the company's first product lines.

(A) late
(B) lateness
(C) lately
(D) later

108. Simpson Incorporated is the nation's leading ------- of high-quality exterior paint.

(A) cause
(B) indicator
(C) source
(D) role

109. Corporate lawyer Jillian Smith can suggest improvements to contract drafts ------- contain vague or confusing language.

(A) than
(B) yet
(C) that
(D) so

110. From June 8, the hotel's sauna room on the ground floor will be ------- open.

(A) immediately
(B) officially
(C) remarkably
(D) sharply

111. While the Jackson Foundation is a major ------- of art education programs, it also makes donations to sports facilities.

(A) supported
(B) supporter
(C) support
(D) supportive

112. The medical center plays music that is soothing and ------- to patients in order to put them at ease.

(A) confidential
(B) familiar
(C) competent
(D) talented

113. The documentary *Circular Path* includes ------- scenes from the exciting world of car racing.

(A) drama
(B) dramatic
(C) dramatically
(D) dramatize

114. When Ms. Broussard arrived at the office in the morning, she ------- the window at the end of the corridor had been left open.

(A) inspected
(B) convinced
(C) noticed
(D) glanced

115. The ad campaign for the new soda from Harness Beverages ------- failed to catch consumer interest.

(A) largest
(B) largely
(C) larger
(D) largeness

116. If the contents of your order are damaged ------- repair when they arrive, you can receive a refund.

(A) across
(B) besides
(C) beyond
(D) except

117. The Manchester Dance Troupe ------- its famous show, *Waltzing Wonderland*, at the Verona Theater on May 29.

(A) will perform
(B) is performed
(C) performing
(D) has been performed

118. Webmax's experts ------- all data from the traffic to your site to help determine the best way to target potential customers.

(A) reassure
(B) attract
(C) possess
(D) analyze

119. The study confirmed that providing more government grants has led directly to higher college -------.

(A) admission
(B) admit
(C) admits
(D) admittedly

120. The handbags were the same brand, but due to being produced at different factories, their quality differed -------.

(A) significantly
(B) lastingly
(C) properly
(D) brightly

GO ON TO THE NEXT PAGE

121. The manager scheduled a last-minute meeting to announce ------- will be promoted to the assistant director position.

(A) who
(B) those
(C) whose
(D) which

122. One of the ------- reasons for voter support of Ms. Grady is her promise to improve public facilities.

(A) rapid
(B) primary
(C) diligent
(D) sensitive

123. If the current sales trends continue, Gilana Autos will have a budget ------- of two million dollars at the end of December.

(A) procedure
(B) surplus
(C) negotiation
(D) assembly

124. How ------- the stain remover works depends on the amount of time it is left on the fabric.

(A) effectiveness
(B) effect
(C) more effective
(D) effectively

125. Faculty members as well as students ------- in classes for the spring term are encouraged to attend the reception.

(A) have enrolled
(B) enrolled
(C) will enroll
(D) enroll

126. The durable power tools created by Nix Industrial are suitable for amateurs and professionals -------.

(A) alike
(B) nearly
(C) very
(D) rightfully

127. Most of the conference's ------- live in the central region of the country.

(A) presenting
(B) presentations
(C) presenters
(D) presented

128. ------- implementation of the new safety policy may take a few weeks or longer.

(A) Evident
(B) Successful
(C) Fortunate
(D) Casual

129. Managers at Sigmund Insurance are more likely to promote employees ------- on the company's mission statement.

(A) focusing
(B) focus
(C) focuses
(D) have focused

130. All businesses operating in the country must ------- with these data protection measures.

(A) combine
(B) interfere
(C) comply
(D) associate

PART 6

Directions: Read the texts that follow. A word, phrase, or sentence is missing in parts of each text. Four answer choices for each question are given below the text. Select the best answer to complete the text. Then mark the letter (A), (B), (C), or (D) on your answer sheet.

Questions 131-134 refer to the following article.

BALTIMORE (April 9)—The fitness club chain Power Gym ------- (**131.**) changes to its membership options. A spokesperson from the company's head office, Frank Jacobs, said they are adjusting their policies based on customer feedback.

------- (**132.**). The new policy will allow people to purchase one-day, one-week, or one-month passes, depending on their needs. This will support the company's commitment to making the gym convenient and ------- (**133.**). A parking garage will also be added to the gym's main site downtown. ------- (**134.**) will begin on that project sometime in June.

131. (A) opposed
(B) collaborated
(C) received
(D) announced

132. (A) Gym users will no longer have to purchase an annual membership.
(B) Power Gym is seeking new employees to keep up with demand.
(C) The chain is well-known on the East Coast for its engaging classes.
(D) Power Gym sells workout gear recommended by its instructors.

133. (A) accessing
(B) access
(C) accessible
(D) accesses

134. (A) Assistance
(B) Construction
(C) Entrance
(D) Specifications

GO ON TO THE NEXT PAGE →

Questions 135-138 refer to the following article.

Model Boats at the Edenton Maritime Museum

From August 1 to August 31, the Edenton Maritime Museum will host *To the Seas*. This -------(135.) features model boats crafted to a high degree of accuracy to their real-life counterparts. It also educates visitors about the fragility of sailors and how their safety relies -------(136.) their understanding of and respect for the sea. Those who visit the museum -------(137.) the new self-guided audio tour equipment. -------(138.). *To the Seas* is included in the regular price of museum admission.

135. (A) exhibit
(B) essay
(C) award
(D) tournament

136. (A) on
(B) with
(C) into
(D) as

137. (A) are also trying
(B) also tried
(C) have also tried
(D) can also try

138. (A) Experienced and friendly guides are welcome to apply.
(B) The closure is expected to be temporary.
(C) Fortunately, the volunteers are very dedicated.
(D) Explore each display at your own pace.

Questions 139-142 refer to the following e-mail.

To: Miyo Kudo <kudom@sebssoaps.com>
From: Sebastian Beneventi <sebastian@applinghealth.com>
Date: July 2
Subject: Pitch meeting

Dear Ms. Kudo,

I have disappointing news about the sales pitch meeting planned for July 12 to discuss your handmade soaps. We must reschedule this ------- (139.) because of other work obligations. Our team has decided to attend the Westbury Trade Fair, so all of our time and effort must be devoted to this ------- (140.) event.

------- (141.). We believe your soaps would complement our current inventory well. The trade fair will take place on July 25, so I plan to ------- (142.) with you after that. I apologize for any inconvenience this may cause.

Sincerely,

Sebastian Beneventi

Purchasing Director, Appling Health

139. (A) appointment
(B) performance
(C) reservation
(D) rehearsal

140. (A) critically
(B) critical
(C) critic
(D) criticize

141. (A) Everyone thought you made a lot of excellent points.
(B) It takes a long time to prepare some sample goods.
(C) As we discussed, previous experience is required.
(D) However, we are still very interested in your product line.

142. (A) agree
(B) reconnect
(C) compete
(D) sympathize

GO ON TO THE NEXT PAGE →

Questions 143-146 refer to the following press release.

WELLINGTON (12 September)—Kerwyn Mart is planning to abandon its 10 P.M. closing time and adopt a 24-hour opening schedule. The ------- (**143.**) hours are set to begin from 1 October. Many customers ------- (**144.**) the change very convenient, especially those who work irregular hours or who need essential items unexpectedly.

"We are excited about having more chances to serve our customers," said Kerwyn Mart spokesperson Paul Yates. "------- (**145.**), this will create employment opportunities, as we need to hire several new workers for the checkout area. The store's lighting and heating are already kept on around the clock for security reasons and for the comfort of our shelf-stocking team. ------- (**146.**)."
Kerwyn Mart has three locations within the Wellington city limits.

143. (A) insignificant
(B) historic
(C) cleaner
(D) longer

144. (A) had found
(B) found
(C) has been finding
(D) will find

145. (A) Nonetheless
(B) For example
(C) At the same time
(D) If not

146. (A) We hope to prevent this from happening again.
(B) Several people are being considered for promotion.
(C) So, this is not expected to greatly increase our utility expenses.
(D) Otherwise, the store layout would have to be changed.

PART 7

Directions: In this part, you will read a selection of texts, such as magazine and newspaper articles, e-mails, and instant messages. Each text or set of texts is followed by several questions. Select the best answer for each question and mark the letter (A), (B), (C), or (D) on your answer sheet.

Questions 147-148 refer to the following e-mail.

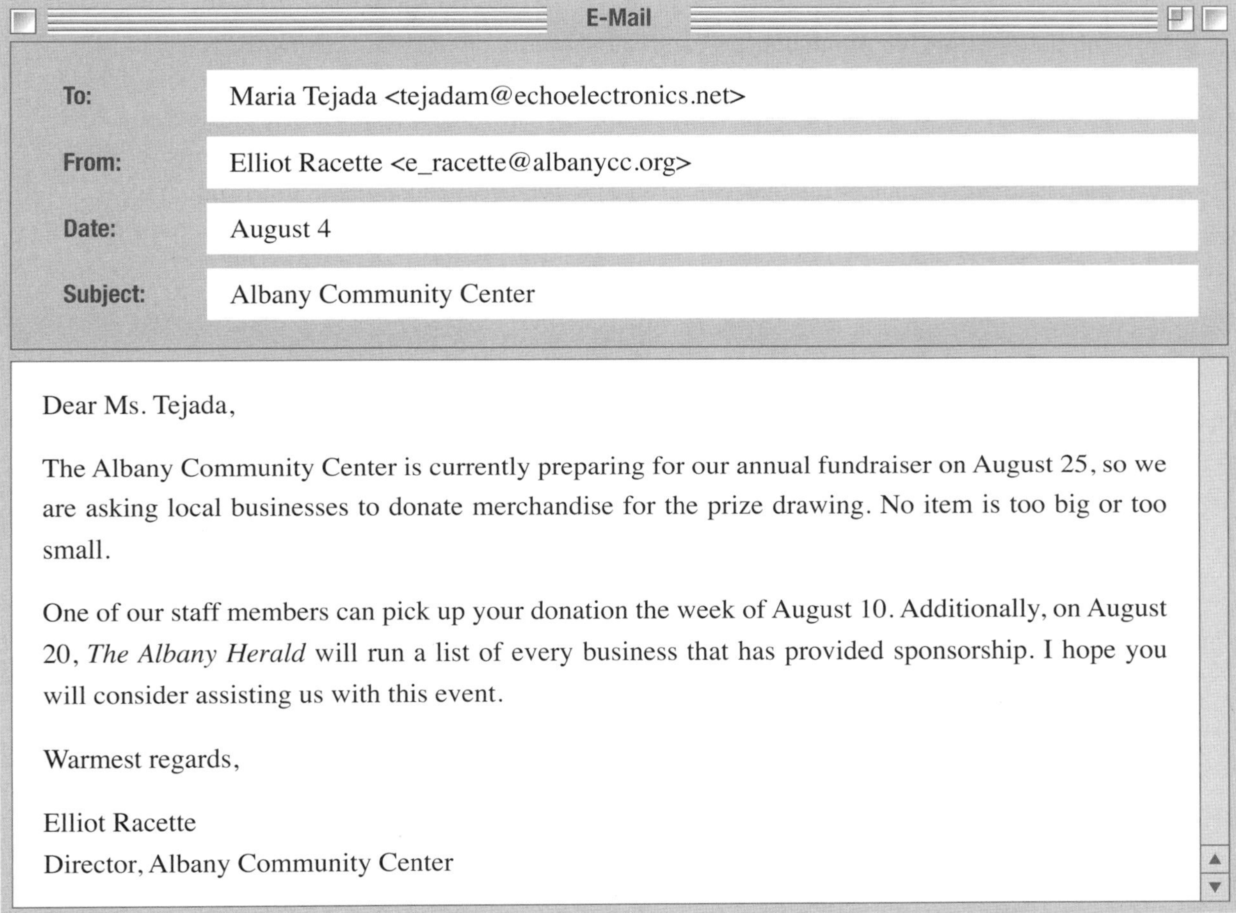

E-Mail

To: Maria Tejada <tejadam@echoelectronics.net>

From: Elliot Racette <e_racette@albanycc.org>

Date: August 4

Subject: Albany Community Center

Dear Ms. Tejada,

The Albany Community Center is currently preparing for our annual fundraiser on August 25, so we are asking local businesses to donate merchandise for the prize drawing. No item is too big or too small.

One of our staff members can pick up your donation the week of August 10. Additionally, on August 20, *The Albany Herald* will run a list of every business that has provided sponsorship. I hope you will consider assisting us with this event.

Warmest regards,

Elliot Racette
Director, Albany Community Center

147. Why did Mr. Racette send the e-mail?
(A) To make a request for goods
(B) To thank a business for a donation
(C) To decline an invitation
(D) To inform a prize winner

148. According to the e-mail, what will happen on August 20?
(A) Some items will be picked up.
(B) A local fundraiser will be held.
(C) A community center will reopen.
(D) A list of sponsors will be publicized.

GO ON TO THE NEXT PAGE

Questions 149-150 refer to the following review.

http://www.merch-review.com/electronics/video_doorbells

Review Category: Electronics
Product: Bessel video doorbell
Reviewer: Heather Arroyo

My friend bought the Chimetime doorbell and raved about it, but I was looking for something more affordable. I tried the Bessel video doorbell on my front door, and I love it. I can check it from my smartphone anytime, and the information can be uploaded wirelessly to the cloud. It is suitable for any kind of weather, and the battery lasts a long time because it only turns on when movement is detected. The setup was easy, too. I would highly recommend this product to anyone looking for a way to monitor the entrance of their property. In fact, I'd love to have one for my back door as well!

149. What is suggested about Bessel doorbells?
(A) They are more expensive than Chimetime doorbells.
(B) They have a fast-charging battery.
(C) They are activated by motion.
(D) They offer a variety of sound options.

150. What did Ms. Arroyo most likely do after posting the review?
(A) She traded a product with her friend.
(B) She requested replacement parts from a manufacturer.
(C) She downloaded a user guide to her phone.
(D) She purchased another Bessel doorbell.

Questions 151-152 refer to the following text-message chain.

Edward Duvall [2:03 P.M.]
Hi, Joan. Since the deadline for returning our customer surveys has passed, I'll start working on analyzing the results of the ones we received.

Joan Salgado [2:05 P.M.]
Thanks! I hope we get better responses this time. The last survey showed that a lot of our guests were disappointed with their stay, especially those in our standard rooms.

Edward Duvall [2:07 P.M.]
Well, the main complaint was about housekeeping issues, and those have been resolved.

Joan Salgado [2:08 P.M.]
That's true.

Edward Duvall [2:10 P.M.]
I'm interested in seeing what people think of the new sofas and chairs we have in the lobby. They are a lot softer and nicer to sit on.

Joan Salgado [2:11 P.M.]
That's what everyone's saying. I haven't had a chance to try them myself yet.

151. Where most likely do the writers work?
(A) At a clothing shop
(B) At a hotel
(C) At a supermarket
(D) At a home furnishings store

152. At 2:11 P.M., what does Ms. Salgado most likely mean when she writes, "That's what everyone's saying"?
(A) She thinks an entrance has a more modern look.
(B) She supposes that some furniture is more comfortable now.
(C) She would like an error to be addressed soon.
(D) She agrees that Mr. Duvall has been working hard.

GO ON TO THE NEXT PAGE

Questions 153-154 refer to the following article.

Recall of Bratton Smartwatches

September 3—Smartwatch manufacturer Bratton has announced the recall of its Dola-9 line of smartwatches after being on the market for only 2 weeks. No serious injuries have been reported, but the product presents a risk of burns to the user, as the battery in the device may get too hot. Customers with a faulty device are eligible for a replacement or a full refund. Those who own a Dola-9 smartwatch are asked to contact the company at 1-800-555-7932. Once connected, you can input the serial number and automatically be informed of what steps to take next. Those with further inquiries can also leave a message for the customer service team.

153. What is indicated about the Dola-9 smartwatch?

(A) Its battery can overheat.
(B) It takes two weeks to be replaced.
(C) Its mileage is not recorded correctly.
(D) It has caused severe injuries.

154. What does the article recommend that Dola-9 owners do first?

(A) Visit a store
(B) Reset the device
(C) Call a helpline
(D) E-mail customer service

Questions 155-157 refer to the following online form.

</>

Quesada Inc.
707 City View Street
Myrtle Beach, SC 29577

Customer Type: [V] New [ ] Existing
Date: April 20
Phone Number: 843-555-4628
Name: Patrick Carter
E-mail Address: p.carter@carterandbrown.com
Best Time of Day to Call: morning

Additional Comments/Notes: I've just bought the office complex on Harahan Street for use by my accounting firm. Through an Internet search, I found many recommendations for your services. I hope you can assist with replanting the front flowerbeds and keeping the grass and bushes tidy. Please provide an estimate on the approximate cost of the initial visit and the ongoing upkeep. Thanks.

155. Why did Mr. Carter complete the form?
(A) To dispute a charge
(B) To request some information
(C) To make a complaint
(D) To recommend a service

156. What is suggested about Mr. Carter?
(A) He is a former Quesada Inc. employee.
(B) He recently purchased a building.
(C) He has changed his phone number.
(D) He closed a business account.

157. What most likely is Quesada Inc.?
(A) A delivery service
(B) An Internet service provider
(C) An accounting firm
(D) A landscaping company

GO ON TO THE NEXT PAGE

Questions 158-160 refer to the following instructions.

Senatobia Appliances

Model: RC-9203

Total Capacity: 5.3 cubic feet
Motor Type: Digital Inverter Motor
Dimensions: 27" W x 38.7" H x 34.5" D

1. Coat the interior of the drum with full-strength white vinegar using a spray bottle.
2. Let it sit for five minutes and then wipe away using a microfiber cloth.
3. Pull out the detergent dispenser drawer, hand wash it in warm soapy water, and replace it.
4. Fill the detergent dispenser with two cups of white vinegar.
5. Sprinkle baking soda around the interior of the drum and then run a cycle on the hottest setting without any clothing in it.
6. Allow the interior to air dry by opening the door and propping something against it so it does not close on its own.
7. Repeat these steps once every few months to ensure all parts are deeply cleaned regularly.

158. For what kind of device are the instructions most likely used?

(A) A washing machine
(B) A vacuum cleaner
(C) An oven
(D) A coffee maker

159. What is NOT a step in the instructions?

(A) Leaving a door open
(B) Spraying a liquid
(C) Removing a drawer
(D) Testing a temperature

160. Why would a user follow the instructions?

(A) To reduce the noise of an appliance
(B) To set up a machine before its first use
(C) To check that some features are working properly
(D) To ensure some components are thoroughly cleaned

Questions 161-163 refer to the following memo.

To: All Staff
From: Adrian Seda
Subject: Coming soon
Date: March 14

As you are aware, we are interested in bringing more traffic to our Web site. —[1]—. In light of this, we will add a travel blog that will be updated weekly. It will include articles about the destinations where we offer packages. —[2]—. This may lead to more bookings.

I'll write the first article, which will be about the tour to Indonesia that I recently led. —[3]—. Others on staff are encouraged to contribute, and we also welcome content from customers, which they can supply to us in exchange for discounts. Any photos included with the articles should look professional, but they can be edited if needed. Further plans will be discussed at the next staff meeting. —[4]—.

161. Why did Mr. Seda send the memo?

(A) To explain a new vacation policy
(B) To remind staff to update their software
(C) To ask for recommendations on where to visit
(D) To announce a new section on a Web site

162. Who most likely is Mr. Seda?

(A) A local journalist
(B) A tour guide
(C) A professional photographer
(D) A magazine editor

163. In which of the positions marked [1], [2], [3], and [4] does the following sentence best belong?

"Ideally, they will generate interest in these places."

(A) [1]
(B) [2]
(C) [3]
(D) [4]

GO ON TO THE NEXT PAGE

Questions 164-167 refer to the following brochure.

Train today for a better tomorrow at the McInnis Institute!

Air Conditioning Repair Course
The McInnis Institute has been training and supporting repair technicians for over 30 years. Air conditioning services are always in high demand, even in the winter months, when routine maintenance is carried out. So, as an air conditioning repair technician, you can enjoy steady work at a reasonable hourly rate.

Study during our evening or weekend courses to avoid any disruptions to your current job. You can complete the program in two years, which includes a six-month apprentice period.

Why choose the McInnis Institute?
- Professional instructors with real-world experience
- All necessary gear is provided and yours to keep, or bring your own and receive a percentage off your course fee
- Students are invited to our quarterly networking dinner so they can meet potential employers
- Graduates have exclusive access to our job database, which is searchable for local, regional, and national jobs
- Monthly payments toward your tuition rather than having to prepare a lump sum

Unlock your earning potential!

	Average Hourly Rate: Recent graduate	Average Hourly Rate: Three years' experience
Regular service	$50	$95
Emergency call-out	$90	$150

Visit our Web site at www.mcinnisinst.com to register for an upcoming course or to get further details.

164. What benefit of working as a repair technician does the brochure mention?
(A) Job stability
(B) Seasonal bonuses
(C) Flexible working hours
(D) Paid vacation time

165. To whom is the institute offering a discount?
(A) People who sign up for the course early
(B) People who have prior work experience
(C) People who join a mailing list
(D) People who supply their own gear

166. According to the brochure, what is included in the course?
(A) Downloads of instructional videos
(B) Access to a list of customers
(C) Invitations to networking events
(D) Coaching on interview strategies

167. What does the McInnis Institute allow students to do?
(A) Take a portion of the course online
(B) Practice on site after hours
(C) Get support for two years after graduating
(D) Pay tuition in installments

Questions 168-171 refer to the following e-mail.

E-Mail

To: Walter Bauman <w_bauman@swindellpost.com>
From: Rachel Helm <rachel@gallowaypark.org>
Date: June 3
Subject: Hike at Galloway National Park

Dear Mr. Bauman,

Thank you for reserving your spot on our upcoming guided hiking tour of Galloway National Park on June 12. As requested, you have been assigned to the "Moderate Pace" group, and the hike is expected to last approximately four and a half hours. —[1]—. We will depart from the Visitors Center at 9 A.M.; we ask that you arrive at least 15 minutes early. If you drive rather than take public transportation, you can get an all-day parking pass at the Visitors Center for $3.00. The hike will include several stops for taking scenic pictures, including a stop at Rosewood Lake, which can only be reached on foot and is not accessible by any roads. —[2]—. You should wear sturdy and comfortable hiking boots. If you have recently purchased new ones, we recommend taking some walks with them in advance to break them in. —[3]—. A packed lunch will be provided, and each hiker will be given a backpack to use. Please note that there are no storage lockers or secure areas for you to leave your belongings, so you will have to carry everything you bring with you. —[4]—.

If you have any questions, please feel free to contact me at this e-mail address.

Sincerely,

Rachel Helm
Activities Director, Galloway National Park

168. What is the purpose of the e-mail?
(A) To explain a change to a schedule
(B) To provide information about an activity
(C) To request some personal details
(D) To give driving directions to a site

169. What is suggested about Rosewood Lake?
(A) It may be too cold for swimming.
(B) It can be seen from the Visitors Center.
(C) It is off limits for part of the year.
(D) It is in a remote area.

170. What does Ms. Helm indicate about personal items?
(A) There are checks that they must undergo.
(B) There is no place to store them.
(C) They should not be too heavy.
(D) They are at risk of getting wet.

171. In which of the positions marked [1], [2], [3], and [4] does the following sentence best belong?

"This will help to prevent discomfort during the hike."

(A) [1]
(B) [2]
(C) [3]
(D) [4]

GO ON TO THE NEXT PAGE

Questions 172-175 refer to the following online chat discussion.

Gerald Lee [9:00 A.M.]	Good morning, Alan and Theresa. I'm so glad that you've agreed to be suppliers for Sunshine Floral. We will begin on a trial basis and proceed from there. We always aim to source our flowers from gardeners in the area to help support the local economy. Did the recent heavy rain affect your first shipment?
Alan Finch [9:02 A.M.]	It wasn't a problem for me because I use a greenhouse. I can make the first delivery as planned.
Gerald Lee [9:03 A.M.]	I'm glad to hear that, Alan.. You'll be our first supplier of the Juliet variety of roses.
Theresa Schaeffer [9:03 A.M.]	Everything is fine on my end as well, so I can stick to the original timeline, sending everything tomorrow. My miniature roses are looking perfect at the moment.
Gerald Lee [9:05 A.M.]	Fantastic! I've sent you both a checklist of what we require. We can only accept flowers that meet our standards.
Alan Finch [9:06 A.M.]	I've taken a close look at it.
Theresa Schaeffer [9:07 A.M.]	So have I.
Gerald Lee [9:08 A.M.]	Great! I'll inform the morning shift workers that they need to clear enough space in our refrigerator for your deliveries.

SEND

172. Who most likely is Mr. Lee?

(A) An event coordinator
(B) A landowner
(C) A professional gardener
(D) A business manager

173. What is true about Mr. Finch's and Ms. Schaeffer's roses?

(A) They have already been shipped.
(B) They will be moved into greenhouses.
(C) They are of the same variety.
(D) They were not affected by the weather.

174. At 9:07 A.M., what does Ms. Schaeffer most likely mean when she writes, "So have I"?

(A) She has reviewed a checklist.
(B) She is interested in working with Mr. Finch.
(C) She has experience dealing with flower shops.
(D) She is willing to try a new growing method.

175. What does Mr. Lee plan to do next?

(A) Inform Mr. Finch and Ms. Schaeffer of a deadline
(B) Check the samples sent by Mr. Finch and Ms. Schaeffer
(C) Provide details about some contract terms
(D) Tell employees to make room for some items

GO ON TO THE NEXT PAGE

Questions 176-180 refer to the following letter and form.

Modern Cycling Monthly

Enjoy the ride!

Nakula Patel
347 Gateway Avenue
Bakersfield, CA 93301
January 13

Dear Mr. Patel,

Thank you for being a *Modern Cycling Monthly* subscriber. We hope you are enjoying our articles on trail selection tips, cycling equipment, original ideas for preparing for races, and more. We are pleased to let you know that you can get free issues of *Modern Cycling Monthly* by referring your friends. To participate in this new program, simply share your unique referral code P2495 with others and ask them to enter it when they order a one-year subscription. For each person who does so, whether they sign up for the print or online version, you'll have another month added to your subscription. Furthermore, if you refer a friend by February 5, we will send you a free *Modern Cycling Monthly* water bottle. Visit our Web site for more information.

Warmest regards,

The *Modern Cycling Monthly* Team

Modern Cycling Monthly

Subscription Status

Name: Nakula Patel

Delivery Address: 347 Gateway Avenue, Bakersfield, CA 93301

Account #: 06478

Subscription: Active

Subscription Expiration: December 20*

*Includes one free month (Referral P2495: processed January 29)

Your subscription will expire on December 20. We will e-mail you one month before this date to remind you to renew your subscription.

176. What is the purpose of the letter?

(A) To offer recommendations for articles
(B) To request a payment for a subscription
(C) To confirm a change of address
(D) To introduce a referral program

177. In the letter, the word "original" in paragraph 1, line 2, is closest in meaning to

(A) occurring
(B) creative
(C) initial
(D) precise

178. What is indicated about *Modern Cycling Monthly* in the letter?

(A) It has hired some new writers.
(B) It is available in two different formats.
(C) It is aimed at bicycle manufacturers.
(D) It offers discounts on equipment.

179. What is suggested about Mr. Patel?

(A) He used a coupon toward his subscription order.
(B) He wants to change his mailing address.
(C) He has recently taken up cycling.
(D) He is eligible for a free gift.

180. What will be sent to Mr. Patel in November?

(A) A reminder to renew
(B) A list of bicycle races
(C) A new cycling gear catalog
(D) A bill for the upcoming year

GO ON TO THE NEXT PAGE

Questions 181-185 refer to the following e-mail and article.

To:	Layla Fiorini ⟨l.fiorini@bradberry.com⟩
From:	Jack Donohue ⟨j.donohue@bradberry.com⟩
Date:	February 18
Subject:	Product demonstrations
Attachment:	demo_article

Hi, Layla,

I read an interesting article in *Retail Trade Magazine*. The author focuses on giving product demonstrations at industry events. However, I believe the contents are applicable to the demonstrations we're running at our department store as well.

Could you please make adjustments to your next demonstration based on the author's tip? I know you're giving one early next month, but it shouldn't take much time to review the details in the article. Let's meet on February 25 to discuss this further.

Thanks!

Jack Donohue
General Manager, Bradberry Department Store

Product Demonstrations Done Right

By Evelyn Taunton

Giving a product demonstration at an industry trade fair or expo is an opportunity to reach hundreds, or even thousands, of new customers. Before you even think about giving a demonstration, make sure that you have enough stock on hand to keep up with a surge in orders. I have seen so many companies provide an excellent demonstration, only to tell customers that they cannot fulfill their orders. It happens all the time.

If you're limited to the number of demonstrations you can give, hold them when the volume of visitors is at its highest. To keep the audience members engaged, let them have hands-on experience using the device. Additionally, it may be helpful to watch the demonstrations of others to get some ideas. Just be sure to note down anything that could be applied to your own demonstration.

181. How does Mr. Donohue want Ms. Fiorini to improve the product demonstrations?

(A) By giving customers a chance to try the product themselves
(B) By including more visual elements in the demonstration
(C) By avoiding the use of too much technical language
(D) By learning about the attendees' needs in advance

182. According to Mr. Donohue, when will Ms. Fiorini's next demonstration most likely take place?

(A) On February 18
(B) On February 25
(C) On March 2
(D) On March 30

183. What mistake does Ms. Taunton say is common regarding demonstrations?

(A) Using an unsuitable venue
(B) Lacking sufficient stock
(C) Making them too long
(D) Skipping important features

184. In the article, the word "volume" in paragraph 2, line 3, is closest in meaning to

(A) issue
(B) amount
(C) dimension
(D) loudness

185. What advice does Ms. Taunton give about attending demonstrations?

(A) People should e-mail their questions.
(B) People should sit near the front.
(C) People should take notes.
(D) People should read a manual.

GO ON TO THE NEXT PAGE →

Questions 186-190 refer to the following advertisement, e-mail, and price list.

Tillie's

www.tilliesservice.com

Give your windows a new look with custom curtains that have a perfect fit! Curtains can reflect your personal taste, and they also have a practical use. Whether you need them to block out light, keep in heat, or protect your privacy, we can help you find the right fabric. And our experienced employees will visit your home in person to ensure the accuracy of the measurements. We have hundreds of colors and patterns in various fabrics such as silk, wool, cotton, and velvet.

Most orders take seven days from measurement to delivery. However, for an additional fee, you can request our express service and get your curtains in just three days. Please note that you must choose the fabric on the day of the measurement in order to take advantage of this service.

Visit our Web site for details. There you can also sign up for our monthly newsletter, which gives customers advance notification of sales, customer testimonials on recent projects, and pictures to help inspire you.

To: Yan Ong <ongyan@harliganmail.com>
From: Tillie's <service@tilliesservice.com>
Date: June 20
Subject: Your Tillie's Order

Dear Ms. Ong,

We are working on processing your express order for the curtains for your living room and bedroom. Eugene Vela, who measured your curtains this morning, forgot to ask whether you plan to pick up the curtains or have them delivered for a fee of $6.95. Your living room curtains with the standard lining will cost $7.00 per square foot. Your bedroom curtains with the blackout lining will cost $10.50 per square foot. I will send you the detailed invoice as soon as you let me know about the delivery. Please feel free to contact us with any questions or concerns.

Sincerely,

Brenda Graves, Customer Service Representative

Tillie's

693 Winslow Avenue
Salt Lake City, UT 84111
www.tilliesservice.com

Customers must pay $20.00 when they place an order and the remaining amount after receiving the curtains.

Price List (per square foot)

With Standard Lining

Cotton	$5.00
Wool	$7.00
Silk	$9.00
Velvet	$10.00

With Blackout Lining

Cotton	$6.50
Wool	$8.50
Silk	$10.50
Velvet	$11.50

186. What does the business specialize in?
(A) Creating custom-made curtains
(B) Designing home interiors
(C) Installing new windows
(D) Printing unique fabrics

187. According to the advertisement, what does the company offer monthly?
(A) New types of fabrics
(B) Comments from customers
(C) Discount coupons
(D) Answers from experts

188. What did Ms. Ong most likely do on June 20?
(A) She selected some fabric.
(B) She e-mailed Mr. Vela some measurements.
(C) She paid a delivery fee.
(D) She signed up for a newsletter.

189. Which fabric will probably be used in Ms. Ong's bedroom?
(A) Cotton
(B) Wool
(C) Silk
(D) Velvet

190. According to the price list, when should Ms. Ong make her first payment?
(A) While receiving a delivery
(B) When scheduling a visit
(C) After receiving a bill by e-mail
(D) Upon placing the order

GO ON TO THE NEXT PAGE

Questions 191-195 refer to the following article, flyer, and advertisement.

DC Footwear

March 19—Toronto-based DC Footwear has announced plans to open new stores across the country, adding locations in Montreal, Vancouver, and Calgary later this year. The Vancouver store is set to open first and will have the largest space of any store in the chain. According to company spokesperson Jennifer Aguilar, the exact grand opening date has not yet been determined, but it will likely be in late summer. Company officials expect to have the other two locations up and running by the start of the holiday shopping season.

DC Footwear's shoes are famous for both their performance and their style. The change is expected to boost profits and improve brand recognition, and company officials hope to eventually open retail outlets in the United States as well.

GREAT OPENING EVENT!

DC Footwear Vancouver
164 Spadina Avenue
Friday, September 8

Store manager Matthew Pomeroy is pleased to welcome you to the grand opening of DC Footwear's Vancouver branch! We will be serving complimentary refreshments all day, and anyone who makes a purchase can enter our drawing to win one of 50 DC Footwear gift certificates. Shoe designer Melanie Pascale will also be in attendance from 9 A.M. to 11 A.M. to answer your questions.

What we have to offer:
- Free foot measuring
- Comfortable seating for you to try on our merchandise
- Displays of protective sprays, polishes, and more to keep your shoes looking great; free samples available

And don't miss our upcoming openings in Montreal (October 6) and Calgary (October 13).

SEEKING SALES ASSOCIATES

DC Footwear Vancouver
164 Spadina Avenue

Duties include:
- Providing outstanding customer service
- Assisting with footwear measuring and selection
- Sharing product knowledge and explaining features clearly
- Processing purchases and returns

Please talk to the store manager when handing in your application.

191. Why was the article written?
(A) To introduce a new brand of shoes
(B) To explain a company's expansion plan
(C) To highlight a trend in Canada
(D) To announce a change in ownership

192. What is suggested in the article about DC Footwear's products?
(A) They are made from environmentally friendly materials.
(B) They are less expensive than competitors' products.
(C) They are endorsed by professional athletes.
(D) They are known for being stylish.

193. What is suggested about DC Footwear?
(A) The chain's largest store opens in September.
(B) All visitors have a chance to win a prize.
(C) The order of store openings was changed.
(D) Snacks will stop being served at 11 A.M.

194. According to the flyer, what is true about the store?
(A) It has not started accepting gift certificates yet.
(B) It offers fitting rooms to shoppers.
(C) It has a selection of shoe care products.
(D) It only sells shoes for sports.

195. Who should people speak to when submitting an application?
(A) Mr. Pomeroy
(B) Ms. Aguilar
(C) Ms. Pascale
(D) A customer service agent

GO ON TO THE NEXT PAGE →

Questions 196-200 refer to the following announcement and e-mails.

Urbina Property Management (UPM)

September 13—Kylie Marzano, Urbina Property Management's administration manager, will be stepping down from her role on September 30. We are grateful for her many years of service, and we are excited that she has decided to remain an important part of our business, as she will consult for the company a few hours a week going forward.

UPM is currently seeking a replacement for Ms. Marzano. The candidate will be responsible for providing legal advice regarding new business initiatives as well as daily operations. Other duties include drafting and negotiating new agreements, reviewing existing property deeds, and communicating with third parties. The candidate must be up to date on regulatory compliance within the industry. Fluency in both English and Spanish is required. Details on the application process can be found at www.urbinapropertymgmt.com.

To:	hiringcommittee@urbinapropertymgmt.com
From:	antoniocastilla@urbinapropertymgmt.com
Date:	October 8
Subject:	Administration Manager

Dear Committee Members,

As our pool of candidates for the administration manager role is quite small, I've reached out to my personal contacts. I believe that a former coworker of mine, Keith Henrich, would be an excellent fit. He meets or exceeds all of the requested qualifications, and he is cooperative and personable. I discussed the role with him, and he was interested. However, he is concerned about applying because he lives in Hartford, making it very time-consuming to get to and from work. We could possibly offer him the opportunity to work from home one day a week to help offset this. Please let me know what you think.

Sincerely,

Antonio Castilla
Chair, Urbina Property Management Hiring Committee

TO:	antoniocastilla@urbinapropertymgmt.com
FROM:	nicoleroman@urbinapropertymgmt.com
DATE:	October 8
SUBJECT:	Committee handbook

Thanks for putting Mr. Henrich forward as a job candidate. On another note, as members have voiced concerns about the level of commitment required to be a part of this committee, we will begin meeting only once a month to free up more time for members' other work tasks. I have updated the handbook as follows:

- The committee will meet on the first Monday of every month to discuss job candidates. Should an urgent need for the committee's advice arise, the head of the relevant department must first get approval from the committee chair to hold a special meeting.

Nicole Roman
Secretary, Urbina Property Management Hiring Committee

196. What does the announcement indicate about Ms. Marzano?
(A) She will assist in the hiring of her replacement.
(B) She will work part time for Urbina Property Management.
(C) She plans to open her own property management firm.
(D) She was a founder of Urbina Property Management.

197. What is suggested about Mr. Henrich?
(A) He is currently working remotely.
(B) He used to be Ms. Marzano's boss.
(C) He is familiar with current regulations.
(D) He is fluent in three languages.

198. Why is Mr. Henrich reluctant to apply for the position?
(A) The job duties are not well defined.
(B) The salary does not meet his expectations.
(C) The company has not been in operation long.
(D) The commute would be difficult.

199. What does Ms. Roman suggest about the hiring committee members?
(A) They are appointed by the business's owner.
(B) They have other responsibilities at the company.
(C) They update their handbook annually.
(D) They would like to expand the group's size.

200. What is indicated about Mr. Castilla?
(A) He can give approval for additional meetings.
(B) He is busy on Mondays.
(C) He wants to hire a recruitment firm.
(D) He is against a proposed policy change.

Stop! This is the end of the test. If you finish before time is called, you may go back to Parts 5, 6, and 7 and check your work.

▶ 정답 및 해설 p. 2

자동 채점 서비스
바로가기

에 듀 윌 토 익 실 전 서

LC+RC

TEST 02

LISTENING TEST

PART 1

PART 2

PART 3

PART 4

READING TEST

PART 5

PART 6

PART 7

LISTENING TEST

In the Listening test, you will be asked to demonstrate how well you understand spoken English. The entire Listening test will last approximately 45 minutes. There are four parts, and directions are given for each part. You must mark your answers on the separate answer sheet. Do not write your answers in your test book.

PART 1

Directions: For each question in this part, you will hear four statements about a picture in your test book. When you hear the statements, you must select the one statement that best describes what you see in the picture. Then find the number of the question on your answer sheet and mark your answer. The statements will not be printed in your test book and will be spoken only one time.

Statement (C), "He's making a phone call," is the best description of the picture, so you should select answer (C) and mark it on your answer sheet.

1.

2.

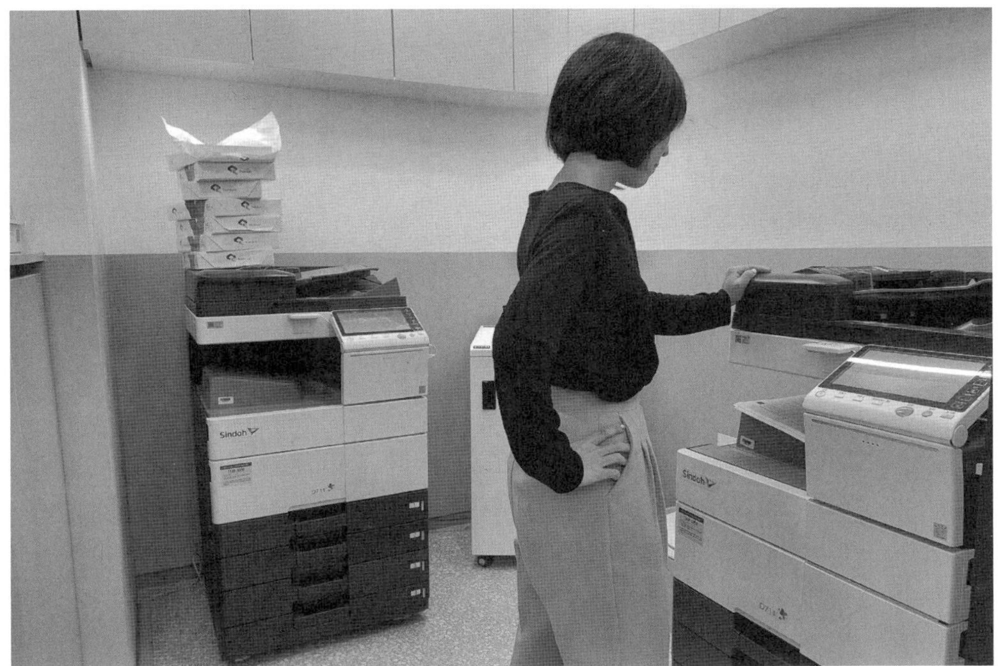

GO ON TO THE NEXT PAGE →

3.

4.

5.

6.

GO ON TO THE NEXT PAGE

PART 2

Directions: You will hear a question or statement and three responses spoken in English. They will not be printed in your test book and will be spoken only one time. Select the best response to the question or statement and mark the letter (A), (B), or (C) on your answer sheet.

7. Mark your answer on your answer sheet.

8. Mark your answer on your answer sheet.

9. Mark your answer on your answer sheet.

10. Mark your answer on your answer sheet.

11. Mark your answer on your answer sheet.

12. Mark your answer on your answer sheet.

13. Mark your answer on your answer sheet.

14. Mark your answer on your answer sheet.

15. Mark your answer on your answer sheet.

16. Mark your answer on your answer sheet.

17. Mark your answer on your answer sheet.

18. Mark your answer on your answer sheet.

19. Mark your answer on your answer sheet.

20. Mark your answer on your answer sheet.

21. Mark your answer on your answer sheet.

22. Mark your answer on your answer sheet.

23. Mark your answer on your answer sheet.

24. Mark your answer on your answer sheet.

25. Mark your answer on your answer sheet.

26. Mark your answer on your answer sheet.

27. Mark your answer on your answer sheet.

28. Mark your answer on your answer sheet.

29. Mark your answer on your answer sheet.

30. Mark your answer on your answer sheet.

31. Mark your answer on your answer sheet.

PART 3

Directions: You will hear some conversations between two or more people. You will be asked to answer three questions about what the speakers say in each conversation. Select the best response to each question and mark the letter (A), (B), (C), or (D) on your answer sheet. The conversations will not be printed in your test book and will be spoken only one time.

32. What is the purpose of the call?
(A) To make a reservation
(B) To request a refund
(C) To get driving directions
(D) To postpone an appointment

33. What does the man ask about?
(A) Arrival times
(B) Color preferences
(C) Payment details
(D) Program membership

34. According to the man, what is now available for free?
(A) A parking area
(B) An overnight service
(C) A fitness facility
(D) A morning meal

---

35. What does the man say is causing a problem?
(A) Heavy traffic
(B) An equipment failure
(C) Severe weather
(D) A power outage

36. What is the woman concerned about?
(A) Some costs may be higher than expected.
(B) Some tickets may not be refunded.
(C) The speakers may be late for a meeting.
(D) The speakers may miss a connection.

37. What does the man suggest doing?
(A) Speaking with a staff member
(B) Waiting for another announcement
(C) Searching for some information online
(D) Sending an urgent message

---

38. What is the woman calling about?
(A) Cutting machines
(B) Shipping containers
(C) Concrete pieces
(D) Power cables

39. What does the woman's company do?
(A) Building roads
(B) Designing gardens
(C) Importing goods
(D) Inspecting bridges

40. What will the woman probably do next?
(A) Check some supplies
(B) Wait on the line
(C) Provide credit card details
(D) Confirm an address

---

41. What does the speakers' company produce?
(A) Office furniture
(B) Sports equipment
(C) Clothing
(D) Automobiles

42. What does the man offer to do?
(A) Visit a branch
(B) Analyze some data
(C) Change a schedule
(D) Provide some instructions

43. Why will the man be busy on Thursday afternoon?
(A) He will be taking a tour of a facility.
(B) He will be interviewing job candidates.
(C) He will be having a consultation.
(D) He will be traveling to a conference.

GO ON TO THE NEXT PAGE

44. What is the purpose of the meeting?
(A) To create a customer survey
(B) To discuss a security upgrade
(C) To develop an advertising strategy
(D) To negotiate a contract

45. What is Kiho concerned about?
(A) Failing an inspection
(B) Losing customers
(C) Spending too much
(D) Confusing employees

46. What does the woman say she will do?
(A) File a complaint
(B) Contact some clients
(C) Place an order
(D) Send a report

---

47. Where most likely are the speakers?
(A) At a hair salon
(B) At a medical clinic
(C) At a library
(D) At a supermarket

48. What does the man imply when he says, "We haven't changed it for years"?
(A) He thinks his business is not modern enough.
(B) He does not plan to buy the products.
(C) He would like to adjust some contract terms.
(D) He has been the woman's loyal customer.

49. What does the woman ask the man to do?
(A) Watch a demonstration
(B) Sign a form
(C) Review a price list
(D) Try some samples

---

50. What most likely is the woman's area of expertise?
(A) Information technology
(B) Graphic arts
(C) International finance
(D) Electrical engineering

51. What is the woman worried about?
(A) Her lack of language skills
(B) Her busy schedule
(C) Her short work history
(D) Her expired certification

52. What does the man ask the woman about?
(A) How she found the job
(B) Whether she will relocate
(C) Who will make a hiring decision
(D) Where an interview will be held

---

53. What problem does the woman mention?
(A) A delivery vehicle broke down.
(B) Some merchandise is out of stock.
(C) A label contained an error.
(D) Some items were damaged.

54. Where does the man most likely work?
(A) At a coffee shop
(B) At a shipping company
(C) At a dry cleaner's
(D) At a clothing store

55. Why does the woman recommend a product?
(A) It is environmentally friendly.
(B) It is affordable.
(C) It is durable.
(D) It is large.

---

56. What does the speakers' company produce?

(A) Outdoor furniture
(B) Power tools
(C) Canned food
(D) Cleaning supplies

57. What does the man say will be given away?

(A) Discount coupons
(B) Gift certificates
(C) Tote bags
(D) Prize money

58. What does the man imply when he says, "The IT team is updating my software"?

(A) He isn't able to comply with her request.
(B) He wants to postpone the meeting with her.
(C) He is planning to complain about a service.
(D) He would like to explain why he missed the deadline.

---

59. What is the conversation about?

(A) A local election
(B) A new sports facility
(C) A research study
(D) A transportation network

60. What does the man say he has done?

(A) Visited some locations
(B) Hired an assistant
(C) Issued a permit
(D) Created a brochure

61. What will take place on October 8?

(A) An annual parade
(B) A training program
(C) A temporary closure
(D) A council meeting

April 7				
	Noon	1 P.M.	2 P.M.	3 P.M.
Luoyang	X	X		
Javier		X		
Bruce			X	
Madri	X		X	X

62. What kind of team do the speakers work on?

(A) Management
(B) Legal
(C) Design
(D) Accounting

63. Why does the woman want to meet on April 7?

(A) To plan a celebration
(B) To assess some software
(C) To assign new work tasks
(D) To review job candidates

64. Look at the graphic. At what time do the speakers plan to have a meeting?

(A) At noon
(B) At 1 P.M.
(C) At 2 P.M.
(D) At 3 P.M.

GO ON TO THE NEXT PAGE

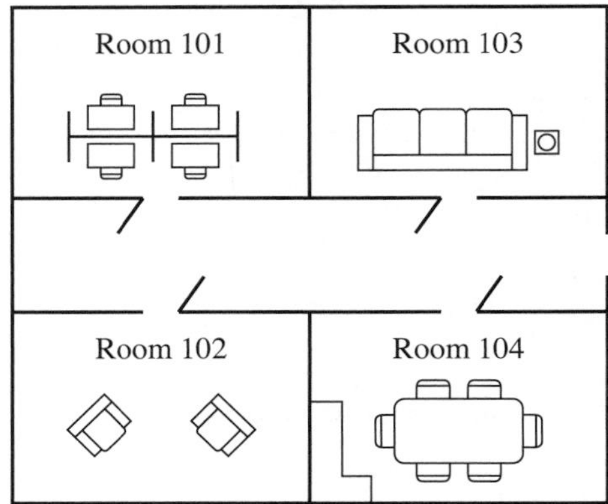

65. What does the man plan to do in June?
(A) Increase some prices
(B) Launch a business
(C) Hire more employees
(D) Redecorate an office

66. Look at the graphic. Which room does the woman talk about?
(A) Room 101
(B) Room 102
(C) Room 103
(D) Room 104

67. What does the man ask the woman to do?
(A) Provide cost-related information
(B) Submit a payment
(C) Set up an appointment
(D) Send him an address

Pre-Tour Checklist

1. Take attendance.
2. Pass out maps.
3. Ask if there are any questions.
4. Write down departure time.

68. Why is the man unable to lead a tour?
(A) He will meet with an important client.
(B) He will attend a medical appointment.
(C) He will participate in an industry event.
(D) He will take a business trip.

69. Look at the graphic. Which task does the man say he sometimes forgets?
(A) Task 1
(B) Task 2
(C) Task 3
(D) Task 4

70. What will the participants do at the end of the tour?
(A) Enjoy some refreshments
(B) Complete some forms
(C) Review a handout
(D) Watch a presentation

PART 4

Directions: You will hear some talks given by a single speaker. You will be asked to answer three questions about what the speaker says in each talk. Select the best response to each question and mark the letter (A), (B), (C), or (D) on your answer sheet. The talks will not be printed in your test book and will be spoken only one time.

71. What is the message mainly about?
(A) Writing an article
(B) Editing some photos
(C) Holding a contest
(D) Attending a trade fair

72. What does the speaker need confirmation about?
(A) A work schedule
(B) A proposed budget
(C) Some complaints
(D) Some judges

73. What does the speaker want to do?
(A) Consult an expert
(B) Place advertisements online
(C) Review some policies
(D) Launch a new Web site

---

74. Who most likely is the speaker?
(A) A news reporter
(B) A charity representative
(C) An event planner
(D) A city official

75. What kind of construction project does the speaker mention?
(A) A parking structure
(B) A library extension
(C) A wind farm
(D) An apartment building

76. Why is the speaker impressed?
(A) A budget was not fully spent.
(B) A task was completed early.
(C) Some materials were reused.
(D) Some profits set a record.

---

77. What is the speaker discussing?
(A) A cleanup project
(B) A security procedure
(C) A road closure
(D) A community picnic

78. Why does the speaker say, "it gets used every day"?
(A) To recruit some volunteers
(B) To recommend a replacement
(C) To explain a delay
(D) To justify a decision

79. What will the listeners most likely do next?
(A) Have a meal together
(B) Share their feedback
(C) View some pictures
(D) Meet an official

---

80. Why is the speaker meeting with the listeners?
(A) To introduce a product
(B) To interview for a job
(C) To offer insurance information
(D) To provide a training workshop

81. What benefit does the speaker mention?
(A) Fewer employee absences
(B) Reducing plastic waste
(C) Increased company profits
(D) Attracting new clients

82. What will the speaker show the listeners?
(A) Current prices
(B) Color options
(C) A size chart
(D) A user manual

GO ON TO THE NEXT PAGE →

83. Why will the speaker travel to Manchester?
(A) To recruit some employees
(B) To negotiate a contract
(C) To present an award
(D) To inspect a facility

84. What did the speaker recently do?
(A) She changed a train ticket.
(B) She upgraded a hotel room.
(C) She submitted some paperwork.
(D) She requested additional funds.

85. What does the speaker invite the listener to attend?
(A) A holiday parade
(B) A food festival
(C) A career fair
(D) An academic lecture

---

86. What is the speaker discussing?
(A) Employee uniforms
(B) Computer accessories
(C) Kitchen appliances
(D) Safety equipment

87. Why does the speaker say, "you know your team members well"?
(A) To express surprise
(B) To give a compliment
(C) To ask for suggestions
(D) To correct a mistake

88. What does the speaker remind the listeners about?
(A) A budget reduction
(B) A holiday party
(C) A training plan
(D) An office closure

---

89. What will the listeners learn about on the tour?
(A) Architectural styles
(B) Leadership styles
(C) Fashion styles
(D) Painting styles

90. What does the speaker mean when he says, "Few people know about this visit"?
(A) A document is missing information.
(B) Some places are very quiet today.
(C) A promotional campaign is not working.
(D) The tour includes a special stop.

91. What does the speaker encourage the listeners to do?
(A) Take a lot of pictures
(B) Read a book
(C) Post reviews online
(D) Pay by check

---

92. Who most likely is the speaker?
(A) A tour guide
(B) An interior decorator
(C) An environmental engineer
(D) A shop owner

93. What will be changed next month?
(A) The work schedule
(B) The type of packaging
(C) A payment procedure
(D) A business location

94. What will the speaker do next?
(A) Give a demonstration
(B) Post a notice
(C) Take a break
(D) Hold a celebration

Price List	
Product Code	Unit Price
D-54	$21
F-12	$38
G-90	$67
L-68	$79

95. What does the speaker's company produce?
(A) Bedding
(B) Hair accessories
(C) Footwear
(D) Furniture

96. Look at the graphic. How much will be added to the speaker's payment?
(A) $21
(B) $38
(C) $67
(D) $79

97. According to the speaker, what will take place in November?
(A) A sports competition
(B) A product launch
(C) A store opening
(D) A trade show

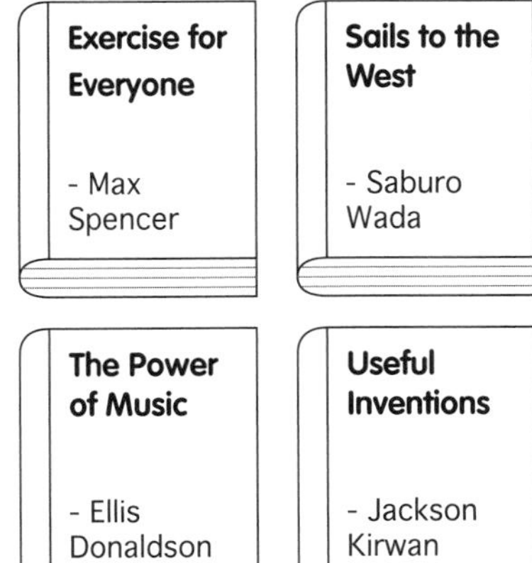

98. Where most likely is the speaker?
(A) At a business institute
(B) At a public library
(C) At a coffee shop
(D) At a bookstore

99. When did the speaker first come up with his book idea?
(A) While reading a magazine article
(B) While volunteering for a charity
(C) While visiting his relatives
(D) While watching a documentary

100. Look at the graphic. Who is the speaker?
(A) Max Spencer
(B) Saburo Wada
(C) Ellis Donaldson
(D) Jackson Kirwan

This is the end of the Listening test. Turn to Part 5 in your test book.

READING TEST

In the Reading test, you will read a variety of texts and answer several different types of reading comprehension questions. The entire Reading test will last 75 minutes. There are three parts, and directions are given for each part. You are encouraged to answer as many questions as possible within the time allowed.

You must mark your answers on the separate answer sheet. Do not write your answers in your test book.

PART 5

Directions: A word or phrase is missing in each of the sentences below. Four answer choices are given below each sentence. Select the best answer to complete the sentence. Then mark the letter (A), (B), (C), or (D) on your answer sheet.

101. Please provide your credit card details ------- a payment.

(A) will submit
(B) to submit
(C) submitted
(D) submit

102. There will be a small group discussion so that people can share their ------- of the facility.

(A) observe
(B) observations
(C) observant
(D) observantly

103. Due to a mechanical fault, the bus ------- the terminal two hours late.

(A) arrived
(B) continued
(C) traveled
(D) reached

104. The interns who will participate in our summer program must complete ------- human resources paperwork in advance.

(A) them
(B) they
(C) their
(D) themselves

105. The architect for the new BV Bank headquarters has ------- based the design on the nearby buildings.

(A) presume
(B) presumed
(C) presumably
(D) presumption

106. The wording of the survey questions should be ------- and easy to comprehend.

(A) exclusive
(B) fresh
(C) simple
(D) able

107. The ------- of its fleet is what makes customers choose Gregson Car Rentals.

(A) rely
(B) reliably
(C) reliable
(D) reliability

108. Masonex has plans to open franchises of its popular restaurant ------- the country.

(A) during
(B) under
(C) against
(D) across

109. Because so few people applied for the job, the hiring manager could not be ------- about filling the position.

(A) selective
(B) selection
(C) selectively
(D) selects

110. The man waiting to check into a room should be informed that ------- will be ready in 15 minutes.

(A) he
(B) his
(C) him
(D) himself

111. This training video is intended for cashiers ------- have never worked in a retail setting.

(A) who
(B) them
(C) what
(D) its

112. Taking flash photography of the artwork is ------- prohibited by the museum.

(A) strictly
(B) tensely
(C) importantly
(D) equally

113. The director of the orchestra believes that the free performances in the park can ------- young musicians.

(A) inspiration
(B) inspiring
(C) inspire
(D) inspirational

114. Because refunds are not offered on clearance merchandise, customers should inspect the items carefully ------- purchasing them.

(A) along
(B) except
(C) whereas
(D) before

115. Mr. Higgins makes contributions to local causes more often than ------- acknowledged.

(A) public
(B) publicized
(C) publication
(D) publicly

116. ------- losing two days' work due to a technical error, the team met the deadline for the report.

(A) Either
(B) Because of
(C) Even as
(D) Despite

117. Mr. Zamora will ------- how to adjust the settings of the optical scanner.

(A) enroll
(B) impress
(C) attempt
(D) demonstrate

118. With 15 ------- located throughout the state, Wright Hardware is the largest chain in Delaware.

(A) references
(B) branches
(C) routines
(D) currencies

119. *The Journal of Social Sciences* reported 10% more annual subscribers this year ------- it did last year.

(A) whenever
(B) only
(C) which
(D) than

120. ------- documents cannot be shared with anyone who is not a staff member without explicit permission from a manager.

(A) Realistic
(B) Internal
(C) Occasional
(D) Improved

GO ON TO THE NEXT PAGE →

121. The news feed will update ------- when your laptop is connected to a Wi-Fi network.

(A) automated
(B) automatically
(C) automation
(D) automatic

122. The new customer contract for Yorkie Video Streaming Services eliminates ------- language.

(A) confusing
(B) to confuse
(C) confuses
(D) confuse

123. Visitors must wash their hands thoroughly and put on gloves ------- entering the food preparation area.

(A) by the time
(B) otherwise
(C) prior to
(D) as long as

124. The shuttle from the Jade Hotel to the Spencer Convention Center departs at half-hour -------.

(A) disposals
(B) intervals
(C) divisions
(D) purposes

125. The goal of the workshop is to increase participants' ------- about food safety and hygienic practices.

(A) knowledgeable
(B) know
(C) knowledgeably
(D) knowledge

126. Unfortunately, the spelling error in the spring catalog ------- by the editor.

(A) overlooked
(B) overlooking
(C) used to overlook
(D) was overlooked

127. If you need to ------- your GC Clothing merchandise for another item, you must show your receipt to the customer service team.

(A) dress
(B) exchange
(C) display
(D) reassure

128. Hendrix Communications is working on increasing cell phone coverage ------- there is demand.

(A) another
(B) although
(C) wherever
(D) quickly

129. The lessons are broken down into short, ------- sections so learners can work on them in their spare time.

(A) manageably
(B) management
(C) manageable
(D) manages

130. Concord Enterprises has ------- from a small accounting firm to a nationally acclaimed financial corporation.

(A) regarded
(B) evolved
(C) determined
(D) transported

PART 6

Directions: Read the texts that follow. A word, phrase, or sentence is missing in parts of each text. Four answer choices for each question are given below the text. Select the best answer to complete the text. Then mark the letter (A), (B), (C), or (D) on your answer sheet.

Questions 131-134 refer to the following product review.

I was ------- (**131.**) to receive a free sample of Meadowlark Shampoo to try at home since I had heard a lot about the brand. To be honest, because the product is made exclusively from natural ingredients, I thought that the results would be mediocre. I was ------- (**132.**) surprised by how effective the shampoo was.

------- (**133.**). After using Meadowlark Shampoo a few times, however, I identified what was causing the problem. ------- (**134.**) was due to not working the product into my hair enough. After I corrected this issue, I was satisfied with the look of my hair. I highly recommend this shampoo because it is gentle on your scalp and also comes in a variety of great scents.

131. (A) delight
(B) delightful
(C) delights
(D) delighted

132. (A) probably
(B) flexibly
(C) pleasantly
(D) tightly

133. (A) Initially, it seemed worse than other brands I was using.
(B) On the contrary, the bottle was quite difficult to open.
(C) You can now find the shampoo at most supermarkets.
(D) Cheaper ingredients would have been a better option.

134. (A) Few
(B) It
(C) Another
(D) Them

GO ON TO THE NEXT PAGE →

Questions 135-138 refer to the following article.

A recent report showed a significant increase in the price of materials used to make solar panels. Over the past few years, new investors have started to reject traditional fuel sources such as petroleum. -------, the renewable energy sector is thriving. The ------- in the demand for solar panels has led to rising prices, as it seems companies and individuals alike want to diversify their energy options. Consumers will likely see an increase in consumer prices on panels soon. -------. The ------- increase is anywhere from 15 to 25%.

(blanks: 135., 136., 137., 138.)

135. (A) In general
(B) Likewise
(C) For instance
(D) In contrast

136. (A) change
(B) placement
(C) decision
(D) clarification

137. (A) Safety inspectors are monitoring the production process.
(B) This is because manufacturers must maintain their profit margins.
(C) Not all buildings are well positioned to take advantage of the panels.
(D) Heavy regulations on imports help to keep consistency in the industry.

138. (A) predicting
(B) predict
(C) prediction
(D) predicted

Questions 139-142 refer to the following article.

Tiger Fashions Opens Shop in Vancouver

Tiger Fashions, a clothing company known for its bold colors and modern designs, has opened a retail store in Vancouver. "Our ------- (139.) of the Canadian market showed that consumers are looking for ways to stand out, and our brand can certainly help them do so," said Jack Palmer, a company representative.

Tiger Fashions began as a small shop in San Francisco, and it quickly grew to 25 locations in its first six years. ------- (140.). "We ------- (141.) excited about reaching an entirely new group of customers," said Mr. Palmer. "This will help us with our plan to eventually bring our brand to shoppers ------- (142.) the world."

139. (A) examiner
(B) examined
(C) examination
(D) examine

140. (A) The Vancouver store will be its first branch outside of the U.S.
(B) Sales of jackets and outerwear are becoming more common.
(C) This change in leadership was better for the company.
(D) The clothing's fabric is made from recycled materials.

141. (A) were
(B) are
(C) have been
(D) being

142. (A) throughout
(B) onto
(C) along
(D) toward

GO ON TO THE NEXT PAGE →

Questions 143-146 refer to the following press release.

FOR IMMEDIATE RELEASE

Contact: Tina Newton, tnewton@sumnermedia.com

NEW YORK (July 18)—WM Publishing ------- (143.) the finalization of its sale to Sumner Media. This move is part of Sumner Media's plan to expand its reach. WM Publishing is best known for its educational materials, an area in which Sumner Media will be working for the first time. WM Publishing's board was seriously considering offers from three different media groups. ------- (144.).

Employees of WM Publishing will not only keep their jobs, ------- (145.) opportunities for further promotion within the company will also be available. Additionally, Sumner Media plans to improve the offices of the WM Publishing branches and devote ------- (146.) investment to technology in order to support the staff.

143. (A) to confirm
(B) will confirm
(C) has confirmed
(D) was confirmed

144. (A) Several others were made but rejected in the early stages.
(B) The publishing process will likely become more efficient.
(C) Sumner Media has recently changed its CEO.
(D) Approval for expansion of the building is pending.

145. (A) for
(B) as
(C) but
(D) or

146. (A) capable
(B) significant
(C) inadequate
(D) comfortable

PART 7

Directions: In this part, you will read a selection of texts, such as magazine and newspaper articles, e-mails, and instant messages. Each text or set of texts is followed by several questions. Select the best answer for each question and mark the letter (A), (B), (C), or (D) on your answer sheet.

Questions 147-148 refer to the following information.

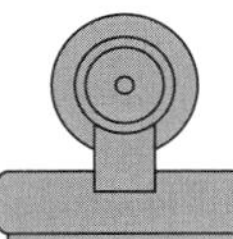

For your convenience, each boat is equipped with a storage container that is lockable and water resistant. Before we depart, if there is anything you would like to place in the container, please speak to your guide. Depending on the weather, the main seating area may get wet, so we highly recommend protecting your items. Please note that there is no fee for using the storage area, but we are not responsible for fragile or valuable items.

147. For whom most likely was the information written?

(A) Maintenance workers
(B) Boat owners
(C) Tour participants
(D) Security guards

148. What is mentioned about the service?

(A) It may be canceled in bad weather.
(B) It is offered at no charge.
(C) It sometimes has a waiting list.
(D) It requires showing an ID.

GO ON TO THE NEXT PAGE

Questions 149-150 refer to the following text-message chain.

Courtney Briggs [8:03 A.M.]
Hi, Luoyang. I'm picking up some extra balloons at the party store for our booth. Fortunately, they have the silver and red colors that we wanted. How is the setup going at the event center?

Luoyang Gu [8:08 A.M.]
Things are going smoothly at our booth. There are so many soda companies here. I hope we find a way to stand out. I think giving away free samples may be a good idea. By the way, I hate to send you on another errand, but would it be possible to get a few strings of lights too?

Courtney Briggs [8:10 A.M.]
I haven't left yet. I think I saw them a few aisles over. See you soon.

149. Where do the writers most likely work?

(A) At a travel agency
(B) At a beverage manufacturer
(C) At a shoe store chain
(D) At a real estate company

150. At 8:10 A.M., what does Ms. Briggs probably mean when she writes, "I haven't left yet"?

(A) She needs directions to a site.
(B) She is unsure about her responsibilities.
(C) She will be late for an event.
(D) She can complete a task.

Questions 151-152 refer to the following brochure.

Haven Fitness

www.myhavenfitness.com

At Haven Fitness, we want to help you look and feel great! Hiring a personal trainer is the best way to meet your goals and improve your health. Not sure personal training is right for you? Purchase our 10-session training package and get a free trial session. You can cancel within one week after the trial.

Personal Training Services

- Initial assessment of your fitness goals and needs
- Experienced trainers who can show you how to do the exercises
- Nutrition advice to accompany and support your training regime

Flexible Services

We are the only gym in the area to offer personal training through video conferencing. This is the perfect way to keep up with your training while traveling or if you don't have time to commute to the gym.

151. What is indicated about the service package?

(A) It includes a free trial session.
(B) It is eligible for a substantial discount.
(C) It can be canceled at any time.
(D) It is for new customers only.

152. According to the brochure, what is special about Haven Fitness?

(A) It is open every day of the year.
(B) It provides food to customers.
(C) It offers training remotely.
(D) It has the most affordable rates.

GO ON TO THE NEXT PAGE →

Questions 153-154 refer to the following job advertisement.

Properties Historian for English Heritage Foundation

The English Heritage Foundation is seeking a full-time properties historian for a two-year contract. The historian will be responsible for undertaking research at a number of the foundation's prehistoric sites in order to create print and digital materials for people visiting our sites. The historian will lead a small research team as well as correspond with external consultants when necessary. The role also includes promoting the foundation at various fundraising events throughout the year.

The candidate must have a degree in archaeology or the equivalent practical experience. A master's degree in a related field is highly desirable but not required. The position requires a considerable amount of travel to our various sites. To apply, visit www.eheritagefoundation.org/careers.

153. What is NOT mentioned as a duty of the properties historian?

(A) Communicating with external experts
(B) Attending fundraisers
(C) Developing content for visitors
(D) Publishing research in journals

154. What is indicated as a requirement of the position?

(A) Ability to travel extensively
(B) Experience in public speaking
(C) A master's degree
(D) A professional network

Questions 155-157 refer to the following e-mail.

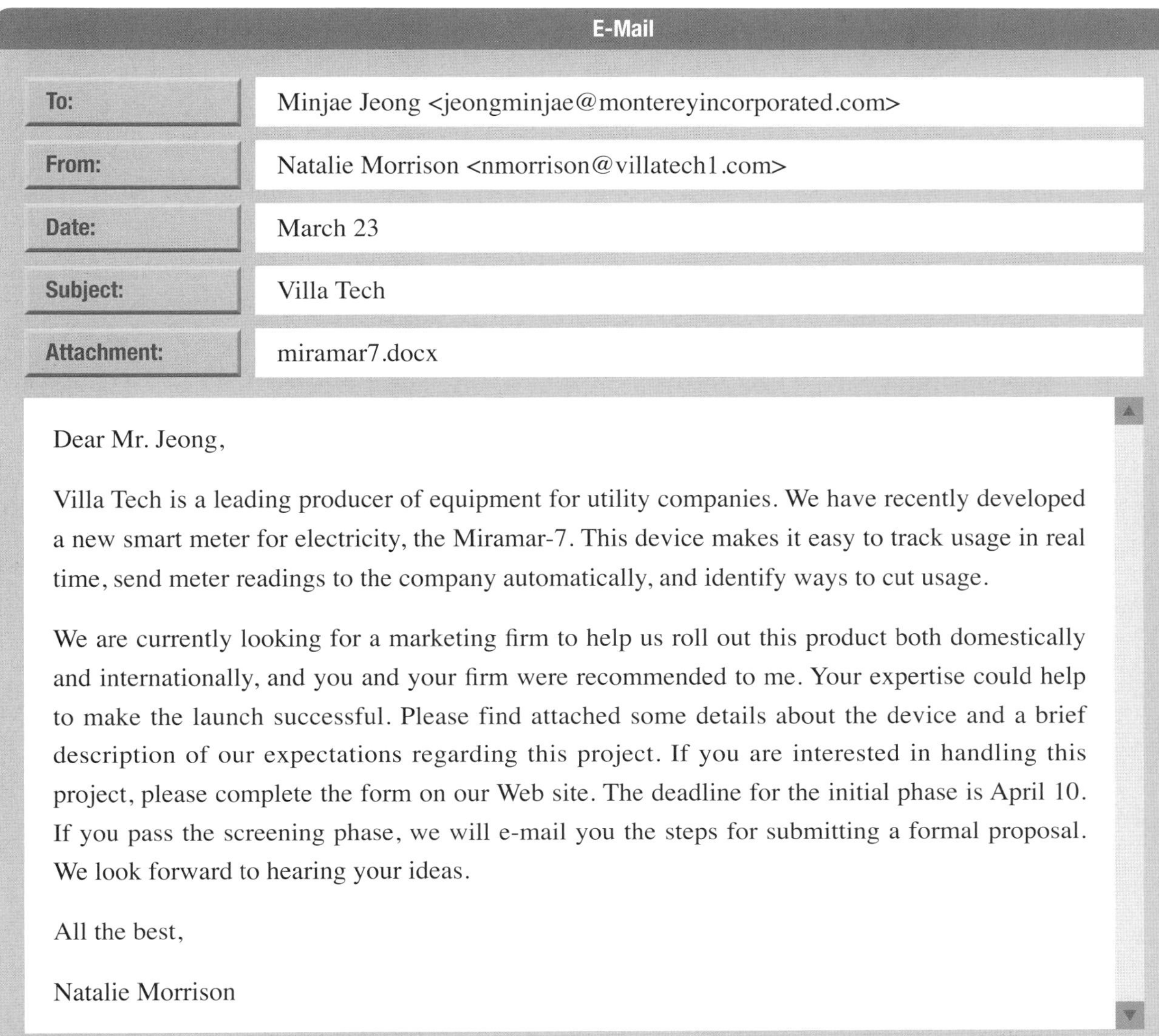

E-Mail

To: Minjae Jeong <jeongminjae@montereyincorporated.com>

From: Natalie Morrison <nmorrison@villatech1.com>

Date: March 23

Subject: Villa Tech

Attachment: miramar7.docx

Dear Mr. Jeong,

Villa Tech is a leading producer of equipment for utility companies. We have recently developed a new smart meter for electricity, the Miramar-7. This device makes it easy to track usage in real time, send meter readings to the company automatically, and identify ways to cut usage.

We are currently looking for a marketing firm to help us roll out this product both domestically and internationally, and you and your firm were recommended to me. Your expertise could help to make the launch successful. Please find attached some details about the device and a brief description of our expectations regarding this project. If you are interested in handling this project, please complete the form on our Web site. The deadline for the initial phase is April 10. If you pass the screening phase, we will e-mail you the steps for submitting a formal proposal. We look forward to hearing your ideas.

All the best,

Natalie Morrison

155. Who most likely is Mr. Jeong?

(A) An electronics manufacturer
(B) A marketing specialist
(C) A board member
(D) A product designer

156. What is the Miramar-7?

(A) A cooling system
(B) A kitchen appliance
(C) A mobile application
(D) An energy-monitoring device

157. What should Mr. Jeong do if he wants to work on a project?

(A) Attend a group interview
(B) Complete an online form
(C) Reply to the e-mail
(D) Print and return the attached document

GO ON TO THE NEXT PAGE

Questions 158-160 refer to the following Web page.

http://www.print4u.com/wait_times

Printing Wait Times

Print4U offers a range of printing services for business as well as personal projects. After you provide us with the file, we guarantee your printed items will be ready within the time frames listed below. You'll receive a text when your order is ready to be picked up. We can hold items for you for up to two weeks. We're open Monday to Wednesday from 8 A.M. to 9 P.M. and Thursday to Saturday from 8 A.M. to 7 P.M.

Product Type	Standard	Express
Documents	1–2 hours	30 minutes
Business Cards	2–3 days	Next day
Brochures and pamphlets	3–5 days	2 days
Banners	5–7 days	X

158. What is NOT indicated about Print4U?
(A) It can complete some projects within the same day.
(B) It closes at the same time on weekdays.
(C) It communicates with customers via text.
(D) Its express service is not available for all products.

159. The word "hold" in paragraph 1, line 3, is closest in meaning to
(A) support
(B) carry
(C) store
(D) restrain

160. What is the longest a customer would have to wait for brochures?
(A) Two days
(B) Three days
(C) Five days
(D) Seven days

Questions 161-164 refer to the following online chat discussion.

Kerry Atkins [9:43 A.M.]	Hi, Levi. I'm wondering if you got the photo of the vases our pottery studio needs to ship. We'll begin boxing them up soon to prepare them for transport.
Levi Marquez [9:44 A.M.]	Hi, Ms. Atkins. Yes, we have packaging big enough for them. Have you decided on what kind of cushioning you'll use?
Kerry Atkins [9:46 A.M.]	That's what's holding things up. I looked into low-density foam, but it's so expensive. There must be something else out there. I'm sure you've seen it all.
Levi Marquez [9:48 A.M.]	In your case, I think you should consider using brown paper. It's great because you can buy it almost anywhere, especially in stationery stores and art shops. Just crumple it up and surround the item with it.
Kerry Atkins [9:49 A.M.]	That sounds great. I'll give it a try. I've also had "Fragile" stickers printed to put on the exterior of the box. Should those just go on the side?
Levi Marquez [9:51 A.M.]	You should put them on the top, bottom, and at all four sides. You want to make sure they're easy to see. They can be easily overlooked otherwise.
Kerry Atkins [9:52 A.M.]	Got it. That's really helpful to know. Thank you!

161. Where most likely does Mr. Marquez work?

(A) At a tour company
(B) At a delivery service
(C) At a print shop
(D) At an accounting firm

162. At 9:46 A.M., what does Ms. Atkins most likely mean when she writes, "I'm sure you've seen it all"?

(A) Mr. Marquez should make a recommendation.
(B) Mr. Marquez has visited a business recently.
(C) Mr. Marquez will receive a new assignment.
(D) Mr. Marquez has made an error.

163. Why does Mr. Marquez recommend brown paper?

(A) It is readily available.
(B) It is environmentally friendly.
(C) It is durable.
(D) It is smooth.

164. What is suggested about the stickers?

(A) They may incur an additional fee.
(B) Their color should be changed.
(C) It is best to put them in multiple places.
(D) It is not necessary to use them for some items.

GO ON TO THE NEXT PAGE →

Questions 165-167 refer to the following e-mail.

E-Mail

To: Shreya Dayal <s_dayal@lingfordmail.com>
From: Reseda Insurance <accounts@resedains.com>
Date: April 8
Subject: Home Insurance

Dear Ms. Dayal,

Thank you for being a Reseda Insurance customer. According to our records, your home insurance (Policy #: 0267855) is set to expire on May 15. Please renew your policy to ensure the uninterrupted protection of your property. We recommend doing so before May 1 to lock in the current price for one more year, as our rates are going up on that date.

You should use our helpline if you have any inquiries. That's because you can get answers more efficiently.

Warmest regards,

Joanne Stroud
Customer Service, Reseda Insurance
Helpline: 1-800-555-1258

165. Why did Ms. Stroud send the e-mail?
(A) To remind Ms. Dayal about an overdue payment
(B) To notify Ms. Dayal of a personnel change
(C) To ask Ms. Dayal for some suggestions
(D) To encourage Ms. Dayal to continue a service

166. According to Ms. Stroud, what will the company do on May 1?
(A) Increase fees for a service
(B) Release a wider range of packages
(C) Send Ms. Dayal a confirmation letter
(D) Assess the value of a property

167. What is Ms. Dayal recommended to do if she has questions?
(A) Send a letter
(B) Reply to the e-mail
(C) Call the business
(D) Visit an office

Questions 168-171 refer to the following article.

Isabella Lenz: Runway Dreams

When Isabella Lenz was just six years old, her parents took her to the runway show of the famous Gauthier Design School; she has wanted to work in the world of fashion ever since. When Ms. Lenz got her first sewing machine, she practiced making clothing non-stop despite not having much money. She got a job in a fabric shop to get discounts on the fabric and always asked for sewing supplies as gifts. —[1]—.

In her early twenties, Ms. Lenz entered a local fashion competition. —[2]—. Although she didn't win, she met several professionals in the field who provided her with valuable career advice.

She borrowed money from the bank to start her own fashion business. It was a risky move, but it gave her the opportunity to build her brand. —[3]—. Her big break came when she designed a stunning gown for her cousin, popular country music singer Stella Perry, to wear at the National Music Awards. Ms. Perry posted photos of the event on social media, and her hundreds of thousands of followers were introduced to Ms. Lenz's talent. —[4]—. Orders poured in, and Ms. Lenz's brand became a household name.

168. What is suggested about Ms. Lenz?
(A) She sells her clothing exclusively online.
(B) She wants to expand her business to other fields.
(C) She studied at a famous fashion design school.
(D) She had the same career goal from a young age.

169. What is NOT indicated as a contributor to Ms. Lenz's success?
(A) Participation in a competition
(B) Support from a scholarship fund
(C) Publicity from a family member
(D) Receipt of a business loan

170. What is suggested about Ms. Perry?
(A) She placed the first order with Ms. Lenz.
(B) She found Ms. Lenz on social media.
(C) She is a successful musician.
(D) She has her own fashion brand.

171. In which of the positions marked [1], [2], [3], and [4] does the following sentence best belong?

"Additionally, she bought clothes from second-hand shops and altered them."

(A) [1]
(B) [2]
(C) [3]
(D) [4]

GO ON TO THE NEXT PAGE

Questions 172-175 refer to the following letter.

Delia Coleman
Coleman Eye Clinic
1090 Miller Street
Northampton, PA 18067

Dear Ms. Coleman,

It was a pleasure meeting you and learning more about your eye clinic's interior design needs. Remodeling your waiting area is a great investment, and we can give it the same modern look that your previous building had. I know that you've just moved in, but this type of project should get underway as soon as possible. —[1]—.

If you choose Beau Interiors, the first step would be for me to draw up some preliminary plans based on the preferences you shared with me. Then I would bring you some fabric and tile samples as well as paint options. —[2]—. You can also visit our showroom, where we have furniture from our partners. We can keep revising the design until you are completely satisfied. After the plans are finalized, our carpenter and electrician will conduct an on-site visit. —[3]—. Finally, we will set up a schedule for each phase of the work. Please let me know if you would like to move forward with this project. —[4]—.

Sincerely,

Kayla Harris
Senior Designer, Beau Interiors

172. What is the purpose of the letter?

(A) To request a document
(B) To outline a process
(C) To announce a decision
(D) To confirm a meeting

173. What is implied about Ms. Coleman?

(A) She requested an express service.
(B) She is seeking investment funds.
(C) She has expanded her staff.
(D) She recently relocated her business.

174. What is indicated about Beau Interiors?

(A) It has several branches in the area.
(B) It displays its partners' merchandise.
(C) It manufactures its own furniture.
(D) It offers a money-back guarantee.

175. In which of the positions marked [1], [2], [3], and [4] does the following sentence best belong?

"Both are experienced with commercial sites."

(A) [1]
(B) [2]
(C) [3]
(D) [4]

GO ON TO THE NEXT PAGE

Questions 176-180 refer to the following review and e-mail.

The Lab

Reviewed by Kevin Collier

The Lab is an intense thriller written and directed by Jackie Montano, in collaboration with producer Shawn Trevino. The film quietly made its debut in independent theaters in March but later gained popularity when it was shown at the Seattle Film Festival. It is now being shown in mainstream theaters across the country and has become so popular that Spark Studios is working on adapting it for a TV series. *The Lab* follows chemist Dr. Christopher Bull, who makes a remarkable scientific discovery but decides to keep it a secret to use for his own ends. With a stunning performance by lead actor Vincent Schiller, *The Lab* will keep you engaged until the very last scene.

E-Mail

TO:	Jackie Montano 〈jackiemontano@montanoproductions.com〉
FROM:	Rosemarie Carey 〈carey_r@woosterinstitute.com〉
DATE:	June 14
SUBJECT:	Class visit

Dear Ms. Montano,

I'd like to thank you once again for agreeing to speak to my class at the Wooster Institute on June 20. My students really enjoyed a speech given by your colleague, Shawn Trevino, a few weeks ago. Everyone has seen *The Lab* at least once as well as read your interview with Gerald Kemp in *Cinema Quarterly Magazine*, so it should be a productive session.

The class begins at 10 A.M. in Room 205 of the Iverson Wing. You should park in the East Parking Lot. It has free parking for up to two hours, which will be plenty of time. If you have any questions before your visit, please let me know.

I look forward to seeing you!

Rosemarie Carey

176. What is true about Ms. Montano's film?

(A) It debuted at a festival in Seattle.
(B) It can be streamed on her Web site.
(C) It was inspired by a true story.
(D) It will be made into a television show.

177. In the review, the word "ends" in paragraph 1, line 7, is closest in meaning to

(A) purposes
(B) finales
(C) closures
(D) borders

178. What is suggested about Ms. Carey's students?

(A) They are nearly finished with the course.
(B) They have met a famous actor.
(C) They will e-mail questions to Ms. Montano.
(D) They heard a talk from a producer.

179. Who most likely is Mr. Kemp?

(A) A course instructor
(B) A journalist
(C) A movie theater owner
(D) A new student

180. What is suggested in the e-mail about Ms. Montano?

(A) She has received a payment from the Wooster Institute.
(B) She has visited the Wooster Institute before.
(C) She will stay at the Wooster Institute for less than two hours.
(D) She will take public transportation to the Wooster Institute.

GO ON TO THE NEXT PAGE

Questions 181-185 refer to the following advertisement and contract.

Supreme Selections

Are you looking for professionally recorded music to enhance your projects? Supreme Selections is right for you! We are a music licensing service with a large collection of songs that can be used in movies, podcasts, commercials, and more. The music comes in a variety of formats, so it works with all major editing software programs on the market.

It's easy to find the music you need with our online catalog's user-friendly search features. Use the complete track or a shorter clip; it's up to you! The music can be added to any kind of project, whether commercial or personal, and can be published anywhere. And, if you're having trouble using our site, you can get help from our tech team 24 hours a day.

Buy more to save more!
Tier 1: One single download per month
Tier 2: Up to 10 downloads per month
Tier 3: Up to 20 downloads per month

LICENSING AGREEMENT

Supreme Selections ("Provider") hereby grants licensing rights to Heather Kane ("Purchaser") under the following terms:

1. Rights of Purchaser. Upon receipt of payment, Purchaser shall be licensed to download 10 audio files from Provider's catalog within each calendar month. Unused downloads will not roll over to the next month. The license for downloaded audio files will be granted in perpetuity.

2. Usage and Responsibilities. Purchaser may use the downloaded audio files for any commercial or personal project, whether the files are used in part or in whole. Projects must include the artist's name and the song title in the credits section. Purchaser must ensure that any use of the audio files does not infringe on the rights of others or break any laws.

Provider: Brenda Mendoza, Supreme Selections Director *Brenda Mendoza*
Purchaser: Heather Kane *Heather Kane*

181. Who would most likely use Supreme Selections?

(A) A translator
(B) A filmmaker
(C) A photographer
(D) A painter

182. What benefit of using Supreme Selections is NOT mentioned?

(A) Access to free editing software
(B) Lack of restrictions on use
(C) Round-the-clock technical support
(D) Ease of searching the catalog

183. In the advertisement, the word "complete" in paragraph 2, line 2, is closest in meaning to

(A) extreme
(B) ample
(C) perfect
(D) entire

184. What is suggested about Ms. Kane?

(A) She would like to renew her contract.
(B) She is ordering on behalf of her company.
(C) She has already paid a deposit.
(D) She signed up for the Tier 2 service.

185. According to the contract, what is Ms. Kane required to do?

(A) Send copies of a project to Supreme Selections
(B) Get changes approved in advance
(C) Cite the source of the music
(D) Give notice prior to canceling the contract

GO ON TO THE NEXT PAGE

Questions 186-190 refer to the following advertisement, e-mail, and customer comment.

Blackwell Security

A trusted name in commercial protection

Blackwell Security can protect your business's assets and confidential information. With everything from premium door locks to a full video monitoring system, we can help.

We've heard what our customers had to say. That's why we now offer installations on weekends so as not to disrupt employees. We can also provide training to your security team on how to use your new security system. Training is available on site at your company in both half-day and two-hour sessions, depending on your staff's experience. We're offering 30% off all training packages in July.

If you would like to have one of our experienced staff members visit your site and provide a free consultation, please e-mail Holly Reinhardt at h.reinhardt@blackwellsec.com to book an appointment.

E-Mail

To: Charles Manadan <cmanadan@eagan-financial.com>
From: Yumeno Shini <y.shini@blackwellsec.com>
Subject: Security
Date: July 2

Dear Mr. Manadan,

I'm glad that you have selected the security plan that I recommended after visiting your site. I believe that the system you ordered will be perfect for your needs. Fortunately, we do have an opening next week, so I've booked the training for your security team for July 12. You mentioned that some of your part-time workers may not be able to attend and that you plan to train them separately yourself. I'm sure that won't be an issue. As head of the security department, you will be able to pick up the concepts easily during my workshop. If there are further updates, I'll let you know.

Sincerely,

Yumeno Shini
Consultant, Blackwell Security

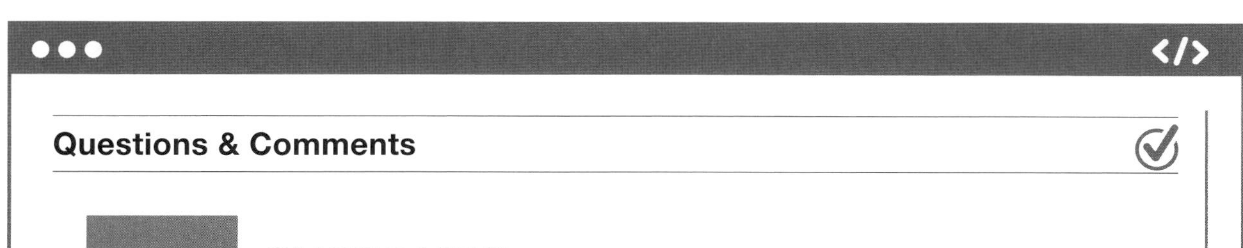

Questions & Comments

CUSTOMER

Jeremy Boldt, July 30

I recently had my first consultation at Eagan Financial, and the whole experience was really great. My financial advisor, Phyllis Jenkins, showed me some great investment packages and explained everything clearly, double checking that I understood everything before signing anything. However, there was a problem when I was entering into the building. My visitor badge set off the alarm, but their security manager resolved it quickly. He mentioned something about a new system they had installed recently. But besides that, everything was great. I highly recommend this business.

SUBMIT

186. Why did Blackwell Security make a change?
(A) To respond to customer feedback
(B) To save money on expenses
(C) To keep up with a competitor
(D) To attract new employees

187. Who most likely is Ms. Reinhardt?
(A) The leader of training workshops
(B) The person who schedules consultations
(C) A supplier of security equipment
(D) A hiring manager for Blackwell Security

188. What is true about Mr. Manadan?
(A) He was displeased with his former security company.
(B) He received advice about security measures.
(C) He is the newest member of the staff.
(D) He had trouble finding a system in his budget.

189. What is probably true about the training on July 12?
(A) It will not be charged at full price.
(B) It will last for half a day.
(C) It will be held at Blackwell Security's offices.
(D) It will be attended by all security staff.

190. What is suggested about Mr. Boldt?
(A) He requested a visitor badge.
(B) He is a long-time customer of Eagan Financial.
(C) He was assisted by the head of a department.
(D) He is an expert in the financial industry.

GO ON TO THE NEXT PAGE

Questions 191-195 refer to the following coupon, receipt, and feedback form.

Corwin Dry Clening

15% OFF

Use this coupon between April 1 and April 30 to get 15% off any of the following services:

- Shortening of pants, shirts, skirts, and jackets
- Zipper repair and replacement
- Button replacement

This coupon cannot be used with any other offer, with the exception of our welcome discount of 5% (WEL5) to new customers. Open daily 7 A.M.–7 P.M. Items for same-day service must be received by 9 A.M.

Corwin Dry Clening

1602 Clay Street, Tampa, FL 33592
(813) 555-8577

Name: Crystal Holcombe
Date: April 9
Phone: (813) 555-9012
Address: 548 Ridge Lane, Tampa, FL 33592

Summary of Services

Shortening: wool pants	$17.00
Zipper repair: leather jacket	$12.00
15% discount (April coupon)	-$4.35
5% discount (WEL5)	-$1.45
Total	**$23.20**

Employee Comments: The customer also brought in a skirt to be shortened. However, we discovered that the lining was badly damaged, so a new one is needed. A cost estimate was provided for this service.

Short on time? Corwin Dry Cleaning delivers completed items to anywhere that is five miles or less from our business. Ask a staff member about our rates.

Corwin Dry Cleaning

Customer Feedback Survey

Thank you for your business! Please take a moment to provide feedback about your experience. This will help us to improve our service.

	Excellent	Good	Average	Poor
Staff	✓			
Cost of service	✓			
Quality of service	✓			
Range of options	✓			

Please describe your experience with us.

Name: Crystal Holcombe

The staff members who assisted me were helpful and friendly. I used the same-day service, and it was very convenient to get my items back so quickly. I was particularly impressed with how well the staff communicated with me. I got a call about an issue with my skirt, and the person explained my options clearly. In addition, I was contacted as soon as my clothes were ready to be picked up. It was nice that there were some comfortable chairs near the entrance for customers who were waiting. The business seemed very modern, and I was relieved that it was easy to find a parking spot near the entrance.

191. What is suggested about Ms. Holcombe?

(A) She requested the service on a weekday.
(B) She is using Corwin Dry Cleaning for the first time.
(C) She signed up for a loyalty program.
(D) She lives near Corwin Dry Cleaning.

192. According to the receipt, what problem did a staff member notice?

(A) A stain could not be removed.
(B) A zipper on a skirt was missing.
(C) Some fabric was too short to work with.
(D) A section of a garment should be replaced.

193. What is true about Corwin Dry Cleaning's delivery service?

(A) It is limited to a certain distance.
(B) It is free for large orders.
(C) It is not available on some days.
(D) It has been launched recently.

194. What did Ms. Holcombe especially like about the business?

(A) The free parking lot
(B) The level of communication
(C) The large waiting area
(D) The modern equipment

195. What is implied about Ms. Holcombe's clothing?

(A) It was dropped off before 9 A.M.
(B) It required a newly offered service.
(C) It was all the same kind of fabric.
(D) It was handled by the manager.

GO ON TO THE NEXT PAGE →

Questions 196-200 refer to the following press release, e-mail, and invitation.

FOR IMMEDIATE RELEASE

September 12

Contact: Florence Knowles, knowlesf@randallproperties.com

ELMSFORD—Randall Properties has announced that work on the new Hudson Tower Office Complex has been finished one month ahead of schedule. About 60 percent of the office units have already been rented, and businesses will begin moving in soon. The complex offers several conference rooms for tenants' use, a cafeteria, and a calming rooftop garden with ample seating in both the shade and the sun. In keeping with Randall Properties' commitment to environmental responsibility, the building has solar panels, a water recovery system, and an energy-efficient design. There is a spacious and inviting lobby from the main entrance on Hatley Street, which also has a small loading/unloading area. Covered parking for employees and visitors is situated by the rear entrance on Cedar Street.

Inquiries regarding renting a space in the building should be directed to Eugene Gallaher at gallahere@randallproperties.com.

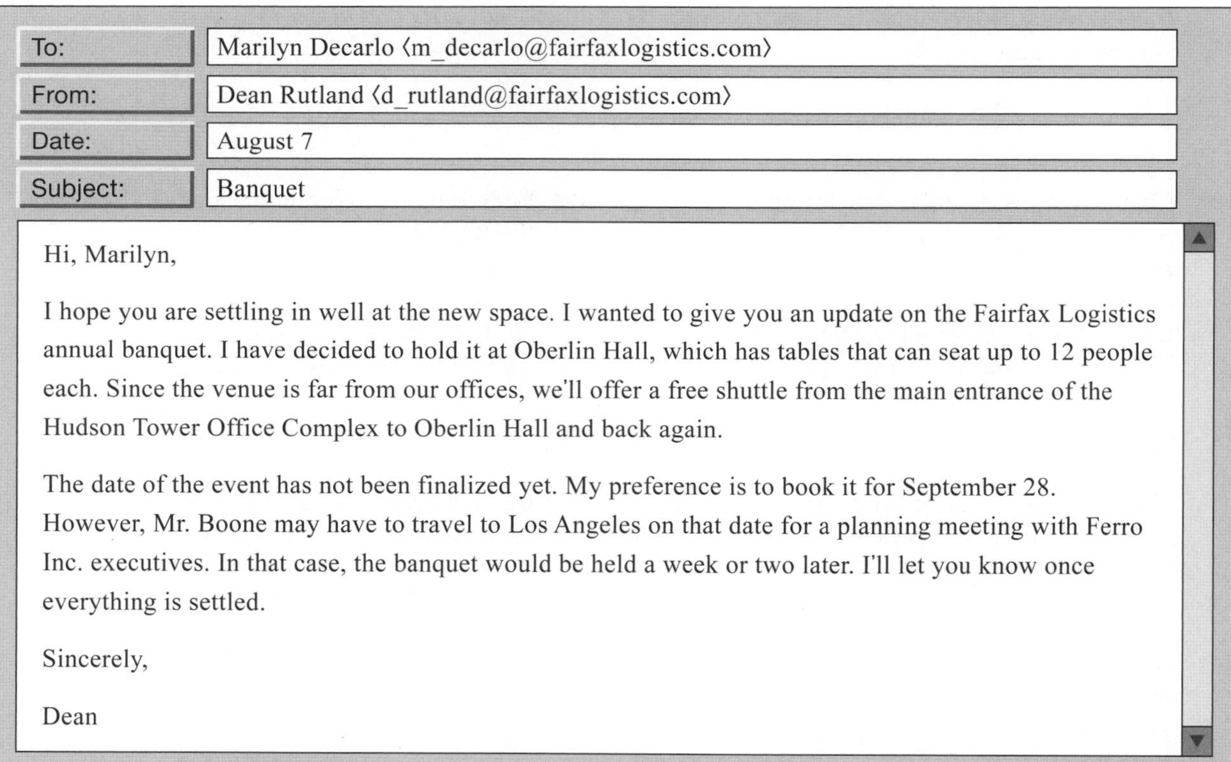

To:	Marilyn Decarlo ⟨m_decarlo@fairfaxlogistics.com⟩
From:	Dean Rutland ⟨d_rutland@fairfaxlogistics.com⟩
Date:	August 7
Subject:	Banquet

Hi, Marilyn,

I hope you are settling in well at the new space. I wanted to give you an update on the Fairfax Logistics annual banquet. I have decided to hold it at Oberlin Hall, which has tables that can seat up to 12 people each. Since the venue is far from our offices, we'll offer a free shuttle from the main entrance of the Hudson Tower Office Complex to Oberlin Hall and back again.

The date of the event has not been finalized yet. My preference is to book it for September 28. However, Mr. Boone may have to travel to Los Angeles on that date for a planning meeting with Ferro Inc. executives. In that case, the banquet would be held a week or two later. I'll let you know once everything is settled.

Sincerely,

Dean

Fairfax Logistics Annual Banquet

You are cordially invited to the Fairfax Logistics Annual Banquet, during which we will recognize our Employee of the Year. Danielle Rojas has dedicated many years of service to the company and is truly deserving of this honor.

Friday, October 5, 7:00 P.M.
Oberlin Hall, Ballroom
914 Rosebud Avenue (free shuttle available from the office)
Hosted by Fairfax Logistics CEO Antonio Boone
Live musical entertainment provided by Sandra Stewart

Please confirm your attendance by e-mailing Dean Rutland at
d_rutland@fairfaxlogistics.com.

196. What is the press release about?
(A) The sale of a commercial property
(B) The relocation of a company's headquarters
(C) The completion of a construction project
(D) The changes to a workshop schedule

197. What feature of the Hudson Tower Office Complex does the press release mention?
(A) An outdoor space
(B) Video conferencing equipment
(C) A secure storage area
(D) Spacious individual offices

198. What is implied about the shuttle for Fairfax Logistics employees?
(A) It will depart from Hatley Street.
(B) It requires a ticket.
(C) It can seat up to 12 people.
(D) It will make several stops on its route.

199. According to the invitation, who will be presented with an award?
(A) Mr. Boone
(B) Ms. Rojas
(C) Mr. Rutland
(D) Ms. Steward

200. What is suggested about Fairfax Logistics?
(A) Its CEO took a business trip in September.
(B) Its entire staff helps select an award winner.
(C) It allows employees to bring guests to a dinner.
(D) It is located near Oberlin Hall.

Stop! This is the end of the test. If you finish before time is called, you may go back to Parts 5, 6, and 7 and check your work.

▶ 정답 및 해설 p. 36

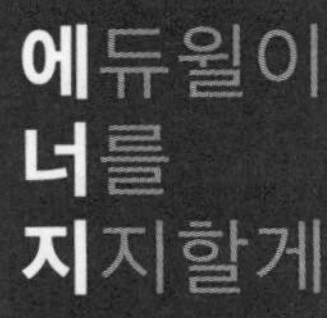

ENERGY

힘이 든다는 건,
앞으로 나아가고 있다는 거야.

– 안정은, 『오늘도 좋아하는 일을 하는 중이야』, 서랍의 날씨

자동 채점 서비스
바로가기

에듀윌 토익 실전서

LC+RC

TEST 03

LISTENING TEST

PART 1

PART 2

PART 3

PART 4

READING TEST

PART 5

PART 6

PART 7

LISTENING TEST

In the Listening test, you will be asked to demonstrate how well you understand spoken English. The entire Listening test will last approximately 45 minutes. There are four parts, and directions are given for each part. You must mark your answers on the separate answer sheet. Do not write your answers in your test book.

PART 1

Directions: For each question in this part, you will hear four statements about a picture in your test book. When you hear the statements, you must select the one statement that best describes what you see in the picture. Then find the number of the question on your answer sheet and mark your answer. The statements will not be printed in your test book and will be spoken only one time.

Statement (C), "He's making a phone call," is the best description of the picture, so you should select answer (C) and mark it on your answer sheet.

1.

2.

TEST 03

GO ON TO THE NEXT PAGE

3.

4.

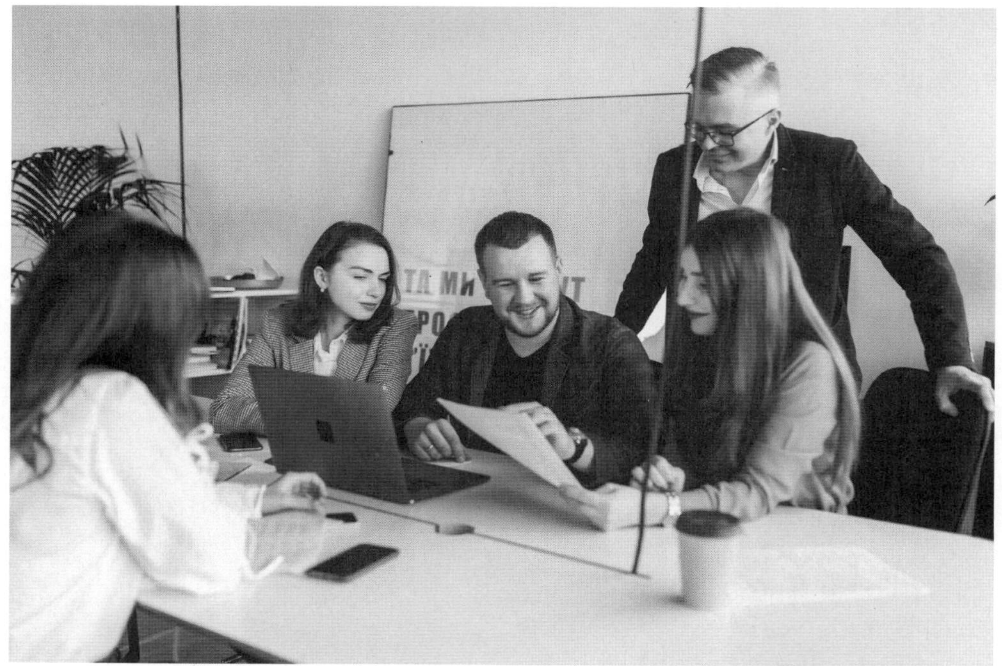

5.

6.

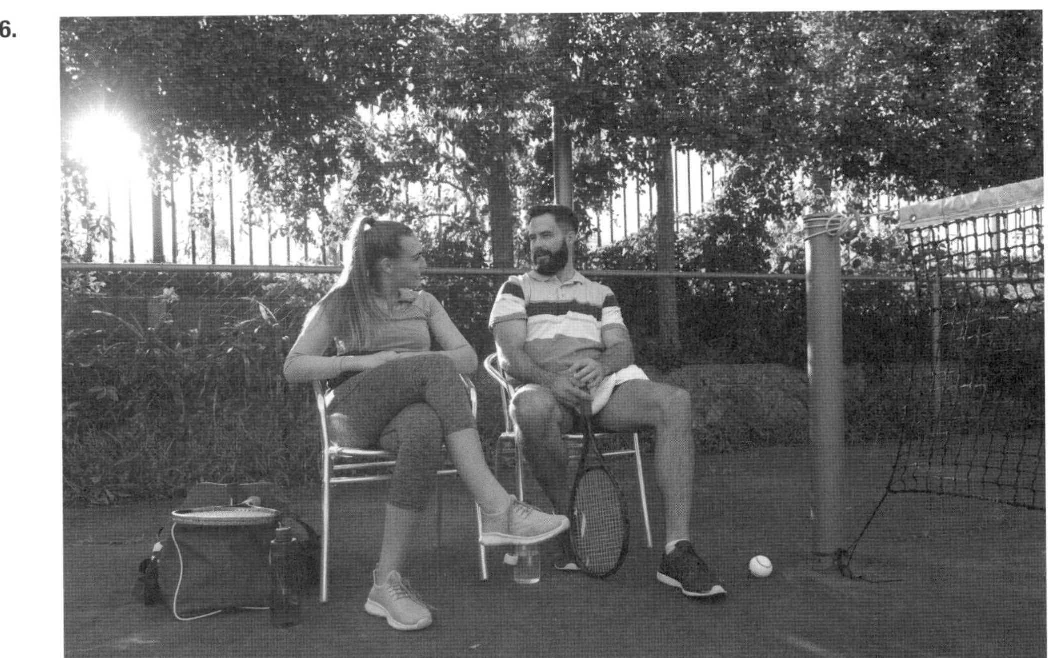

GO ON TO THE NEXT PAGE

PART 2

Directions: You will hear a question or statement and three responses spoken in English. They will not be printed in your test book and will be spoken only one time. Select the best response to the question or statement and mark the letter (A), (B), or (C) on your answer sheet.

7. Mark your answer on your answer sheet.

8. Mark your answer on your answer sheet.

9. Mark your answer on your answer sheet.

10. Mark your answer on your answer sheet.

11. Mark your answer on your answer sheet.

12. Mark your answer on your answer sheet.

13. Mark your answer on your answer sheet.

14. Mark your answer on your answer sheet.

15. Mark your answer on your answer sheet.

16. Mark your answer on your answer sheet.

17. Mark your answer on your answer sheet.

18. Mark your answer on your answer sheet.

19. Mark your answer on your answer sheet.

20. Mark your answer on your answer sheet.

21. Mark your answer on your answer sheet.

22. Mark your answer on your answer sheet.

23. Mark your answer on your answer sheet.

24. Mark your answer on your answer sheet.

25. Mark your answer on your answer sheet.

26. Mark your answer on your answer sheet.

27. Mark your answer on your answer sheet.

28. Mark your answer on your answer sheet.

29. Mark your answer on your answer sheet.

30. Mark your answer on your answer sheet.

31. Mark your answer on your answer sheet.

PART 3

Directions: You will hear some conversations between two or more people. You will be asked to answer three questions about what the speakers say in each conversation. Select the best response to each question and mark the letter (A), (B), (C), or (D) on your answer sheet. The conversations will not be printed in your test book and will be spoken only one time.

32. Where does the man most likely work?
(A) At a financial institution
(B) At a dental clinic
(C) At a warehouse
(D) At a restaurant

33. What did the woman recently do?
(A) She moved to a new neighborhood.
(B) She rescheduled an appointment.
(C) She launched a business nearby.
(D) She returned from a trip.

34. What problem does the man mention?
(A) A time slot has been double-booked.
(B) A credit card payment was rejected.
(C) A document is incomplete.
(D) A label contained an error.

---

35. What department does Makito most likely work in?
(A) Research and development
(B) Technical support
(C) Human resources
(D) Public relations

36. What will the man do on Friday morning?
(A) Attend a conference
(B) Reserve a room
(C) Take food orders
(D) Lead a team meeting

37. Why does the woman recommend speaking to Leo?
(A) To share gift suggestions
(B) To review an agenda
(C) To apply for a promotion
(D) To make a financial donation

---

38. What is the conversation mainly about?
(A) Planning a banquet
(B) Sending some invitations
(C) Editing a training video
(D) Checking employees' qualifications

39. Why does the woman apologize?
(A) She changed an assignment.
(B) She left out some information.
(C) She disagrees with an opinion.
(D) She missed a meeting.

40. What does the man say he is surprised about?
(A) The design of a Web site
(B) The number of participants
(C) The feedback from employees
(D) The speed of completing a project

---

41. What problem does the woman mention?
(A) A customer made a complaint.
(B) A job opening has not been filled.
(C) Some fees will increase.
(D) Some damage was caused.

42. Why does the man say, "they only serve residential properties"?
(A) To give reassurance
(B) To explain a decision
(C) To show surprise
(D) To reject a suggestion

43. What does the woman ask the man to do?
(A) Adjust a budget
(B) Arrange some furniture
(C) Schedule a meeting
(D) Review a policy

GO ON TO THE NEXT PAGE →

44. What products are the speakers preparing?
(A) Automobile parts
(B) Power tools
(C) Sporting goods
(D) Kitchen appliances

45. According to the woman, what is the problem?
(A) A delivery charge has increased.
(B) A machine has stopped working.
(C) Some containers are the wrong size.
(D) Some employees are late for the shift.

46. Why is the woman worried?
(A) Some instructions are confusing.
(B) An employee is inexperienced.
(C) A deadline cannot be changed.
(D) A room cannot be unlocked.

---

47. What is Jessica disappointed about?
(A) The lack of samples
(B) The price of admission fees
(C) The end of a discount
(D) The size of the crowd

48. What does the man's company sell?
(A) Reusable mugs
(B) Digital scales
(C) Coffee grinders
(D) Display cases

49. What does the man ask the women to do?
(A) Complete a feedback questionnaire
(B) Provide the location of their business
(C) Take a business card
(D) Read an informational pamphlet

---

50. What did the woman recently do?
(A) She requested a branch transfer.
(B) She published a book.
(C) She moved to a new team.
(D) She returned from a business trip.

51. What does the man encourage the woman to consider?
(A) Taking a training course
(B) Attending a group meal
(C) Reviewing an employee handbook
(D) Opening a social media account

52. What will the man do this afternoon?
(A) Conduct some interviews
(B) Take a trip
(C) Place an order
(D) Make an announcement

---

53. What are the speakers discussing?
(A) Upcoming assignments
(B) Policy changes
(C) Production goals
(D) Staffing needs

54. What is Francesca doing next week?
(A) Negotiating a contract
(B) Sending a document
(C) Watching a presentation
(D) Leading a workshop

55. What will be discussed at the next meeting?
(A) Creating an informational video
(B) Recruiting new customers
(C) Using a different company's services
(D) Changing the layout of an office

---

56. Who most likely is the man?
(A) A bus driver
(B) A city official
(C) An auto mechanic
(D) A security guard

57. What are the women frustrated about?
(A) Difficulty in finding experienced workers
(B) Problems with a newly purchased item
(C) Increases in service fees
(D) Unfair complaints from customers

58. According to the man, why will a task be finished quickly?
(A) He has recently completed some training.
(B) He brought the component he needs.
(C) He has an assistant to help him.
(D) He has solved similar problems before.

---

59. Where do the speakers most likely work?
(A) At an art museum
(B) At a newspaper publisher
(C) At a print shop
(D) At a technical institute

60. What does the woman imply when she says, "the list is very long"?
(A) Some other staff members should help.
(B) She needs more time to complete a task.
(C) She thinks the man has worked hard.
(D) Some information should be removed.

61. What will be changed in March?
(A) The hiring policies
(B) A site manager
(C) The opening hours
(D) A logo

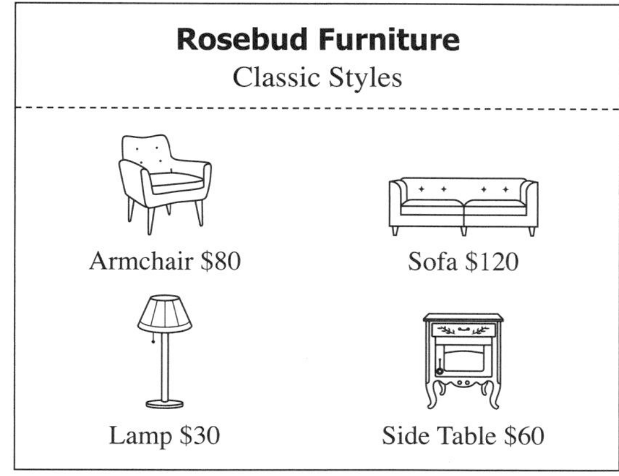

Rosebud Furniture
Classic Styles
Armchair $80
Sofa $120
Lamp $30
Side Table $60

62. What problem does the man have?
(A) A credit card has been canceled.
(B) A web page is not loading.
(C) Some merchandise is out of stock.
(D) Some furniture has been damaged.

63. According to the woman, what will happen in three days?
(A) A catalog will be sent.
(B) A price will change.
(C) An order will arrive.
(D) An employee will call the man.

64. Look at the graphic. How much will the man be charged?
(A) $80
(B) $120
(C) $30
(D) $60

TEST 03

GO ON TO THE NEXT PAGE

Employee Orientation
May 11th

Paperwork:	9:00 A.M.
Building tour:	11:00 A.M.
Department lunch:	12:30 P.M.
Training videos:	2:00 P.M.

65. What industry do the speakers work in?
(A) Engineering
(B) Finance
(C) Manufacturing
(D) Medicine

66. Look at the graphic. When will the woman meet Susan McNeil?
(A) At 9:00 A.M.
(B) At 11:00 A.M.
(C) At 12:30 P.M.
(D) At 2:00 P.M.

67. What will the speakers most likely do next?
(A) Select menu options
(B) Review a plan
(C) Print out a schedule
(D) Go to the security office

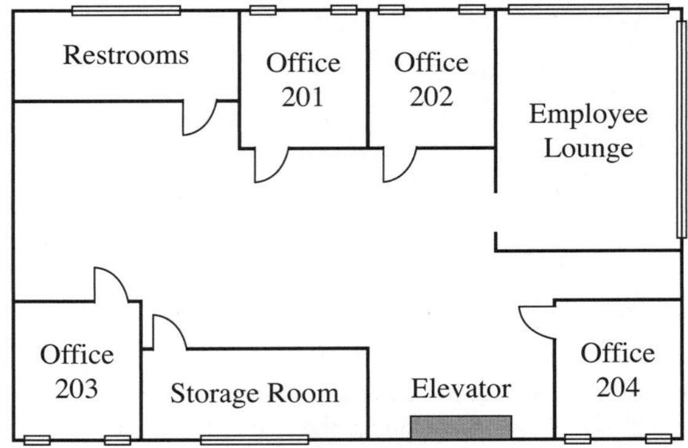

68. Where do the speakers work?
(A) At a software company
(B) At an accounting firm
(C) At an Internet service provider
(D) At an architecture firm

69. What must the man do at two o'clock?
(A) Learn to use some software
(B) Go to a parking lot
(C) Pick up some paperwork
(D) Complete a feedback form

70. Look at the graphic. Where is the woman's office?
(A) Office 201
(B) Office 202
(C) Office 203
(D) Office 204

PART 4

Directions: You will hear some talks given by a single speaker. You will be asked to answer three questions about what the speaker says in each talk. Select the best response to each question and mark the letter (A), (B), (C), or (D) on your answer sheet. The talks will not be printed in your test book and will be spoken only one time.

71. Who most likely is the speaker?
(A) A building owner
(B) A tour guide
(C) A salesperson
(D) An art instructor

72. What does the speaker say about the vases with handles?
(A) They are expensive to make.
(B) They are becoming more popular.
(C) They have recently been added to the inventory.
(D) They have a complex production process.

73. What will the speaker do next?
(A) Show a video
(B) Distribute some coupons
(C) Answer some questions
(D) Prepare some refreshments

---

74. What product is the speaker introducing?
(A) A portable music device
(B) A tablet computer
(C) A paper shredder
(D) A digital camera

75. What feature of the product does the speaker highlight?
(A) Affordability
(B) Durability
(C) A small size
(D) A warranty

76. What will the listeners do next?
(A) Receive a handout
(B) Download some files
(C) Move to another room
(D) Watch a demonstration

---

77. What is the topic of the workshop?
(A) How to manage others
(B) How to create presentations
(C) How to take pictures
(D) How to handle investments

78. What field do the listeners most likely work in?
(A) Law
(B) Transportation
(C) Education
(D) Real estate

79. What does the speaker ask the listeners to do?
(A) Attend another workshop
(B) Form small groups
(C) E-mail some information
(D) Introduce themselves

---

80. Who is the speaker?
(A) A graphic designer
(B) A branch manager
(C) A journalist
(D) A construction supervisor

81. What does the speaker mean when she says, "there's almost always a line"?
(A) A service is used frequently.
(B) An exchange process is confusing.
(C) A deadline extension is needed.
(D) A layout should be changed.

82. What does the speaker want some advice about?
(A) Market trends
(B) Transfer policies
(C) Investment opportunities
(D) Potential solutions

GO ON TO THE NEXT PAGE →

83. What is the speaker pleased about?
(A) New regulations
(B) Factory output
(C) A budget surplus
(D) An industry award

84. According to the speaker, what is the problem with the testing room?
(A) It is not secure.
(B) It is too small.
(C) It failed a recent inspection.
(D) Its temperature is uncomfortable.

85. What will some listeners most likely do next?
(A) Introduce some employees
(B) Recommend a company
(C) Volunteer for a task
(D) Give a presentation

---

86. Who most likely are the listeners?
(A) Restaurant employees
(B) Marketing executives
(C) Trade fair employees
(D) Interior designers

87. What does the speaker imply when he says, "the weather will be a factor"?
(A) He has not finalized a schedule.
(B) He needs help selecting a location.
(C) He is not expecting a good turnout.
(D) He may change some uniforms.

88. What does the speaker instruct the listeners to do?
(A) Keep some items organized
(B) Print out a schedule
(C) Arrive at a site early
(D) Update their availability

---

89. What did Dempsey Transportation announce this morning?
(A) It has added more routes.
(B) It plans to increase its fares.
(C) It will merge with another company.
(D) It is under new leadership.

90. According to the speaker, what will new drivers receive?
(A) Extra vacation time
(B) Free training
(C) A cash bonus
(D) Overtime pay

91. What will take place in August?
(A) A baking contest
(B) A sports tournament
(C) A political debate
(D) A music festival

---

92. What is the speaker planning?
(A) A fund-raiser
(B) An awards ceremony
(C) A writing competition
(D) A book-signing event

93. What does the speaker imply when she says, "I nearly spilled my coffee"?
(A) A beverage was too hot.
(B) A product has not been designed well.
(C) She was in a rush in the morning.
(D) She was excited about some news.

94. What does the speaker ask the listener to do?
(A) Design some invitations
(B) Send a receipt
(C) Check a Web site
(D) Contact a manufacturer

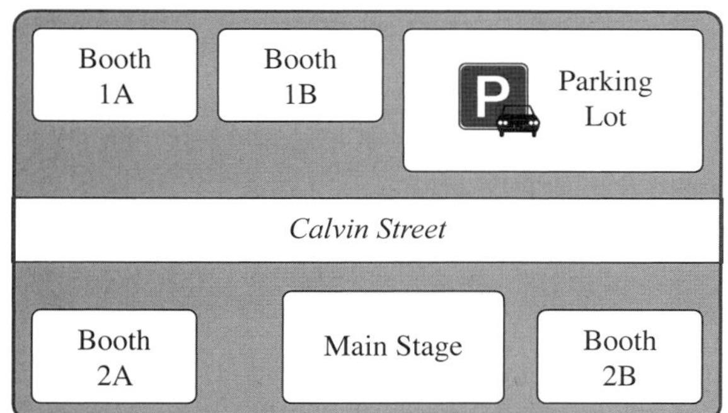

95. What type of products does the company sell?
(A) Vitamin supplements
(B) Healthy snacks
(C) Handmade jewelry
(D) Exercise machines

96. What does the speaker ask the listeners to do?
(A) Label some merchandise
(B) Sign an attendance sheet
(C) Load a truck
(D) Call some customers

97. Look at the graphic. Which booth will the company use?
(A) Booth 1A
(B) Booth 1B
(C) Booth 2A
(D) Booth 2B

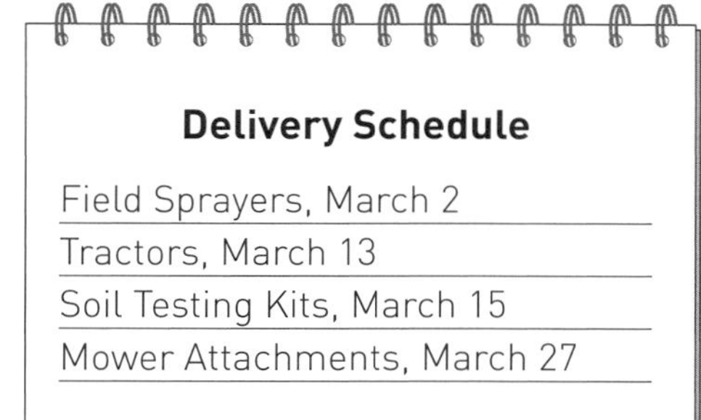

Delivery Schedule
Field Sprayers, March 2
Tractors, March 13
Soil Testing Kits, March 15
Mower Attachments, March 27

98. What does the speaker say happened last week?
(A) Some inspection results were confirmed.
(B) The business was featured in a magazine.
(C) A loan from the bank was approved.
(D) Some renovations were completed.

99. Why will some equipment be replaced?
(A) To help the environment
(B) To keep up with competitors
(C) To reduce expenses
(D) To improve safety

100. Look at the graphic. When will the speaker conduct a training session?
(A) On March 2
(B) On March 13
(C) On March 15
(D) On March 27

This is the end of the Listening test. Turn to Part 5 in your test book.

READING TEST

In the Reading test, you will read a variety of texts and answer several different types of reading comprehension questions. The entire Reading test will last 75 minutes. There are three parts, and directions are given for each part. You are encouraged to answer as many questions as possible within the time allowed.

You must mark your answers on the separate answer sheet. Do not write your answers in your test book.

PART 5

Directions: A word or phrase is missing in each of the sentences below. Four answer choices are given below each sentence. Select the best answer to complete the sentence. Then mark the letter (A), (B), (C), or (D) on your answer sheet.

101. Ms. Dalton read an excerpt from ------- book at the event last Saturday.

(A) her
(B) hers
(C) herself
(D) she

102. We hope that your ------- into the matter helps to resolve the issue quickly.

(A) investigate
(B) investigation
(C) investigates
(D) investigated

103. Anyone who ------- to volunteer at the annual marathon should call City Hall.

(A) wishes
(B) requires
(C) declares
(D) fulfills

104. Mr. Gardner will introduce his replacement ------- the company dinner on Friday.

(A) off
(B) onto
(C) at
(D) as

105. Ms. Nelson's physician advised her to eat a high-protein -------.

(A) dieter
(B) dietary
(C) diet
(D) dieted

106. Customers were ------- encouraged to give the new electric vehicle a test drive.

(A) broadly
(B) evenly
(C) rapidly
(D) strongly

107. Please attend the reception on Monday ------- the newest members of the staff to our company.

(A) welcomes
(B) welcomed
(C) to welcome
(D) will welcome

108. The ------- of 12 golf clubs comes with a leather bag on wheels for easy transportation.

(A) panel
(B) fit
(C) game
(D) set

109. Phoenix Inc. is offering 15% off all carpet cleaning services ------- August.

(A) while
(B) during
(C) because
(D) than

110. ------- the weather was rainy, a record number of people attended the parade.

(A) Nevertheless
(B) If
(C) Regarding
(D) Although

111. The new air conditioner turns ------- off automatically once the set temperature has been reached.

(A) itself
(B) himself
(C) oneself
(D) themselves

112. The transition to an all-digital news platform was ------- by the management last week.

(A) located
(B) discussed
(C) subscribed
(D) entitled

113. Kirk's Moving Service has a reputation for transporting extremely fragile items with ------- damage.

(A) minimizes
(B) minimized
(C) minimize
(D) minimal

114. Fenway Hair Salon experienced no drop in the number of patrons ------- it raised its prices by 50 percent.

(A) prior to
(B) even though
(C) however
(D) likewise

115. Thanks to the growth in the hospitality industry, the new hotel is expected to be a ------- venture.

(A) structural
(B) compact
(C) profitable
(D) voluntary

116. The new advertising campaign did not have the dramatic effect on sales that Mr. Yates ------- it would.

(A) assumed
(B) assuming
(C) assumption
(D) assume

117. The representative from VC Roofing said we must wait until the ------- to book an inspection.

(A) days
(B) summer
(C) weather
(D) month

118. The leaders of ------- team in the department should complete these evaluation forms.

(A) each
(B) whose
(C) much
(D) its

119. Many audience members had already visited the exhibit ------- during Professor Dorsey's lecture.

(A) accomplished
(B) occurred
(C) mentioned
(D) qualified

120. Our sales staff is confident in making improvements to any ------- that has not been finalized yet.

(A) negotiator
(B) negotiable
(C) negotiation
(D) negotiated

GO ON TO THE NEXT PAGE

121. In addition to a hot meal at lunchtime, passengers will ------- be served snacks and beverages throughout the flight.

(A) also
(B) nonetheless
(C) although
(D) therefore

122. The Provost Gallery had an impressive turnout for its grand opening event with ------- 500 people in attendance.

(A) again
(B) many
(C) toward
(D) over

123. Mountainside Resort will open for the season in November and is now seeking ------- ski instructors.

(A) complimentary
(B) durable
(C) elaborate
(D) enthusiastic

124. Now that a new manager has been hired, the team has started to follow regulations more -------.

(A) strict
(B) stricter
(C) strictly
(D) strictness

125. Daffodil Supermarket has been working ------- the goal of eliminating 50% of plastic from its packaging.

(A) between
(B) toward
(C) across
(D) except

126. Edelmira Fashion's ------- gifts to clients at their contract renewal time made the business stand out.

(A) thoughtful
(B) thought
(C) thoughtfully
(D) thinks

127. The school board voted to build an extension to the Merriam Art Building ------- the increase in construction costs.

(A) in spite of
(B) on the contrary
(C) so that
(D) even so

128. Drayson Antiques can help customers ------- their furniture pieces to their original condition.

(A) restorer
(B) restored
(C) restore
(D) restorable

129. Ms. Nelson sought ------- from the head librarian, who made copies of old city maps from the archives.

(A) activities
(B) permits
(C) materials
(D) suggestions

130. In order to provide accurate legal advice, the client must explain his property dispute -------.

(A) specified
(B) specify
(C) specific
(D) more specifically

PART 6

Directions: Read the texts that follow. A word, phrase, or sentence is missing in parts of each text. Four answer choices for each question are given below the text. Select the best answer to complete the text. Then mark the letter (A), (B), (C), or (D) on your answer sheet.

Questions 131-134 refer to the following information.

Thank you for shopping at Gift-Max online store, where you can have unique gifts sent right to your ------- **131.** Please note that members can get discounted gift-wrapping and free delivery. To start ------- **132.** from the membership program, simply visit our Web site, click the "Membership" button, and complete the form. ------- **133.** We hope you will continue to use Gift-Max and have the ------- **134.** of giving special gifts to your friends and family.

131. (A) inquiry
(B) market
(C) doorstep
(D) credit

132. (A) benefited
(B) beneficent
(C) beneficial
(D) benefiting

133. (A) Please settle the overdue bill.
(B) It only takes a few minutes.
(C) Our employees are highly knowledgeable.
(D) The new product is very popular.

134. (A) enjoy
(B) enjoyment
(C) enjoying
(D) enjoyed

GO ON TO THE NEXT PAGE

Questions 135-138 refer to the following e-mail.

To: Shawn Ayala <shawnayala@regalado.com>
From: Varner Communications <billing@varnercomm.com>
Date: October 19
Subject: Phone bill

Dear Mr. Ayala,

Thank you for signing up for the automated billing ------- (135.) for your Varner Communications phone bill. ------- (136.) on November 1, a payment of $79.99 will be deducted from your bank account on the 1st of every month. Please note that if you do not have enough funds in the account at the time of withdrawal, you may ------- (137.) a late fee. ------- (138.). In that case, we would resume sending paper bills to your address every month.

Sincerely,

Varner Communications

135. (A) occasion
(B) value
(C) option
(D) attempt

136. (A) Beginning
(B) Only
(C) Along
(D) Through

137. (A) to incur
(B) incur
(C) incurring
(D) incurred

138. (A) We will send you a copy of the contract.
(B) You can cancel the direct debit at any time.
(C) The package includes unlimited texts and data.
(D) It would be helpful to restart your phone.

Questions 139-142 refer to the following memo.

To: All Longoria Staff
From: Althea Panadio
Subject: Safety record
Date: July 3
Attachment: Q2_Safety_Report

Congratulations on our new safety record at our production facility! No injuries have been reported this quarter. ------- (139.), we need to continue to follow all safety rules carefully. For this reason, we are launching a monthly ------- (140.) program. It has been designed by Carmen Riley, who has closely ------- (141.) our operations, looking for areas of improvement. Through learning about the industry's best practices, you can help to ensure a positive working environment for everyone. ------- (142.). Meanwhile, keep up the good work!

139. (A) Rather
(B) Otherwise
(C) Even if
(D) Nevertheless

140. (A) training
(B) voucher
(C) exercise
(D) treatment

141. (A) observing
(B) to observe
(C) been observed
(D) observed

142. (A) Demand for our products is growing.
(B) We have decided to extend the registration deadline.
(C) The session dates will be announced next week.
(D) Basic first aid kits are available in the main office.

GO ON TO THE NEXT PAGE

Questions 143-146 refer to the following e-mail.

To: Thornton Sales Management Team
From: Farah Bakir
Date: September 22
Subject: Natasha Brannon's retirement

Dear Sales Management Team,

The planning committee is looking for a few people from our team to make brief speeches at the ------- (143.) retirement party for Natasha Brannon. ------- (144.).

The speeches will take place at the beginning of the party, which starts at 4 P.M. on October 6. ------- (145.) willing to share some memories of her time at our company is asked to contact a committee member. We also want to leave enough time for Ms. Brannon to say a few words herself. ------- (146.), we will only have a few speeches from other people.

Sincerely,

Farah Bakir

143. (A) upcoming
(B) assorted
(C) prosperous
(D) enthusiastic

144. (A) Therefore, I need someone to train her replacement.
(B) We think this would help to make the event special.
(C) Alternatively, she may become a part-time consultant.
(D) Committee members are discussing a theme for next year.

145. (A) Whoever
(B) One another
(C) Anyone
(D) Ours

146. (A) For instance
(B) Since then
(C) On the contrary
(D) For this reason

PART 7

Directions: In this part, you will read a selection of texts, such as magazine and newspaper articles, e-mails, and instant messages. Each text or set of texts is followed by several questions. Select the best answer for each question and mark the letter (A), (B), (C), or (D) on your answer sheet.

Questions 147-148 refer to the following information.

Campbell County Fish and Wildlife Department

Job Openings

Fish and Wildlife Technician (#8020C): Enjoy the great outdoors while helping to maintain the health and diversity of wildlife in water habitats in both nature reserves and tourism sites throughout Campbell County. The position includes recording water sample data in a database, checking and reporting the number of various fish species and how that figure changes over time, and distributing new fish into certain areas. Attention to detail is required, as the guidelines must be followed carefully. No experience is necessary. Apply at www.campbellcounty.gov/jobs/8020C.

147. What is suggested about the position?

(A) It is intended for seasonal work only.
(B) It requires working at multiple locations.
(C) It is only open to Campbell County residents.
(D) It is intended for experienced technicians.

148. What is mentioned as a duty of the position?

(A) Recording park attendance figures
(B) Making repairs to boats
(C) Monitoring fish populations
(D) Leading guided tours

GO ON TO THE NEXT PAGE

Questions 149-150 refer to the following notice.

Thank you for your Topeka Carpeting purchase!

At Topeka Carpeting, we strive to provide high-quality floor coverings at affordable prices. Please note that colors on our online store may not look the same on your computer screen, so please check your product carefully before installing it. If you have any questions or comments, you can speak to a Topeka Carpeting representative by calling our helpline at 1-800-555-7826. We ask that you have the manufacturer's name and the product number ready when you call so that we may better assist you.

149. What is suggested about Topeka Carpeting?

(A) It regularly adds new products.
(B) It does not accept exchanges.
(C) It sells merchandise on a Web site.
(D) It charges a fee for installation.

150. According to the notice, what should customers prepare before calling the helpline?

(A) The address of the manufacturer
(B) The customer's order number
(C) The location of where the item was purchased
(D) The product identification number

Questions 151-152 refer to the following e-mail.

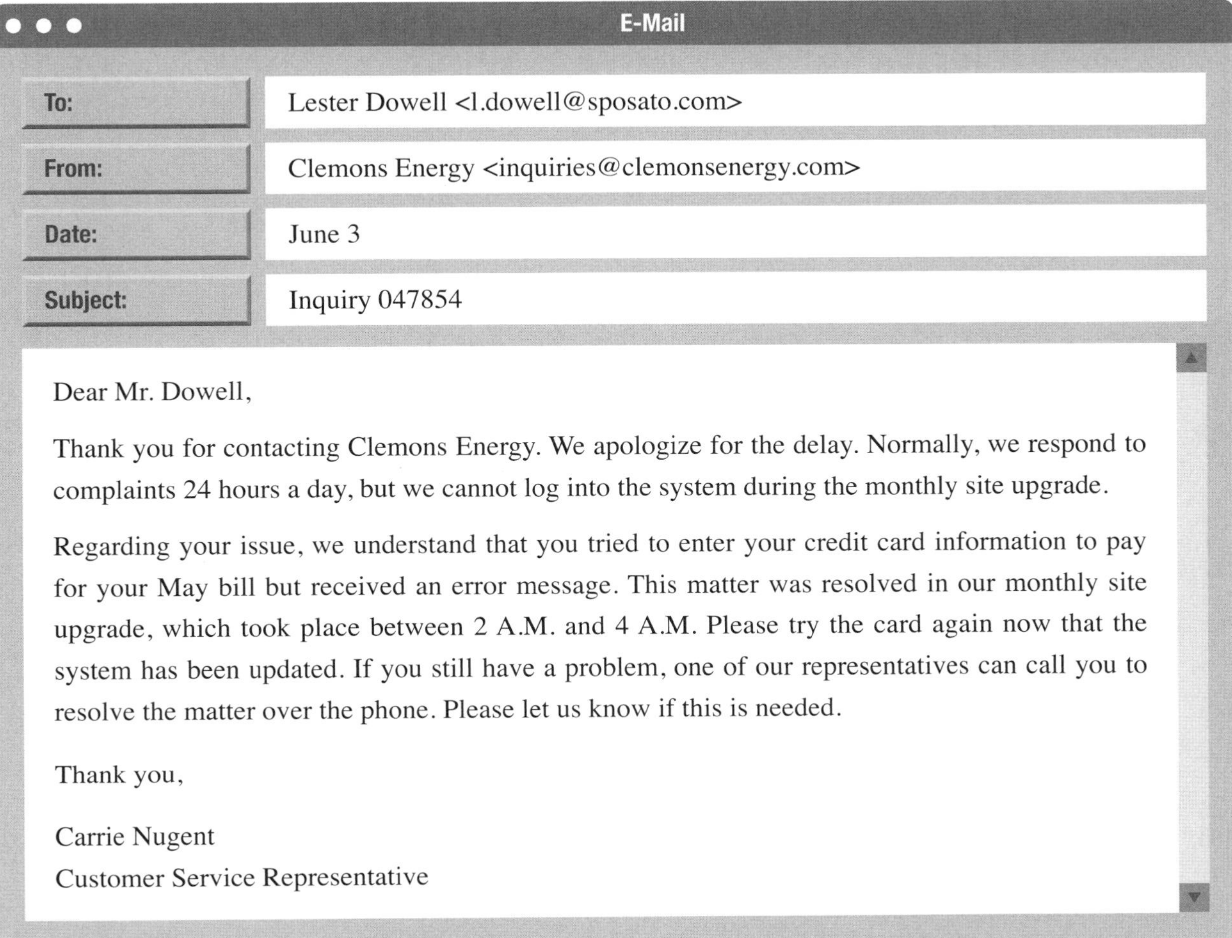

E-Mail

To: Lester Dowell <l.dowell@sposato.com>

From: Clemons Energy <inquiries@clemonsenergy.com>

Date: June 3

Subject: Inquiry 047854

Dear Mr. Dowell,

Thank you for contacting Clemons Energy. We apologize for the delay. Normally, we respond to complaints 24 hours a day, but we cannot log into the system during the monthly site upgrade.

Regarding your issue, we understand that you tried to enter your credit card information to pay for your May bill but received an error message. This matter was resolved in our monthly site upgrade, which took place between 2 A.M. and 4 A.M. Please try the card again now that the system has been updated. If you still have a problem, one of our representatives can call you to resolve the matter over the phone. Please let us know if this is needed.

Thank you,

Carrie Nugent
Customer Service Representative

151. Why most likely did Mr. Dowell contact Clemons Energy?

(A) He moved to a new address in May.
(B) He wanted to upgrade his account.
(C) He had difficulty making a payment.
(D) He was overcharged for a service.

152. What is suggested about Ms. Nugent?

(A) She could not access a system for two hours.
(B) She plans to call Mr. Dowell later.
(C) Her work shift ended at 2 A.M.
(D) Her first message contained an error.

GO ON TO THE NEXT PAGE

Questions 153-155 refer to the following e-mail.

E-Mail

To: Paula Ortiz <p.ortiz@metzfinancial.com>
From: Edwin Ramsay <ramsayed@quillypost.com>
Date: July 25
Subject: Financial advisor position

Dear Ms. Ortiz,

My name is Edwin Ramsay, and I am a senior portfolio manager at Cullins Investments. I am writing on behalf of a member of my staff, Rico Alston, who has recently applied for your financial advisor position. I have worked with Mr. Alston for the past three years, and I can confirm that he would be an amazing asset to your team. In my 10 years working for this company, I have never seen someone with so much dedication to the job. In addition, he is able to build relationships with customers quickly. I would be happy to answer any detailed questions you may have about Mr. Alston's time with our company. Please feel free to contact my office at 746-555-8306.

Edwin Ramsay

153. What is the purpose of the e-mail?
(A) To promote a company
(B) To announce a job opening
(C) To offer an applicant a position
(D) To recommend a colleague

154. What is indicated about Mr. Ramsay?
(A) He is managing Ms. Ortiz's investment portfolio.
(B) He has met with Ms. Ortiz in person before.
(C) He has worked at Cullins Investments for a decade.
(D) He is the founder of Cullins Investments.

155. What does Mr. Ramsay offer to do?
(A) Have a phone conversation
(B) Send some updated figures
(C) Visit Ms. Ortiz's office
(D) Change his working hours

Questions 156-157 refer to the following text-message chain.

Curtis Burnett [1:18 P.M.]
Hi, Fiona. I'm working on the schedule for the fall. Originally, you said you could teach two of the Saturday workshops each month. Is that still the case?

Fiona Ervin [1:21 P.M.]
That's fine for September, but I don't think it would be possible for the other months. I've been assigned a lot of extra tasks.

Curtis Burnett [1:22 P.M.]
Yeah, everyone is overloaded with work. We need to hire a few more people.

Fiona Ervin [1:23 P.M.]
That's for sure. If you can find someone else to do it, they're welcome to use my slides from last year. They have good tips for creating a plot, developing characters, and using descriptive language.

Curtis Burnett [1:24 P.M.]
Thanks! That would be really useful. For now, I'll schedule you for the first and third Saturday in September.

Fiona Ervin [1:25 P.M.]
I can make that work.

156. At 1:23 P.M., what does Ms. Ervin mean when she writes, "That's for sure"?

(A) She agrees that an assignment was confusing.
(B) She thinks the company should employ more staff members.
(C) She plans to work overtime with Mr. Burnett.
(D) She will look for a new job in September.

157. What kind of classes will most likely take place on Saturdays?

(A) Music
(B) Writing
(C) Art
(D) Fitness

GO ON TO THE NEXT PAGE

Questions 158-160 refer to the following letter.

Erica Sutton
Norfolk Tower, Unit 304
372 Chamberlain Avenue
Atlanta, GA 30306

Dear Ms. Sutton,

I am the event planner for the National Engineering Conference (NEC) hosted by Houston-based firm Waddell Engineering. —[1]—. This year, the event is scheduled for October 16 and 17 at the Marietta Center in Sacramento. The theme is Responsive Design for Improved Well-Being.

Dr. Ayaan Vadekar, of the University of Charlotte, will be the keynote speaker. —[2]—. We also need other experts in the field to share their insights with our attendees. Therefore, I would like to invite you to be a speaker at the event. I recently saw your talk at the Smart Cities Summit. —[3]—. I hope you could do the same for our event.

We would pay for your flight from Atlanta to the conference site, provide free accommodations near the Marietta Center, and supply you with meal vouchers. If you are interested, I would like to discuss the matter further at your convenience. —[4]—.

Warmest regards,

Pauline Faber
Pauline Faber
Waddell Engineering
832-555-4219, ext. 16

158. What is the purpose of the letter?

(A) To recruit a presenter for an event
(B) To confirm registration at a conference
(C) To announce a change in venue
(D) To ask for theme suggestions

159. Where will this year's NEC take place?

(A) In Atlanta
(B) In Charlotte
(C) In Houston
(D) In Sacramento

160. In which of the positions marked [1], [2], [3], and [4] does the following sentence best belong?

"I was impressed with how you kept the audience so engaged."

(A) [1]
(B) [2]
(C) [3]
(D) [4]

Questions 161-163 refer to the following Web page.

www.sasba.org/survey/07562

Your opinions matter!

Thank you for your interest in the annual survey conducted by the San Antonio Small Business Association (SASBA). The SASBA is dedicated to influencing local and state politicians to provide a supportive framework for small business owners. This survey is intended for small business owners in San Antonio. Your answers will help us to determine which area to focus on.

The online survey takes about ten minutes to complete. You can select to have your name included with your answers or have your name removed so you cannot be identified. The link to the survey will work until November 7. We will publish a summary of our findings on our Web site on November 30. Questions or comments should be directed to Molly Steele at msteele@sasba.org.

Thank you for your participation.

Survey: #07562
Name: Audrey Walsh

161. What is true about Ms. Walsh?

(A) She runs a business in San Antonio.
(B) She works for SASBA.
(C) She completed last year's survey.
(D) She had a problem with the first link.

162. Why most likely is SASBA conducting the survey?

(A) To evaluate the effectiveness of a membership program
(B) To determine which businesses should win an award
(C) To identify policy changes that are needed
(D) To develop an educational program for business owners

163. What is indicated about the survey?

(A) Its questions were developed by Ms. Steele.
(B) It will be available until November 30.
(C) Its answers can be changed after submission.
(D) It can be submitted anonymously.

GO ON TO THE NEXT PAGE

Questions 164-167 refer to the following notice.

Notice to All Preston Insurance Employees:

May 4

From June 1, Preston Insurance will begin requiring parking passes for all vehicles in the lot. Currently, although the lot is intended for our employees only, it is often used by members of the public without authorization. Therefore, we will be issuing barcode parking permits to all employees who drive to work. The passes are easily scannable, so they will save the company a lot of time on running the parking lot.

There are two options for passes—a stick-on decal or a plastic tag. The adhesive of the decal is designed not to leave any residue behind, so it can be peeled off easily. As for the tag, it hangs from the rearview mirror so must be removed while driving. While we recommend the decal, we will leave it up to individual employees, so please let us know which one you would like. We already have your license plate numbers and other necessary information on record. Please contact Reggie Norris at extension 41 to get a pass.

164. Why was the notice written?

(A) To warn employees about a parking lot closure
(B) To explain an increase in a parking fee
(C) To announce changes to a parking system
(D) To ask people not to use a company parking lot

165. The word "running" in paragraph 1, line 5, is closest in meaning to

(A) flowing
(B) operating
(C) participating
(D) competing

166. What benefit of the decal is mentioned?

(A) It is easy to remove.
(B) It is a small size.
(C) It can be printed inexpensively.
(D) It is visible from far away.

167. What information should people provide to Mr. Norris?

(A) A driver's license number
(B) A pass type preference
(C) A license plate number
(D) A selected parking spot

Questions 168-171 refer to the following online chat discussion.

Darlene Gray [10:40 A.M.]	Hi, Karen and Owen. I wanted to let you know that Morland Hall has been confirmed for the April 4 workshop for our employees here at Falcon Data.
Karen Ralston [10:41 A.M.]	That's great. Do I need to meet the instructor, Clair Wallace, at the airport?
Darlene Gray [10:42 A.M.]	Actually, she plans to rent a car at the airport and drive to the venue from there. Morland Hall has tables and chairs for us to use, but we must arrange them ourselves. We can borrow presentation equipment from the venue as well.
Karen Ralston [10:44 A.M.]	All right. Owen is going to set everything up. I've already sent him a drawing of what we discussed.
Owen Foley [10:45 A.M.]	That's right. Also, I found out that the catering company can deliver, but the fee for that is quite high. It's just boxed lunches, so I'll stop by and get them on the way to the venue that morning.
Darlene Gray [10:47 A.M.]	That's perfect, Owen. Thank you! I've already paid the bill in full, so there will be nothing due.

168. What is the purpose of the online chat discussion?

(A) To assign some writing tasks
(B) To book a venue for an event
(C) To discuss plans for a workshop
(D) To find instructors for training

169. What is indicated about Ms. Wallace?

(A) She is a Morland Hall employee.
(B) She has met Ms. Ralston before.
(C) She attended an event last year.
(D) She is traveling from out of town.

170. Who will prepare a room?

(A) Ms. Ralston
(B) Ms. Gray
(C) Ms. Wallace
(D) Mr. Foley

171. At 10:47 A.M., what does Ms. Gray most likely mean when she writes, "That's perfect, Owen"?

(A) She would like to order boxed lunches for an event.
(B) She thinks Owen should meet Ms. Wallace early.
(C) She agrees that Mr. Foley should pick up some food.
(D) She is pleased with catering company's services.

GO ON TO THE NEXT PAGE

Questions 172-175 refer to the following letter.

October 15

Mr. Craig Jenkins
General Manager
Barrington Hotel
4667 Ward Street
Philadelphia, PA 19108

Dear Mr. Jenkins,

As the Accommodation Manager for Modoc Airlines, it is my responsibility to procure overnight accommodations for our pilots and flight attendants when they are staying in a city for work-related reasons. Many of our staff members have praised the high quality of the Barrington Hotel. —[1]—. However, I've been told numerous times that you offer excellent customer service and that the rooms are clean and comfortable. —[2]—. It is also convenient that you have an on-site gym and that there is a world-class restaurant within walking distance.

I believe that our businesses could help each other. —[3]—. What I would suggest is having us book a block of rooms at a discounted price. These would be guaranteed to be booked and paid for every month, even on the days we do not use them. That way, we could get affordable accommodations while your business receives a steady income. —[4]—. Modoc Airlines is growing steadily, and we increased our staff by 10% last year. This means we can offer you stability and a long-time partnership. Additionally, if this works in Philadelphia, we could possibly do the same in other branches in your chain of hotels. Enclosed you will find a list of the routes that our airline serves. Please call me at 327-555-1888 to discuss this matter further.

Sincerely,

Raul Flores
Raul Flores, Accommodation Manager
Modoc Airlines

172. Why did Mr. Flores write the letter?

(A) To introduce a job opening
(B) To propose a business arrangement
(C) To review his hotel stay
(D) To make a hotel reservation

173. What is indicated about the Barrington Hotel?

(A) It has a fitness facility.
(B) Its guests can dine on-site.
(C) It offers spacious guest rooms.
(D) Its staff grew by 10% last year.

174. What has been included with the letter?

(A) A discount voucher
(B) A staff directory
(C) A sample contract
(D) A list of travel routes

175. In which of the positions marked [1], [2], [3], and [4] does the following sentence best belong?

"I haven't had the opportunity to stay there myself."

(A) [1]
(B) [2]
(C) [3]
(D) [4]

TEST 03

GO ON TO THE NEXT PAGE

Questions 176-180 refer to the following schedule and e-mail.

Cooking Demonstrations at Delamore Department Store
September Schedule
Theme: Vegetarian Food

- Saturday, September 4 — Amber Paschal of The Wave, author of *Hearty Home Meals*
- Saturday, September 11 — Loni McIntyre and Jerome Kellum of BT Bistro
- Sunday, September 19 — Ralph Scherr of Eagleway Restaurant
- Thursday, September 23 — Patricia Marquez of Carmine Café, author of *Very Veggie*

All demonstrations begin at 2 P.M. in our Kitchenware section.

If you are a professional chef and are available to give a demonstration in October, please contact Kent Briggs at k.briggs@delamore.com. The theme for October will be Indian Food. Demonstrations should last 60 to 90 minutes. We will supply the necessary cooking equipment as well as the ingredients, so please let us know what is needed for your recipe.

E-Mail

TO:	Loni McIntyre
FROM:	Anthony Ulrich
DATE:	September 25
SUBJECT:	Demonstration

Dear Ms. McIntyre,

I work for *The Colton Times*, writing articles for its Food and Dining section. I attended the demonstration that you and your coworker, Jerome Kellum, gave at the Delamore Department Store. I was very impressed with your techniques, and I thought the samples you gave out were simply delicious. I would like to feature you and your restaurant in an upcoming article. Are you available for a phone call sometime this week? I'm sure my readers would be very interested in how you develop your recipes and what originally inspired you to become a chef. In addition to being helpful for my column, it would be excellent publicity for your restaurant. I've already made arrangements with Mr. Kellum, who said he would give another demonstration at the department store in October.

If you are interested, please let me know. I can work around your schedule.

Warmest regards,

Anthony Ulrich

176. What is indicated about the demonstration events?

(A) They will continue to be held in October.
(B) Their presenters include published authors only.
(C) They should not be longer than an hour.
(D) Their participants can receive a discount.

177. What should chefs include in their e-mail?

(A) Information about hourly rates
(B) Details of recipe steps
(C) A résumé of career history
(D) A list of required ingredients

178. Why did Mr. Ulrich send the e-mail?

(A) To request food samples for an event
(B) To propose an interview for a publication
(C) To introduce his promotional services
(D) To hire Ms. McIntyre for a private event

179. When did Mr. Ulrich see Ms. McIntyre give a demonstration?

(A) On September 4
(B) On September 11
(C) On September 19
(D) On September 23

180. What is suggested about Mr. Kellum?

(A) He wants to open a new restaurant.
(B) He is able to cook Indian food.
(C) He plans to write a cookbook.
(D) He was too busy to help Mr. Ulrich.

GO ON TO THE NEXT PAGE

Questions 181-185 refer to the following Web page and e-mail.

</>

Gifts Galore—Custom promotional items to help you stand out!

Are you looking for a way to thank customers or employees? Do you want to promote your business? Gifts Galore has a wide range of items for corporate gifts, trade fairs, contests, or any time you want to make your business memorable. Get your logo or other image printed on water bottles, tote bags, pens, calendars, and more. We follow customers' purchasing habits and change our inventory accordingly. We can even wrap your items in paper and ribbons to ensure they are beautifully presented. And, there's no need to make a bulk purchase, as we can process orders with a minimum of just 5 items.

If you need advice about your design, you will be assigned a graphic designer to make sure everything looks good. We ship anywhere in the world, but please note that because items are custom printed, it can take up to three weeks to receive your order. All sales are final. However, since customers cannot send items back, we are willing to provide samples in advance for your checking.

E-Mail

To: Courtney Fitch <cfitch@gifts-galore.com>
From: Warren Evans <evansw@serranofinance.net>
Date: January 9
Subject: Thanks!

I would like to let you know that I had a very positive experience with the first order I placed with your company. It was so helpful to have Howard Lopez providing design advice on an individual level. I was impressed that Gifts Galore had so many options for different items, so I decided to give it a chance. I'm glad that I did! We hope to place a large order soon, as your bulk discount pricing is definitely a consideration in making Gifts Galore the right choice for us.

All the best,

Warren Evans
Client Relations Manager

181. What is true about Gifts Galore?

(A) Its goods meet high quality control standards.
(B) It sponsors various trade fairs.
(C) It adjusts its stock based on trends.
(D) It specializes in domestically produced goods.

182. What is NOT indicated about Gifts Galore's products?

(A) They feature the Gifts Galore logo.
(B) They can be made in small orders.
(C) They are not eligible for returns.
(D) They can be gift-wrapped.

183. Who most likely is Howard Lopez?

(A) A company owner
(B) A graphic designer
(C) A finance manager
(D) A delivery driver

184. In the e-mail, the word "consideration" in paragraph 1, line 5, is closest in meaning to

(A) deposit
(B) factor
(C) outcome
(D) kindness

185. What is suggested about Mr. Evans?

(A) He thinks Gifts Galore has a good variety.
(B) He was surprised by the fast service.
(C) He ordered items in different sizes.
(D) He is still waiting for his first order.

GO ON TO THE NEXT PAGE →

Questions 186-190 refer to the following sign, receipt, and e-mail.

Cicero Auction House

Information for Auction Winners

1. Payment must be made within three business days. If not, the item will be put up for the next auction.
2. Paid items are dispatched for delivery within one week. Local delivery is free. Speak to a staff member regarding other locations.
3. Oversized items (exceeding 3 feet in any direction) are stored in our secure basement rather than the ground floor storage room.
4. All purchases include insurance for the item.
5. Returns are not accepted.

Open: Tues.–Fri. 8 A.M.–6 P.M.
Sat.–Sun. 10 A.M.–4 P.M.

Cicero Auction House Customer Receipt

Item Number: 06251
Artist Name: Antone Vinson
Total Payment: $385
Previous Owner: Daniel Bartholomew
Dimensions: 3.5 ft. x 4 ft.

Customer Name: Beatrice Mueller
Auction Date: January 9
Pick up/Delivery: To be delivered on January 14

E-Mail

To:	Cicero Auction House <contact@ciceroauctionhouse.com>
From:	Beatrice Mueller <bmueller@wilmar-inc.com>
Date:	January 12
Subject:	Auction Item Inquiry

Hello,

I recently won an auction at your site and paid for the item the same day. I had originally planned to have the painting sent to my office, as it matched an antique vase and a rug that I have there. However, I have now decided that I would like it in my home instead, which is at 324 Osborne Street, as I want to hang it above a sculpture in my living room. I hope this is possible. Please let me know.

Sincerely,

Beatrice Mueller

186. What does the sign indicate about items that are not paid for on time?

(A) They will incur an additional fee.
(B) They will be added to a future event.
(C) They will be donated to a charity.
(D) They will be sold to the second-highest bidder.

187. What is true about Cicero Auction House?

(A) It is closed on Mondays.
(B) It has more than one location.
(C) It only delivers locally.
(D) It is a family-owned business.

188. What is indicated about Ms. Mueller's item?

(A) It was purchased on January 14.
(B) It was sold for more than 500 dollars.
(C) It was classified as oversized.
(D) It was created by Daniel Bartholomew.

189. What kind of item most likely is 06251?

(A) A sculpture
(B) A vase
(C) A painting
(D) A rug

190. Why did Ms. Mueller write the e-mail?

(A) To request a change in delivery location
(B) To report a problem with a payment
(C) To postpone receiving a purchase
(D) To get advice about cleaning an item

GO ON TO THE NEXT PAGE →

Questions 191-195 refer to the following Web page, advertisement, and e-mail.

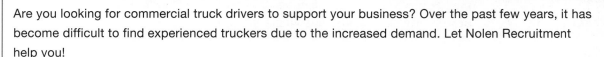

http://www.nolenrecruitment.com 

Are you looking for commercial truck drivers to support your business? Over the past few years, it has become difficult to find experienced truckers due to the increased demand. Let Nolen Recruitment help you!

We have been a leader in the recruitment of commercial truck drivers for trucking and construction for the past decade. We screen all of our job candidates carefully, verifying licenses and checking the professional references that we require. Our team will also ensure that any driver we recommend to your company has a clean driving record, helping to keep your insurance rates low.

To find out how we can help you, e-mail our customer service team today!

COMMERCIAL TRUCKERS WANTED

Lakeland Trucking is expanding our staff after being purchased by CW Industries.

Job Description: Long-haul truck drivers needed for the transportation of retail goods. Must be able to meet delivery deadlines, work full-time hours, and adhere to all road safety practices.

Job Requirements: Must hold valid commercial driver's license and submit two letters of recommendation from a current or previous employer. At least two years' experience. Must attend a two-week orientation before first assignment.

Compensation: $45,000–$55,000 starting salary, depending on experience. Quarterly performance bonuses.

Application Process: Please bring your résumé to our recruitment event anytime on October 3 from 8 A.M. to 8 P.M. at the Fulton Convention Center.

To: contact@nolenrecruitment.com
From: d_williford@lakelandtrucking.com
Date: October 13
Subject: Recruitment request

To Whom It May Concern:

I am interested in using your services to hire 5–10 experienced commercial truck drivers. Our company held a recruitment event earlier this month. However, not as many people showed up as we expected, so we had difficulty finding enough suitable candidates. We accept drivers with at least two years' experience, and they should be able to start work as soon as possible. We will have all new recruits attend a one-week orientation. Please let me know your commission rates as well as how soon you can get me a list of prospective candidates.

Warm regards,

Diana Williford

191. According to the Web page, what has changed?

(A) The cost of fuel
(B) The need for truck drivers
(C) The regulations for transportation
(D) The price of vehicles

192. What is suggested about Lakeland Trucking in the advertisement?

(A) It has started offering a new service.
(B) It has part-time job openings.
(C) It is under new ownership.
(D) It runs road safety courses.

193. What do Nolen Recruitment and Lakeland Trucking have in common?

(A) They provide insurance for drivers.
(B) They have both developed driving tests.
(C) They pay bonuses to employees.
(D) They require professional references.

194. What does Ms. Williford mention about a recruitment event?

(A) It was canceled unexpectedly.
(B) It needs a new event planner.
(C) It had a low turnout.
(D) It is held every year.

195. What was adjusted for the positions at Lakeland Trucking?

(A) The orientation period
(B) The required experience
(C) The annual salary
(D) The number of working hours

GO ON TO THE NEXT PAGE

Questions 196-200 refer to the following article, schedule, and e-mail.

Brenton Industries to Offer New Grant

(April 9)—In a press conference held yesterday, startup technology firm Brenton Industries announced that it will offer five private grants to individuals working in a variety of industries and fields. The grants are aimed at encouraging innovation through individual research. Those awarded the grants will also be invited to attend the Bright Future Conference for free.

"The future depends on the creativity of workers, and we want to reward those who have the potential to achieve major breakthroughs," said Ruth Gillis, the vice president of Brenton Industries. "Through these funds, we hope to facilitate inspiration within the workforce."

Applicants must be currently taking classes at the master's or Ph.D. level. They should provide examples of previous projects demonstrating their ideas. More information is available at www.brentonind.com/grant.

Bright Future Conference

Concord Convention Center

Below is the schedule of this year's conference activities. A final list of speakers will be sent to participants once it is finalized, no later than July 3.

❑ 8:00 A.M.	Reception and networking breakfast — Lobby
❑ 9:00 A.M.	Welcome speech and Brenton Industries mission statement
❑ 9:30 A.M. – 10:30 A.M.	Panel discussion — Main Hall
❑ 10:30 A.M. – 12:30 P.M.	Presentations — Various Rooms
❑ 12:30 P.M. – 1:30 P.M.	Lunch — Buffet lunch in Room 103. Attendees should show their conference pass for admission.
❑ 1:30 P.M. – 4:30 P.M.	Workshops — Various Rooms
❑ 4:30 P.M. – 5:00 P.M.	Feedback session

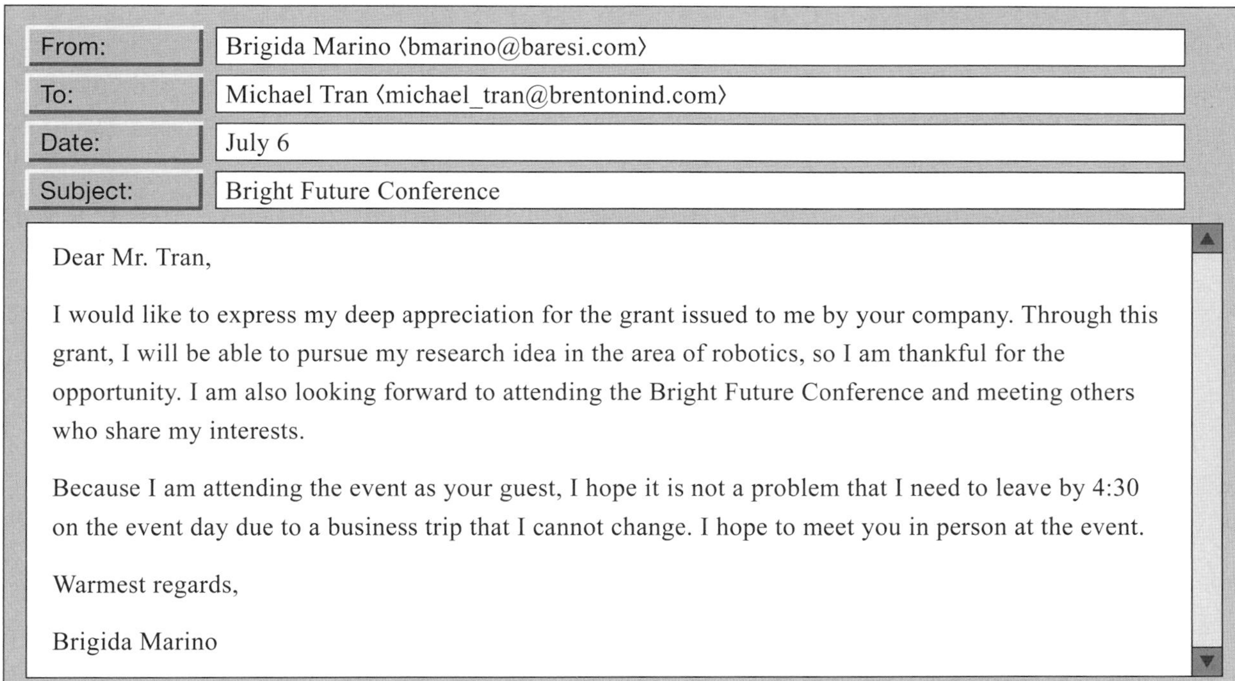

From:	Brigida Marino ⟨bmarino@baresi.com⟩
To:	Michael Tran ⟨michael_tran@brentonind.com⟩
Date:	July 6
Subject:	Bright Future Conference

Dear Mr. Tran,

I would like to express my deep appreciation for the grant issued to me by your company. Through this grant, I will be able to pursue my research idea in the area of robotics, so I am thankful for the opportunity. I am also looking forward to attending the Bright Future Conference and meeting others who share my interests.

Because I am attending the event as your guest, I hope it is not a problem that I need to leave by 4:30 on the event day due to a business trip that I cannot change. I hope to meet you in person at the event.

Warmest regards,

Brigida Marino

196. What does Brenton Industries want to support with the grant?
(A) Job creation
(B) Creative ideas
(C) Cultural diversity
(D) Environmental protection

197. According to the article, what does Brenton Industries require of applicants?
(A) Enrollment in higher education courses
(B) Participation in an online questionnaire
(C) Specialization in a certain industry
(D) Experience with public speaking

198. What is suggested about the conference in the schedule?
(A) Most activities will take place in the Main Hall.
(B) A panel discussion will be filmed.
(C) Attendees should order their lunch in advance.
(D) Some presenters have not been confirmed.

199. What is implied about Ms. Marino?
(A) She will travel to the event from overseas.
(B) She submitted samples of her work.
(C) She will give a talk at the conference.
(D) She is an employee of Brenton Industries.

200. Which part of the conference will Ms. Marino be unable to attend?
(A) One of the presentations
(B) The networking breakfast
(C) One of the workshops
(D) The feedback session

Stop! This is the end of the test. If you finish before time is called, you may go back to Parts 5, 6, and 7 and check your work.

▶ 정답 및 해설 p. 70

자동 채점 서비스
바로가기

에 듀 윌 토 익 실 전 서

LC+RC

TEST 04

LISTENING TEST

PART 1

PART 2

PART 3

PART 4

READING TEST

PART 5

PART 6

PART 7

LISTENING TEST

In the Listening test, you will be asked to demonstrate how well you understand spoken English. The entire Listening test will last approximately 45 minutes. There are four parts, and directions are given for each part. You must mark your answers on the separate answer sheet. Do not write your answers in your test book.

PART 1

Directions: For each question in this part, you will hear four statements about a picture in your test book. When you hear the statements, you must select the one statement that best describes what you see in the picture. Then find the number of the question on your answer sheet and mark your answer. The statements will not be printed in your test book and will be spoken only one time.

Statement (C), "He's making a phone call," is the best description of the picture, so you should select answer (C) and mark it on your answer sheet.

1.

2.

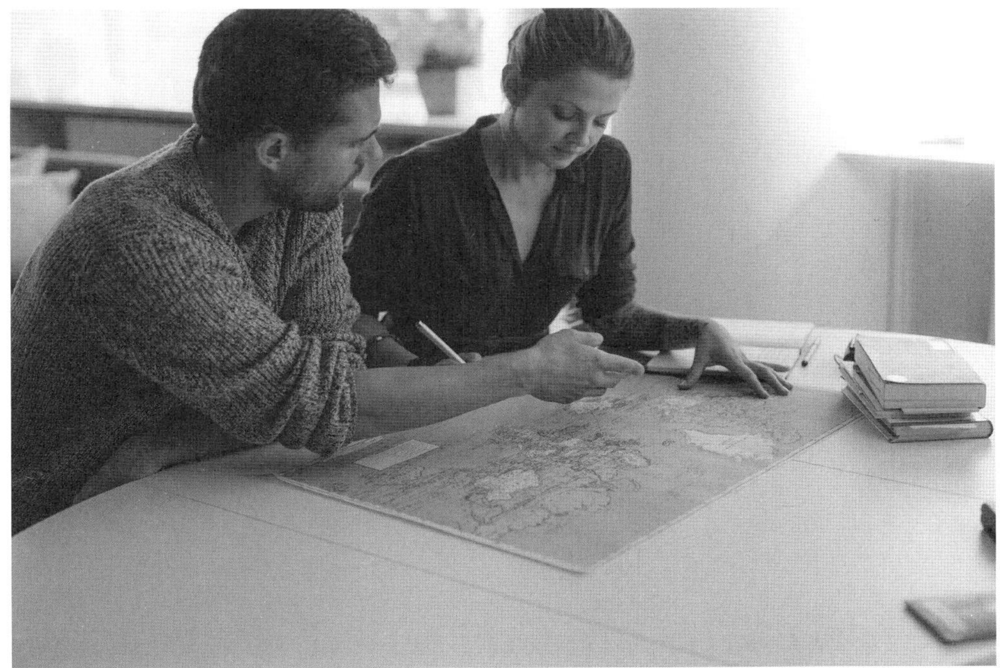

TEST 04

GO ON TO THE NEXT PAGE

3.

4.

5.

6.

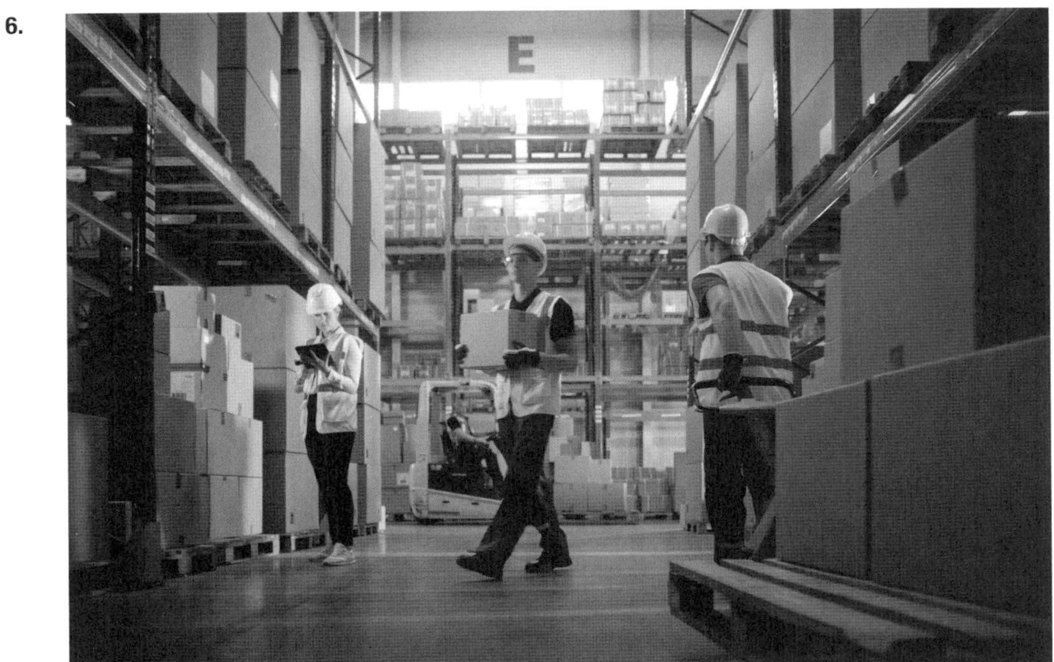

GO ON TO THE NEXT PAGE

PART 2

Directions: You will hear a question or statement and three responses spoken in English. They will not be printed in your test book and will be spoken only one time. Select the best response to the question or statement and mark the letter (A), (B), or (C) on your answer sheet.

7. Mark your answer on your answer sheet.
8. Mark your answer on your answer sheet.
9. Mark your answer on your answer sheet.
10. Mark your answer on your answer sheet.
11. Mark your answer on your answer sheet.
12. Mark your answer on your answer sheet.
13. Mark your answer on your answer sheet.
14. Mark your answer on your answer sheet.
15. Mark your answer on your answer sheet.
16. Mark your answer on your answer sheet.
17. Mark your answer on your answer sheet.
18. Mark your answer on your answer sheet.
19. Mark your answer on your answer sheet.
20. Mark your answer on your answer sheet.
21. Mark your answer on your answer sheet.
22. Mark your answer on your answer sheet.
23. Mark your answer on your answer sheet.
24. Mark your answer on your answer sheet.
25. Mark your answer on your answer sheet.
26. Mark your answer on your answer sheet.
27. Mark your answer on your answer sheet.
28. Mark your answer on your answer sheet.
29. Mark your answer on your answer sheet.
30. Mark your answer on your answer sheet.
31. Mark your answer on your answer sheet.

PART 3

Directions: You will hear some conversations between two or more people. You will be asked to answer three questions about what the speakers say in each conversation. Select the best response to each question and mark the letter (A), (B), (C), or (D) on your answer sheet. The conversations will not be printed in your test book and will be spoken only one time.

32. What are the speakers mainly discussing?
(A) Some marketing plans
(B) Some company investors
(C) An upcoming trip
(D) An award nomination

33. Why has the woman been very busy?
(A) She returned from taking time off.
(B) She has been planning an event.
(C) She has been preparing a show.
(D) She completed a quarterly report.

34. What does the man suggest doing?
(A) Talking to a supervisor
(B) Checking a policy carefully
(C) Making a reservation
(D) Downloading a mobile application

---

35. Where does the woman most likely work?
(A) At a newspaper publisher
(B) At a tour company
(C) At a car dealership
(D) At an employment agency

36. What does the man inquire about?
(A) A return policy
(B) A job opportunity
(C) A discount offer
(D) A new product

37. What does the woman invite the man to do?
(A) Attend an event
(B) Take a brochure
(C) Sign up for an account
(D) Visit a Web site

---

38. Where do the men work?
(A) At a graphic design company
(B) At an accounting firm
(C) At a medical clinic
(D) At a law firm

39. What are the men having trouble doing?
(A) Implementing new technology
(B) Keeping existing customers
(C) Finding experienced staff
(D) Identifying reliable suppliers

40. What does the woman suggest doing?
(A) Expanding the business hours
(B) Providing further training
(C) Placing advertisements online
(D) Adjusting a benefits package

---

41. What is sold at the speakers' business?
(A) Photography equipment
(B) Cleaning products
(C) Art supplies
(D) Computer accessories

42. What does the woman mean when she says, "I think he needs a signature"?
(A) A contract will go into effect soon.
(B) A delivery has not been completed.
(C) A check is not valid yet.
(D) A schedule change was not approved.

43. According to the man, what do customers forget to do?
(A) Read signs
(B) Show an ID card
(C) Keep sales receipts
(D) Use coupons

GO ON TO THE NEXT PAGE

44. Who most likely are the men?

(A) Plumbers
(B) Fitness instructors
(C) Physicians
(D) Travel agents

45. What are the men frustrated about?

(A) A building was locked.
(B) A form was not updated.
(C) A colleague is absent.
(D) A package was not labeled.

46. What will the woman show to the men?

(A) A supplemental estimate
(B) A revised contract
(C) A product catalog
(D) A system layout

---

47. What project does the woman propose?

(A) Planting flowers in a field
(B) Renovating a city building
(C) Adding a tennis court
(D) Expanding a parking lot

48. What does the man say will be difficult?

(A) Securing enough funds
(B) Raising a parking fee
(C) Getting a building permit
(D) Finding a suitable space

49. What does the man advise the woman to do?

(A) Contact local businesses
(B) Attend a meeting
(C) Visit the city's Web site
(D) Train as a volunteer

---

50. What industry does the man most likely work in?

(A) Transportation
(B) Agriculture
(C) Food service
(D) Healthcare

51. What did the man do last month?

(A) He published a book.
(B) He gave a speech.
(C) He won an award.
(D) He launched a business.

52. What will the man probably talk about next?

(A) Resolving staff complaints
(B) Attracting new customers
(C) Choosing the right tools
(D) Applying for businesses loans

---

53. Where do the speakers work?

(A) At a home improvement store
(B) At an advertising agency
(C) At a real estate agency
(D) At an investment bank

54. What does the woman suggest purchasing?

(A) Some computer equipment
(B) Some furniture
(C) Some company vehicles
(D) Some carpets

55. Why does the man say, "Last time, it took two weeks"?

(A) To make a guess
(B) To register a complaint
(C) To offer an excuse
(D) To reject a proposal

---

56. Who most likely is the woman?
(A) The man's previous classmate
(B) The man's former customer
(C) The man's supervisor
(D) The man's coworker

57. What does the man plan to do in a few weeks?
(A) Run for city council
(B) Submit a bid for a project
(C) Teach a workshop at the library
(D) Visit the woman's home

58. What does the man need?
(A) A company directory
(B) A budget summary
(C) A safety certification
(D) A letter of reference

---

59. Where do the speakers most likely work?
(A) At a construction company
(B) At an automobile factory
(C) At a radio station
(D) At a ferry terminal

60. What does the woman say about Warner Road?
(A) It passes by a stadium.
(B) It needs significant repairs.
(C) It has reopened to traffic.
(D) It has heavy traffic today.

61. How can the listeners learn more about a new project?
(A) By signing up for a mailing list
(B) By attending a meeting
(C) By calling a business
(D) By downloading a brochure

Sonora Community Center Spring Schedule				
Mon	Tue	Wed	Thu	Fri
Baking	Sewing	Ceramics	Painting	Spanish

62. Why is the woman calling?
(A) To ask for driving directions
(B) To inquire about making a payment
(C) To volunteer to teach a class
(D) To confirm that on-site parking is available

63. Look at the graphic. Which class does the woman want to attend?
(A) Baking
(B) Sewing
(C) Ceramics
(D) Painting

64. What will the woman do in Atlanta?
(A) Give a speech
(B) Attend an interview
(C) See a musical performance
(D) Go to a retirement party

GO ON TO THE NEXT PAGE

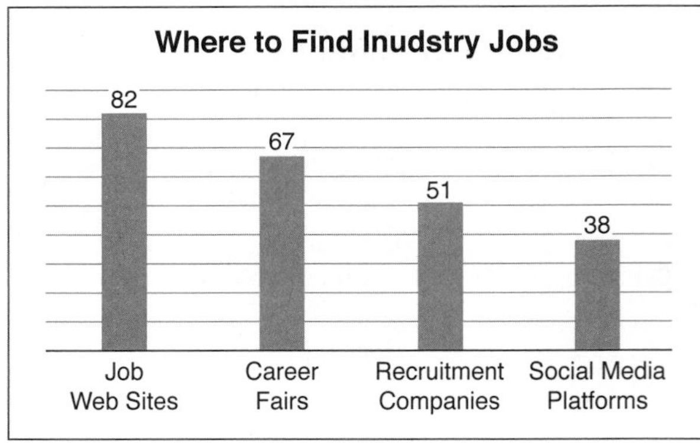

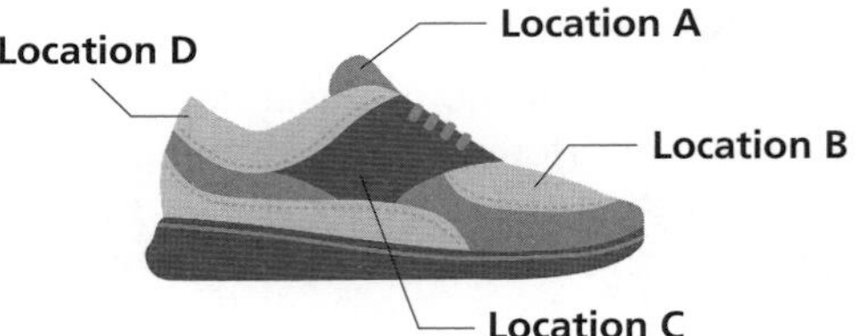

65. Where do the speakers most likely work?

(A) At a graphic design firm
(B) At a cleaning service
(C) At an appliance manufacturer
(D) At a property management company

66. Look at the graphic. What category will the company spend money on?

(A) Job Web Sites
(B) Career Fairs
(C) Recruitment Companies
(D) Social Media Platforms

67. What does the man offer to do?

(A) Write a job description
(B) Look for upcoming events
(C) Approve a budget change
(D) Review some résumés

68. What is the woman having trouble deciding about the shoes?

(A) The fabric type
(B) The launch date
(C) The colors
(D) The prices

69. According to the woman, why does a design need to be changed?

(A) To reduce the manufacturing costs
(B) To attract younger consumers
(C) To avoid looking similar to a competitor
(D) To respond to some customer feedback

70. Look at the graphic. Where will the logo be placed?

(A) Location A
(B) Location B
(C) Location C
(D) Location D

PART 4

Directions: You will hear some talks given by a single speaker. You will be asked to answer three questions about what the speaker says in each talk. Select the best response to each question and mark the letter (A), (B), (C), or (D) on your answer sheet. The talks will not be printed in your test book and will be spoken only one time.

71. What did the speaker order from the company?
(A) A set of golf clubs
(B) A collection of dishes
(C) A piece of luggage
(D) A pair of eyeglasses

72. What problem does the speaker tell the listener about?
(A) A size was incorrect.
(B) A part was damaged.
(C) A Web site is not loading.
(D) A bill was too high.

73. What does the speaker inquire about?
(A) A processing time
(B) An e-mail address
(C) A delivery route
(D) A store location

---

74. What kind of award does the speaker announce?
(A) Lifetime Achievement
(B) Best Graphic Design
(C) Employee of the Year
(D) Outstanding Salesperson

75. What will be given to the winner?
(A) An office party
(B) A cash bonus
(C) An extra day off
(D) A trophy

76. According to the speaker, what can the listeners see next week?
(A) A new Web site
(B) A completed book
(C) A group photograph
(D) A nomination form

---

77. What does the speaker's company sell?
(A) Office software
(B) Mobile phones
(C) Light fixtures
(D) Power tools

78. What will the listeners do next?
(A) Tour a site
(B) Watch a video
(C) Take a test
(D) Sign a contract

79. Why does the speaker say, "So far, no one has done so"?
(A) To assign a task
(B) To reassure the listeners
(C) To make a complaint
(D) To adjust the schedule

---

80. What is the main topic of the meeting?
(A) Improving product packaging
(B) Complying with new regulations
(C) Reducing transportation costs
(D) Simplifying a training process

81. What will the company do next month?
(A) Hire more mechanics
(B) Partner with another firm
(C) Apply for a business loan
(D) Change a type of packaging

82. What should listeners do to make a recommendation?
(A) Call the speaker later
(B) Complete an online form
(C) Contact an HR employee
(D) Submit reference letters

GO ON TO THE NEXT PAGE

83. Who most likely are the listeners?
(A) Teachers
(B) Reporters
(C) Nurses
(D) Lawyers

84. What does the speaker mean when she says, "volunteers will be there until 3 P.M."?
(A) There has been an unexpected change in the schedule.
(B) Some people will be available to answer questions.
(C) Participants can collect a gift in the afternoon.
(D) Tours will be given to new members.

85. What does the speaker say she is looking forward to?
(A) Watching a presentation
(B) Enjoying a meal
(C) Upgrading a ticket
(D) Announcing a winner

---

86. Who is Asano Tanaka?
(A) A university professor
(B) A medical researcher
(C) A business owner
(D) A magazine editor

87. What is Ms. Tanaka's work most likely used for?
(A) Encouraging healthy lifestyles
(B) Evaluating industry trends
(C) Developing new products
(D) Protecting the environment

88. According to the speaker, what can be done on a Web site today?
(A) Signing up for an event
(B) Asking Ms. Tanaka questions
(C) Applying for funding
(D) Requesting a free book

---

89. Where do the speakers most likely work?
(A) At a movie theater
(B) At a clothing store
(C) At a furniture manufacturer
(D) At an advertising agency

90. What problem does the speaker mention?
(A) Competition has increased.
(B) The business received poor reviews.
(C) A lease will expire soon.
(D) Some employees have quit.

91. What will happen next week?
(A) Some investors will visit the business.
(B) The speaker will conduct a training session.
(C) Some new products will be launched.
(D) An advertisement will be filmed.

---

92. What kind of event are the listeners attending?
(A) A community fund-raiser
(B) An award ceremony
(C) A press conference
(D) A theater performance

93. What does the speaker apologize for?
(A) A lack of seating
(B) A change of venue
(C) Some unexpected delays
(D) Some noise disturbances

94. What does the speaker suggest when he says, "It has to be open during the day"?
(A) She cannot resolve an issue.
(B) She has demanded a change.
(C) A schedule contained an error.
(D) More workers are needed.

Dining Room Layout

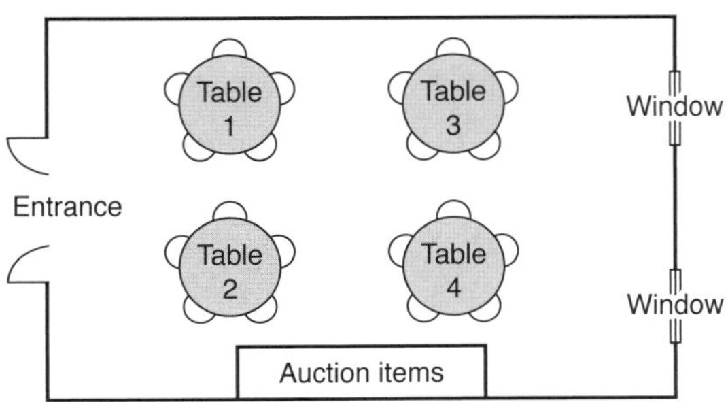

95. What will take place this Saturday?
(A) A birthday party
(B) A fund-raising event
(C) An orientation ceremony
(D) A retirement party

96. Look at the graphic. Where does the speaker want a podium to be placed?
(A) Next to Table 1
(B) Next to Table 2
(C) Next to Table 3
(D) Next to Table 4

97. What has the speaker shipped to the hotel?
(A) Some cups
(B) Some decorations
(C) Some pamphlets
(D) Some aprons

3D-Printed Models	
Machine Number	**Output per 24 Hours**
1	33
2	32
3	28
4	35

98. According to the speaker, what did the company do last month?
(A) It changed to another supplier.
(B) It hired a consultant.
(C) It purchased new equipment.
(D) It updated some software.

99. Look at the graphic. Which machine will Joseph check?
(A) Machine 1
(B) Machine 2
(C) Machine 3
(D) Machine 4

100. What does the speaker say she wants to do?
(A) Increase the production capacity
(B) Experiment with different materials
(C) Complain to a manufacturer
(D) Attend a board gaming convention

This is the end of the Listening Test. Turn to Part 5 in your test book.

READING TEST

In the Reading test, you will read a variety of texts and answer several different types of reading comprehension questions. The entire Reading test will last 75 minutes. There are three parts, and directions are given for each part. You are encouraged to answer as many questions as possible within the time allowed.

You must mark your answers on the separate answer sheet. Do not write your answers in your test book.

PART 5

Directions: A word or phrase is missing in each of the sentences below. Four answer choices are given below each sentence. Select the best answer to complete the sentence. Then mark the letter (A), (B), (C), or (D) on your answer sheet.

101. We will begin boarding procedures now for anyone who ------- additional time getting on the plane.

(A) need
(B) to need
(C) needs
(D) needing

102. Each pair of Banyan sunglasses comes ------- a protective carrying case.

(A) before
(B) along
(C) upon
(D) with

103. The northbound lanes of Highway 13 will be closed tomorrow for ------- maintenance.

(A) delinquent
(B) routine
(C) constant
(D) legal

104. To get assistance with any technical issues, you can call ------- support team at 1-800-555-9733.

(A) they
(B) their
(C) them
(D) themselves

105. The dance studio became successful through ------- advertising the center on local media channels.

(A) aggressiveness
(B) aggressive
(C) aggression
(D) aggressively

106. The hardware store's 35th anniversary ------- last month with a party for customers.

(A) celebrated
(B) to celebrate
(C) was celebrated
(D) was celebrating

107. The main ------- for the bookkeeping role is the ability to work with accounting software.

(A) beneficiary
(B) advice
(C) assistant
(D) requirement

108. ------- will participate in the building's safety drill at 4 P.M. on Saturday to learn the evacuation procedure.

(A) Occupants
(B) Occupying
(C) Occupancy
(D) Occupational

109. Because the restaurant is ------- new management, changes will be made to the interior.

(A) regarding
(B) toward
(C) under
(D) across

110. ------- participants in the Avery Bay Tour must wear a life vest while on board the boat.

(A) Another
(B) Entire
(C) All
(D) Each

111. Regularly collecting feedback helps Wesley Shoes to improve customer -------.

(A) platform
(B) satisfaction
(C) production
(D) outcome

112. The bus drivers ------- are scheduled to work on the national holiday will receive a higher hourly wage.

(A) who
(B) what
(C) these
(D) whose

113. A room service option is ------- from the hotel's restaurant 24 hours a day.

(A) subsequent
(B) available
(C) urgent
(D) practical

114. Among other -------, the property's neighborhood can greatly affect its market value.

(A) factor
(B) factors
(C) factored
(D) factoring

115. To hire a new manager, the first step is ------- a job description online.

(A) post
(B) posts
(C) posting
(D) posted

116. The Reyna electric car ------- its first appearance on the market after the Vehicle Trade Show last spring.

(A) seemed
(B) drew
(C) felt
(D) made

117. Business owners can get a 30-day free trial of Office-Tech's latest payroll ------- tax software.

(A) for
(B) that
(C) yet
(D) and

118. The final design of the product brochure was ------- different from what was requested by the client.

(A) noticeably
(B) noticeable
(C) notice
(D) noticing

119. The motors on the golf carts at Rigsby Resort are strong ------- to carry up to six people and their equipment.

(A) quite
(B) enough
(C) still
(D) much

120. Poor communication among airline check-in staff can cause ------- experiences for travelers.

(A) frustrated
(B) frustrate
(C) frustration
(D) frustrating

GO ON TO THE NEXT PAGE

121. Shoppers can find out more about ------- body lotions by speaking with a sales representative.

(A) each
(B) our
(C) whose
(D) while

122. The Sea Shanty singing group gives ------- performances throughout the summer at various sites.

(A) publicize
(B) will publicize
(C) publicly
(D) public

123. BC Transportation offers a shuttle from the Arbor Hotel to the airport, which is priced ------- at $18.

(A) eagerly
(B) partially
(C) reasonably
(D) instantly

124. Because ------- renters are looking for housing at the moment, prices on monthly rates have gone up significantly.

(A) due to
(B) so many
(C) for which
(D) that much

125. Blaze Marketing has experts that can create the ------- campaign to promote your business.

(A) success
(B) successfully
(C) more successfully
(D) most successful

126. Vincent Art Museum's board of directors is looking for activities that will ------- to younger visitors.

(A) vary
(B) appeal
(C) result
(D) oversee

127. The Health Department ------- that the restaurant needed to upgrade its refrigeration facilities was considered fair.

(A) assessing
(B) assessed
(C) assessment
(D) assessor

128. ------- damage from last week's severe storm, Rainbow Coffee Shop will be closed for the next two weeks.

(A) Those
(B) Due to
(C) If only
(D) While

129. Fullerton Insurance rewards its hard-working employees with ------- and annual bonuses.

(A) promotions
(B) promotional
(C) promotionally
(D) promotes

130. The ------- who recruit athletes for professional sports teams look for talented individuals across the country.

(A) agents
(B) artists
(C) vendors
(D) announcers

PART 6

Directions: Read the texts that follow. A word, phrase, or sentence is missing in parts of each text. Four answer choices for each question are given below the text. Select the best answer to complete the text. Then mark the letter (A), (B), (C), or (D) on your answer sheet.

Questions 131-134 refer to the following notice.

Notice of Committee Meeting

The Kennewick Parade Planning Committee will hold a meeting on April 3 at 7:30 P.M. at the Kennewick Community Center. All members are expected to ------- **131.**. Accompanying the floats from local businesses, we will design our own float based on this year's theme, ------- **132.** "By the Seaside." At the meeting, Rhonda Delgado will show some pictures from last year's event. ------- **133.**, she will talk about the most common materials used for making floats.

After the meeting, members should share their ideas with Rhonda via e-mail before the next meeting on April 17. ------- **134.**.

131. (A) secure
(B) retain
(C) attend
(D) donate

132. (A) been
(B) be
(C) what must be
(D) which is

133. (A) Nevertheless
(B) Alternatively
(C) In addition
(D) Provided that

134. (A) Participants' questions will be answered promptly.
(B) New members should complete this paperwork.
(C) On that day, we will vote on the best one.
(D) The event is popular with locals and tourists alike.

TEST 04

GO ON TO THE NEXT PAGE →

Questions 135-138 refer to the following e-mail.

To: All Sales Clerks
From: Elaine Spangler
Date: March 10
Subject: Products

In order to best serve our customers, it is essential that all employees have sufficient product knowledge. -------(**135.**), we have created a fun way to help employees review the details about our merchandise. Later this week, each of you -------(**136.**) with a catalog that contains all of the information that you need to memorize.

Then, on March 22, we will reserve a venue -------(**137.**) we can have a quiz night. Employees can compete in teams of up to four people. You will earn points for correctly answering questions about our products. We have prepared prizes for the top-scoring teams. We hope that everyone will have a great time. -------(**138.**).

Elaine Spangler
Nature Health Foods

135. (A) Unfortunately
(B) For that reason
(C) Even so
(D) For example

136. (A) has to provide
(B) was provided
(C) will be provided
(D) is providing

137. (A) following
(B) when
(C) where
(D) from

138. (A) The catalogs can be taken home with you.
(B) We plan to announce the winners tomorrow.
(C) Customers noticed the improvements right away.
(D) If successful, we plan to do similar events in the future.

Questions 139-142 refer to the following e-mail.

To: Stephen Gilden <s.gilden@meade-marketing.com>
From: Cory Dixon <dixonc@wardcommunications.com>
Date: November 3
Subject: Internet service

Dear Mr. Gilden,

I would like to confirm that one of our technicians can ------- (139.) a high-speed Internet line at your office on November 12 as you requested. The technician ------- (140.) the best place for the router, depending on your needs and office setup. The visit is scheduled to take place at 9:30 A.M. and is expected to be completed no later than 11:30 A.M. ------- (141.). If you need to cancel or postpone the ------- (142.) for any reason, please let us know.

Warmest regards,

Cory Dixon
Ward Communications

139. (A) highlight
(B) inspect
(C) enforce
(D) install

140. (A) identified
(B) was identifying
(C) will identify
(D) would have identified

141. (A) This service is becoming more popular.
(B) You can go online anytime after that.
(C) Our staff works in a variety of neighborhoods.
(D) Please let us know your preferred date.

142. (A) appointment
(B) instruction
(C) membership
(D) solution

TEST 04

GO ON TO THE NEXT PAGE →

Questions 143-146 refer to the following e-mail.

To: Vega Supermarket Employees
From: Charles Siems
Date: 6 August
Subject: Environment

Dear Staff Members,

As one of Canada's largest grocery store chains, we ------- (143.) to minimize our negative effect on the environment. We recently changed to a different design for the packaging of products with the Vega Supermarket brand. ------- (144.).

From next month, we will no longer offer plastic bags for produce. Customers can purchase items without a bag or bring one from home. This will help them to make a ------- (145.) effort to change their habits. ------- (146.), we are encouraging our suppliers to only use eco-friendly packaging for their products.

Sincerely,

Charles Siems
Supply Manager, Vega Supermarket

143. (A) consult
(B) remember
(C) strive
(D) accomplish

144. (A) The store's own products are usually cheaper than national brands.
(B) The city collects a wide range of recyclable items.
(C) Customers are returning items that do not meet their standards.
(D) Thus we reduced plastic waste for those items by 15 percent.

145. (A) determine
(B) determines
(C) determining
(D) determined

146. (A) For instance
(B) Instead
(C) Additionally
(D) Therefore

PART 7

Directions: In this part, you will read a selection of texts, such as magazine and newspaper articles, e-mails, and instant messages. Each text or set of texts is followed by several questions. Select the best answer for each question and mark the letter (A), (B), (C), or (D) on your answer sheet.

Questions 147-148 refer to the following advertisement.

Commercial Space for Rent

Previously used as a hair salon, Unit 109 of the Coleman Building will be available for rent from September 1. The site comprises 1,500 square feet and is offered under a two-year lease at a rate of $1,800 per month. The building's large display windows are perfect for showcasing your business, and they are well insulated to reduce heating and cooling costs. The building is within walking distance of the waterfront and several popular restaurants. Tenants enjoy a private parking lot that is covered for vehicles' protection. There is also a security team on site 24 hours a day. To book a viewing, call 555-7820.

147. What is suggested about the Coleman Building?

(A) It has energy-efficient windows.
(B) It was completed two years ago.
(C) It houses several hair salons.
(D) It is near public transportation.

148. What is NOT indicated as an amenity?

(A) Proximity to dining facilities
(B) A view of the waterfront
(C) A covered parking area
(D) Round-the-clock security

GO ON TO THE NEXT PAGE

Questions 149-150 refer to the following notice.

Thank you for your interest in Tirado Whale-Watching Tours at Miramar Bay! As a ticket holder, you are about to experience the adventure of a lifetime. Our experienced captains will bring you to the best areas for finding whales, and you'll get to see these amazing animals up-close. Please note that we cannot issue refunds on cancellations made less than 7 days before your scheduled tour.

For the safety of our passengers, we sometimes need to cancel tours due to inclement weather. In this case, you will receive a full refund. As announcements of cancellations can sometimes come at the last minute, please double-check that you have provided us with the right phone number and e-mail address.

149. Who most likely is the intended audience of the notice?

(A) People who are training for a captain job
(B) People who have purchased tickets
(C) People who work for Tirado Whale-Watching Tours
(D) People who provide transportation to Miramar Bay

150. What is recommended in the notice?

(A) Ensuring contact information is correct
(B) Bringing special clothing for bad weather
(C) Calling the business to check on cancellations
(D) Receiving a newsletter by e-mail

Questions 151-152 refer to the following text-message chain.

Sheila Engel (12:51 P.M.)
How are things going? Where are you?

Frederick Kocher (12:53 P.M.)
We've almost finished cleaning the guest rooms on the 6th floor. When I was stocking the cart this morning, I noticed that the stain remover was running low. Could you please order more?

Sheila Engel (12:55 P.M.)
Sure. I'm taking inventory of our department's supplies and placing an order today.

Frederick Kocher (12:56 P.M.)
Great. Dana and I will move to the 7th floor next, and everything should be done by 1:50 at the latest.

Sheila Engel (12:58 P.M.)
That doesn't leave much time. We have guests checking into those rooms at two o'clock.

Frederick Kocher (1:00 P.M.)
I understand that, but Beth called in sick this morning, so we are short-staffed.

Sheila Engel (1:01 P.M.)
Fair enough. If any other teams finish early, I'll send them to the 7th floor.

151. What most likely is Ms. Engel's job?
(A) Travel agent
(B) Event planner
(C) Housekeeping manager
(D) Delivery person

152. At 1:01 P.M., what does Ms. Engel most likely mean when she writes, "Fair enough"?
(A) She agrees that more workers should be hired.
(B) She understands why a task is not completed.
(C) She knows that Mr. Kocher is not feeling well.
(D) She remembers why the supplies are low.

GO ON TO THE NEXT PAGE

Questions 153-154 refer to the following advertisement.

Valley Lighting Clearance Sale!

282 Sigley Road

Valley Lighting is holding a Clearance Sale from June 1 to June 8. We're selling hundreds of fixtures and fittings. You can get huge discounts—up to 80% off! Some of the items are former display models and do not have their original packaging. However, everything we sell is in working order.

Valley Lighting will be moving to the Baldwin Mall next month, so we need to reduce our inventory to accommodate the reduced storage and display space at the new location. Don't miss your chance to pick up a great deal!

153. What is indicated about the clearance items?

(A) They are all sold with their original packaging.
(B) They are from a discontinued brand.
(C) They are not allowed to be returned.
(D) They are all functioning properly.

154. What is suggested about Valley Lighting's new shop?

(A) It will have longer operating hours.
(B) It will be smaller than the current site.
(C) It will be under new ownership.
(D) It will continue the clearance sale.

Questions 155-157 refer to the following newsletter.

Arroyo Theater Preservation Society (ATPS)

Quarterly Newsletter

ATPS members have been busy this past quarter! We continue to be dedicated to preserving the beautiful and historic Arroyo Theater. Our main accomplishments are listed below.

- In April, we created a display in the lobby of old photographs of the theater to show how it has changed through the years.
- In May, we recognized the theater's 125th anniversary with special performances by local musicians and dancers.
- In June, we created a list of the most-needed improvements based on the inspection summary submitted by fellow member Thomas Lewis. We will begin to work on these from July.

In the upcoming months, we plan to:

- Begin fundraising efforts for necessary repairs
- Hold a teleconference with similar preservation groups across the nation
- Launch a Children's Theater Program
- Recruit more drama groups for performances at the theater

New members are welcome anytime. If you would like to join ATPS, please send an e-mail to Shirley Deleon at sdeleon@trmail.com. Our next meeting will be Tuesday, July 11, at noon. We also appreciate any financial support that the community can provide. Go to www.atps.org to make a donation. It only takes a few minutes!

155. When did the ATPS hold an anniversary celebration?

(A) In April
(B) In May
(C) In June
(D) In July

156. Where did the ATPS get information about improvements to be made?

(A) From an interview
(B) From a report
(C) From a Web site
(D) From a news article

157. How can someone donate to the ATPS?

(A) By attending the July 11 meeting
(B) By stopping by the theater
(C) By e-mailing Ms. Deleon
(D) By visiting a Web site

GO ON TO THE NEXT PAGE →

Questions 158-160 refer to the following advertisement.

Lunsford Properties is Seeking Senior Property Managers!

Lunsford Properties is a well-respected property management firm operating in Philadelphia. We are growing rapidly and would like to add two more senior property managers to our team.

The Role

The ideal candidate would have a complete understanding of the property sector and its current regulations. Responsibilities include acting as the main point of contact between tenants and landlords, addressing maintenance issues promptly, and coordinating dates for moving in/out of the properties. You would also carry out inspections to assess property damage and building improvement needs.

What Our Employees Have to Say

"It's great working with such a friendly team, keeping the Web site running and uploading the latest property photos. When I've been working from home for a few days, I always enjoy returning to the office and seeing my coworkers." —Maria Carter

"Although I don't work with the properties directly, I feel connected to Lunsford Properties' mission and can contribute through my accounting services. It's nice to have a telecommuting option two days a week, and I was pleased to be able to manage a small team and gain leadership experience. I would highly recommend this company to anyone." —Felix Diaz

158. The word "complete" in paragraph 2, line 1, is closest in meaning to

(A) achieved
(B) finished
(C) thorough
(D) pure

159. What most likely is Mr. Diaz's job?

(A) Office manager
(B) Photographer
(C) Web developer
(D) Accountant

160. What do Ms. Carter and Mr. Diaz have in common?

(A) They both manage other employees.
(B) They both work remotely sometimes.
(C) They are both working directly with properties.
(D) They are both long-term staff members.

Questions 161-163 refer to the following letter.

September 3

Nellie Tomberlin
City Dental Clinic
854 Seneca Avenue
Portland, OR 97204

Dear Ms. Tomberlin,

I am writing on behalf of Victoria Lowell, one of the applicants for the dental assistant position at the City Dental Clinic. —[1]—. I have had the pleasure of working with Ms. Lowell for the past four years at Hermes Dental, and I believe she would be an excellent asset to your clinic. Throughout her time working with us, she has demonstrated a high level of professionalism at all times. She has had training in handling patient records with discretion and confidentiality. —[2]—.

I always felt confident delegating work to Ms. Lowell, as she can easily handle projects independently. —[3]—. For example, I have to submit bills to insurance companies regularly. —[4]—. Whenever I got behind on this task, Ms. Lowell was able to assist me with completing the necessary documents in a timely manner.

I would be happy to discuss Ms. Lowell's experience further.

Sincerely,

Maxine Blake
Manager, Hermes Dental
(479) 555-0863

161. Who most likely is Ms. Tomberlin?

(A) A representative of Hermes Dental
(B) An applicant for a position
(C) An employee at City Dental Clinic
(D) A training manager

162. What is true about Ms. Blake?

(A) She is responsible for hiring employees.
(B) She used to work for an insurance company.
(C) She has to supply forms to other businesses.
(D) She founded a dental clinic four years ago.

163. In which of the positions marked [1], [2], [3], and [4] does the following sentence best belong?

"Therefore, I am confident in Ms. Lowell's ability to deal with sensitive information."

(A) [1]
(B) [2]
(C) [3]
(D) [4]

GO ON TO THE NEXT PAGE

Questions 164-167 refer to the following document.

Morrison Research

Following all safety procedures is a critical part of limiting the risk of injury to our workers in the lab. Please keep the guidelines below in mind while you are carrying out experiments.

Wear Proper Lab Attire

- Lab coats, gloves, and eye protection must be worn at all times.
- Used coats should be left in the basket by the door.

Maintain the Work Area

- Wipe down counters regularly to avoid cross-contamination.
- Make sure no residue is left on the floor or on all tables before you leave.
- All containers should be labeled with the precise contents, date, and any known hazards.

Prohibited Items

- Do not bring food or beverages into the lab and do not consume anything on the premises.
- Lighters and other fire-related items are not allowed in the lab.

Good Hygiene

- Wash your hands when you arrive, after handling materials, and before leaving the lab.
- Sterilize equipment between each use.

164. For whom was the document most likely written?

(A) Safety inspectors
(B) Delivery personnel
(C) Laboratory technicians
(D) Company investors

165. The word "critical" in paragraph 1, line 1, is closest in meaning to

(A) doubtful
(B) essential
(C) urgent
(D) dangerous

166. What is suggested in the document?

(A) Some safety rules may change soon.
(B) It takes a long time to sterilize equipment.
(C) Lab coats can be taken home by staff.
(D) It is important to keep surfaces clean.

167. What is NOT a safety measure mentioned in the document?

(A) Labeling containers accurately
(B) Avoiding eating and drinking
(C) Storing items off site
(D) Washing hands regularly

Questions 168-171 refer to the following article.

Issues at Collins Park

NEWTON (August 2)—Adding a decorative fountain to Collins Park seemed like a good idea when first proposed, and last year the Newton City Council quickly approved the $280,000 budget needed to make it a reality. Unfortunately, since that time, numerous issues have surrounded the project. —[1]—.

The fountain was designed by architectural firm Luu Designs. —[2]—. Most residents responded favorably to the look of the initial drawings posted on the city's Web site. However, they did not take into account the scale of the fountain, and many expressed opposition to the project after they saw how large the completed fountain was.

As Collins Park is the city's smallest park, smaller than a soccer field, people were worried that the existing benches in the park would have to be taken out to make space for the fountain. —[3]—. "I live right next to the park, and people are constantly sitting on my garden wall because there's nowhere to do so in the actual park," said Iris Bailey, a long-time resident. —[4]—.

Warren Pursell, head of the Parks and Recreation Department, said that the original work was completed on time and that the $320,000 spent on the project was worthwhile. However, he recognizes the shortcomings of the project and has already hired Luu Designs to put a ring of chairs around the fountain, which will be incorporated into the design.

168. According to the article, what do residents dislike about the fountain?

(A) Its noise
(B) Its materials
(C) Its cost
(D) Its size

169. What is suggested about the city of Newton?

(A) It canceled plans for other fountains.
(B) It exceeded a budget on a project.
(C) Its residents want a new basketball court.
(D) Its parks are small compared to those of other cities.

170. How will the problem at Collins Park be addressed?

(A) By adding a seating area
(B) By hiring a different design firm
(C) By putting up more signs
(D) By enforcing the local laws

171. In which of the positions marked [1], [2], [3], and [4] does the following sentence best belong?

"That is exactly what happened."

(A) [1]
(B) [2]
(C) [3]
(D) [4]

GO ON TO THE NEXT PAGE

Questions 172-175 refer to the following online chat discussion.

Levi Avila 10:09 A.M.		Thank you for contacting Scenic Shuttles customer service. How may I help you?
Eleanor Worley 10:11 A.M.		My company, Landeros, has booked one of your shuttle buses to take our employees to the National Engineering Conference in Sacramento. Our booking number is T7893. We plan to bring a mini-refrigerator on board, so I just wanted to make sure there is an outlet for that.
Levi Avila 10:12 A.M.		According to your reservation, you reserved a 21-seater shuttle. It doesn't have any outlets.
Eleanor Worley 10:14 A.M.		No way! I thought that was standard on shuttles of that size. We need to bring drinks and packed lunches for everyone, and we don't want to use a cooler with ice, as that would be too messy. Could I speak to your supervisor about this?
Rafael Duke 10:18 A.M.		Good morning, Ms. Worley. I'm sorry that you are disappointed with the features offered on the 21-seater shuttle for your upcoming trip. You could upgrade to the 37-seater, which has outlets as well as a built-in refrigerator. It's $85 more per day, but I could give you a discount and only charge $60 more per day.
Eleanor Worley 10:19 A.M.		I think that would be better, thanks. But I'd have to get the extra cost approved. Let me check on that and get back to you.

172. Why will Ms. Worley's company use the services of Scenic Shuttles?

(A) To enjoy local tourist attractions
(B) To relocate to a new office
(C) To visit another company branch
(D) To attend a professional conference

173. At 10:14 A.M., what does Ms. Worley suggest when she writes, "No way"?

(A) She is surprised that a feature is not included.
(B) She thought that the shuttle would seat more people.
(C) She does not agree to a proposed price.
(D) She is frustrated that a reservation has been lost.

174. Who most likely is Mr. Duke?

(A) Mr. Avila's assistant
(B) Mr. Avila's manager
(C) A shuttle bus driver
(D) A tour guide

175. What does Ms. Worley plan to do?

(A) Cancel a service contract
(B) Request a budget increase
(C) Confirm a head count
(D) Make a bank transfer

GO ON TO THE NEXT PAGE →

Questions 176-180 refer to the following e-mail and article.

E-Mail Message

To: Laura Navarre
From: Max Stallworth
Date: February 17
Subject: Exercise trail

Dear Ms. Navarre,

As confirmed in my last e-mail, Mayor Cole plans to attend the upcoming event to celebrate the March 3 grand opening of the city's new multi-use exercise trail built by Primrose Construction. However, he would also like to be accompanied by Sandra Krone, if possible. We ask that you make room for this additional attendee in the event's VIP seating section.

As you may know, Ms. Krone helped to negotiate an agreement between the project's lead designer, Gregory Burkett, and the president of the environmental group Eco-Friends, Marian Conroy, when the group expressed opposition to the proposal.

Warmest regards,

Max Stallworth
Assistant to Mayor Roger Cole
Kerrville City Hall

Exercise Options Increase for Locals

KERRVILLE (March 4)—At a ceremony held yesterday, city officials celebrated the opening of a multi-use exercise trail in Kerrville. The trail, which stretches over 10 miles and is suitable for biking, jogging, and walking, was finished on time and within the estimated budget. Some parts of the trail were redirected to keep existing trees rather than cut them down to make room for the trail. The ceremony included a speech by the trail's designer as well as the head of the city's Parks and Recreation Department.

The project's planners were so pleased with the construction company that carried out the work that they have already hired the company to build a tennis court at Spencer Park. Updates of these plans can be found on the city's Web site. There you can also see a map of the new trail.

176. What is the purpose of the e-mail?

(A) To suggest an activity
(B) To congratulate the recipient
(C) To adjust a guest list
(D) To modify some overnight accommodations

177. How did Ms. Krone assist with a project?

(A) By providing funds for an event
(B) By founding an environmental group
(C) By recommending a construction firm
(D) By helping to resolve a complaint

178. Why was the article written?

(A) To recognize some award winners
(B) To announce the completion of a project
(C) To confirm the results of a vote
(D) To report a change in city personnel

179. What is implied about Primrose Construction?

(A) It will work on a project at Spencer Park.
(B) It removed some trees from an area.
(C) It is owned by Mr. Stallworth.
(D) Its contract details are on the city's Web site.

180. Who gave a speech at the March 3 event?

(A) Ms. Conroy
(B) Mr. Cole
(C) Ms. Krone
(D) Mr. Burkett

GO ON TO THE NEXT PAGE →

Questions 181-185 refer to the following letter and receipt.

July 27

Lisa Alford, Computer Department Manager
Hickory Electronics
3179 Terrell Street
Houston, TX 77056

Dear Ms. Alford,

I visited your store earlier this week to purchase a new desktop computer. Mr. Bradshaw assisted me and helped me figure out how much memory I would need. He also recommended an antivirus program. However, I was disappointed by the limited selection of graphics cards sold at your store, as I need a very powerful one for online gaming.

I found a graphics card online that would be suitable for my needs. I'm wondering if one of your employees could install it even though I purchased it from a third party. Please let me know. You can reach me at 832-555-6541. I also plan to write to Steven Noguera, your general manager, to suggest expanding the inventory.

Sincerely,

Evan Irving

Evan Irving

CYBER PARTS INC.
www.cyberpartsinc.com

Date of order:	July 29
Order #:	0456218
Processed by:	Sarah Lombardo
Customer:	Evan Irving, 966 Highland View, Houston, TX 77102
Description:	12GB Loomis RX Graphics Card (Item #G97002)
Price:	$525.00, charged to Maxxo Credit Card XXXX XXXX XXXX 9032
Deliver to:	Computer Department Manager, Hickory Electronics, 3179 Terrell Street, Houston, TX 77056
Delivery type:	Standard
Estimated delivery:	August 3
Notes:	Signature required upon receipt of item.

181. What is one purpose of the letter?

(A) To inquire about a job opening
(B) To request a special service
(C) To complain about a damaged item
(D) To introduce a new product

182. Where does Mr. Bradshaw most likely work?

(A) At an electronics store
(B) At an online retail shop
(C) At a video game developer
(D) At a delivery company

183. What is suggested about Hickory Electronics?

(A) It will add new items to its inventory soon.
(B) It sells some of its products online.
(C) It will install a component not sold at its store.
(D) It offers a wide range of graphics cards.

184. Who will receive the package from Cyber Parts Inc.?

(A) Ms. Alford
(B) Mr. Noguera
(C) Mr. Irving
(D) Ms. Lombardo

185. What is true about the order?

(A) It will be shipped from Houston.
(B) It is expected to be delivered on July 29.
(C) A discounted item was included in it.
(D) A credit card was used to pay for it.

TEST 04

GO ON TO THE NEXT PAGE

Questions 186-190 refer to the following Web page, schedule, and e-mail.

http://www.senoiamovingservices.com 

Senoia Moving Services

1161 Crenshaw Avenue, Akron, Ohio 44310

Whether you're moving within Akron or to another city, Senoia Moving Services can help. Our experienced movers will treat your belongings with care. We serve both individuals and businesses, and we can provide secure storage if needed. It's easy to book our services!

1. Contact us at 330-555-8522 to schedule a moving date.
2. One of our employees will assess your items and provide a cost estimate.
3. After we confirm the moving date, you should pay a deposit. We will then give you all the boxes and packaging supplies you need.
4. Our crew will carry out the move at the agreed date and time.

Senoia Moving Services

March 22 Crew Pick-Up Assignments

Crew / # of Crew Members	Vehicle Size	Pick-Up Location	Time
Robin Crew / 2 members	Van	247 Albany Lane	9:00 A.M.
Dove Crew / 5 members	26-foot truck	432 Java Street	9:00 A.M.
Canary Crew / 2 members	12-foot truck	950 Columbia Building, Unit 309, 2746 Rochelle Street	10:30 A.M.
Sparrow Crew / 3 members	16-foot truck	1614 Caxon Street	10:00 A.M.
Robin Crew / 2 members	Van	30 Whitman Avenue	1:00 P.M.

Further details are available from your crew leader. Please note that one more person will be added to the Sparrow Crew (16-foot truck) from April 1.

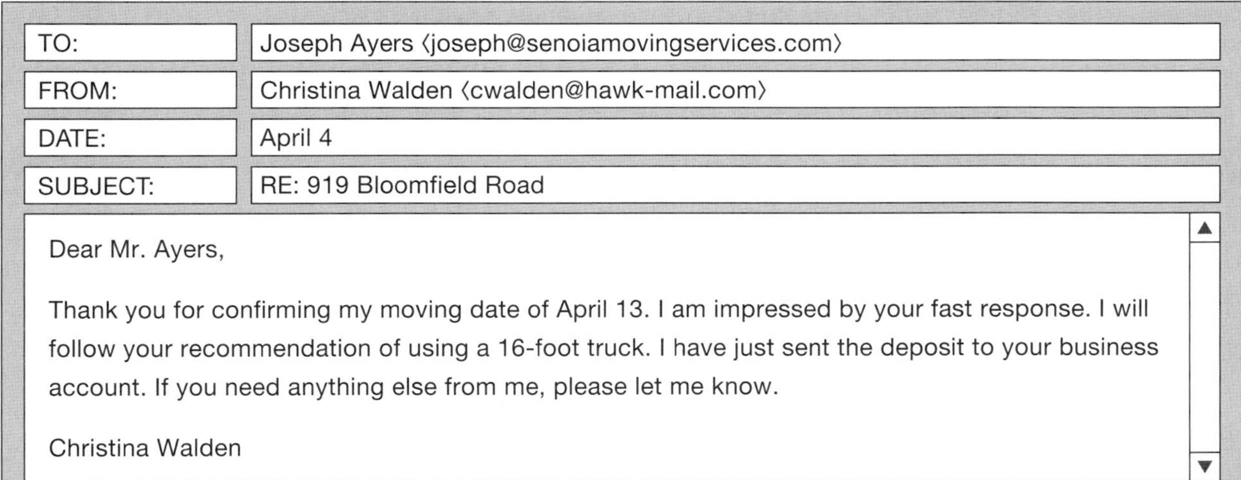
TO: Joseph Ayers ⟨joseph@senoiamovingservices.com⟩
FROM: Christina Walden ⟨cwalden@hawk-mail.com⟩
DATE: April 4
SUBJECT: RE: 919 Bloomfield Road

Dear Mr. Ayers,

Thank you for confirming my moving date of April 13. I am impressed by your fast response. I will follow your recommendation of using a 16-foot truck. I have just sent the deposit to your business account. If you need anything else from me, please let me know.

Christina Walden

186. What is true about Senoia Moving Services?
(A) It only serves commercial customers.
(B) It provides services outside of Akron.
(C) It has recently been sold to a competitor.
(D) It is currently seeking experienced movers to hire.

187. For whom was the schedule written?
(A) Investors in Senoia Moving Services
(B) Clients of Senoia Moving Services
(C) Senoia Moving Services job applicants
(D) Senoia Moving Services employees

188. Where should the Dove Crew report on March 22?
(A) Albany Lane
(B) Java Street
(C) Caxon Street
(D) Whitman Avenue

189. What will Senoia Moving Services employees most likely do in response to the e-mail?
(A) Drop off some packing materials
(B) Measure some personal belongings
(C) Correct an error in an invoice
(D) Check a schedule for open time slots

190. How many people will most likely assist with Ms. Walden's move?
(A) 2
(B) 3
(C) 4
(D) 5

GO ON TO THE NEXT PAGE

Questions 191-195 refer to the following menu, invoice, and e-mail.

Pasta Buffet: $20.00 per person

Build a custom menu of five dishes with the following combinations:

Pasta type: spaghetti, fettuccine, penne

Meat/Vegetarian: chicken, beef, shrimp, tofu, beans

Sauce: tomato, garlic and oil, cream

The buffet fee includes coffee, tea, soda, glasses, ceramic plates, as well as silver forks, spoons, and knives.

Extra Dishes: priced per person, see our Web site for options in each category

Soup: $2.00

Appetizer: $2.25

Salad: $1.50

Cheese Plate: $2.50

Dessert Buffet: priced per person

Served with coffee and tea. Choose among Italian ice cream, tiramisu (coffee-soaked cake), fresh fruit salad, lemon cheesecake, and chocolate cake

3 choices: $8.00

4 choices: $10.50

5 choices: $12.00

Contact our event coordinator, Camelia Rossi, at 555-7019 to place an order. You can also inquire about our rental options for chairs, tablecloths, centerpieces, and more.

Nicolette Italian Catering Invoice

Customer: Aaron Kendall

Item Description	**Cost per Unit**	**Quantity**	**Subtotal**
Pasta Buffet	$20.00	35	$700.00
Extra Dish	$2.00	35	$70.00
Delivery [to 792 Oak Lane, 5:30 P.M. April 19]			$15.00
Dessert Buffet	$10.50	20	$210.00
Delivery [to 1960 Stratford Avenue, 8:00 P.M. April 19]			$15.00
Subtotal			$1,010.00
Tax (7.25%)			$73.23
Total Due (by April 12)			**$1,083.23**

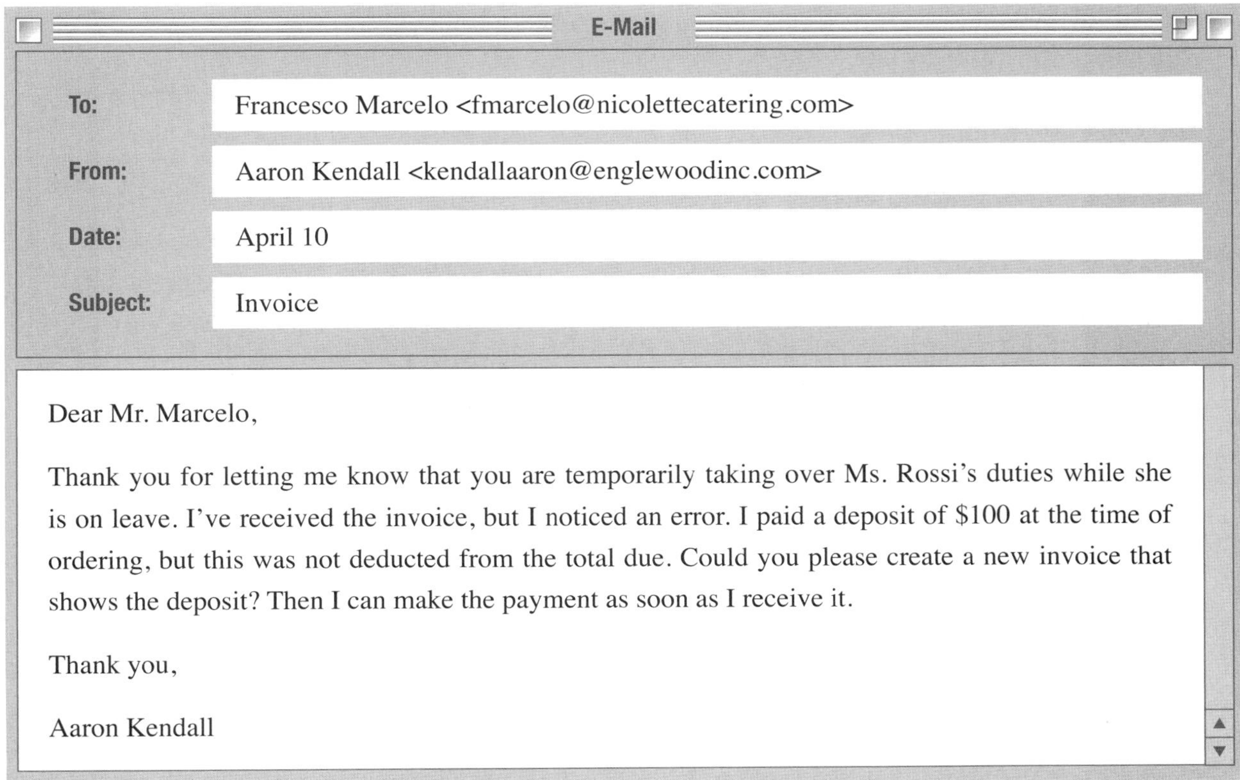

To: Francesco Marcelo <fmarcelo@nicolettecatering.com>

From: Aaron Kendall <kendallaaron@englewoodinc.com>

Date: April 10

Subject: Invoice

Dear Mr. Marcelo,

Thank you for letting me know that you are temporarily taking over Ms. Rossi's duties while she is on leave. I've received the invoice, but I noticed an error. I paid a deposit of $100 at the time of ordering, but this was not deducted from the total due. Could you please create a new invoice that shows the deposit? Then I can make the payment as soon as I receive it.

Thank you,

Aaron Kendall

191. What is NOT indicated as part of the Pasta Buffet package?

(A) Utensils
(B) Glassware
(C) Tablecloths
(D) Plates

192. What does the invoice indicate about the delivery?

(A) It has a delivery window of one hour.
(B) It will be made to two separate locations.
(C) Its fee has been reduced.
(D) It is scheduled for two different dates.

193. Which extra dish did Mr. Kendall order?

(A) Soup
(B) Appetizer
(C) Salad
(D) Cheese Plate

194. Who is Mr. Marcelo covering for?

(A) The business owner
(B) The head chef
(C) The event coordinator
(D) The accountant

195. What most likely does Mr. Kendall expect Mr. Marcelo to do?

(A) Adjust the number of guests
(B) Issue a refund
(C) Provide a new menu
(D) Send an updated invoice

GO ON TO THE NEXT PAGE

Questions 196-200 refer to the following article, press release, and e-mail.

Petersburg Business Highlights

April 9—With the fierce competition in the cosmetics industry, business leaders are always looking for ways to provide growth and stability for their brand. An increasingly popular strategy is selling small sample-sized versions of products to luxury hotel chains for their guests. This means that the products are sampled by a wider range of potential customers.

Marketing consultant Eric Weiss explains why this approach can be effective. "Customers are using the products in a relaxed environment, so they don't feel pressured to make a purchasing decision. It doesn't feel like an advertisement, even though the effect is the same."

Companies such as Farland Cosmetics and Arrowood have already formed such partnerships with the Grant Hotel and the Terra Hotel, respectively. More high-end brands are expected to follow suit.

FOR IMMEDIATE RELEASE

August 2

Contact: Sarah Calderon, scalderon@farlandcosmetics.com

(Petersburg)—Farland Cosmetics announced that Jia Zheng will take over as CEO from August 15. After months of negotiations beginning in March, the company was finally purchased by the Fieldcrest Group last month. Duane Baur, the current CEO, stayed on temporarily to assist with the transition. Ms. Zheng plans to continue all current partnerships as well as explore other opportunities for expansion.

Investors at the Fieldcrest Group are confident in Ms. Zheng's business experience. After studying business management at university, Ms. Zheng and her university friend Marilyn Burks launched a vitamin supplement company that grew quickly. It was sold at a substantial profit after three years. Ms. Zheng has also worked as CFO at Valentine Inc. and CEO at Womack International.

E-Mail

To: Jia Zheng <jzheng@farlandcosmetics.com>
From: Fabian Cattaneo <fabianc@truemail.com>
Date: October 11
Subject: Congratulations!

Dear Ms. Zheng,

I recently read about your new position at Farland Cosmetics, and I wanted to congratulate you. When I worked for you a few years ago, I thought you were an excellent CEO, so I'm sure you'll do a great job in your new role as well.

All the best,

Fabian Cattaneo

196. How can businesses benefit from the strategy explained in the article?
(A) By getting more people to try their products
(B) By avoiding regulations on imports
(C) By retaining experienced staff members
(D) By reducing some delivery costs

197. When did Farland Cosmetics have a change of ownership?
(A) In March
(B) In July
(C) In August
(D) In October

198. What is implied about Ms. Zheng?
(A) She plans to move to a new city to take on work.
(B) She led the company's negotiations team.
(C) She will maintain a business relationship with the Grant Hotel.
(D) She is a former employee of the Terra Hotel.

199. According to the press release, what did Ms. Burks do?
(A) She recruited Ms. Zheng to Farland Cosmetics.
(B) She co-founded a successful company.
(C) She invented a new kind of vitamin.
(D) She sold a business to Valentine Inc.

200. What is suggested about Mr. Cattaneo?
(A) He previously worked at Womack International.
(B) He is currently employed in the cosmetics industry.
(C) He wants to write an article about Ms. Zheng.
(D) He is seeking a role on Ms. Zheng's team.

Stop! This is the end of the test. If you finish before time is called, you may go back to Parts 5, 6, and 7 and check your work.

▶ 정답 및 해설 p. 104

자동 채점 서비스
바로가기

에 듀 윌 토 익 실 전 서

LC+RC

TEST 05

LISTENING TEST

PART 1

PART 2

PART 3

PART 4

READING TEST

PART 5

PART 6

PART 7

LISTENING TEST

In the Listening test, you will be asked to demonstrate how well you understand spoken English. The entire Listening test will last approximately 45 minutes. There are four parts, and directions are given for each part. You must mark your answers on the separate answer sheet. Do not write your answers in your test book.

PART 1

Directions: For each question in this part, you will hear four statements about a picture in your test book. When you hear the statements, you must select the one statement that best describes what you see in the picture. Then find the number of the question on your answer sheet and mark your answer. The statements will not be printed in your test book and will be spoken only one time.

Statement (C), "He's making a phone call," is the best description of the picture, so you should select answer (C) and mark it on your answer sheet.

1.

2.

GO ON TO THE NEXT PAGE

3.

4.

5.

6.

TEST 05

GO ON TO THE NEXT PAGE →

PART 2

Directions: You will hear a question or statement and three responses spoken in English. They will not be printed in your test book and will be spoken only one time. Select the best response to the question or statement and mark the letter (A), (B), or (C) on your answer sheet.

7. Mark your answer on your answer sheet.

8. Mark your answer on your answer sheet.

9. Mark your answer on your answer sheet.

10. Mark your answer on your answer sheet.

11. Mark your answer on your answer sheet.

12. Mark your answer on your answer sheet.

13. Mark your answer on your answer sheet.

14. Mark your answer on your answer sheet.

15. Mark your answer on your answer sheet.

16. Mark your answer on your answer sheet.

17. Mark your answer on your answer sheet.

18. Mark your answer on your answer sheet.

19. Mark your answer on your answer sheet.

20. Mark your answer on your answer sheet.

21. Mark your answer on your answer sheet.

22. Mark your answer on your answer sheet.

23. Mark your answer on your answer sheet.

24. Mark your answer on your answer sheet.

25. Mark your answer on your answer sheet.

26. Mark your answer on your answer sheet.

27. Mark your answer on your answer sheet.

28. Mark your answer on your answer sheet.

29. Mark your answer on your answer sheet.

30. Mark your answer on your answer sheet.

31. Mark your answer on your answer sheet.

PART 3

Directions: You will hear some conversations between two or more people. You will be asked to answer three questions about what the speakers say in each conversation. Select the best response to each question and mark the letter (A), (B), (C), or (D) on your answer sheet. The conversations will not be printed in your test book and will be spoken only one time.

32. Why does the man want to buy Ms. Gupta some flowers?
(A) She is retiring.
(B) She is switching companies.
(C) She got a promotion.
(D) She received an award.

33. According to the woman, where is Alice's Flower Shop?
(A) Next to the train station
(B) In a department store
(C) Across from a school
(D) Near the library

34. What does the man say he will do before he leaves the office?
(A) Send some e-mails
(B) Make a phone call
(C) Attend a meeting
(D) Finalize a project

35. What did the man do for the woman?
(A) He arranged her flight.
(B) He found her accomodations.
(C) He bought her conference ticket.
(D) He found her a driver.

36. What does the man remind the woman to do?
(A) Bring her presentation slides
(B) Save her receipts
(C) Arrive at the conference early
(D) Pack her luggage carefully

37. What does the woman ask the man about?
(A) A computer room
(B) A hotel gym
(C) A conference center
(D) A restaurant

38. What industry do the speakers most likely work in?
(A) Gardening
(B) Finance
(C) Advertising
(D) Fashion

39. What does the man suggest doing?
(A) Expanding current offerings
(B) Changing the fabric choice
(C) Opening a new store
(D) Attending a formal event

40. What is the woman worried about?
(A) A plan is too expensive.
(B) A pattern is too distracting.
(C) Some customers might complain.
(D) Some items have not been selling well.

41. What issue is being discussed?
(A) A copier is not working properly.
(B) A meeting room is already in use.
(C) A shipment was not fulfilled on time.
(D) Some employees cannot access their accounts.

42. Who most likely is the man?
(A) A company executive
(B) An advertising manager
(C) A computer specialist
(D) A new intern

43. What are the women most likely planning to do next?
(A) Have a meeting
(B) Go visit a client
(C) Go to the airport
(D) Sign an agreement

TEST 05

GO ON TO THE NEXT PAGE

44. Where does the woman work?
(A) At a hair salon
(B) At a tour agency
(C) At a restaurant
(D) At a car dealership

45. Why can't the man make a reservation for next Wednesday?
(A) Some facilities will be cleaned.
(B) All the staff will be on vacation.
(C) A calendar is fully booked.
(D) Some equipment is being replaced.

46. What will the man most likely do next?
(A) Call back again
(B) Find a different venue
(C) Give his name
(D) Write an online review

---

47. Who is the man?
(A) An interpreter
(B) An editor-in-chief
(C) A writer
(D) A sales representative

48. Why does the woman say, "The issue has already gone to the printer"?
(A) To make a complaint
(B) To reject an offer
(C) To apologize for a mistake
(D) To reschedule an appointment

49. What does the woman ask the man to do?
(A) Write a new assignment
(B) Recruit more writers
(C) Come in for an interview
(D) Appear on a magazine cover

---

50. What kind of business do the speakers most likely work for?
(A) A construction firm
(B) A doctor's office
(C) A toy company
(D) A government agency

51. What problem do the women describe?
(A) A payment was not received.
(B) Some facilities need to be repaired.
(C) A supplier did not deliver the correct goods.
(D) Prospective clients have not answered back.

52. What does the man recommend?
(A) Opening a new branch
(B) Searching for other clients
(C) Offering a discounted rate
(D) Finding a new vendor

---

53. What has the woman agreed to do?
(A) Purchase a keyboard
(B) Lead a conference
(C) Test out some products
(D) Design a new ad campaign

54. What does the man ask from the woman?
(A) A consent form
(B) Her full name
(C) Her identification card
(D) A copy of her résumé

55. What will the woman most likely do next?
(A) Return to her home
(B) Follow the man
(C) Accept a job offer
(D) Make a phone call

---

56. What is the woman waiting for?
(A) A manager to answer a question
(B) A customer to place an order
(C) Some employees to come to work
(D) Some utensils to be cleaned

57. Why does the woman say, "They seem to have fewer customers, though"?
(A) To emphasize the success of this branch
(B) To justify higher expenses
(C) To suggest changing the strategy
(D) To deny the previous claim

58. What will happen later today?
(A) A staff meeting will be held.
(B) A promotion will begin.
(C) A new item will be released.
(D) A cleaning crew will visit.

---

59. Which industry do the speakers most likely work in?
(A) Finance
(B) Fashion
(C) Engineering
(D) Tourism

60. What does the man say he is concerned about?
(A) Sunshine duration
(B) Initial costs
(C) Environmental pollution
(D) Safety procedures

61. What does the man agree to do?
(A) Call the client
(B) Carry out some research
(C) Plan a conference
(D) Cut the budget

CALTON EXITS

Goodman Drive	Exit 21
Kingsley Lane	Exit 22
Rosebud Street	Exit 23
Marcus Road	Exit 24

62. What does the woman remind the man about?
(A) She is leading a seminar.
(B) She is an experienced driver.
(C) She used to live in the area.
(D) She must return home for her purse.

63. Look at the graphic. Which exit will the speakers take?
(A) Goodman Drive
(B) Kingsley Lane
(C) Rosebud Street
(D) Marcus Road

64. What will the man ask his coworkers to do?
(A) Save an extra seat
(B) Record the seminar
(C) Return to the office
(D) Prepare for the presentation

GO ON TO THE NEXT PAGE

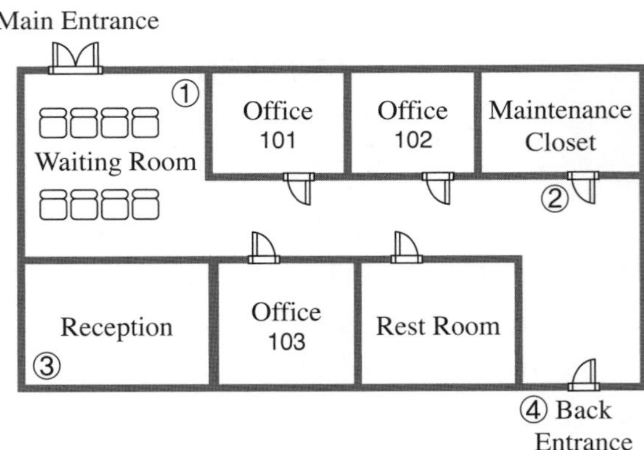

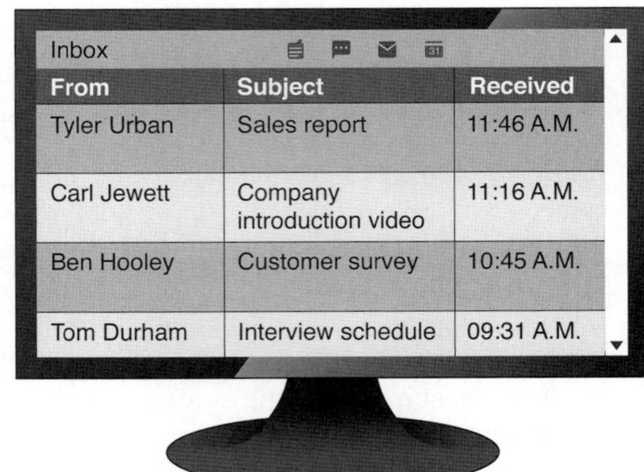

65. Where does the conversation most likely take place?
(A) At a university
(B) At a law firm
(C) At a healthcare organization
(D) At a publishing company

66. Look at the graphic. Where will the man put the documents?
(A) At area 1
(B) At area 2
(C) At area 3
(D) At area 4

67. What will the man do next?
(A) Print some documents
(B) Bring some equipment
(C) Order some shelves
(D) Complete an online form

68. What problem are the speakers discussing?
(A) A video file is not working.
(B) A product launch has been delayed.
(C) An event location is unavailable.
(D) A project deadline has passed.

69. Look at the graphic. Whose e-mail does the woman mention?
(A) Tyler Urban's
(B) Carl Jewett's
(C) Ben Hooley's
(D) Tom Durham's

70. What event will happen on Wednesday?
(A) A product demonstration
(B) A fund-raiser
(C) An investor meeting
(D) A theater show

PART 4

Directions: You will hear some talks given by a single speaker. You will be asked to answer three questions about what the speaker says in each talk. Select the best response to each question and mark the letter (A), (B), (C), or (D) on your answer sheet. The talks will not be printed in your test book and will be spoken only one time.

71. What did Brittany's Corner recently do?
(A) It started a new product line.
(B) It hired a celebrity sponsor.
(C) It opened up a new store.
(D) It conducted an audit.

72. What type of products does Brittany's Corner make?
(A) Cosmetics
(B) Electronics
(C) Clothing
(D) Furniture

73. What will be available on a Web site?
(A) An updated schedule
(B) A job application
(C) An exclusive interview
(D) A listener survey

---

74. What kind of event is taking place?
(A) A welcome ceremony
(B) A film award ceremony
(C) A retirement party
(D) A magazine launch

75. What kind of business do the listeners work for?
(A) A newspaper company
(B) A film studio
(C) An art gallery
(D) A magazine publisher

76. What will the new recruits receive?
(A) Some uniforms
(B) A training manual
(C) An employee ID badge
(D) An electronic device

---

77. What does the speaker's company produce?
(A) Children's toys
(B) Medication
(C) Electric cars
(D) Sporting goods

78. What are listeners reminded to do?
(A) Read a manual
(B) Wear specific equipment
(C) Log in their hours
(D) Attend a training session

79. What can be found online?
(A) Software updates
(B) A product list
(C) A floor plan
(D) A handbook

---

80. What will the speaker most likely do at a park?
(A) Get some exercise
(B) Reserve a campsite
(C) Take photographs
(D) Sell pottery

81. Why does the speaker say, "the sky looks a little cloudy"?
(A) To state a concern
(B) To give a warning
(C) To provide reassurance
(D) To express frustration

82. What does the speaker remind the listener to do?
(A) To bring some equipment
(B) To purchase some materials
(C) To register for a competition
(D) To send an e-mail

GO ON TO THE NEXT PAGE

83. Where is the announcement being made?

(A) At a clothing factory
(B) At a department store
(C) At an advertising agency
(D) At a software company

84. Where should the listeners go at the end of their shifts?

(A) To the employee break room
(B) To Customer Service
(C) To the manager's office
(D) To the parking lot

85. What will most likely happen tomorrow?

(A) A computer program will be fixed.
(B) A store-wide sale will begin.
(C) New merchandise will be delivered.
(D) Office supplies will be ordered.

---

86. Where do the listeners work?

(A) At a law firm
(B) At an employment agency
(C) At a community center
(D) At a repair shop

87. What does the speaker imply when she says, "she will be away on business"?

(A) Some events will be canceled.
(B) A virtual meeting needs to be held.
(C) Some plans should be reviewed.
(D) A replacement needs to be found.

88. What will the listeners most likely do next?

(A) Go to a job fair
(B) Have a discussion
(C) Fill out a form
(D) Call their clients

---

89. What is scheduled for Wednesday?

(A) A community health fair
(B) A retirement party
(C) A client meeting
(D) A welcome breakfast

90. Why does the speaker say, "the consulting business is very competitive"?

(A) To reassure his coworker
(B) To justify seeking new recruits
(C) To suggest the listener redo the work
(D) To ask the listener to lower the price

91. What does the speaker say about Kento?

(A) He will help the woman with her presentation.
(B) He will arrange the woman's flight.
(C) He is familiar with HJC Industries.
(D) He wants to speak to the listener.

---

92. What is the purpose of the meeting?

(A) To introduce a new employee
(B) To celebrate a manager's retirement
(C) To plan a new marketing strategy
(D) To teach professional skills

93. What is causing a delay?

(A) The speaker misplaced some notes.
(B) There is an issue with the projector.
(C) A microphone stopped working.
(D) There was a power outage.

94. What are the listeners encouraged to do?

(A) Write a grant proposal
(B) Attend an international conference
(C) Participate in a feedback session
(D) Draw up a financing strategy

List of Fees & Taxes		Paid	Unpaid
Deposit	$25.00	✓	
Base rental fee ($24 x 5 days)	$120.00		✓
Facility fee	$15.00		✓
State tax	$6.90		✓

95. Who most likely is the speaker?
(A) A car rental agent
(B) An auto engineer
(C) A tax accountant
(D) An airline employee

96. Look at the graphic. Which charge must be paid in cash?
(A) Deposit
(B) Base rental fee
(C) Facility fee
(D) State tax

97. What service does the speaker remind the listener about?
(A) An interest-free payment
(B) A shuttle service
(C) Gas coupons
(D) Maintenance reminders

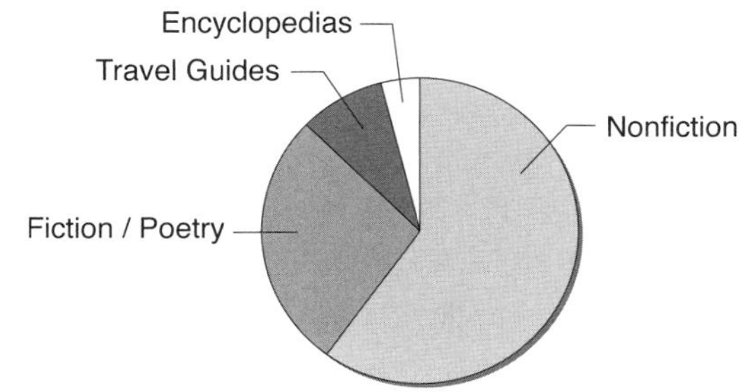

98. Who most likely is the speaker?
(A) A travel guide
(B) A local poet
(C) A book author
(D) A store manager

99. What event will take place every other Saturday?
(A) A talent show
(B) A music performance
(C) A poetry reading
(D) A charity event

100. Look at the graphic. Which type of book does the speaker focus on?
(A) Nonfiction
(B) Fiction and poetry
(C) Travel guides
(D) Encyclopedias

This is the end of the Listening Test. Turn to Part 5 in your test book.

READING TEST

In the Reading test, you will read a variety of texts and answer several different types of reading comprehension questions. The entire Reading test will last 75 minutes. There are three parts, and directions are given for each part. You are encouraged to answer as many questions as possible within the time allowed.

You must mark your answers on the separate answer sheet. Do not write your answers in your test book.

PART 5

Directions: A word or phrase is missing in each of the sentences below. Four answer choices are given below each sentence. Select the best answer to complete the sentence. Then mark the letter (A), (B), (C), or (D) on your answer sheet.

101. A ------- examination of the contract terms is needed before signing it.

(A) care
(B) cared
(C) carefully
(D) careful

102. Artist Wayne Frazer ------- teaches free painting classes at the community center.

(A) together
(B) regularly
(C) sooner
(D) extremely

103. Event planners have been tracking the rate of ------- each year to see if the event is becoming more popular.

(A) attendee
(B) attendance
(C) attendant
(D) attending

104. To cancel an -------, patients of Watson Dental Clinic should call the front desk as early as possible.

(A) appointment
(B) example
(C) origin
(D) issue

105. Benson Automotive provides a bonus to the top salesperson at the end of ------- month.

(A) but
(B) whom
(C) each
(D) now

106. A highly experienced translator is needed for this document ------- it is a business contract.

(A) otherwise
(B) whereas
(C) unless
(D) because

107. In NC Enterprises' offices, wearing casual clothing to work is perfectly -------.

(A) acceptable
(B) accepting
(C) accepts
(D) accept

108. Customer service representatives are reminded that merchandise can only be returned if ------- its original packaging.

(A) onto
(B) except
(C) when
(D) in

109. ------- the peak season, the number of staff members at Herron Golf Resort will be significantly reduced.

(A) Now that
(B) Such as
(C) After
(D) Furthermore

110. Participants in the nature hike ------- before a difficult part of the trail.

(A) resting
(B) rest
(C) rests
(D) restful

111. When leaving the restaurant, customers should be ------- of their noise levels, as residential apartments are nearby.

(A) mindful
(B) exclusive
(C) particular
(D) responsible

112. Bakers should allow the bread to cool ------- prior to putting it into plastic bags.

(A) complete
(B) most complete
(C) more complete
(D) completely

113. Please ------- Laurel Bank the next time you are thinking about getting a loan.

(A) perceive
(B) balance
(C) consider
(D) insure

114. September will be a good month for ------- to carry out some renovations at the hotel.

(A) us
(B) we
(C) ours
(D) our

115. Photographers, ------- to capture the beauty of the waterfall at sunrise, always arrive at the site early in the morning.

(A) eager
(B) tender
(C) voluntary
(D) secure

116. Ainsley Construction ------- the contract terms when the initial 12-month period is over.

(A) modification
(B) to modify
(C) will modify
(D) modifying

117. Diners ------- complained about the long wait time for getting their main course.

(A) primarily
(B) flexibly
(C) ideally
(D) incredibly

118. ------- the bank transfer request is made before 3 P.M., the funds will be sent that day.

(A) In spite of
(B) As long as
(C) Rather than
(D) Ever since

119. The HR team plans to ------- a team-building session on Friday afternoon.

(A) meet
(B) hold
(C) motivate
(D) depart

120. ------- working environments result in employees with a higher job satisfaction rating.

(A) Cooperatively
(B) Cooperative
(C) Cooperate
(D) Cooperates

GO ON TO THE NEXT PAGE

121. Thanks to the teleconferencing software used by the company, team members can easily collaborate ------- leaving their homes.

(A) although
(B) until
(C) among
(D) without

122. People ------- materials that are under copyright could face a fine if they do not have permission to do so.

(A) duplicate
(B) duplication
(C) duplicable
(D) duplicating

123. Midland Communications has a manager handle customer complaints ------- possible.

(A) despite
(B) anyhow
(C) whenever
(D) always

124. As the parking lot at the Rockford Building is small, the building owner has decided to place a ------- of three hours for guest parking.

(A) remark
(B) limit
(C) procedure
(D) concept

125. In the case of temporary employees, ID badges will be disabled when ------- contract ends.

(A) theirs
(B) them
(C) themselves
(D) their

126. Robert Holley, the CEO of technology firm Vidalia, is ------- to announce his resignation at the press conference.

(A) inquired
(B) analyzed
(C) strategized
(D) expected

127. Although the new laptop from Phoenix Electronics has a large screen, it is ------- lightweight.

(A) surprise
(B) surprisingly
(C) surprises
(D) to surprise

128. The new sports arena in Murphyville was designed to be used by ------- athletes.

(A) spare
(B) tangible
(C) visible
(D) amateur

129. The new measures passed by the government are intended to contribute to the ------- of the economy.

(A) stabilize
(B) stability
(C) stable
(D) stabilizes

130. Stand up and stretch your legs ------- throughout your work shift to improve blood flow.

(A) periodically
(B) evidently
(C) mutually
(D) reluctantly

PART 6

Directions: Read the texts that follow. A word, phrase, or sentence is missing in parts of each text. Four answer choices for each question are given below the text. Select the best answer to complete the text. Then mark the letter (A), (B), (C), or (D) on your answer sheet.

Questions 131-134 refer to the following notice.

Palm Tree Amusement Park is hiring workers ------- **131.** the summer season. ------- **132.**. In addition, employees may need to check passes for customers re-entering the park and answer questions regarding park activities. No previous experience is necessary, but we are looking for polite and ------- **133.** people. If you are interested in applying, please visit www.palmtreepark.com. The ------- **134.** is March 22.

131. (A) notwithstanding
(B) as
(C) for
(D) about

132. (A) The parking area near the main entrance is very spacious.
(B) The main responsibilities include selling tickets to customers.
(C) We are a popular tourist attraction for families.
(D) Our park also has live performances by musical groups.

133. (A) consider
(B) considerately
(C) considerate
(D) consideration

134. (A) installation
(B) venture
(C) celebration
(D) deadline

GO ON TO THE NEXT PAGE →

Questions 135-138 refer to the following article.

Lakeside Town to Become Tech Hub

BROOKFIELD—The small town of Brookfield is positioned to become a major site for the technology industry. Thanks to greater ------- (135.) in the town, more tech companies are showing interest in the area. Town officials are spending millions on digital infrastructure. These funds ------- (136.) support the operations of modern businesses. For example, a high-speed Internet network has been added. ------- (137.).

Some residents are concerned that an influx of new businesses could be problematic. ------- (138.), the majority of people in the area welcome the economic growth that will likely accompany these operations.

135. (A) investment
(B) merger
(C) tourism
(D) treatment

136. (A) are meant for
(B) are meant to
(C) mean to
(D) meaning to

137. (A) Brookfield officials are re-elected every four years.
(B) Others think the city's Web site is functional.
(C) This project provides an essential tool for businesses.
(D) Programmers are adjusting the software.

138. (A) Otherwise
(B) In case
(C) Consequently
(D) Nonetheless

Questions 139-142 refer to the following advertisement.

Explore underwater worlds at the Abia Aquarium! Located at 1605 Sherman Avenue, we're open daily all year round, excluding national holidays. At the Abia Aquarium, you can not only learn about a wide variety of amazing sea creatures ------- (139.) immerse yourself in sea life with our underwater tunnel. In addition, you'll love our newest ------- (140.). The Abia Touch Pool is an open tank where you can touch, and even feed, stingrays, eels, and more.

We're proud to offer a variety of educational opportunities for school groups. ------- (141.). For a unique experience, we ------- (142.) after-hours tours to community groups. You can even hold a private party at our site. If you're looking for a unique experience, don't miss a visit to the Abia Aquarium.

139. (A) in addition to
(B) but also
(C) if only
(D) while

140. (A) attraction
(B) transaction
(C) member
(D) statement

141. (A) If you are a teacher, check our Web site for more information.
(B) Some of these species are in danger of becoming extinct.
(C) Contact our site manager to inquire about job openings.
(D) We have not raised our admission fees for many years.

142. (A) were providing
(B) to be provided
(C) will be provided
(D) provide

GO ON TO THE NEXT PAGE

Questions 143-146 refer to the following letter.

Winfrey Snow Removal
602 Vernon Street
Irvington, NJ 07111

February 13

Daniel Roldan

9141 Bingamon Road

Irvington, NJ 07111

Dear Mr. Roldan,

As you know, we -------(143.) a seasonal snow removal business every winter for the past 8 years. -------(144.), we understand that it is difficult for employees like you to find work the rest of the year. We were recently contacted by Garner Construction about using our equipment during the spring and summer months. It is needed for -------(145.) work on repairing roads. Since we already have employees experienced in operating this equipment, such as trucks for hauling materials, the company is willing to hire people based on our recommendation. We will pass along your contact details if you are interested, so please let us know. -------(146.).

Sincerely,

Jeremy Winfrey

143. (A) operate
(B) were operating
(C) have operated
(D) could operate

144. (A) However
(B) At that time
(C) For example
(D) Rather

145. (A) her
(B) what
(C) our
(D) its

146. (A) Customers rely on prompt clearance of driveways.
(B) You should do so quickly so you don't miss this opportunity.
(C) Some storms result in more snowfall than others.
(D) We hope you will celebrate with us at the retirement party.

PART 7

Directions: In this part, you will read a selection of texts, such as magazine and newspaper articles, e-mails, and instant messages. Each text or set of texts is followed by several questions. Select the best answer for each question and mark the letter (A), (B), (C), or (D) on your answer sheet.

Questions 147-148 refer to the following text-message chain.

Janet Woodall [11:43 A.M.]
Hi, Patrick. I've just finished boxing up the cookies and cupcakes for Mr. Howard. Is there anything else?

Patrick Ladner [11:45 A.M.]
Thanks. Someone from Reno Accounting is picking up their cake at 4 P.M. today, so we'd better make sure it is done on time. Also, the Summer Food Festival date has been confirmed for July 22.

Janet Woodall [11:46 A.M.]
What a shame. That doesn't work for me.

Patrick Ladner [11:47 A.M.]
Oh really? I was hoping that you could run the booth like you did last year.

Janet Woodall [11:49 A.M.]
I'll be on vacation in Los Angeles that week, remember? But Nora helped me last year, and I'm sure she can handle it. Anyway, I'll begin the work on the Reno Accounting order now. It will take a while to complete.

Patrick Ladner [11:50 A.M.]
All right.

147. What will Ms. Woodall most likely work on next?

(A) Some cookies
(B) Some cupcakes
(C) A cake
(D) A loaf of bread

148. At 11:46 A.M., what does Ms. Woodall mean when she writes, "That doesn't work for me"?

(A) She is unable to give Mr. Ladner advice.
(B) She is having trouble with some machinery.
(C) She is not available for an event.
(D) She does not have time to meet with Nora.

TEST 05

GO ON TO THE NEXT PAGE →

Questions 149-150 refer to the following notice.

Thank you for using the Yogtastic smartphone application! You are currently signed in as a Basic member. This allows you to stream up to two yoga videos per day and access our guide of over 50 yoga poses. To help meet your fitness goals, why not upgrade to our Platinum membership? You can try this membership level for 30 days without making a payment. With the Platinum membership, you can download an unlimited number of videos, track your progress, get advice from experts, and more. You can see everything offered under the new membership on the Platinum Members page.

149. What are readers of the notice encouraged to do?

(A) Report streaming problems
(B) Sign up for a free trial
(C) Upload their yoga videos
(D) Try a new pose each day

150. According to the notice, what is available on a Web page?

(A) A list of features
(B) A tracking number
(C) Payment information
(D) Product reviews

Questions 151-152 refer to the following e-mail.

To: Audrey Swenson <a.swenson@ardito.ca>
From: Herman Bray <brayherman@bclandscaping.com>
Date: March 25
Subject: Services at 468 Trujillo Street

Dear Ms. Swenson,

Thank you for signing up for a three-month contract for lawn care services at your property. As agreed, our team will mow your lawn twice a month and trim the bushes once a month. Our first visit will be on April 3, and we will bring all of our own equipment. Could you please let me know whether you have garden collection bins at your property or whether you need us to remove the grass and bush trimmings? This will help us to plan ahead. Also, after our first visit, you will be e-mailed a brief questionnaire about the service. If you complete it, you will be given a 15% discount on the next service visit.

Warmest regards,

Herman Bray
BC Landscaping

151. What is Ms. Swenson asked to confirm?

(A) Where some equipment should be stored
(B) What should be done with some waste
(C) How often a lawn should be mowed
(D) What kind of bushes should be planted

152. How can Ms. Swenson get a discount on a service?

(A) By recommending the business to others
(B) By paying for the work up front
(C) By signing a three-month contract
(D) By providing some feedback

GO ON TO THE NEXT PAGE

Questions 153-154 refer to the following e-mail.

To: Kevin Moore
From: Mona Russell
Date: 14 October
Subject: Meeting

Hi Kevin,

Unfortunately, I've run into an issue with our meeting scheduled for tomorrow at 11:30 at our office. I'm wondering if you would be able to come to the Galindo Restaurant in the Mosquera neighborhood instead. I have a morning meeting with Rowe Manufacturing in that neighborhood, and then I need to visit Eugene Conner, also in that neighborhood, at one o'clock. I don't think I'd be able to get all the way back to the office for our meeting and then back to Mr. Conner's office by one.

Galindo Restaurant has a big parking lot as well as private booths, so we can enjoy lunch while going through the job applications and decide who should be invited to an interview. If this works for you, please let me know.

Thanks!

Mona

153. Why does Ms. Russell want to change a meeting place?

(A) She is concerned about a lack of parking in the area.
(B) She found out that the original place was fully booked.
(C) She will not have time to travel very far.
(D) She would like a client to attend.

154. What most likely will be discussed at the meeting with Mr. Moore?

(A) Preparing for a presentation
(B) Improving the manufacturing process
(C) Selecting job candidates
(D) Boosting staff productivity

Questions 155-157 refer to the following comment card.

Gateway Housewares Customer Comment Card

The company has recently been purchased by a third party, so we are looking for ways to improve the shopping experience for all of our customers. Your honest opinions are greatly appreciated, and we will do our best to implement changes that address your feedback. If you would like to be entered into our monthly prize drawing, please include your contact details below.

Name (optional): *Alanna Bianco*
E-mail address (optional): *abianco@perineenterprises.com*
Date of visit: *February 8*

Comments: *I visited your store to purchase a gift for a relative. One of your sales clerks, Elizabeth, answered questions about the products. She explained that my coupon had expired, but she still helped me find something that was within my price range. It was a luxury candle that seemed to be of high quality. In fact, I liked it so much that I bought one for myself as well. Overall, I would recommend your store to others.*

155. What is indicated about Gateway Housewares?

(A) It has recently relocated.
(B) It had a change of ownership.
(C) It changes its inventory monthly.
(D) It is training staff members.

156. The word "address" in paragraph 1, line 4, is closest in meaning to

(A) deal with
(B) speak to
(C) send
(D) label

157. What does Ms. Bianco suggest about her shopping experience?

(A) She visited the store based on a recommendation.
(B) She bought more items than originally intended.
(C) She used a coupon for her purchase.
(D) She was surprised by the price of the merchandise.

GO ON TO THE NEXT PAGE

Questions 158-160 refer to the following e-mail.

E-Mail

To:	staff@vasquezpharma.com
From:	tphillips@vasquezpharma.com
Date:	August 15
Subject:	Notice

Please note that the software program for our research database will be updated this Friday, August 19. Members of the IT team will carry out the necessary work after you leave for the day on Friday. —[1]—.

Following the update, your log-in details will remain the same. —[2]—. However, you will see that some confidential files cannot be accessed without the proper authorization. In addition, there will be more search functions than before. This will help you narrow down your search results more quickly. —[3]—.

Your computer may take longer than usual to start on Monday, but this is a normal part of the process and will only happen one time. Should you have any questions or comments, please contact the IT team directly by calling extension 30. —[4]—. Thank you for your patience and cooperation in this matter.

Sincerely,

Thomas Phillips

158. What is the purpose of the e-mail?

(A) To explain how to request a database upgrade
(B) To inform employees about some software changes
(C) To give instructions on maintaining confidential records
(D) To remind employees to update their log-in details

159. According to Mr. Phillips, what will users experience after August 19?

(A) Results will be displayed alphabetically.
(B) The authorization code will be adjusted.
(C) More search options will be available.
(D) The home page will load more quickly.

160. In which of the positions marked [1], [2], [3], and [4] does the following sentence belong?

"Please leave your computer on to speed up the process."

(A) [1]
(B) [2]
(C) [3]
(D) [4]

Questions 161-163 refer to the following Web page.

https://www.salvoelectronics.com/recall

Salvo Electronics Recall of Delima-XR Smartphone

Salvo Electronics is issuing a voluntary recall of certain Delima-XR Smartphones due to a design flaw. Our quality control team has determined that the battery may overheat. If you purchased this phone model between January 1 and March 31, please check the serial number. If the number begins with 56 or 57, the device is eligible for the recall. You can return the phone to any Salvo Electronics store for a full refund. We do not require the original packaging or a receipt to do so. Alternatively, you may request a return box by calling our customer helpline at 1-800-555-7932. A return box will be sent to you, and the postage will be prepaid. Please note that the box is designated as "Ground Transport Only".

161. For whom is the Web page most likely intended?

(A) Salvo Electronics salespeople
(B) Salvo Electronics customers
(C) Product designers
(D) Quality control inspectors

162. What is suggested about Delima-XR smartphones?

(A) They can be returned without a receipt.
(B) They were discontinued after March 31.
(C) Their battery can be replaced.
(D) They are not selling well.

163. What is indicated about the return boxes?

(A) They are available in several different sizes.
(B) Their postage must be paid upon receipt.
(C) They should not be transported by air.
(D) They will arrive within two days.

GO ON TO THE NEXT PAGE

Questions 164-167 refer to the following online chat discussion.

Teresa Juarez [12:32 P.M.] Hi, Chen and Bonnie. Is either of you back from lunch yet? I'm on my way back to the office now for the meeting with the representatives from Strauss Logistics, but my bus is stuck in traffic. It starts at 1 P.M., so I won't have much time to prepare.

Chen Xuan [12:33 P.M.] I didn't go out for lunch. What can I help you with, Teresa?

Bonnie Eley [12:34 P.M.] I'm here, too. Do you need the Juniper Room set up for the meeting? The projection screen is already in there, and there's a podium at the front.

Teresa Juarez [12:36 P.M.] Actually, the Juniper Room won't work because it only has space for 12 people. There's a sign on my desk directing the visitors to the Spruce Room. I need someone to hang it up at the entrance so they know where to go when they arrive.

Bonnie Eley [12:37 P.M.] Sure thing. That won't take me long.

Chen Xuan [12:39 P.M.] The coffee machine on that floor is working fine, but do you have anything else to serve? I could buy a fruit plate and some pastries at the grocery store across the street.

Teresa Juarez [12:41 P.M.] That would be great, Chen. Thank you! You can use the company card. And thanks to you, too, Bonnie. I'll be there as soon as possible. It looks like traffic is clearing up a bit now.

SEND

164. Why did Ms. Juarez contact Mr. Xuan and Ms. Eley?

(A) To take their lunch orders
(B) To apologize for an error
(C) To invite them to a meeting
(D) To ask for assistance

165. What is suggested about the meeting with the Strauss Logistics representatives?

(A) It will be led by Ms. Eley.
(B) It will be held in the Juniper Room.
(C) It will include a product demonstration.
(D) It will have more than 12 participants.

166. At 12:37 P.M., what does Ms. Eley most likely mean when she writes, "Sure thing"?

(A) She will greet some visitors.
(B) She will post information online.
(C) She will put up a sign.
(D) She will unlock an entrance.

167. What does Mr. Xuan offer to do?

(A) Move a projection screen
(B) Purchase some refreshments
(C) Print some documents
(D) Bring in more chairs

Questions 168-171 refer to the following e-mail.

To: staff@elswicksoftware.com
From: gferraz@elswicksoftware.com
Date: October 6
Subject: For your information

Dear Elswick Software Staff,

As our company continues to thrive, you can expect to see some new faces around the office. Lara Yi will be taking over as the Berrini branch's marketing director starting on October 12. She joins us from Brasilia Tech.

Nicole Rocha is also part of the staff expansion at Berrini. She will perform administrative services and will be supported by Diego Barbosa, who is currently assigned to Berrini on Mondays, Wednesdays, and Fridays, and Ibirapuera on Tuesdays and Thursdays.

At Ibirapuera, Julio Azevedo has been hired as the new office manager. He has worked in the software industry for over 20 years. Luisa Sousa at the Moema branch suggested hiring him, and he impressed everyone on the interview panel. He will hold a question-and-answer session on his first day, October 19, so that employees have the chance to get to know him.

I will keep you updated on any other personnel changes. We are expecting a large number of transfers from the Moema branch once it is no longer in operation. We are still finalizing what will happen to each employee there.

Gustavo Ferraz

168. Why did Mr. Ferraz send the e-mail?

(A) To thank employees for their hard work
(B) To introduce some new employees
(C) To discuss some upcoming visitors
(D) To summarize branch achievements

169. Who works at more than one branch?

(A) Ms. Yi
(B) Ms. Rocha
(C) Mr. Barbosa
(D) Mr. Ferraz

170. What is NOT mentioned about Mr. Azevedo?

(A) He will respond to questions from staff.
(B) He has two decades of experience.
(C) He was recommended by a company employee.
(D) He will sign his contract on October 19.

171. What does Mr. Ferraz suggest about the Moema branch?

(A) It will be relocated to another building.
(B) It has the largest number of employees.
(C) It is scheduled to permanently close.
(D) It is the site of his new office.

GO ON TO THE NEXT PAGE

Questions 172-175 refer to the following Web page.

http://www.gilletthistorymuseum.org

HOME | **ABOUT** | PHOTO GALLERY | CONTACT US

The Gillett County History Museum

The Gillett County History Museum was founded as a non-profit organization in 1963 in a small building in downtown Clousson. —[1]—. After 25 years, it moved to its current and permanent home in Greenwood. The site is dedicated to preserving historical artifacts related to the county's history as well as providing educational programs for the public.

—[2]—. The museum is fighting to remain relevant and help people understand the importance of staying connected to the past. Through the well-organized presentation of documents, photographs, handmade items, and more, the museum's team of employees and volunteers hope to create a picture of what Gillett County was like in the past. By understanding where we've been, we can understand where we're going.

The museum has hosted lectures with speakers from as far away as Ketchikan, Alaska, screenings of relevant documentaries, and debates on historical discoveries. —[3]—. All special events take place in the Bryant Room, which is decorated with art donated by the family of Leonard Bryant. The most popular special event at the museum in recent years has been the Annual Gillett Fashion Workshop. Participants learned to recreate traditional styles of clothing based on photos from the museum's archives.

Whether you want to learn about the history of the military base in Logan, changes to law enforcement, agriculture methods, or more, the museum is likely to have something of interest. —[4]—. Everyone is invited to explore the museum for free during its opening hours, which are Tuesday through Saturday, 10 A.M. to 4 P.M.

172. What is the purpose of the Web page?

(A) To promote a museum exhibit
(B) To highlight a local museum
(C) To announce a museum's opening
(D) To introduce a volunteer recruitment project

173. Where is the Gillett County History Museum located?

(A) In Clousson
(B) In Greenwood
(C) In Ketchikan
(D) In Logan

174. What is indicated about the Bryant Room?

(A) It was recently redecorated.
(B) Its displays are changed regularly.
(C) It is where rare documents are stored.
(D) It has been the site of a workshop.

175. In which of the positions marked [1], [2], [3], and [4] does the following sentence best belong?

"It's no surprise that people value modern technology and experiences these days."

(A) [1]
(B) [2]
(C) [3]
(D) [4]

GO ON TO THE NEXT PAGE

Questions 176-180 refer to the following brochure and e-mail.

At Carolina Solar, we believe that energy efficiency can be achieved through transitioning to sustainable energy sources. No matter which utility company you are currently using, you can do your part to help the environment, and save money in the long run, by having a solar panel system installed at your home. You may or may not need a permit to do so, depending on your property type and neighborhood, so visit www.carolinasolar.net to find out more.

There are four steps in our process for new customers.

Step 1: Call us at (919) 555-5228, and a technician will visit your home, take measurements, and discuss your energy needs.

Step 2: A technician will send you a virtual 3D design of the recommended solar panel array in place on your rooftop. This will be accompanied by a projected energy savings report.

Step 3: Once a contract is signed, one of our experienced crews will install the panels at your home for a fixed fee. Please note that June to August is our busy season.

Step 4: Two weeks after the installation, a company representative will visit your home to ensure everything is working adequately and to answer any follow-up questions you may have.

E-Mail

To: Theresa Ruiz <t_ruiz@rochestermail.com>
From: Alan Knox <alan@carolinasolar.net>
Date: August 8
Subject: 192 Holland Street Project
Attachments: Ruiz1.doc, Ruiz2.doc

Dear Ms. Ruiz,

Please find attached the design drawings for the solar panels and the summary of what you are likely to save on energy based on your usage. I know you had wanted to use a Nuzum battery for the system. However, I would recommend a Girard Co. battery instead. It is a bit more expensive up front, but it is scalable, which means you would have the option of adding more battery power in the coming years without replacing the unit. It has the same warranty period as the Nuzum battery.

Please let me know if you approve of the plan and whether you have any questions. I look forward to hearing from you!

Warmest regards,

Alan Knox

176. What does the brochure suggest about the company's solar panels?

(A) They are checked carefully for defects at the factory.
(B) They are made from environmentally friendly materials.
(C) They can be easily maintained by the homeowner.
(D) They can be used with any energy supplier.

177. According to the brochure, why should readers visit the company's Web site?

(A) To upload photos of their roof
(B) To read comments from current customers
(C) To get information about permit requirements
(D) To estimate the size of the necessary system

178. What is true about Carolina Solar?

(A) It does not have appointments available after August.
(B) It has more than one installation crew.
(C) It calculates fees based on installation time.
(D) It aims to use domestic suppliers only.

179. On which step of the process is Ms. Ruiz?

(A) Step 1
(B) Step 2
(C) Step 3
(D) Step 4

180. Why does Mr. Knox suggest changing a battery?

(A) To use a more reliable product
(B) To take advantage of an extended warranty
(C) To reduce the cost of the project
(D) To provide more flexibility in the future

GO ON TO THE NEXT PAGE

Questions 181-185 refer to the following notice and e-mail.

Gloversville Association of Farmers
Public Notice

Following an extensive feedback survey of both vendors and members of the public, the Gloversville Association of Farmers will be making the following changes to our local farmers markets, effective immediately:

Flower Market: The market will be moved from Lance Park to Grove Plaza to make space for more stalls and to gain outdoor access to electricity. It will be open on Tuesdays and Saturdays as usual.

Mixed Market: Vendors can still sell jams, fruits, vegetables, and herbs at this market at Renner Park, and we are now allowing potted plants. We have added Mondays as an opening day in addition to Wednesdays and Saturdays as before.

Meat & More Market: This market selling locally produced meat, fish, and dairy products will remain in operation at Sunset Hall on Saturdays and Sundays. However, it will open one hour earlier than before, at 7 A.M.

Produce Market: We will distribute free shopping bags to those coming to purchase fresh fruits and vegetables at this market, which runs on Thursdays, Fridays, and Saturdays at Crosswind Field.

E-Mail

TO:	Lisa Jordan
FROM:	Joe Cawthorn
DATE:	July 14
SUBJECT:	Farmers Market

Hi Lisa,

I've checked my schedule, and it's no problem for me to cover Olivia's shift at the market this Saturday. I'm already familiar with the various fish varieties we sell, so I should be able to help customers. Thanks for offering to secure a parking pass for me. However, I won't need it because my car is currently in the shop. Please let me know exactly what time you need me to turn up.

All the best,

Joe

181. Why was the notice written?

(A) To announce improvements to local markets
(B) To invite vendors to participate in some events
(C) To gather feedback about shoppers' needs
(D) To promote membership in the Gloversville Association of Farmers

182. What is suggested about the Mixed Market?

(A) It is open both weekend days.
(B) It used to operate only twice a week.
(C) It is the most-visited market.
(D) It no longer allows plants to be sold.

183. Where will Mr. Cawthorn most likely work this Saturday?

(A) At Grove Plaza
(B) At Renner Park
(C) At Sunset Hall
(D) At Crosswind Field

184. In the e-mail, the phrase "turn up" in paragraph 1, line 4, is closest in meaning to

(A) arrive
(B) discover
(C) increase
(D) adapt

185. What does Mr. Cawthorn suggest in his e-mail?

(A) He thinks a pass has not expired.
(B) He does not plan to drive to an event.
(C) He would like to shop after his work shift.
(D) He will get product information from Olivia.

GO ON TO THE NEXT PAGE

Questions 186-190 refer to the following flyer, brochure, and e-mail.

Community Plus Workshop Series

Wakefield residents are invited to improve their skills in a variety of areas by taking part in the Community Plus Workshop Series on March 28. Why not try something new like unlocking your creativity while writing? Or go for something more practical, such as learning how to use less water in your garden by collecting rainwater. We're sure you'll be impressed with our instructors, such as Erica Cantrell, who will show you how to make interesting crafts from used materials.

There is no fee for participating in the workshops, and advance registration is not required. Seating is available on a first-come, first-served basis, so we recommend arriving early to get a good seat. Please direct any inquiries to Ralph Quinn at quinnr@wakefieldcomm.org.

Community Plus Workshop Series – Final Schedule
March 28

9:00 A.M.	**Kitchen Cuts** – Just because you're cooking on a budget doesn't mean you have to sacrifice on taste! Make delicious dinners with affordable ingredients. **Insects That Help** – Grow plants that will attract bees and other garden-friendly insects to your garden. Choose the right varieties for the amount of shade you have.
11:00 A.M.	**Nature Made** – Learn how to set up a rainwater collection system for your roof and get tips on how to maintain your supply.
2:00 P.M.	**Perfect Plots** – Hone your creative writing skills by practicing plot development and getting tips for keeping readers engaged. **Turning Inward** – Learn simple yoga poses and breathing exercises that will help to put you in a calm and relaxed state anytime.
3:30 P.M.	**Trash to Treasure** – Reuse ordinary materials that you would normally throw away and convert them into beautiful gifts and decorations. Taught by an award-winning artist on this topic.

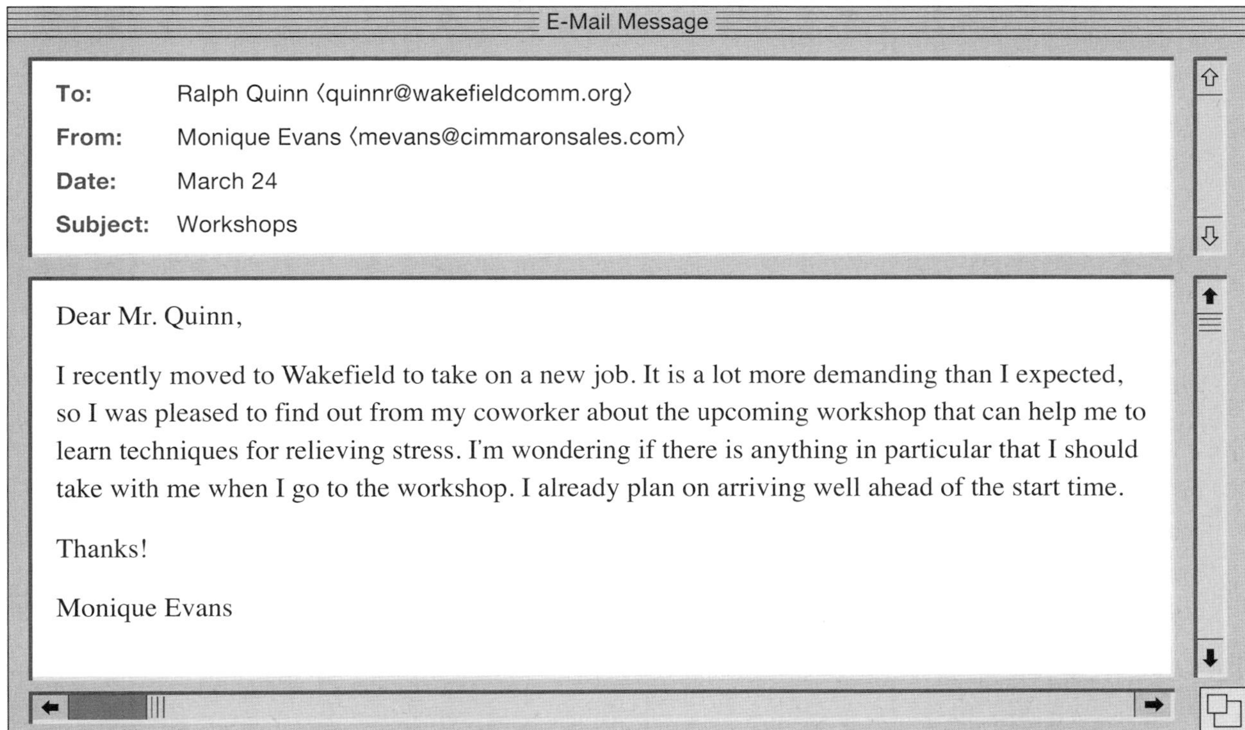
E-Mail Message

To: Ralph Quinn 〈quinnr@wakefieldcomm.org〉
From: Monique Evans 〈mevans@cimmaronsales.com〉
Date: March 24
Subject: Workshops

Dear Mr. Quinn,

I recently moved to Wakefield to take on a new job. It is a lot more demanding than I expected, so I was pleased to find out from my coworker about the upcoming workshop that can help me to learn techniques for relieving stress. I'm wondering if there is anything in particular that I should take with me when I go to the workshop. I already plan on arriving well ahead of the start time.

Thanks!

Monique Evans

186. According to the flyer, what is one topic that will be covered in the workshops?
(A) Renovating a home
(B) Starting a business
(C) Saving water
(D) Improving listening skills

187. What is probably true about Ms. Cantrell?
(A) She has won an award for her work.
(B) She will teach more than one workshop.
(C) She founded the Community Plus Workshop Series.
(D) She is a long-time resident of Wakefield.

188. When can participants learn about saving money on meals?
(A) At 9:00 A.M.
(B) At 11:00 A.M.
(C) At 2:00 P.M.
(D) At 3:30 P.M.

189. What does Ms. Evans want to know about a workshop?
(A) Where to go
(B) What to bring
(C) How to enroll
(D) When to arrive

190. Which workshop will Ms. Evans most likely attend?
(A) Insects That Help
(B) Nature Made
(C) Perfect Plots
(D) Turning Inward

GO ON TO THE NEXT PAGE

Questions 191-195 refer to the following e-mail, chart, and online review.

To: All Dawson Horse-Riding Center Staff
From: Suzan Salazar
Date: February 6
Subject: Notes

Thank you all for your active participation this morning. As we will be busy with the annual horse show on the first Monday of March, we won't have another all-staff meeting until the first Monday of April.

In the meantime, we will go forward with our plans to add a picnic shelter to our gardens so people can enjoy lunch or a snack while waiting for their turn to ride the horses. Alfonso Miller's landscaping firm will take out two flower beds from that section to make space. Esther Francis is going to research the expenses for building the shelter. In addition, Glenn Lopez will hire someone to repave the parking lot and carry out the other improvements there.

We're excited about the changes ahead at Dawson Horse-Riding Center!

Thanks,

Suzan Salazar
Dawson Horse-Riding Center

PICNIC SHELTER CONSTRUCTION COSTS

Company	Cost	Estimated Completion Date
Dillon Construction	$8,550	June 27
Edgewood	$7,800	July 11
Hale Construction	$8,200	June 4
Outdoor Shelters Inc.	$7,995	July 31

Comments: Dillon Construction and Hale Construction have consistently had top ratings from customers.

I visited Dawson Horse-Riding Center with my family yesterday. My children had a great time riding the horses. The center has a wide range of horses in its stables that are suitable for riders of different ages and experience levels. I'm surprised that they have started charging for parking at the site, although the fee is minimal. I was impressed with the new picnic shelter in the gardens, and I plan to bring a packed lunch the next time I visit. This facility is a great place to spend your free time!

Reviewed by Clara Hamilton, June 15

191. According to the e-mail, how often does Dawson Horse-Riding Center most likely have an all-staff meeting?

(A) Once a week
(B) Once a month
(C) Twice a month
(D) Once a quarter

192. What does Ms. Salazar indicate about the business's gardens?

(A) They are a popular site with visitors.
(B) Some of their flowers will be sold.
(C) They will be planted by a landscaping firm.
(D) Some of the flower beds will be removed.

193. Who most likely prepared the chart?

(A) Mr. Miller
(B) Ms. Francis
(C) Mr. Lopez
(D) Ms. Salazar

194. What does Ms. Hamilton suggest about Dawson Horse-Riding Center in her review?

(A) It previously offered free parking.
(B) It sells food on site.
(C) It provides free tours of the stables.
(D) It holds special activities for children.

195. Which company did Dawson Horse-Riding Center most likely hire to build a picnic area?

(A) Dillon Construction
(B) Edgewood
(C) Hale Construction
(D) Outdoor Shelters Inc.

GO ON TO THE NEXT PAGE

Questions 196-200 refer to the following brochure, chart, and e-mail.

Grand Canyon Adventures (GCA)

Day tours throughout the Grand Canyon National Park!

Enjoy a guided, narrated tour led by an experienced guide. We provide free pickup and return from Carabello Hotel. Please contact us at (928) 555-4983 for more information.

Explorer Tour — 2 hours, $450 per person
See breathtaking views of the canyon from a helicopter on this unforgettable tour! Please wear long pants and closed-toed shoes. Lunch included.

West Rim Tour — 4 hours, $150 per person
Take a bus ride through the West Rim area of the park, where you can see famous sites like Eagle Point, a rock formation that is said to look like an eagle. Breakfast and lunch included.

South Rim Tour — 3 hours, $110 per person
Photographers especially will love the stunning views of the South Rim. The bus will make multiple stops at scenic spots, including Mather Point. Lunch included.

Valley Tour — 3 hours, $175 per person
Get into the heart of the canyon with this unique boat trip. You'll descend by bus all the way to the canyon floor, nearly 4,000 feet, and take a boat down the Colorado River. Lunch included.

GCA Summary of June Tours

Tour Type	Tours per Week	Average Profit per Tour	Average Profit per Week	Average Rating
Explorer Tour	7	$217	$1,519	4.9
West Rim Tour	12	$725	$8,700	3.7
South Rim Tour	14	$454	$6,356	4.2
Valley Tour	9	$83	$747	4.0

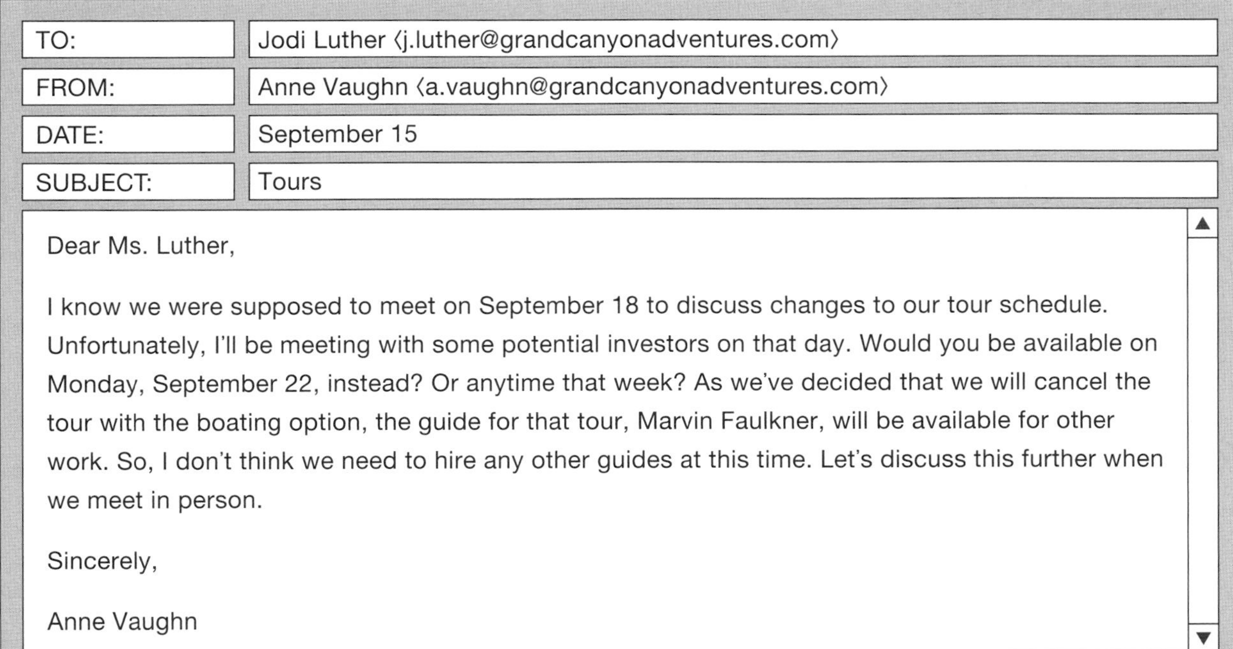

TO:	Jodi Luther <j.luther@grandcanyonadventures.com>
FROM:	Anne Vaughn <a.vaughn@grandcanyonadventures.com>
DATE:	September 15
SUBJECT:	Tours

Dear Ms. Luther,

I know we were supposed to meet on September 18 to discuss changes to our tour schedule. Unfortunately, I'll be meeting with some potential investors on that day. Would you be available on Monday, September 22, instead? Or anytime that week? As we've decided that we will cancel the tour with the boating option, the guide for that tour, Marvin Faulkner, will be available for other work. So, I don't think we need to hire any other guides at this time. Let's discuss this further when we meet in person.

Sincerely,

Anne Vaughn

196. What does the brochure suggest is the same about all of the tours?

(A) The fee per participant
(B) The transportation from a hotel
(C) The duration of the tour
(D) The number of meals included

197. According to the chart, what is true about the West Rim Tour?

(A) It received a lower rating than the Explorer Tour.
(B) It is the most frequently offered tour.
(C) It is less profitable per tour than the South Rim Tour.
(D) It is the second-most profitable tour per week.

198. How many times per week does GCA give tours to Mather Point?

(A) 7
(B) 9
(C) 12
(D) 14

199. Why did Ms. Vaughn write the e-mail?

(A) To reschedule a meeting
(B) To apologize for an error in a tour schedule
(C) To recommend a new tour guide for hire
(D) To introduce some investors

200. What tour does Mr. Faulkner lead?

(A) The Explorer Tour
(B) The West Rim Tour
(C) The South Rim Tour
(D) The Valley Tour

TEST 05

Stop! This is the end of the test. If you finish before time is called, you may go back to Parts 5, 6, and 7 and check your work.

▶ 정답 및 해설 p. 139

삶의 순간순간이
아름다운 마무리이며
새로운 시작이어야 한다.

– 법정 스님

ANSWER SHEET

ACTUAL TEST

LISTENING(Part I ~ IV)

NO.	A	B	C	D	NO.	A	B	C	D	NO.	A	B	C	D	NO.	A	B	C	D	NO.	A	B	C	D
1	a	b	c	d	21	a	b	c		41	a	b	c	d	61	a	b	c	d	81	a	b	c	d
2	a	b	c	d	22	a	b	c		42	a	b	c	d	62	a	b	c	d	82	a	b	c	d
3	a	b	c	d	23	a	b	c		43	a	b	c	d	63	a	b	c	d	83	a	b	c	d
4	a	b	c	d	24	a	b	c		44	a	b	c	d	64	a	b	c	d	84	a	b	c	d
5	a	b	c	d	25	a	b	c		45	a	b	c	d	65	a	b	c	d	85	a	b	c	d
6	a	b	c	d	26	a	b	c		46	a	b	c	d	66	a	b	c	d	86	a	b	c	d
7	a	b	c		27	a	b	c		47	a	b	c	d	67	a	b	c	d	87	a	b	c	d
8	a	b	c		28	a	b	c		48	a	b	c	d	68	a	b	c	d	88	a	b	c	d
9	a	b	c		29	a	b	c		49	a	b	c	d	69	a	b	c	d	89	a	b	c	d
10	a	b	c		30	a	b	c		50	a	b	c	d	70	a	b	c	d	90	a	b	c	d
11	a	b	c		31	a	b	c		51	a	b	c	d	71	a	b	c	d	91	a	b	c	d
12	a	b	c		32	a	b	c	d	52	a	b	c	d	72	a	b	c	d	92	a	b	c	d
13	a	b	c		33	a	b	c	d	53	a	b	c	d	73	a	b	c	d	93	a	b	c	d
14	a	b	c		34	a	b	c	d	54	a	b	c	d	74	a	b	c	d	94	a	b	c	d
15	a	b	c		35	a	b	c	d	55	a	b	c	d	75	a	b	c	d	95	a	b	c	d
16	a	b	c		36	a	b	c	d	56	a	b	c	d	76	a	b	c	d	96	a	b	c	d
17	a	b	c		37	a	b	c	d	57	a	b	c	d	77	a	b	c	d	97	a	b	c	d
18	a	b	c		38	a	b	c	d	58	a	b	c	d	78	a	b	c	d	98	a	b	c	d
19	a	b	c		39	a	b	c	d	59	a	b	c	d	79	a	b	c	d	99	a	b	c	d
20	a	b	c		40	a	b	c	d	60	a	b	c	d	80	a	b	c	d	100	a	b	c	d

* 문제를 다 풀고 채점한 후 점수로 환산해 봅니다. 점수 환산표는 16페이지에 있습니다.

READING(Part V ~ VII)

NO.	A	B	C	D	NO.	A	B	C	D	NO.	A	B	C	D	NO.	A	B	C	D	NO.	A	B	C	D
101	a	b	c	d	121	a	b	c	d	141	a	b	c	d	161	a	b	c	d	181	a	b	c	d
102	a	b	c	d	122	a	b	c	d	142	a	b	c	d	162	a	b	c	d	182	a	b	c	d
103	a	b	c	d	123	a	b	c	d	143	a	b	c	d	163	a	b	c	d	183	a	b	c	d
104	a	b	c	d	124	a	b	c	d	144	a	b	c	d	164	a	b	c	d	184	a	b	c	d
105	a	b	c	d	125	a	b	c	d	145	a	b	c	d	165	a	b	c	d	185	a	b	c	d
106	a	b	c	d	126	a	b	c	d	146	a	b	c	d	166	a	b	c	d	186	a	b	c	d
107	a	b	c	d	127	a	b	c	d	147	a	b	c	d	167	a	b	c	d	187	a	b	c	d
108	a	b	c	d	128	a	b	c	d	148	a	b	c	d	168	a	b	c	d	188	a	b	c	d
109	a	b	c	d	129	a	b	c	d	149	a	b	c	d	169	a	b	c	d	189	a	b	c	d
110	a	b	c	d	130	a	b	c	d	150	a	b	c	d	170	a	b	c	d	190	a	b	c	d
111	a	b	c	d	131	a	b	c	d	151	a	b	c	d	171	a	b	c	d	191	a	b	c	d
112	a	b	c	d	132	a	b	c	d	152	a	b	c	d	172	a	b	c	d	192	a	b	c	d
113	a	b	c	d	133	a	b	c	d	153	a	b	c	d	173	a	b	c	d	193	a	b	c	d
114	a	b	c	d	134	a	b	c	d	154	a	b	c	d	174	a	b	c	d	194	a	b	c	d
115	a	b	c	d	135	a	b	c	d	155	a	b	c	d	175	a	b	c	d	195	a	b	c	d
116	a	b	c	d	136	a	b	c	d	156	a	b	c	d	176	a	b	c	d	196	a	b	c	d
117	a	b	c	d	137	a	b	c	d	157	a	b	c	d	177	a	b	c	d	197	a	b	c	d
118	a	b	c	d	138	a	b	c	d	158	a	b	c	d	178	a	b	c	d	198	a	b	c	d
119	a	b	c	d	139	a	b	c	d	159	a	b	c	d	179	a	b	c	d	199	a	b	c	d
120	a	b	c	d	140	a	b	c	d	160	a	b	c	d	180	a	b	c	d	200	a	b	c	d

자르는 선

ANSWER SHEET

ACTUAL TEST

LISTENING(Part I ~ IV)

NO.	A	B	C	D	NO.	A	B	C	D	NO.	A	B	C	D	NO.	A	B	C	D	NO.	A	B	C	D
1	ⓐ	ⓑ	ⓒ	ⓓ	21	ⓐ	ⓑ	ⓒ		41	ⓐ	ⓑ	ⓒ	ⓓ	61	ⓐ	ⓑ	ⓒ	ⓓ	81	ⓐ	ⓑ	ⓒ	ⓓ
2	ⓐ	ⓑ	ⓒ	ⓓ	22	ⓐ	ⓑ	ⓒ		42	ⓐ	ⓑ	ⓒ	ⓓ	62	ⓐ	ⓑ	ⓒ	ⓓ	82	ⓐ	ⓑ	ⓒ	ⓓ
3	ⓐ	ⓑ	ⓒ	ⓓ	23	ⓐ	ⓑ	ⓒ		43	ⓐ	ⓑ	ⓒ	ⓓ	63	ⓐ	ⓑ	ⓒ	ⓓ	83	ⓐ	ⓑ	ⓒ	ⓓ
4	ⓐ	ⓑ	ⓒ	ⓓ	24	ⓐ	ⓑ	ⓒ		44	ⓐ	ⓑ	ⓒ	ⓓ	64	ⓐ	ⓑ	ⓒ	ⓓ	84	ⓐ	ⓑ	ⓒ	ⓓ
5	ⓐ	ⓑ	ⓒ	ⓓ	25	ⓐ	ⓑ	ⓒ		45	ⓐ	ⓑ	ⓒ	ⓓ	65	ⓐ	ⓑ	ⓒ	ⓓ	85	ⓐ	ⓑ	ⓒ	ⓓ
6	ⓐ	ⓑ	ⓒ	ⓓ	26	ⓐ	ⓑ	ⓒ		46	ⓐ	ⓑ	ⓒ	ⓓ	66	ⓐ	ⓑ	ⓒ	ⓓ	86	ⓐ	ⓑ	ⓒ	ⓓ
7	ⓐ	ⓑ	ⓒ		27	ⓐ	ⓑ	ⓒ		47	ⓐ	ⓑ	ⓒ	ⓓ	67	ⓐ	ⓑ	ⓒ	ⓓ	87	ⓐ	ⓑ	ⓒ	ⓓ
8	ⓐ	ⓑ	ⓒ		28	ⓐ	ⓑ	ⓒ		48	ⓐ	ⓑ	ⓒ	ⓓ	68	ⓐ	ⓑ	ⓒ	ⓓ	88	ⓐ	ⓑ	ⓒ	ⓓ
9	ⓐ	ⓑ	ⓒ		29	ⓐ	ⓑ	ⓒ		49	ⓐ	ⓑ	ⓒ	ⓓ	69	ⓐ	ⓑ	ⓒ	ⓓ	89	ⓐ	ⓑ	ⓒ	ⓓ
10	ⓐ	ⓑ	ⓒ		30	ⓐ	ⓑ	ⓒ		50	ⓐ	ⓑ	ⓒ	ⓓ	70	ⓐ	ⓑ	ⓒ	ⓓ	90	ⓐ	ⓑ	ⓒ	ⓓ
11	ⓐ	ⓑ	ⓒ		31	ⓐ	ⓑ	ⓒ		51	ⓐ	ⓑ	ⓒ	ⓓ	71	ⓐ	ⓑ	ⓒ	ⓓ	91	ⓐ	ⓑ	ⓒ	ⓓ
12	ⓐ	ⓑ	ⓒ		32	ⓐ	ⓑ	ⓒ	ⓓ	52	ⓐ	ⓑ	ⓒ	ⓓ	72	ⓐ	ⓑ	ⓒ	ⓓ	92	ⓐ	ⓑ	ⓒ	ⓓ
13	ⓐ	ⓑ	ⓒ		33	ⓐ	ⓑ	ⓒ	ⓓ	53	ⓐ	ⓑ	ⓒ	ⓓ	73	ⓐ	ⓑ	ⓒ	ⓓ	93	ⓐ	ⓑ	ⓒ	ⓓ
14	ⓐ	ⓑ	ⓒ		34	ⓐ	ⓑ	ⓒ	ⓓ	54	ⓐ	ⓑ	ⓒ	ⓓ	74	ⓐ	ⓑ	ⓒ	ⓓ	94	ⓐ	ⓑ	ⓒ	ⓓ
15	ⓐ	ⓑ	ⓒ		35	ⓐ	ⓑ	ⓒ	ⓓ	55	ⓐ	ⓑ	ⓒ	ⓓ	75	ⓐ	ⓑ	ⓒ	ⓓ	95	ⓐ	ⓑ	ⓒ	ⓓ
16	ⓐ	ⓑ	ⓒ		36	ⓐ	ⓑ	ⓒ	ⓓ	56	ⓐ	ⓑ	ⓒ	ⓓ	76	ⓐ	ⓑ	ⓒ	ⓓ	96	ⓐ	ⓑ	ⓒ	ⓓ
17	ⓐ	ⓑ	ⓒ		37	ⓐ	ⓑ	ⓒ	ⓓ	57	ⓐ	ⓑ	ⓒ	ⓓ	77	ⓐ	ⓑ	ⓒ	ⓓ	97	ⓐ	ⓑ	ⓒ	ⓓ
18	ⓐ	ⓑ	ⓒ		38	ⓐ	ⓑ	ⓒ	ⓓ	58	ⓐ	ⓑ	ⓒ	ⓓ	78	ⓐ	ⓑ	ⓒ	ⓓ	98	ⓐ	ⓑ	ⓒ	ⓓ
19	ⓐ	ⓑ	ⓒ		39	ⓐ	ⓑ	ⓒ	ⓓ	59	ⓐ	ⓑ	ⓒ	ⓓ	79	ⓐ	ⓑ	ⓒ	ⓓ	99	ⓐ	ⓑ	ⓒ	ⓓ
20	ⓐ	ⓑ	ⓒ		40	ⓐ	ⓑ	ⓒ	ⓓ	60	ⓐ	ⓑ	ⓒ	ⓓ	80	ⓐ	ⓑ	ⓒ	ⓓ	100	ⓐ	ⓑ	ⓒ	ⓓ

* 문제를 다 풀고 채점한 후 점수로 환산해 봅니다. 점수 환산표는 16페이지에 있습니다.

READING(Part V ~ VII)

NO.	A	B	C	D	NO.	A	B	C	D	NO.	A	B	C	D	NO.	A	B	C	D	NO.	A	B	C	D
101	ⓐ	ⓑ	ⓒ	ⓓ	121	ⓐ	ⓑ	ⓒ	ⓓ	141	ⓐ	ⓑ	ⓒ	ⓓ	161	ⓐ	ⓑ	ⓒ	ⓓ	181	ⓐ	ⓑ	ⓒ	ⓓ
102	ⓐ	ⓑ	ⓒ	ⓓ	122	ⓐ	ⓑ	ⓒ	ⓓ	142	ⓐ	ⓑ	ⓒ	ⓓ	162	ⓐ	ⓑ	ⓒ	ⓓ	182	ⓐ	ⓑ	ⓒ	ⓓ
103	ⓐ	ⓑ	ⓒ	ⓓ	123	ⓐ	ⓑ	ⓒ	ⓓ	143	ⓐ	ⓑ	ⓒ	ⓓ	163	ⓐ	ⓑ	ⓒ	ⓓ	183	ⓐ	ⓑ	ⓒ	ⓓ
104	ⓐ	ⓑ	ⓒ	ⓓ	124	ⓐ	ⓑ	ⓒ	ⓓ	144	ⓐ	ⓑ	ⓒ	ⓓ	164	ⓐ	ⓑ	ⓒ	ⓓ	184	ⓐ	ⓑ	ⓒ	ⓓ
105	ⓐ	ⓑ	ⓒ	ⓓ	125	ⓐ	ⓑ	ⓒ	ⓓ	145	ⓐ	ⓑ	ⓒ	ⓓ	165	ⓐ	ⓑ	ⓒ	ⓓ	185	ⓐ	ⓑ	ⓒ	ⓓ
106	ⓐ	ⓑ	ⓒ	ⓓ	126	ⓐ	ⓑ	ⓒ	ⓓ	146	ⓐ	ⓑ	ⓒ	ⓓ	166	ⓐ	ⓑ	ⓒ	ⓓ	186	ⓐ	ⓑ	ⓒ	ⓓ
107	ⓐ	ⓑ	ⓒ	ⓓ	127	ⓐ	ⓑ	ⓒ	ⓓ	147	ⓐ	ⓑ	ⓒ	ⓓ	167	ⓐ	ⓑ	ⓒ	ⓓ	187	ⓐ	ⓑ	ⓒ	ⓓ
108	ⓐ	ⓑ	ⓒ	ⓓ	128	ⓐ	ⓑ	ⓒ	ⓓ	148	ⓐ	ⓑ	ⓒ	ⓓ	168	ⓐ	ⓑ	ⓒ	ⓓ	188	ⓐ	ⓑ	ⓒ	ⓓ
109	ⓐ	ⓑ	ⓒ	ⓓ	129	ⓐ	ⓑ	ⓒ	ⓓ	149	ⓐ	ⓑ	ⓒ	ⓓ	169	ⓐ	ⓑ	ⓒ	ⓓ	189	ⓐ	ⓑ	ⓒ	ⓓ
110	ⓐ	ⓑ	ⓒ	ⓓ	130	ⓐ	ⓑ	ⓒ	ⓓ	150	ⓐ	ⓑ	ⓒ	ⓓ	170	ⓐ	ⓑ	ⓒ	ⓓ	190	ⓐ	ⓑ	ⓒ	ⓓ
111	ⓐ	ⓑ	ⓒ	ⓓ	131	ⓐ	ⓑ	ⓒ	ⓓ	151	ⓐ	ⓑ	ⓒ	ⓓ	171	ⓐ	ⓑ	ⓒ	ⓓ	191	ⓐ	ⓑ	ⓒ	ⓓ
112	ⓐ	ⓑ	ⓒ	ⓓ	132	ⓐ	ⓑ	ⓒ	ⓓ	152	ⓐ	ⓑ	ⓒ	ⓓ	172	ⓐ	ⓑ	ⓒ	ⓓ	192	ⓐ	ⓑ	ⓒ	ⓓ
113	ⓐ	ⓑ	ⓒ	ⓓ	133	ⓐ	ⓑ	ⓒ	ⓓ	153	ⓐ	ⓑ	ⓒ	ⓓ	173	ⓐ	ⓑ	ⓒ	ⓓ	193	ⓐ	ⓑ	ⓒ	ⓓ
114	ⓐ	ⓑ	ⓒ	ⓓ	134	ⓐ	ⓑ	ⓒ	ⓓ	154	ⓐ	ⓑ	ⓒ	ⓓ	174	ⓐ	ⓑ	ⓒ	ⓓ	194	ⓐ	ⓑ	ⓒ	ⓓ
115	ⓐ	ⓑ	ⓒ	ⓓ	135	ⓐ	ⓑ	ⓒ	ⓓ	155	ⓐ	ⓑ	ⓒ	ⓓ	175	ⓐ	ⓑ	ⓒ	ⓓ	195	ⓐ	ⓑ	ⓒ	ⓓ
116	ⓐ	ⓑ	ⓒ	ⓓ	136	ⓐ	ⓑ	ⓒ	ⓓ	156	ⓐ	ⓑ	ⓒ	ⓓ	176	ⓐ	ⓑ	ⓒ	ⓓ	196	ⓐ	ⓑ	ⓒ	ⓓ
117	ⓐ	ⓑ	ⓒ	ⓓ	137	ⓐ	ⓑ	ⓒ	ⓓ	157	ⓐ	ⓑ	ⓒ	ⓓ	177	ⓐ	ⓑ	ⓒ	ⓓ	197	ⓐ	ⓑ	ⓒ	ⓓ
118	ⓐ	ⓑ	ⓒ	ⓓ	138	ⓐ	ⓑ	ⓒ	ⓓ	158	ⓐ	ⓑ	ⓒ	ⓓ	178	ⓐ	ⓑ	ⓒ	ⓓ	198	ⓐ	ⓑ	ⓒ	ⓓ
119	ⓐ	ⓑ	ⓒ	ⓓ	139	ⓐ	ⓑ	ⓒ	ⓓ	159	ⓐ	ⓑ	ⓒ	ⓓ	179	ⓐ	ⓑ	ⓒ	ⓓ	199	ⓐ	ⓑ	ⓒ	ⓓ
120	ⓐ	ⓑ	ⓒ	ⓓ	140	ⓐ	ⓑ	ⓒ	ⓓ	160	ⓐ	ⓑ	ⓒ	ⓓ	180	ⓐ	ⓑ	ⓒ	ⓓ	200	ⓐ	ⓑ	ⓒ	ⓓ

✂ 자르는 선

ANSWER SHEET

ACTUAL TEST

LISTENING(Part I ~ IV)

NO.	ANSWER				NO.	ANSWER				NO.	ANSWER				NO.	ANSWER				NO.	ANSWER			
	A	B	C	D		A	B	C	D		A	B	C	D		A	B	C	D		A	B	C	D
1	a	b	c	d	21	a	b	c		41	a	b	c	d	61	a	b	c	d	81	a	b	c	d
2	a	b	c	d	22	a	b	c		42	a	b	c	d	62	a	b	c	d	82	a	b	c	d
3	a	b	c	d	23	a	b	c		43	a	b	c	d	63	a	b	c	d	83	a	b	c	d
4	a	b	c	d	24	a	b	c		44	a	b	c	d	64	a	b	c	d	84	a	b	c	d
5	a	b	c	d	25	a	b	c		45	a	b	c	d	65	a	b	c	d	85	a	b	c	d
6	a	b	c	d	26	a	b	c		46	a	b	c	d	66	a	b	c	d	86	a	b	c	d
7	a	b	c		27	a	b	c		47	a	b	c	d	67	a	b	c	d	87	a	b	c	d
8	a	b	c		28	a	b	c		48	a	b	c	d	68	a	b	c	d	88	a	b	c	d
9	a	b	c		29	a	b	c		49	a	b	c	d	69	a	b	c	d	89	a	b	c	d
10	a	b	c		30	a	b	c		50	a	b	c	d	70	a	b	c	d	90	a	b	c	d
11	a	b	c		31	a	b	c		51	a	b	c	d	71	a	b	c	d	91	a	b	c	d
12	a	b	c		32	a	b	c	d	52	a	b	c	d	72	a	b	c	d	92	a	b	c	d
13	a	b	c		33	a	b	c	d	53	a	b	c	d	73	a	b	c	d	93	a	b	c	d
14	a	b	c		34	a	b	c	d	54	a	b	c	d	74	a	b	c	d	94	a	b	c	d
15	a	b	c		35	a	b	c	d	55	a	b	c	d	75	a	b	c	d	95	a	b	c	d
16	a	b	c		36	a	b	c	d	56	a	b	c	d	76	a	b	c	d	96	a	b	c	d
17	a	b	c		37	a	b	c	d	57	a	b	c	d	77	a	b	c	d	97	a	b	c	d
18	a	b	c		38	a	b	c	d	58	a	b	c	d	78	a	b	c	d	98	a	b	c	d
19	a	b	c		39	a	b	c	d	59	a	b	c	d	79	a	b	c	d	99	a	b	c	d
20	a	b	c		40	a	b	c	d	60	a	b	c	d	80	a	b	c	d	100	a	b	c	d

* 문제를 다 풀고 채점한 후 점수로 환산해 봅니다. 점수 환산표는 16페이지에 있습니다.

READING(Part V ~ VII)

NO.	ANSWER				NO.	ANSWER				NO.	ANSWER				NO.	ANSWER				NO.	ANSWER			
	A	B	C	D		A	B	C	D		A	B	C	D		A	B	C	D		A	B	C	D
101	a	b	c	d	121	a	b	c	d	141	a	b	c	d	161	a	b	c	d	181	a	b	c	d
102	a	b	c	d	122	a	b	c	d	142	a	b	c	d	162	a	b	c	d	182	a	b	c	d
103	a	b	c	d	123	a	b	c	d	143	a	b	c	d	163	a	b	c	d	183	a	b	c	d
104	a	b	c	d	124	a	b	c	d	144	a	b	c	d	164	a	b	c	d	184	a	b	c	d
105	a	b	c	d	125	a	b	c	d	145	a	b	c	d	165	a	b	c	d	185	a	b	c	d
106	a	b	c	d	126	a	b	c	d	146	a	b	c	d	166	a	b	c	d	186	a	b	c	d
107	a	b	c	d	127	a	b	c	d	147	a	b	c	d	167	a	b	c	d	187	a	b	c	d
108	a	b	c	d	128	a	b	c	d	148	a	b	c	d	168	a	b	c	d	188	a	b	c	d
109	a	b	c	d	129	a	b	c	d	149	a	b	c	d	169	a	b	c	d	189	a	b	c	d
110	a	b	c	d	130	a	b	c	d	150	a	b	c	d	170	a	b	c	d	190	a	b	c	d
111	a	b	c	d	131	a	b	c	d	151	a	b	c	d	171	a	b	c	d	191	a	b	c	d
112	a	b	c	d	132	a	b	c	d	152	a	b	c	d	172	a	b	c	d	192	a	b	c	d
113	a	b	c	d	133	a	b	c	d	153	a	b	c	d	173	a	b	c	d	193	a	b	c	d
114	a	b	c	d	134	a	b	c	d	154	a	b	c	d	174	a	b	c	d	194	a	b	c	d
115	a	b	c	d	135	a	b	c	d	155	a	b	c	d	175	a	b	c	d	195	a	b	c	d
116	a	b	c	d	136	a	b	c	d	156	a	b	c	d	176	a	b	c	d	196	a	b	c	d
117	a	b	c	d	137	a	b	c	d	157	a	b	c	d	177	a	b	c	d	197	a	b	c	d
118	a	b	c	d	138	a	b	c	d	158	a	b	c	d	178	a	b	c	d	198	a	b	c	d
119	a	b	c	d	139	a	b	c	d	159	a	b	c	d	179	a	b	c	d	199	a	b	c	d
120	a	b	c	d	140	a	b	c	d	160	a	b	c	d	180	a	b	c	d	200	a	b	c	d

자르는 선

ANSWER SHEET

ACTUAL TEST

LISTENING(Part I ~ IV)																								
NO.	ANSWER				NO.	ANSWER				NO.	ANSWER				NO.	ANSWER				NO.	ANSWER			
	A	B	C	D		A	B	C	D		A	B	C	D		A	B	C	D		A	B	C	D
1	ⓐ	ⓑ	ⓒ	ⓓ	21	ⓐ	ⓑ	ⓒ		41	ⓐ	ⓑ	ⓒ	ⓓ	61	ⓐ	ⓑ	ⓒ	ⓓ	81	ⓐ	ⓑ	ⓒ	ⓓ
2	ⓐ	ⓑ	ⓒ	ⓓ	22	ⓐ	ⓑ	ⓒ		42	ⓐ	ⓑ	ⓒ	ⓓ	62	ⓐ	ⓑ	ⓒ	ⓓ	82	ⓐ	ⓑ	ⓒ	ⓓ
3	ⓐ	ⓑ	ⓒ	ⓓ	23	ⓐ	ⓑ	ⓒ		43	ⓐ	ⓑ	ⓒ	ⓓ	63	ⓐ	ⓑ	ⓒ	ⓓ	83	ⓐ	ⓑ	ⓒ	ⓓ
4	ⓐ	ⓑ	ⓒ	ⓓ	24	ⓐ	ⓑ	ⓒ		44	ⓐ	ⓑ	ⓒ	ⓓ	64	ⓐ	ⓑ	ⓒ	ⓓ	84	ⓐ	ⓑ	ⓒ	ⓓ
5	ⓐ	ⓑ	ⓒ	ⓓ	25	ⓐ	ⓑ	ⓒ		45	ⓐ	ⓑ	ⓒ	ⓓ	65	ⓐ	ⓑ	ⓒ	ⓓ	85	ⓐ	ⓑ	ⓒ	ⓓ
6	ⓐ	ⓑ	ⓒ	ⓓ	26	ⓐ	ⓑ	ⓒ		46	ⓐ	ⓑ	ⓒ	ⓓ	66	ⓐ	ⓑ	ⓒ	ⓓ	86	ⓐ	ⓑ	ⓒ	ⓓ
7	ⓐ	ⓑ	ⓒ		27	ⓐ	ⓑ	ⓒ		47	ⓐ	ⓑ	ⓒ	ⓓ	67	ⓐ	ⓑ	ⓒ	ⓓ	87	ⓐ	ⓑ	ⓒ	ⓓ
8	ⓐ	ⓑ	ⓒ		28	ⓐ	ⓑ	ⓒ		48	ⓐ	ⓑ	ⓒ	ⓓ	68	ⓐ	ⓑ	ⓒ	ⓓ	88	ⓐ	ⓑ	ⓒ	ⓓ
9	ⓐ	ⓑ	ⓒ		29	ⓐ	ⓑ	ⓒ		49	ⓐ	ⓑ	ⓒ	ⓓ	69	ⓐ	ⓑ	ⓒ	ⓓ	89	ⓐ	ⓑ	ⓒ	ⓓ
10	ⓐ	ⓑ	ⓒ		30	ⓐ	ⓑ	ⓒ		50	ⓐ	ⓑ	ⓒ	ⓓ	70	ⓐ	ⓑ	ⓒ	ⓓ	90	ⓐ	ⓑ	ⓒ	ⓓ
11	ⓐ	ⓑ	ⓒ		31	ⓐ	ⓑ	ⓒ		51	ⓐ	ⓑ	ⓒ	ⓓ	71	ⓐ	ⓑ	ⓒ	ⓓ	91	ⓐ	ⓑ	ⓒ	ⓓ
12	ⓐ	ⓑ	ⓒ		32	ⓐ	ⓑ	ⓒ	ⓓ	52	ⓐ	ⓑ	ⓒ	ⓓ	72	ⓐ	ⓑ	ⓒ	ⓓ	92	ⓐ	ⓑ	ⓒ	ⓓ
13	ⓐ	ⓑ	ⓒ		33	ⓐ	ⓑ	ⓒ	ⓓ	53	ⓐ	ⓑ	ⓒ	ⓓ	73	ⓐ	ⓑ	ⓒ	ⓓ	93	ⓐ	ⓑ	ⓒ	ⓓ
14	ⓐ	ⓑ	ⓒ		34	ⓐ	ⓑ	ⓒ	ⓓ	54	ⓐ	ⓑ	ⓒ	ⓓ	74	ⓐ	ⓑ	ⓒ	ⓓ	94	ⓐ	ⓑ	ⓒ	ⓓ
15	ⓐ	ⓑ	ⓒ		35	ⓐ	ⓑ	ⓒ	ⓓ	55	ⓐ	ⓑ	ⓒ	ⓓ	75	ⓐ	ⓑ	ⓒ	ⓓ	95	ⓐ	ⓑ	ⓒ	ⓓ
16	ⓐ	ⓑ	ⓒ		36	ⓐ	ⓑ	ⓒ	ⓓ	56	ⓐ	ⓑ	ⓒ	ⓓ	76	ⓐ	ⓑ	ⓒ	ⓓ	96	ⓐ	ⓑ	ⓒ	ⓓ
17	ⓐ	ⓑ	ⓒ		37	ⓐ	ⓑ	ⓒ	ⓓ	57	ⓐ	ⓑ	ⓒ	ⓓ	77	ⓐ	ⓑ	ⓒ	ⓓ	97	ⓐ	ⓑ	ⓒ	ⓓ
18	ⓐ	ⓑ	ⓒ		38	ⓐ	ⓑ	ⓒ	ⓓ	58	ⓐ	ⓑ	ⓒ	ⓓ	78	ⓐ	ⓑ	ⓒ	ⓓ	98	ⓐ	ⓑ	ⓒ	ⓓ
19	ⓐ	ⓑ	ⓒ		39	ⓐ	ⓑ	ⓒ	ⓓ	59	ⓐ	ⓑ	ⓒ	ⓓ	79	ⓐ	ⓑ	ⓒ	ⓓ	99	ⓐ	ⓑ	ⓒ	ⓓ
20	ⓐ	ⓑ	ⓒ		40	ⓐ	ⓑ	ⓒ	ⓓ	60	ⓐ	ⓑ	ⓒ	ⓓ	80	ⓐ	ⓑ	ⓒ	ⓓ	100	ⓐ	ⓑ	ⓒ	ⓓ

READING(Part V ~ VII)																								
NO.	ANSWER				NO.	ANSWER				NO.	ANSWER				NO.	ANSWER				NO.	ANSWER			
	A	B	C	D		A	B	C	D		A	B	C	D		A	B	C	D		A	B	C	D
101	ⓐ	ⓑ	ⓒ	ⓓ	121	ⓐ	ⓑ	ⓒ	ⓓ	141	ⓐ	ⓑ	ⓒ	ⓓ	161	ⓐ	ⓑ	ⓒ	ⓓ	181	ⓐ	ⓑ	ⓒ	ⓓ
102	ⓐ	ⓑ	ⓒ	ⓓ	122	ⓐ	ⓑ	ⓒ	ⓓ	142	ⓐ	ⓑ	ⓒ	ⓓ	162	ⓐ	ⓑ	ⓒ	ⓓ	182	ⓐ	ⓑ	ⓒ	ⓓ
103	ⓐ	ⓑ	ⓒ	ⓓ	123	ⓐ	ⓑ	ⓒ	ⓓ	143	ⓐ	ⓑ	ⓒ	ⓓ	163	ⓐ	ⓑ	ⓒ	ⓓ	183	ⓐ	ⓑ	ⓒ	ⓓ
104	ⓐ	ⓑ	ⓒ	ⓓ	124	ⓐ	ⓑ	ⓒ	ⓓ	144	ⓐ	ⓑ	ⓒ	ⓓ	164	ⓐ	ⓑ	ⓒ	ⓓ	184	ⓐ	ⓑ	ⓒ	ⓓ
105	ⓐ	ⓑ	ⓒ	ⓓ	125	ⓐ	ⓑ	ⓒ	ⓓ	145	ⓐ	ⓑ	ⓒ	ⓓ	165	ⓐ	ⓑ	ⓒ	ⓓ	185	ⓐ	ⓑ	ⓒ	ⓓ
106	ⓐ	ⓑ	ⓒ	ⓓ	126	ⓐ	ⓑ	ⓒ	ⓓ	146	ⓐ	ⓑ	ⓒ	ⓓ	166	ⓐ	ⓑ	ⓒ	ⓓ	186	ⓐ	ⓑ	ⓒ	ⓓ
107	ⓐ	ⓑ	ⓒ	ⓓ	127	ⓐ	ⓑ	ⓒ	ⓓ	147	ⓐ	ⓑ	ⓒ	ⓓ	167	ⓐ	ⓑ	ⓒ	ⓓ	187	ⓐ	ⓑ	ⓒ	ⓓ
108	ⓐ	ⓑ	ⓒ	ⓓ	128	ⓐ	ⓑ	ⓒ	ⓓ	148	ⓐ	ⓑ	ⓒ	ⓓ	168	ⓐ	ⓑ	ⓒ	ⓓ	188	ⓐ	ⓑ	ⓒ	ⓓ
109	ⓐ	ⓑ	ⓒ	ⓓ	129	ⓐ	ⓑ	ⓒ	ⓓ	149	ⓐ	ⓑ	ⓒ	ⓓ	169	ⓐ	ⓑ	ⓒ	ⓓ	189	ⓐ	ⓑ	ⓒ	ⓓ
110	ⓐ	ⓑ	ⓒ	ⓓ	130	ⓐ	ⓑ	ⓒ	ⓓ	150	ⓐ	ⓑ	ⓒ	ⓓ	170	ⓐ	ⓑ	ⓒ	ⓓ	190	ⓐ	ⓑ	ⓒ	ⓓ
111	ⓐ	ⓑ	ⓒ	ⓓ	131	ⓐ	ⓑ	ⓒ	ⓓ	151	ⓐ	ⓑ	ⓒ	ⓓ	171	ⓐ	ⓑ	ⓒ	ⓓ	191	ⓐ	ⓑ	ⓒ	ⓓ
112	ⓐ	ⓑ	ⓒ	ⓓ	132	ⓐ	ⓑ	ⓒ	ⓓ	152	ⓐ	ⓑ	ⓒ	ⓓ	172	ⓐ	ⓑ	ⓒ	ⓓ	192	ⓐ	ⓑ	ⓒ	ⓓ
113	ⓐ	ⓑ	ⓒ	ⓓ	133	ⓐ	ⓑ	ⓒ	ⓓ	153	ⓐ	ⓑ	ⓒ	ⓓ	173	ⓐ	ⓑ	ⓒ	ⓓ	193	ⓐ	ⓑ	ⓒ	ⓓ
114	ⓐ	ⓑ	ⓒ	ⓓ	134	ⓐ	ⓑ	ⓒ	ⓓ	154	ⓐ	ⓑ	ⓒ	ⓓ	174	ⓐ	ⓑ	ⓒ	ⓓ	194	ⓐ	ⓑ	ⓒ	ⓓ
115	ⓐ	ⓑ	ⓒ	ⓓ	135	ⓐ	ⓑ	ⓒ	ⓓ	155	ⓐ	ⓑ	ⓒ	ⓓ	175	ⓐ	ⓑ	ⓒ	ⓓ	195	ⓐ	ⓑ	ⓒ	ⓓ
116	ⓐ	ⓑ	ⓒ	ⓓ	136	ⓐ	ⓑ	ⓒ	ⓓ	156	ⓐ	ⓑ	ⓒ	ⓓ	176	ⓐ	ⓑ	ⓒ	ⓓ	196	ⓐ	ⓑ	ⓒ	ⓓ
117	ⓐ	ⓑ	ⓒ	ⓓ	137	ⓐ	ⓑ	ⓒ	ⓓ	157	ⓐ	ⓑ	ⓒ	ⓓ	177	ⓐ	ⓑ	ⓒ	ⓓ	197	ⓐ	ⓑ	ⓒ	ⓓ
118	ⓐ	ⓑ	ⓒ	ⓓ	138	ⓐ	ⓑ	ⓒ	ⓓ	158	ⓐ	ⓑ	ⓒ	ⓓ	178	ⓐ	ⓑ	ⓒ	ⓓ	198	ⓐ	ⓑ	ⓒ	ⓓ
119	ⓐ	ⓑ	ⓒ	ⓓ	139	ⓐ	ⓑ	ⓒ	ⓓ	159	ⓐ	ⓑ	ⓒ	ⓓ	179	ⓐ	ⓑ	ⓒ	ⓓ	199	ⓐ	ⓑ	ⓒ	ⓓ
120	ⓐ	ⓑ	ⓒ	ⓓ	140	ⓐ	ⓑ	ⓒ	ⓓ	160	ⓐ	ⓑ	ⓒ	ⓓ	180	ⓐ	ⓑ	ⓒ	ⓓ	200	ⓐ	ⓑ	ⓒ	ⓓ

* 문제를 다 풀고 채점한 후 점수로 환산해 봅니다. 점수 환산표는 16페이지에 있습니다.

✂ 자르는 선

ANSWER SHEET

ACTUAL TEST

LISTENING(Part I ~ IV)

NO.	A	B	C	D	NO.	A	B	C	D	NO.	A	B	C	D	NO.	A	B	C	D	NO.	A	B	C	D
1	a	b	c	d	21	a	b	c		41	a	b	c	d	61	a	b	c	d	81	a	b	c	d
2	a	b	c	d	22	a	b	c		42	a	b	c	d	62	a	b	c	d	82	a	b	c	d
3	a	b	c	d	23	a	b	c		43	a	b	c	d	63	a	b	c	d	83	a	b	c	d
4	a	b	c	d	24	a	b	c		44	a	b	c	d	64	a	b	c	d	84	a	b	c	d
5	a	b	c	d	25	a	b	c		45	a	b	c	d	65	a	b	c	d	85	a	b	c	d
6	a	b	c	d	26	a	b	c		46	a	b	c	d	66	a	b	c	d	86	a	b	c	d
7	a	b	c		27	a	b	c		47	a	b	c	d	67	a	b	c	d	87	a	b	c	d
8	a	b	c		28	a	b	c		48	a	b	c	d	68	a	b	c	d	88	a	b	c	d
9	a	b	c		29	a	b	c		49	a	b	c	d	69	a	b	c	d	89	a	b	c	d
10	a	b	c		30	a	b	c		50	a	b	c	d	70	a	b	c	d	90	a	b	c	d
11	a	b	c		31	a	b	c		51	a	b	c	d	71	a	b	c	d	91	a	b	c	d
12	a	b	c		32	a	b	c	d	52	a	b	c	d	72	a	b	c	d	92	a	b	c	d
13	a	b	c		33	a	b	c	d	53	a	b	c	d	73	a	b	c	d	93	a	b	c	d
14	a	b	c		34	a	b	c	d	54	a	b	c	d	74	a	b	c	d	94	a	b	c	d
15	a	b	c		35	a	b	c	d	55	a	b	c	d	75	a	b	c	d	95	a	b	c	d
16	a	b	c		36	a	b	c	d	56	a	b	c	d	76	a	b	c	d	96	a	b	c	d
17	a	b	c		37	a	b	c	d	57	a	b	c	d	77	a	b	c	d	97	a	b	c	d
18	a	b	c		38	a	b	c	d	58	a	b	c	d	78	a	b	c	d	98	a	b	c	d
19	a	b	c		39	a	b	c	d	59	a	b	c	d	79	a	b	c	d	99	a	b	c	d
20	a	b	c		40	a	b	c	d	60	a	b	c	d	80	a	b	c	d	100	a	b	c	d

* 문제를 다 풀고 채점한 후 점수로 환산해 봅니다. 점수 환산표는 16페이지에 있습니다.

READING(Part V ~ VII)

NO.	A	B	C	D	NO.	A	B	C	D	NO.	A	B	C	D	NO.	A	B	C	D	NO.	A	B	C	D
101	a	b	c	d	121	a	b	c	d	141	a	b	c	d	161	a	b	c	d	181	a	b	c	d
102	a	b	c	d	122	a	b	c	d	142	a	b	c	d	162	a	b	c	d	182	a	b	c	d
103	a	b	c	d	123	a	b	c	d	143	a	b	c	d	163	a	b	c	d	183	a	b	c	d
104	a	b	c	d	124	a	b	c	d	144	a	b	c	d	164	a	b	c	d	184	a	b	c	d
105	a	b	c	d	125	a	b	c	d	145	a	b	c	d	165	a	b	c	d	185	a	b	c	d
106	a	b	c	d	126	a	b	c	d	146	a	b	c	d	166	a	b	c	d	186	a	b	c	d
107	a	b	c	d	127	a	b	c	d	147	a	b	c	d	167	a	b	c	d	187	a	b	c	d
108	a	b	c	d	128	a	b	c	d	148	a	b	c	d	168	a	b	c	d	188	a	b	c	d
109	a	b	c	d	129	a	b	c	d	149	a	b	c	d	169	a	b	c	d	189	a	b	c	d
110	a	b	c	d	130	a	b	c	d	150	a	b	c	d	170	a	b	c	d	190	a	b	c	d
111	a	b	c	d	131	a	b	c	d	151	a	b	c	d	171	a	b	c	d	191	a	b	c	d
112	a	b	c	d	132	a	b	c	d	152	a	b	c	d	172	a	b	c	d	192	a	b	c	d
113	a	b	c	d	133	a	b	c	d	153	a	b	c	d	173	a	b	c	d	193	a	b	c	d
114	a	b	c	d	134	a	b	c	d	154	a	b	c	d	174	a	b	c	d	194	a	b	c	d
115	a	b	c	d	135	a	b	c	d	155	a	b	c	d	175	a	b	c	d	195	a	b	c	d
116	a	b	c	d	136	a	b	c	d	156	a	b	c	d	176	a	b	c	d	196	a	b	c	d
117	a	b	c	d	137	a	b	c	d	157	a	b	c	d	177	a	b	c	d	197	a	b	c	d
118	a	b	c	d	138	a	b	c	d	158	a	b	c	d	178	a	b	c	d	198	a	b	c	d
119	a	b	c	d	139	a	b	c	d	159	a	b	c	d	179	a	b	c	d	199	a	b	c	d
120	a	b	c	d	140	a	b	c	d	160	a	b	c	d	180	a	b	c	d	200	a	b	c	d

자르는 선

ANSWER SHEET

ACTUAL TEST

LISTENING(Part I ~ IV)

NO.	ANSWER				NO.	ANSWER				NO.	ANSWER				NO.	ANSWER				NO.	ANSWER			
	A	B	C	D		A	B	C	D		A	B	C	D		A	B	C	D		A	B	C	D
1	ⓐ	ⓑ	ⓒ	ⓓ	21	ⓐ	ⓑ	ⓒ		41	ⓐ	ⓑ	ⓒ	ⓓ	61	ⓐ	ⓑ	ⓒ	ⓓ	81	ⓐ	ⓑ	ⓒ	ⓓ
2	ⓐ	ⓑ	ⓒ	ⓓ	22	ⓐ	ⓑ	ⓒ		42	ⓐ	ⓑ	ⓒ	ⓓ	62	ⓐ	ⓑ	ⓒ	ⓓ	82	ⓐ	ⓑ	ⓒ	ⓓ
3	ⓐ	ⓑ	ⓒ	ⓓ	23	ⓐ	ⓑ	ⓒ		43	ⓐ	ⓑ	ⓒ	ⓓ	63	ⓐ	ⓑ	ⓒ	ⓓ	83	ⓐ	ⓑ	ⓒ	ⓓ
4	ⓐ	ⓑ	ⓒ	ⓓ	24	ⓐ	ⓑ	ⓒ		44	ⓐ	ⓑ	ⓒ	ⓓ	64	ⓐ	ⓑ	ⓒ	ⓓ	84	ⓐ	ⓑ	ⓒ	ⓓ
5	ⓐ	ⓑ	ⓒ	ⓓ	25	ⓐ	ⓑ	ⓒ		45	ⓐ	ⓑ	ⓒ	ⓓ	65	ⓐ	ⓑ	ⓒ	ⓓ	85	ⓐ	ⓑ	ⓒ	ⓓ
6	ⓐ	ⓑ	ⓒ	ⓓ	26	ⓐ	ⓑ	ⓒ		46	ⓐ	ⓑ	ⓒ	ⓓ	66	ⓐ	ⓑ	ⓒ	ⓓ	86	ⓐ	ⓑ	ⓒ	ⓓ
7	ⓐ	ⓑ	ⓒ		27	ⓐ	ⓑ	ⓒ		47	ⓐ	ⓑ	ⓒ	ⓓ	67	ⓐ	ⓑ	ⓒ	ⓓ	87	ⓐ	ⓑ	ⓒ	ⓓ
8	ⓐ	ⓑ	ⓒ		28	ⓐ	ⓑ	ⓒ		48	ⓐ	ⓑ	ⓒ	ⓓ	68	ⓐ	ⓑ	ⓒ	ⓓ	88	ⓐ	ⓑ	ⓒ	ⓓ
9	ⓐ	ⓑ	ⓒ		29	ⓐ	ⓑ	ⓒ		49	ⓐ	ⓑ	ⓒ	ⓓ	69	ⓐ	ⓑ	ⓒ	ⓓ	89	ⓐ	ⓑ	ⓒ	ⓓ
10	ⓐ	ⓑ	ⓒ		30	ⓐ	ⓑ	ⓒ		50	ⓐ	ⓑ	ⓒ	ⓓ	70	ⓐ	ⓑ	ⓒ	ⓓ	90	ⓐ	ⓑ	ⓒ	ⓓ
11	ⓐ	ⓑ	ⓒ		31	ⓐ	ⓑ	ⓒ		51	ⓐ	ⓑ	ⓒ	ⓓ	71	ⓐ	ⓑ	ⓒ	ⓓ	91	ⓐ	ⓑ	ⓒ	ⓓ
12	ⓐ	ⓑ	ⓒ		32	ⓐ	ⓑ	ⓒ	ⓓ	52	ⓐ	ⓑ	ⓒ	ⓓ	72	ⓐ	ⓑ	ⓒ	ⓓ	92	ⓐ	ⓑ	ⓒ	ⓓ
13	ⓐ	ⓑ	ⓒ		33	ⓐ	ⓑ	ⓒ	ⓓ	53	ⓐ	ⓑ	ⓒ	ⓓ	73	ⓐ	ⓑ	ⓒ	ⓓ	93	ⓐ	ⓑ	ⓒ	ⓓ
14	ⓐ	ⓑ	ⓒ		34	ⓐ	ⓑ	ⓒ	ⓓ	54	ⓐ	ⓑ	ⓒ	ⓓ	74	ⓐ	ⓑ	ⓒ	ⓓ	94	ⓐ	ⓑ	ⓒ	ⓓ
15	ⓐ	ⓑ	ⓒ		35	ⓐ	ⓑ	ⓒ	ⓓ	55	ⓐ	ⓑ	ⓒ	ⓓ	75	ⓐ	ⓑ	ⓒ	ⓓ	95	ⓐ	ⓑ	ⓒ	ⓓ
16	ⓐ	ⓑ	ⓒ		36	ⓐ	ⓑ	ⓒ	ⓓ	56	ⓐ	ⓑ	ⓒ	ⓓ	76	ⓐ	ⓑ	ⓒ	ⓓ	96	ⓐ	ⓑ	ⓒ	ⓓ
17	ⓐ	ⓑ	ⓒ		37	ⓐ	ⓑ	ⓒ	ⓓ	57	ⓐ	ⓑ	ⓒ	ⓓ	77	ⓐ	ⓑ	ⓒ	ⓓ	97	ⓐ	ⓑ	ⓒ	ⓓ
18	ⓐ	ⓑ	ⓒ		38	ⓐ	ⓑ	ⓒ	ⓓ	58	ⓐ	ⓑ	ⓒ	ⓓ	78	ⓐ	ⓑ	ⓒ	ⓓ	98	ⓐ	ⓑ	ⓒ	ⓓ
19	ⓐ	ⓑ	ⓒ		39	ⓐ	ⓑ	ⓒ	ⓓ	59	ⓐ	ⓑ	ⓒ	ⓓ	79	ⓐ	ⓑ	ⓒ	ⓓ	99	ⓐ	ⓑ	ⓒ	ⓓ
20	ⓐ	ⓑ	ⓒ		40	ⓐ	ⓑ	ⓒ	ⓓ	60	ⓐ	ⓑ	ⓒ	ⓓ	80	ⓐ	ⓑ	ⓒ	ⓓ	100	ⓐ	ⓑ	ⓒ	ⓓ

READING(Part V ~ VII)

NO.	ANSWER				NO.	ANSWER				NO.	ANSWER				NO.	ANSWER				NO.	ANSWER			
	A	B	C	D		A	B	C	D		A	B	C	D		A	B	C	D		A	B	C	D
101	ⓐ	ⓑ	ⓒ	ⓓ	121	ⓐ	ⓑ	ⓒ	ⓓ	141	ⓐ	ⓑ	ⓒ	ⓓ	161	ⓐ	ⓑ	ⓒ	ⓓ	181	ⓐ	ⓑ	ⓒ	ⓓ
102	ⓐ	ⓑ	ⓒ	ⓓ	122	ⓐ	ⓑ	ⓒ	ⓓ	142	ⓐ	ⓑ	ⓒ	ⓓ	162	ⓐ	ⓑ	ⓒ	ⓓ	182	ⓐ	ⓑ	ⓒ	ⓓ
103	ⓐ	ⓑ	ⓒ	ⓓ	123	ⓐ	ⓑ	ⓒ	ⓓ	143	ⓐ	ⓑ	ⓒ	ⓓ	163	ⓐ	ⓑ	ⓒ	ⓓ	183	ⓐ	ⓑ	ⓒ	ⓓ
104	ⓐ	ⓑ	ⓒ	ⓓ	124	ⓐ	ⓑ	ⓒ	ⓓ	144	ⓐ	ⓑ	ⓒ	ⓓ	164	ⓐ	ⓑ	ⓒ	ⓓ	184	ⓐ	ⓑ	ⓒ	ⓓ
105	ⓐ	ⓑ	ⓒ	ⓓ	125	ⓐ	ⓑ	ⓒ	ⓓ	145	ⓐ	ⓑ	ⓒ	ⓓ	165	ⓐ	ⓑ	ⓒ	ⓓ	185	ⓐ	ⓑ	ⓒ	ⓓ
106	ⓐ	ⓑ	ⓒ	ⓓ	126	ⓐ	ⓑ	ⓒ	ⓓ	146	ⓐ	ⓑ	ⓒ	ⓓ	166	ⓐ	ⓑ	ⓒ	ⓓ	186	ⓐ	ⓑ	ⓒ	ⓓ
107	ⓐ	ⓑ	ⓒ	ⓓ	127	ⓐ	ⓑ	ⓒ	ⓓ	147	ⓐ	ⓑ	ⓒ	ⓓ	167	ⓐ	ⓑ	ⓒ	ⓓ	187	ⓐ	ⓑ	ⓒ	ⓓ
108	ⓐ	ⓑ	ⓒ	ⓓ	128	ⓐ	ⓑ	ⓒ	ⓓ	148	ⓐ	ⓑ	ⓒ	ⓓ	168	ⓐ	ⓑ	ⓒ	ⓓ	188	ⓐ	ⓑ	ⓒ	ⓓ
109	ⓐ	ⓑ	ⓒ	ⓓ	129	ⓐ	ⓑ	ⓒ	ⓓ	149	ⓐ	ⓑ	ⓒ	ⓓ	169	ⓐ	ⓑ	ⓒ	ⓓ	189	ⓐ	ⓑ	ⓒ	ⓓ
110	ⓐ	ⓑ	ⓒ	ⓓ	130	ⓐ	ⓑ	ⓒ	ⓓ	150	ⓐ	ⓑ	ⓒ	ⓓ	170	ⓐ	ⓑ	ⓒ	ⓓ	190	ⓐ	ⓑ	ⓒ	ⓓ
111	ⓐ	ⓑ	ⓒ	ⓓ	131	ⓐ	ⓑ	ⓒ	ⓓ	151	ⓐ	ⓑ	ⓒ	ⓓ	171	ⓐ	ⓑ	ⓒ	ⓓ	191	ⓐ	ⓑ	ⓒ	ⓓ
112	ⓐ	ⓑ	ⓒ	ⓓ	132	ⓐ	ⓑ	ⓒ	ⓓ	152	ⓐ	ⓑ	ⓒ	ⓓ	172	ⓐ	ⓑ	ⓒ	ⓓ	192	ⓐ	ⓑ	ⓒ	ⓓ
113	ⓐ	ⓑ	ⓒ	ⓓ	133	ⓐ	ⓑ	ⓒ	ⓓ	153	ⓐ	ⓑ	ⓒ	ⓓ	173	ⓐ	ⓑ	ⓒ	ⓓ	193	ⓐ	ⓑ	ⓒ	ⓓ
114	ⓐ	ⓑ	ⓒ	ⓓ	134	ⓐ	ⓑ	ⓒ	ⓓ	154	ⓐ	ⓑ	ⓒ	ⓓ	174	ⓐ	ⓑ	ⓒ	ⓓ	194	ⓐ	ⓑ	ⓒ	ⓓ
115	ⓐ	ⓑ	ⓒ	ⓓ	135	ⓐ	ⓑ	ⓒ	ⓓ	155	ⓐ	ⓑ	ⓒ	ⓓ	175	ⓐ	ⓑ	ⓒ	ⓓ	195	ⓐ	ⓑ	ⓒ	ⓓ
116	ⓐ	ⓑ	ⓒ	ⓓ	136	ⓐ	ⓑ	ⓒ	ⓓ	156	ⓐ	ⓑ	ⓒ	ⓓ	176	ⓐ	ⓑ	ⓒ	ⓓ	196	ⓐ	ⓑ	ⓒ	ⓓ
117	ⓐ	ⓑ	ⓒ	ⓓ	137	ⓐ	ⓑ	ⓒ	ⓓ	157	ⓐ	ⓑ	ⓒ	ⓓ	177	ⓐ	ⓑ	ⓒ	ⓓ	197	ⓐ	ⓑ	ⓒ	ⓓ
118	ⓐ	ⓑ	ⓒ	ⓓ	138	ⓐ	ⓑ	ⓒ	ⓓ	158	ⓐ	ⓑ	ⓒ	ⓓ	178	ⓐ	ⓑ	ⓒ	ⓓ	198	ⓐ	ⓑ	ⓒ	ⓓ
119	ⓐ	ⓑ	ⓒ	ⓓ	139	ⓐ	ⓑ	ⓒ	ⓓ	159	ⓐ	ⓑ	ⓒ	ⓓ	179	ⓐ	ⓑ	ⓒ	ⓓ	199	ⓐ	ⓑ	ⓒ	ⓓ
120	ⓐ	ⓑ	ⓒ	ⓓ	140	ⓐ	ⓑ	ⓒ	ⓓ	160	ⓐ	ⓑ	ⓒ	ⓓ	180	ⓐ	ⓑ	ⓒ	ⓓ	200	ⓐ	ⓑ	ⓒ	ⓓ

* 문제를 다 풀고 채점한 후 점수로 환산해 봅니다. 점수 환산표는 16페이지에 있습니다.

자르는 선

ANSWER SHEET

ACTUAL TEST

LISTENING(Part I ~ IV)																								
NO.	ANSWER				NO.	ANSWER				NO.	ANSWER				NO.	ANSWER				NO.	ANSWER			
	A	B	C	D		A	B	C	D		A	B	C	D		A	B	C	D		A	B	C	D
1	a	b	c	d	21	a	b	c		41	a	b	c	d	61	a	b	c	d	81	a	b	c	d
2	a	b	c	d	22	a	b	c		42	a	b	c	d	62	a	b	c	d	82	a	b	c	d
3	a	b	c	d	23	a	b	c		43	a	b	c	d	63	a	b	c	d	83	a	b	c	d
4	a	b	c	d	24	a	b	c		44	a	b	c	d	64	a	b	c	d	84	a	b	c	d
5	a	b	c	d	25	a	b	c		45	a	b	c	d	65	a	b	c	d	85	a	b	c	d
6	a	b	c	d	26	a	b	c		46	a	b	c	d	66	a	b	c	d	86	a	b	c	d
7	a	b	c		27	a	b	c		47	a	b	c	d	67	a	b	c	d	87	a	b	c	d
8	a	b	c		28	a	b	c		48	a	b	c	d	68	a	b	c	d	88	a	b	c	d
9	a	b	c		29	a	b	c		49	a	b	c	d	69	a	b	c	d	89	a	b	c	d
10	a	b	c		30	a	b	c		50	a	b	c	d	70	a	b	c	d	90	a	b	c	d
11	a	b	c		31	a	b	c		51	a	b	c	d	71	a	b	c	d	91	a	b	c	d
12	a	b	c		32	a	b	c	d	52	a	b	c	d	72	a	b	c	d	92	a	b	c	d
13	a	b	c		33	a	b	c	d	53	a	b	c	d	73	a	b	c	d	93	a	b	c	d
14	a	b	c		34	a	b	c	d	54	a	b	c	d	74	a	b	c	d	94	a	b	c	d
15	a	b	c		35	a	b	c	d	55	a	b	c	d	75	a	b	c	d	95	a	b	c	d
16	a	b	c		36	a	b	c	d	56	a	b	c	d	76	a	b	c	d	96	a	b	c	d
17	a	b	c		37	a	b	c	d	57	a	b	c	d	77	a	b	c	d	97	a	b	c	d
18	a	b	c		38	a	b	c	d	58	a	b	c	d	78	a	b	c	d	98	a	b	c	d
19	a	b	c		39	a	b	c	d	59	a	b	c	d	79	a	b	c	d	99	a	b	c	d
20	a	b	c		40	a	b	c	d	60	a	b	c	d	80	a	b	c	d	100	a	b	c	d

READING(Part V ~ VII)																								
NO.	ANSWER				NO.	ANSWER				NO.	ANSWER				NO.	ANSWER				NO.	ANSWER			
	A	B	C	D		A	B	C	D		A	B	C	D		A	B	C	D		A	B	C	D
101	a	b	c	d	121	a	b	c	d	141	a	b	c	d	161	a	b	c	d	181	a	b	c	d
102	a	b	c	d	122	a	b	c	d	142	a	b	c	d	162	a	b	c	d	182	a	b	c	d
103	a	b	c	d	123	a	b	c	d	143	a	b	c	d	163	a	b	c	d	183	a	b	c	d
104	a	b	c	d	124	a	b	c	d	144	a	b	c	d	164	a	b	c	d	184	a	b	c	d
105	a	b	c	d	125	a	b	c	d	145	a	b	c	d	165	a	b	c	d	185	a	b	c	d
106	a	b	c	d	126	a	b	c	d	146	a	b	c	d	166	a	b	c	d	186	a	b	c	d
107	a	b	c	d	127	a	b	c	d	147	a	b	c	d	167	a	b	c	d	187	a	b	c	d
108	a	b	c	d	128	a	b	c	d	148	a	b	c	d	168	a	b	c	d	188	a	b	c	d
109	a	b	c	d	129	a	b	c	d	149	a	b	c	d	169	a	b	c	d	189	a	b	c	d
110	a	b	c	d	130	a	b	c	d	150	a	b	c	d	170	a	b	c	d	190	a	b	c	d
111	a	b	c	d	131	a	b	c	d	151	a	b	c	d	171	a	b	c	d	191	a	b	c	d
112	a	b	c	d	132	a	b	c	d	152	a	b	c	d	172	a	b	c	d	192	a	b	c	d
113	a	b	c	d	133	a	b	c	d	153	a	b	c	d	173	a	b	c	d	193	a	b	c	d
114	a	b	c	d	134	a	b	c	d	154	a	b	c	d	174	a	b	c	d	194	a	b	c	d
115	a	b	c	d	135	a	b	c	d	155	a	b	c	d	175	a	b	c	d	195	a	b	c	d
116	a	b	c	d	136	a	b	c	d	156	a	b	c	d	176	a	b	c	d	196	a	b	c	d
117	a	b	c	d	137	a	b	c	d	157	a	b	c	d	177	a	b	c	d	197	a	b	c	d
118	a	b	c	d	138	a	b	c	d	158	a	b	c	d	178	a	b	c	d	198	a	b	c	d
119	a	b	c	d	139	a	b	c	d	159	a	b	c	d	179	a	b	c	d	199	a	b	c	d
120	a	b	c	d	140	a	b	c	d	160	a	b	c	d	180	a	b	c	d	200	a	b	c	d

* 문제를 다 풀고 채점한 후 점수로 환산해 봅니다. 점수 환산표는 16페이지에 있습니다.

자르는 선

ANSWER SHEET

ACTUAL TEST

LISTENING(Part I ~ IV)																								
NO.	ANSWER				NO.	ANSWER				NO.	ANSWER				NO.	ANSWER				NO.	ANSWER			
	A	B	C	D		A	B	C	D		A	B	C	D		A	B	C	D		A	B	C	D
1	ⓐ	ⓑ	ⓒ	ⓓ	21	ⓐ	ⓑ	ⓒ		41	ⓐ	ⓑ	ⓒ	ⓓ	61	ⓐ	ⓑ	ⓒ	ⓓ	81	ⓐ	ⓑ	ⓒ	ⓓ
2	ⓐ	ⓑ	ⓒ	ⓓ	22	ⓐ	ⓑ	ⓒ		42	ⓐ	ⓑ	ⓒ	ⓓ	62	ⓐ	ⓑ	ⓒ	ⓓ	82	ⓐ	ⓑ	ⓒ	ⓓ
3	ⓐ	ⓑ	ⓒ	ⓓ	23	ⓐ	ⓑ	ⓒ		43	ⓐ	ⓑ	ⓒ	ⓓ	63	ⓐ	ⓑ	ⓒ	ⓓ	83	ⓐ	ⓑ	ⓒ	ⓓ
4	ⓐ	ⓑ	ⓒ	ⓓ	24	ⓐ	ⓑ	ⓒ		44	ⓐ	ⓑ	ⓒ	ⓓ	64	ⓐ	ⓑ	ⓒ	ⓓ	84	ⓐ	ⓑ	ⓒ	ⓓ
5	ⓐ	ⓑ	ⓒ	ⓓ	25	ⓐ	ⓑ	ⓒ		45	ⓐ	ⓑ	ⓒ	ⓓ	65	ⓐ	ⓑ	ⓒ	ⓓ	85	ⓐ	ⓑ	ⓒ	ⓓ
6	ⓐ	ⓑ	ⓒ	ⓓ	26	ⓐ	ⓑ	ⓒ		46	ⓐ	ⓑ	ⓒ	ⓓ	66	ⓐ	ⓑ	ⓒ	ⓓ	86	ⓐ	ⓑ	ⓒ	ⓓ
7	ⓐ	ⓑ	ⓒ		27	ⓐ	ⓑ	ⓒ		47	ⓐ	ⓑ	ⓒ	ⓓ	67	ⓐ	ⓑ	ⓒ	ⓓ	87	ⓐ	ⓑ	ⓒ	ⓓ
8	ⓐ	ⓑ	ⓒ		28	ⓐ	ⓑ	ⓒ		48	ⓐ	ⓑ	ⓒ	ⓓ	68	ⓐ	ⓑ	ⓒ	ⓓ	88	ⓐ	ⓑ	ⓒ	ⓓ
9	ⓐ	ⓑ	ⓒ		29	ⓐ	ⓑ	ⓒ		49	ⓐ	ⓑ	ⓒ	ⓓ	69	ⓐ	ⓑ	ⓒ	ⓓ	89	ⓐ	ⓑ	ⓒ	ⓓ
10	ⓐ	ⓑ	ⓒ		30	ⓐ	ⓑ	ⓒ		50	ⓐ	ⓑ	ⓒ	ⓓ	70	ⓐ	ⓑ	ⓒ	ⓓ	90	ⓐ	ⓑ	ⓒ	ⓓ
11	ⓐ	ⓑ	ⓒ		31	ⓐ	ⓑ	ⓒ		51	ⓐ	ⓑ	ⓒ	ⓓ	71	ⓐ	ⓑ	ⓒ	ⓓ	91	ⓐ	ⓑ	ⓒ	ⓓ
12	ⓐ	ⓑ	ⓒ		32	ⓐ	ⓑ	ⓒ	ⓓ	52	ⓐ	ⓑ	ⓒ	ⓓ	72	ⓐ	ⓑ	ⓒ	ⓓ	92	ⓐ	ⓑ	ⓒ	ⓓ
13	ⓐ	ⓑ	ⓒ		33	ⓐ	ⓑ	ⓒ	ⓓ	53	ⓐ	ⓑ	ⓒ	ⓓ	73	ⓐ	ⓑ	ⓒ	ⓓ	93	ⓐ	ⓑ	ⓒ	ⓓ
14	ⓐ	ⓑ	ⓒ		34	ⓐ	ⓑ	ⓒ	ⓓ	54	ⓐ	ⓑ	ⓒ	ⓓ	74	ⓐ	ⓑ	ⓒ	ⓓ	94	ⓐ	ⓑ	ⓒ	ⓓ
15	ⓐ	ⓑ	ⓒ		35	ⓐ	ⓑ	ⓒ	ⓓ	55	ⓐ	ⓑ	ⓒ	ⓓ	75	ⓐ	ⓑ	ⓒ	ⓓ	95	ⓐ	ⓑ	ⓒ	ⓓ
16	ⓐ	ⓑ	ⓒ		36	ⓐ	ⓑ	ⓒ	ⓓ	56	ⓐ	ⓑ	ⓒ	ⓓ	76	ⓐ	ⓑ	ⓒ	ⓓ	96	ⓐ	ⓑ	ⓒ	ⓓ
17	ⓐ	ⓑ	ⓒ		37	ⓐ	ⓑ	ⓒ	ⓓ	57	ⓐ	ⓑ	ⓒ	ⓓ	77	ⓐ	ⓑ	ⓒ	ⓓ	97	ⓐ	ⓑ	ⓒ	ⓓ
18	ⓐ	ⓑ	ⓒ		38	ⓐ	ⓑ	ⓒ	ⓓ	58	ⓐ	ⓑ	ⓒ	ⓓ	78	ⓐ	ⓑ	ⓒ	ⓓ	98	ⓐ	ⓑ	ⓒ	ⓓ
19	ⓐ	ⓑ	ⓒ		39	ⓐ	ⓑ	ⓒ	ⓓ	59	ⓐ	ⓑ	ⓒ	ⓓ	79	ⓐ	ⓑ	ⓒ	ⓓ	99	ⓐ	ⓑ	ⓒ	ⓓ
20	ⓐ	ⓑ	ⓒ		40	ⓐ	ⓑ	ⓒ	ⓓ	60	ⓐ	ⓑ	ⓒ	ⓓ	80	ⓐ	ⓑ	ⓒ	ⓓ	100	ⓐ	ⓑ	ⓒ	ⓓ

READING(Part V ~ VII)																								
NO.	ANSWER				NO.	ANSWER				NO.	ANSWER				NO.	ANSWER				NO.	ANSWER			
	A	B	C	D		A	B	C	D		A	B	C	D		A	B	C	D		A	B	C	D
101	ⓐ	ⓑ	ⓒ	ⓓ	121	ⓐ	ⓑ	ⓒ	ⓓ	141	ⓐ	ⓑ	ⓒ	ⓓ	161	ⓐ	ⓑ	ⓒ	ⓓ	181	ⓐ	ⓑ	ⓒ	ⓓ
102	ⓐ	ⓑ	ⓒ	ⓓ	122	ⓐ	ⓑ	ⓒ	ⓓ	142	ⓐ	ⓑ	ⓒ	ⓓ	162	ⓐ	ⓑ	ⓒ	ⓓ	182	ⓐ	ⓑ	ⓒ	ⓓ
103	ⓐ	ⓑ	ⓒ	ⓓ	123	ⓐ	ⓑ	ⓒ	ⓓ	143	ⓐ	ⓑ	ⓒ	ⓓ	163	ⓐ	ⓑ	ⓒ	ⓓ	183	ⓐ	ⓑ	ⓒ	ⓓ
104	ⓐ	ⓑ	ⓒ	ⓓ	124	ⓐ	ⓑ	ⓒ	ⓓ	144	ⓐ	ⓑ	ⓒ	ⓓ	164	ⓐ	ⓑ	ⓒ	ⓓ	184	ⓐ	ⓑ	ⓒ	ⓓ
105	ⓐ	ⓑ	ⓒ	ⓓ	125	ⓐ	ⓑ	ⓒ	ⓓ	145	ⓐ	ⓑ	ⓒ	ⓓ	165	ⓐ	ⓑ	ⓒ	ⓓ	185	ⓐ	ⓑ	ⓒ	ⓓ
106	ⓐ	ⓑ	ⓒ	ⓓ	126	ⓐ	ⓑ	ⓒ	ⓓ	146	ⓐ	ⓑ	ⓒ	ⓓ	166	ⓐ	ⓑ	ⓒ	ⓓ	186	ⓐ	ⓑ	ⓒ	ⓓ
107	ⓐ	ⓑ	ⓒ	ⓓ	127	ⓐ	ⓑ	ⓒ	ⓓ	147	ⓐ	ⓑ	ⓒ	ⓓ	167	ⓐ	ⓑ	ⓒ	ⓓ	187	ⓐ	ⓑ	ⓒ	ⓓ
108	ⓐ	ⓑ	ⓒ	ⓓ	128	ⓐ	ⓑ	ⓒ	ⓓ	148	ⓐ	ⓑ	ⓒ	ⓓ	168	ⓐ	ⓑ	ⓒ	ⓓ	188	ⓐ	ⓑ	ⓒ	ⓓ
109	ⓐ	ⓑ	ⓒ	ⓓ	129	ⓐ	ⓑ	ⓒ	ⓓ	149	ⓐ	ⓑ	ⓒ	ⓓ	169	ⓐ	ⓑ	ⓒ	ⓓ	189	ⓐ	ⓑ	ⓒ	ⓓ
110	ⓐ	ⓑ	ⓒ	ⓓ	130	ⓐ	ⓑ	ⓒ	ⓓ	150	ⓐ	ⓑ	ⓒ	ⓓ	170	ⓐ	ⓑ	ⓒ	ⓓ	190	ⓐ	ⓑ	ⓒ	ⓓ
111	ⓐ	ⓑ	ⓒ	ⓓ	131	ⓐ	ⓑ	ⓒ	ⓓ	151	ⓐ	ⓑ	ⓒ	ⓓ	171	ⓐ	ⓑ	ⓒ	ⓓ	191	ⓐ	ⓑ	ⓒ	ⓓ
112	ⓐ	ⓑ	ⓒ	ⓓ	132	ⓐ	ⓑ	ⓒ	ⓓ	152	ⓐ	ⓑ	ⓒ	ⓓ	172	ⓐ	ⓑ	ⓒ	ⓓ	192	ⓐ	ⓑ	ⓒ	ⓓ
113	ⓐ	ⓑ	ⓒ	ⓓ	133	ⓐ	ⓑ	ⓒ	ⓓ	153	ⓐ	ⓑ	ⓒ	ⓓ	173	ⓐ	ⓑ	ⓒ	ⓓ	193	ⓐ	ⓑ	ⓒ	ⓓ
114	ⓐ	ⓑ	ⓒ	ⓓ	134	ⓐ	ⓑ	ⓒ	ⓓ	154	ⓐ	ⓑ	ⓒ	ⓓ	174	ⓐ	ⓑ	ⓒ	ⓓ	194	ⓐ	ⓑ	ⓒ	ⓓ
115	ⓐ	ⓑ	ⓒ	ⓓ	135	ⓐ	ⓑ	ⓒ	ⓓ	155	ⓐ	ⓑ	ⓒ	ⓓ	175	ⓐ	ⓑ	ⓒ	ⓓ	195	ⓐ	ⓑ	ⓒ	ⓓ
116	ⓐ	ⓑ	ⓒ	ⓓ	136	ⓐ	ⓑ	ⓒ	ⓓ	156	ⓐ	ⓑ	ⓒ	ⓓ	176	ⓐ	ⓑ	ⓒ	ⓓ	196	ⓐ	ⓑ	ⓒ	ⓓ
117	ⓐ	ⓑ	ⓒ	ⓓ	137	ⓐ	ⓑ	ⓒ	ⓓ	157	ⓐ	ⓑ	ⓒ	ⓓ	177	ⓐ	ⓑ	ⓒ	ⓓ	197	ⓐ	ⓑ	ⓒ	ⓓ
118	ⓐ	ⓑ	ⓒ	ⓓ	138	ⓐ	ⓑ	ⓒ	ⓓ	158	ⓐ	ⓑ	ⓒ	ⓓ	178	ⓐ	ⓑ	ⓒ	ⓓ	198	ⓐ	ⓑ	ⓒ	ⓓ
119	ⓐ	ⓑ	ⓒ	ⓓ	139	ⓐ	ⓑ	ⓒ	ⓓ	159	ⓐ	ⓑ	ⓒ	ⓓ	179	ⓐ	ⓑ	ⓒ	ⓓ	199	ⓐ	ⓑ	ⓒ	ⓓ
120	ⓐ	ⓑ	ⓒ	ⓓ	140	ⓐ	ⓑ	ⓒ	ⓓ	160	ⓐ	ⓑ	ⓒ	ⓓ	180	ⓐ	ⓑ	ⓒ	ⓓ	200	ⓐ	ⓑ	ⓒ	ⓓ

* 문제를 다 풀고 채점한 후 점수로 환산해 봅니다. 점수 환산표는 16페이지에 있습니다.

자르는 선

에듀윌 토익 실전 LC + RC Vol.2

발 행 일	2022년 11월 28일 초판
저 자	에듀윌 어학연구소
펴 낸 이	권대호, 김재환
펴 낸 곳	(주)에듀윌
등록번호	제25100-2002-000052호
주 소	08378 서울특별시 구로구 디지털로34길 55 코오롱싸이언스밸리 2차 3층

www.eduwill.net

대표전화 1600-6700

여러분의 작은 소리
에듀윌은 크게 듣겠습니다.

본 교재에 대한 여러분의 목소리를 들려주세요.
공부하시면서 어려웠던 점, 궁금한 점,
칭찬하고 싶은 점, 개선할 점, 어떤 것이라도 좋습니다.

에듀윌은 여러분께서 나누어 주신 의견을
통해 끊임없이 발전하고 있습니다.

에듀윌 도서몰 book.eduwill.net

- 부가학습자료 및 정오표: 에듀윌 도서몰 → 도서자료실
- 교재 문의: 에듀윌 도서몰 → 문의하기 → 교재(내용, 출간) / 주문 및 배송

취업, 공무원, 자격증 시험준비의 흐름을 바꾼 화제작!

에듀윌 히트교재 시리즈

에듀윌 교육출판연구소가 만든 히트교재 시리즈!
YES 24, 교보문고, 알라딘, 인터파크, 영풍문고 등 전국 유명 온/오프라인 서점에서 절찬 판매 중!

12년간 1위
2022. 11월
에듀윌 공인중개사
6년간 아무도 깨지 못한 기록 합격자 수 1위를 만든 교재
13년간 1위
2022. 11월
에듀윌 주택관리사
1,710명 최종 합격생 중 1,103명이 에듀윌!
공인중개사 기초입문서/기본서/핵심요약집/문제집/기출문제집/실전모의고사 외 다수
주택관리사 기초서/기본서/핵심요약집/문제집/기출문제집/실전모의고사/네컷회계

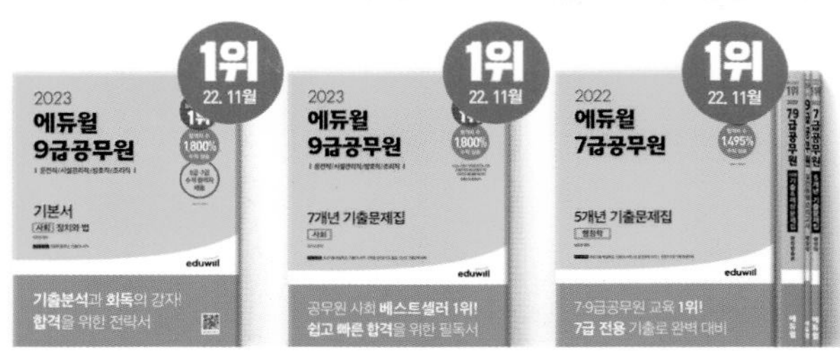

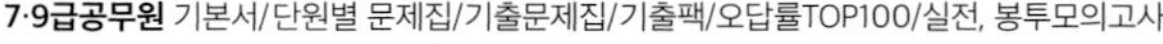

7·9급공무원 기본서/단원별 문제집/기출문제집/기출팩/오답률TOP100/실전, 봉투모의고사

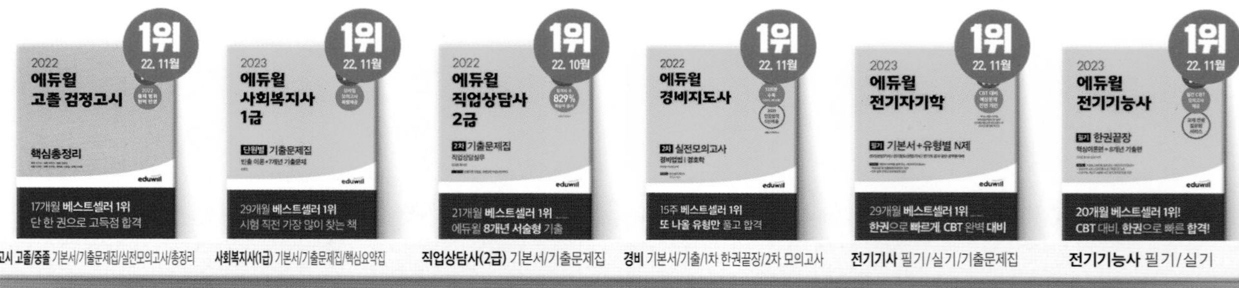

※ YES24 수험서 자격증 공인중개사 베스트셀러 1위 (2011년 12월, 2012년 1월, 12월, 2013년 1월~5월, 8월~12월, 2014년 1월~5월, 7월~8월, 12월, 2015년 2월~4월, 2016년 2월, 4월, 6월, 12월, 2017년 1월~12월, 2018년 1월~12월, 2019년 1월~12월, 2020년 1월~12월, 2021년 1월~12월, 2022년 1월~11월 월별 베스트, 매월 1위 교재는 다름)
※ YES24 국내도서 해당분야 월별, 주별 베스트 기준

에듀윌 토익 실전 LC+RC Vol.2

정답 및 해설

eduwill

에듀윌 토익 실전 LC+RC Vol.2

정답 및 해설

에듀윌 토익

실전 LC+RC

Vol.2

정답 및 해설

TEST 01

LISTENING TEST

1. (B)	**2.** (C)	**3.** (A)	**4.** (D)	**5.** (B)
6. (D)	**7.** (C)	**8.** (B)	**9.** (A)	**10.** (B)
11. (A)	**12.** (C)	**13.** (C)	**14.** (A)	**15.** (B)
16. (A)	**17.** (C)	**18.** (A)	**19.** (B)	**20.** (A)
21. (B)	**22.** (B)	**23.** (A)	**24.** (C)	**25.** (C)
26. (B)	**27.** (A)	**28.** (A)	**29.** (B)	**30.** (C)
31. (A)	**32.** (D)	**33.** (A)	**34.** (B)	**35.** (A)
36. (B)	**37.** (C)	**38.** (B)	**39.** (D)	**40.** (C)
41. (B)	**42.** (A)	**43.** (D)	**44.** (D)	**45.** (B)
46. (D)	**47.** (B)	**48.** (C)	**49.** (A)	**50.** (C)
51. (B)	**52.** (B)	**53.** (C)	**54.** (A)	**55.** (C)
56. (B)	**57.** (D)	**58.** (C)	**59.** (B)	**60.** (A)
61. (C)	**62.** (D)	**63.** (A)	**64.** (C)	**65.** (A)
66. (B)	**67.** (C)	**68.** (C)	**69.** (C)	**70.** (A)
71. (C)	**72.** (A)	**73.** (B)	**74.** (D)	**75.** (A)
76. (B)	**77.** (B)	**78.** (C)	**79.** (D)	**80.** (C)
81. (D)	**82.** (A)	**83.** (B)	**84.** (C)	**85.** (C)
86. (B)	**87.** (A)	**88.** (D)	**89.** (C)	**90.** (C)
91. (A)	**92.** (A)	**93.** (B)	**94.** (A)	**95.** (D)
96. (B)	**97.** (C)	**98.** (D)	**99.** (C)	**100.** (D)

READING TEST

101. (B)	**102.** (B)	**103.** (D)	**104.** (A)	**105.** (A)
106. (B)	**107.** (D)	**108.** (C)	**109.** (C)	**110.** (B)
111. (B)	**112.** (B)	**113.** (B)	**114.** (C)	**115.** (B)
116. (C)	**117.** (A)	**118.** (D)	**119.** (A)	**120.** (A)
121. (A)	**122.** (B)	**123.** (B)	**124.** (D)	**125.** (B)
126. (A)	**127.** (C)	**128.** (B)	**129.** (A)	**130.** (C)
131. (D)	**132.** (A)	**133.** (C)	**134.** (B)	**135.** (A)
136. (A)	**137.** (D)	**138.** (D)	**139.** (A)	**140.** (B)
141. (D)	**142.** (B)	**143.** (D)	**144.** (D)	**145.** (C)
146. (C)	**147.** (A)	**148.** (D)	**149.** (C)	**150.** (D)
151. (B)	**152.** (B)	**153.** (A)	**154.** (C)	**155.** (B)
156. (B)	**157.** (D)	**158.** (A)	**159.** (D)	**160.** (D)
161. (D)	**162.** (B)	**163.** (B)	**164.** (A)	**165.** (D)
166. (C)	**167.** (D)	**168.** (B)	**169.** (D)	**170.** (B)
171. (C)	**172.** (D)	**173.** (D)	**174.** (A)	**175.** (D)
176. (D)	**177.** (B)	**178.** (B)	**179.** (D)	**180.** (A)
181. (A)	**182.** (C)	**183.** (B)	**184.** (B)	**185.** (C)
186. (A)	**187.** (B)	**188.** (A)	**189.** (C)	**190.** (D)
191. (B)	**192.** (D)	**193.** (A)	**194.** (C)	**195.** (A)
196. (B)	**197.** (C)	**198.** (D)	**199.** (B)	**200.** (A)

PART 1

1. 호남

(A) She's pulling books off a shelf.
(B) She's photocopying a document.
(C) She's plugging in some equipment.
(D) She's lifting a stack of papers.

(A) 그녀는 책꽂이에서 책을 꺼내고 있다.
(B) 그녀는 문서를 복사하고 있다.
(C) 그녀는 장비의 플러그를 꽂고 있다.
(D) 그녀는 서류 더미를 들어 올리고 있다.

어휘 pull 끌어당기다, 빼다 shelf 책꽂이, 선반 photocopy 복사하다 (= make a photocopy) plug in ~의 플러그를 꽂다, 전원을 연결하다 lift 들어 올리다 stack 더미

2. 영녀

(A) Some people are standing in a doorway.
(B) Some people are entering a shop.
(C) Some people are going down an escalator.
(D) Some people are waiting in line at a bus stop.

(A) 몇몇 사람들이 현관에 서 있다.
(B) 몇몇 사람들이 가게에 들어가고 있다.
(C) 몇몇 사람들이 에스컬레이터를 타고 내려가고 있다.
(D) 몇몇 사람들이 버스 정류장에서 줄을 서서 기다리고 있다.

어휘 doorway 현관 wait in line 줄을 서서 기다리다

3. 미남

(A) They're walking bicycles down a path.
(B) They're jogging along a walkway.
(C) They're mounting bicycles onto a vehicle.
(D) They're putting on protective gear.

(A) 그들은 자전거를 끌면서 길을 걸어가고 있다.
(B) 그들은 산책로를 따라 조깅하고 있다.
(C) 그들은 자전거를 차량 위에 올리고 있다.
(D) 그들은 보호 장비를 착용하는 중이다.

어휘 path 길 walkway 산책로, 보도 mount 올려놓다, 올라타다 vehicle 차량 put on ~을 착용하다 protective gear 보호 장비

4. 미녀

(A) Some books are stacked on the floor.
(B) A bookshelf is positioned by a window.
(C) The woman is labeling a box.
(D) The woman has a book in each hand.

(A) 책 몇 권이 바닥에 쌓여 있다.
(B) 책장이 창가에 놓여 있다.
(C) 여자가 상자에 라벨을 붙이고 있다.
(D) 여자가 양손에 책을 들고 있다.

어휘 stack 쌓다 floor 바닥 bookshelf 책장, 책꽂이 position 놓다, ~의 위치를 정하다 label 라벨을 붙이다

5. 영녀

(A) One of the men is setting up a music stand.
(B) One of the men is holding an instrument.
(C) Some microphones are in a display case.
(D) Some musicians are exiting the stage.

(A) 남자들 중 한 명이 악보대를 설치하고 있다.
(B) 남자들 중 한 명이 악기를 들고 있다.
(C) 마이크 몇 개가 진열장 안에 있다.
(D) 몇몇 음악가들이 무대에서 퇴장하고 있다.

어휘 set up 설치하다, 준비하다 music stand 악보대 instrument 악기, 기구 display case 진열장 musician 음악가 exit 퇴장하다

6. 미남

(A) Some people are strolling on the dock.
(B) A pier is being built in a harbor.
(C) A boat has been taken out of the water.
(D) The surface of the water is calm.

(A) 몇몇 사람들이 선착장을 거닐고 있다.
(B) 항구에 부두가 건설되고 있다.
(C) 배 한 척이 물에서 건져졌다.
(D) 수면이 잔잔하다.

어휘 stroll 거닐다 dock 선착장, 부두 pier 부두 harbor 항구 surface 표면 calm 잔잔한, 고요한

PART 2

7. 호남 영녀

When's the grand opening?
(A) Take a seat.
(B) What a nice venue!
(C) In the evening.

개업식이 언제인가요?
(A) 자리에 앉으세요.
(B) 정말 좋은 장소네요!
(C) 저녁이에요.

어휘 grand opening 개업식 venue (행사의) 장소

8. 영녀 미남

> Where can I find some envelopes?
> (A) For about a week.
> **(B) In aisle three.**
> (C) Yes, I'll buy one.

봉투는 어디에서 찾을 수 있나요?
(A) 약 일주일 동안이요.
(B) 3번 통로에서요.
(C) 네, 하나 살게요.

어휘 envelope 봉투 aisle 통로

9. 미녀 호남

> How much will the parking fees be?
> **(A) Around twenty dollars.**
> (B) What was the traffic like?
> (C) By the parking meter.

주차 요금은 얼마나 나올까요?
(A) 20달러 정도요.
(B) 교통이 어땠어요?
(C) 주차 요금 징수기 옆에요.

어휘 parking fee 주차 요금 traffic 교통 parking meter 주차 요금 징수기

10. 미남 미녀

> Which branch will you transfer to?
> (A) A few days ago.
> **(B) I'll move to the Seattle office.**
> (C) Yes, it's been successful.

당신은 어느 지점으로 전근 가시나요?
(A) 며칠 전에요.
(B) 전 시애틀 지사로 옮길 거예요.
(C) 네, 그건 성공적이었습니다.

어휘 branch 지점, 지사 transfer 전근 가다, 이동하다 successful 성공적인

11. 미녀 호남

> Would you prefer coffee or a soda with your meal?
> **(A) I'll have some coffee.**
> (B) She always does.
> (C) No, I'm not hungry.

식사와 함께 커피를 드시겠어요, 아니면 탄산음료를 드시겠어요?
(A) 커피로 할게요.
(B) 그녀는 항상 그래요.
(C) 아니요, 저는 배고프지 않아요.

어휘 prefer 더 좋아하다, 선호하다 meal 식사

12. 미남 영녀

> Don't you have to replace the battery for the camera?
> (A) Thanks for the camera.
> (B) The same place as usual, please.
> **(C) Cheryl handled that this morning.**

당신은 카메라 배터리를 교체해야 하지 않나요?
(A) 카메라 고마워요.
(B) 평소와 같은 장소로 부탁합니다.
(C) 셰릴이 오늘 아침에 그걸 처리했어요.

어휘 replace 교체하다 handle 처리하다

13. 영녀 미남

> How can I get a new photo ID badge issued?
> (A) Yes, that's for visitors.
> (B) The access to restricted areas.
> **(C) You can visit the security desk.**

사진이 부착된 새로운 신분증을 어떻게 발급받을 수 있나요?
(A) 네, 그건 방문객용이에요.
(B) 제한 구역 출입이요.
(C) 보안 창구에 방문하시면 돼요.

어휘 badge 신분증, 명찰 issue 발급하다 access 출입, 접근 restricted 출입이 제한되는 security 보안

14. 호남 미녀

> Where can I leave my suitcase?
> **(A) At the front desk.**
> (B) It's a first-class ticket.
> (C) I think it suits you.

제 여행 가방을 어디에 둘 수 있나요?
(A) 안내 데스크에요.
(B) 그건 일등석 표입니다.
(C) 그게 당신에게 어울리는 것 같아요.

어휘 suitcase 여행 가방 first-class 일등석의 suit 어울리다

15. 영녀 미남

> The facilities at this hotel are amazing, aren't they?
> (A) No, I'm not sure where he is.
> **(B) Yes, I love staying here.**
> (C) Here, use this parking pass.

이 호텔의 편의 시설은 놀랍군요, 그렇지 않나요?

(A) 아니요, 저는 그가 어디 있는지 잘 모르겠어요.
(B) 네, 저는 여기 머무는 게 정말 좋아요.
(C) 여기요, 이 주차권을 사용하세요.

어휘 facilities 편의 시설 amazing 놀라운

16. 영녀 미녀

Do you prefer going to the aquarium or the art museum?
(A) I'd rather visit the museum.
(B) For the entire weekend.
(C) She is very talented.

당신은 수족관에 가는 게 좋으세요, 아니면 미술관에 가는 게 좋으세요?
(A) 미술관을 방문하는 편이 낫겠어요.
(B) 주말 내내요.
(D) 그녀는 매우 재능이 있어요.

어휘 aquarium 수족관 entire 전체의 talented 재능이 있는

17. 미녀 호남

Did you send in the forms to renew the insurance?
(A) That's exactly how I feel.
(B) Protection of our property.
(C) No, but I'll do it today.

당신은 보험을 갱신하기 위한 양식을 제출했나요?
(A) 그게 바로 제가 느끼는 거예요.
(B) 우리 재산 보장이요.
(C) 아니요, 하지만 오늘 할 거예요.

어휘 send in 제출하다 form 양식, 서식 renew 갱신하다 insurance 보험 protection (보험) 보장 property 재산, 부동산

18. 미남 미녀

You brought some product samples for the investors, didn't you?
(A) Yes, definitely.
(B) On the Web site.
(C) A significant investment.

당신이 투자자들을 위해 제품 샘플을 몇 개 가져왔죠, 그렇지 않나요?
(A) 네, 물론이죠.
(B) 웹사이트에요.
(C) 중요한 투자입니다.

어휘 investor 투자자 definitely 분명히 significant 중요한 investment 투자

19. 호남 미남

When did we last have the air conditioner inspected?
(A) That model isn't for sale.
(B) There should be a note in the manual.
(C) No, I'm busy for the rest of the day.

언제 우리가 마지막으로 에어컨 점검을 받았죠?
(A) 그 모델은 판매용이 아닙니다.
(B) 설명서에 메모가 있을 거예요.
(C) 아니요, 저는 남은 하루 동안 바빠요.

어휘 inspect 점검하다 manual 설명서

20. 미남 영녀

Didn't that singer used to be an actress?
(A) Yes, she was in a few films.
(B) When does the concert start?
(C) I don't use it very well.

저 가수는 예전에 배우 아니었나요?
(A) 네, 그녀는 몇 편의 영화에 출연했어요.
(B) 콘서트는 언제 시작하나요?
(C) 저는 그걸 잘 안 써요.

21. 호남 미녀

Would you like to grab something to eat at the café?
(A) Thank you for your help.
(B) The meeting starts in five minutes.
(C) I made copies of the report.

카페에서 뭐 좀 드실래요?
(A) 도와주셔서 감사합니다.
(B) 회의가 5분 뒤에 시작해요.
(C) 제가 보고서를 복사했어요.

22. 영녀 호남

Will you sign up for the leadership workshop on Friday?
(A) A memo from the manager.
(B) I'm planning to be out of town.
(C) Usually twice a day.

당신은 금요일 리더십 워크숍을 신청할 건가요?
(A) 관리자가 보낸 메모예요.
(B) 저는 출장 갈 계획입니다.
(C) 보통은 하루에 두 번이요.

어휘 sign up for ~을 신청하다 be out of town 출장 가다

23. 미남 영녀

Are beverages allowed here?
(A) The guide didn't say anything.
(B) He's buying snacks for the party.
(C) It's been very hot.

여기서 음료 허용되나요?
(A) 가이드가 아무 말도 안 했어요.
(B) 그는 파티를 위해 간식을 사고 있어요.
(C) 날씨가 너무 더워요.

24. 영녀 호남

Why was the fence taken down?
(A) The boundary of the property.
(B) No, I planted a garden.
(C) Because of the broken boards.

왜 울타리가 철거되었나요?
(A) 토지의 경계입니다.
(B) 아니요, 저는 정원을 가꿨어요.
(C) 깨진 판자 때문에요.

어휘 fence 울타리 take down (구조물을 해체하여) 치우다 boundary 경계 board 판자

25. 미녀 미남

Can you please unload these boxes?
(A) The display rack looks great.
(B) Fifteen boxes of paper.
(C) My lunch break just started.

이 상자들을 내려 주시겠어요?
(A) 진열 선반이 멋져 보여요.
(B) 종이 15상자요.
(C) 저는 이제 막 점심시간이 시작됐어요.

어휘 unload 짐을 내리다 display 진열 rack 선반

26. 호남 영녀

The public relations director is holding a press conference.
(A) It's too heavy for me.
(B) I didn't know that.
(C) An urgent announcement.

홍보 담당 이사가 기자 회견을 하고 있어요.
(A) 그건 저한테 너무 무거워요.
(B) 저는 몰랐어요.
(C) 긴급 공지입니다.

어휘 public relations 홍보 press conference 기자 회견 urgent 긴급한

27. 미남 미녀

Who did the electrical repairs?
(A) I'll give you their business card.
(B) My car is not working.
(C) Once every two weeks.

누가 전기 수리를 했나요?
(A) 제가 그들의 명함을 드릴게요.
(B) 제 차가 작동하지 않아요.
(C) 2주마다 한 번이요.

어휘 electrical 전기의

28. 미녀 미남

Why don't we buy floor tickets for the concert?
(A) They seem rather expensive.
(B) One of my favorite bands.
(C) According to the theater's policy.

우리 콘서트 티켓을 스탠딩석으로 사는 게 어때요?
(A) 그것들은 꽤 비싼 것 같아요.
(B) 제가 가장 좋아하는 밴드 중 하나예요.
(C) 극장의 방침에 따라서요.

29. 호남 영녀

Where did you buy this lamp?
(A) Let's find a desk lamp.
(B) I've got the catalog.
(C) This room needs better lighting.

당신은 이 램프를 어디에서 샀나요?
(A) 탁상용 램프를 찾아봅시다.
(B) 제가 카탈로그를 가져왔어요.
(C) 이 방에는 더 나은 조명이 필요해요.

어휘 lighting 조명

30. 미녀 호남

Dr. Robinson is looking for a research assistant.
(A) There's an excellent view.
(B) No, I'm still searching for it.
(C) Has he tried contacting the university?

로빈슨 박사가 연구 조교를 찾고 있어요.
(A) 경치가 아주 좋아요.
(B) 아니요, 저는 아직 찾고 있어요.
(C) 대학에 연락해 보셨대요?

31. 미남 영녀

Why was the staff picnic canceled?
(A) It's only been postponed.
(B) We picked the perfect spot.
(C) Did you pay the cancellation fee?

왜 직원 야유회가 취소되었나요?
(A) 연기된 것뿐이에요.
(B) 우리는 완벽한 장소를 골랐어요.
(C) 당신은 취소 수수료를 지불했나요?

어휘 postpone 연기하다 pick 고르다 spot 장소, 자리 cancellation fee 취소 수수료

PART 3

호남 미녀

Questions 32-34 refer to the following conversation.

M Hello. [32]I'd like to sign up for the historic district bike tour. When does the next one depart?

W At eleven o'clock… um… about twenty minutes from now. And there are still a few spots left.

M Oh, that's great. I'd like one ticket, please.

W All right. And we provide all participants with a helmet and a safety vest. [33]Please choose which size would be best for you.

M Sure. I'll take a medium.

W [34]You might also want to buy something to drink to take with you. There's a convenience store right across the street.

남 안녕하세요. [32]저는 역사 지구 자전거 투어를 신청하고 싶어요. 다음 편은 언제 출발하나요?

여 11시에요... 음... 지금부터 약 20분 후네요. 그리고 아직 몇 자리가 남아 있어요.

남 아, 잘됐네요. 표 한 장 주세요.

여 알겠습니다. 그리고 저희는 모든 참가자들에게 헬멧과 안전 조끼를 제공합니다. [33]당신에게 가장 적합한 사이즈를 골라 주세요.

남 알겠습니다. 저는 미디움으로 할게요.

여 [34]또한 마실 것을 사가지고 가시는 게 좋을 거예요. 바로 길 건너편에 편의점이 있습니다.

어휘 historic 역사적인 district 지구, 구역 depart 출발하다, 떠나다 spot 자리, 장소 provide A with B A에게 B를 제공하다 participant 참가자 convenience store 편의점

32. 대화는 주로 무엇에 관한 것인가?
(A) 보트 타기
(B) 역사 강의
(C) 자연 탐사 도보 여행
(D) 자전거 투어

33. 여자는 남자에게 무엇을 해 달라고 요청하는가?
(A) 사이즈 고르기
(B) 영수증 보여 주기
(C) 전화번호 제공하기
(D) 신분증 보여 주기

패러프레이징 choose which size would be best for you → Select a size

34. 여자는 무엇을 구매할 것을 제안하는가?
(A) 지도
(B) 음료
(C) 상품권
(D) 주차권

패러프레이징 something to drink → A beverage

미남 미녀

Questions 35-37 refer to the following conversation.

M Hi, Lorene. [35]I've added another task to your work schedule today. Ms. Kerrick needs her washing machine fixed. She lives at 461 Andell Road.

W Alright. I actually have another job in that neighborhood this morning, so [36]it would be better to visit Ms. Kerrick right after that and move Mr. Perry to the afternoon. Could you please call him to change the time?

M Of course. And I'm placing an order for spare parts. [37]I've got the catalog here. Is there anything you need?

남 안녕하세요, 로린. [35]오늘 당신의 업무 일정에 다른 일을 추가했어요. 케릭 씨가 세탁기 수리를 요청했어요. 그녀는 안델로 461번지에 살아요.

여 알았어요. 사실은 제가 오늘 아침에 그 동네에서 다른 일이 있어서, [36]그 후에 바로 케릭 씨를 찾아가고 페리 씨를 오후로 옮기는 게 좋을 것 같아요. 당신이 그에게 시간을 변경해 달라고 전화해 주시겠어요?

남 물론이죠. 그리고 제가 예비 부품을 주문할 건데요. [37]여기에 카탈로그가 있어요. 당신이 필요한 게 있나요?

어휘 task 일, 과업 neighborhood 근처, 인근 place an order ~을 주문하다 spare part 예비 부품

35. 화자들은 어디에서 일하는 것 같은가?

(A) 가전제품 수리업체에서

(B) 치과에서

(C) 관공서에서

(D) 드라이클리닝 회사에서

36. 여자는 남자에게 무엇을 해 달라고 요청하는가?

(A) 부동산 점검하기

(B) 방문 일정 변경하기

(C) 출장에 그녀와 동행하기

(D) 목록 출력하기

패러프레이징 change the time → Reschedule

37. 여자는 다음에 무엇을 할 것 같은가?

(A) 전화 회의에 참여하기

(B) 양식에 서명하기

(C) 카탈로그 보기

(D) 가구 재배치하기

영녀 미남

Questions 38-40 refer to the following conversation.

W Do you have a moment, Oliver?

M [38]I'm just stocking the organic produce section, and then I need to check the shelves of low-fat snacks. What's up?

W Well, our business has been invited to participate in the city's Health and Wellness Expo on June 18. [39]Would you be interested in giving a talk?

M I wouldn't mind doing it, but [39]could you tell me what it should be about?

W The theme is healthy habits.

M Oh, great. [40]I did a slideshow presentation on that last year. I could make some adjustments to that tomorrow and use it.

W Perfect. I'll let the event planner know.

여 올리버, 시간 좀 있어요?

남 [38]저는 유기농 제품 코너를 채우고 있는데, 그 다음에 저지방 스낵 진열대를 확인해야 해요. 무슨 일이죠?

여 음, 우리 회사는 6월 18일에 열리는 시의 건강 박람회에 참가하도록 초대받았어요. [39]강연하는 데 관심 있으세요?

남 강연하는 건 괜찮은데, [39]어떤 내용이어야 하는지 말씀해 주실래요?

여 주제는 건강한 습관입니다.

남 아, 잘됐네요. [40]저는 작년에 그것에 관한 슬라이드쇼 프레젠테이션을 했거든요. 내일 그것을 수정해서 사용할 수 있을 것 같아요.

여 완벽해요. 행사 기획자에게 알려 드리겠습니다.

어휘 stock 채우다, 비축하다 organic 유기농의 produce 생산물, 농작물 low-fat 저지방의 participate in ~에 참가하다 wellness 건강 give a talk 강연하다 theme 주제, 테마 make adjustments to ~을 조정하다

38. 화자들은 어디에서 일하는 것 같은가?

(A) 행사 기획사에서

(B) 건강식품점에서

(C) 댄스 학원에서

(D) 파티용품점에서

39. 남자는 여자에게 무엇을 확인해 달라고 요청하는가?

(A) 행사 장소

(B) 참가자 수

(C) 일정 최신 정보

(D) 강연 주제

40. 남자는 내일 무엇을 할 것인가?

(A) 회사 조사하기

(B) 시청에 연락하기

(C) 슬라이드 편집하기

(D) 일찍 출근하기

패러프레이징 make some adjustments → Edit

호남 미남 영녀

Questions 41-43 refer to the following conversation with three speakers.

M1 Hi, Danielle and Cedric. [41]I just got a call from Mr. Powell at McVaney Incorporated. He said several of the pairs of headphones in their latest order were broken.

M2 [42]Our electronics are known for their quality. We've never had a problem like this before.

W I doubt it was an issue with the production line. They must have been damaged in transit.

M1 Hmm... but we've used the same delivery company for years.

W You know, [43]we did just change our shipping boxes recently. The cardboard isn't as thick. That's probably the reason why this happened.

남1 안녕하세요, 다니엘, 세드릭. [41]방금 맥베니 주식회사의 파월 씨로부터 전화를 받았어요. 그는 가장 최근에 주문한 헤드폰 몇 쌍

이 고장 났다고 말했어요.

남2 [42]우리 전자제품은 품질 면에서 유명합니다. 우리는 전에 이와 같은 문제를 겪어 본 적이 없어요.

여 생산 라인에 문제가 있었을 것 같지는 않아요. 운송 중에 손상된 게 틀림없어요.

남1 흠… 하지만 우리는 몇 년 동안 같은 배송 업체를 이용했어요.

여 알다시피, [43]우리는 최근에 배송 상자를 바꿨어요. 판지가 그렇게 두껍지 않더라고요. 그것이 아마도 이런 일이 일어난 이유일 거예요.

어휘 electronics 전자제품 quality 품질 doubt 의심하다 issue 문제, 사안 production line 생산 라인 damage 손상시키다 in transit 운송 중에 thick 두꺼운

41. 파월 씨는 왜 전화했는가?

(A) 잘못된 청구서에 이의를 제기하기 위해
(B) 손상된 물품에 대해 불평하기 위해
(C) 웹사이트의 오류를 보고하기 위해
(D) 배송 지연에 대해 문의하기 위해

42. 화자들은 어디에서 일하는 것 같은가?

(A) 전자제품 매장에서
(B) 캠핑용품 회사에서
(C) 의류 매장에서
(D) 도자기 공장에서

43. 여자는 무엇이 문제를 일으켰다고 생각하는가?

(A) 빠듯한 기한
(B) 컴퓨터 오류
(C) 미숙한 직원
(D) 용기 변경

패러프레이징 shipping boxes → containers

호남 미녀

Questions 44-46 refer to the following conversation.

M Thanks for seeing me, Katie. You said you have some comments about my home?

W That's right. Since [44]I'll be the one selling your house, I wanted to make sure it is ready to be put on the market. [45]The front yard needs some attention.

M Yeah, [45]I haven't done much with the garden. But I'm not sure how much I should invest in upgrading the flower beds and making everything look better.

W It's important to make a positive first impression on potential buyers. Just a few inexpensive changes could make a big difference.

M What did you have in mind?

W Well, [46]I've made some rough sketches of my recommended changes. Here, why don't you take a look?

남 만나 줘서 고마워요, 케이티. 저희 집에 대해 하실 말씀이 있다고 하셨죠?

여 맞아요. [44]제가 당신의 집을 팔 거라서, 집이 시장에 나올 준비가 되었는지 확인하고 싶었어요. [45]앞마당은 관리가 필요해요.

남 네, [45]제가 정원 손질을 별로 안 했어요. 하지만 저는 화단을 업그레이드하고 모든 게 더 나아 보이게 하기 위해 얼마나 투자해야 하는지 잘 모르겠어요.

여 잠재적 구매자들에게 긍정적인 첫인상을 주는 게 중요해요. 비용이 많이 들지 않는 몇 가지 변화만으로도 큰 차이를 만들 수 있어요.

남 생각해 두신 게 있나요?

여 음, [46]제가 추천한 변경 사항들에 대한 스케치를 대강 해 봤어요. 여기, 한 번 보실래요?

어휘 front yard 앞마당 attention 주의 invest in ~에 투자하다 flower bed 화단 positive 긍정적인 first impression 첫인상 potential 잠재적인 buyer 구매자 inexpensive 값싼, 비용이 많이 들지 않는 rough 대강의

44. 여자는 누구인 것 같은가?

(A) 건설 노동자
(B) 행사 기획자
(C) 정원사
(D) 부동산 중개인

45. 대화는 주로 무엇에 관한 것인가?

(A) 정책 변경 사항
(B) 부동산 개선
(C) 수수료 인상
(D) 자료 순서

46. 여자는 다음에 무엇을 할 것인가?

(A) 동료에게 연락하기
(B) 예산 검토하기
(C) 남자를 위해 계약서 인쇄하기
(D) 남자에게 그림 보여 주기

패러프레이징 some rough sketches → some drawings

영녀 미남

Questions 47-49 refer to the following conversation.

W Hi, Samuel. [47]I'm getting excited about our runway show.

M Me, too. [47]I think the audience is going to love our clothing. There's just one issue.

W What's happened?

M I've realized that all the clothes will need to stay hanging up while in transit. So, [48]we've got to rent a van on short notice.

W Harlan Rentals has a big fleet.

M So... you've used them before?

W Yes, and, actually, [49]I just got a discount code e-mailed to me yesterday. I'll forward it to you.

여 안녕하세요, 사무엘. [47]우리 런웨이 쇼를 기대하고 있어요.

남 저도 그래요. [47]관객들이 우리 옷을 정말 좋아할 것 같아요. 딱 한 가지 문제가 있어요.

여 뭐죠?

남 모든 옷들이 운송 중에 걸어 놓은 채로 있어야 한다는 걸 알았어요. 그래서, 급하게 [48]승합차를 빌려야 해요.

여 할란 렌털은 차를 많이 갖고 있어요.

남 그래서... 전에 이용해 보셨어요?

여 네, 그리고 사실, [49]어제 할인 코드를 이메일로 받았어요. 당신한테 그걸 전달해 드릴게요.

어휘 audience 관객, 청중 hang up 걸다 on short notice 촉박하게 forward 전달하다

47. 화자들은 누구인 것 같은가?

(A) 전문 사진작가
(B) 패션 디자이너
(C) 유지 보수 담당자
(D) 미술 강사

48. 남자는 그들이 무엇을 해야 한다고 말하는가?

(A) 조수 고용하기
(B) 부품 주문하기
(C) 차량 대여하기
(D) 프레젠테이션 만들기

패러프레이징 van → vehicle

49. 여자는 남자에게 무엇을 줄 것인가?

(A) 할인 코드
(B) 명함
(C) 운전 경로
(D) 여분 티켓

미녀 호남

Questions 50-52 refer to the following conversation.

W Excuse me, [50]I work on this floor, in suite 105.

M Oh, yes. I've seen you in the lobby before. Can I help you with something?

W Actually, yes. You're having a work crew do some renovations, right?

M That's right. [51]We are updating all of the rooms in our recruiting firm.

W Well, [52]I noticed that their trucks are blocking the main doors. That'll make it difficult for my customers to get in and out.

M I think that's just temporary while they're unloading, but I'll make sure they move them as soon as possible.

W Thank you.

여 실례합니다. [50]저는 이 층 105호실에서 일합니다.

남 아, 그래요. 전에 로비에서 당신을 본 적이 있어요. 제가 뭘 도와드릴까요?

여 사실, 네. 당신이 섭외한 작업반이 지금 보수 작업을 하고 있죠?

남 맞아요. [51]우리 채용 대행사의 모든 사무실을 개선하고 있어요.

여 음, [52]그들의 트럭이 정문을 막고 있다는 걸 알았어요. 그렇게 하면 제 고객들이 출입하기 어려울 거예요.

남 그건 그들이 짐을 내리는 동안 일시적인 것 같은데, 그들이 가능한 빨리 그것들을 옮기도록 제가 확실히 할게요.

여 감사합니다.

어휘 renovation 수리, 수선 notice 알다, 알아차리다 block 막다 temporary 일시적인, 임시의 unload (짐을) 내리다

50. 화자들은 어디에 있는 것 같은가?

(A) 공항에
(B) 슈퍼마켓에
(C) 사무실 건물에
(D) 호텔에

51. 남자는 어떤 종류의 업체에서 일하는가?

(A) 건축 회사
(B) 직업 소개소
(C) 마케팅 회사
(D) 여행사

패러프레이징 recruiting firm → An employment agency

52. 여자는 무엇에 대해 걱정하는가?

(A) 소음으로 인한 차질
(B) 출입구로의 접근
(C) 현장이 정전되는 것
(D) 저장 옵션의 부족

패러프레이징 get in and out → Access to an entrance

미남 영녀

Questions 53-55 refer to the following conversation.

M Hello. [53]I saw your advertisement on the community Web site about the microwave oven for sale. I'm wondering if it's been sold.

W No, not yet.

M Wonderful! Are there any problems with it?

W [54]It's working fine. I've had it for a few years, but I rarely eat at home, so I've hardly touched it. I'm moving, so I didn't want to bring it with me.

M I see. Could I meet you tomorrow to pick it up?

W Actually, [55]I'll be working at my office quite late tomorrow. How about Thursday?

남 안녕하세요. [53]저는 커뮤니티 웹사이트에서 당신의 전자레인지 판매 광고를 봤어요. 그게 팔렸는지 궁금해요.

여 아니요, 아직이요.

남 잘됐네요! 그것에 무슨 문제라도 있나요?

여 [54]그건 잘 작동되고 있어요. 제가 그걸 몇 년 동안 갖고 있었는데, 제가 집에서 거의 안 먹어서 거의 손도 안 댔어요. 저는 이사할 예정이라 그걸 갖고 가고 싶지 않았어요.

남 그렇군요. 내일 만나서 그걸 가져가도 될까요?

여 사실, [55]내일은 제가 사무실에서 꽤 늦게까지 일할 거예요. 목요일은 어때요?

어휘 for sale 판매하는 rarely 거의 ~하지 않는 hardly 거의 ~ 아니다

53. 남자는 왜 전화하고 있는가?

(A) 제품을 소개하기 위해
(B) 프로젝트에 자원하기 위해
(C) 물품의 이용 가능성을 확인하기 위해
(D) 행사를 홍보하기 위해

54. 여자는 "거의 손도 안 댔어요"라고 말할 때 무엇을 의미하는가?

(A) 전자레인지의 상태가 아주 좋다.
(B) 전자레인지에 데운 음식은 건강에 좋지 않을 수 있다.
(C) 그녀는 장치를 작동하는 법을 모른다.
(D) 그녀는 제품의 디자인이 마음에 들지 않았다.

패러프레이징 working fine → in excellent condition

55. 여자는 내일 무엇을 할 계획인가?

(A) 출장 가기
(B) 이삿짐 업체 고용하기
(C) 늦게까지 일하기
(D) 식사 준비하기

미남 호남 미녀

Questions 56-58 refer to the following conversation with three speakers.

M1 Good morning, Alison. [56]Thanks for meeting with us today.

M2 [56]You've been doing such a great job in your temporary role here at Stratford Power Company, that we'd like to offer you a permanent position.

M1 You'd have similar job duties to what you're doing now.

W Thank you so much! I'm very interested. [57]Would I need to take a certification course?

M1 That's not necessary because of your career experience.

W Great!

M2 And, [58]you can choose which hours you work as long as they add up to forty per week.

남1 안녕하세요, 앨리슨. [56]오늘 저희와 만나 주셔서 감사합니다.

남2 [56]당신은 이곳 스트랫퍼드 전력 회사에서 임시로 맡은 역할을 아주 훌륭히 해내고 계시기 때문에, 저희는 당신에게 정규직을 제안하고 싶습니다.

남1 당신은 지금 하고 있는 것과 비슷한 업무를 하게 될 겁니다.

여 정말 고맙습니다! 굉장히 흥미가 있습니다. [57]제가 자격증 과정을 들어야 할까요?

남1 당신의 경력 덕에 그럴 필요는 없습니다.

여 잘됐네요!

남1 그리고, [58]주당 40시간이 되기만 하면 어느 시간에 일할지 선택할 수 있습니다.

어휘 role 역할 offer 제안하다 permanent 정규직의, 영구적인 duty 업무 certification 증명서 career 경력 add up to 합계 ~이 되다

56. 남자들은 어떤 업계에서 일하는가?

(A) 배송
(B) 에너지
(C) 연예

(D) 금융

패러프레이징 Power → Energy

57. 여자는 무엇에 대해 문의하는가?

(A) 새로운 직무 책임에 무엇이 포함되는지
(B) 직책이 언제 시작되는지
(C) 월급이 얼마인지
(D) 교육 과정이 필요한지 아닌지

패러프레이징 a certification course → a training course

58. 역할의 어떤 이점이 언급되는가?

(A) 연간 성과급
(B) 법인 카드 사용
(C) 유연한 근무 시간
(D) 승진 기회

패러프레이징 which hours you work → work hours

영녀 호남

Questions 59-61 refer to the following conversation.

W Welcome to Bryson Home Improvement Center. How can I help you?

M [59]I just completed a paving project in my backyard. Now that the concrete is finished, [60]I'd like to put tiles on top to create a patio.

W [60]What kind of tiles did you have in mind?

M I'd like something durable, but I've never worked with outdoor tiles.

W That's no problem. We have a range of products that are suitable for any kind of weather. Would you consider natural stone tiles?

M That sounds nice.

W All right. [61]We have our stone tiles at the back, and you can see and feel them for yourself. Right this way.

여 브라이슨 주택 개조 센터에 오신 걸 환영합니다. 어떻게 도와드릴까요?

남 [59]제 뒤뜰에 포장 공사를 막 끝냈어요. 콘크리트 작업이 끝났으니, [60]그 위에 타일을 깔아 테라스를 만들고 싶습니다.

여 [60]어떤 종류의 타일을 생각하고 계셨나요?

남 내구성이 있는 것이 좋겠지만, 야외 타일로는 작업해 본 적이 없어요.

여 아무 문제 없습니다. 저희는 어떤 날씨에도 적합한 다양한 제품들을 갖고 있어요. 자연석 타일을 고려해 보시겠어요?

남 그거 좋군요.

여 알겠습니다. [61]뒤쪽에 돌 타일이 있으니, 그것들을 직접 보고 만져 보실 수 있습니다. 이쪽으로 오세요.

어휘 improvement 개량, 개선 complete 끝내다 pave 포장하다 patio (옥외) 테라스 durable 내구성이 있는 a range of 다양한 suitable 적합한

59. 남자는 최근에 무엇을 했는가?

(A) 그는 새집으로 이사했다.
(B) 그는 자신의 소유지 일부에 포장 작업을 했다.
(C) 그는 테라스 가구를 구입했다.
(D) 그는 조경 사업을 시작했다.

패러프레이징 completed a paving project in my backyard → paved a section of his property

60. 남자는 왜 "야외 타일로는 작업해 본 적이 없어요"라고 말하는가?

(A) 조언을 구하기 위해
(B) 추가 시간을 요청하기 위해
(C) 일자리 제안을 거절하기 위해
(D) 예산을 설명하기 위해

61. 화자들은 다음에 무엇을 할 것 같은가?

(A) 가격표 보기
(B) 관리자 기다리기
(C) 몇 가지 제품 보기
(D) 설치 예약하기

패러프레이징 see → Look at

호남 영녀

Questions 62-64 refer to the following conversation and map.

M Hi, Sandy. I noticed that the lights went out in our store's demonstration area. [62]We're supposed to show how to use the Syracuse camp stove today at three.

W I've called an electrician, but I don't think they'll be fixed by then. [63]We'll have to move the activity to a different part of the store.

M Hmm... [63]we could easily make space by taking down some display items in the tent section. And I could move the chairs there, too.

W Good idea. Thanks. Oh, and [64]I'd better get some signs printed to tell people about the change.

M [64]Joanne has a printer in her office.

남 안녕하세요, 샌디. 우리 매장 시연 구역에 조명이 나갔던데요. [62]우리는 오늘 3시에 시러큐스 캠프용 휴대 난로 사용법을 보여 주기로 되어 있어요.

여 전기 기술자를 불렀는데, 그때까지는 수리되지 않을 것 같아요. [63]그 행사를 매장의 다른 곳으로 옮겨야 할 거예요.

남 흠… [63]텐트 구역에 진열된 물건들을 치우면 쉽게 공간을 만들 수 있어요. 그리고 제가 의자를 거기로 옮길 수도 있고요.

여 좋은 생각이에요. 고마워요. 아, 그리고 [64]사람들에게 변경 사항을 알리기 위해 제가 게시물을 인쇄하는 게 낫겠어요.

남 [64]조앤 사무실에 프린터가 있어요.

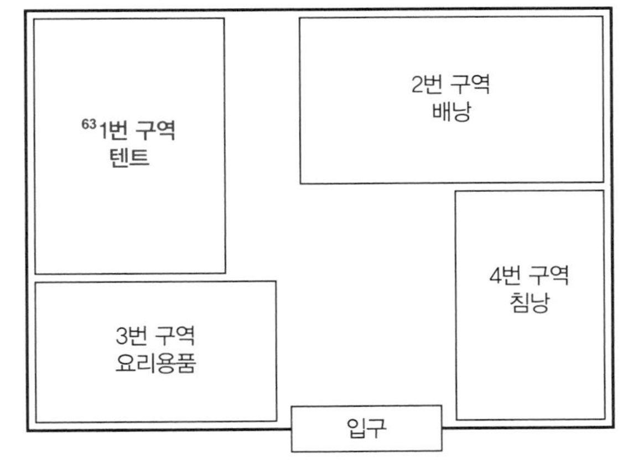

어휘 be supposed to do ~하기로 되어 있다 electrician 전기 기술자

62. 화자들은 누구인 것 같은가?

(A) 건축물 검사관
(B) 공장 근로자
(C) 여행 가이드
(D) 판매원

63. 시각 자료를 보시오. 오늘 특별 행사는 어디에서 열릴 것인가?

(A) 1번 구역에서
(B) 2번 구역에서
(C) 3번 구역에서
(D) 4번 구역에서

64. 여자는 왜 조앤의 사무실에 방문할 것 같은가?

(A) 수리공을 호출하기 위해
(B) 용품을 주문하기 위해
(C) 게시물을 인쇄하기 위해
(D) 설명서를 확인하기 위해

패러프레이징 get some signs printed → print some signs

미녀 미남

Questions 65-67 refer to the following conversation and chart.

W Carlos, here are the analytics for our Web site traffic last month. [65]I was glad that our paid ads have been bringing in so much traffic. That was a good use of our budget.

M I agree. [66]I hope we can get more people to volunteer for our charity and support our environmental conservation efforts.

W Well, [67]it's a lot easier for volunteers to sign up now because they can do it by phone and e-mail too, not just through the Web site.

여 카를로스 씨, 여기 지난달 우리 웹사이트 트래픽에 대한 분석 자료가 있습니다. [65]우리 유료 광고가 이렇게 많은 트래픽을 가져와서 기뻤습니다. 거기에 예산 쓰기를 잘했네요.

남 저도 동의해요. [66]저는 더 많은 사람들이 우리 자선 단체를 위해 자원봉사하고 우리의 환경 보전 노력을 지지할 수 있길 바라요.

여 음, [67]자원봉사자들은 웹사이트뿐만 아니라 전화와 이메일로도 가입할 수 있기 때문에 이제 가입하는 게 훨씬 더 쉬워요.

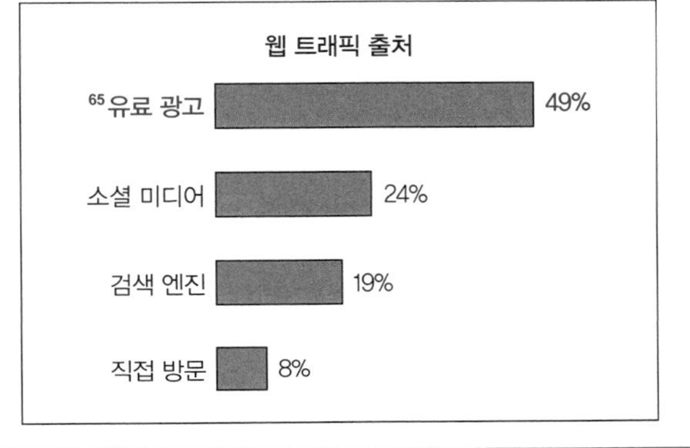

어휘 analytics 분석 정보 bring in ~을 가져오다, 생기게 하다 budget 예산 charity 자선 단체 environmental 환경의 conservation 보전, 보존

65. 시각 자료를 보시오. 여자는 어떤 비율에 대해 기뻐하는가?

(A) 49%
(B) 24%
(C) 19%
(D) 8%

66. 화자들의 자선 단체는 무엇에 초점을 맞추는가?

(A) 동물을 보호하는 것
(B) 환경을 돕는 것
(C) 재해 지역을 복구하는 것
(D) 교육을 증진시키는 것

패러프레이징 environmental conservation efforts → Helping the environment

67. 가입 절차가 어떻게 변경되었는가?

(A) 그것은 더 이상 요금이 없다.
(B) 그것은 기한이 더 길다.
(C) 그것은 다른 수단을 통해 이용할 수 있다.
(D) 그것은 자원봉사자 패널에 의해 검토된다.

패러프레이징 by phone and e-mail → through different methods

호남 미녀

Questions 68-70 refer to the following conversation and price tag.

M Hi, Maria. [68]How are things coming along for the launch of our new running shoes tomorrow?

W We're ready to stock the shelves with this merchandise after the store closes.

M Great. Oh, [69]it seems there's a mistake on this tag. Aren't these shoes eighty-five dollars?

W Oh, you're right. [69]I'll change that. Do you think we'll be busy tomorrow?

M Yes, so [70]I'm actually going to talk to some of the team members today to see if they can work longer shifts.

남 안녕하세요, 마리아. [68]내일 우리 새 운동화 출시 준비는 어떻게 돼 가고 있어요?

여 우리는 매장 문을 닫은 뒤에 이 상품으로 선반을 채울 준비가 되어 있어요.

남 좋습니다. 아, [69]이 가격표에 오류가 있는 것 같아요. 이 신발은 85 달러 아니에요?

여 아, 그러네요. [69]바꿀게요. 우리가 내일 바쁠 것 같나요?

남 네, 그래서 [70]저는 사실 오늘 몇몇 팀원들이 좀 더 오래 근무할 수 있는지 이야기해 보려고요.

1행. 브랜드: 브라보
2행. 색상: 짙은 갈색
[69]3행. 가격: 95달러
4행. 사이즈: 7

어휘 launch 출시 merchandise 상품 tag 가격표, 꼬리표 shift 교대 근무

68. 내일 무슨 일이 예정되어 있는가?

(A) 매장 점검
(B) 기자 회견
(C) 제품 출시
(D) 지점 개점

패러프레이징 the launch of our new running shoes → A product launch

69. 시각 자료를 보시오. 여자는 몇 행을 변경할 것이라고 말하는가?

(A) 1행
(B) 2행
(C) 3행
(D) 4행

70. 남자는 무엇을 할 계획인가?

(A) 동료들과 이야기하기
(B) 업데이트된 일정을 이메일로 보내기
(C) 면접 진행하기
(D) 제조사에 전화하기

패러프레이징 talk to some of the team members → Speak to some coworkers

PART 4

미녀

Questions 71-73 refer to the following announcement.

Attention, passengers. [71]We're about half an hour from the final station. I apologize for the delay earlier, which was caused by a fallen tree on the tracks. In just a moment, we'll be passing by Bloomfield Valley. [72]Don't miss your chance to catch a great view of the beautiful landscape out of the windows on the right-hand side. Usually there is a thick blanket of fog in the valley. But [73]today, luckily for you, the fog has been cleared away by the strong winds. So, it's a great day to be passing through.

승객 여러분, 주목하십시오. [71]우리는 종착역까지 약 30분 남았습니다. 선로에 쓰러진 나무로 인해 초래된 앞선 지연에 대해 사과드립니다. 잠시 후에 우리는 블룸필드 계곡을 지나갈 것입니다. [72]오른쪽 창밖으로 아름답고 멋진 풍경을 볼 수 있는 기회를 놓치지 마세요. 보통 계곡에는 짙은 안개가 끼어 있습니다. 하지만 [73]오늘은 운 좋게도, 강풍으로 인해 안개가 걷혔습니다. 그래서 지나가기에 좋은 날입니다.

어휘 apologize for ~에 대해 사과하다 valley 계곡 landscape 풍경, 경치 fog 안개 luckily 운 좋게 clear away ~을 제거하다

71. 공지는 어디에서 일어나고 있는가?

(A) 여객선에서
(B) 택시에서
(C) 기차에서
(D) 비행기에서

72. 화자는 무엇을 할 것을 추천하는가?

(A) 경치를 보는 것
(B) 추가로 업데이트되는 것을 듣는 것
(C) 개인 물품을 확인하는 것
(D) 티켓 영수증을 보관하는 것

패러프레이징 catch a great view of the beautiful landscape → Looking at the scenery

73. 화자에 따르면, 청자들은 왜 운이 좋은가?

(A) 방문객이 적다.
(B) 안개가 걷혔다.
(C) 기차가 일찍 도착했다.
(D) 좌석 업그레이드를 이용할 수 있다.

패러프레이징 the fog has been cleared away → The fog has lifted

호남

Questions 74-76 refer to the following telephone message.

Hello, my name is Sherman Gilliam, and [74]I'm the owner of Odessa Catering. I'm looking for someone to create a professional-looking logo for my business. [75]My friend, Lucia Kraus, loved the one you designed for her, so she said I should hire you. Of course, the logo should match our brand identity and goals. [76]More details about our company can be found on the company introduction page of our Web site. I can e-mail you the link to the webpage. Please call me back at 555-4863.

여보세요, 제 이름은 셔먼 길리엄이고, [74]오데사 출장 음식 업체의 대표입니다. 저는 제 사업체를 위해 전문적으로 보이는 로고를 제작해 줄 사람을 찾고 있습니다. [75]제 친구인 루시아 크라우스가 당신이 그녀에게 디자인해 준 것을 매우 마음에 들어한 터라, 당신을 적극 추천하더군요. 물론, 로고는 우리 브랜드 정체성과 목표에 어울려야 합니다. [76]우리 회사에 대한 더 자세한 사항은 웹사이트의 회사 소개 페이지에서 찾으실 수 있습니다. 제가 당신에게 이메일로 웹페이지 링크를 보내 드릴 수 있습니다. 555-4863번으로 전화 부탁드려요.

어휘 match 어울리다, 일치하다 identity 정체성 introduction 소개

74. 화자는 어떤 종류의 업체를 소유하고 있는가?

(A) 인테리어 디자인 회사
(B) 서점
(C) 기술 회사
(D) 출장 음식 회사

75. 루시아 크라우스는 화자를 어떻게 도왔는가?

(A) 거래처를 추천함으로써
(B) 사업에 투자함으로써
(C) 용품을 제공함으로써
(D) 추가 시간을 근무함으로써

76. 화자는 청자가 무엇을 보길 원하는가?

(A) 일부 의류 품목
(B) 웹사이트
(C) 일부 직원들의 의견
(D) 제안된 계약서

영녀

Questions 77-79 refer to the following announcement.

As you take your seats, I have a quick announcement. [77, 78]We are supposed to have some bottled water and snacks for the journey. My colleague is bringing them now, so the bus will depart about five minutes late. This won't be a problem, though, as traffic is very light at this time of day, so I can still drive your group to the first stop on time. [79]I also printed extra copies of today's itinerary. If you didn't pick one up when you boarded, please come forward and do that now. Thank you.

자리에 앉으시는 동안 잠시 안내 말씀 드리겠습니다. [77, 78]우리는 여행을 위해 생수와 간식을 준비하기로 되어 있습니다. 제 동료가 지금 그것들을 가져오고 있어서, 버스가 5분 정도 늦게 출발할 것입니다. 하지만 하루 중 이 시간에는 교통이 매우 원활해서 제가 여전히 여러분 단체를 첫 번째 목적지까지 제시간에 모셔다 드릴 수 있으니 이는 문제가 되지 않을 겁니다. [79]제가 오늘 여행 일정표 사본도 추가로 인쇄했습니다. 탑승하실 때 가져가지 않으셨다면, 앞으로 나오셔서 지금 가져가시기 바랍니다. 감사합니다.

어휘 take a seat 자리에 앉다 journey 여행 colleague 동료 depart 출발하다, 떠나다 itinerary 여행 일정표 pick up ~을 찾아가다 board 탑승하다 forward 앞으로

77. 화자는 누구인 것 같은가?

(A) 식당 종업원
(B) 버스 기사
(C) 극장 주인
(D) 피트니스 강사

78. 화자는 왜 기다릴 계획인가?

(A) 그 지역에 교통이 혼잡할 것으로 예상된다.
(B) 참가자가 부재 중이다.
(C) 보급품이 오는 중이다.
(D) 차량이 점검되고 있다.

패러프레이징 some bottled water and snacks → Some supplies

79. 청자들 중 일부는 무엇을 하도록 권장되는가?

(A) 신분증 제시하기
(B) 화면에 주목하기
(C) 단체 사진 찍기
(D) 일정표 찾아가기

패러프레이징 itinerary → schedule

미남 🎧

Questions 80-82 refer to the following podcast.

Welcome to another episode in this podcast series. [80]As usual, we're going to take a look at another quirky building design. This one is found in the Astoria neighborhood of New York. [81]It was designed by architect Ken Morgan. I was actually not familiar with Morgan's work at all until one of our listeners e-mailed us with a request to talk about his buildings. The structure we're going to discuss today is an apartment building that was inspired by the shape of a beehive. But before we dive into the details, [82]let me tell you what you'll hear about on the podcast next week. I think you'll be excited about it.

이 팟캐스트 시리즈의 또 다른 에피소드에 오신 것을 환영합니다. [80]여느 때처럼, 우리는 또 다른 기발한 건물 디자인을 볼 것입니다. 이것은 뉴욕의 아스토리아 인근에 있습니다. [81]이것은 건축가 켄 모건이 디자인했습니다. 저는 사실 우리 청취자들 중 한 분이 그의 건물에 대해 이야기해 달라는 요청을 우리에게 이메일로 보내기 전까지는 모건의 작품을 전혀 알지 못했습니다. 오늘 우리가 이야기할 건축물은 벌집 모양에서 영감을 받은 아파트 건물입니다. 하지만 더 자세히 들여다보기 전에, [82]다음 주 팟캐스트에서 여러분이 듣게 될 내용을 말씀드리겠습니다. 여러분은 그것에 대해 흥미를 느끼실 것 같습니다.

어휘 quirky 기발한 be found ~에 존재하다 architect 건축가 be familiar with 잘 알다, ~에 익숙하다 structure 구조, 건축물 inspire 영감을 주다 dive into ~으로 뛰어들다

80. 팟캐스트 시리즈는 무엇에 관한 것인가?

(A) 획기적인 과학적 성과
(B) 여행지
(C) 독특한 건축 양식
(D) 야생과 자연

패러프레이징 quirky building design → Unique architecture

81. 화자는 켄 모건의 작품에 대해 어떻게 알게 되었는가?

(A) 이전의 게스트로부터
(B) 온라인 검색으로
(C) 잡지 기사에서
(D) 팟캐스트 청취자로부터

82. 청자들은 다음에 무엇을 들을 것인가?

(A) 프로그램 주제
(B) 노래
(C) 광고
(D) 일기 예보

미녀 🎧

Questions 83-85 refer to the following excerpt from a meeting.

Thanks to the high demand for our products, our company is expanding rapidly. As you know, [83]we will move our company headquarters to a larger building in August. We've hired a company to do all of the packing and transportation. [84]I've assigned Melissa Collins the task of creating an itemized list of all of our equipment on site. Please help her by letting her know exactly what devices your department is currently using. [85]If you have any questions about that process, please speak to Melissa directly. However, keep in mind that <u>we've never had to do this before</u>.

우리 제품에 대한 높은 수요 덕분에, 우리 회사는 빠르게 확장하고 있습니다. 여러분도 알다시피, [83]우리는 8월에 본사를 더 큰 건물로 이전할 것입니다. 우리는 포장과 운송을 모두 맡을 회사를 고용했습니다. [84]저는 멜리사 콜린스에게 현장에 있는 우리 장비를 모두 항목별 목록으로 작성하는 일을 배정했습니다. 여러분의 부서가 현재 어떤 기기를 사용하고 있는지 그녀에게 정확히 알려서 그녀를 도와주세요. [85]그 과정에 대해 궁금한 점이 있으면, 멜리사에게 직접 이야기하세요. 하지만, <u>우리가 전에는 이것을 할 필요가 없었다</u>는 걸 명심하세요.

어휘 demand 수요 expand 확장되다 rapidly 빠르게 headquarters 본사 transportation 운송 assign 배정하다, 맡기다 itemize 항목별로 적다 on site 현장에 있는, 현지의 keep in mind 명심하다

83. 화자에 따르면, 8월에 무슨 일이 일어날 것인가?

(A) 재고 정리 세일이 열릴 것이다.
(B) 회사 이전이 이루어질 것이다.
(C) 새로운 관리자가 고용될 것이다.
(D) 기업 합병이 마무리될 것이다.

패러프레이징 move our company headquarters → A company relocation

84. 멜리사 콜린스는 무엇을 담당하는가?

(A) 장비를 주문하는 것
(B) 수리하는 것
(C) 재고를 조사하는 것
(D) 지원자를 심사하는 것

패러프레이징 creating an itemized list of all of our equipment on site → Taking inventory

85. 화자는 "우리가 전에는 이것을 할 필요가 없었다"라고 말할 때 무엇을 암시하는가?

(A) 과정이 검토되어야 한다.
(B) 요청이 부당하다고 간주된다.
(C) 몇 가지 질문에 대답을 하지 못할 수 있다.

(D) 일부 정보가 업데이트되지 않았다.

호남

Questions 86-88 refer to the following speech.

[86]It's wonderful to see such a great turnout for this year's conference on hotel management. I'd like to welcome not only the people in the audience but also [87]those who are streaming the video live from our Web site. This is the first year we've offered that option. We hope that today's lectures on strategies and trends will be useful. The first presentation will begin in about ten minutes. And [88]please note that we still have a few spots left for the workshop led by Clyde Jones at one o'clock. If you're interested, you can still register for it at the table near the entrance.

[86]올해 호텔 경영 학회에 이렇게 많은 참가자가 몰리다니 정말 대단하네요. 저는 관객들뿐만 아니라 [87]우리 웹사이트에서 영상을 라이브로 스트리밍하고 계신 분들도 환영하고자 합니다. [87]올해는 우리가 그 옵션을 제공한 첫 해입니다. 전략과 동향에 관한 오늘 강의가 유용하길 바랍니다. 첫 번째 발표는 약 10분 뒤에 시작될 겁니다. 그리고 [88]1시에 클라이드 존스가 진행할 워크숍에 아직 몇 자리가 남아 있다는 걸 알려드립니다. 관심이 있으시면, 입구 근처의 테이블에서 등록하실 수 있습니다.

어휘 turnout 참가자의 수 strategy 전략 spot 자리 register for ~에 등록하다 entrance 입구

86. 청자들은 어떤 업계에서 일하는 것 같은가?

(A) 통신
(B) 접객
(C) 제조
(D) 보건 의료

패러프레이징 hotel management → Hospitality

87. 화자에 따르면, 올해 학회에 대해 무엇이 다른가?

(A) 그것은 온라인으로 볼 수 있다.
(B) 강사들이 다른 나라에서 왔다.
(C) 참가자들이 피드백을 줄 수 있다.
(D) 발표자들이 질문을 받을 시간이 더 많다.

88. 일부 청자들은 무엇을 하도록 권장되는가?

(A) 이름표 달기
(B) 관련 도서 구입하기
(C) 다과 마음껏 먹기
(D) 교육 과정에 등록하기

패러프레이징 register for → Sign up for

영녀

Questions 89-91 refer to the following talk.

[89]I'd like to bring your attention to an issue that happened in the laboratory this morning. Unfortunately, one of the test batches got contaminated, so it can't be used in our final results. We need to run another test on Saturday. I know that you weren't planning to work that day, but [90]we must finish the project on time, so it's important that there aren't delays at any stage. Now, [91]the building's entrances are kept locked on the weekend, and only a few of you have keys. Well, I'll be here with my phone on.

[89]저는 여러분이 오늘 아침 연구실에서 발생한 문제에 주목해 주셨으면 합니다. 유감스럽게도, 실험한 세트 중 하나가 오염되어, 우리 최종 결과에 사용될 수 없습니다. 우리는 토요일에 한 차례 더 실험을 해야 합니다. 여러분이 그날 일할 계획이 아니었던 건 알지만, [90]우리는 그 프로젝트를 제시간에 끝내야 하므로 어떤 단계에서도 지연이 없도록 하는 게 중요합니다. 자, [91]건물 출입구가 주말에는 잠겨 있고, 여러분 중 몇 명만이 열쇠를 갖고 있습니다. 음, 제가 전화를 켜 놓고 여기 있을게요.

어휘 laboratory 연구실, 실험실 batch 한 묶음, 1회분 contaminate 오염시키다 run 행하다, 실시하다 lock 잠그다

89. 청자들은 어디에서 일하는 것 같은가?

(A) 창고에서
(B) 자동차 공장에서
(C) 연구 시설에서
(D) 관공서에서

패러프레이징 the laboratory → a research facility

90. 화자는 무엇에 대해 걱정하는가?

(A) 새로운 정책을 시행하는 것
(B) 장비를 손상시키는 것
(C) 예정보다 늦는 것
(D) 일자리 공석을 채우는 것

91. 화자는 왜 "제가 전화를 켜 놓고 여기 있을게요"라고 말하는가?

(A) 해결책을 제안하기 위해
(B) 방해에 대해 사과하기 위해
(C) 피드백을 장려하기 위해
(D) 긴급성을 나타내기 위해

미녀

Questions 92-94 refer to the following telephone message.

Hi, Stanley. Thanks for the list of specialists for [92]the restoration and building project we're doing for

Hartford Enterprises. It's essential that we keep the changes historically accurate. [93]Hartford Enterprises has agreed to pay a deposit of twenty percent instead of our usual fifteen percent, as this project is very complex. [94]I know it requires a lot of effort and that we don't usually take on projects with such difficult requirements. However, they could become a regular client.

안녕하세요, 스탠리. [92]우리가 하트포드 산업을 위해 진행하고 있는 복구 및 건설 프로젝트에 대한 전문가 명단을 보내 주셔서 감사합니다. 우리는 변화를 줄 때 역사적 정확성을 유지하는 것이 필수적입니다. 이 프로젝트는 매우 복잡하기 때문에 [93]하트포드 산업은 보통의 15퍼센트 대신에 20퍼센트의 계약금을 지불하기로 합의했습니다. [94]저는 그것이 많은 노력을 필요로 하는 것을 알고 있고 우리는 보통은 그렇게 어려운 요구 사항이 있는 프로젝트는 맡지 않습니다. 하지만, 그들은 고정 거래처가 될 수 있습니다.

어휘 specialist 전문가 restoration 복구 essential 필수적인 historically 역사적으로 accurate 정확한 deposit 계약금, 보증금 complex 복잡한 take on (일 등을) 맡다 requirement 요구되는 것 regular client 고정 거래처, 단골 고객

92. 화자는 어디에서 일하는가?

(A) 건설 회사에서
(B) 광고 대행사에서
(C) 인쇄소에서
(D) 박물관에서

93. 하트포드 산업은 무엇을 제공하기로 합의했는가?

(A) 기사 초안
(B) 더 많은 계약금
(C) 현재 카탈로그
(D) 측정값 목록

94. 화자는 왜 "그들은 고정 거래처가 될 수 있습니다"라고 말하는가?

(A) 결정 이유를 설명하기 위해
(B) 할인을 정당화하기 위해
(C) 놀라움을 나타내기 위해
(D) 오류를 바로잡기 위해

미남

Questions 95-97 refer to the following excerpt from a meeting and price list.

Let's get this meeting started, everyone. [95]I know that some of you were scheduled to have the day off, so thank you for coming in anyway. We need everyone's help to complete this order on time. [96]We'll be making a delivery of flowers to the Towson Art Gallery this afternoon. They've placed a large order for bouquets of lilies to celebrate a new exhibition. This will make a big enough profit to make up for last month's sluggish sales. And as a token of my appreciation, [97]I'll buy you all lunch from Connie's Pizza around the corner at noon.

여러분, 회의를 시작합시다. [95]여러분 중 몇 분은 오늘 휴무였던 걸로 알고 있는데, 그럼에도 와 주셔서 감사합니다. 우리는 이 주문을 제시간에 완료하기 위해 모두의 도움이 필요합니다. [96]우리는 오늘 오후에 타우슨 미술관에 꽃을 배달할 것입니다. 그들은 새로운 전시를 축하하기 위해 백합 꽃다발을 대량으로 주문했습니다. 이는 지난달의 판매 부진을 만회할 만큼 충분히 큰 수익을 낼 것입니다. 그리고 감사의 표시로 [97]제가 정오에 근처에 있는 코니스 피자에서 여러분 모두에게 점심을 사겠습니다.

한 다스당 가격	
해바라기 32달러	[96]백합 30달러
장미 25달러	튤립 18달러

어휘 complete 완료하다, 끝마치다 make a delivery 배달하다 place an order 주문하다 celebrate 축하하다, 기념하다 exhibition 전시회 profit 이익, 이윤 make up for ~을 만회하다 sluggish 부진한, 느릿느릿 움직이는 as a token of ~의 표시로 appreciation 감사

95. 화자는 왜 청자들 몇 명에게 감사하는가?

(A) 오류를 알아차린 것에 대해
(B) 늦게까지 남은 것에 대해
(C) 공급업체를 추천해 준 것에 대해
(D) 추가 근무를 한 것에 대해

96. 시각 자료를 보시오. 타우슨 미술관에서는 주문에서 한 다스당 얼마를 지불할 것인가?

(A) 32달러
(B) 30달러
(C) 25달러
(D) 18달러

97. 화자는 정오에 무엇을 할 것인가?

(A) 진열하기
(B) 용기에 라벨 붙이기
(C) 식사 제공하기
(D) 가구 주문하기

패러프레이징 buy you all lunch → Provide a meal

미녀

Questions 98-100 refer to the following speech and list.

Welcome to this book-signing event for *Key to the Forest*. [98]Many readers are calling it the best mystery novel in a generation. [99]The book has been nominated for several awards, including the prestigious Cervantes Literary Award, whose winner will be made public at a ceremony next week. We have several special guests in attendance this evening, and they are ready to answer your questions. However, [100]the cover artist missed a connecting flight and will not be here in time. So, if you're interested in the cover creation process, I'm afraid we won't be addressing that topic.

이곳 〈숲으로 가는 열쇠〉 도서 사인회에 오신 걸 환영합니다. [98]많은 독자들이 이 책을 이 세대 최고의 추리 소설이라고 부르고 있습니다. [99]이 책은 명망 있는 세르반테스 문학상을 포함한 여러 상의 후보에 올랐는데, 그 수상자는 다음 주 시상식에서 공개될 것입니다. 우리는 오늘 저녁에 특별 손님 몇 분을 모셨고, 그들은 여러분의 질문에 대답할 준비가 되어 있습니다. 하지만 [100]표지 화가가 연결 항공편을 놓쳐서 이곳에 제시간에 도착하지 못할 것입니다. 따라서 표지 창작 과정에 관심이 있는 분들께는 유감이지만 그 주제는 다루지 못할 것 같습니다.

특별 손님	
저자	파비아노 바레시
편집자	웨이 창
저작권 대리인	마드리 카말
[100]표지 화가	이네스 파우스트

어휘 generation 세대 nominate (후보로) 지명하다 award 상 prestigious 명망 있는, 일류의 literary 문학의 make public 일반에게 알리다, 공표하다 ceremony 의식, 식 in attendance 참석한 connecting flight 연결 항공편 creation 창작 address 다루다

98. 어떤 종류의 책이 홍보되고 있는가?

(A) 시
(B) 공상 과학 소설
(C) 연애 소설
(D) 추리 소설

99. 화자에 따르면, 다음 주에 무슨 일이 일어날 것인가?

(A) 글짓기 대회가 시작될 것이다.
(B) 책값이 인상될 것이다.
(C) 수상자가 발표될 것이다.
(D) 수업이 제공될 것이다.

패러프레이징 be made public → be announced

100. 시각 자료를 보시오. 누가 행사에 참석할 수 없겠는가?

(A) 파비아노 바레시
(B) 웨이 창
(C) 마드리 카말
(D) 이네스 파우스트

PART 5

101. 부사 자리

퍼레이드가 정확하게 계획대로 진행된다면 기획 위원회 회원들은 기뻐할 것이다.

해설 빈칸이 없어도 완전한 절이 성립하므로 빈칸은 부사 자리이다. 따라서 (B) precisely가 정답이다.

어휘 go as planned 계획대로 진행되다 committee 위원회

102. 전치사 어휘 at

미술관의 VIP 손님들은 오후 7시에 화가들과 함께 관람하도록 초청된다.
(A) ~의 (B) ~에 (C) ~을 위한 (D) ~에

해설 빈칸 뒤에 7 P.M.으로 특정 시각이 명시되어 있으므로 (B) at이 정답이다. at은 특정 시각/시점/지점/위치 등을 구체적으로 나타낼 때 쓴다.

어휘 take a tour 견학하다, 둘러보다

103. 소유한정사

Mr. Latham은 연례 회의에서 합병 거래를 성사시킨 노력을 인정받았다.

해설 빈칸 앞에 전치사 for가 있고 뒤에는 명사 efforts가 있으므로 빈칸은 명사를 수식하는 자리이다. 따라서 소유한정사인 (D) his가 정답이다.

어휘 recognize 알아보다, 인정하다 secure 얻어 내다, 확보하다 merger 합병 deal 거래

104. 전치사 어휘 for

Felosa Media는 자사의 동영상 스트리밍 서비스에 대한 월 사용료를 인상할 것이라고 발표했다.
(A) ~에 대한 (B) ~을 따라 (C) ~ 근처에 (D) ~로서

해설 빈칸 앞뒤에 명사구가 있는 것으로 보아 빈칸은 전치사 자리이므로 형용사 또는 부사인 (C) nearby는 오답이다.

어휘 announce 발표하다 raise 올리다, 인상하다 monthly fee 월 사용료

105. 접속사 어휘 before

휴가철이 시작되기 전에 브레몬드 베이의 부두는 수리될 것이다.
(A) ~ 하기 전에 (B) ~한 반면에 (C) 마치 ~인 것처럼 (D) ~하기 위해서

어휘 tourist season 휴가철, 여행 시즌 repair 수리, 보수 pier 부두

106. 명사 어휘 delivery

Ms. Revilla가 Office World에서 주문한 인쇄용지는 금요일 오후에 배송될 예정이다.
(A) 상태 (B) 배송 (C) 보증 (D) 계좌

어휘 be scheduled for ~로 예정되어 있다

107. 형용사 자리+어휘

소비자 대부분은 나중에 나온 모델이 그 회사의 첫 제품군보다 더 효율적이라고 평가했다.

해설 빈칸 앞에 동사 rated가 있고 뒤에는 명사 models가 있으므로 빈칸은 명사를 수식하는 형용사 자리이다. (A) late와 (D) later가 정답 후보인데 문맥상 나중에 나온 모델이 더 낫다는 내용이 되는 게 자연스러우므로 (D) later가 정답이다.

어휘 consumer 소비자 rate 평가하다 efficient 효율적인

108. 명사 어휘 source

Simpson Incorporated는 국내 유수의 고품질 외부 도장용 페인트 공급업체이다.

(A) 원인 (B) 지표 (C) 공급원 (D) 역할

어휘 leading 선두의, 주요한, 가장 중요한 high-quality 고품질의 exterior 외부의

109. 관계대명사 [주격]

사내 변호사인 Jillian Smith는 모호하거나 헷갈리는 언어를 포함하고 있는 계약서 초안에 개선을 제안할 수 있다.

해설 빈칸 앞에 사물을 나타내는 명사구 contract drafts가 있고 뒤에는 동사 contain이 바로 이어지므로 빈칸은 주격 관계대명사 자리이다. 따라서 (C) that이 정답이다.

어휘 corporate 회사의, 기업의 suggest 제안하다 improvement 개선 contract 계약(서) draft 원고, 초안 contain 포함하다 vague 모호한, 애매한 confusing 혼란스러운

110. 부사 어휘 officially

6월 8일부터 1층에 있는 호텔 사우나실이 공식적으로 문을 열 것이다.

(A) 즉시 (B) 공식적으로 (C) 현저하게 (D) (비판 등을) 신랄하게; 급격히

어휘 ground floor 1층

111. 명사 자리+가산/불가산명사

Jackson Foundation은 예술 교육 프로그램의 주요 후원자인 동시에 스포츠 시설에 기부도 한다.

해설 빈칸 앞에 부정관사 a와 형용사 major가 있고 뒤에는 전치사 of가 있으므로 빈칸은 형용사의 수식을 받는 명사 자리이다. 따라서 (B) supporter가 정답이다. (C) support가 '지원, 지지'를 뜻할 때는 불가산명사이므로 부정관사와 함께 쓸 수 없기 때문에 오답이다.

어휘 foundation 재단 major 주요한 supporter 지지자, 후원자 make a donation 기부하다 facility 시설

112. 형용사 어휘 familiar

그 의료 센터는 환자들을 편안하게 해 주기 위해 조용하고 그들에게 친숙한 음악을 틀어 준다.

(A) 비밀의, 기밀의 (B) 익숙한, 친숙한 (C) 유능한 (D) 재능 있는

어휘 soothing 진정시키는, 위로하는 in order to do ~하기 위해 put ~ at ease ~을 편안하게 해 주다

113. 형용사 자리

다큐멘터리 〈Circular Path〉에는 흥미진진한 자동차 경주 세계의 극적인 장면들이 나온다.

해설 빈칸 앞에 동사 includes가 있고 뒤에는 명사 scenes가 있으므로 빈칸은 명사를 수식하는 형용사 자리이다. 따라서 (B) dramatic이 정답이다.

어휘 documentary 다큐멘터리 include 포함하다 dramatic 극적인 scene 장면 exciting 신나는, 흥미진진한

114. 동사 어휘 notice

아침에 Ms. Broussard가 사무실에 도착했을 때 그녀는 복도 끝에 있는 창문이 열려 있었다는 걸 알아차렸다.

(A) 검사하다 (B) 납득시키다 (C) 알아차리다 (D) 흘끗 보다

어휘 corridor 복도

115. 부사 자리

Harness Beverages에서 새로 나온 탄산음료 광고는 소비자의 관심을 사로잡는 데 대체로 실패했다.

해설 빈칸은 동사 failed를 수식하는 자리이므로 선택지 중 부사인 (B) largely가 정답이다.

어휘 ad campaign 광고 캠페인 largely 대체로, 크게 fail 실패하다 interest 관심, 흥미

116. 전치사 어휘 beyond

주문하신 물건들이 도착했을 때 내용물이 수리할 수 없을 정도로 파손되어 있다면 환불을 받을 수 있습니다.

(A) ~을 가로질러 (B) ~ 외에도 (C) ~을 넘어서 (D) ~을 제외하고

해설 빈칸 뒤의 repair와 함께 쓰여 수리할 수 없을 정도로 파손되었다는 내용이 되는 게 자연스러우므로 (C) beyond가 정답이다.

어휘 contents 내용물 damaged 손상된, 파손된 beyond repair 수리가 불가능한 receive a refund 환불을 받다

117. 능동태

Manchester Dance Troupe은 5월 29일에 Verona Theater에서 인기 공연인 〈Waltzing Wonderland〉를 선보일 것이다.

해설 빈칸 뒤에 목적어(its famous show)가 있으므로 빈칸에는 능동태가 들어가야 한다. 따라서 (A) will perform이 정답이다.

어휘 troupe 공연단 perform 공연하다

118. 동사 어휘 analyze

Webmax의 전문가들은 귀하의 사이트로 유입되는 모든 트래픽 데이터를 분석하여 잠재 고객을 공략할 최고의 방법을 결정하는 데 도움을 드립니다.

(A) 안심시키다 (B) 끌어들이다 (C) 소유하다 (D) 분석하다

어휘 traffic 전산망에서 전송되는 정보의 양[흐름]; 교통(량) determine 결정하다 target 대상으로 삼다, 겨냥하다 potential 잠재적인

119. 명사 자리

그 연구는 더 많은 정부 보조금 제공이 더 높은 대학 진학률에 직접 기여했다는 것을 확인해 주었다.

해설 빈칸에는 college와 결합하여 전치사 to의 목적어 역할을 할 수 있는 말이 들어가야 한다. 따라서 선택지 중 명사인 (A) admission이 정답이다.

어휘 confirm 확인해 주다 government grant 정부 보조금 lead to ~로 이어지다 directly 직접적으로

120. 부사 어휘 significantly

그 핸드백들은 같은 브랜드였지만 다른 공장에서 생산되었기 때문에 품질이 상당히 달랐다.

(A) 상당히, 크게 (B) 지속적으로 (C) 적절히 (D) 밝게

어휘 due to ~ 때문에 produce 생산하다 quality 품질 differ 다르다

121. 의문 대명사 who

부장은 누가 차장직으로 승진될 것인지 발표하기 위해 막판에 회의를 잡았다.

해설 빈칸에는 동사 announce의 목적어인 명사절을 이끄는 접속사가 들어가야 한다. 빈칸 뒤에 주어가 없는 불완전한 절이 이어지므로 명사절을 이끄는 의문 대명사인 (A) who가 정답이다.

어휘 schedule 일정을 잡다, 예정하다 last-minute 마지막 순간의, 막바지의 promote 승진하다; 홍보하다 assistant director 차장

122. 형용사 어휘 primary

유권자들이 Ms. Grady를 지지하는 주요 이유 중 하나는 공공시설을 개선하겠다는 그녀의 약속 때문이다.

(A) 신속한 (B) 주요한 (C) 근면한 (D) 민감한

어휘 voter 투표자, 유권자 support 지지 improve 개선하다 public facilities 공공시설

123. 명사 어휘 surplus

현재 판매 추세가 계속된다면 Gilana Autos는 12월 말에 200만 달러의 예산 흑자를 낼 것이다.

(A) 절차 (B) 흑자, 잉여 (C) 협상 (D) 조립

어휘 current 현재의 trend 추세, 동향 budget 예산 at the end of ~의 말에

124. 부사 자리

얼룩 제거제가 얼마나 효과적으로 작용하는지는 그것이 직물에 남아 있는 시간에 의해 결정된다.

해설 빈칸은 명사절을 이끄는 의문 부사 How를 수식하는 자리이므로 빈칸에는 형용사나 부사가 들어갈 수 있다. 이때 how 이하의 절이 불완전하면 형용사, 완전하면 부사를 쓰는데, 〈주어(the stain remover)+자동사(works)〉 구조로 완전한 절이 이어지므로 부사인 (D) effectively가 정답이다.

어휘 stain remover 얼룩 제거제 work 작동하다, 작용하다 depend on ~에 의존하다, ~에 따라 결정되다 fabric 천, 직물

125. 분사 자리

봄 학기 수업에 등록한 학생들뿐 아니라 교수진도 환영회에 참석하는 것이 권장된다.

해설 빈칸 뒤에 본동사인 are encouraged가 있는 것으로 보아 '------- in classes for the spring term'은 students를 수식하는 역할을 한다는 걸 알 수 있다. 따라서 선택지 중 형용사 역할을 할 수 있는 과거분사인 (B) enrolled가 정답이다. 여기에서 enroll은 '등록시키다'라는 뜻의 타동사로 쓰였으며, 학생들 및 교수진이 '등록되었다'는 수동의 의미가 되어야 하므로 who were enrolled에서 〈관계대명사+be동사〉인 who were가 생략되고 과거분사 enrolled만 남은 축약관계사절로 볼 수 있다.

어휘 faculty member 교수진 term 학기; 용어 be encouraged to do ~하도록 장려되다 attend 참석하다 reception 환영회; (호텔의) 프런트

126. 부사 어휘 alike

Nix Industrial이 만든 내구성 있는 전동 공구는 아마추어와 전문가 모두에게 적합하다.

(A) 둘 다, 똑같이 (B) 거의 (C) 매우 (D) 정당하게

어휘 durable 내구성이 있는, 오래가는 power tool 전동 공구 suitable for ~에 적합한 amateur 아마추어, 비전문가 professional 전문가; 전문적인

127. 명사 자리+어휘

학회 발표자 대부분은 그 나라의 중부 지역에 살고 있다.

해설 빈칸 앞에 소유한정사 conference's가 있고 뒤에는 동사 live가 있으므로 빈칸은 한정사의 수식을 받는 명사 자리이다. (B) presentations와 (C) presenters가 정답 후보인데 문맥상 특정 지역에 사는 주체는 사람이어야 하므로 '발표자'를 뜻하는 (C) presenters가 정답이다.

어휘 conference 학회, 회의 central 중앙의 region 지역

128. 형용사 어휘 successful

새로운 안전 정책의 성공적인 이행은 몇 주 또는 그 이상이 걸릴 수 있다.

(A) 명백한 (B) 성공적인 (C) 운이 좋은 (D) 우연한

어휘 implementation 이행, 실행 policy 정책, 방침

129. 분사 자리

Sigmund Insurance의 관리자들은 회사 비전에 집중한 직원들을 승진시킬 가능성이 더 높다.

해설 빈칸에는 employees를 뒤에서 수식할 수 있는 말이 들어가야 한다. 따라서 선택지 중 형용사 역할을 할 수 있는 현재분사인 (A) focusing이 정답이다.

어휘 insurance 보험 be likely to do ~할 것 같다 focus on ~에 초점을 맞추다 mission statement 강령, 사명 선언

130. 동사 어휘 comply

국내에서 운영되는 모든 기업은 이러한 데이터 보호 조치를 준수해야 한다.

(A) 결합하다 (B) 방해하다 (C) 따르다, 준수하다 (D) 연상하다, 관련시키다

어휘 operate 운영하다 protection 보호 measure 조치

PART 6

131-134 기사

볼티모어 (4월 9일)—헬스클럽 체인점인 Power Gym은 회원권 옵션의 변경 사항을 [131]발표했다. 이 회사의 본사 대변인인 Frank Jacobs는 고객 의견을 바탕으로 정책을 조정하고 있다고 말했다.

[132]헬스클럽 이용자들은 더 이상 연간 회원권을 구매할 필요가 없을 것이다. 새로운 정책으로 인해 사람들은 필요에 따라 하루, 일주일, 또는 한 달 정기권을 구매할 수 있게 된다. 이는 헬스클럽을 편리하고 [133]이용하기 쉽게 만들겠다는 회사의 약속을 뒷받침할 것이다. 시내에 있는 헬스클럽의 주요 부지에 주차장도 추가될 것이다. 프로젝트 [134]공사는 6월 중에 시작될 것이다.

어휘 fitness club 헬스클럽 membership 회원 자격, 회원권 spokesperson 대변인 head office 본사 adjust 조정하다 based on ~에 근거하여 pass 출입증, 통행증 commitment 약속; 전념 convenient 편리한 parking garage 주차장 site 현장, 부지 downtown 시내에

131. 동사 어휘 announce

(A) 반대하다 (B) 협력하다 (C) 받다 (D) 발표하다

132. 알맞은 문장 고르기

(A) 헬스클럽 이용자들은 더 이상 연간 회원권을 구매할 필요가 없을 것이다.
(B) Power Gym은 수요를 따라잡기 위해 새로운 직원을 구하고 있다.
(C) 그 체인점은 회원들을 사로잡는 수업으로 동부 해안 지역에서 잘 알려져 있다.
(D) Power Gym에서는 강사들이 추천하는 운동 기구를 판매한다.

해설 빈칸 앞에서 정책을 조정하고 있다고 했고 뒤에서는 새로운 정책을 구체적으로 설명하고 있으므로 빈칸에는 새로운 정책이 무엇인지 소개하는 내용이 들어가야 한다. 따라서 (A)가 정답이다.

어휘 keep up with ~에 뒤지지 않다 demand 수요 engaging 남을 매혹하는 workout 운동 gear 장비 instructor 강사

133. 형용사 자리

해설 빈칸 앞에 형용사 convenient가 등위접속사 and로 병렬 연결되어 있으므로 빈칸에도 동일한 품사가 들어가야 한다. 따라서 형용사인 (C) accessible이 정답이다.

134. 명사 어휘 construction

(A) 도움 (B) 공사 (C) 입장, 입구 (D) 사양

135-138 기사

이든턴 해양 박물관의 모형 보트

8월 1일부터 8월 31일까지 이든턴 해양 박물관에서 〈To the Seas〉를 주최할 예정이다. 이 [135]전시회에서는 실제로 쓰는 것과 매우 유사하게 제작된 모형 보트를 선보인다. 전시회는 선원들이 (바다에서는) 나약한 존재라는 것과 어떻게 그들의 안전이 바다에 대한 이해와 존중[136]에 달려 있는지에 관해 방문객들에게 교육도 진행한다. 박물관을 방문하는 사람들은 새로운 자동 안내 오디오 관람 장비를 [137]써 볼 수도 있다. [138]각 전시품을 자신의 속도로 관람해 보라. 〈To the Seas〉는 박물관 입장료 정가에 포함되어 있다.

어휘 maritime 바다의, 해양의 host 주최하다 feature 특징으로 하다, 특별히 선보이다 craft (특히 손으로) 공예품을 만들다 counterpart (동일한 지위의) 상대편, 대응물 fragility 부서지기 쉬움 rely on ~에 의존하다 admission 입장료

135. 명사 어휘 exhibit

(A) 전시회 (B) 수필 (C) 상 (D) 토너먼트

136. 전치사 어휘 on

(A) ~에 (B) ~와 함께 (C) ~ 안으로 (D) ~로서

해설 빈칸 앞의 동사 relies와 함께 쓰여 선원들의 안전이 바다에 대한 이해와 존중에 달려 있다는 내용이 되는 게 자연스러우므로 (A) on이 정답이다.

137. 조동사 can

해설 문맥상 장비를 써 볼 수 있다는 '가능성'을 나타내는 게 적절하므로 (D) can also try가 정답이다. 또한 첫 문장에서 미래 시제(will host)로 8월에 전시회가 있을 것이라고 했으며, 이후 이어지는 내용은 모두 그 전시회에 대한 설명이므로 현재진행 시제인 (A)와 과거 시제인 (B), 현재완료 시제인 (C)는 모두 답이 될 수 없다.

138. 알맞은 문장 고르기

(A) 경험이 풍부하고 상냥한 가이드의 지원을 환영한다.
(B) 폐쇄는 일시적일 것으로 예상된다.
(C) 다행히도 자원봉사자들은 매우 헌신적이다.
(D) 각 전시품을 자신의 속도로 관람해 보라.

해설 빈칸 앞에서 박물관 방문객들은 자동 안내 오디오 관람 장비를 써 볼 수 있다고 한 것으로 보아 방문객들은 스스로 전시품을 감상할 수 있음을 추론할 수 있다. 따라서 빈칸에는 방문객들이 각자의 속도대로 전시품을 탐색하라는 내용인 (D)가 들어가는 게 적절하다.

어휘 experienced 경험 많은, 노련한 closure 폐쇄 temporary 일시적인 dedicated 헌신적인 explore 탐구하다, 알아보다

139-142 이메일

수신: Miyo Kudo
발신: Sebastian Beneventi
날짜: 7월 2일
제목: 상품 제안 회의

Ms. Kudo께,

당신의 수제 비누를 논의하기 위해 7월 12일로 예정된 상품 제안 회의에 관한 실망스러운 소식이 있습니다. 우리는 다른 피치 못할 일 때문에 이 [139]약속을 다시 잡아야 합니다. 우리 팀은 웨스트베리 무역 박람회에 참가하기로 결정했기 때문에 우리의 모든 시간과 노력을 이 [140]중

요한 행사에 쏟아야 합니다.

[141]하지만 우리는 여전히 당신의 제품군에 관심이 많습니다. 우리는 당신의 비누가 우리의 현재 상품 목록을 잘 보완할 것이라고 믿습니다. 무역 박람회는 7월 25일에 열리기 때문에 그 후에 당신에게 [142]다시 연락할 계획입니다. 이로 인해 불편을 끼쳐 드려 죄송합니다.

Sebastian Beneventi
Appling Health 구매 담당자

어휘 pitch meeting (상품, 서비스 등의) 제안 회의, (아이디어 등을 보여 주는) 발표회 reschedule 일정을 다시 잡다 obligation 의무, 책무 trade fair 무역 박람회 be devoted to ~에 전념하다 complement 보완하다 inventory 상품 목록, 재고 품목 take place 열리다, 일어나다 apologize 사과하다 inconvenience 불편 cause 일으키다, 야기하다

139. 명사 어휘 appointment

(A) 약속 (B) 공연 (C) (호텔 방, 좌석 등의) 예약 (D) 리허설

140. 형용사 자리

해설 빈칸 앞에 지시형용사 this가 있고 뒤에는 명사 event가 있으므로 빈칸은 명사를 수식하는 형용사 자리이다. 따라서 (B) critical이 정답이다.

141. 알맞은 문장 고르기

(A) 다들 당신이 훌륭한 아이디어를 많이 냈다고 생각했습니다.
(B) 견본 제품을 준비하는 데 시간이 오래 걸립니다.
(C) 우리가 논의한 바와 같이 경력이 요구됩니다.
(D) 하지만 우리는 여전히 당신의 제품군에 관심이 많습니다.

해설 빈칸 앞에 모든 시간과 노력을 무역 박람회에 쏟아야 해서 회의 일정을 다시 잡아야 한다는 내용이 나오고, 빈칸 뒤에는 Ms. Kudo의 비누가 상품 목록을 잘 보완할 것이라는 상반된 내용이 나오므로 빈칸에는 Ms. Kudo의 제품에 관심이 없는 게 아니라는 내용이 들어가는 게 적절하다. 따라서 (D)가 정답이다.

어휘 make a point 생각을 밝히다 previous 예전의

142. 동사 어휘 reconnect

(A) 동의하다 (B) 다시 연락하다 (C) 경쟁하다 (D) 동정하다

143-146 보도 자료

웰링턴 (9월 12일)—Kerwyn Mart는 오후 10시 폐점을 하지 않고 24시간 영업 일정을 채택할 계획이다. [143]더 길어진 영업시간은 10월 1일부터 시작될 예정이다. 많은 고객들은 이같은 변화가 매우 편리하다는 것을 [144]알게 될 텐데, 특히 불규칙적으로 일하거나 갑자기 생필품이 필요한 고객들이 그러할 것이다.

"우리는 고객들에게 서비스를 제공할 수 있는 기회를 더 많이 갖게 되어 기쁩니다."라고 Kerwyn Mart의 대변인인 Paul Yates가 말했다. "우리는 계산대에 새로운 직원을 몇 명 고용해야 하기 때문에 이는 [145]동시에 고용 기회를 창출할 것입니다. 매장의 조명과 난방은 보안상의 이유와 우리 진열대 비축 팀의 편의를 위해 이미 24시간 내내 켜져 있습니다. [146]따라서 이것은 우리의 관리비를 크게 증가시키지 않을 것으로 예상됩니다."

Kerwyn Mart는 웰링턴 시에 3개의 지점이 있다.

어휘 abandon 포기하다, 버리다 adopt 채택하다 be set to do ~하도록 예정되어 있다 convenient 편리한 irregular 불규칙한 essential 필수적인 unexpectedly 뜻밖에, 갑자기 employment 고용 opportunity 기회 hire 고용하다 checkout 계산대 around the clock 24시간 내내 security 보안 comfort 안락, 편안 shelf 선반 stock 상품을 채우다 location 지점; 위치, 장소 limit (장소 등의) 경계; 한계

143. 형용사 어휘 longer

(A) 사소한 (B) 역사적인 (C) 더 깨끗한 (D) 더 긴

144. 미래 시제

해설 빈칸 앞에 보도 자료 작성 날짜는 9월 12일이고 24시간 영업 시작일은 10월 1일부터라는 내용이 있다. 따라서 주어인 Many customers는 영업시간의 변화로 인한 효과를 앞으로 알게 될 것이므로 미래 시제인 (D) will find가 정답이다.

145. 접속부사 어휘 at the same time

(A) 그럼에도 불구하고 (B) 예를 들어 (C) 동시에 (D) 그렇지 않다면

해설 빈칸 뒤에 첫 번째 절이 있고 그 뒤에 접속사 as로 두 번째 절이 연결되어 있는 것으로 보아 빈칸은 접속부사 자리이므로 접속사 if로 시작하는 (D) If not은 오답이다.

146. 알맞은 문장 고르기

(A) 우리는 이런 일이 다시 발생하는 걸 방지하고 싶습니다.
(B) 몇 사람이 승진 대상으로 고려되고 있습니다.
(C) 따라서 이것은 우리의 관리비를 크게 증가시키지 않을 것으로 예상됩니다.
(D) 그렇지 않으면 매장 배치를 변경해야 할 것입니다.

해설 빈칸 앞에서 가게의 조명과 난방이 이미 24시간 내내 켜져 있다고 했으므로 빈칸에는 영업시간 연장이 관리비 증가에 큰 영향을 주지 않을 것이라는 내용이 들어가는 게 적절하다. 따라서 (C)가 정답이다.

어휘 consider 고려하다 promotion 승진 utility 공공요금 otherwise 그렇지 않으면 layout 배치

PART 7

147-148 이메일

수신: Maria Tejada
발신: Elliot Racette
날짜: 8월 4일
제목: 올버니 주민 센터

Ms. Tejada께,

올버니 주민 센터는 현재 8월 25일에 열리는 연례 모금 행사를 준비 중이며 [147]지역 업체들에 경품 추첨에 사용할 물품 기증을 요청하고 있습니다. 물품의 크기는 상관이 없습니다.

저희 직원 중 한 명이 8월 10일이 있는 주에 귀하의 기증품을 가지러 갈 수 있습니다. 덧붙여 [148]8월 20일에 〈The Albany Herald〉는 후원한 모든 업체의 목록을 게재할 것입니다. 이 행사에서 저희를 돕는 것을 고려해 주시기 바랍니다.

Elliot Racette
올버니 주민 센터, 책임자

어휘 fundraiser 모금 행사 donate 기부하다, 기증하다 merchandise 물품, 상품 prize drawing 경품 추첨 pick up ~을 찾아오다, ~을 수령하다 additionally 덧붙여, 게다가 run (광고나 기사 등을) 싣다, 게재하다 sponsorship 후원 consider 고려하다 assist 돕다

147. Mr. Racette가 이메일을 보낸 이유는 무엇인가?

(A) 물품을 요청하기 위해
(B) 기증품에 대해 업체에 감사하기 위해
(C) 초대를 거절하기 위해
(D) 수상자에게 알리기 위해

해설 주제/목적
경품 추첨에 사용할 물품 기증을 요청하고 있으므로 (A)가 정답이다.

148. 이메일에 따르면, 8월 20일에 무슨 일이 일어날 것인가?

(A) 몇 가지 물품을 수령할 것이다.
(B) 지역 모금 행사가 열릴 것이다.
(C) 주민 센터가 다시 문을 열 것이다.
(D) 후원자 명단이 공개될 것이다.

해설 세부 사항
8월 20일에 〈The Albany Herald〉가 후원 업체 목록을 게재할 것이라고 했으므로 (D)가 정답이다.

패러프레이징 will run a list of every business that has provided sponsorship → A list of sponsors will be publicized.

어휘 publicize 알리다, 공표하다

149-150 후기

후기 카테고리: 전자 제품
제품: Bessel 비디오폰 초인종
후기 작성자: Heather Arroyo

제 친구가 Chimetime 초인종을 구입하고서 극찬을 했지만 저는 좀 더 저렴한 것을 찾고 있었습니다. 저희 집 현관에 Bessel 비디오폰 초인종을 달아 봤는데 마음에 드네요. 언제든지 스마트폰에서 확인할 수 있고 정보를 클라우드에 무선으로 업로드할 수 있습니다. 날씨에 구애받지 않으며 [149]움직임이 감지될 때만 켜지기 때문에 배터리가 오래갑니다. 설치도 쉬웠습니다. 저는 이 제품을 건물 입구를 감시할 방법을 찾는 사람들에게 강력히 추천하고 싶어요. 사실 [150]저는 뒷문에도 하나 설치하고 싶어요!

어휘 electronics 전자 제품 doorbell 초인종 rave 극찬하다 affordable (가격이) 알맞은, 저렴한 wirelessly 무선으로 suitable for ~에 적합한 last 지속되다 movement 움직임 detect 감지하다 setup 설치 recommend 추천하다 monitor 감시하다 property 건물, 소유지

149. Bessel 초인종에 대해 암시된 것은 무엇인가?

(A) Chimetime 초인종보다 비싸다.
(B) 고속 충전되는 배터리가 있다.
(C) 움직임에 의해 작동된다.
(D) 다양한 사운드 옵션을 제공한다.

해설 추론/암시
움직임이 감지될 때만 켜진다고 했으므로 (C)가 정답이다.

패러프레이징 it only turns on when movement is detected → They are activated by motion.

150. 후기를 게시한 후 Ms. Arroyo가 했을 것 같은 일은 무엇인가?

(A) 친구와 제품을 교환했다.
(B) 제조업체에 교체 부품을 요청했다.
(C) 자신의 전화기에 사용 설명서를 다운로드했다.
(D) 또 다른 Bessel 초인종을 구입했다.

해설 추론/암시
뒷문에도 Bessel 초인종을 설치하고 싶다고 했으므로 후기를 게시한 후 하나 더 샀을 것임을 유추할 수 있다. 따라서 (D)가 정답이다.

151-152 문자 메시지

Edward Duvall [오후 2:03] 안녕하세요, Joan. 고객 설문 조사 제출 기한이 지났으니 우리가 받은 설문 조사 결과를 분석하는 작업을 시작할게요.

Joan Salgado [오후 2:05] 고마워요! 이번에는 좀 더 좋은 반응을 얻었으면 좋겠어요. 지난 설문 조사에 따르면 [151]많은 손님이 투숙에 실망했는데, 특히 일반실에 묵었던 분들이 그랬지요.

Edward Duvall [오후 2:07] 음, 주된 불만은 객실 관리 문제였는데 그건 해결되었어요.

Joan Salgado [오후 2:08] 맞아요.

Edward Duvall [오후 2:10] [152]저는 로비에 가져다 놓은 새 소파와 의자에 대해 사람들이 어떻게 생각하는지 알아보는 것에 관심이 있어요. 그것들은 앉기에 훨씬 더 푹신하고 좋거든요.

Joan Salgado [오후 2:11] 다들 그렇게 말하고 있어요. 저는 아직 직접 앉아 볼 기회가 없었지만요.

어휘 deadline 기한 survey 설문 조사 work on ~을 작업하다 analyze 분석하다 result 결과 response 대답, 반응 be disappointed with ~에 실망하다 especially 특히 standard room 일반실 main 주된 complaint 불평, 불만 housekeeping (호텔의) 시설 관리 issue 문제, 사안 resolve 해결하다

151. 메시지 작성자들은 어디에서 근무하겠는가?

(A) 옷 가게에서

(B) 호텔에서
(C) 슈퍼마켓에서
(D) 가정용품점에서

해설 추론/암시
일반실에 묵은 사람들이 투숙에 실망했다고 하는 것으로 보아 두 사람은 호텔에서 근무하고 있음을 추론할 수 있다. 따라서 (B)가 정답이다.

152. 오후 2시 11분에 Ms. Salgado가 "다들 그렇게 말하고 있어요"라고 쓸 때 그녀가 의미하는 것은 무엇이겠는가?

(A) 입구가 더 현대적으로 보인다고 생각한다.
(B) 몇 가지 가구가 이제 더 안락해졌다고 생각한다.
(C) 오류가 빨리 해결되기를 바란다.
(D) Mr. Duvall이 열심히 일했다는 것에 동의한다.

해설 의도 파악
오후 2시 10분에 Mr. Duvall이 새로운 소파와 의자가 더 푹신하다고 한 말에 대한 답변이다. 또한 Ms. Salgado가 자신은 아직 앉아 본 적이 없다고 덧붙인 것으로 보아 새 가구가 예전 것보다 더 좋아졌다고 추측하는 것이므로 (B)가 정답이다.

패러프레이징 They are a lot softer and nicer to sit on. → some furniture is more comfortable now

153-154 기사

> **Bratton 스마트워치 리콜**
>
> 9월 3일—스마트워치 제조업체인 Bratton이 출시한 지 불과 2주 만에 Dola-9 스마트워치 제품군을 리콜한다고 발표했다. 심각한 부상은 보고되지 않았지만 [153]기기의 배터리가 너무 뜨거워질 수 있기 때문에 사용자에게 화상 위험이 있다.
>
> 결함이 있는 기기를 가진 고객은 교환 또는 전액 환불을 받을 수 있다. [154]Dola-9 스마트워치를 가지고 있는 사람은 1-800-555-7932로 회사에 연락해야 한다. 연결되고 나서 일련번호를 입력하면 다음에 무슨 절차를 거쳐야 하는지 자동으로 안내된다. 추가로 문의 사항이 있는 사람들 또한 고객 서비스 팀에 메시지를 남길 수 있다.

어휘 recall 리콜, 회수 manufacturer 제조업체 serious 심각한 injury 부상 present (문제 등을) 야기하다 burn 화상 device 기기, 장치 faulty 결함이 있는 be eligible for ~할 자격이 있다 replacement 교체, 교환 full refund 전액 환불 contact 연락하다 connect 연결하다 input 입력하다 serial number 일련번호 inform 알리다 further 추가의 inquiry 문의

153. Dola-9 스마트워치에 대해 시사된 것은 무엇인가?

(A) 배터리가 과열될 수 있다.
(B) 교체하는 데 2주가 걸린다.
(C) 이동 거리가 올바르게 기록되지 않는다.
(D) 심각한 부상을 초래했다.

해설 NOT/True
스마트워치의 배터리가 너무 뜨거워질 수 있다고 했으므로 (A)가 정답이다.

패러프레이징 may get too hot → can overheat

154. 기사는 Dola-9 소유자들에게 먼저 무엇을 할 것을 권하는가?

(A) 매장 방문하기
(B) 기기 초기화하기
(C) 고객 상담 번호로 전화하기
(D) 고객 서비스에 이메일 보내기

해설 세부 사항
Dola-9 스마트워치를 갖고 있는 사람들은 회사에 연락하라고 했는데, 연결되면 어떤 조치를 취해야 할지 안내받을 수 있다고 했으므로 (C)가 정답이다.

155-157 온라인 양식

> Quesada Inc.
> 707 시티 뷰 스트리트
> 머틀 비치, 사우스캐롤라이나 29577
>
> **고객 유형:** [V] 신규 [ ] 기존 **이름:** Patrick Carter
> **날짜:** 4월 20일 **이메일 주소:** p.carter@carterandbrown.com
> **전화번호:** 843-555-4628 **하루 중 통화하기 가장 좋은 시간:** 오전
>
> **추가 의견/메모:** [156]제 회계 회사에서 사용하기 위해 해러핸 스트리트에 있는 사무실 단지를 얼마 전에 매입했습니다. 인터넷 검색을 통해 귀사의 서비스에 대한 많은 추천글을 찾았습니다. [157]앞쪽 화단에 식물을 옮겨 심고 잔디와 덤불을 깔끔하게 유지하는 것을 도와주셨으면 합니다. [155]첫 방문 비용과 지속적인 유지비에 대한 대략적인 견적을 제시해 주십시오. 감사합니다.

어휘 comment 의견, 논평 complex (건물) 단지 recommendation 추천 assist with ~을 돕다 replant 옮겨 심다 flowerbed 화단 tidy 정돈된 estimate 견적(서) approximate 대략의 initial 처음의, 초기의 ongoing 진행 중인 upkeep 유지(비)

155. Mr. Carter가 양식을 작성한 이유는 무엇인가?

(A) 요금에 이의를 제기하기 위해
(B) 어떤 정보를 요청하기 위해
(C) 불평을 하기 위해
(D) 서비스를 추천하기 위해

해설 주제/목적
Mr. Carter는 견적 정보를 요청하기 위해 양식을 작성했으므로 (B)가 정답이다.

어휘 dispute 이의를 제기하다 charge 요금 make a complaint 불평하다, 민원을 제기하다

156. Mr. Carter에 대해 암시된 것은 무엇인가?

(A) Quesada Inc.의 예전 직원이다.
(B) 최근에 건물을 구입했다.
(C) 전화번호를 바꿨다.
(D) 법인 계좌를 해지했다.

해설 추론/암시
사무실 단지를 얼마 전에 매입했다고 했으므로 (B)가 정답이다.

패러프레이징 have just bought the office complex → recently purchased a building

157. Quesada Inc.는 무엇이겠는가?

(A) 택배 회사
(B) 인터넷 서비스 공급업체
(C) 회계 회사
(D) 조경 회사

해설 추론/암시
화단에 식물을 심고 잔디와 덤불 관리를 도와 달라고 했으므로 Quesada Inc.는 조경 회사임을 추론할 수 있다. 따라서 (D)가 정답이다.

158-160 설명서

Senatobia Appliances
모델: RC-9203

최대 용량: 5.3 세제곱피트
모터 유형: 디지털 인버터 모터
규격: 폭 27인치 x 높이 38.7인치 x 깊이 34.5인치

1. [159B]**분무기를 이용하여** [158]**드럼의 내부에 농도가 강한 백식초를 도포하세요.**
2. 5분간 그대로 두었다가 극세사 천으로 닦아 내세요.
3. [158]**세제통** [159C]**서랍을** 꺼내 따뜻한 비눗물을 이용해 손으로 닦은 후 제자리에 놓으세요.
4. 세제통에 백식초 두 컵을 채우세요.
5. 드럼 내부에 베이킹 소다를 골고루 뿌린 후 [158]**안에 옷가지를 넣지** 않고 가장 뜨거운 물 설정으로 한 번 돌리세요.
6. [159A]**문을 열고 무언가를 받쳐 문이 저절로 닫히지 않도록 하여 내부**가 자연 건조되도록 하세요.
7. [160]**이 과정을 몇 달에 한 번 반복하여 모든 부품이 정기적으로 철저히 청소되도록 하세요.**

어휘 capacity 용량 cubic 세제곱의 dimension 크기, 치수 coat 도포하다, 칠하다 interior 내부 drum 드럼, 원통 strength 농도, 함량 vinegar 식초 spray bottle 분무기 wipe 닦다 microfiber 극세사 pull out ~을 빼다, ~을 꺼내다 detergent 세제 replace 제자리에 두다 fill A with B A를 B로 채우다 sprinkle 뿌리다 cycle (기계 작동 등에서의) 주기, 사이클 air dry 자연 건조하다 prop 받치다 on one's own 자기 스스로, 혼자서 ensure 확실하게 하다 deeply 깊이, 철저히 regularly 정기적으로

158. 설명서는 어떤 종류의 장치에 사용되겠는가?

(A) 세탁기
(B) 진공청소기
(C) 오븐
(D) 커피 메이커

해설 추론/암시
드럼, 세제통, 옷가지 등을 통해 세탁기와 관련된 설명서라는 걸 알 수 있으므로 (A)가 정답이다.

159. 설명서에 나온 단계가 아닌 것은 무엇인가?

(A) 문 열어 두기
(B) 액체 뿌리기
(C) 서랍 제거하기
(D) 온도 테스트하기

해설 NOT/True
온도를 테스트하는 것과 관련된 내용은 없으므로 (D)가 정답이다.

패러프레이징 (A) opening the door and propping something against it so it does not close → Leaving a door open
(C) Pull out the detergent dispenser drawer → Removing a drawer

160. 사용자가 설명서를 따를 이유는 무엇이겠는가?

(A) 가전제품의 소음을 줄이기 위해
(B) 기계를 처음 사용하기 전에 설정하기 위해
(C) 일부 기능이 제대로 작동하는지 확인하기 위해
(D) 몇몇 부품이 철저히 청소되도록 하기 위해

해설 세부 사항
이 과정을 몇 달에 한 번 반복하여 모든 부품이 철저히 청소되도록 하라고 했으므로 (D)가 정답이다.

161-163 회람

수신: 전 직원
발신: Adrian Seda
제목: 개봉 박두
날짜: 3월 14일

아시다시피 우리는 [161]웹사이트에 더 많은 트래픽을 유입시키는 것에 관심이 있습니다. 이 점을 고려하여 우리는 매주 업데이트되는 [161]여행 블로그를 추가할 예정입니다. [163]블로그에는 우리가 패키지 상품을 제공하는 여행지에 대한 기사가 포함될 것입니다. 이상적으로는 그것들이 이러한 장소들에 대한 관심을 불러일으킬 것입니다. 이렇게 하면 예약이 더 늘어날 수 있습니다.

[162]제가 첫 번째 기사를 쓸 텐데, 그것은 제가 최근에 인솔했던 인도네시아 투어에 관한 내용이 될 겁니다. 다른 직원들도 기고해 주시기를 장려하는 바이며 고객들로부터의 콘텐츠도 환영하는데, 고객들은 콘텐츠를 제공하는 대가로 할인을 받을 수 있습니다. 기사에 포함된 모든 사진은 전문적으로 보여야 하지만 필요한 경우 편집할 수 있습니다. 추가 계획은 다음 직원 회의에서 논의될 것입니다.

어휘 in light of ~에 비추어, ~을 고려하여 include 포함하다 article 글, 기사 destination 목적지 package 패키지 상품 lead to ~로 이어지다 be encouraged to do ~하도록 장려되다 contribute 기고하다, 기여하다 supply 공급하다 in exchange for ~ 대신에, ~와 교환하여 professional 전문가의, 전문적인 edit 편집하다

161. Mr. Seda가 회람을 보낸 이유는 무엇인가?

(A) 새로운 휴가 정책을 설명하기 위해
(B) 직원들에게 소프트웨어를 업데이트할 것을 상기시키기 위해
(C) 어디를 방문할지 추천을 요청하기 위해
(D) 웹사이트의 새로운 섹션을 알리기 위해

해설 주제/목적
웹사이트에 여행 블로그를 추가할 것이라고 했으므로 (D)가 정답이다.

162. Mr. Seda는 누구이겠는가?

(A) 지역 언론인
(B) 여행 가이드
(C) 전문 사진작가
(D) 잡지 편집자

해설 추론/암시
최근에 인도네시아 투어를 인솔했다고 한 것으로 보아 여행 가이드임을 유추할 수 있다. 따라서 (B)가 정답이다.

163. [1], [2], [3], [4]로 표시된 위치 중 다음 문장이 들어가기에 가장 적절한 곳은?

"이상적으로는 그것들이 이러한 장소들에 대한 관심을 불러일으킬 것입니다."

해설 문장 삽입
주어진 문장의 they는 기사(articles)를, these places는 패키지 상품으로 제공하는 여행지(the destinations where we offer packages)를 각각 가리키므로, 주어진 문장은 해당 내용이 언급되고 난 다음에 들어가는 것이 적절하다. 따라서 (B)가 정답이다.

164-167 안내 책자

더 나은 내일을 위해 McInnis Institute에서 오늘 교육을 받으세요!

에어컨 수리 과정
McInnis Institute는 30년 이상 수리 기사들을 교육하고 지원해 왔습니다. [164]**에어컨 서비스는 항상 수요가 많은데, 정기적인 유지 보수가 이루어지는 겨울철에도 그러합니다.** 따라서 에어컨 수리 기사로서 여러분은 합리적인 시급에 [164]**꾸준한 일감을 누릴 수 있습니다.**

현재 업무에 지장을 주지 않도록 저녁 또는 주말 과정 중에 공부하세요. 프로그램을 2년 안에 마칠 수 있고, 6개월 수습 기간이 포함되어 있습니다.

왜 McInnis Institute를 선택할까요?
– 실무 경험이 있는 전문 강사들
– 필요한 모든 장비가 제공되며 가지셔도 됩니다. 또는 [165]**본인의 장비를 가져와서 수업료의 1퍼센트를 할인받으세요.**
– [166]**학생들은 분기별 네트워킹 만찬에 초대되어 잠재 고용주를 만날 수 있습니다.**
– 졸업생들은 지역, 지구 및 전국 단위의 일자리를 검색할 수 있는 우리의 일자리 데이터베이스에 독점적으로 접속할 수 있습니다.
– 일시불을 준비할 필요 없이 [167]**수업료를 월납할 수 있습니다.**

당신의 수입 잠재력을 이끌어 내세요!

	평균 시급: 최근 졸업생	평균 시급: 3년 경력직
일반 서비스	50달러	95달러
긴급 출동	90달러	150달러

곧 있을 과정에 등록하시거나 자세한 내용을 알아보시려면 저희 웹사이트 www.mcinnisinst.com을 방문해 주십시오.

어휘 technician 기사, 기술자 be in high demand 수요가 많다 routine maintenance 정기 유지 보수 carry out ~을 수행하다 steady 꾸준한 reasonable 합리적인 hourly rate 시급 avoid 피하다 disruption 방해, 지장 complete 완료하다, 끝마치다 apprentice 견습생 instructor 강사 gear 장비 quarterly 분기별의 networking 인맥 형성 potential 잠재적인; 잠재력 graduate 졸업생 exclusive 독점적인 searchable 검색이 가능한 monthly payment 할부, 월별 지불 tuition 수업료 lump sum 일시불 unlock 열다, 드러내다 emergency 비상 (사태), 긴급 call-out 호출, 출장 서비스 register for ~에 등록하다 upcoming 다가오는, 곧 있을 details 상세 정보

164. 안내 책자에서 수리 기사로 일하는 것의 이점으로 언급하는 것은 무엇인가?

(A) 직업 안정성
(B) 계절별 상여금
(C) 탄력적인 근로 시간
(D) 유급 휴가

해설 세부 사항
에어컨 서비스는 겨울철에도 수요가 많고, 꾸준히 일을 할 수 있다고 했으므로 (A)가 정답이다.

어휘 stability 안정(성) flexible 탄력적인

165. 기관은 누구에게 할인을 제공하는가?

(A) 강좌에 조기 등록하는 사람들
(B) 예전 업무 경력이 있는 사람들
(C) 우편물 수신자 명단에 등록하는 사람들
(D) 자신의 장비를 제공하는 사람들

해설 세부 사항
자신의 장비를 가져오면 수업료의 1퍼센트를 할인해 준다고 했으므로 (D)가 정답이다.

어휘 sign up for ~을 신청하다 prior 이전의 mailing list 우편물 수신자 명단 supply 공급하다

166. 안내 책자에 따르면, 강좌에는 무엇이 포함되어 있는가?

(A) 교육용 비디오 다운로드
(B) 고객 목록 접근권
(C) 네트워킹 행사 초대
(D) 면접 전략 코칭

해설 세부 사항
학생들은 분기별 네트워킹 만찬에 초대된다고 했으므로 (C)가 정답이다.

167. McInnis Institute는 학생들이 무엇을 하는 것을 허용하는가?

(A) 과정의 일부를 온라인으로 수강하는 것
(B) 근무 시간 후에 현장 실습을 하는 것
(C) 졸업 후 2년간 지원을 받는 것
(D) 수업료를 분할 납부하는 것

해설 세부 사항
수업료를 월납할 수 있다고 했으므로 (D)가 정답이다.

패러프레이징 Monthly payments toward your tuition → Pay tuition in installments

어휘 portion 부분, 일부 installment 할부(금)

168-171 이메일

수신: Walter Bauman
발신: Rachel Helm
날짜: 6월 3일
제목: Galloway National Park에서의 하이킹

Mr. Bauman께,

6월 12일 Galloway National Park의 가이드 동반 하이킹 투어에 자리를 예약해 주셔서 감사합니다. 요청하신 대로 [168]귀하는 'Moderate Pace' 그룹에 배정되었으며, 하이킹은 약 4시간 30분 동안 진행될 것으로 예상됩니다. 우리는 오전 9시에 방문자 센터에서 출발할 것입니다. 최소 15분 일찍 도착하시기 바랍니다. 대중교통을 이용하지 않고 차를 갖고 오신다면 방문자 센터에서 종일 주차권을 3달러에 구매하실 수 있습니다. 하이킹에는 Rosewood Lake를 포함하여 멋진 풍경 사진을 찍을 만한 몇몇 장소가 포함되어 있는데, [169]Rosewood Lake는 도보로만 갈 수 있고 차량으로는 접근할 수 없습니다.

튼튼하고 편안한 등산화를 신고 오셔야 합니다. [171]최근에 새로 등산화를 구입하셨다면 미리 신고 걸어서 신발을 길들이는 것을 추천합니다. 이것은 하이킹 중에 불편함을 방지하는 데 도움이 될 것입니다. 도시락이 제공되고 각 하이킹 참가자에게 사용할 배낭이 제공됩니다. [170]소지품을 둘 수 있는 보관함이나 안전한 공간이 없으므로 가져오신 모든 것을 휴대해야 한다는 것을 유념하시기 바랍니다.

궁금한 점이 있으시면 이 이메일 주소로 편하게 연락 주세요.

Rachel Helm
Galloway National Park, 활동 책임자

어휘 reserve 예약하다 spot 장소, 자리 upcoming 다가오는, 곧 있을 hiking 하이킹, 도보 여행 assign 배정하다 moderate 적당한, 보통의 pace 속도 approximately 약, 대략 depart 출발하다 public transportation 대중교통 scenic 경치가 좋은 accessible 접근할 수 있는 sturdy 튼튼한, 견고한 in advance 미리, 사전에 break in (신발 등을) 신어서 길들이다 storage 저장, 보관 locker 물품 보관함 secure 안전한 belongings 소지품

168. 이메일의 목적은 무엇인가?

(A) 일정 변경을 설명하기 위해
(B) 활동에 관한 정보를 제공하기 위해
(C) 몇 가지 개인 정보를 요청하기 위해
(D) 어떤 장소로 가는 운전 경로를 알려 주기 위해

해설 주제/목적
가이드 동반 하이킹 투어를 예약한 사람에게 하이킹과 관련된 여러 정보를 알려 주고 있으므로 (B)가 정답이다.

169. Rosewood Lake에 대해 암시된 것은 무엇인가?

(A) 수영하기에 너무 추울지도 모른다.
(B) 방문자 센터에서 보인다.
(C) 일 년 중 일부분은 출입이 금지된다.
(D) 외딴 지역에 있다.

해설 추론/암시
Rosewood Lake는 걸어서만 갈 수 있고 차량으로는 접근할 수 없다고 했으므로 외딴 지역에 있음을 유추할 수 있다. 따라서 (D)가 정답이다.

어휘 off limits 출입 금지의 remote 외딴

170. Ms. Helm이 개인 물품에 대해 시사하는 것은 무엇인가?

(A) 거쳐야 하는 검사가 있다.
(B) 보관할 장소가 없다.
(C) 너무 무거우면 안 된다.
(D) 젖을 위험이 있다.

해설 추론/암시
소지품을 둘 수 있는 곳이 없다고 했으므로 (B)가 정답이다.

어휘 check 점검, 확인 undergo 겪다, 받다 be at risk of doing ~할 위험에 처해 있다

171. [1], [2], [3], [4]로 표시된 위치 중 다음 문장이 들어가기에 가장 적절한 곳은?

"이것은 하이킹 중에 불편함을 방지하는 데 도움이 될 것입니다."

해설 문장 삽입
주어진 문장의 This가 가리키는 것은 새 등산화를 미리 신어서 길들이라는 것이므로 주어진 문장은 [3]에 들어가는 것이 적절하다. 따라서 (C)가 정답이다.

172-175 온라인 채팅

Gerald Lee [오전 9:00] 좋은 아침입니다, Alan, Theresa. [172]여러분이 Sunshine Floral의 공급처가 되는 것에 동의해 주셔서 정말 기쁩니다. 우리는 시험 삼아 시작해 보고 거기서부터 진행할 거예요. 우리는 지역 경제를 돕기 위해 항상 지역 내 원예업자들로부터 꽃을 수급받는 것을 목표로 합니다. [173]최근에 내린 폭우가 여러분의 첫 번째 출하에 영향을 미쳤나요?

Alan Finch [오전 9:02] [173]저는 온실을 이용하기 때문에 문제가 되지 않았습니다. 저는 계획대로 첫 번째 배송을 할 수 있어요.

Gerald Lee [오전 9:03] 그 말씀을 들으니 기쁘네요, Alan. 당신은 우리에게 줄리엣 품종의 장미를 공급하는 첫 번째 공급업자가 될 거예요.

Theresa Schaeffer [오전 9:03] [173]저도 모든 것이 순조로워서 원래 일정대로 내일 모든 것을 보낼 수 있습니다. 제 미니어처 장미는 지금 완벽해 보입니다.

Gerald Lee [오전 9:05] 아주 좋습니다! 두 분에게 우리가 요구하는 것들의 체크 리스트를 보내 드렸습니다. 우리는 기준에 맞는 꽃들만 받을 수 있어서요.

Alan Finch [오전 9:06] [174]자세히 읽어 봤습니다.

Theresa Schaeffer [오전 9:07] 저도요.

Gerald Lee [오전 9:08] 좋아요! [175]오전 근무자들에게 여러분이 보내는 물품을 넣을 수 있도록 냉장고에 충분한 공간을 확보해야 한다고 알리겠습니다.

어휘 supplier 공급자, 공급사 on a trial basis 시험 삼아 proceed 진행하다, 나아가다 aim 목표로 하다 source 얻다, 공급자를 찾다 recent 최근의

affect 영향을 미치다 shipment 출하, 선적 greenhouse 온실 variety (식물의) 품종 stick to ~을 고수하다 original 원래의 timeline 스케줄, 시간표 miniature 아주 작은, 소형의 at the moment 지금 standard 기준 take a look at ~을 보다

172. Mr. Lee는 누구이겠는가?

(A) 행사 진행자
(B) 토지 소유자
(C) 전문 원예사
(D) 업체 관리자

해설 추론/암시
Sunshine Floral에 꽃을 공급하는 공급업자들에게 작업 진행 방식에 대해 알리고 있으므로 해당 업체의 관리자임을 유추할 수 있다. 따라서 (D)가 정답이다.

173. Mr. Finch와 Ms. Schaeffer의 장미에 대해 사실인 것은 무엇인가?

(A) 이미 출하되었다.
(B) 온실로 옮겨질 것이다.
(C) 같은 품종이다.
(D) 날씨에 영향을 받지 않았다.

해설 NOT/True
Mr. Lee가 최근의 폭우로 상품 출하에 영향을 받았는지 묻자 두 사람 모두 괜찮다고 답했으므로 (D)가 정답이다.

174. 오전 9시 7분에, Ms. Schaeffer가 "저도요"라고 쓸 때 그녀가 의미하는 것은 무엇이겠는가?

(A) 그녀는 체크 리스트를 검토했다.
(B) 그녀는 Mr. Finch와 함께 일하는 데 관심이 있다.
(C) 그녀는 꽃집과 거래한 경험이 있다.
(D) 그녀는 새로운 재배법을 기꺼이 시도하려고 한다.

해설 의도 파악
"So have I"는 '저도요'라는 뜻으로 상대의 말에 동감한다는 걸 나타낼 때 쓰는 표현이다. Mr. Finch가 체크 리스트를 자세히 살펴보았다고 한 말에 Ms. Schaeffer가 한 말이므로, Ms. Schaeffer 역시 체크 리스트를 살펴보았다는 것을 의미한다. 따라서 (A)가 정답이다.

어휘 method 방법

175. Mr. Lee가 다음에 하려고 계획하는 일은 무엇인가?

(A) Mr. Finch와 Ms. Schaeffer에게 마감 기한 알려 주기
(B) Mr. Finch와 Ms. Schaeffer가 보낸 견본 확인하기
(C) 일부 계약 조건에 대한 세부 정보 제공하기
(D) 직원들에게 일부 품목을 위한 공간을 만들라고 말하기

해설 세부 사항
오전 9시 8분에 Mr. Lee가 Mr. Finch와 Ms. Schaeffer로부터 받는 꽃을 보관할 수 있도록 근무자들에게 냉장고 공간을 마련하라고 말하겠다고 했으므로 (D)가 정답이다.

패러프레이징 to clear enough space in our refrigerator for your deliveries → to make room for some items

어휘 inform A of B A에게 B를 알리다 terms (계약의) 조건 make room for ~을 위한 공간을 만들다

176-180 편지 & 양식

Modern Cycling Monthly
즐겁게 타세요!

Nakula Patel
347 게이트웨이 애비뉴
베이커스필드, 캘리포니아 93301
1월 13일

Mr. Patel께,

〈Modern Cycling Monthly〉의 구독자가 되어 주셔서 감사합니다. 코스 선택 요령, 사이클링 장비, 경주 준비에 대한 [177]창의적인 아이디어 등에 관한 저희 기사를 즐기시기 바랍니다. [176]친구들을 소개해 주시면 〈Modern Cycling Monthly〉를 무료로 받으실 수 있다는 것을 알려 드리게 되어 기쁩니다. 이 새로운 프로그램에 참여하시려면 귀하의 고유 추천 코드인 P2495를 다른 분들과 공유하시고, 그분들이 1년 구독을 신청할 때 그 코드를 입력하라고 요청하시기만 하면 됩니다. [178]책자든 온라인 버전이든 상관없이, 그렇게 하는 사람 한 명당 귀하의 구독 기간에 한 달이 추가될 겁니다. 또한 [179]2월 5일까지 친구 한 명을 소개해 주시면 〈Modern Cycling Monthly〉 물병을 무료로 보내 드리겠습니다. 좀 더 자세한 정보를 원하시면 저희 웹사이트를 방문해 주세요.

〈Modern Cycling Monthly〉 팀

어휘 subscriber 구독자 article 기사 trail 코스, 루트 selection 선택, 선정 equipment 장비 issue (정기 간행물의) 호 refer 언급하다, 인용하다 participate in ~에 참여하다 unique 독특한, 고유의 referral 소개, 추천 enter 입력하다 subscription 구독 sign up for ~을 신청하다

Modern Cycling Monthly
구독 상태

이름: Nakula Patel
배송 주소: 347 게이트웨이 애비뉴, 베이커스필드, 캘리포니아 93301
계정 번호: 06478
구독: 유효
구독 만료: 12월 20일*

[179]*무료 1개월 포함 (추천 P2495: 1월 29일 처리)

[180]귀하의 구독은 12월 20일에 만료됩니다. 구독 갱신을 상기시켜 드리기 위해 이 날짜보다 한 달 전에 이메일을 보내 드리겠습니다.

어휘 status 상태 account 계정 expiration 만료 process 처리하다 expire 만료되다 renew 갱신하다

176. 편지의 목적은 무엇인가?

(A) 기사에 몇 가지 권고를 하기 위해
(B) 구독에 대한 대금 지불을 요청하기 위해
(C) 주소 변경을 확인하기 위해

(D) 추천 프로그램을 안내하기 위해

해설 주제/목적

친구를 소개하면 잡지를 무료로 받을 수 있는 프로그램을 알려 주고 있으므로 (D)가 정답이다.

어휘 recommendation 권고; 추천 confirm 확인하다, 확정하다

177. 편지에서, 첫 번째 단락 두 번째 줄의 어휘 "original"과 의미상 가장 가까운 것은?

(A) 일어나고 있는
(B) 창의적인
(C) 초기의
(D) 정밀한

해설 동의어 찾기

original이 있는 original ideas for preparing for races는 '경주 준비에 대한 창의적인 아이디어'라는 의미이며, 여기서 original은 '창의적인, 독창적인'이라는 뜻으로 쓰였다. 따라서 (B) creative가 정답이다.

178. 편지에서 〈Modern Cycling Monthly〉에 대해 시사된 것은 무엇인가?

(A) 새로운 작가 몇 명을 채용했다.
(B) 두 가지 다른 포맷으로 이용할 수 있다.
(C) 자전거 제조사들을 겨냥한 것이다.
(D) 장비를 할인해 준다.

해설 NOT/True

책자와 온라인 버전의 형태로 제공된다고 했으므로 (B)가 정답이다.

패러프레이징 the print or online version → two different formats

어휘 hire 고용하다 available 이용할 수 있는, 구할 수 있는 format 포맷, 형식 aim 목표로 하다, 겨냥하다 manufacturer 제조사

179. Mr. Patel에 대해 암시된 것은 무엇인가?

(A) 구독 신청에 할인권을 사용했다.
(B) 우편 주소를 변경하고 싶어 한다.
(C) 최근에 자전거 타기를 시작했다.
(D) 무료 선물을 받을 자격이 있다.

해설 두 지문 연계_추론/암시

첫 번째 지문에 2월 5일까지 친구를 소개해 주면 무료 물병을 준다는 내용이 있고, 두 번째 지문에는 1월 29일에 추천이 처리되어 무료 1개월 구독을 받은 것으로 되어 있다. 이를 통해 Mr. Patel은 2월 5일 전에 친구를 소개했으므로 무료 물병, 즉 사은품을 받을 수 있다는 사실을 유추할 수 있으므로 (D)가 정답이다.

어휘 coupon 할인권, 쿠폰 mailing (우편물) 발송 take up (직장, 취미 등을) 시작하다 be eligible for ~을 받을 자격이 있다

180. 11월에 Mr. Patel에게 보낼 예정인 것은 무엇인가?

(A) 갱신 알림
(B) 자전거 경주 목록
(C) 새로운 자전거 장비 카탈로그
(D) 다음 연도의 청구서

해설 세부 사항

두 번째 지문에서 Mr. Patel의 구독이 12월 20일에 만료되며, 구독 만료 한 달 전에 이메일로 구독 갱신을 상기시켜 주겠다고 했으므로 (A)가 정답이다.

어휘 reminder 상기시키는 것, 독촉장 gear 장비 bill 청구서

181-185 이메일 & 기사

수신: Layla Fiorini
발신: Jack Donohue
[182]날짜: 2월 18일
제목: 제품 시연
첨부 파일: demo_article

안녕하세요, Layla.

제가 〈Retail Trade Magazine〉에서 흥미로운 기사를 읽었습니다. 기사 작성자는 업계 행사에서 제품 시연을 하는 것에 초점을 맞추고 있습니다. 하지만 저는 그 내용이 우리 백화점에서 진행하고 있는 시연회에도 적용될 수 있다고 생각합니다.

[181]기사 작성자의 조언을 바탕으로 당신의 다음 시연회를 수정해 주시겠습니까? [182]다음 달 초에 시연회를 하실 예정이라는 것은 알지만 기사의 세부 사항을 검토하는 데 많은 시간이 걸리지는 않을 겁니다. 2월 25일에 만나서 이 문제를 더 논의합시다.

고마워요!

Jack Donohue
Bradberry 백화점 총책임자

어휘 author 작가, 저자 focus on ~에 초점을 맞추다 give a demonstration 시연하다 industry 산업, 업계 applicable 적용되는, 해당되는 make adjustments to ~을 수정하다 based on ~을 바탕으로 review 검토하다; 복습하다 details 세부 사항

제품 시연 제대로 하기
Evelyn Taunton 작성

산업 박람회나 엑스포에서 제품 시연회를 하는 것은 수백 심지어 수천 명의 신규 고객에게 접근할 수 있는 기회이다. 시연할 생각을 하기 전에 주문 급증을 따라잡을 수 있을 만큼 충분한 재고가 있는지 확인해야 한다. **[183]나는 많은 회사가 훌륭한 시연을 했지만 결국 고객들에게 주문을 맞추기 어렵다고 말하는 것을 보았다.** 그런 일은 항상 일어나기 마련이다.

만약 여러분이 할 수 있는 시연 횟수에 제한이 있다면 방문자 [184]수가 가장 많을 때 시연회를 개최하라. **[181]청중들의 관심을 유지하기 위해 그들이 제품을 사용하여 직접 체험하게 하라.** 덧붙여 아이디어를 얻기 위해 다른 사람들의 시연을 보는 것이 도움이 될 수 있다. **[185]여러분 자신의 시연에 적용될 수 있는 모든 것을 꼭 적어 두어야 한다.**

어휘 expo 엑스포, 국제 박람회 stock on hand 재고품 keep up with ~을 따라잡다 surge 급증 fulfill 이행하다, 만족시키다 all the time 늘, 항상 engaged 몰두해 있는 hands-on 직접 해 보는 note down ~을 적어 두다 apply to A to B A를 B에 적용시키다

181. Mr. Donohue는 Ms. Fiorini가 제품 시연회를 어떻게 개선하기를 원하는가?

(A) 고객들이 제품을 직접 사용해 볼 기회를 줌으로써
(B) 시연회에 더 많은 시각적 요소를 포함시킴으로써
(C) 지나친 전문 용어의 사용을 피함으로써
(D) 참석자의 요구를 사전에 파악함으로써

해설 두 지문 연계_세부 사항
첫 번째 지문에서 Mr. Donohue는 〈Retail Trade Magazine〉에 실린 기사의 작성자가 제안한 내용을 바탕으로 시연회를 수정해 달라고 했다. 두 번째 지문에서 해당 기사의 작성자는 청중들의 관심을 유지하기 위해 그들이 제품을 사용하여 직접 체험하게 하라고 했으므로 (A)가 정답이다.

어휘 visual 시각적인 element 요소 attendee 참가자 in advance 미리, 사전에

182. Mr. Donohue에 따르면, Ms. Fiorini의 다음 시연은 언제 있을 것 같은가?

(A) 2월 18일
(B) 2월 25일
(C) 3월 2일
(D) 3월 30일

해설 추론/암시
Mr. Donohue는 Ms. Fiorini의 제품 시연이 다음 달 초라는 걸 알고 있다고 언급했는데, 이메일을 보낸 날짜가 2월 18일인 것으로 보아 3월 초에 시연회가 있을 것임을 추론할 수 있다. 따라서 (C)가 정답이다.

183. Ms. Taunton은 시연과 관련해 어떤 실수가 흔하다고 말하는가?

(A) 부적절한 장소를 사용하는 것
(B) 충분한 재고가 없는 것
(C) 너무 길게 하는 것
(D) 중요한 기능을 건너뛰는 것

해설 세부 사항
시연을 잘하고도 재고가 부족하여 주문을 이행할 수 없다고 말하는 회사들이 많은데 이는 항상 일어나는 일이라고 언급했으므로 (B)가 정답이다.

어휘 unsuitable 부적당한 venue 장소 lack 없다, 부족하다 skip 건너뛰다, 생략하다

184. 기사에서, 두 번째 단락 세 번째 줄의 어휘 "volume"과 의미상 가장 가까운 것은?

(A) 문제
(B) 양
(C) 크기
(D) 음량

해설 동의어 찾기
volume이 있는 when the volume of visitors is at its highest는 '방문자 수가 가장 많을 때'라는 의미이며, 여기서 volume은 '양'이라는 뜻으로 쓰였다. 따라서 (B) amount가 정답이다.

185. Ms. Taunton은 시연회 참석에 관해 어떤 조언을 하는가?

(A) 질문을 이메일로 보내야 한다.
(B) 앞쪽에 앉아야 한다.
(C) 메모를 해야 한다.
(D) 설명서를 읽어야 한다.

해설 세부 사항
자신의 시연에 적용될 수 있는 걸 적어 두라고 했으므로 (C)가 정답이다.

186-190 광고 & 이메일 & 가격표

Tillie's
www.tilliesservice.com

[186]꼭 맞는 맞춤 커튼으로 창문에 새로운 모습을 연출하세요! 커튼은 여러분의 개인적인 취향을 반영할 수 있고 실용성도 있습니다. 빛을 차단하거나, 온기를 유지하거나, 혹은 프라이버시를 보호하기 위해 커튼이 필요한 경우에 우리는 여러분이 적절한 직물 소재를 찾도록 도울 수 있습니다. 그리고 우리의 노련한 직원들이 직접 댁을 방문하여 치수의 정확성을 보장할 것입니다. 우리는 실크, 울, 면, 벨벳과 같은 다양한 직물에 수백 가지의 색깔과 무늬를 보유하고 있습니다.

대부분의 주문은 치수 측정부터 배송까지 7일이 걸립니다. 그러나 추가 요금을 지불하시면 [188]우리의 속달 서비스를 요청하시어 단 3일 만에 커튼을 받으실 수 있습니다. 이 서비스를 이용하시려면 측정 당일에 직물을 선택하셔야 한다는 것을 유념해 주십시오.

보다 자세한 내용은 저희 웹사이트를 방문해 주십시오. [187]웹사이트에서는 우리의 월간 소식지를 신청하실 수도 있는데, 소식지는 고객에게 세일에 대한 사전 알림, [187]최근 프로젝트에 대해 고객이 작성한 추천의 글, 그리고 여러분에게 영감을 주는 사진 등을 제공합니다.

어휘 custom 맞춤의 reflect 반영하다 taste 취향 practical 실용적인 block out (빛, 소리를) 차단하다 fabric 직물, 천 in person 직접 measurement 측정, 치수 additional 추가의 take advantage of ~을 이용하다 newsletter 소식지 advance 사전의 notification 알림 testimonial 추천의 글 inspire 영감을 주다

수신: Yan Ong
발신: Tillie's
[188]날짜: 6월 20일
제목: 귀하의 Tillie's 주문

Ms. Ong께,

[188]저희는 귀하의 거실과 침실에 설치할 커튼에 대한 속달 주문을 처리하고 있습니다. 오늘 오전에 귀하의 커튼 크기를 잰 Eugene Vela는 귀하께서 커튼을 찾으러 오실 것인지, 아니면 6.95달러의 요금을 내고 커튼을 배송받으실 것인지 여쭤 보는 것을 잊었습니다. 표준 안감이 있는 귀하의 거실 커튼은 제곱피트당 7달러입니다. [189]암막 안감이 있는 귀하의 침실 커튼은 제곱피트당 10.50달러입니다. 배송에 대해 알려 주시는 대로 상세한 청구서를 보내 드리겠습니다. 문의 사항이나 우려되는 점이 있으시면 편하게 연락 주세요.

고객 서비스 담당자 Brenda Graves

어휘 process 처리하다 measure 측정하다 lining 안감 square foot 제곱피트 blackout 암막 invoice 청구서, 송장 concern 우려, 걱정

representative 대표자, 담당 직원

Tillie's

693 윈슬로 애비뉴
솔트레이크시티, 유타 84111
www.tilliesservice.com
[190]고객 여러분은 주문 시 20달러를 지불하셔야 하며, 커튼을 수령하신 후 남은 금액을 지불하셔야 합니다.

가격표 (제곱피트당)

표준 안감 포함

면	5달러
울	7달러
실크	9달러
벨벳	10달러

[189]암막 안감 포함

면	6.50달러
울	8.50달러
[189]실크	10.50달러
벨벳	11.50달러

어휘 place an order 주문하다

186. 업체가 전문으로 하는 것은 무엇인가?

(A) 맞춤 커튼 제작
(B) 홈 인테리어 디자인
(C) 새 창문 설치
(D) 패턴이 독특한 직물 인쇄

해설 세부 사항
첫 번째 지문에서 맞춤 커튼을 광고하고 있으므로 (A)가 정답이다.

어휘 install 설치하다 print 인쇄하다 unique 독특한

187. 광고에 따르면, 회사가 매달 제공하는 것은 무엇인가?

(A) 새로운 종류의 직물
(B) 고객들의 의견
(C) 할인 쿠폰
(D) 전문가들의 답변

해설 세부 사항
고객이 작성한 추천의 글이 들어 있는 월간 소식지를 제공한다고 했으므로 (B)가 정답이다.

188. Ms. Ong이 6월 20일에 한 일은 무엇이겠는가?

(A) 어떤 직물을 선택했다.
(B) Mr. Vela에게 몇 가지 치수를 이메일로 보냈다.
(C) 배송비를 지불했다.
(D) 소식지를 신청했다.

해설 두 지문 연계_추론/암시
두 번째 지문을 보면 이메일을 보낸 날짜가 6월 20일인데 Tillie's의 직원이 Ms. Ong의 속달 주문을 처리하고 있으며 Mr. Vela가 오전에 커튼 크기를 측정했다고 언급했다. 첫 번째 지문에서 속달 서비스를 이용하려면 측정 당일에 직물을 선택해야 한다고 했으므로 Ms. Ong은 6월 20일에 직물을 선택했음을 알 수 있다. 따라서 (A)가 정답이다.

189. 어떤 직물이 Ms. Ong의 침실에 사용되겠는가?

(A) 면
(B) 울
(C) 실크
(D) 벨벳

해설 두 지문 연계_추론/암시
두 번째 지문에서 Ms. Ong이 선택한 침실 커튼은 암막 안감이 있으며 제곱피트당 10.50달러임을 알 수 있다. 세 번째 지문에서 암막 안감 중 제곱피트당 가격이 10.50달러인 것은 실크라고 나와 있으므로 Ms. Ong이 침실 커튼으로 고른 직물은 실크이다. 따라서 (C)가 정답이다.

190. 가격표에 따르면, Ms. Ong이 첫 결제를 해야 하는 때는 언제인가?

(A) 배송 도중
(B) 방문 일정을 잡을 때
(C) 이메일로 청구서를 받은 후
(D) 주문하자마자

해설 세부 사항
고객은 주문 시 20달러를 지불해야 한다고 했으므로 (D)가 정답이다.

어휘 bill 청구서, 고지서 place an order 주문하다

191-195 기사 & 전단지 & 광고

DC Footwear

3월 19일—[191]토론토에 본사를 둔 DC Footwear는 올해 하반기에 몬트리올, 밴쿠버, 캘거리에 지점을 추가하며 전국적으로 새로운 매장을 연다는 계획을 발표했다. [193]밴쿠버 매장이 제일 먼저 문을 열 예정이고 체인점 중에서 가장 넓은 공간을 차지할 것이다. 회사 대변인인 Jennifer Aguilar에 따르면 정확한 개점 날짜는 아직 정해지지 않았지만 늦은 여름이 될 가능성이 높다. 회사 관계자들은 연말연시 쇼핑 시즌이 시작될 때까지 나머지 두 개 지점도 정상 운영할 수 있을 것으로 기대하고 있다.

[192]DC Footwear의 신발은 성능과 스타일 모두로 유명하다. 그 변화는 이익을 증진시키고 브랜드 인지도를 향상시킬 것으로 기대되며, 회사 관계자들은 궁극적으로 미국 내에도 소매점을 열 수 있기를 희망한다.

어휘 spokesperson 대변인 exact 정확한 grand opening 개장, 개점 official 관계자, 임원 up and running 운영 중인 performance 성능 boost 증진시키다 recognition 알아봄, 인식 eventually 결국, 궁극적으로 retail outlet 소매점 as well 또한, 역시

성대한 개업 행사!
[193 195]DC Footwear 밴쿠버
[195]164 스파다이나 애비뉴
[193]9월 8일 금요일

[195]Matthew Pomeroy 점장이 DC Footwear 밴쿠버 지점의 개업식에

오시는 여러분을 환영합니다! 저희는 하루 종일 무료 다과를 제공할 예정이며, 구매를 하시는 분은 경품 추첨 행사에 참여하시어 DC Footwear 상품권 50장 중 하나를 받으실 수 있습니다. 신발 디자이너인 Melanie Pascale도 오전 9시부터 11시까지 참석하여 여러분의 질문에 답할 것입니다.

저희는 다음과 같은 것들을 제공합니다.
– 무료 발 크기 측정
– 상품을 신어 볼 수 있는 편안한 좌석
– [194]신발을 멋지게 보이게 하기 위한 보호 스프레이, 광택제 등의 제품 전시: 무료 샘플 증정

그리고 곧 있을 몬트리올(10월 6일)과 캘거리(10월 13일) 개업식도 놓치지 마세요.

어휘 complimentary 무료의 refreshments 다과 make a purchase 구매하다 drawing 추첨 gift certificate 상품권 be in attendance 참석하다 display 전시(품) protective 보호용의 polish 광택제 miss 놓치다

판매 사원 모집
[195]DC Footwear 밴쿠버
[195]164 스파다이나 애비뉴

직무 소개:
• 탁월한 고객 서비스 제공
• 신발 측정 및 선택에 도움 제공
• 제품 정보를 공유하고 기능을 명확하게 설명
• 구매 및 반품 처리

[195]지원서를 제출할 때 매장 관리자에게 말씀하세요.

어휘 sales associate 판매[영업] 사원 outstanding 뛰어난 feature 특징, 기능 hand in ~을 제출하다 application 지원서, 신청서

191. 기사가 작성된 이유는 무엇인가?
(A) 새로운 신발 브랜드를 소개하기 위해
(B) 회사의 확장 계획을 설명하기 위해
(C) 캐나다 내의 트렌드를 강조하기 위해
(D) 소유권 변경 사실을 공지하기 위해

해설 주제/목적
DC Footwear가 몇 개의 신규 지점을 추가하여 전국에 새로운 매장을 열 계획을 발표했다고 했으므로 (B)가 정답이다.

패러프레이징 plans to open new stores across the country → expansion plan

어휘 expansion 확장 highlight 강조하다 ownership 소유(권)

192. DC Footwear의 제품에 대해 기사에서 암시된 것은 무엇인가?
(A) 친환경 소재로 만들어졌다.
(B) 경쟁사의 제품보다 저렴하다.
(C) 프로 운동선수들이 홍보를 하고 있다.
(D) 스타일리시한 것으로 알려져 있다.

해설 추론/암시
성능과 스타일 모두로 유명하다고 했으므로 (D)가 정답이다.

어휘 environmentally friendly 환경 친화적인 material 재료 competitor 경쟁자 endorse (유명인이 특정 상품을) 홍보하다 athlete 운동선수

193. DC Footwear에 대해 암시된 것은 무엇인가?
(A) 체인점의 가장 큰 매장이 9월에 개장한다.
(B) 모든 방문객들은 상품을 받을 기회가 있다.
(C) 매장 개점 순서가 변경되었다.
(D) 간식 제공은 오전 11시에 중단될 것이다.

해설 두 지문 연계_추론/암시
첫 번째 지문에서 밴쿠버 매장이 체인점 중에서 가장 클 것이라고 했는데, 두 번째 지문을 보면 밴쿠버 매장은 9월 8일에 개점 행사를 연다고 나와 있다. 따라서 제일 큰 매장이 9월에 개장한다고 한 (A)가 정답이다.

194. 전단지에 따르면, 매장에 대해 사실인 것은 무엇인가?
(A) 아직 상품권을 받고 있지 않다.
(B) 쇼핑객들에게 탈의실을 제공한다.
(C) 다양한 신발 관리 제품을 갖추고 있다.
(D) 스포츠용 신발만 판매한다.

해설 NOT/True
보호 스프레이, 광택제 등을 판매한다고 했으므로 (C)가 정답이다.

패러프레이징 protective sprays, polishes, and more to keep your shoes looking great → a selection of shoe care products

195. 지원서를 제출할 때 사람들은 누구에게 말해야 하는가?
(A) Mr. Pomeroy
(B) Ms. Aguilar
(C) Ms. Pascale
(D) 고객 서비스 담당자

해설 두 지문 연계_세부 사항
세 번째 지문인 DC Footwear 밴쿠버 지점의 판매 사원 모집 공고에서 지원서를 제출할 때 매장 관리자에게 말하라는 내용을 찾을 수 있다. 두 번째 지문을 보면 해당 매장의 점장은 Matthew Pomeroy라는 것을 알 수 있으므로 (A)가 정답이다.

196-200 발표 & 이메일 & 이메일

Urbina Property Management (UPM)

9월 13일—Urbina Property Management의 관리 책임자인 Kylie Marzano가 9월 30일에 직책에서 물러나게 됩니다. 우리는 그녀가 다년간 수고한 것에 감사하며 [196]그녀가 우리 사업의 중요한 부분으로 남기로 결정했다는 사실에 매우 기쁩니다. 그녀는 앞으로 일주일에 몇 시간씩 회사 고문으로 일할 것이기 때문입니다.

UPM은 현재 Ms. Marzano의 후임자를 찾고 있습니다. 후보자는 일상적인 업무뿐만 아니라 신사업 계획에 대한 법률 자문 제공을 담당하게 됩니다. 다른 업무에는 새로운 계약서 초안 작성 및 협상, 기존 부동산 증서의 검토, 제3자와의 소통 등이 있습니다. [197]후보자는 업계 내 규정

준수에 대한 최신 정보를 잘 알고 있어야 합니다. 영어와 스페인어를 모두 유창하게 구사해야 합니다. 지원 절차에 대한 자세한 내용은 www.urbinapropertymgmt.com에서 확인할 수 있습니다.

어휘 property 자산, 부동산 administration 관리, 행정 step down from ~에서 사임하다 consult 상담하다 going forward 앞으로(의) replacement 후임자 candidate 후보자 legal 법률(상)의 regarding ~에 관하여 initiative 계획 draft 초안을 작성하다 negotiate 협상하다 agreement 협정, 계약 deed (부동산) 증서 third party 제3자 regulatory 규정하는 compliance 준수 fluency 유창(함) application 지원

수신: hiringcommittee@urbinapropertymgmt.com
발신: antoniocastilla@urbinapropertymgmt.com
날짜: 10월 8일
제목: 관리 책임자

위원회 여러분께,

우리가 보유한 관리 책임자의 후보군이 상당히 적기 때문에 제가 개인적으로 아는 사람들에게 연락을 취했습니다. 저의 예전 동료인 Keith Henrich가 아주 적합한 사람일 수 있다고 생각합니다. [197]그는 모든 자격 요건을 충족하거나 초과하며, 협력적이고 매력적입니다. 제가 그와 그 직위에 대해 논의했는데 제법 관심을 보였습니다. 하지만 그는 하트퍼드에 살고 있어 [198]출퇴근에 시간이 오래 걸리기 때문에 지원하는 것을 염려하고 있습니다. 이 문제를 상쇄하기 위해 그에게 일주일에 하루는 재택근무를 할 기회를 줄 수 있지 않을까 싶습니다. 어떻게 생각하시는지 알려 주세요.

[200]Antonio Castilla
[200]Urbina Property Management 고용 위원회 의장

어휘 committee 위원회 pool 이용 가능 인력, 인력 풀 reach out to ~에게 접근하다 contact 연줄, 인맥 meet 충족시키다 exceed 초과하다 qualification 자격 cooperative 협력적인 personable (잘생기고 성격이 좋아서) 매력적인 be concerned about ~에 대해 걱정하다 time-consuming 시간이 많이 걸리는 work from home 재택근무하다 offset 상쇄하다, 보완하다

수신: antoniocastilla@urbinapropertymgmt.com
발신: nicoleroman@urbinapropertymgmt.com
날짜: 10월 8일
제목: 위원회 편람

Mr. Henrich를 입사 지원자로 제안해 주셔서 감사합니다. 다른 이야기인데, 위원들이 이 위원회의 일원이 되기 위해 필요한 시간 투입 수준에 대해 우려의 목소리를 냈기 때문에 [199]우리는 위원들의 다른 업무를 위한 더 많은 시간을 확보하기 위해 한 달에 한 번만 만날 것입니다. 저는 다음과 같이 편람을 업데이트했습니다.

- 위원회는 매월 첫째 주 월요일에 만나서 입사 지원자들을 논의할 것이다. 위원회의 긴급한 자문이 필요한 경우 [200]관련 부서장은 먼저 위원회 의장의 승인을 받아야 임시 회의를 개최할 수 있다.

Nicole Roman
Urbina Property Management 고용 위원회 간사

어휘 handbook 편람, 안내서 put A forward as B A를 B로 추천[지명]하다 on another note 다른 이야기인데, 그건 그렇고 voice 의견을 내다; 목소리 commitment (돈, 시간 등의) 투입; 전념 free up ~을 마련하다 urgent 긴급한 arise 생기다, 발생하다 relevant 관련 있는 approval 승인 secretary 간사, 비서

196. 발표는 Ms. Marzano에 대해서 무엇을 시사하는가?

(A) 자신의 후임자 고용을 도울 것이다.
(B) Urbina Property Management에서 파트타임으로 일할 것이다.
(C) 자산 관리 회사를 차릴 계획이다.
(D) Urbina Property Management 창립자였다.

해설 **NOT/True**
일주일에 몇 시간씩 회사 고문으로 일할 것이라고 했으므로 (B)가 정답이다.

어휘 assist 돕다 replacement 후임자; 대체물 founder 설립자, 창립자

197. Mr. Henrich에 대해 암시된 것은 무엇인가?

(A) 현재 원격으로 일하고 있다.
(B) 전에 Ms. Marzano의 상사였다.
(C) 현재의 규정을 잘 알고 있다.
(D) 3개 국어가 유창하다.

해설 두 지문 연계_추론/암시
두 번째 지문에서 Mr. Castilla는 자신이 추천한 Mr. Henrich가 모든 자격을 충족하거나 초과한다고 했다. 첫 번째 지문에서는 Ms. Marzano의 후임자가 될 사람이 업계 내 규정 준수에 대해 최신 정보를 잘 알고 있어야 한다고 했으므로 (C)가 정답이다.

패러프레이징 up to date on regulatory compliance → familiar with current regulations

198. Mr. Henrich가 그 자리에 지원하기를 주저하는 이유는 무엇인가?

(A) 직무가 잘 정의되어 있지 않다.
(B) 급여가 그의 기대에 미치지 못한다.
(C) 회사가 운영된 지 얼마 되지 않았다.
(D) 통근이 어려울 것이다.

해설 세부 사항
두 번째 지문에서 출퇴근 시간이 오래 걸리기 때문에 지원하는 것을 염려하고 있다고 했으므로 (D)가 정답이다.

어휘 define 정의하다 meet one's expectations ~의 기대를 충족시키다 be in operation 운영하다, 가동 중이다 commute 통근 (시간)

199. Ms. Roman이 고용 위원회 위원들에 대해 암시하는 것은 무엇인가?

(A) 사업주에 의해 임명된다.
(B) 회사에서 다른 책무가 있다.
(C) 매년 편람을 업데이트한다.
(D) 조직의 규모를 확장하고 싶어 한다.

해설 추론/암시
세 번째 지문에서 위원들의 다른 업무를 위한 더 많은 시간을 확보하기 위해 한 달에 한 번만 만날 것이라고 한 것으로 보아 위원들은 위원회 업무 외에 다른 업무도 한다는 것을 유추할 수 있다. 따라서 (B)가 정답이다.

어휘 appoint 임명하다 annually 매년, 해마다 expand 확대하다, 확장하다

200. Mr. Castilla에 대해 시사된 것은 무엇인가?

(A) 추가 회의를 승인할 수 있다.
(B) 월요일마다 바쁘다.
(C) 채용 대행사를 고용하기를 원한다.
(D) 제안된 정책 변경에 반대한다.

해설 두 지문 연계_**NOT/True**
세 번째 지문에 위원회 의장의 승인을 받아야 임시 회의를 개최할 수 있다는 정보가 나오는데, 두 번째 지문을 보면 Mr. Castilla가 고용 위원회 의장이라는 걸 알 수 있다. 따라서 (A)가 정답이다.

어휘 give approval 승인하다 additional 추가의 recruitment 모집 policy 정책, 방침

TEST 02

LISTENING TEST

1. (C)	**2.** (D)	**3.** (B)	**4.** (A)	**5.** (B)
6. (A)	**7.** (C)	**8.** (A)	**9.** (C)	**10.** (B)
11. (A)	**12.** (C)	**13.** (B)	**14.** (C)	**15.** (B)
16. (B)	**17.** (A)	**18.** (C)	**19.** (B)	**20.** (A)
21. (C)	**22.** (B)	**23.** (A)	**24.** (C)	**25.** (B)
26. (A)	**27.** (A)	**28.** (A)	**29.** (A)	**30.** (C)
31. (C)	**32.** (A)	**33.** (D)	**34.** (C)	**35.** (B)
36. (D)	**37.** (C)	**38.** (C)	**39.** (A)	**40.** (B)
41. (D)	**42.** (A)	**43.** (C)	**44.** (B)	**45.** (C)
46. (D)	**47.** (A)	**48.** (B)	**49.** (D)	**50.** (C)
51. (A)	**52.** (B)	**53.** (D)	**54.** (A)	**55.** (C)
56. (D)	**57.** (C)	**58.** (A)	**59.** (B)	**60.** (A)
61. (D)	**62.** (C)	**63.** (B)	**64.** (B)	**65.** (C)
66. (D)	**67.** (A)	**68.** (B)	**69.** (D)	**70.** (A)
71. (C)	**72.** (D)	**73.** (B)	**74.** (B)	**75.** (C)
76. (B)	**77.** (A)	**78.** (D)	**79.** (C)	**80.** (A)
81. (A)	**82.** (B)	**83.** (B)	**84.** (A)	**85.** (D)
86. (A)	**87.** (C)	**88.** (D)	**89.** (A)	**90.** (D)
91. (B)	**92.** (D)	**93.** (B)	**94.** (A)	**95.** (C)
96. (A)	**97.** (D)	**98.** (C)	**99.** (B)	**100.** (C)

READING TEST

101. (B)	**102.** (B)	**103.** (D)	**104.** (C)	**105.** (C)
106. (C)	**107.** (D)	**108.** (D)	**109.** (A)	**110.** (B)
111. (A)	**112.** (A)	**113.** (C)	**114.** (D)	**115.** (D)
116. (D)	**117.** (D)	**118.** (B)	**119.** (D)	**120.** (B)
121. (B)	**122.** (A)	**123.** (C)	**124.** (B)	**125.** (D)
126. (D)	**127.** (B)	**128.** (C)	**129.** (C)	**130.** (B)
131. (D)	**132.** (C)	**133.** (A)	**134.** (B)	**135.** (D)
136. (A)	**137.** (B)	**138.** (D)	**139.** (C)	**140.** (A)
141. (B)	**142.** (A)	**143.** (C)	**144.** (A)	**145.** (C)
146. (B)	**147.** (C)	**148.** (B)	**149.** (B)	**150.** (D)
151. (A)	**152.** (C)	**153.** (D)	**154.** (A)	**155.** (B)
156. (D)	**157.** (B)	**158.** (B)	**159.** (C)	**160.** (C)
161. (B)	**162.** (A)	**163.** (A)	**164.** (C)	**165.** (D)
166. (A)	**167.** (C)	**168.** (D)	**169.** (B)	**170.** (C)
171. (A)	**172.** (B)	**173.** (D)	**174.** (B)	**175.** (C)
176. (D)	**177.** (A)	**178.** (D)	**179.** (B)	**180.** (C)
181. (B)	**182.** (A)	**183.** (D)	**184.** (D)	**185.** (C)
186. (A)	**187.** (B)	**188.** (B)	**189.** (A)	**190.** (C)
191. (B)	**192.** (D)	**193.** (A)	**194.** (B)	**195.** (A)
196. (C)	**197.** (A)	**198.** (A)	**199.** (B)	**200.** (A)

PART 1

1. 미녀

(A) He's typing on a keyboard.
(B) He's reading a book.
(C) He's facing a computer monitor.
(D) He's watering a plant.

(A) 그는 키보드로 타자를 치고 있다.
(B) 그는 책을 읽고 있다.
(C) 그는 컴퓨터 화면을 마주 보고 있다.
(D) 그는 식물에 물을 주고 있다.

어휘 face ~을 마주 보다, 향하다 water 물을 주다

2. 미남

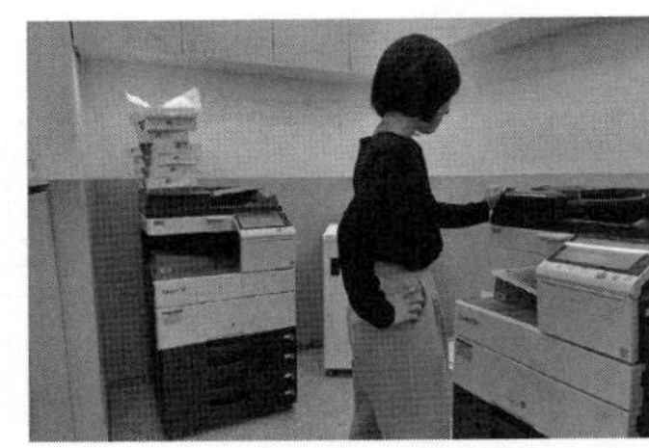

(A) She's putting some papers in a file.
(B) She's emptying out a paper shredder.
(C) She's stapling some documents together.
(D) She's resting her hand on a copy machine.

(A) 그녀가 서류를 철하고 있다.
(B) 그녀가 종이 분쇄기를 비우고 있다.
(C) 그녀는 서류를 스테이플러로 고정하고 있다.
(D) 그녀는 복사기에 손을 얹고 있다.

어휘 empty out 비우다 shredder 분쇄기 staple 스테이플러로 고정하다 rest one's hand on ~ 손을 ~ 위에 얹다

3. 미녀

(A) Containers are stacked in a truck.
(B) They are holding a box.
(C) They are examining some documents.
(D) A cart is leaning against a building.

(A) 용기들이 트럭 안에 쌓여 있다.
(B) 그들은 상자를 들고 있다.
(C) 그들은 몇 가지 서류를 검토하고 있다.
(D) 손수레가 건물에 기대어 있다.

어휘 container 용기, 컨테이너 be stacked 쌓여 있다 examine 검토하다 lean against ~에 기대다

4. 미남

(A) A touch screen monitor has been placed on a stand.
(B) Some televisions have been arranged in a circle.
(C) She's looking through a window.
(D) She's sweeping the floor in a shop.

(A) 터치스크린 모니터가 스탠드 위에 놓여 있다.
(B) 텔레비전 몇 대가 원형으로 배열되어 있다.
(C) 그녀는 창 너머를 바라보고 있다.
(D) 그녀는 상점에서 바닥을 쓸고 있다.

어휘 place 놓다, 두다 arrange 배열하다, 배치하다 in a circle 원형을 이루어 sweep 쓸다

5. 미녀

(A) Some workers are climbing a stairway.
(B) A portion of the roof is unfinished.
(C) A ladder is lying across the street.
(D) Some building materials are being unloaded from a vehicle.

(A) 작업자 몇 명이 계단을 오르고 있다.
(B) 지붕의 일부가 완성되지 않았다.
(C) 사다리가 길에 놓여 있다.
(D) 건축 자재가 차량에서 내려지고 있다.

어휘 stairway 계단 portion 일부, 부분 unfinished 완성되지 않은 lie 놓여 있다, 누워 있다 material 자재 unload (짐을) 내리다 vehicle 차량

6. 호남

(A) Tools are propped against a wall.
(B) Some bricks are piled in the corner.
(C) A shovel has been stored on a rack.
(D) A railing is being repaired.

(A) 도구들이 벽에 기대어 있다.
(B) 벽돌 몇 개가 구석에 쌓여 있다.
(C) 삽이 선반 위에 보관되어 있다.
(D) 난간이 수리되고 있다.

어휘 tool 연장, 도구 be propped against ~에 기대어 있다 brick 벽돌 pile 쌓다 shovel 삽 rack 선반 railing 난간 repair 수리하다

PART 2

7. 미남 미녀

Can you change the size of the text on these flyers?
(A) We need to promote the event.
(B) The keypad code has changed.
(C) Yes, I'll do it right away.

당신이 이 전단에 있는 글씨 크기를 변경할 수 있나요?
(A) 우리는 행사를 홍보해야 합니다.
(B) 키패드 암호가 변경되었습니다.
(C) 네, 바로 하겠습니다.

어휘 flyer 전단 promote 홍보하다

8. 호남 미녀

Does your gym have any dance classes?
(A) Yes, every Tuesday evening.
(B) Thanks, I'll sign up soon.
(C) He's in good shape.

당신의 체육관에 댄스 수업이 있나요?
(A) 네, 매주 화요일 저녁입니다.
(B) 고마워요, 곧 등록할게요.
(C) 그는 체격이 좋아요.

어휘 sign up 등록하다 be in good shape (몸의) 상태가 좋다

9. 영녀 미남

Who is in charge of the interview process?
(A) Around half an hour.
(B) A new phone charger.
(C) Priya's supposed to handle it.

누가 면접 과정을 담당하죠?
(A) 30분 쯤이요.
(B) 새 휴대폰 충전기요.
(C) 프리야가 처리하기로 되어 있어요.

어휘 be in charge of ~을 담당하다 process 과정 charger 충전기 be supposed to do ~하기로 되어 있다 handle 처리하다, 다루다

10. 미녀 호남

Why is the post office closed today?
(A) I live close to it.
(B) Because there's a training event.
(C) On Montgomery Street.

왜 오늘 우체국이 문을 닫았나요?
(A) 저는 그 근처에 살아요.
(B) 교육 행사가 있기 때문이에요.
(C) 몽고메리 거리에요.

11. 미남 영녀

Which desk is yours?
(A) The one in the corner.
(B) Until about 6 P.M.
(C) The catalog shows a variety.

어느 책상이 당신 것인가요?
(A) 구석에 있는 거요.
(B) 오후 6시 정도까지요.
(C) 그 카탈로그는 다양한 것을 보여 줘요.

어휘 variety 여러 가지, 다양성

12. 호남 미녀

Should we attend the afternoon show or the evening show?
(A) Ten would be enough.
(B) It received great reviews.
(C) The afternoon show is cheaper.

우리 오후 공연을 갈까요, 아니면 저녁 공연을 갈까요?
(A) 10개면 충분할 거예요.
(B) 그것은 좋은 평가를 받았어요.
(C) 오후 공연이 더 저렴해요.

어휘 attend 참석하다 receive 받다

13. 호남 미녀

When will the quarterly bonuses be paid?
(A) He received his paycheck.
(B) Ms. Campbell probably knows.
(C) A generous cash bonus.

분기별 보너스는 언제 지급될까요?
(A) 그는 봉급을 받았어요.
(B) 아마 캠벨 씨가 아실 거예요.
(C) 후한 현금 보너스요.

어휘 quarterly 분기별의, 4분의 1의 paycheck 봉급, 급료 generous 후한, 관대한

14. 미남 영녀

Who has the guest list for the fund-raising banquet?
(A) Yes, I'd love to come.
(B) Near the bank.
(C) Eliana has it.

누가 모금 연회의 손님 명단을 갖고 있나요?
(A) 네, 가고 싶어요.
(B) 은행 근처에요.
(C) 엘리아나가 갖고 있어요.

어휘 fund-raising 모금의; 모금 banquet 연회

15. 영녀 호남

The delivery truck will be here in about ten minutes.
(A) Several times each day.
(B) I'll get some help for unloading.
(C) The new line of winter sweaters.

배달 트럭이 약 10분 뒤에 이곳에 도착할 거예요.
(A) 매일 몇 번이요.
(B) 제가 짐 내리는 데 도움을 청할게요.
(C) 겨울 스웨터 신상품이요.

어휘 unload (짐을) 내리다 line 제품, (상품의) 종류

16. 미녀 호남

Where's the nearest public parking lot?
(A) In the vice president's briefcase.
(B) The closest one is behind the Reeves Building.
(C) An energy-efficient car is best.

가장 가까운 공영 주차장이 어디죠?
(A) 부사장님의 서류 가방 안에요.
(B) 가장 가까운 곳은 리브스 빌딩 뒤에 있습니다.
(C) 연비 좋은 차가 가장 좋습니다.

어휘 public 공영의, 공공의 parking lot 주차장 vice president 부사장, 부통령 briefcase 서류 가방 energy-efficient 연료 효율이 좋은

17. 미남 미녀

What else do we need for the trade fair booth?
(A) The pens with our company logo.
(B) All weekend long.
(C) Yes, I still need them.

무역 박람회 부스를 위해 그 밖에 또 뭐가 우리에게 필요하죠?
(A) 우리 회사 로고가 있는 펜이요.
(B) 주말 내내요.
(C) 네, 저는 아직 그것들이 필요해요.

18. 호남 영녀

How often do you change your password?
(A) We passed the inspection.
(B) Some supply chain issues.
(C) At least once a quarter.

당신은 얼마나 자주 비밀번호를 바꾸나요?
(A) 우리는 검사를 통과했어요.
(B) 일부 공급망 문제요.
(C) 적어도 분기마다 한 번씩이요.

어휘 inspection 검사 supply chain 공급망 issue 문제, 사안

19. 영녀 호남

Would you like to see our dessert menu?
(A) Of course, the reservation is for seven.
(B) Yes, I was just going to request one.
(C) I'll save you a seat.

저희 디저트 메뉴를 보시겠어요?
(A) 물론이죠, 7명 예약되어 있습니다.
(B) 네, 이제 막 하나 요청하려고 했어요.
(C) 제가 당신 자리를 맡아 놓을게요.

20. 미녀 미남

Why is Peter absent today?
(A) There's an event in San Diego.
(B) Show your ticket, please.
(C) Monday through Friday.

피터는 오늘 왜 결석했나요?
(A) 샌디에이고에서 행사가 있어요.
(B) 표를 보여 주세요.
(C) 월요일에서 금요일까지요.

어휘 absent 결석한, 없는

21. 미남 영녀

Would you prefer to use the regular or express service?
(A) Within two days.
(B) Yes, at the press conference.
(C) I'm not in a hurry.

일반 서비스를 이용하시겠어요, 아니면 특급 서비스를 이용하시겠어요?
(A) 이틀 안에요.
(B) 네, 기자 회견에서요.
(C) 저는 급하지 않아요.

어휘 prefer ~을 (더) 좋아하다, 선호하다 regular 일반적인, 규칙적인

express 급행의 press conference 기자 회견 in a hurry 급히, 서둘러

22. 호남 미녀

Could I borrow your laptop?
(A) Sure, he could lead the meeting.
(B) Valerie's using it for a presentation.
(C) How much money did you lend?

제가 당신의 노트북 컴퓨터를 빌려도 될까요?
(A) 그럼요, 그가 회의를 진행할 수 있어요.
(B) 발레리가 발표를 위해 그걸 사용하고 있어요.
(C) 당신은 돈을 얼마나 빌려줬어요?

어휘 borrow 빌리다 lead 이끌다, 안내하다 lend 빌려주다

23. 영녀 미남

How should we improve the presentation slides?
(A) We should add more graphics.
(B) For the slide show.
(C) Yes, she proved it was true.

우리가 프레젠테이션 슬라이드를 어떻게 개선해야 할까요?
(A) 우리는 그래픽을 더 추가해야 해요.
(B) 슬라이드 쇼를 위해서요.
(C) 네, 그녀가 그게 사실이라는 걸 증명했어요.

어휘 improve 개선하다, 향상시키다 prove 증명하다

24. 미남 미녀

Are there enough handouts for the workshop?
(A) Yes, I took the trash cans out.
(B) You can choose your own hours.
(C) I'll check with the speaker.

워크숍 유인물이 충분한가요?
(A) 네, 제가 쓰레기통을 내놨어요.
(B) 당신은 시간을 고를 수 있어요.
(C) 제가 연사에게 문의해 볼게요.

25. 미녀 호남

Has the building manager been by to repair the air conditioner?
(A) A few degrees cooler, please.
(B) I haven't seen anyone.
(C) Yes, you can send it by e-mail.

건물 관리인이 에어컨을 수리하러 들렀나요?
(A) 몇 도 더 시원하게 해 주세요.
(B) 아무도 못 봤어요.
(C) 네, 이메일로 그걸 보내시면 돼요.

어휘 degree (각도 · 온도 단위인) 도, 학위

26. 미남 영녀

Who's replacing the assistant manager?
(A) The hiring process just began.
(B) In the Walton Building.
(C) I can assist you with the files.

누가 대리를 대신할 건가요?
(A) 채용 절차가 이제 막 시작되었어요.
(B) 월턴 빌딩에서요.
(C) 제가 파일 정리하는 걸 도와드릴 수 있어요.

해설 (A) 대리를 대신할 사람을 뽑는 채용 절차가 이제 막 시작되었다는 의미이다.

27. 미남 미녀

The renovations look fantastic, don't they?
(A) That's what I was thinking.
(B) What's wrong with it?
(C) No, I can't afford one.

보수한 것이 정말 멋져 보여요, 그렇지 않나요?
(A) 저도 그렇게 생각하고 있었어요.
(B) 뭐가 문제인가요?
(C) 아니요, 하나 살 여유가 없어요.

어휘 renovation 보수, 수리 fantastic 멋진, 환상적인 afford ~할 여유가 되다

28. 영녀 호남

Wouldn't it be better to store these paper boxes in the basement?
(A) There's plenty of room down there.
(B) The store has good prices.
(C) We print on both sides.

이 종이 상자들을 지하실에 보관하는 게 낫지 않을까요?
(A) 저 아래에는 공간이 많아요.
(B) 그 가게는 가격이 좋아요.
(C) 우리는 양면으로 인쇄해요.

어휘 basement 지하실 plenty of 많은 room 공간, 자리

29. 미녀 미남

Have you been to the restaurant's new location?
(A) My reservation isn't until Saturday.
(B) You make a good point.
(C) A healthy recipe.

그 식당의 새로운 지점에 가 보셨나요?
(A) 전 토요일 이후로 예약했어요.
(B) 당신 말이 맞아요.
(C) 건강에 좋은 조리법이요.

어휘 location 장소, 위치 recipe 조리법, 요리법

30. 영녀 호남

What do you plan to do on your day off tomorrow?
(A) That sounds very relaxing.
(B) Thanks, I hope so.
(C) It depends on the weather.

당신은 내일 쉬는 날에 무엇을 할 계획이에요?
(A) 아주 편안할 것 같네요.
(B) 고마워요, 그러면 좋겠네요.
(C) 그건 날씨에 달려 있어요.

어휘 relaxing 편안한 depend on ~에 달려 있다, 의존하다

31. 미남 영녀

When will the updated software be on the market?
(A) No, it's too soft for that purpose.
(B) She's a talented programmer.
(C) Didn't you read the memo?

업데이트된 소프트웨어는 언제 시장에 출시될까요?
(A) 아니요, 그건 그런 용도로는 너무 부드러워요.
(B) 그녀는 재능 있는 프로그래머예요.
(C) 메모 안 읽었어요?

어휘 be on the market (물건이) 시장에 나와 있다 purpose 용도, 목적 talented 재능이 있는

PART 3

호남 영녀

Questions 32-34 refer to the following conversation.

M You've reached the Lyndon Hotel. How can I help you?

W Hello. [32]I'd like to reserve a standard room from June 6 to 9. Can I do that over the phone?

M Of course. [33]Are you a member of our loyalty program?

W No, because I don't usually use your hotel chain.

M I understand. If you change your mind about signing up, there's information about the benefits on our Web site. Also, [34]we've just opened an on-site gym that all guests can use for free.

W That's something I might be interested in. Thanks for letting me know.

남 린든 호텔에 전화하셨습니다. 무엇을 도와드릴까요?

여 안녕하세요. [32]6월 6일부터 9일까지 일반실을 예약하고 싶습니다. 전화로 할 수 있나요?

남 물론입니다. [33]저희 고객 보상 프로그램 회원이십니까?

여 아니요, 보통은 귀사의 호텔 체인을 사용하지 않아서요.

남 알겠습니다. 가입하는 것에 대해 마음을 바꾸신다면, 저희 웹사이트에 혜택에 대한 정보가 있습니다. 또한, [34]저희는 모든 손님이 무료로 이용하실 수 있는 호텔 내 헬스장을 열었습니다.

여 그건 제가 관심을 가질 수도 있는 거네요. 알려 주셔서 감사합니다.

어휘 reserve 예약하다 over the phone 전화로 loyalty program 고객 보상 프로그램 sign up 가입하다 benefit 혜택, 이득 on-site 현장의, 건물 내의 for free 무료로

32. 전화의 목적은 무엇인가?
(A) 예약을 하기 위해
(B) 환불을 요청하기 위해
(C) 운전 경로 정보를 얻기 위해
(D) 예약을 미루기 위해

패러프레이징 reserve → make a reservation

33. 남자는 무엇에 대해 물어보는가?
(A) 도착 시간
(B) 선호 색상
(C) 결제 정보
(D) 프로그램 회원 여부

34. 남자에 따르면, 무엇이 현재 무료로 이용 가능한가?
(A) 주차장
(B) 야간 서비스
(C) 피트니스 시설
(D) 조식

패러프레이징 an on-site gym → A fitness facility

미녀 미남

Questions 35-37 refer to the following conversation.

W I didn't catch that announcement, Jeff. Did they say something about a delay?

M Yes, the train will remain stopped at this station for at least half an hour. [35]One of the compressors isn't working, so that machinery has to be fixed before we can move on.

W Oh, no! [36]We're supposed to catch our connecting train in Plymouth at 5:45. We might not get there in time.

M [37]Why don't we look up the train schedule on the rail line's Web site to see what our options are if that happens?

여 제가 안내 방송을 못 들었어요, 제프. 지연에 대해서 무언가 말하던가요?

남 네, 기차가 적어도 30분 동안 이 역에 정차해 있을 거래요. [35]압축기 한 대가 작동하지 않아서, 이동하기 전에 그 기계가 수리되어야 한대요.

여 아, 이런! [36]5시 45분에 플리머스에서 연결편 기차를 타기로 되어 있잖아요. 우리가 거기 제시간에 도착하지 못할 수도 있어요.

남 그럴 경우 우리가 선택할 수 있는 게 뭔지 알아보기 위해 [37]우리가 철도 웹사이트에서 기차 시간표를 찾아보는 게 어때요?

어휘 announcement 알림, 발표 delay 지연 remain (~의 상태로) 여전히 있다 at least 적어도, 최소한 machinery 기계(류) be supposed to do ~하기로 되어 있다 rail line 철도

35. 남자는 무엇이 문제를 일으키고 있다고 말하는가?

(A) 교통 체증
(B) 장비 고장
(C) 혹독한 날씨
(D) 정전

패러프레이징 One of the compressors isn't working → An equipment failure

36. 여자는 무엇에 대해 걱정하는가?

(A) 비용이 예상보다 높을지도 모른다.
(B) 티켓은 환불되지 않을지도 모른다.
(C) 화자들은 회의에 늦을지도 모른다.
(D) 화자들은 연결편을 놓칠지도 모른다.

37. 남자는 무엇을 할 것을 제안하는가?

(A) 직원과 이야기하는 것
(B) 다른 안내를 기다리는 것
(C) 온라인으로 정보를 검색하는 것
(D) 긴급 메시지를 보내는 것

패러프레이징 look up the train schedule on the rail line's Web site → Searching for some information online

미남 영녀

Questions 38-40 refer to the following conversation.

M Good morning, Molina Construction.

W Hi. [38]I'm calling to find out if you sell any of your construction waste to other companies.

M Sometimes. Is there something specific that you're interested in?

W [38]Any pieces of concrete that you have.

M Does the size matter?

W Not at all. [39]I own a company that constructs roads, and we can use the concrete as part of our paving materials. We're looking for ways to cut costs as well as be more environmentally friendly.

M [40]Let me transfer you to our supply manager. Please hold a moment.

남 안녕하세요, 몰리나 건설입니다.

여 안녕하세요. [38]귀사에서 다른 회사에 건설 폐기물을 판매하시는지 알아보려고 전화드립니다.

남 가끔이요. 특별히 관심 있으신 것이 있나요?

여 [38]갖고 계신 콘크리트 조각들이요.

남 크기가 관계있나요?

여 전혀요. [39]저는 도로를 건설하는 회사를 소유하고 있는데, 포장재의 일부로 콘크리트를 사용할 수 있어요. 우리는 더 환경친화적일 뿐만 아니라 비용도 절감할 방법을 찾고 있어요.

남 [40]저희 공급 담당자를 연결해 드리겠습니다. 잠시만 기다려 주세요.

어휘 construction 건설, 공사 waste 폐기물, 쓰레기 specific 특정한 piece 조각 matter 중요하다 own 소유하다 construct 건설하다 pave (길을) 포장하다 material 재료, 자재 environmentally friendly 환경친화적인 transfer 넘겨주다, 옮기다

38. 여자는 무엇에 대해 전화하고 있는가?

(A) 절단기
(B) 선적 컨테이너
(C) 콘크리트 조각
(D) 전원 케이블

39. 여자의 회사는 무엇을 하는가?

(A) 도로를 건설하는 것
(B) 정원을 설계하는 것
(C) 제품을 수입하는 것
(D) 교량을 점검하는 것

패러프레이징 constructs roads → Building roads

40. 여자는 아마도 다음에 무엇을 할 것인가?

(A) 공급품 확인하기
(B) 전화 끊지 않고 기다리기
(C) 신용 카드 정보 제공하기
(D) 주소 확인해 주기

패러프레이징 hold → Wait on the line

호남 미녀

Questions 41-43 refer to the following conversation.

M I got your message, Melanie. You said you had an update on the sales of [41]our new hybrid car?

W Yes. Overall, we're meeting or exceeding our targets, with one exception. The branch in Portland is far behind the others. I'm not sure what's going on.

M [42]Do you need me to go there in person to monitor their procedures? I could do it on Friday.

W That would be great. Then [43]let's meet on Thursday to go over what you need to look for.

M OK, but [43]could we do it in the morning? I'm consulting Mr. Brecker about our department strategies via video conference in the afternoon.

남 당신의 메시지를 받았어요, 멜라니. 당신은 [41]우리 신형 하이브리드 자동차 판매에 대한 최신 정보가 있다고 말씀하셨죠?

여 네. 전반적으로, 우리는 한 가지를 제외하고는 우리 목표액을 달성하거나 초과하고 있습니다. 포틀랜드에 있는 지점이 다른 곳보다 훨씬 뒤처져 있어요. 무슨 일인지 잘 모르겠어요.

남 [42]제가 직접 가서 그들의 절차를 모니터하기를 원하시나요? 제가 금요일에 시간이 돼요.

여 그게 좋겠네요. 그럼 [43]목요일에 만나서 당신이 뭘 알아봐야 할지 검토해 봅시다.

남 알았어요. 하지만 [43]오전에 할 수 있을까요? 제가 오후에는 화상 회의로 우리 부서의 전략에 관해 브레커 씨와 상담할 거라서요.

어휘 overall 전반적으로 meet one's target 목표를 달성하다 exceed 초과하다 exception 예외 branch 지점, 지사 in person 직접 monitor 감시하다, 조사하다 procedure 절차, 과정 go over 검토하다 consult 상담하다 strategy 전략 via 통하여, 경유하여 video conference 화상 회의

41. 화자들의 회사는 무엇을 생산하는가?

(A) 사무용 가구
(B) 스포츠 장비
(C) 의류
(D) 자동차

패러프레이징 hybrid car → Automobiles

42. 남자는 무엇을 해 주겠다고 제안하는가?

(A) 지점 방문하기
(B) 데이터 분석하기
(C) 일정 변경하기
(D) 지침 제공하기

패러프레이징 go there in person → Visit

43. 남자는 왜 목요일 오후에 바쁠 것인가?

(A) 그는 시설을 둘러볼 것이다.
(B) 그는 구직자들과 면접을 볼 것이다.
(C) 그는 상담을 받을 것이다.
(D) 그는 학회를 위해 출장을 갈 것이다.

패러프레이징 consulting → having a consultation

미남 미녀 호남

Questions 44-46 refer to the following conversation with three speakers.

M1 Let's get this meeting started, Suzanne and Kiho. [44]We need to discuss how we are going to improve security at our building.

W Right. There is too much free movement into and within the building. We'll need to give employees new photo IDs and have keycard access on all doors. That way, we can restrict access to some areas. [45]Don't you agree, Kiho?

M2 Hmm... That would be ideal, but it would involve purchasing a lot of new equipment. [45]It's going to cost quite a lot.

W The improvements would attract new commercial tenants, so it would be worth it. [46]I'll e-mail you a copy of the financial report, which contains the projections.

남1 수잔, 기호, 이번 회의를 시작합시다. [44]우리가 건물의 보안을 어떻게 개선할지 논의할 필요가 있습니다.

여 맞아요. 건물 안으로도 건물 내부에서도 자유로운 이동이 너무 많아요. 직원들에게 사진이 부착된 새로운 신분증을 지급하고 모든 출입구에 키 카드로 접근하도록 해야 할 거예요. 그렇게 하면 일부 지역에 대한 접근을 제한할 수 있습니다. [45]안 그래요, 기호?

남2 음... 이상적이긴 하겠지만, 새 장비를 많이 구입해야 할 거예요. [45]그건 비용이 꽤 많이 들 거고요.

여 그러한 개선은 신규 입주 기업들을 끌어들일 것이므로 가치가 있을 겁니다. 추정치가 포함된 [46]재무 보고서 사본을 제가 이메일로 보내 드릴게요.

어휘 security 보안 site 현장, 장소 access 접근, 출입 restrict 제한하다

ideal 이상적인 involve 수반하다, 포함하다 purchase 구입하다 equipment 장비 attract 끌어들이다 worth ~의 가치가 있는 financial 재무의, 재정의 contain 포함하다 projection 추정, 예상

44. 회의의 목적은 무엇인가?

(A) 고객 설문 조사를 작성하기 위해

(B) 보안 개선을 논의하기 위해

(C) 광고 전략을 개발하기 위해

(D) 계약을 협상하기 위해

패러프레이징 improve security → a security upgrade

45. 기호는 무엇에 대해 걱정하는가?

(A) 검사에 불합격하는 것

(B) 고객을 잃는 것

(C) 너무 많이 지출하는 것

(D) 직원들을 혼란스럽게 만드는 것

패러프레이징 cost quite a lot → Spending too much

46. 여자는 무엇을 할 것이라고 말하는가?

(A) 항의 제기하기

(B) 고객에게 연락하기

(C) 주문하기

(D) 보고서 보내기

패러프레이징 e-mail → Send

영녀 미남

Questions 47-49 refer to the following conversation.

W Thanks for making time for my visit, Mr. Riley. [47]My company has recently released some haircare products that I think would be perfect for the customers at your salon.

M This is the line of hot oil treatments, right?

W That's right. After just one use, there is a noticeable improvement in the texture.

M [48]There's a hot oil brand that we always have in stock. We haven't changed it for years.

W You might change your mind once you see how well it works. [49]I'll leave some samples with you. Please give them a try to see if you like them.

여 저의 방문을 위해 시간 내 주셔서 감사합니다, 라일리 씨. [47]저희 회사에서 당신의 미용실 손님들에게 딱 맞을 것 같은 모발 관리 제품을 최근에 출시했습니다.

남 이건 핫 오일 트리트먼트 제품이죠, 그렇죠?

여 맞아요. 한 번만 사용해도 감촉이 눈에 띄게 개선된답니다.

남 [48]저희가 항상 구비해 놓는 핫 오일 브랜드가 있어요. 저희는 몇 년 동안 그걸 바꾸지 않았죠.

여 일단 그게 얼마나 효과가 있는지 보시면 마음이 바뀌실지도 몰라요. [49]샘플 몇 개를 남겨 드릴게요. 한번 써 보시고 판단해 보세요.

어휘 recently 최근에 release 출시하다 noticeable 눈에 띄는, 현저한 improvement 개선, 향상 texture 감촉, 질감 have ~ in stock ~의 재고가 있다 give it a try 한번 해 보다

47. 화자들은 어디에 있는 것 같은가?

(A) 미용실에

(B) 병원에

(C) 도서관에

(D) 슈퍼마켓에

48. 남자는 "저희는 몇 년 동안 그걸 바꾸지 않았죠"라고 말할 때 무엇을 암시하는가?

(A) 그는 그의 사업체가 충분히 현대적이지 않다고 생각한다.

(B) 그는 그 제품을 구입할 계획이 없다.

(C) 그는 몇 가지 계약 조건을 조정하고 싶어 한다.

(D) 그는 그 여자의 단골 고객이었다.

49. 여자는 남자에게 무엇을 해 달라고 요청하는가?

(A) 시연 보기

(B) 양식에 서명하기

(C) 가격표 검토하기

(D) 샘플 사용해 보기

패러프레이징 give them a try → Try

미녀 호남

Questions 50-52 refer to the following conversation.

W I got some good news this morning, Mickey. I've been invited to an interview at Pompey Enterprises.

M That's fantastic! Do you feel prepared for it?

W Yes, [50]I'm sure I can speak knowledgeably about the banking systems and investment opportunities in many countries around the world. I have a lot of experience in those areas.

M You'll do great.

W Thanks. [51]The only thing I'm worried about is that I don't speak any foreign languages. But it's not a requirement.

M I'm sure you can still perform the work well. [52]Would you have to move to a new city if you got the job?

여 미키, 오늘 아침에 제게 좋은 소식이 있었어요. 제가 폼페이 사의 면접 요청을 받았어요.

남 굉장하네요! 면접 준비는 되셨어요?

여 네. [50]저는 세계 여러 나라의 은행 시스템과 투자 기회에 대해 박식하게 이야기할 수 있다고 확신해요. 저는 그 분야에 경험이 많거든요.

남 당신은 잘할 거예요.

여 고마워요. [51]제가 유일하게 걱정하는 건 제가 외국어를 전혀 못 한다는 거예요. 하지만 그게 필요조건은 아니에요.

남 당신은 그래도 틀림없이 그 일을 잘 할 수 있을 거예요. [52]그 일자리를 얻으면 새로운 도시로 이사 가야 하나요?

어휘 knowledgeably 박식하게 investment 투자 opportunity 기회 area 분야, 지역 requirement 필요조건, 요건 perform 행하다

50. 여자의 전문 분야는 무엇인 것 같은가?

(A) 정보 기술
(B) 그래픽 아트
(C) 국제 금융
(D) 전기 공학

패러프레이징 the banking systems and investment opportunities in many countries around the world → International finance

51. 여자는 무엇에 대해 걱정하는가?

(A) 자신의 언어 능력 부족
(B) 자신의 바쁜 일정
(C) 자신의 짧은 근무 경력
(D) 자신의 만료된 증명서

패러프레이징 don't speak any foreign languages → lack of language skills

52. 남자는 여자에게 무엇에 대해 물어보는가?

(A) 어떻게 그녀가 그 일자리를 찾았는지
(B) 그녀가 이주할지 아닐지
(C) 누가 채용 결정을 내릴지
(D) 어디에서 면접이 열릴지

패러프레이징 move to a new city → relocate

영녀 호남

Questions 53-55 refer to the following conversation.

W Mr. Avery, [53]I noticed that one of the boxes in your weekly supply order got crushed in transit. The contents inside were dented. I'll bring a replacement tomorrow, if that's all right.

M Okay. [54]A lot of our customers are having their drinks on site these days anyway, so we don't need a lot of cups for to-go coffee.

W Great. Oh, that reminds me. [55]We have a new extra thick cup that you should try. It's very sturdy, so it's perfect for hot beverages. Shall I leave you a few samples?

M I'd appreciate that.

여 에이버리 씨, [53]당신의 주간 납품 주문에 있는 상자들 중 하나가 수송 중에 찌그러졌더라구요. 안의 내용물이 움푹 들어갔어요. 괜찮으시다면 내일 대체품을 가져오겠습니다.

남 알았어요. [54]어차피 요즘 많은 손님들이 매장에서 음료를 마시기 때문에, 저희는 포장 커피 컵이 많이 필요하지는 않아요.

여 좋아요. 아, 그러고 보니 생각나네요. [55]당신이 사용해 봐야 할 새로 나온 특별 두께의 컵이 있어요. 그건 매우 견고해서 뜨거운 음료에 제격이죠. 제가 샘플 몇 개 두고 갈까요?

남 그래 주시면 고맙죠.

어휘 get crushed 찌부러지다 in transit 수송 중에 contents 내용물 dent 움푹 들어가게 만들다 replacement 대체물 to-go 포장의 remind 생각나게 하다, 상기시키다 thick 두꺼운 sturdy 견고한 appreciate 고맙게 생각하다

53. 여자는 어떤 문제를 언급하는가?

(A) 배달 차량이 고장 났다.
(B) 일부 상품이 품절되었다.
(C) 라벨에 오류가 있었다.
(D) 일부 품목이 훼손되었다.

패러프레이징 The contents inside were dented → Some items were damaged

54. 남자는 어디에서 일하는 것 같은가?

(A) 커피숍에서
(B) 운송 회사에서
(C) 세탁소에서
(D) 옷가게에서

55. 여자는 왜 제품을 추천하는가?

(A) 그것은 환경친화적이다.
(B) 그것은 저렴하다.
(C) 그것은 내구성이 있다.
(D) 그것은 크다.

패러프레이징 sturdy → durable

미녀 미남

Questions 56-58 refer to the following conversation.

W Hi, Jordan. [56]I'm calling to find out how the promotions for our new carpet cleaning spray are going.

M People have been showing a lot of interest in the prize drawing.

W That's great! I hope this will help improve our brand recognition.

M I think it will. [57]We're giving away one hundred tote bags. They'll have our logo, so that's another way to promote the product.

W Perfect. How have sales been? [58]How about you give me the figures over the phone?

M The IT team is updating my software.

W OK. Then please e-mail me later.

여 안녕하세요, 조던. [56]새로 나온 우리 카펫 청소 스프레이 판촉 활동이 어떻게 진행되고 있는지 알아보려고 전화드립니다.

남 사람들이 경품 추첨에 많은 관심을 보이고 있어요.

여 잘됐네요! 이것이 우리 브랜드 인지도를 높이는 데 도움이 되길 바랍니다.

남 그럴 것 같아요. [57]우리는 토트백 100개를 증정할 거예요. 그것에 우리 로고가 있을 테니, 그것도 제품을 홍보하는 또 다른 방법이지요.

여 완벽하네요. 판매는 좀 어때요? [58]제게 전화로 수치를 알려 주시는 게 어떨까요?

남 IT 팀이 제 소프트웨어를 업데이트하고 있어요.

여 알았어요. 그러면 나중에 제게 이메일을 보내 주세요.

어휘 promotion 판촉 (활동) prize drawing 경품 추첨 recognition 인지, 알아봄 give away 나눠 주다 promote 홍보하다 figures 수치

56. 화자들의 회사는 무엇을 생산하는가?

(A) 옥외 가구
(B) 전동 공구
(C) 통조림 식품
(D) 청소용품

패러프레이징 carpet cleaning spray → Cleaning supplies

57. 남자는 무엇이 증정될 것이라고 말하는가?

(A) 할인 쿠폰
(B) 상품권
(C) 토트백
(D) 상금

58. 남자가 "IT 팀이 제 소프트웨어를 업데이트하고 있어요"라고 말할 때 무엇을 의미하는가?

(A) 그는 그녀의 요구를 들어 줄 수 없다.
(B) 그는 그녀와의 회의를 미루고 싶어 한다.
(C) 그는 서비스에 대해 불만을 제기할 계획이다.
(D) 그는 왜 마감일을 놓쳤는지 설명하고 싶어 한다.

영녀 미남 미녀

Questions 59-61 refer to the following conversation with three speakers.

W1 Good afternoon, Toby and Satya. [59]I wanted to talk to you briefly to find out how things are going with the proposal to build a baseball stadium here in Meadowville. As we discussed last time, this could be a great opportunity to attract more tourists.

M Right. [60]I've visited a few different spots that might be right for our project. The one on Monroe Street is particularly promising.

W1 That's great. And will you present your findings to the city council members?

W2 Yes. [61]They're meeting on October 8 to give the preliminary approval. I'll give a presentation then. I'd appreciate your help in getting ready for that.

여1 토비, 사티야, 안녕하세요. [59]이곳 메도우빌에 야구 경기장을 건설하는 제안서가 어떻게 진행되고 있는지 알기 위해 여러분과 간단히 이야기를 하고 싶었습니다. 우리가 지난번에 논의했듯이, 이것은 더 많은 관광객을 유치할 수 있는 좋은 기회가 될 거예요.

남 맞아요. [60]제가 우리 프로젝트에 적합할지도 모르는 장소들을 몇 군데 방문했어요. 먼로 거리에 있는 곳이 특히 유망해요.

여1 잘됐네요. 그리고 당신은 시 의회 의원들에게 조사 결과를 발표할 건가요?

여2 네. [61]그들은 10월 8일에 예비 승인을 하기 위해 모일 거예요. 제가 그때 발표를 할 거예요. 그걸 준비하는 데 도움을 주시면 감사하겠습니다.

어휘 briefly 간단히, 간략하게 proposal 제안(서) attract 유치하다, 끌어들이다 spot 장소, 자리 particularly 특히 promising 유망한 present 발표하다, 제시하다 findings 조사 결과 city council 시 의회 preliminary 예비의 approval 승인

59. 대화는 무엇에 관한 것인가?

(A) 지방 선거
(B) 새로운 스포츠 시설
(C) 연구 조사
(D) 교통망

패러프레이징 a baseball stadium → sports facility

60. 남자는 무엇을 했다고 말하는가?

(A) 몇몇 장소를 방문했다
(B) 조수를 고용했다
(C) 허가증을 발급했다
(D) 안내 책자를 제작했다

61. 10월 8일에 무슨 일이 일어날 것인가?

(A) 연례 퍼레이드
(B) 연수 프로그램
(C) 임시 휴업
(D) 의회 회의

영녀 호남

Questions 62-64 refer to the following conversation and schedule.

W [62]We've been getting a lot of positive feedback on the work our design team did for the product launch.

M I'm glad to hear that. It took a lot of effort.

W That's true, but things might get easier. I've signed up for a 30-day trial of some new software that may help us. [63]I'd like the team to meet so that we can evaluate the features together. How is the schedule for April 7 looking?

M Let's see... [64]it looks like Madri is the busiest person.

W Then [64]let's schedule the meeting when Madri is available. You and I were supposed to work on some brochures then, but that can be easily postponed.

여 [62]제품 출시를 위해 우리 디자인 팀이 한 일에 대해 긍정적인 피드백을 많이 받고 있어요.

남 그 말을 들으니 기쁘네요. 그것에는 많은 노력이 들었어요.

여 그건 사실이지만, 일이 더 쉬워질 수도 있어요. 제가 우리에게 도움이 될 만한 새로운 소프트웨어 30일 체험판을 신청했어요. [63]팀이 모여서 함께 그 기능들을 평가해 봤으면 좋겠어요. 4월 7일 일정이 어때 보여요?

남 어디 볼게요... [64]마드리가 가장 바쁜 사람인 것 같네요.

여 그러면 [64]마드리가 시간이 될 때 회의 일정을 잡읍시다. 당신과 나는 그때 안내 책자 작업을 하기로 되어 있었지만, 그건 쉽게 미룰 수 있어요.

4월 7일				
	정오	[64]오후 1시	오후 2시	오후 3시
뤄양	X	X		
자비에르		X		
브루스			X	
[64]마드리	X		X	X

어휘 positive 긍정적인 launch 출시 take effort 노력을 필요로 하다 trial 시험, 시도 evaluate 평가하다 feature 기능, 특징 available 시간이 있는 brochure 안내 책자 postpone 미루다, 연기하다

62. 화자들은 어떤 종류의 팀에서 일하는가?

(A) 관리
(B) 법무
(C) 디자인
(D) 회계

63. 여자는 왜 4월 7일에 만나고 싶어 하는가?

(A) 축하 행사를 계획하기 위해
(B) 소프트웨어를 평가하기 위해
(C) 새로운 업무를 할당하기 위해
(D) 입사 지원자들을 검토하기 위해

패러프레이징 evaluate → assess

64. 시각 자료를 보시오. 화자들은 몇 시에 회의를 할 계획인가?

(A) 정오에
(B) 오후 1시에
(C) 오후 2시에
(D) 오후 3시에

미녀 미남

Questions 65-67 refer to the following conversation and floor plan.

W Hi, Mr. Garvin. This is Jean. I think I've found the perfect office space based on your requirements.

M That's great! [65]I really need to move to a new office before I hire additional staff members in June.

W Well, I think you'll like this office unit. It's in the Tatum Building. [66]On the first floor, it has a spacious employee lounge with an L-shaped countertop and a table in the middle.

M [67]Could you please tell me how much the monthly rent would be and the average cost of utilities?

여 안녕하세요, 가빈 씨. 진이에요. 당신의 요구에 따라 완벽한 사무실 공간을 찾은 것 같아요.

남 잘됐네요! [65]저는 6월에 직원을 추가로 채용하기 전에 새 사무실로 꼭 이전해야 해요.

여 음, 이 사무실이 마음에 드실 거예요. 이곳은 테이텀 빌딩에 있어요. [66]1층에는 L자형 조리대와 중앙에 테이블이 있는 널찍한 직원 휴게실이 있고요.

남 [67]월세가 얼마일지와 공공요금의 평균 비용을 말씀해 주시겠어요?

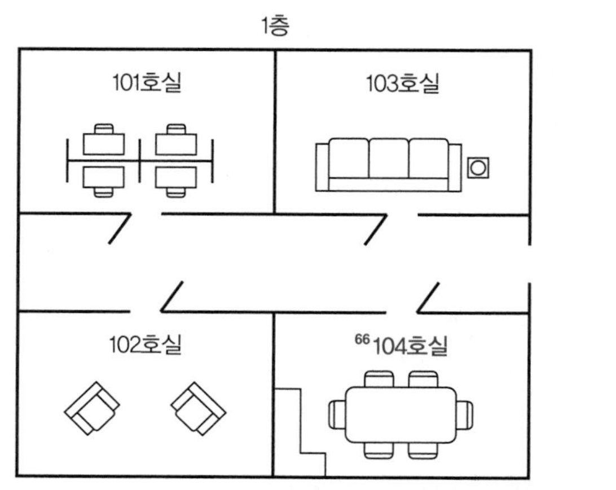

어휘 based on ~에 근거하여 additional 추가의 unit 구성 단위, 한 가구 spacious 널찍한 countertop 주방용 조리대 monthly rent 월 임대료 average 평균의 utilities 공공요금

65. 남자는 6월에 무엇을 할 계획인가?

(A) 일부 가격 인상하기
(B) 사업 시작하기
(C) 직원 더 채용하기
(D) 사무실 다시 꾸미기

패러프레이징 additional staff members → more employees

66. 시각 자료를 보시오. 여자는 어떤 방에 대해 이야기하는가?

(A) 101호실
(B) 102호실
(C) 103호실
(D) 104호실

67. 남자는 여자에게 무엇을 해 달라고 요청하는가?

(A) 비용 관련 정보 제공하기
(B) 대금 결제하기
(C) 약속 정하기
(D) 그에게 주소 보내기

패러프레이징 tell me how much the monthly rent would be and the average cost of utilities → Provide cost-related information

호남 영녀

Questions 68-70 refer to the following conversation and checklist.

M I have a favor to ask, Jillian. [68]Could you lead the building tour with the representatives from Odell Enterprises at two o'clock? I was supposed to do it, but I forgot that I have a checkup at the doctor's office at that time.

W Hmm... I've never led a tour before.

M It'll be easy. You just have to show them each department. And I've prepared a pre-tour checklist. One thing I'd like to point out, [69]I sometimes forget to write down the exact departure time. But this is important for our records.

W Okay. And [70]the tour usually ends at the conference room, right?

M [70]Yes. There will be some snacks and drinks there for them.

남 부탁이 있어요, 질리언. [68]당신이 2시에 오델 사의 대표들과 함께 건물 투어를 진행해 주실 수 있나요? 제가 그걸 하기로 되어 있었는데, 저는 그때 병원에서 검진이 있는 걸 잊어버렸어요.

여 흠... 저는 전에 투어를 진행해 본 적이 없어요.

남 쉬울 거예요. 당신은 그들에게 각 부서를 안내해 주기만 하면 돼요. 그리고 제가 투어 전 체크 리스트를 준비했어요. 한 가지 언급하고 싶은 것은, [69]제가 가끔 정확한 출발 시각을 적어 두는 걸 잊는다는 거예요. 하지만 꼭 기록해 둘 필요가 있어요.

여 알았어요. 그리고 [70]투어는 보통 회의실에서 끝나죠, 맞죠?

남 [70]네. 그곳에 그들을 위한 간식과 음료가 있을 거예요.

투어 전 체크 리스트

1. 출석을 확인하세요.
2. 지도를 나눠 주세요.
3. 질문이 있는지 물어보세요.
[69]4. 출발 시각을 적어 두세요.

어휘 favor 부탁 lead 이끌다 representative 대표 point out 언급하다, 지적하다 departure 출발 record 기록

68. 남자는 왜 투어를 이끌 수 없는가?

(A) 그는 중요한 고객을 만날 것이다.
(B) 그는 진료 예약에 갈 것이다.
(C) 그는 업계 행사에 참가할 것이다.
(D) 그는 출장을 갈 것이다.

패러프레이징 checkup at the doctor's office → medical appointment

69. 시각 자료를 보시오. 남자는 그가 가끔 어떤 업무를 잊어버린다고 말하는가?

(A) 1번 업무
(B) 2번 업무
(C) 3번 업무
(D) 4번 업무

70. 참가자들은 투어 마지막에 무엇을 할 것인가?

(A) 다과 즐기기
(B) 양식 작성하기
(C) 유인물 검토하기
(D) 발표 보기

패러프레이징 snacks and drinks → refreshments

PART 4

영녀

Questions 71-73 refer to the following telephone message.

Hi, Raymond. [71]I'm calling about the photography contest we're holding next month. I know you suggested nature as the theme, but that's what we used a few years ago. Also, [72]I need to find out who will participate in our judging panel. Could you please let me know if it's the same three people as last year? [73]I've forwarded you our advertisement for the event. I'd like to put it on social media as well as other popular Web sites to get more people interested. This will help to reach a wider range of people.

안녕하세요, 레이먼드. [71]우리가 다음 달에 개최할 사진 대회 때문에 전화 드렸습니다. 당신이 주제로 자연을 제안한 건 알지만, 그건 몇 년 전에 썼던 거예요. 그리고 [72]저는 우리 심사위원단에 누가 참여할지 알아봐야 해요. 혹시 작년과 같은 세 명인지 제게 알려 주실 수 있나요? [73]제가 그 행사를 위한 광고를 당신에게 보냈습니다. 저는 더 많은 사람들이 관심을 갖도록 [73]다른 대중적인 웹사이트뿐만 아니라 소셜 미디어에도 그걸 게시하고 싶어요. 이렇게 하면 더 다양한 사람들에게 전달되는 데 도움이 될 것입니다.

어휘 photography 사진 촬영(술) theme 주제 participate in ~에 참여하다 panel 위원단 forward 보내다, 전달하다 advertisement 광고 a wide range of 다양한, 광범위한

71. 메시지는 주로 무엇에 관한 것인가?

(A) 기사를 쓰는 것
(B) 사진을 편집하는 것
(C) 대회를 개최하는 것
(D) 무역 박람회에 참석하는 것

72. 화자는 무엇에 관해 확인이 필요한가?

(A) 작업 일정
(B) 제안된 예산
(C) 불만 사항
(D) 심사자

패러프레이징 who will participate in our judging panel → judges

73. 화자는 무엇을 하고 싶어 하는가?

(A) 전문가와 상담하기
(B) 온라인에 광고 게시하기
(C) 일부 정책 검토하기
(D) 신규 웹사이트 출시하기

패러프레이징 put it on social media as well as other popular Web sites → Place advertisements online

미남

Questions 74-76 refer to the following broadcast.

Good afternoon. Let's get this press conference started. My name is Arthur Cooper, and [74]I'm the spokesperson for the Ruston Foundation. Our nonprofit organization is dedicated to funding projects that help the environment. [75]We are proud to have contributed to this wind farm, which will supply clean energy to hundreds of households in the area. [76]We were expecting the construction to take six months, but the construction company finished it in just four. That's really impressive!

안녕하세요. 이번 기자 회견을 시작합시다. 제 이름은 아서 쿠퍼이고, [74]러스턴 재단의 대변인입니다. 우리 비영리 단체는 환경을 돕는 프로젝트에 자금을 제공하는 데 전념하고 있습니다. 우리는 이 지역의 수백 가구에 청정에너지를 공급할 [75]이 풍력 발전소에 기여한 것을 자랑스럽게 생각합니다. [76]우리는 공사가 6개월 걸릴 것이라 예상했지만, 건설 회사는 단 4개월 만에 그것을 끝냈습니다. 그건 정말 인상적입니다!

어휘 press conference 기자 회견 spokesperson 대변인 foundation 재단 nonprofit organization 비영리 단체 be dedicated to ~에 전념하다 fund ~에 자금을 제공하다 environment 환경 contribute to ~에 기여하다 wind farm 풍력 발전 시설 supply 공급하다 household 가구, 가정 impressive 인상적인

74. 화자는 누구인 것 같은가?

(A) 뉴스 기자
(B) 자선 단체 대변인
(C) 행사 기획자
(D) 시 공무원

패러프레이징 the spokesperson for the Ruston Foundation → A charity representative

75. 화자는 어떤 종류의 건설 프로젝트를 언급하는가?

(A) 주차 빌딩
(B) 도서관 확장
(C) 풍력 발전소
(D) 아파트 건물

76. 화자는 왜 감명받았는가?

(A) 예산이 전부 사용되지 않았다.
(B) 작업이 일찍 완료되었다.
(C) 일부 자재가 재사용되었다.
(D) 수익이 기록을 세웠다.

호남

Questions 77-79 refer to the following speech.

Good morning, and welcome to Sunset Lake. It's a pleasure to see such a great turnout for the grand reopening. During the closure, [77]we removed an extensive amount of litter from the shoreline as well as from the water itself. [78]I know that many people were surprised and even upset that the city council invested so heavily in this site. However, it gets used every day. And I think you'll all agree that the recreational facilities here look much better. [79]I'd like to show you some before-and-after photos to highlight the differences.

안녕하세요, 선셋 호수에 오신 걸 환영합니다. 이 재개장에 이렇게 많은 분들이 모인 걸 보게 되어 기쁩니다. 폐쇄 기간 동안, [77]우리는 호수 물 자체뿐만 아니라 호숫가에서 엄청난 양의 쓰레기를 치웠습니다. [78]저는 시 의회가 이 부지에 이렇게 많이 투자를 한 것에 많은 분들이 놀라고 심지어 속상해하셨다는 걸 알고 있습니다. 하지만, 이곳은 매일 사용됩니다. 그리고 저는 이곳 휴양 시설이 훨씬 더 좋아 보인다는 것에 여러분 모두 동의하실 거라고 생각합니다. [79]그 차이점을 강조하기 위해 제가 여러분에게 전후 사진을 보여드리고자 합니다.

어휘 turnout 참가자 수 closure 폐쇄 remove 치우다, 제거하다 extensive (수량 · 규모 · 정도 따위가) 큰, 엄청난 litter 쓰레기 shoreline 물가, 해안가 upset 속상한 city council 시 의회 invest 투자하다 recreational 휴양의, 오락의 facilities 시설 highlight 강조하다

77. 화자는 무엇에 관해 이야기하고 있는가?

(A) 정화 작업
(B) 보안 절차
(C) 도로 폐쇄
(D) 지역 야유회

78. 화자는 왜 "이곳은 매일 사용됩니다"라고 말하는가?

(A) 자원봉사자를 모집하기 위해
(B) 대체품을 추천하기 위해
(C) 지연을 설명하기 위해
(D) 결정을 정당화하기 위해

79. 청자들은 다음에 무엇을 할 것 같은가?

(A) 함께 식사하기
(B) 피드백 공유하기
(C) 사진 보기
(D) 관계자 만나기

패러프레이징 some before-and-after photos → some pictures

영녀

Questions 80-82 refer to the following talk.

Thank you for inviting me to this management meeting here at your office. [80]I'm happy to tell you about Malona Furniture's new office chair. It is specially designed to support the back and help the user to maintain the correct posture. Studies show that using this kind of chair can lead to better health, so it means that [81]your staff will not take time off for illness as often. Now, if you take a look at the screen, [82]you'll see which colors we offer.

귀사의 이 경영 회의에 저를 초대해 주셔서 감사합니다. [80]저는 말로나 가구의 새 사무용 의자에 대해 여러분에게 말씀드리게 되어 기쁩니다. 이것은 등을 받쳐 주고 사용자가 올바른 자세를 유지하는 걸 돕기 위해 특별히 고안되었습니다. 연구들은 이런 종류의 의자를 사용하는 것이 건강에 기여한다는 걸 보여주는데, 그래서 그것은 [81]여러분의 직원이 그렇게 자주 병가를 내지 않게 될 것이라는 걸 의미합니다. 자, 화면을 보시면 [82]저희가 어떤 색상을 제공하는지 아실 수 있을 겁니다.

어휘 management 경영 support 받치다 maintain 유지하다 correct 올바른 posture 자세 lead to ~로 이끌다 take time off 휴가를 내다 take a look at ~을 보다 offer 제공하다

80. 화자는 왜 청자들과 만나고 있는가?

(A) 제품을 소개하기 위해
(B) 구직 면접을 보기 위해
(C) 보험 정보를 주기 위해
(D) 교육 워크숍을 제공하기 위해

81. 화자는 어떤 이점을 언급하는가?

(A) 직원 결근 감소
(B) 플라스틱 폐기물 감소
(C) 회사 이익 증가
(D) 신규 고객 유치

패러프레이징 take time off → absences

82. 화자는 청자들에게 무엇을 보여줄 것인가?

(A) 현재 가격
(B) 색상 옵션
(C) 사이즈 표
(D) 사용 설명서

패러프레이징 which colors we offer → Color options

미녀

Questions 83-85 refer to the following telephone message.

Hi, Anthony. It's Carolyn. I'm calling about the travel arrangements for [83]our business trip to Manchester, the one where we'll be negotiating the sales contract with Kuhn Logistics. [84]I just changed my return ticket for the train journey so that I could come back late in the evening instead of mid-afternoon. That's because [85]there's a lecture on advances in medical technology at the Barnes Institute that I'd like to attend. I know you're interested in this topic as well, so why don't you come with me? Please let me know.

안녕하세요, 앤서니. 캐롤린입니다. [83]우리가 쿤 물류와 판매 계약을 협상할 맨체스터 출장 준비 때문에 전화드렸습니다. 저는 오후 중반이 아니라 저녁 늦게 돌아올 수 있도록 [84]방금 기차 여행 왕복표를 바꿨습니다. [85]반스 연구소에서 의료 기술의 진보에 관한 강의가 있어서 참석하고 싶어서요. [85]당신도 이 주제에 관심 있는 걸 아는데, 저랑 같이 가시는 게 어때요? 제게 알려 주세요.

어휘 arrangement 준비 negotiate 협상하다 contract 계약(서) return ticket 왕복표 advance 진보 medical 의료의 technology 기술 institute 연구소, 협회 attend 참석하다

83. 화자는 왜 맨체스터로 갈 것인가?

(A) 직원을 모집하기 위해
(B) 계약을 협상하기 위해
(C) 상을 주기 위해
(D) 시설을 시찰하기 위해

84. 화자는 최근에 무엇을 했는가?

(A) 그녀는 기차표를 바꿨다.
(B) 그녀는 호텔 객실을 업그레이드했다.
(C) 그녀는 몇몇 서류를 제출했다.
(D) 그녀는 추가 자금을 요청했다.

85. 화자는 청자가 무엇에 참석할 것을 청하는가?

(A) 휴일 퍼레이드
(B) 음식 축제
(C) 취업 박람회
(D) 학술 강의

패러프레이징 a lecture on advances in medical technology → An academic lecture

호남

Questions 86-88 refer to the following excerpt from a meeting.

Let's get this managers' meeting started. First on the agenda, [86]I'd like to talk about getting new uniforms for our staff. We want our business to have a more professional look, so it's time for a change. I've got the Snyder Supplies catalog here, and [87]there are a few outfits that I think would look great and be comfortable, but you know your team members well. I'd like to place the order this week, but [88]just remember that our office is closed on Friday for the national holiday.

이번 간부 회의를 시작합시다. 첫 번째 안건으로, [86]저는 우리 직원들을 위해 새 유니폼을 받는 것에 대해 이야기하려고 합니다. 우리는 사업체가 더 전문적으로 보이길 원하기 때문에, 이제 변화가 필요한 때입니다. 저에게 여기 스나이더 용품의 카탈로그가 있어요. [87]멋져 보이고 편안할 것 같은 의상이 몇 개 있긴 하지만, 여러분이 팀원들을 잘 아시잖아요. 저는 이번 주에 주문을 하고 싶은데, [88]금요일은 공휴일이라서 우리 사무실이 휴무라는 것만 기억하세요.

어휘 agenda 안건 professional 전문적인 outfit 의상 comfortable 편안한 place an order 주문하다 national holiday 공휴일, 국경일

86. 화자는 무엇에 관해 이야기하고 있는가?

(A) 직원 유니폼
(B) 컴퓨터 부속품
(C) 주방용품
(D) 안전 장비

87. 화자는 왜 "여러분이 팀원들을 잘 아시잖아요"라고 말하는가?

(A) 놀라움을 나타내기 위해
(B) 칭찬을 하기 위해
(C) 제안을 요청하기 위해
(D) 실수를 바로잡기 위해

88. 화자는 청자들에게 무엇에 관해 상기시키는가?

(A) 예산 삭감
(B) 휴일 파티
(C) 연수 계획
(D) 사무실 폐쇄

미남

Questions 89-91 refer to the following tour information.

Welcome to this tour of the Worcester historic district. [89]As we walk through this beautiful neighborhood, I'll tell you about the styles of architecture used in the buildings around us. You'll be able to see first-hand how materials and structures changed over time. [90]You'll also get the chance to visit a unique house designed by Finlay Weston. Few people know about this visit. Mr. Weston was a world-renowned architect who designed several buildings in this area, and he had a fascinating career history. If you're interested in learning more about it, [91]I recommend the book *Brick by Brick*, which is about his life.

이번 우스터 역사 지구 투어에 오신 걸 환영합니다. [89]이 아름다운 동네를 거닐면서, 저는 여러분에게 우리 주변의 건물들에 사용된 건축 양식에 대해 말씀드리겠습니다. 여러분은 시간이 지남에 따라 자재와 구조가 어떻게 변했는지 직접 보실 수 있을 것입니다. [90]여러분은 또한 핀레이 웨스턴이 설계한 독특한 집을 방문할 기회도 얻게 될 것입니다. 이 방문에 대해 아는 사람은 거의 없습니다. 웨스턴 씨는 이 지역의 여러 건물을 설계한 세계적으로 유명한 건축가였고, 대단히 흥미로운 이력을 가졌습니다. 만약 여러분이 그것에 대해 더 알아보는 데 관심이 있다면, [91]그의 삶에 대한 책 〈브릭 바이 브릭〉을 추천합니다.

어휘 historic 역사적인 district 지구, 구역 neighborhood 동네, 이웃 architecture 건축 first-hand 직접 material 재료 structure 구조 unique 독특한 world-renowned 세계적으로 유명한 architect 건축가 fascinating 대단히 흥미로운, 매력적인

89. 청자들은 투어에서 무엇에 대해 알게 될 것인가?

(A) 건축 양식
(B) 리더십 유형
(C) 패션 스타일
(D) 화풍

패러프레이징 styles of architecture → Architectural styles

90. 화자는 "이 방문에 대해 아는 사람은 거의 없습니다"라고 말할 때 무엇을 의미하는가?

(A) 문서에 정보가 빠져 있다.
(B) 몇몇 장소는 오늘 매우 조용하다.
(C) 판촉 캠페인이 효과가 없다.
(D) 투어에는 특별한 장소가 포함된다.

91. 화자는 청자들이 무엇을 하도록 권하는가?

(A) 사진 많이 찍기
(B) 책 읽기
(C) 온라인에 후기 게시하기
(D) 수표로 지불하기

미녀

Questions 92-94 refer to the following talk.

I'd like to inform you all of an upcoming change. [92]When I opened this flower shop five years ago, my goal was to help people celebrate the special occasions in their lives. These days, I'm starting to look for ways to reduce our environmental impact. That's why, [93]from next month, we'll stop wrapping flowers in plastic and will instead package them in a plant-based wrap. This material can be composted with regular garden waste. Now, you should know that the material is a bit more difficult to work with than plastic. I've got some samples here. [94]Let me show you a wrapping technique that I think you should use.

여러분 모두에게 곧 있을 변경 사항에 대해 알려드리고자 합니다. [92]제가 5년 전에 이 꽃집을 열었을 때, 제 목표는 사람들이 그들의 삶에서 특별한 날들을 기념하는 걸 돕는 것이었습니다. 요즘, 저는 우리가 환경에 미치는 영향을 줄일 방법을 찾기 시작했습니다. 그렇기 때문에, [93]다음 달부터 우리는 꽃을 비닐로 포장하는 걸 중단하고 대신에 식물성 포장지로 꽃을 포장할 것입니다. 이 재료는 일반 정원 폐기물과 함께 퇴비가 될 수 있습니다. 자, 여러분은 그 재료가 작업하기에 비닐보다 조금 더 어렵다는 걸 아셔야 합니다. 여기 샘플이 몇 개 있어요. 여러분이 이용하셔야 하는 [94]포장 기법을 제가 보여 드릴게요.

어휘 inform 알리다 upcoming 곧 있을, 다가오는 celebrate 기념하다, 축하하다 occasion (특별한) 행사, 경우 reduce 줄이다 environmental 환경의 impact 영향 wrap 포장하다, 싸다; 포장지 package 포장하다 plant-based 식물성의 compost 퇴비가 되다 waste 폐기물

92. 화자는 누구인 것 같은가?

(A) 여행 가이드
(B) 실내 장식가
(C) 환경 공학자
(D) 가게 주인

93. 다음 달에 무엇이 변경될 것인가?

(A) 근무 일정
(B) 포장 종류
(C) 지불 절차
(D) 업체 장소

94. 화자는 다음에 무엇을 할 것인가?

(A) 시연하기
(B) 공지 게시하기
(C) 휴식 취하기
(D) 기념 행사 열기

패러프레이징 show you a wrapping technique → Give a demonstration

호남

Questions 95-97 refer to the following telephone message and price list.

Good morning, [95]this is Aiden Becker from Lennox Shoes. We're working on the first batch of our new running shoes. I placed an order earlier today, but [96]I've just realized that I forgot one of the items we need. It's the heavy-duty cotton thread in white... um... product code D-54. I hope it's not too late to add that to the order so we get everything at the same time. That way, there won't be any delays. We're on a tight deadline because we want plenty of finished products ready for [97]the Vancouver Trade Show in November. Thank you!

안녕하세요. [95]저는 레녹스 슈즈의 에이든 베커입니다. 저희는 새 운동화의 1차분을 만들고 있어요. 제가 오늘 일찍 주문을 넣었는데, [96]필요한 물품 중 하나를 깜박한 걸 이제야 깨달았어요. 그건 흰색으로 된 튼튼한 면사인데... 음... 제품 코드 D-54입니다. 저희가 모든 걸 동시에 받을 수 있도록 [96]그걸 주문에 추가하는 게 너무 늦지 않았기를 바랍니다. 그렇게 하면 지연되는 게 없을 거예요. 저희는 [97]11월 밴쿠버 무역 박람회를 위해 완제품이 많이 준비되길 원하기 때문에 마감일이 촉박합니다. 감사합니다!

가격표	
제품 코드	단가
[96]D-54	21달러
F-12	38달러
G-90	67달러
L-68	79달러

어휘 batch 1회분, 한 묶음 heavy-duty 튼튼한 cotton thread 면사 at the same time 동시에 tight 빠듯한, 단단한 finished product 완제품

95. 화자의 회사는 무엇을 생산하는가?

(A) 침구
(B) 헤어 액세서리
(C) 신발
(D) 가구

패러프레이징 running shoes → Footwear

96. 시각 자료를 보시오. 화자의 지불금에 얼마가 추가될 것인가?

(A) 21달러
(B) 38달러
(C) 67달러
(D) 79달러

97. 화자에 따르면, 11월에 무슨 일이 일어날 것인가?

(A) 스포츠 경기
(B) 제품 출시
(C) 가게 개업
(D) 무역 박람회

미남

Questions 98-100 refer to the following speech and books.

Good afternoon. I'm delighted to be here today to read an excerpt from my new book. Actually, [98]this is a special place for me, as I often came here to order breakfast and a hot drink while working on my book. I'd like to thank the owner, Mindy Lee, for arranging this event. [99]I got the idea for my book from an unexpected place. I was doing volunteer work for a nonprofit organization that supports schools overseas. [100]I saw what an important role music played in helping to keep children interested in their lessons. I started researching the topic further and found it to be very interesting.

안녕하세요. 저는 오늘 제 신간 도서의 발췌문을 읽기 위해 이 자리에 있게 되어 기쁩니다. 사실, [98]이곳은 제가 책을 쓰면서 아침 식사와 따뜻한 음료를 주문하기 위해 자주 왔기 때문에 제게 있어 특별한 장소입니다. 이 행사를 마련해 준 주인이신 민디 리 님께 감사드리고 싶습니다. [99]저는 예상치 못한 곳에서 제 책에 대한 아이디어를 얻었습니다. 저는 해외 학교를 후원하는 비영리 단체에서 자원봉사를 하고 있었습니다. [100]저는 음악이 아이들이 수업에 흥미를 가지도록 돕는 데 얼마나 중요한 역할을 하는지 보았습니다. 저는 그 주제를 더 연구하기 시작했고 그게 매우 흥미롭다는 걸 알았습니다.

어휘 excerpt 발췌 (부분) arrange 마련하다, 준비하다 unexpected 예상 밖의 do volunteer work 자원봉사를 하다 support 후원하다, 지지하다 overseas 해외에 play a role 역할을 하다

98. 화자는 어디에 있는 것 같은가?

(A) 기업 연구소에
(B) 공공 도서관에
(C) 커피숍에
(D) 서점에

99. 화자는 그의 책 아이디어를 언제 처음 생각해 냈는가?

(A) 잡지 기사를 읽으면서
(B) 자선 단체를 위해 자원봉사하면서
(C) 친척을 방문하면서
(D) 다큐멘터리를 시청하면서

패러프레이징 doing volunteer work for a nonprofit organization → volunteering for a charity

100. 시각 자료를 보시오. 화자는 누구인가?

(A) 맥스 스펜서
(B) 사부로 와다
(C) 엘리스 도널드슨
(D) 잭슨 커완

PART 5

101. to부정사 [부사 역할]

대금을 결제하려면 신용 카드 정보를 제공하십시오.

해설 빈칸 앞이 완전한 절이므로 빈칸 이하는 부사 역할을 해야 한다. 선택지에서 부사 역할을 할 수 있는 것은 to부정사인 (B) to submit뿐이다.

어휘 provide 제공하다 credit card 신용 카드 details 세부 사항 submit 제출하다 payment 지불, 대금

102. 명사 자리

사람들이 그 시설에 대한 의견을 공유할 수 있도록 소그룹 토론이 있을 것이다.

해설 빈칸 앞에 소유한정사 their가 있고 뒤에는 전치사 of가 있으므로 빈칸은 소유한정사의 수식을 받는 명사 자리이다. 따라서 명사인 (B) observations가 정답이다.

어휘 discussion 토론 share 공유하다 observation (관찰에 따른) 논평, 의견 facility 시설

103. 동사 어휘 reach

기계적 결함 때문에 버스는 터미널에 두 시간 늦게 도착했다.
(A) 도착하다 (B) 계속하다 (C) 이동하다 (D) 도착하다

해설 문맥상 '도착하다'를 뜻하는 (A) arrived와 (D) reached가 정답 후보인데 빈칸 뒤에 목적어가 있으므로 타동사인 (D)가 정답이다.

어휘 due to ~ 때문에 mechanical 기계적인 fault 결함, 잘못

104. 소유한정사

우리의 여름 프로그램에 참가할 인턴들은 미리 인사 서류 작성을 완료해야 한다.

해설 빈칸 앞에 동사 must complete가 있고 뒤에는 명사구 human resources paperwork가 있으므로 빈칸은 명사를 수식하는 자리이다. 따라서 소유한정사인 (C) their가 정답이다.

어휘 participate in ~에 참가하다 complete 완료하다 human resources 인적 자원, 인사부 paperwork 서류 작업 in advance 미리, 사전에

105. 부사 자리 [동사 수식]

새로운 BV 은행 본점의 건축가는 아마도 인근 건물들을 참고하여 디자인을 한 것 같다.

해설 빈칸은 조동사(has)와 과거분사(based) 사이의 부사 자리이므로 선택지 중 부사인 (C) presumably가 정답이다.

어휘 architect 건축가 headquarters 본사 presumably 아마 base A on B A의 기초[근거]를 B에 두다 nearby 근처의, 인근의

106. 형용사 어휘 simple

설문 조사 문항의 표현은 단순하고 이해하기 쉬워야 한다.
(A) 독점적인 (B) 새로운 (C) 단순한 (D) 유능한

어휘 wording 표현 survey 설문 조사 comprehend 이해하다

107. 명사 자리

모든 보유 차량에 대한 신뢰도는 고객들이 Gregson Car Rentals를 선택하게 하는 요소이다.

해설 빈칸 앞에 정관사 The가 있고 뒤에는 전치사 of가 있으므로 빈칸은 명사 자리이다. 따라서 (D) reliability가 정답이다.

어휘 reliability 신뢰도 fleet (기관이나 회사 등이 소유한) 모든 차량

108. 전치사 어휘 across

Masonex는 전국에 인기 있는 레스토랑 체인점을 열 계획이다.
(A) ~ 동안 (B) ~ 아래에 (C) ~에 반대하여 (D) ~ 전역에

109. 형용사 자리

그 일자리에 지원한 사람들이 너무 적어서 인사 부장은 그 자리를 충원하는 데 있어서 까다로울 수 없었다.

해설 빈칸은 be동사 뒤의 주격 보어 자리로 주어인 the hiring manager의 상태나 상황을 나타낼 수 있는 말이 들어가야 한다. 따라서 선택지 중 형용사인 (A) selective가 정답이다. 명사인 (B) selection은 주어와 동격 관계일 때만 주격 보어 자리에 위치할 수 있기 때문에 오답이다.

어휘 apply for ~에 지원하다 hiring manager 인사 부장 selective 선별적인, 까다로운 fill 채우다 position (일)자리, 직위

110. 소유대명사

객실에 체크인하기 위해 기다리고 있는 그 남자분께 그분의 방이 15분 후에 준비된다는 걸 알려 드려야 합니다.

해설 빈칸 앞에 명사절 접속사 that이 있고 뒤에는 동사 will be가 있으므로 빈칸은 주어 자리이다. 주격 대명사인 (A) he와 소유대명사인 (B) his가 정답 후보인데 문맥상 그가 준비되는 것이 아니라 그가 묵을 방이 준비된다는 내용이 되는 게 자연스러우므로 (B)가 정답이다. 여기서 his는 his room을 의미한다.

어휘 check into ~에 체크인하다 inform 알리다, 통지하다

111. 관계대명사 [주격]

이 교육 동영상은 소매점 환경에서 일해 본 적이 없는 계산원들을 위한 것이다.

해설 빈칸 앞에 사람을 나타내는 명사 cashiers가 있고 뒤에는 조동사 have가 바로 이어지므로 빈칸은 주격 관계대명사 자리이다. 따라서 (A) who가 정답이다.

어휘 be intended for ~을 위한 것이다 cashier 계산원 retail 소매 setting 환경, 설정

112. 부사 어휘 strictly

플래시를 켜고 전시품 사진을 찍는 것은 미술관에 의해 엄격히 금지되어 있다.
(A) 엄격하게 (B) 긴장하여; 팽팽하게 (C) 중요하게 (D) 동일하게

어휘 take photography 사진을 찍다 artwork 미술품 prohibit 금지하다

113. 동사 자리

오케스트라의 지휘자는 공원에서 무료 공연을 하는 것이 젊은 음악가들에게 영감을 줄 수 있다고 믿는다.

해설 빈칸 앞에 조동사 can이 있으므로 빈칸에는 동사원형이 들어가야 한다. 따라서 (C) inspire가 정답이다.

어휘 performance 공연 inspire 영감을 주다

114. 전치사 어휘 before

재고 정리 세일 상품은 환불되지 않기 때문에 고객들은 물품을 구매하기 전에 꼼꼼히 살펴야 한다.
(A) ~을 따라 (B) ~을 제외하고 (C) ~한 반면에 (D) ~하기 전에

해설 빈칸 뒤에 동명사 purchasing이 있는 것으로 보아 빈칸은 전치사 자리이므로 접속사인 (C) whereas는 오답이다.

어휘 refund 환불 offer 제공하다 clearance 재고 정리 세일 merchandise 제품 inspect 면밀히 살피다, 검사하다

115. 부사 자리

Mr. Higgins는 공식적으로 알려진 것보다 더 자주 지역 발전에 기여한다.

해설 빈칸은 과거분사 acknowledged를 수식하는 자리이므로 선택지 중 부사인 (D) publicly가 정답이다.

어휘 make a contribution 기여하다, 기부하다 cause 대의; 원인, 이유 publicly 공개적으로, 공식적으로 acknowledge (사실임을) 인정하다, 받아들이다

116. 전치사 자리+어휘

기술적 오류 때문에 이틀 동안 작업한 것을 날렸음에도 불구하고 그 팀은 보고서 마감일을 맞추었다.

해설 빈칸 뒤에 동명사 losing이 있으므로 빈칸은 전치사 자리이다. (B) Because of와 (D) Despite가 정답 후보인데 문맥상 이틀 동안 일을 하지 못했음에도 마감일을 맞췄다는 내용이 되는 게 자연스러우므로 (D) Despite가 정답이다.

어휘 lose 잃어버리다, 분실하다 technical 기술적인 meet the deadline 마감일을 맞추다

117. 동사 어휘 demonstrate

Mr. Zamora가 광 스캐너의 설정을 조정하는 방법을 시연할 것이다.
(A) 등록하다 (B) 깊은 인상을 주다 (C) 시도하다 (D) 시연하다

어휘 adjust 조정하다 setting 설정 optical scanner 광 스캐너

118. 명사 어휘 branch

주 전역에 15개의 지점이 있는 Wright Hardware는 델라웨어에서 가장 큰 체인점이다.
(A) 참고 문헌 (B) 지점 (C) 일과 (D) 통화, 화폐

어휘 locate 위치시키다, (특정 위치에) 두다 throughout ~ 전역에

119. 접속사 자리+어휘

〈The Journal of Social Sciences〉는 올해 연간 구독자가 작년보다 10% 더 많다고 알렸다.

해설 빈칸 앞뒤에 완전한 절이 있으므로 빈칸은 두 절을 연결하는 접속사 자리이다. (A) whenever와 (D) than이 정답 후보인데 문맥상 올해 연간 구독자가 작년보다 더 많다는 내용이 되는 게 자연스러우므로 (D) than이 정답이다.

어휘 report 보고하다, 알리다 annual 연간의 subscriber 구독자

120. 형용사 어휘 internal

내부 문서는 관리자의 명시적인 허가 없이는 외부인과 공유할 수 없다.
(A) 현실적인 (B) 내부의 (C) 가끔의 (D) 개선된

어휘 document 문서 share 공유하다 explicit 명시적인 permission 허가

121. 부사 자리 [동사 수식]

노트북 컴퓨터가 와이파이 네트워크에 연결되면 뉴스 피드가 자동으로 업데이트될 것이다.

해설 빈칸이 없어도 완전한 절이 성립하므로 빈칸은 부사 자리이다. 따라서 (B) automatically가 정답이다.

어휘 news feed 뉴스 피드 automatically 자동으로 laptop 노트북 컴퓨터 connect 연결하다

122. 형용사 자리

Yorkie Video Streaming Services의 새로운 고객 계약서에는 혼란스러운 표현이 없다.

해설 빈칸 앞에 동사 eliminates가 있고 뒤에는 명사 language가 있으므로 빈칸은 명사를 수식하는 형용사 자리이다. 따라서 (A) confusing이 정답이다.

어휘 contract 계약(서) eliminate 제거하다 confusing 혼란스러운 language 언어, 표현

123. 전치사 자리

방문객들은 음식 준비 구역에 들어가기에 앞서 손을 철저하게 씻고 장갑을 껴야 한다.

해설 빈칸 앞에 완전한 절이 있고 뒤에는 동명사구가 이어지므로 빈칸은 전치사 자리이다. 따라서 (C) prior to가 정답이다.

어휘 thoroughly 철저히 put on ~을 입다[쓰다/끼다/걸치다] preparation 준비

124. 명사 어휘 interval

Jade Hotel에서 Spencer Convention Center로 가는 왕복 교통편은 30분 간격으로 출발한다.
(A) 처분, 폐기 (B) 간격 (C) 분할; 부서 (D) 목적

어휘 shuttle 왕복 교통 기관 depart 출발하다

125. 명사 자리

워크숍의 목표는 식품 안전과 위생 습관에 대한 참가자들의 지식을 늘리는 것이다.

해설 빈칸 앞에 소유한정사 participants'가 있고 뒤에는 전치사 about이 있으므로 빈칸은 명사 자리이다. 따라서 (D) knowledge가 정답이다.

어휘 goal 목표 increase 늘리다 knowledge 지식 hygienic 위생의 practice 실행; 관행

126. 수동태

안타깝게도 편집자는 봄철 카탈로그에 있는 철자 오류를 놓쳤다.

해설 주어 the spelling error는 타동사 overlook의 행위를 받는 대상이고 빈칸 뒤에 〈by+행위 주체〉인 by the editor도 있으므로 동사는 〈be+과거분사〉 형태의 수동태가 적절하다. 따라서 (D) was overlooked가 정답이다.

어휘 unfortunately 안타깝게도, 유감스럽게도 spelling error 철자 오류 overlook 간과하다 editor 편집자

127. 동사 어휘 exchange

GC Clothing 상품을 다른 상품으로 교환해야 할 경우 고객 서비스 팀에 영수증을 보여 주셔야 합니다.

(A) 옷을 입다 (B) 교환하다 (C) 전시하다 (D) 안심시키다

어휘 merchandise 상품 receipt 영수증

128. 접속사 자리+어휘

Hendrix Communications는 수요가 있는 곳은 어디든 휴대폰 서비스 구역을 늘리는 데 노력을 들이고 있다.

해설 빈칸 앞뒤에 완전한 절이 있으므로 빈칸은 두 절을 연결하는 접속사 자리이다. (B) although와 (C) wherever가 정답 후보인데 문맥상 수요가 있는 곳은 어디든 휴대폰 서비스 구역을 늘리기 위해 노력하고 있다는 내용이 되는 게 자연스러우므로 (C) wherever가 정답이다.

어휘 work on ~에 노력을 들이다 coverage 범위, 서비스 구역 demand 수요

129. 형용사 자리

그 수업은 학습자들이 남는 시간에 들을 수 있도록 짧으면서도 감당할 수 있는 분량으로 나누어져 있다.

해설 빈칸 앞에 형용사 short가 콤마로 병렬 연결되어 있으므로 빈칸에도 동일한 품사가 들어가야 한다. 따라서 형용사인 (C) manageable이 정답이다.

어휘 break A down into B A를 B로 나누다 manageable 처리하기 쉬운

130. 동사 어휘 evolve

Concord Enterprises는 작은 회계 법인에서 전국적으로 호평을 받는 금융사로 발전했다.

(A) 간주하다 (B) 발전하다 (C) 결정하다 (D) 운송하다

어휘 nationally 전국적으로 acclaimed 호평을 받은 financial 금융의

PART 6

131-134 제품 후기

> 브랜드에 대해 많이 들어 봤기 때문에 집에서 써 볼 수 있는 Meadowlark Shampoo 샘플을 무료로 받게 되어 [131]기뻤습니다. 솔직히 말하면 그 제품은 오로지 천연 재료로 만들어졌기 때문에 결과가 평범할 거라고 생각했어요. 저는 그 샴푸가 매우 효과적이어서 [132]기분 좋게 놀랐습니다. [133]처음에는 제가 사용하고 있는 다른 브랜드보다 더 안 좋은 것 같았습니다. 하지만 Meadowlark Shampoo를 몇 번 사용해 보니 저는 무엇이 문제를 야기했는지 알아냈습니다. [134]그것은 제품을 제 머리카락에 충분히 묻히지 않았기 때문이었어요. 이 문제를 바로잡고 나서는 제 머리 모양에 만족하게 되었습니다. 이 샴푸는 두피에 순하고 여러 좋은 향으로 출시되기 때문에 강력 추천합니다.

어휘 to be honest 솔직히 말하면 exclusively 오로지, 독점적으로 natural 천연의 ingredient 재료, 성분 mediocre 보통의, 평범한 effective 효과적인 identify 확인하다, 밝히다 cause 일으키다, 야기하다 correct 바로잡다, 정정하다 be satisfied with ~에 만족하다 highly 대단히, 매우 recommend 추천하다 gentle 부드러운, 순한 scalp 두피 a variety of 여러 가지의, 다양한 scent 향기

131. 분사 자리

해설 빈칸은 be동사 was 뒤의 주격 보어 자리로 주어인 I의 상태나 상황을 나타낼 수 있는 말이 들어가야 한다. 따라서 선택지 중 형용사인 (B) delightful과 (D) delighted가 정답 후보인데, I는 기쁨을 주는 주체가 아니라 기쁨을 느끼는 대상이므로 과거분사인 (D)가 정답이다.

132. 부사 어휘 pleasantly

(A) 아마 (B) 융통성 있게 (C) 기분 좋게 (D) 단단히

133. 알맞은 문장 고르기

(A) 처음에는 제가 사용하고 있는 다른 브랜드보다 더 안 좋은 것 같았습니다.
(B) 그와는 반대로, 병을 여는 것은 꽤 어려웠습니다.
(C) 이제 대부분의 슈퍼마켓에서 그 샴푸를 찾을 수 있습니다.
(D) 더 저렴한 재료들이 더 나은 선택권이었을 것입니다.

해설 빈칸 뒤에서 샴푸를 제대로 사용해 보니 효과가 있었다고 언급했으므로 빈칸에는 다른 브랜드보다 안 좋은 샴푸인 줄 알았다는 내용이 들어가는 게 가장 자연스럽다. 따라서 (A)가 정답이다.

어휘 initially 처음에, 애초에 on the contrary 그와는 반대로 option 선택권, 옵션

134. 대명사 it

해설 빈칸에는 문장의 주어 역할을 하는 동시에 앞에서 언급된 문제의 원인(what was causing the problem)을 가리키는 대명사가 들어가야 하므로 3인칭 대명사인 (B) It이 정답이다. It은 앞에 이미 언급되었거나 현재 이야기되고 있는 사물, 동물, 또는 상황을 가리킬 때 쓴다.

135-138 기사

> 최근 한 보고서는 태양 전지판을 만드는 데 사용되는 재료 가격의 상당한 상승을 보여 주었다. 지난 몇 년 동안 새로운 투자자들은 석유와 같은 전통적인 연료원을 거부하기 시작했다. [135]이와는 대조적으로 재생 에너지 부문은 번창하고 있다. 태양 전지판 수요의 [136]변화가 가격 상승으로 이어졌는데, 기업과 개인 모두 다양한 에너지 선택권을 원하기 때문인 것으로 보인다. 소비자들은 곧 전지판의 소비자 가격 상승을 보게 될 것이다. [137]제조사들이 마진을 남겨야 하기 때문이다. [138]예상 증가율은 15~25% 사이이다.

어휘 recent 최근의 significant 중요한, 상당한 material 재료 solar panel 태양 전지판 investor 투자자 reject 거부하다 traditional 전통적인 fuel source 연료원 such as ~와 같은 petroleum 석유 renewable 재생 가능한 sector 부문 thrive 번창하다 lead to ~로 이어지다 individual 개인 alike 둘 다, 똑같이 diversify 다양화하다 consumer 소비자 likely 아마

135. 접속부사 어휘 in contrast

(A) 일반적으로 (B) 마찬가지로 (C) 예를 들면 (D) 대조적으로

136. 명사 어휘 change

(A) 변화 (B) 배치 (C) 결정 (D) (명확한) 설명

137. 알맞은 문장 고르기

(A) 안전 검사관들이 생산 과정을 감시하고 있다.
(B) 제조사들이 마진을 남겨야 하기 때문이다.
(C) 모든 건물이 전지판을 이용하기에 좋은 위치에 있는 것은 아니다.
(D) 엄격한 수입 규제는 산업의 일관성을 유지하는 데 도움이 된다.

해설 빈칸 앞에서 소비자들이 곧 전지판 가격 상승을 보게 될 것이라고 했으므로 빈칸에는 이것을 This is because로 받아 이유를 설명하는 내용이 들어가는 게 자연스럽다. 따라서 (B)가 정답이다.

어휘 inspector 검사자, 조사관 monitor 감시하다, 모니터링하다 manufacturer 제조업체 position 두다, 위치를 정하다 regulation 규제, 통제 consistency 일관성

138. 분사 자리 [과거분사]

해설 빈칸 앞에 정관사 The가 있고 뒤에는 명사 increase가 있으므로 빈칸은 명사를 수식하는 자리이다. 선택지 중 명사를 수식할 수 있는 것은 현재분사 (A) predicting과 과거분사 (D) predicted인데, 수식 대상인 increase는 행위자에 의해 '예측되는' 대상이기 때문에 빈칸과 수동 관계이므로 (D) predicted가 정답이다.

139-142 기사

> **Tiger Fashions가 밴쿠버에 매장을 오픈하다**
>
> 과감한 색상과 현대적인 디자인으로 유명한 의류 회사인 Tiger Fashions가 밴쿠버에 소매점을 열었다. "우리가 캐나다 시장을 [139]관찰한 결과, 소비자들은 남들 눈에 띄는 방법을 찾고 있기에 우리 브랜드는 확실히 그들이 그렇게 하는 것을 도울 수 있습니다."라고 회사의 대표인 Jack Palmer가 말했다.
>
> Tiger Fashions는 샌프란시스코의 작은 상점으로 시작했고, 첫 6년 동안 25개 지점으로 빠르게 성장했다. [140]밴쿠버 매장은 미국 이외의 지역에서 오픈하는 첫 번째 지점이 될 것이다. "우리는 완전히 새로운 고객군에 도달하게 되어 [141]기쁩니다."라고 Mr. Palmer가 말했다. "이것은 궁극적으로는 우리의 브랜드를 [142]전 세계 쇼핑객들에게 이르게 하겠다는 우리의 계획에 도움이 될 것입니다."

어휘 bold 대담한 retail 소매 stand out 눈에 띄다, 두드러지다 representative 대표(자) location 지점; 장소, 위치 reach 이르다, 도달하다 entirely 완전히 eventually 결국, 궁극적으로

139. 명사 자리+어휘

해설 빈칸 앞에 소유한정사 Our가 있고 뒤에는 전치사 of가 있으므로 빈칸은 소유한정사의 수식을 받는 명사 자리이다. (A) examiner와 (C) examination이 정답 후보인데 문맥상 캐나다 시장을 관찰하여 그들의 성향을 파악했다는 내용이 되는 게 자연스러우므로 '조사, 검토'를 뜻하는 (C)가 정답이다.

140. 알맞은 문장 고르기

(A) 밴쿠버 매장은 미국 이외의 지역에서 오픈하는 첫 번째 지점이 될 것이다.
(B) 재킷과 외투의 판매가 점점 보편화되고 있다.
(C) 이 같은 지도부의 변화는 회사에는 더 좋은 것이었다.
(D) 옷감은 재활용 재료로 만들어진다.

해설 빈칸 앞에서 Tiger Fashions가 캐나다 시장 분석 결과를 바탕으로 밴쿠버에 지점을 낸다고 한 것으로 보아 빈칸 뒤에서 완전히 새로운 고객군에 도달한다고 언급한 것은 Tiger Fashions가 처음 진출하는 캐나다 시장의 고객과 만난다는 걸 의미한다. 따라서 밴쿠버 매장이 미국 이외의 지역에 오픈하는 첫 지점이 될 거라는 내용의 (A)가 정답이다.

어휘 branch 지점, 지사 outerwear 겉옷, 외투 common 흔한 leadership 지도부, 지도력 fabric 천, 옷감 recycled 재활용된 material 재료, 직물

141. 현재 시제

해설 밴쿠버 사람들에게 도달하게 된 현재의 상황이 기쁘다는 내용이 되는 게 자연스러우므로 현재 시제인 (B) are가 정답이다.

142. 전치사 어휘 throughout

(A) ~ 전역에 (B) ~ 위에 (C) ~을 따라 (D) ~을 향해

해설 빈칸 뒤의 the world와 함께 쓰여 전 세계 쇼핑객에게 선보이겠다는 내용이 되는 게 자연스러우므로 (A) throughout이 정답이다.

143-146 보도 자료

> 즉시 배포용
> 연락처: Tina Newton, tnewton@sumnermedia.com
>
> 뉴욕 (7월 18일)—WM Publishing이 Sumner Media로의 매각 완료를 [143]확인해 주었다. 이번 매각은 Sumner Media가 저변을 확장하려는 계획의 일환이다. WM Publishing은 Sumner Media가 처음으로 진출하게 될 분야인 교육물로 가장 잘 알려져 있다. WM Publishing의 이사회는 세 개의 다른 미디어 그룹에게서 받은 제안을 진지하게 고려하고 있었다. [144]다른 제안도 몇 개 있었지만 초기에 거절되었다.
>
> WM Publishing의 직원들은 일자리를 유지할 뿐만 아니라 회사 내에서 더욱 승진할 수 있는 기회[145]도 있을 것이다. 덧붙여 Sumner Media는 WM Publishing 지사의 사무실을 개선하고 직원들을 지원하기 위해 기술에 [146]상당한 투자를 할 계획이다.

어휘 immediate 즉각적인 release 발표, 공개 finalization 완결, 마무리 move 조치, 움직임 expand 넓히다, 확장하다 reach 범위, 구역 be known for ~로 알려져 있다 educational material 교육 자료 board 이사회

seriously 진지하게 consider 고려하다 promotion 승진 additionally 덧붙여, 게다가 improve 개선하다 support 지원하다

143. 능동태+현재완료 시제

해설 빈칸 뒤에 목적어(the finalization)가 있으므로 빈칸에는 능동태가 들어가야 한다. (B) will confirm과 (C) has confirmed가 정답 후보인데, 뒤에 이어지는 내용을 보면 매각 협상이 이미 끝난 상황에서 할 수 있는 이야기들이 이어지므로 현재완료 시제인 (C)가 정답이다.

144. 알맞은 문장 고르기

(A) 다른 제안도 몇 개 있었지만 초기에 거절되었다.
(B) 출판 과정이 더 효율적으로 진행될 것 같다.
(C) Sumner Media는 최근에 최고 경영자가 바뀌었다.
(D) 건물 증축 승인이 계류 중이다.

해설 빈칸 앞에서 세 개의 다른 미디어 그룹에게서 받은 제안을 진지하게 고려하고 있었다고 했으므로 빈칸에는 다른 제안도 있었지만 거절되었다는 내용이 들어가는 게 가장 자연스럽다. 따라서 (A)가 정답이다. 참고로 Several others는 Several other offers를 의미한다.

어휘 efficient 효율적인 approval 승인 pending 계류 중인, 미완의

145. 상관 접속사 자리

해설 빈칸은 앞에 있는 not only와 짝을 이루는 말이 들어갈 자리이므로 (C) but이 정답이다.

146. 형용사 어휘 significant

(A) ~을 할 수 있는; 유능한 (B) 상당한, 중요한 (C) 충분하지 않은 (D) 편안한, 쾌적한

PART 7

147-148 안내문

> 여러분의 편의를 위해 각 보트에는 열쇠로 잠글 수 있고 방수가 되는 수납공간이 마련되어 있습니다. [147]출발하기 전에 수납공간에 넣고 싶은 것이 있으면 여러분의 가이드에게 말씀하세요. 날씨에 따라 주요 좌석 구역이 젖을 수 있으니 여러분의 물품을 보호할 것을 적극 권장합니다. [148]수납공간 이용료는 없지만 깨지기 쉬운 물품이나 귀중품은 책임지지 않는다는 것을 알아 두시기 바랍니다.

어휘 convenience 편리, 편의 be equipped with ~을 갖추고 있다 storage 보관, 저장 container 용기, 컨테이너 lockable 열쇠로 잠글 수 있는 water resistant 방수의 depart 출발하다 place 놓다, 두다 depending on ~에 따라 fee 수수료, 요금 fragile 깨지기 쉬운 valuable 귀중한

147. 안내문이 작성된 대상은 누구이겠는가?

(A) 유지 보수 작업자
(B) 보트 소유자
(C) 투어 참가자
(D) 경비원

해설 추론/암시
수납공간에 넣고 싶은 게 있으면 가이드에게 말하라고 한 것으로 보아 투어 참가자를 대상으로 작성된 정보임을 유추할 수 있다. 따라서 (C)가 정답이다.

148. 서비스에 대해 언급된 것은 무엇인가?

(A) 날씨가 안 좋으면 취소될 수 있다.
(B) 무료로 제공된다.
(C) 가끔 대기자 명단이 있다.
(D) 신분증을 제시해야 한다.

해설 NOT/True
수납공간 이용료는 없다고 했으므로 (B)가 정답이다.

어휘 cancel 취소하다 at no charge 무료로

149-150 문자 메시지

> **Courtney Briggs** [오전 8:03]
> 안녕하세요, Luoyang. 저는 파티용품점에서 우리 부스에 쓸 여분의 풍선을 몇 개 사고 있어요. 다행히 우리가 원했던 은색과 빨간색이 있네요. 행사장의 설치 작업은 어떻게 되어 가고 있나요?
>
> **Luoyang Gu** [오전 8:08]
> 우리 부스에서는 순조롭게 진행 중입니다. [149]이곳에는 탄산음료 회사가 정말 많네요. 우리가 돋보일 수 있는 방법을 찾았으면 좋겠어요. 무료 샘플을 나눠 주는 것이 좋은 아이디어일 수 있다고 생각해요. [150]그런데, 당신에게 또 심부름을 시키기는 싫지만 줄 조명 몇 개도 구할 수 있을까요?
>
> **Courtney Briggs** [오전 8:10]
> <u>저는 아직 출발하지 않았어요.</u> [150]그것들을 저쪽 통로에서 본 것 같아요. 이따 봐요.

어휘 pick up ~을 사다 extra 추가의, 여분의 booth (전시회장의) 부스 setup 설치 stand out 눈에 띄다 give away ~을 나누어 주다 send ~ on an errand ~을 심부름 보내다 string 끈, 줄 light 전등, 불 aisle 통로, 복도

149. 메시지 작성자들은 어디서 근무하겠는가?

(A) 여행사
(B) 음료 제조업체
(C) 신발 체인점
(D) 부동산 회사

해설 추론/암시
오전 8시 8분에 행사장에 탄산음료 회사가 많다고 말하면서 자신들이 돋보일 수 있는 방법을 찾고 싶다고 한 것으로 보아 메시지 작성자들은 해당 업계 종사자들이라는 걸 추론할 수 있다. 따라서 (B)가 정답이다.

패러프레이징 soda companies → a beverage manufacturer

150. 오전 8시 10분에, Ms. Briggs가 "저는 아직 출발하지 않았어요"라고 쓸 때 그녀는 무엇을 의미하겠는가?

(A) 현장으로 가는 길 안내가 필요하다.

(B) 자신의 책임에 대해 확신이 없다.
(C) 행사에 늦을 것이다.
(D) 일을 끝낼 수 있다.

해설 의도 파악
줄 조명을 구해다 달라는 부탁에 이렇게 답하며 그것을 본 것 같다고 말했으므로, 아직 현장을 떠나지 않았으니 조명을 구할 수 있다는 의미로 답했다는 것을 알 수 있다. 따라서 (D)가 정답이다.

151-152 안내 책자

> Haven Fitness
> www.myhavenfitness.com
>
> Haven Fitness에서 우리는 여러분이 멋진 외모와 최상의 컨디션을 만드는 걸 돕고 싶습니다! 개인 트레이너를 고용하는 것은 여러분의 목표를 달성하고 건강을 증진시키는 가장 좋은 방법입니다. 개인 트레이닝이 여러분에게 맞을지 확신이 들지 않나요? [151]10회 트레이닝 패키지 상품을 구입해서 1회 무료 체험을 해 보세요. 체험 후 일주일 이내에 취소할 수 있습니다.
>
> 개인 트레이닝 서비스
> • 건강에 관한 목표 및 필요성 첫 진단
> • 운동 방법을 알려 줄 수 있는 숙련된 트레이너들
> • 트레이닝 식이요법을 병행하고 지원하기 위한 영양 조언
>
> 유연한 서비스
> [152]우리는 지역 내에서 화상 회의로 개인 트레이닝을 제공하는 유일한 헬스클럽입니다. 이것은 여행을 하거나 헬스클럽에 올 시간이 없을 때 여러분이 트레이닝을 꾸준히 할 수 있는 완벽한 방법입니다.

어휘 meet a goal 목표를 달성하다 session (어느 활동의) 시간 trial 시도, 시험 cancel 취소하다 initial 처음의, 초기의 assessment 평가 experienced 경험 있는, 숙련된 nutrition 영양 accompany 동반하다, 동행하다 regime 식이요법 (= regimen) flexible 유연한 video conferencing 화상 회의 keep up with ~을 따라잡다, ~에 뒤처지지 않다 commute 통근하다

151. 서비스 패키지에 대해 시사된 것은 무엇인가?
(A) 무료 체험 시간이 포함되어 있다.
(B) 상당한 할인을 받을 수 있다.
(C) 언제든지 취소할 수 있다.
(D) 신규 고객들만을 위한 것이다.

해설 NOT/True
10회 트레이닝 패키지를 구입하면 무료 체험을 할 수 있다고 했으므로 (A)가 정답이다. 체험 후 일주일 이내에 취소할 수 있다고 했으므로 (C)는 오답이다.

어휘 be eligible for ~을 받을 자격이 있다 substantial 상당한

152. 안내 책자에 따르면, Haven Fitness에 대해 특별한 것은 무엇인가?
(A) 연중무휴로 운영된다.
(B) 고객들에게 음식을 제공한다.
(C) 원격으로 트레이닝을 제공한다.
(D) 요금이 가장 저렴하다.

해설 세부 사항
화상 회의로 개인 트레이닝을 제공하는 유일한 헬스클럽이라고 했으므로 (C)가 정답이다.

패러프레이징 through video conferencing → remotely

153-154 채용 공고

> **영국 헤리티지 재단에서 일할 건축사학자**
>
> 영국 헤리티지 재단은 2년 계약의 전임 건축사학자를 구하고 있습니다. 역사학자는 [153C]우리 현장을 방문하는 사람들을 위한 인쇄물과 디지털 자료를 만들기 위해 재단의 많은 선사 유적지에서 연구를 수행하는 책임을 맡게 됩니다. 역사학자는 필요한 경우 [153A]외부의 자문 위원들과 서신을 주고받을 뿐만 아니라 소규모 연구팀을 이끌 것입니다. 업무에는 연중 [153B]다양한 모금 행사에서 재단을 홍보하는 일도 포함됩니다.
>
> 후보자는 고고학 학위 또는 이와 동등한 실무 경력이 있어야 합니다. 관련 분야의 석사 학위를 우대하지만 필수는 아닙니다. [154]이 자리는 우리의 다양한 현장에 대한 상당한 횟수의 출장을 요구합니다. 지원하려면 www.eheritagefoundation.org/careers를 방문하세요.

어휘 property 건물; 부동산, 재산 historian 역사학자 foundation 재단 seek 찾다, 구하다 undertake 맡다, 착수하다 prehistoric 선사 시대의 lead 이끌다 correspond with ~와 서신을 주고받다 external 외부의 consultant 자문 위원, 상담가 promote 홍보하다 fundraising 모금 candidate 지원자, 후보자 degree 학위 archaeology 고고학 equivalent 동등한 practical 실제적인, 실무의 master's degree 석사 학위 related 관련된 field 분야 desirable 바람직한 position (일)자리, 직위 considerable 상당한 apply 지원하다, 신청하다

153. 건축사학자의 업무로 언급되지 않은 것은 무엇인가?
(A) 외부 전문가들과 소통하기
(B) 모금 행사에 참석하기
(C) 방문객들을 위한 콘텐츠 개발하기
(D) 학술지에 연구 결과 게재하기

해설 NOT/True
학술지에 연구 결과를 게재해야 한다는 내용은 언급되어 있지 않으므로 (D)가 정답이다.

패러프레이징 (A) correspond with external consultants → Communicating with external experts
(C) create print and digital materials → Developing content

어휘 communicate with ~와 연락하다 expert 전문가 fundraiser 모금 행사 journal 학술지, 저널

154. 직무 요건으로 시사된 것은 무엇인가?
(A) 광범위한 출장 능력
(B) 대중 연설 경험
(C) 석사 학위
(D) 전문적 네트워크

해설 NOT/True
상당한 횟수의 현장 출장을 요구한다고 했으므로 (A)가 정답이다.

패러프레이징 a considerable amount of travel to our various sites → travel extensively

어휘 extensively 광범위하게, 폭넓게 public speaking 대중 연설 professional 전문적인

155-157 이메일

> 수신: Minjae Jeong
> 발신: Natalie Morrison
> 날짜: 3월 23일
> 제목: Villa Tech
> 첨부 파일: miramar7.docx
>
> Mr. Jeong께,
>
> Villa Tech는 공공 기업들을 위한 장비의 선도적인 생산업체입니다. [156]우리는 최근에 새로운 스마트 전기 계량기인 Miramar-7을 개발했습니다. 이 장치는 실시간으로 사용량을 추적하고, 계량기 숫자를 회사에 자동으로 전송하고, 사용량을 줄일 수 있는 방법을 알아내는 것을 쉽게 해 줍니다.
>
> [155]우리는 현재 이 제품을 국내외에 출시하는 걸 도와줄 마케팅 회사를 찾고 있는데, 제가 귀하와 귀하의 회사를 추천받았습니다. 귀하의 전문 지식이 성공적인 출시에 도움이 될 수 있습니다. 장치에 대한 몇 가지 세부 사항과 이 프로젝트에 우리가 기대하는 바를 간단히 정리하여 첨부했습니다. [157]이 프로젝트를 하는 것에 관심이 있다면 우리 웹사이트에서 양식을 작성해 주십시오. 첫 단계의 마감일은 4월 10일입니다. 심사 단계를 통과하시면 정식 제안서를 제출하는 과정을 이메일로 보내드리겠습니다. 우리는 귀하의 의견을 듣기를 고대합니다.
>
> Natalie Morrison

어휘 leading 선도적인 utility company (수도, 전기, 가스 등의 사업을 하는) 공공 기업 meter 계량기, 미터기 track 추적하다 usage 사용(량) in real time 실시간으로 reading (계량기 등에 표시된) 측정값 identify 알아내다 roll out (신상품을) 출시하다 domestically 국내에서 expertise 전문 지식 launch 출시 brief 간단한 description 설명, 묘사 expectation 기대 regarding ~에 대하여 handle 처리하다, 취급하다 complete 작성하다 form 서식, 양식 screening phase 심사 단계 formal 정식의 proposal 제안 look forward to ~을 고대하다

155. Mr. Jeong은 누구이겠는가?

(A) 전자 제품 제조업자
(B) 마케팅 전문가
(C) 이사
(D) 제품 디자이너

해설 추론/암시
Villa Tech는 마케팅 회사를 찾고 있다고 했는데 Mr. Jeong의 전문 지식이 도움이 될 수 있다고 했으므로 이메일 수신자인 Mr. Jeong은 마케팅 전문가임을 유추할 수 있다. 따라서 (B)가 정답이다.

어휘 electronics 전자 제품 manufacturer 제조업체 specialist 전문가 board 이사회

156. Miramar-7은 무엇인가?

(A) 냉각 장치
(B) 주방 기기
(C) 모바일 애플리케이션
(D) 에너지 모니터링 장치

해설 세부 사항
Miramar-7은 전기 계량기라고 했으므로 (D)가 정답이다.

어휘 appliance 가전제품, 기기 application 애플리케이션, 앱 monitor 감시하다, 모니터링하다 device 기기

157. 프로젝트를 작업하고 싶다면 Mr. Jeong은 무엇을 해야 하는가?

(A) 그룹 면접에 참석하기
(B) 온라인 양식 작성하기
(C) 이메일에 회신하기
(D) 첨부된 문서를 인쇄하여 반송하기

해설 세부 사항
프로젝트에 관심이 있다면 웹사이트에서 양식을 작성하라고 했으므로 (B)가 정답이다.

패러프레이징 complete the form on our Web site → Complete an online form

158-160 웹페이지

> **인쇄 대기 시간**
>
> Print4U는 개인적인 프로젝트뿐만 아니라 기업체에도 다양한 인쇄 서비스를 제공합니다. 저희에게 파일을 주시면 인쇄된 품목이 아래 나열된 기간 내에 준비될 것을 보장합니다. 주문품이 수령 준비가 되면 문자를 받으실 겁니다. 저희는 최대 2주까지 물품을 [159]보관할 수 있습니다. [158]월요일부터 수요일까지는 오전 8시부터 오후 9시까지, 목요일부터 토요일까지는 오전 8시부터 오후 7시까지 영업합니다.

제품 종류	표준	특급
문서	1-2시간	30분
명함	2-3일	익일
[160]안내 책자 및 팸플릿	3-5일	2일
현수막	5-7일	X

어휘 a range of 다양한 personal 개인의, 개인적인 guarantee 보장하다 time frame 시간, 기간 pick up ~을 찾다, ~을 수령하다 hold 유지하다, 보유하다 banner 현수막

158. Print4U에 대해 시사되지 않은 것은 무엇인가?

(A) 당일에 일부 프로젝트를 완료할 수 있다.
(B) 평일에는 같은 시간에 문을 닫는다.
(C) 고객들과 문자로 연락을 주고받는다.
(D) 특급 서비스를 모든 제품에 이용할 수는 없다.

해설 NOT/True
월요일부터 수요일까지는 오후 9시까지, 목요일부터 토요일까지는 오후 7시까지 영업한다고 했으므로 평일에는 같은 시간에 문을 닫지 않는다는 것을 알 수 있다. 따라서 (B)가 정답이다.

어휘 weekday 평일 via ~을 통하여 text 문자 메시지 available 이용할 수 있는

159. 첫 번째 단락 세 번째 줄의 어휘 "hold"와 의미상 가장 가까운 것은?

(A) 지지하다
(B) 운반하다
(C) 보관하다
(D) 저지하다

해설 동의어 찾기
hold가 있는 hold items는 물품을 보관한다는 의미이며, 여기서 hold는 '보관하다'라는 뜻으로 쓰였다. 따라서 (C) store가 정답이다.

160. 고객이 안내 책자를 받기 위해 기다려야 하는 가장 긴 시간은 얼마인가?

(A) 2일
(B) 3일
(C) 5일
(D) 7일

해설 세부 사항
표준은 최소 3일에서 최대 5일, 특급은 2일이 걸린다고 나와 있으므로 (C)가 정답이다.

161-164 온라인 채팅

Kerry Atkins [오전 9:43] 안녕하세요, Levi. [161]저희 도예 공방에서 선적해야 하는 꽃병 사진을 받으셨는지 궁금해요. 우리는 수송 준비를 할 수 있도록 곧 그것들을 상자에 넣기 시작할 거예요.

Levi Marquez [오전 9:44] 안녕하세요, Ms. Atkins. [161]네, 그것들을 넣을 만큼 충분히 큰 포장재가 있습니다. 어떤 종류의 완충재를 사용할지 결정하셨나요?

Kerry Atkins [오전 9:46] 그 문제가 상황을 지연시키고 있어요. [162]저밀도 스펀지를 알아봤는데 너무 비싸네요. 뭔가 다른 게 있을 거예요. 당신이 아는 게 좀 있을 것 같아요.

Levi Marquez [오전 9:48] 당신의 경우에는 갈색 포장지 사용을 고려해야 할 것 같아요. [163]거의 모든 곳, 특히 문구점이나 미술용품점에서 살 수 있다는 게 제일 좋죠. 종이를 구겨서 물품을 둘둘 싸기만 하면 돼요.

Kerry Atkins [오전 9:49] 그거 괜찮네요. 한번 해 볼게요. [164]상자 겉면에 붙이기 위해 '취급 주의' 스티커도 인쇄했거든요. 그냥 옆에 붙이면 될까요?

Levi Marquez [오전 9:51] [164]위, 아래, 그리고 사면에 모두 붙여야 합니다. 눈에 잘 띄도록 확실히 하는 것이 좋아요. 그렇지 않으면 쉽게 간과될 수 있습니다.

Kerry Atkins [오전 9:52] 알겠어요. 알아 두니 정말 도움이 되네요. 감사해요!

어휘 pottery 도자기, 도예 ship 선적하다, 배에 싣다 box up ~을 상자에 넣다 transport 수송, 운송 packaging 포장(재) cushioning 완충재 hold ~ up ~을 지연시키다, 방해하다 look into ~을 조사하다, ~을 살펴보다 low-density 저밀도의 foam 스펀지, (침대 매트리스 등에 쓰는) 발포 고무 stationery store 문구점 crumple 구기다 surround 둘러싸다 give it a try 한번 해 보다 exterior 외부, 겉면 bottom 바닥

161. Mr. Marquez는 어디서 근무하겠는가?

(A) 여행사
(B) 배송 업체
(C) 인쇄소
(D) 회계 법인

해설 추론/암시
Ms. Atkins가 Mr. Marquez에게 선적할 꽃병 사진을 받았는지 물어본 것과 Mr. Marquez가 꽃병을 넣을 만한 포장재가 있다고 말한 것으로 보아 Ms. Atkins는 물건을 보내려는 고객이고, Mr. Marquez는 운송하는 일을 담당하고 있음을 추론할 수 있다. 따라서 (B)가 정답이다.

162. 오전 9시 46분에 Ms. Atkins가 "당신이 아는 게 좀 있을 것 같아요"라고 쓸 때 그녀는 무엇을 의미하는가?

(A) Mr. Marquez는 추천을 해 줘야 한다.
(B) Mr. Marquez는 최근에 업체를 방문했다.
(C) Mr. Marquez는 새로운 과제를 받게 될 것이다.
(D) Mr. Marquez는 실수를 했다.

해설 의도 파악
have seen it all은 경험이나 아는 것이 많다는 걸 나타낼 때 쓰는 표현이다. 여기서는 Ms. Atkins가 저밀도 스펀지는 너무 비싸다며 다른 대체물이 있을 것 같다고 한 다음 이 말을 했으므로 Mr. Marquez가 아는 게 많으니 저밀도 스펀지를 대신할 만한 것을 추천해 달라는 의도로 한 말이라는 걸 알 수 있다. 따라서 (A)가 정답이다.

어휘 make a recommendation 추천하다 assignment 과제, 임무 make an error 실수하다

163. Mr. Marquez는 왜 갈색 포장지를 추천하는가?

(A) 쉽게 구할 수 있다.
(B) 환경친화적이다.
(C) 내구성이 있다.
(D) 부드럽다.

해설 세부 사항
거의 모든 곳에서 구할 수 있어서 좋다고 했으므로 (A)가 정답이다.

패러프레이징 you can buy it almost anywhere → It is readily available.

어휘 readily 손쉽게 available 구할 수 있는, 이용할 수 있는 durable 내구성이 있는

164. 스티커에 대해 암시된 것은 무엇인가?

(A) 추가 요금을 발생시킬 수 있다.
(B) 색깔이 바뀌어야 한다.
(C) 여러 곳에 붙이는 것이 가장 좋다.
(D) 일부 품목에는 사용할 필요가 없다.

해설 추론/암시
Ms. Atkins가 스티커를 상자 옆면에 붙이면 되는지 묻자 Mr. Marquez가

위, 아래, 그리고 사면에 모두 붙이라고 했으므로 스티커를 여러 곳에 붙이는 게 가장 좋다는 것을 유추할 수 있다. 따라서 (C)가 정답이다.

어휘 incur 초래하다, 발생시키다 additional 추가적인 fee 요금, 수수료 multiple 다수의, 복수의

165-167 이메일

수신: Shreya Dayal
발신: Reseda Insurance
날짜: 4월 8일
제목: 주택 보험

Ms. Dayal께,

Reseda Insurance의 고객이 되어 주셔서 감사합니다. 저희 기록에 따르면 귀하의 주택 보험(증권 번호: 0267855)은 5월 15일에 만료될 예정입니다. [165]차질 없는 부동산 보호를 위해 보험을 갱신해 주십시오. [166]현재의 요금을 1년 더 고정시키기 위해 5월 1일 전에 그렇게 하실 것을 추천합니다. 저희 요금이 그 날짜에 인상될 예정이기 때문입니다.

[167]문의 사항이 있으시면 저희 상담 전화를 이용하셔야 합니다. 보다 효율적으로 답을 얻으실 수 있기 때문입니다.

Joanne Stroud
Reseda Insurance, 고객 서비스
상담 전화: 1-800-555-1258

어휘 insurance 보험 policy 보험 증권 be set to do ~하도록 예정되어 있다 expire 만료되다 renew 갱신하다 uninterrupted 중단되지 않는, 연속된 protection 보호 property 재산, 부동산 lock in (가격 등을) 고정시키다 rate 요금, 요율 helpline 고객 상담 전화 inquiry 문의 efficiently 효율적으로

165. Ms. Stroud가 이메일을 보낸 이유는 무엇인가?
(A) Ms. Dayal에게 연체 요금에 대해 상기시키기 위해
(B) Ms. Dayal에게 직원 변경을 알리기 위해
(C) Ms. Dayal에게 몇 가지 제안을 요청하기 위해
(D) Ms. Dayal이 서비스를 연장하도록 권유하기 위해

해설 주제/목적
주택 보험을 갱신하라고 했으므로 (D)가 정답이다.

어휘 remind 상기시키다 overdue 기한이 지난 notify 알리다, 통지하다 personnel 인원, 직원 encourage 장려하다

166. Ms. Stroud에 따르면, 회사는 5월 1일에 무엇을 할 것인가?
(A) 서비스 요금 인상하기
(B) 더 다양한 패키지 상품 출시하기
(C) Ms. Dayal에게 확인서 보내기
(D) 부동산 가치 평가하기

해설 세부 사항
5월 1일에 보험료가 오를 것이라고 했으므로 (A)가 정답이다.

패러프레이징 our rates are going up → Increase fees for a service

어휘 fee 요금, 수수료 release 출시하다, 공개하다 a wide range of 광범위한, 다양한 package 패키지 상품 confirmation 확인 assess 평가하다 value 가치

167. Ms. Dayal은 질문이 있으면 무엇을 하라고 추천받는가?
(A) 편지 보내기
(B) 이메일에 회신하기
(C) 업체에 전화하기
(D) 사무실 방문하기

해설 세부 사항
문의 사항이 있으면 상담 전화를 이용하라고 했으므로 (C)가 정답이다.

168-171 기사

Isabella Lenz: 런웨이의 꿈

[168]Isabella Lenz가 겨우 6살이었을 때, 그녀의 부모님은 그녀를 유명한 Gauthier Design School의 런웨이 쇼에 데려갔다. 그녀는 그 이후로 패션계에서 일하기를 원했다. Ms. Lenz에게 처음으로 재봉틀이 생겼을 때 [171]그녀는 돈이 많지 않았음에도 불구하고 쉬지 않고 옷 만드는 연습을 했다. 그녀는 원단에 할인을 받기 위해 원단 가게에 취직했고, 항상 선물로 재봉 용품을 요구했다. <u>게다가 그녀는 중고 매장에서 옷을 사서 수선했다.</u>

[169A]20대 초반에 Ms. Lenz는 지역 패션 대회에 참가했다. 그녀는 우승하지는 못했지만 그녀에게 귀중한 직업 관련 조언을 해 준 그 분야의 전문가 몇 명을 만났다.

[169D]그녀는 자신의 패션 사업을 시작하기 위해 은행에서 돈을 대출했다. 그것은 위험한 행보였지만 그녀에게 자신의 브랜드를 만들 기회를 주었다. [169C 170]그녀의 사촌이자 유명 컨트리 음악 가수인 Stella Perry가 National Music Awards에서 입을 멋진 드레스를 그녀가 디자인했을 때 큰 기회가 찾아왔다. Ms. Perry가 소셜 미디어에 행사 사진들을 올렸는데 [170]수십만 명의 팔로워들이 Ms. Lenz의 재능을 접하게 된 것이다. 주문이 쇄도했고 Ms. Lenz의 브랜드는 누구나 아는 브랜드가 되었다.

어휘 runway 런웨이, (패션쇼) 무대 sewing machine 재봉틀 risky 위험한 big break (특히 직업과 관련된) 큰 기회[행운] stunning 굉장히 아름다운 gown 드레스, 가운 post 올리다, 게시하다 introduce 소개하다, 접하게 하다 household name 누구나 아는 이름

168. Ms. Lenz에 대해 암시된 것은 무엇인가?
(A) 온라인으로만 옷을 판매한다.
(B) 사업을 다른 분야로 확장하기를 원한다.
(C) 유명한 패션 디자인 학교에서 공부했다.
(D) 어릴 때부터 같은 직업 목표를 갖고 있었다.

해설 추론/암시
6살 때 런웨이 쇼를 본 이후로 패션계에서 일하고 싶어 했다고 나와 있으므로 어릴 때부터 직업 목표가 동일했음을 추론할 수 있다. 따라서 (D)가 정답이다.

어휘 exclusively 배타적으로, 독점적으로 expand 확장하다

169. Ms. Lenz의 성공에 기여한 것으로 시사되지 않은 것은 무엇인가?

(A) 대회 참가
(B) 장학 자금 지원
(C) 가족 구성원의 홍보
(D) 사업 대출금 수령

해설 **NOT/True**
장학금을 받았다는 내용은 없으므로 (B)가 정답이다.

패러프레이징 (A) entered a local fashion competition → Participation in a competition
(D) borrowed money from the bank → Receipt of a business loan

어휘 scholarship fund 장학 기금 publicity 홍보, (매스컴의) 관심

170. Ms. Perry에 대해 암시된 것은 무엇인가?

(A) Ms. Lenz에게 첫 번째 주문을 했다.
(B) 소셜 미디어에서 Ms. Lenz를 찾았다.
(C) 성공한 음악가이다.
(D) 자신만의 패션 브랜드를 갖고 있다.

해설 추론/암시
National Music Awards에 참석했고 수십만 명의 팔로워들이 있는 것으로 보아 성공한 음악가임을 유추할 수 있다. 따라서 (C)가 정답이다.

어휘 place an order 주문하다

171. [1], [2], [3], [4]로 표시된 위치 중 다음 문장이 들어가기에 가장 적절한 곳은?

"게다가 그녀는 중고 매장에서 옷을 사서 수선했다."

해설 문장 삽입
주어진 문장은 중고 매장에서 옷을 사다가 고쳤다는 의미인데, 부가 의미가 있는 접속부사 Additionally(게다가)가 있는 것으로 보아 주어진 문장 앞에 이와 비슷한 내용이 서술되어야 한다는 걸 알 수 있다. 따라서 Ms. Lenz는 없는 형편에도 옷 만드는 연습을 계속했고, 원단 할인을 받으려고 원단 가게에 취직했다는 내용 바로 뒤에 이어지는 게 가장 자연스러우므로 (A)가 정답이다.

172-175 편지

Delia Coleman
Coleman Eye Clinic
1090 밀러 스트리트
노샘프턴, 펜실베이니아 18067

Ms. Coleman께,

귀하를 만나고, 귀하의 안과에서 필요로 하는 인테리어 디자인에 대해 더 많이 알게 되어 즐거웠습니다. 대기실을 리모델링하는 것은 훌륭한 투자이며, [173]저희는 귀하의 예전 건물에 있었던 현대적인 느낌을 똑같이 낼 수 있습니다. 귀하께서 입주한 지 얼마 되지 않은 것은 알지만 이런 종류의 프로젝트는 가능한 한 빨리 진행되어야 합니다.

[172]Beau Interiors를 선택하신다면 첫 번째 단계는 제게 공유해 주신 선호를 기반으로 하여 몇 가지 예비 계획을 세우는 것입니다. 그런 다음 제가 페인트뿐만 아니라 원단과 타일 샘플도 가져다 드리겠습니다. [174]협력업체의 가구가 비치되어 있는 저희 전시장도 방문하실 수 있습니다. 귀하께서 완전히 만족하실 때까지 디자인을 계속 수정해 드릴 수 있습니다. 계획이 확정되면 [175]목수와 전기 기술자가 현장을 방문할 것입니다. 둘 다 상가 현장에 경험이 있습니다. 마지막으로 저희는 작업 단계별로 일정을 잡을 것입니다. 이 프로젝트를 진행하기를 원하신다면 저에게 알려 주세요.

Kayla Harris
Beau Interiors, 선임 디자이너

어휘 clinic 의원, 병원 investment 투자 previous 이전의, 예전의 get underway 시작하다 draw up (계획을) 작성하다 preliminary 예비의 preference 선호(도) showroom 전시장 revise 변경하다, 수정하다 completely 완전히 finalize 마무리 짓다 carpenter 목수 electrician 전기 기사 conduct (특정한 활동을) 하다 on-site 현장의 set up (일정 등을) 수립하다 phase 단계 move forward 전진하다, 추진하다

172. 편지의 목적은 무엇인가?

(A) 문서를 요청하기 위해
(B) 과정을 간략하게 설명하기 위해
(C) 결정을 발표하기 위해
(D) 회의를 확정하기 위해

해설 주제/목적
리모델링의 각 단계를 순차적으로 설명하고 있는 것으로 보아 리모델링 과정을 설명하기 위한 편지임을 알 수 있다. 따라서 (B)가 정답이다.

어휘 outline (간략하게) 설명하다 process 과정 confirm 확정하다

173. Ms. Coleman에 대해 암시된 것은 무엇인가?

(A) 속달 서비스를 요청했다.
(B) 투자금을 구하고 있다.
(C) 직원을 늘렸다.
(D) 최근에 업체를 이전했다.

해설 추론/암시
Ms. Coleman의 예전 건물에 대한 언급이 있고 입주한 지 얼마 안 되었다고 했으므로 최근에 이사했다는 것을 유추할 수 있다. 따라서 (D)가 정답이다.

패러프레이징 you've just moved in → recently relocated her business

어휘 seek 찾다, 구하다 investment 투자 expand 확장하다, 확대하다 staff 직원 relocate 이전하다, 옮기다

174. Beau Interiors에 대해 시사된 것은 무엇인가?

(A) 지역에 지점이 몇 개 있다.
(B) 협력업체의 상품을 전시한다.
(C) 자체 가구를 제작한다.
(D) 환불 보증을 해 준다.

해설 **NOT/True**
협력업체의 가구가 비치되어 있는 전시장도 방문할 수 있다고 했으므로 (B)가 정답이다.

어휘 branch 지점 display 전시하다 merchandise 상품 money-back guarantee 환불 보장

175. [1], [2], [3], [4]로 표시된 위치 중 다음 문장이 들어가기에 가장 적절한 곳은?

"둘 다 상가 현장에 경험이 있습니다."

해설 문장 삽입
주어진 문장의 Both가 가리키는 것을 찾아야 한다. 상가 현장에 경험이 있다는 것으로 보아 Both는 리모델링 현장에서 일할 예정인 사람들이라고 유추할 수 있다. 따라서 주어진 문장은 목수와 전기 기술자가 현장을 방문할 것이라는 내용 뒤에 위치하는 것이 적절하므로 (C)가 정답이다.

176-180 후기 & 이메일

〈The Lab〉
Kevin Collier 후기 작성

〈The Lab〉은 Jackie Montano가 각본 및 감독을 맡았고, [178]프로듀서인 Shawn Trevino와 합작하여 만든 강렬한 스릴러물이다. 영화는 3월에 독립 극장에서 조용히 첫선을 보였지만 후에 시애틀 영화제에서 상영되었을 때 인기를 얻었다. 그것은 현재 전국의 주류 극장에서 상영되고 있으며, 대단한 인기를 끌게 되어 [176]Spark Studios가 그것을 각색하여 TV 시리즈로 만드는 작업을 하고 있다. 〈The Lab〉은 놀라운 과학적 발견을 하지만 자신의 [177]목적을 위해 그것을 비밀로 하기로 결심하는 화학자인 Christopher Bull 박사를 추적한다. 주연 배우 Vincent Schiller의 놀라운 연기와 더불어 〈The Lab〉은 마지막 장면까지 여러분을 몰두하게 만들 것이다.

어휘 intense 강렬한 in collaboration with ~와 협력하여 producer 제작자 make one's debut 데뷔하다, 처음 등장하다 independent 독립된 gain 얻다 popularity 인기 mainstream 주류의 adapt 각색하다 chemist 화학자 remarkable 놀라운 for one's own ends 자신의 목적을 위해 engaged 몰두하는 scene 장면

수신: Jackie Montano
발신: Rosemarie Carey
날짜: 6월 14일
제목: 학급 방문

Ms. Montano께,

6월 20일에 Wooster Institute의 저희 반에서 강연하는 데 동의해 주셔서 다시 한번 감사드립니다. [178]제 학생들은 몇 주 전에 당신의 동료인 Shawn Trevino가 한 강연을 정말 즐겁게 들었습니다. [179]모두가 당신이 〈Cinema Quarterly Magazine〉에서 Gerald Kemp와 한 인터뷰를 읽었을 뿐만 아니라 적어도 한 번은 〈The Lab〉을 봤기 때문에 강연은 생산적인 시간이 될 겁니다.

수업은 오전 10시에 Iverson Wing 205호에서 시작됩니다. [180]동쪽 주차장에 주차해야 합니다. 최대 2시간까지 무료 주차가 가능하여 시간은 넉넉할 겁니다. 방문하기 전에 궁금한 점이 있으면 알려 주세요.

만나 뵙기를 고대합니다!

Rosemarie Carey

어휘 institute 전문 교육원, (과학, 교육 등을 목적으로 하는) 협회 give a speech 연설하다 productive 생산적인 session (특정 활동을 위한) 시간 wing 부속 건물 up to ~까지 plenty of 많은

176. Ms. Montano의 영화에 대해 사실인 것은 무엇인가?

(A) 시애틀의 한 축제에서 첫선을 보였다.
(B) 그녀의 웹사이트에서 스트리밍할 수 있다.
(C) 실화에서 영감을 받았다.
(D) 텔레비전 프로그램으로 만들어질 것이다.

해설 NOT/True
첫 번째 지문에서 TV 시리즈로 각색되고 있다고 했으므로 (D)가 정답이다.

어휘 debut 처음으로 공개하다, 데뷔하다 inspire 영감을 주다

177. 후기에서, 첫 번째 단락 일곱 번째 줄의 어휘 "ends"와 의미상 가장 가까운 것은?

(A) 목적
(B) 피날레
(C) 폐쇄
(D) 경계

해설 동의어 찾기
ends가 있는 to use for his own ends는 자기 자신의 목적을 위해 사용한다는 의미이며, 여기서 ends는 '목적'이라는 뜻으로 쓰였다. 따라서 (A) purposes가 정답이다.

178. Ms. Carey의 학생들에 대해 암시된 것은 무엇인가?

(A) 과정을 거의 끝마쳤다.
(B) 유명한 배우를 만났다.
(C) Ms. Montano에게 이메일로 질문을 보낼 것이다.
(D) 프로듀서의 강연을 들었다.

해설 두 지문 연계_추론/암시
두 번째 지문에서 학생들이 Shawn Trevino가 한 강연을 정말 즐겁게 들었다고 했는데, 첫 번째 지문을 보면 Shawn Trevino가 프로듀서라고 언급되어 있다. 따라서 학생들은 프로듀서의 강연을 들었다는 걸 알 수 있으므로 (D)가 정답이다.

179. Mr. Kemp는 누구이겠는가?

(A) 강좌의 강사
(B) 기자
(C) 영화관 소유주
(D) 신입생

해설 추론/암시
두 번째 지문에 Gerald Kemp에 대한 언급이 있는데 Ms. Montano가 〈Cinema Quarterly Magazine〉에서 Gerald Kemp와 인터뷰했다고 한 것으로 보아 그는 해당 잡지의 기자임을 유추할 수 있다. 따라서 (B)가 정답이다.

180. 이메일에서 Ms. Montano에 대해 암시되는 것은 무엇인가?

(A) Wooster Institute에서 돈을 지불받았다.
(B) 전에 Wooster Institute를 방문한 적이 있다.
(C) Wooster Institute에서 2시간도 채 머물지 않을 것이다.
(D) 대중교통을 이용하여 Wooster Institute로 갈 것이다.

해설 추론/암시

Ms. Montano가 주차해야 하는 동쪽 주차장은 최대 2시간까지 무료 주차라서 시간이 넉넉할 것이라고 했다. 이를 통해 Ms. Montano가 2시간이 안 되는 시간 동안 Wooster Institute에 머물 것임을 유추할 수 있으므로 (C)가 정답이다.

어휘 public transportation 대중교통

181-185 광고 & 계약서

> **Supreme Selections**
>
> 당신의 프로젝트를 돋보이게 하기 위해 전문적으로 녹음된 음악을 찾고 계신가요? Supreme Selections가 당신에게 적합합니다! [181]**저희는 영화, 팟캐스트, 광고 등에서 사용할 수 있는 많은 노래를 보유한 음악 라이선스 회사입니다.** 음악은 다양한 포맷으로 제공되기 때문에 시중의 모든 주요 편집 소프트웨어 프로그램에서 작동됩니다.
>
> [182D]**사용이 용이한 저희 온라인 카탈로그의 검색 기능으로 당신이 필요한 음악을 쉽게 찾을 수 있습니다.** 곡 [183]**전체를 사용하시거나 짧은** 클립을 사용하세요. 그것은 당신에게 달려 있습니다! [182B]**음악은 상업적인 것이든 개인적인 것이든 어떤 종류의 프로젝트에나 추가될 수 있고, 어디서든 출시될 수 있습니다.** 그리고 저희 사이트를 이용하시는 데 어려움이 있다면 [182C]**저희 기술팀의 도움을 24시간 받으실 수 있습니다.**
>
> 더 많이 구입하셔서 더 절약하세요!
> 1단계: 월 1회 다운로드
> [184]2단계: 최대 월 10회 다운로드
> 3단계: 최대 월 20회 다운로드

어휘 professionally 전문적으로 record 녹음하다 enhance 강화하다, 향상시키다 license 출판을 허가하다, 면허를 주다 collection (시, 이야기, 노래 등의) 모음집 commercial 광고 (방송); 상업적인 format 형식, 형태 on the market 시중에 나온 user-friendly 사용하기 쉬운 feature 기능 tier (조직, 시스템 등의) 단계

> **사용권 계약**
>
> Supreme Selections('공급자')는 이로써 Heather Kane('구매자')에게 다음 조건에 따라 사용 권한을 부여한다.
>
> 1. 구매자의 권리. 대금을 받는 즉시 [184]**구매자는 매월 공급자의 카탈로그에서 10개의 오디오 파일을 다운로드할 수 있는 허가를 받게 된다.** 사용하지 않은 다운로드는 다음 달로 이월되지 않는다. 다운로드한 오디오 파일에 대한 라이선스는 영구히 부여된다.
>
> 2. 사용 및 책임. 구매자는 다운로드한 오디오 파일을 부분적으로든 전체적으로 사용하든 상관없이 모든 상업적 또는 개인적인 프로젝트에 사용할 수 있다. [185]**프로젝트의 저작자 부분에는 아티스트의 이름과 노래 제목이 포함되어야 한다.** 구매자는 오디오 파일 사용이 타인의 권리를 침해하거나 어떤 법률도 위반하지 않도록 해야 한다.
>
> 공급자: Brenda Mendoza, Supreme Selections 이사 *Brenda Mendoza*
>
> 구매자: Heather Kane *Heather Kane*

어휘 agreement 계약 hereby 이로써 grant 부여하다 terms (계약) 조건 upon receipt of ~을 받는 즉시 calendar month 달력상의 월 roll over 이월되다 in perpetuity 영구히, 영원히 credit 저작자 infringe on ~을 침해하다

181. 누가 Supreme Selections를 이용하겠는가?

(A) 번역가
(B) 영화 제작자
(C) 사진작가
(D) 화가

해설 추론/암시

첫 번째 지문에서 Supreme Selections는 영화, 팟캐스트, 광고 등에서 사용할 수 있는 많은 노래를 보유하고 있다고 했으므로 영화 제작자가 해당 서비스를 사용할 것임을 유추할 수 있다. 따라서 (B)가 정답이다.

182. Supreme Selections를 이용하는 것의 이점으로 언급되지 않은 것은 무엇인가?

(A) 무료 편집 소프트웨어 이용
(B) 사용 제한 없음
(C) 24시간 기술 지원
(D) 카탈로그 검색의 용이성

해설 NOT/True

시중의 모든 주요 편집 소프트웨어 프로그램에서 작동된다고 했을 뿐, 무료 편집 소프트웨어 이용에 대한 내용은 언급되지 않았으므로 (A)가 정답이다.

패러프레이징 (C) get help from our tech team 24 hours a day → Round-the-clock technical support
(D) online catalog's user-friendly search features → Ease of searching the catalog

어휘 access 접근, 이용 lack 결핍, 부족 restriction 제한 round-the-clock 24시간의 ease 쉬움, 용이함

183. 광고에서, 두 번째 단락 두 번째 줄의 어휘 "complete"와 의미상 가장 가까운 것은?

(A) 극도의
(B) 충분한
(C) 완벽한
(D) 전체의

해설 동의어 찾기

complete track은 '완전한 곡'이라는 의미이며, 여기서 complete는 '전부의, 완전한'이라는 뜻으로 쓰였다. 따라서 (D) entire가 정답이다.

184. Ms. Kane에 대해 암시된 것은 무엇인가?

(A) 계약을 갱신하고 싶어 한다.
(B) 회사를 대표하여 주문하고 있다.
(C) 이미 보증금을 지불했다.
(D) 2단계 서비스에 가입했다.

해설 두 지문 연계_추론/암시

두 번째 지문에 구매자인 Ms. Kane은 매월 10개의 오디오 파일을 다운로드할 수 있다고 나와 있다. 첫 번째 지문을 보면 2단계에 해당하는 서비스로 최대 월 10회 다운로드가 가능하다는 정보를 찾을 수 있다. 따라서 (D)가

정답이다.

어휘 renew 갱신하다 contract 계약(서) on behalf of ~을 대신하여 deposit 보증금 sign up for ~을 신청하다

185. 계약서에 따르면, Ms. Kane은 무엇을 해야 하는가?

(A) Supreme Selections에 프로젝트 사본 보내기
(B) 변경 사항을 사전에 승인받기
(C) 음악 출처 언급하기
(D) 계약 해지 전에 통보하기

해설 세부 사항
'사용 및 책임' 항목에 프로젝트의 저작자 부분에는 아티스트의 이름과 노래 제목이 포함되어야 한다고 되어 있으므로 (C)가 정답이다.

패러프레이징 include the artist's name and the song title in the credits section → Cite the source of the music

어휘 approve 승인하다 in advance 사전에, 미리 cite 언급하다 source 출처, 원천 prior to ~에 앞서

186-190 광고 & 이메일 & 고객 의견

> **Blackwell Security**
> 상업 보안에서 신뢰할 수 있는 이름
>
> Blackwell Security는 귀사의 자산과 기밀 정보를 보호할 수 있습니다. 프리미엄 현관 잠금 장치에서부터 상시 비디오 감시 시스템에 이르기까지 모든 것에 저희가 도움을 드릴 수 있습니다.
>
> [186]저희는 고객님들의 의견을 귀담아 들었습니다. 그래서 이제는 직원들에게 방해가 되지 않도록 주말에 설치 서비스를 제공하고 있습니다. 또한 귀사의 보안 팀에 새 보안 시스템 사용법에 대한 교육도 제공할 수 있습니다. 교육은 귀사에서 받으실 수 있으며 직원들의 경력에 따라 반나절 또는 두 시간 동안 진행될 수 있습니다. [189]7월 중에는 모든 교육 패키지 상품을 30% 할인해 드립니다.
>
> 경험이 풍부한 저희 직원 중 한 명이 귀사를 방문하여 무료 상담을 제공하기를 원하시면 [187]h.reinhardt@blackwellsec.com으로 Holly Reinhardt에게 이메일을 보내 약속을 잡아 주십시오.

어휘 security 보안 commercial 상업의 asset 자산 confidential 기밀의 installation 설치 disrupt 방해하다 depending on ~에 따라 consultation 상담 book an appointment 약속을 잡다

> [190]수신: Charles Manadan
> 발신: Yumeno Shini
> 제목: 보안
> 날짜: 7월 2일
>
> Mr. Manadan께,
>
> [188]제가 귀하의 현장을 방문한 후 추천드린 보안 계획을 선택해 주셔서 감사합니다. 주문하신 시스템이 귀사의 필요성에 완벽히 맞을 거라고 생각합니다. 다행히도 저희가 다음 주에 빈 시간이 있어서 [189]7월 12일에 귀하의 보안팀을 위한 교육을 예약했습니다. 귀하는 일부 시간제 근로자들이 참석하지 못할 수도 있다고 하셨고, 귀하께서 그들을 별도로 교육하실 계획이라고 말씀하셨습니다. 그건 문제가 되지 않을 거라고 생각합니다. [190]보안 부서의 책임자로서, 귀하께서는 제 워크숍에서 개념을 쉽게 습득할 수 있을 것입니다. 새로운 소식이 있으면 알려 드리겠습니다.
>
> Yumeno Shini
> Blackwell Security 컨설턴트

어휘 select 선택하다 site 장소, 현장 opening 빈자리 separately 별도로 pick up ~을 습득하다, ~을 배우다 concept 개념 update 최신 정보

> Jeremy Boldt, 7월 30일
> 얼마 전에 Eagan Financial에서 처음으로 상담을 받았는데, 모든 경험이 정말 좋았습니다. 저의 재무 상담역인 Phyllis Jenkins는 제게 몇 가지 훌륭한 투자 패키지 상품을 보여 주었고, 제가 서명하기 전에 모든 부분을 이해했는지 재차 확인하며 모든 것을 명확하게 설명해 주셨습니다. 하지만 제가 그 건물에 들어갈 때 문제가 있었습니다. [190]제 방문증이 경보를 작동시켰는데, 그 회사의 보안 관리자가 그 문제를 빠르게 해결했습니다. 그는 회사에서 얼마 전에 설치한 새로운 시스템에 대해 뭔가를 말씀하시더군요. 하지만 그것 말고는 모든 것이 훌륭했습니다. 저는 이 업체를 강력 추천합니다.

어휘 recently 최근에, 얼마 전에 consultation 상담 financial 재무의, 재정의 whole 전체의, 모든 investment 투자 package 패키지 (상품) double check 재차 확인하다 visitor badge 방문증 set off (경보를) 울리다 resolve 해결하다 mention 말하다, 언급하다 besides ~ 외에 highly 매우 recommend 추천하다

186. Blackwell Security가 변화를 꾀한 이유는 무엇인가?

(A) 고객 의견을 반영하기 위해
(B) 비용을 절약하기 위해
(C) 경쟁업체에 뒤지지 않기 위해
(D) 신입 사원을 모집하기 위해

해설 세부 사항
첫 번째 지문에서 고객의 의견을 반영하여 고객의 업무를 방해하지 않기 위해 설치 서비스를 주말에 제공하는 것으로 바꾸었다고 했으므로 (A)가 정답이다.

패러프레이징 have heard what our customers had to say → respond to customer feedback

어휘 respond to ~에 대응하다 keep up with ~에 뒤지지 않다 competitor 경쟁자 attract 끌어모으다

187. Ms. Reinhardt는 누구이겠는가?

(A) 교육 워크숍 리더
(B) 상담 일정 담당자
(C) 보안 장비 공급자
(D) Blackwell Security 인사 부장

해설 추론/암시
첫 번째 지문에서 무료 상담을 원한다면 Holly Reinhardt에게 이메일을 보

내 약속을 잡으라고 한 것으로 보아 Ms. Reinhardt는 상담 일정을 관리하는 사람임을 유추할 수 있다. 따라서 (B)가 정답이다.

어휘 schedule 일정을 잡다 supplier 공급자

188. Mr. Manadan에 대해 사실인 것은 무엇인가?

(A) 예전 보안 회사에 불만이 있었다.
(B) 보안 대책에 대한 조언을 받았다.
(C) 가장 최근에 입사한 직원이다.
(D) 예산 안에 들어오는 시스템을 찾는 데 어려움을 겪었다.

해설 **NOT/True**
두 번째 지문에서 이메일의 수신인인 Mr. Manadan이 발신인이자 Blackwell Security의 컨설턴트인 Yumeno Shini가 추천한 보안 계획을 받아들였다고 했으므로 (B)가 정답이다.

어휘 displeased 마음에 들지 않는 former 이전의 measure 대책, 조치 budget 예산

189. 7월 12일의 교육에 대한 사실은 무엇이겠는가?

(A) 전액이 청구되지는 않을 것이다.
(B) 반나절 동안 계속될 것이다.
(C) Blackwell Security 사무실에서 열릴 것이다.
(D) 모든 보안 직원이 참석할 것이다.

해설 두 지문 연계_추론/암시
첫 번째 지문에서 7월에는 모든 교육 패키지가 30% 할인된다고 했고, 두 번째 지문에서는 7월 12일에 보안팀 교육을 예약했다고 했다. 따라서 할인된 가격으로 교육을 받는다는 걸 알 수 있으므로 (A)가 정답이다.

어휘 charge 청구하다, (비용을) 부과하다 last 지속되다, 계속되다

190. Mr. Boldt에 대해 암시된 것은 무엇인가?

(A) 방문증을 요청했다.
(B) Eagan Financial의 오랜 고객이다.
(C) 부서장의 도움을 받았다.
(D) 금융업계의 전문가이다.

해설 두 지문 연계_추론/암시
세 번째 지문에서 방문증에 문제가 있었지만 보안 관리자의 도움을 받았다고 했는데, 두 번째 지문에서 수신인인 Charles Manadan은 보안 부서의 책임자라고 언급되어 있다. 따라서 (C)가 정답이다.

191-195 쿠폰 & 영수증 & 의견 양식

Corwin Dry Cleaning
15% 할인

4월 1일부터 4월 30일 사이에 이 쿠폰을 사용하여 다음 서비스 중 아무것이나 15% 할인을 받으세요.

- 바지, 셔츠, 스커트, 재킷 기장 줄이기
- 지퍼 수선 및 교체
- 단추 교체

이 쿠폰은 [191]신규 고객에 대한 5% 환영 할인(WEL5)을 제외하고 다른 할인과 함께 사용할 수 없습니다. 매일 오전 7시부터 오후 7시까지 영업합니다. [195]당일 서비스를 위한 물품은 오전 9시까지 접수되어야 합니다.

어휘 shorten 길이를 줄이다 replacement 교체 offer 가격 할인 with the exception of ~을 제외하고

Corwin Dry Cleaning
1602 클레이 스트리트, 탬파, 플로리다 33592
(813) 555-8577

이름: Crystal Holcombe
날짜: 4월 9일
전화: (813) 555-9012
주소: 548 리지 레인, 탬파, 플로리다 33592

서비스 요약

기장 수선: 모직 바지	17.00달러
지퍼 수선: 가죽 재킷	12.00달러
15% 할인 (4월 쿠폰)	−4.35달러
[191]5% 할인 (WEL5)	−1.45달러
합계	23.20달러

직원 의견: 이 손님은 기장 수선을 위해 스커트도 가지고 오셨습니다. 하지만 [192]안감이 심하게 손상된 것을 발견하여 새로운 안감이 필요합니다. 이 서비스에 대한 비용 견적이 제공되었습니다.

시간이 촉박하세요? [193]Corwin Dry Cleaning은 완성된 품목을 당사 사업장에서 5마일 이내 거리에 있다면 어디든지 배달합니다. 직원에게 요금에 대해 문의하세요.

어휘 summary 요약 comment 의견 lining 안감 badly 심하게 damaged 손상을 입은 estimate 견적(서) short on ~가 부족한

Corwin Dry Cleaning
고객 의견 설문 조사

귀하의 거래에 감사드립니다! 잠시 시간을 내어 귀하의 경험에 대한 의견을 제공해 주십시오. 귀하의 의견은 저희 서비스를 향상시키는 데 도움이 됩니다.

	훌륭함	우수함	보통	나쁨
직원	✓			
서비스 비용	✓			
서비스 품질	✓			
옵션 범위	✓			

저희에게서 경험한 바를 설명해 주십시오.
이름: Crystal Holcombe
저를 도와준 직원들은 도움이 되었고 친절했습니다. [195]저는 당일 서비스를 이용했는데 아주 빨리 물건을 돌려받을 수 있어서 정말 편리했어요. [194]특히 직원들과 소통이 너무나 잘 되어서 깊은 인상을 받았습니다. 제 스커트에 문제가 있다는 전화를 받았는데, 그분이 제 선택지에 대해 명확하게 설명해 주셨어요. 게다가 저는 제 옷이 되찾아갈 준비가 되자마자 연락을 받았습니다. 대기하는 손님들을 위해 입구 근처에 편

안한 의자가 몇 개 있어서 좋았습니다. 업체는 매우 현대적으로 보였고 입구 근처에 주차할 곳을 쉽게 찾을 수 있어서 안심했습니다.

어휘 survey 설문 조사 average 보통의, 평균의 quality 품질 range 범위 describe 설명하다, 묘사하다 assist 돕다 helpful 도움이 되는 convenient 편리한 be impressed with ~에 깊은 감명을 받다 particularly 특히 communicate 의사소통하다 contact 연락하다 entrance 입구 relieved 안심한

191. Ms. Holcombe에 대해 암시된 것은 무엇인가?

(A) 평일에 서비스를 요청했다.
(B) Corwin Dry Cleaning을 처음 이용하고 있다.
(C) 고객 보상 프로그램을 신청했다.
(D) Corwin Dry Cleaning 근처에 산다.

해설 두 지문 연계_추론/암시
첫 번째 지문에서 신규 고객에 대한 5% 환영 할인(WEL5)이 있다고 했는데, 두 번째 지문인 Ms. Holcombe의 영수증에 5% 할인(WEL5) 항목이 있는 것으로 보아 Ms. Holcombe은 Corwin Dry Cleaning의 신규 고객임을 유추할 수 있다. 따라서 (B)가 정답이다.

어휘 sign up for ~을 신청하다 loyalty program (구매 금액에서 일정 비율의 할인이나 포인트 등을 제공하는) 고객 보상 프로그램

192. 영수증에 따르면, 직원이 알아차린 문제점은 무엇인가?

(A) 얼룩을 제거할 수 없었다.
(B) 스커트 지퍼가 없어졌다.
(C) 어떤 천은 너무 짧아서 작업할 수 없었다.
(D) 의복의 한 부분을 교체해야 한다.

해설 세부 사항
스커트 안감이 심하게 손상되어 새로운 안감이 필요하다고 했으므로 (D)가 정답이다.

패러프레이징 the lining → A section of a garment

193. Corwin Dry Cleaning의 배달 서비스에 대해 사실인 것은 무엇인가?

(A) 일정 거리로 제한되어 있다.
(B) 대량 주문 시 무료이다.
(C) 어떤 날에는 이용할 수 없다.
(D) 최근에 개시되었다.

해설 NOT/True
두 번째 지문에서 사업장에서 5마일 이내 거리에 있다면 어디든지 배달한다고 했으므로 (A)가 정답이다.

194. Ms. Holcombe이 업체에 대해 특히 좋아한 것은 무엇인가?

(A) 무료 주차장
(B) 의사소통의 수준
(C) 넓은 대기실
(D) 현대적인 장비

해설 세부 사항
Ms. Holcombe이 작성한 의견 양식에서 그녀는 Corwin Dry Cleaning 직원들과 소통이 잘 되어서 깊은 인상을 받았다고 했으므로 (B)가 정답이다.

195. Ms. Holcombe의 의류에 대해 암시된 것은 무엇인가?

(A) 오전 9시 전에 맡겨졌다.
(B) 새로 제공되는 서비스가 필요했다.
(C) 모두 같은 종류의 천이었다.
(D) 관리자가 처리했다.

해설 두 지문 연계 문제_추론/암시
첫 번째 지문에서 당일 서비스를 위한 물품은 오전 9시까지 접수되어야 한다고 했고, 세 번째 지문에서 Ms. Holcombe은 당일 서비스를 이용했다고 했다. 따라서 Ms. Holcombe은 오전 9시 전에 의류를 맡겼을 것으로 유추할 수 있으므로 (A)가 정답이다.

196-200 보도 자료 & 이메일 & 초대장

즉시 배포 요망
9월 12일
연락처: Florence Knowles, knowlesf@randallproperties.com

엘름스포드—Randall Properties는 [196]**새로운 허드슨 타워 오피스 단지 공사가 예정보다 한 달 일찍 완료되었다고 발표했다.** 사무실의 약 60%가 이미 임대되어 곧 업체들이 입주하기 시작할 것이다. 단지는 입주자들이 이용할 수 있는 여러 개의 회의실과 카페테리아, 그리고 그늘과 햇빛이 잘 드는 곳 모두에 충분한 좌석이 있는 [197]**안락한 옥상 정원을 제공한다.** Randall Properties의 환경적 책임에 대한 공약 이행을 위해 그 건물은 태양 전지판, 물 회수 장치, 그리고 에너지 효율적인 디자인을 갖추고 있다. [198]**하틀리 스트리트에 접한 정문에서부터** 넓고 매력적인 로비가 있는데, 로비에는 작은 하역 공간도 있다. 직원과 방문객을 위한 지붕이 덮인 주차장은 시더 스트리트에 접한 후문 옆에 있다.

건물 내 공간 임대 관련 문의는 gallahere@randallproperties.com으로 Eugene Gallaher에게 해야 한다.

어휘 ahead of schedule 예정보다 일찍 conference room 회의실 tenant 세입자, 임차인 calm 진정시키다, 달래다 rooftop 옥상 ample 충분한 commitment 약속, 헌신 solar panel 태양 전지판 recovery 회수, 회복 spacious 넓은 inviting 매력적인 situate 위치시키다 rear 뒤쪽의 inquiry 문의 space 공간 direct ~로 향하다

수신: Marilyn Decarlo
발신: Dean Rutland
날짜: 8월 7일
제목: 연회

안녕하세요, Marilyn,

당신이 새로운 공간에서 잘 적응하고 있기를 바랍니다. Fairfax Logistics의 연례 연회에 대한 최신 정보를 알려 드리고자 합니다. 저는 그 행사를 오벌린 홀에서 열기로 결정했는데, 홀에 있는 테이블은 하나당 12명까지 앉을 수 있어요. 장소가 우리 사무실에서 멀기 때문에 [198]**허드슨 타워 오피스 단지 정문에서 오벌린 홀까지 갔다가 다시 돌아오는 무료 왕복 교통편을 제공할 것입니다.**

행사 날짜는 아직 확정되지 않았습니다. [200]**저는 9월 28일로 예약했으면 합니다.** 하지만 Mr. Boone이 Ferro Inc. 임원들과의 기획 회의를 위해 그날 로스앤젤레스로 출장을 가야 할 수도 있습니다. 그럴 경우

연회는 1~2주 뒤에 개최될 것입니다. 모든 것이 확정되면 알려 드리겠습니다.

Dean

어휘 banquet 연회, 만찬 settle in 적응하다, 익숙해지다 give A an update on B A에게 B에 대한 최신 정보를 제공하다 seat (특정 수의) 좌석이 있다 venue 장소 finalize 마무리 짓다 preference 선호(도) executive 임원

Fairfax Logistics 연례 연회

귀하를 Fairfax Logistics의 연례 연회에 초대합니다. 연회가 열리는 동안 [199]우리는 올해의 직원을 축하할 것입니다. Danielle Rojas는 수년간 회사에 헌신하여 진정으로 이 영광을 누릴 자격이 있습니다.

[200]10월 5일 금요일 오후 7시
오벌린 홀, 연회장
914 로즈버드 애비뉴 (사무실에서 무료 왕복 교통편 이용 가능)
[200]Fairfax Logistics 최고 경영자 Antonio Boone 주최
Sandra Stewart의 라이브 음악 연주

d_rutland@fairfaxlogistics.com으로 Dean Rutland에게 이메일을 보내서 귀하의 참석 여부를 확정해 주십시오.

어휘 cordially 진심으로 recognize (공로를) 인정하다, 표창하다 dedicate 헌신하다 be deserving of ~을 받을 자격이 있다 honor 영광 host 주최하다 entertainment 오락, 여흥 attendance 참석

196. 보도 자료는 무엇에 관한 것인가?

(A) 상업용 부동산 매매
(B) 회사의 본사 이전
(C) 건설 공사의 완료
(D) 워크숍 일정 변경

해설 주제/목적
오피스 단지 건설 공사가 예정보다 한 달 일찍 완료되었다고 했으므로 (C)가 정답이다.

어휘 commercial 상업의 property 부동산 relocation 이전 headquarters 본사 completion 완성, 완공

197. 보도 자료에서 허드슨 타워 오피스 단지의 어떤 특징을 언급하는가?

(A) 야외 공간
(B) 화상 회의 장비
(C) 안전한 보관실
(D) 넓은 개별 사무실

해설 세부 사항
안락한 옥상 정원이 있다고 했으므로 (A)가 정답이다.

패러프레이징 rooftop garden → outdoor space

어휘 outdoor 야외의 video conferencing 화상 회의 equipment 장비, 기기 secure 안전한 storage 보관, 저장 individual 개별적인

198. Fairfax Logistics 직원들을 위한 왕복 교통편에 대해 암시되는 것은 무엇인가?

(A) 하틀리 스트리트에서 출발할 것이다.
(B) 티켓이 필요하다.
(C) 12명까지 앉을 수 있다.
(D) 도중에 몇 차례 정차할 것이다.

해설 두 지문 연계_추론/암시
두 번째 지문에 허드슨 타워 오피스 단지 정문에서 출발하는 왕복 교통편을 제공할 것이라는 언급이 있다. 첫 번째 지문에는 허드슨 타워 오피스 단지의 정문이 하틀리 스트리트에 접해 있다고 나와 있으므로 (A)가 정답이다.

199. 초대장에 따르면, 누가 상을 받을 것인가?

(A) Mr. Boone
(B) Ms. Rojas
(C) Mr. Rutland
(D) Ms. Steward

해설 세부 사항
Danielle Rojas가 올해의 직원이 될 것이라고 했으므로 (B)가 정답이다.

200. Fairfax Logistics에 대해 암시된 것은 무엇인가?

(A) 최고 경영자가 9월에 출장을 갔다.
(B) 전 직원이 수상자 선정을 돕는다.
(C) 직원들이 손님을 저녁 식사에 데려오는 것을 허용한다.
(D) 오벌린 홀 근처에 위치해 있다.

해설 두 지문 연계_추론/암시
세 번째 지문에 10월 5일 금요일에 열리는 연회의 주최자가 최고 경영자인 Antonio Boone이라는 정보가 있다. 두 번째 지문에서 9월 28일에 연회를 했으면 좋겠지만 Mr. Boone이 로스앤젤레스로 출장을 가게 되면 연회가 1~2주 뒤에 개최될 것이라고 한 것으로 보아 최고 경영자가 9월에 출장을 갔다는 걸 추론할 수 있으므로 (A)가 정답이다.

어휘 take a business trip 출장을 가다 entire 전체의 be located 위치해 있다

TEST 03

LISTENING TEST

1. (C)	**2.** (D)	**3.** (C)	**4.** (A)	**5.** (C)
6. (B)	**7.** (A)	**8.** (C)	**9.** (C)	**10.** (C)
11. (A)	**12.** (B)	**13.** (A)	**14.** (B)	**15.** (B)
16. (C)	**17.** (B)	**18.** (A)	**19.** (A)	**20.** (A)
21. (B)	**22.** (C)	**23.** (A)	**24.** (B)	**25.** (C)
26. (A)	**27.** (C)	**28.** (B)	**29.** (A)	**30.** (B)
31. (C)	**32.** (B)	**33.** (A)	**34.** (C)	**35.** (D)
36. (C)	**37.** (A)	**38.** (C)	**39.** (B)	**40.** (D)
41. (C)	**42.** (D)	**43.** (B)	**44.** (B)	**45.** (C)
46. (C)	**47.** (A)	**48.** (D)	**49.** (B)	**50.** (C)
51. (A)	**52.** (A)	**53.** (D)	**54.** (A)	**55.** (C)
56. (C)	**57.** (B)	**58.** (B)	**59.** (A)	**60.** (D)
61. (C)	**62.** (B)	**63.** (C)	**64.** (A)	**65.** (B)
66. (C)	**67.** (D)	**68.** (B)	**69.** (A)	**70.** (D)
71. (B)	**72.** (D)	**73.** (A)	**74.** (A)	**75.** (B)
76. (D)	**77.** (C)	**78.** (D)	**79.** (B)	**80.** (B)
81. (A)	**82.** (D)	**83.** (B)	**84.** (D)	**85.** (C)
86. (A)	**87.** (A)	**88.** (D)	**89.** (A)	**90.** (C)
91. (D)	**92.** (A)	**93.** (D)	**94.** (C)	**95.** (B)
96. (C)	**97.** (B)	**98.** (A)	**99.** (D)	**100.** (B)

READING TEST

101. (A)	**102.** (B)	**103.** (A)	**104.** (C)	**105.** (C)
106. (D)	**107.** (C)	**108.** (D)	**109.** (B)	**110.** (D)
111. (A)	**112.** (B)	**113.** (D)	**114.** (B)	**115.** (C)
116. (A)	**117.** (B)	**118.** (A)	**119.** (C)	**120.** (C)
121. (A)	**122.** (D)	**123.** (D)	**124.** (C)	**125.** (B)
126. (A)	**127.** (A)	**128.** (C)	**129.** (C)	**130.** (D)
131. (C)	**132.** (D)	**133.** (B)	**134.** (B)	**135.** (C)
136. (A)	**137.** (B)	**138.** (B)	**139.** (D)	**140.** (A)
141. (D)	**142.** (C)	**143.** (A)	**144.** (B)	**145.** (C)
146. (D)	**147.** (B)	**148.** (C)	**149.** (C)	**150.** (D)
151. (C)	**152.** (A)	**153.** (D)	**154.** (C)	**155.** (A)
156. (B)	**157.** (B)	**158.** (A)	**159.** (D)	**160.** (C)
161. (A)	**162.** (C)	**163.** (D)	**164.** (C)	**165.** (B)
166. (A)	**167.** (B)	**168.** (C)	**169.** (D)	**170.** (D)
171. (C)	**172.** (B)	**173.** (A)	**174.** (D)	**175.** (A)
176. (A)	**177.** (D)	**178.** (B)	**179.** (B)	**180.** (B)
181. (C)	**182.** (A)	**183.** (B)	**184.** (B)	**185.** (A)
186. (B)	**187.** (A)	**188.** (C)	**189.** (C)	**190.** (A)
191. (B)	**192.** (C)	**193.** (D)	**194.** (C)	**195.** (A)
196. (B)	**197.** (A)	**198.** (D)	**199.** (B)	**200.** (D)

PART 1

1. 미녀

(A) She's walking down the hallway.
(B) She's polishing some glass.
(C) She's adjusting a window shade.
(D) She's looking at a computer screen.

(A) 그녀는 복도를 따라 걸어가고 있다.
(B) 그녀는 유리를 닦고 있다.
(C) 그녀는 블라인드를 조정하고 있다.
(D) 그녀는 컴퓨터 화면을 보고 있다.

어휘 hallway 복도 polish 닦다, 광을 내다 adjust 조정하다 window shade 블라인드, 차양

2. 미남

(A) One of the people is cooking some food.
(B) One of the people is opening a door.
(C) One of the people is turning on the lights.
(D) One of the people is dining alone.

(A) 사람들 중 한 명이 음식을 요리하고 있다.
(B) 사람들 중 한 명이 문을 열고 있다.
(C) 사람들 중 한 명이 불을 켜고 있다.
(D) 사람들 중 한 명이 혼자 식사하고 있다.

어휘 turn on (전기 · 가스 · 수도 등을) 켜다 (↔ turn off) dine 식사를 하다

3. 미녀

(A) A sidewalk is being painted.
(B) A ladder is lying on the ground.
(C) He's cleaning up some debris.
(D) He's reaching for a broom.

(A) 보도가 페인트칠되고 있다.
(B) 사다리가 땅에 놓여 있다.
(C) 그는 잔해를 치우고 있다.
(D) 그는 빗자루에 손을 뻗고 있다.

어휘 sidewalk 보도, 인도 ladder 사다리 lie 놓여 있다, 누워 있다 debris 잔해, 파편 reach for ~을 잡으려고 손을 뻗다 broom 빗자루

4. 미남

(A) Some of the people are examining a document.
(B) One of the men is writing on a whiteboard.
(C) A woman is putting a laptop computer away.
(D) They're printing copies of some paperwork.

(A) 사람들 중 몇 명이 문서를 검토하고 있다.
(B) 남자들 중 한 명이 화이트보드에 무언가를 쓰고 있다.
(C) 여자가 노트북 컴퓨터를 치우고 있다.
(D) 그들은 몇몇 서류의 사본을 인쇄하고 있다.

어휘 examine 검토하다, 조사하다 put away ~을 치우다 paperwork 서류, 서류 작업

5. 호남

(A) There's a bag hanging from a railing.
(B) Several drawers have been left open.
(C) Some boxes are stacked on the shelf.
(D) Some clothing is being folded.

(A) 가방이 난간에 걸려 있다.
(B) 서랍 몇 개가 열려 있다.
(C) 상자 몇 개가 선반 위에 쌓여 있다.
(D) 옷 몇 벌이 개어지고 있다.

어휘 hang 걸다, 매달다 railing 난간 drawer 서랍 stack 쌓다 shelf 선반 clothing 옷, 의복 fold 개다, 접다

6. 미남

(A) The people are playing a game outdoors.
(B) The people are seated facing the same direction.
(C) A tennis net is being set up.
(D) Some chairs are arranged in a circle.

(A) 사람들이 야외에서 경기를 하고 있다.
(B) 사람들이 같은 방향을 향해 앉아 있다.
(C) 테니스 네트가 설치되고 있다.
(D) 의자 몇 개가 원형으로 배열되어 있다.

어휘 outdoors 야외에서 be seated 앉아 있다 face ~을 향하다 direction 방향 set up 설치하다, 준비하다 arrange 배열하다, 정리하다 in a circle 원형을 이루어

PART 2

7. 영녀 미남

When can I drop off my car?
(A) Any time after 9 A.M.
(B) At a rental company.
(C) She dropped it by accident.

제가 차를 언제 갖다 놓으면 될까요?
(A) 오전 9시 이후 아무 때나요.
(B) 대여 회사예요.
(C) 그녀가 실수로 그걸 떨어뜨렸어요.

어휘 drop off 갖다 주다, 내려 주다 rental 대여, 임대 drop 떨어뜨리다 by accident 잘못해서, 우연히

8. 미남 영녀

How much money do you hope to raise at the event?
(A) On the event calendar.
(B) The art museum downtown.
(C) Enough to cover some repairs.

그 행사에서 돈을 얼마나 모으길 희망하세요?
(A) 행사 달력에요.
(B) 시내에 있는 미술관이요.
(C) 몇 가지 수리를 충당할 수 있을 만큼이요.

어휘 raise (자금을) 모으다, 들어올리다 downtown 시내에

9. 미녀 미남

Who approved the purchase of these smartphones?
(A) To improve communication.
(B) Yes, a few days ago.
(C) I heard it was Victor.

누가 이 스마트폰의 구매를 승인했나요?
(A) 의사소통을 증진하기 위해서요.
(B) 네, 며칠 전에요.
(C) 빅터라고 들었어요.

어휘 approve 승인하다 purchase 구매; 구매하다

10. 미남 미녀

Would you like to carpool to the company retreat together?
(A) Use Highway 27.
(B) The CEO's speech.
(C) That would be nice.

회사 야유회에 카풀해서 같이 가실래요?
(A) 27번 고속도로를 이용하세요.
(B) 대표님 연설이요.
(C) 그러면 좋겠네요.

어휘 company retreat 회사 야유회 highway 고속도로 speech 연설

11. 미녀 영녀

Should we buy metal file cabinets or wooden ones?
(A) I'd like to have metal.
(B) Some confidential documents.
(C) I couldn't check for errors.

금속 서류 캐비닛을 사야 하나요, 아니면 나무로 된 것을 사야 하나요?
(A) 금속으로 하고 싶어요.
(B) 일부 기밀 문서요.
(C) 저는 오류를 확인할 수 없었어요.

어휘 metal 금속 confidential 기밀의, 비밀의

12. 미남 영녀

Will you be able to submit your loan application soon?
(A) She usually works alone.
(B) Yes, I'm almost done filling it out.
(C) A job application form.

당신의 대출 신청서를 곧 제출할 수 있겠어요?
(A) 그녀는 보통 혼자 일해요.
(B) 네, 거의 다 작성했어요.
(C) 입사 지원서요.

어휘 submit 제출하다 loan 대출 application 신청(서), 지원(서) fill out 작성하다, 기입하다 form 서식, 양식

13. 미녀 호남

Aren't these winter jackets supposed to be in the clearance area?
(A) I have no idea.
(B) It's a medium size.
(C) Yes, I found him.

이 겨울 재킷들은 창고 세일 구역에 있어야 하는 거 아니에요?
(A) 저도 모르겠어요.
(B) 그건 중간 사이즈예요.
(C) 네, 그를 찾았어요.

어휘 be supposed to do ~하기로 되어 있다 medium 중간의

14. 미남 영녀

How long does it take to install a washing machine?
(A) I think I'll go downstairs.
(B) About an hour.
(C) This needs to be dry cleaned.

세탁기를 설치하는 데 얼마나 걸리나요?
(A) 저는 아래층으로 내려가야겠어요.
(B) 한 시간 정도요.
(C) 이건 드라이클리닝을 해야 돼요.

어휘 install 설치하다 go downstairs 아래층으로 내려가다

15. 호남 미녀

These figures don't look right.
(A) She figured out who sent it.
(B) Several team members reviewed them.
(C) Please line up on the left.

이 수치들은 안 맞는 것 같아요.

(A) 그녀는 누가 그것을 보냈는지 알아냈어요.
(B) 몇몇 팀원들이 그걸 검토했어요.
(C) 왼쪽에 줄을 서 주세요.

어휘 figure 수치, 숫자 figure out 알아내다, 이해하다 line up 줄을 서다

16. 미남 호남

The class isn't full yet, is it?
(A) Thanks, I'm full now.
(B) I studied about modern classic writers.
(C) No, there are still a few spaces.

그 수업은 정원이 아직 다 차지 않았죠, 그렇죠?
(A) 고마워요, 전 이제 배불러요.
(B) 저는 현대 고전 작가들에 대해 공부했어요.
(C) 네, 아직 자리가 몇 개 있어요.

어휘 full 가득 찬, 배부른 modern 현대의 classic 고전의 space 자리, 공간

17. 호남 영녀

Why do I need to create a new password?
(A) By the end of the day.
(B) Because the first one was temporary.
(C) No, my pass hasn't expired.

제가 왜 암호를 새로 만들어야 하나요?
(A) 오늘 중으로요.
(B) 첫 번째 것은 임시였기 때문이에요.
(C) 아니요, 제 출입증은 만료되지 않았어요.

어휘 temporary 임시의, 일시적인 expire 만료되다

18. 미남 미녀

What is required for exchanging merchandise?
(A) We need the receipt and the item.
(B) The store changed its business hours.
(C) I have a shopping cart.

상품을 교환하려면 무엇이 필요한가요?
(A) 영수증과 물건이 필요합니다.
(B) 가게가 영업시간을 변경했어요.
(C) 저한테 쇼핑 카트가 있어요.

어휘 require 필요로 하다, 요구하다 exchange 교환하다 merchandise 상품, 물품 receipt 영수증 business hours 영업시간

19. 영녀 미남

When did you assign the article to our junior reporter?
(A) She just received the assignment.
(B) About the city's annual parade.
(C) No, it's been written.

당신은 언제 우리 수습 기자에게 기사를 배정했나요?
(A) 그녀는 방금 업무를 받았어요.
(B) 시의 연례 퍼레이드에 대해서요.
(C) 아니요, 그건 쓰여 있어요.

어휘 assign 배정하다, 부과하다 article 기사, 글 assignment 과제, 임무 annual 연례의

20. 호남 미남

Where should I put up the flyers about our band?
(A) I can suggest a few good places.
(B) Any time after 4 P.M.
(C) No, please take it down.

저는 우리 밴드에 대한 전단을 어디에 붙여야 하나요?
(A) 제가 몇 군데 좋은 장소를 제안할 수 있어요.
(B) 오후 4시 이후에 아무 때나요.
(C) 아니요, 그것을 치워 주세요.

어휘 put up 내붙이다, 게시하다 flyer 전단 take down 치우다, 내리다

21. 영녀 미남

We're all out of the air filters, right?
(A) That seems fair to me.
(B) Yes, I've checked the inventory.
(C) An energy-efficient appliance.

우리 공기 정화 필터가 다 떨어졌죠, 맞죠?
(A) 제게는 그것이 공평해 보여요.
(B) 네, 제가 재고를 확인했어요.
(C) 에너지 효율이 좋은 가전제품이요.

어휘 be out of 떨어지다, 동나다 fair 공평한 inventory 재고(품) energy-efficient 에너지 효율이 좋은 appliance 가전제품

22. 미녀 호남

Who ordered the business cards with our new titles?
(A) Congratulations on your promotion!
(B) One hundred per box.
(C) Didn't yours arrive yet?

누가 우리의 새 직함이 있는 명함을 주문했나요?
(A) 승진을 축하합니다!
(B) 한 상자당 100장이요.
(C) 당신 것이 아직 도착하지 않았나요?

어휘 title 직함, 제목 promotion 승진, 홍보 arrive 도착하다

23. 호남 미녀

This window doesn't close all the way.
(A) Mr. Huntly is handling all repairs.
(B) I like the green curtains.
(C) Just before the closing time.

이 창문이 계속 닫히지 않아요.
(A) 헌틀리 씨가 모든 수리를 처리해요.
(B) 저는 녹색 커튼이 마음에 들어요.
(C) 폐점 시간 직전에요.

어휘 all the way 줄곧, 내내 handle 처리하다, 다루다

24. 호남 미녀

Where can I hand in this comment card?
(A) Yes, I rented a car.
(B) We will collect them.
(C) No, it's very common.

이 의견 카드를 어디에 제출하면 되나요?
(A) 네, 제가 차를 빌렸어요.
(B) 저희가 걷을 거예요.
(C) 아니요, 그건 아주 흔해요.

어휘 hand in 제출하다 comment 의견, 논평 collect 모으다, 수집하다 common 흔한

25. 미녀 영녀

What floor is the human resources department on?
(A) The layout of the rooms.
(B) To screen job applicants.
(C) Eduardo is headed there now.

인사부는 몇 층에 있나요?
(A) 방 배치도요.
(B) 입사 지원자들을 심사하기 위해서요.
(C) 에두아르도가 지금 거기로 가고 있어요.

어휘 human resources department 인사부 layout 배치(도) screen 심사하다, 가려내다 applicant 지원자 be headed ~로 향하여 가다

26. 미남 미녀

Can I see the photo on your new passport?
(A) I don't carry it with me.
(B) No, I've never watched that.
(C) Where was your vacation?

당신의 새 여권에 있는 사진을 볼 수 있을까요?
(A) 저는 그걸 가지고 다니지 않아요.
(B) 아니요, 저는 그걸 본 적이 없어요.
(C) 당신은 휴가를 어디서 보냈나요?

27. 미녀 호남

Doesn't the awards ceremony start at seven?
(A) Yes, they're offering a reward.
(B) I thought it was quite spacious.
(C) There's time for networking beforehand.

시상식이 7시에 시작하지 않나요?
(A) 네, 그들은 보상금을 주고 있어요.
(B) 저는 그곳이 꽤 널찍하다고 생각했어요.
(C) 사전에 인맥을 쌓기 위한 시간이 있어요.

어휘 awards ceremony 시상식 spacious 널찍한, 넓은 beforehand 사전에

28. 영녀 미남

Will you contact me if the pipe starts leaking again?
(A) Turn this handle tightly.
(B) Your number's saved on my phone.
(C) The hardware store is called Henderson's.

배관에서 다시 새기 시작하면 제게 연락해 주실래요?
(A) 이 손잡이를 단단히 조이세요.
(B) 당신의 번호가 제 전화기에 저장되어 있어요.
(C) 그 철물점 이름은 헨더슨이에요.

어휘 leak (액체 · 기체가) 새다 tightly 꽉, 단단히 hardware store 철물점

29. 미녀 미남

I haven't seen Mr. Larkin at his desk.
(A) He's off today.
(B) The new assistant director.
(C) Oh, I'll give you directions.

라킨 씨가 자리에 없던데요.
(A) 그는 오늘 휴가예요.
(B) 새로운 조감독이요.
(C) 아, 제가 길을 알려 드릴게요.

어휘 assistant director 조감독 directions 길 안내

30. 미녀 미남

Why don't we practice the sales presentation a few more times?
(A) Yes, the medical practice is open.
(B) Our presentation style could be improved.
(C) Did you use a discount coupon?

우리 제품 소개를 몇 번 더 연습하는 게 어때요?

(A) 네, 그 의원은 열려 있어요.
(B) 우리 발표 스타일이 더 나아질 수 있어요.
(C) 할인 쿠폰을 사용하셨나요?

어휘 practice 연습하다; (의사 · 변호사 등의) 개업 장소

31. 영녀 호남

Will the managers from the Tokyo branch arrive on Thursday or Friday?
(A) Sign up for the management seminar.
(B) That brand is very popular.
(C) They haven't bought their tickets yet.

도쿄 지사의 관리자들이 목요일에 도착하나요, 아니면 금요일에 도착하나요?
(A) 경영 세미나에 등록하세요.
(B) 그 브랜드는 매우 인기 있어요.
(C) 그들은 아직 표를 사지 않았어요.

PART 3

호남 미녀

Questions 32-34 refer to the following conversation.

M Oh, I'm sorry if you've been waiting long. [32]I was discussing an order of tools with the dentist. How may I help you?

W Good morning. [33]I just moved to this neighborhood, and I've booked an appointment as a new customer. My name is Lucy Nixon. I was asked to bring my old dental records.

M Hmm... [34]it looks like the last page is missing. We'll need that before we can continue your previous treatment. But you can still get a cleaning during today's appointment.

남 아, 오래 기다리셨다면 죄송합니다. [32]치과 의사 선생님과 도구 주문에 대해 의논하고 있었어요. 무엇을 도와드릴까요?

여 안녕하세요. [33]저는 얼마 전에 이 동네로 이사 왔는데, 신규 고객으로 진료 예약을 했어요. 제 이름은 루시 닉슨입니다. 저는 이전의 치과 기록을 가져오라는 요청을 받았어요.

남 흠... [34]마지막 페이지가 빠져 있는 것 같아요. 저희가 당신의 이전 치료를 이어서 하기 전에 그게 필요할 거예요. 하지만 그래도 오늘 진료에서 클리닝은 받으실 수 있습니다.

어휘 discuss 의논하다 neighborhood 근처, 이웃 book an appointment 예약하다 dental 치과의 record 기록 missing 빠진, 없어진 previous 이전의

32. 남자는 어디에서 일하는 것 같은가?
(A) 금융 기관에서
(B) 치과에서
(C) 창고에서
(D) 식당에서

33. 여자는 최근에 무엇을 했는가?
(A) 그녀는 새로운 동네로 이사했다.
(B) 그녀는 예약 일정을 변경했다.
(C) 그녀는 근처에서 사업을 시작했다.
(D) 그녀는 여행에서 돌아왔다.

34. 남자는 어떤 문제를 언급하는가?
(A) 시간대가 이중으로 예약되었다.
(B) 신용 카드 결제가 거부되었다.
(C) 서류가 불완전하다.
(D) 라벨에 오류가 있었다.

패러프레이징 the last page is missing → A document is incomplete

미녀 미남

Questions 35-37 refer to the following conversation.

W Did you hear that [35]Makito got promoted? [35]He'll be the assistant manager of our public relations team.

M Good for him! He's the perfect person for the job.

W I agree. I thought we could all have lunch together on Friday in the conference room to celebrate. I could order food from Tino's.

M That sounds good. [36]How about I find out what everyone wants on Friday morning to save you some time?

W Great, thanks! And [37]Leo is going to buy a small gift for Makito. If you have any ideas, please talk to him sometime today.

여 [35]마키토가 승진했다는 소식 들었어요? [35]그는 우리 홍보팀의 대리가 될 거예요.

남 잘됐네요! 그는 그 자리에 딱 맞는 사람이에요.

여 동의해요. 축하를 위해 금요일에 회의실에서 우리 모두 함께 점심을 먹으면 어떨까 생각했어요. 제가 티노스에서 음식을 주문할 수도 있어요.

남 그게 좋겠네요. [36]당신이 시간을 아낄 수 있도록 제가 금요일 아침에 모두 무엇을 원하는지 알아보는 게 어떨까요?

여 좋아요, 고마워요! 그리고 [37]레오가 마키토를 위해 작은 선물을 살 거예요. 아이디어가 있으면, 오늘 중으로 그에게 이야기해 주세요.

어휘 get promoted 승진하다 public relations 홍보 conference room 회의실 celebrate 축하하다

35. 마키토는 어떤 부서에서 일하는 것 같은가?

(A) 연구 개발
(B) 기술 지원
(C) 인사
(D) 홍보

36. 남자는 금요일 아침에 무엇을 할 것인가?

(A) 학회 참석하기
(B) 방 예약하기
(C) 음식 주문 받기
(D) 팀 회의 이끌기

37. 여자는 왜 레오와 이야기할 것을 추천하는가?

(A) 선물 제안을 공유하기 위해
(B) 안건을 검토하기 위해
(C) 승진을 신청하기 위해
(D) 금전적 기부를 하기 위해

패러프레이징 ideas → suggestions

호남 영녀

Questions 38-40 refer to the following conversation.

M Hi, Cassie. Thanks for sending me [38]the first cut of the video you're editing to train new employees.

W Is it what you had in mind?

M Yes. The pace of each section is perfect, and I like the background music you chose. But [39]there was supposed to be a list of department heads at the end.

W [39]Sorry about that! I forgot to add it. I can do that now.

M Thanks. Then it'll be ready to go. [40]I'm surprised at how quickly you were able to finish the work. I appreciate it.

남 안녕하세요, 캐시. [38]신입 사원을 교육하기 위해 당신이 편집하고 있는 영상의 첫 번째 컷을 제게 보내 주셔서 고맙습니다.

여 그게 당신이 생각하고 있던 건가요?

남 네. 각 부분의 속도가 완벽하고, 당신이 선택한 배경 음악이 마음에 들어요. 그런데 [39]마지막에 부서장 명단이 있어야 하는데요.

여 [39]미안해요! 그걸 추가하는 걸 잊었어요. 지금 그걸 할 수 있어요.

남 고마워요. 그럼 그건 준비가 끝나겠네요. [40]당신이 그 일을 얼마나 빨리 끝낼 수 있었는지가 놀랍네요. 감사합니다.

어휘 edit 편집하다 have ~ in mind ~을 생각하다, 염두에 두다 pace 속도 section 부분, 구역 background 배경 add 추가하다 appreciate 고마워하다

38. 대화는 주로 무엇에 관한 것인가?

(A) 연회를 계획하는 것
(B) 초대장을 보내는 것
(C) 교육용 영상을 편집하는 것
(D) 직원들의 자격을 확인하는 것

39. 여자는 왜 사과하는가?

(A) 그녀는 업무를 변경했다.
(B) 그녀는 몇 가지 정보를 빠뜨렸다.
(C) 그녀는 의견에 동의하지 않는다.
(D) 그녀는 회의에 불참했다.

패러프레이징 a list of department heads → some information

40. 남자는 무엇에 대해 놀랐다고 말하는가?

(A) 웹사이트의 디자인
(B) 참가자의 수
(C) 직원들의 피드백
(D) 프로젝트 완료의 속도

패러프레이징 how quickly you were able to finish the work → The speed of completing a project

미녀 미남

Questions 41-43 refer to the following conversation.

W Michael, I've just received a letter from Farrow Incorporated regarding our insurance.

M Is there a problem?

W [41]They are going to raise our company's monthly fees by fifteen percent starting in August when our current policy expires. We can probably find a better deal somewhere else. [42]How about getting a policy with Edsel Insurance?

M As far as I know, they only serve residential properties.

W Oh, I see. I'll keep looking. In the meantime, [43]could you set up the chairs and tables in the conference room to get ready for the meeting?

M No problem.

여 마이클, 방금 패로 사로부터 우리 보험에 관한 서한을 받았어요.

남 무슨 문제가 있나요?

여 그들은 현재 보험이 만료되는 8월부터 [41]우리 회사의 월 보험료를 15퍼센트 인상할 예정이에요. 우리는 아마도 다른 곳에서 더 나은 거래를 찾을 수 있을 거예요. [42]에드셀 보험사에 보험을 드는 게

어때요?

남 제가 알기로는, 그들은 주거용 부동산만 취급해요.

여 아, 그렇군요. 계속 찾아볼게요. 그러는 동안에, [43]회의 준비를 하기 위해 회의실에 의자와 테이블을 준비해 주실래요?

남 그럼요.

어휘 insurance 보험 fee 요금, 수수료 current 현재의 deal 거래 as far as ~하는 한 policy 보험 증권 serve 취급하다, 다루다 residential 주거의 property 부동산, 재산 in the meantime 그 동안에 set up 준비하다, 마련하다

41. 여자는 어떤 문제를 언급하는가?

(A) 고객이 항의했다.
(B) 일자리 공석이 채워지지 않았다.
(C) 일부 요금이 인상될 것이다.
(D) 약간의 손해를 입었다.

패러프레이징 raise our company's monthly fees → fees will increase

42. 남자는 왜 "그들은 주거용 부동산만 취급해요"라고 말하는가?

(A) 안심시키기 위해
(B) 결정에 대해 설명하기 위해
(C) 놀라움을 나타내기 위해
(D) 제안을 거절하기 위해

43. 여자는 남자에게 무엇을 해 달라고 요청하는가?

(A) 예산 조정하기
(B) 몇몇 가구 배치하기
(C) 회의 일정 잡기
(D) 보험 증권 검토하기

패러프레이징 set up the chairs and tables → Arrange some furniture

영녀 미남

Questions 44-46 refer to the following conversation.

W Ayush, [44]we need to get the electric screwdrivers ready to ship to the Sherman Department Store warehouse, but I've got some bad news.

M Oh, no. What's happened?

W [45]I've just checked the boxes we've ordered for the screwdrivers, and they're too small.

M Are there any others in the storage room that we can use?

W I'm afraid not. And the goods are due to be there by Thursday. [46]We can't make any adjustments to that schedule.

여 아유시, 셔먼 백화점 창고로 보낼 [44]전기 드라이버를 준비해야 하는데, 안 좋은 소식이 있어요.

남 이런, 무슨 일이죠?

여 [45]우리가 주문한 드라이버 상자들을 방금 확인했는데, 너무 작아요.

남 창고에 사용할 수 있는 다른 것들이 있나요?

여 없는 것 같아요. 그리고 물건은 목요일까지 거기 도착하기로 되어 있어요. [46]우리는 그 일정을 조정할 수 없어요.

어휘 electric 전기의 ship ~을 보내다, 부치다 warehouse 창고 goods 물건, 상품 make adjustments to ~을 조정하다

44. 화자들은 어떤 제품을 준비하고 있는가?

(A) 자동차 부품
(B) 전동 공구
(C) 스포츠 용품
(D) 주방용품

패러프레이징 electric screwdrivers → Power tools

45. 여자에 따르면, 무엇이 문제인가?

(A) 배송료가 인상되었다.
(B) 기계가 작동을 멈췄다.
(C) 일부 용기의 크기가 잘못되었다.
(D) 몇몇 직원들이 교대 근무 시간에 늦었다.

패러프레이징 the boxes → Some containers

46. 여자는 왜 걱정하는가?

(A) 몇 가지 설명이 헷갈린다.
(B) 직원이 경험이 부족하다.
(C) 기한을 변경할 수 없다.
(D) 방이 열리지 않는다.

패러프레이징 can't make any adjustments → cannot be changed

미녀 영녀 호남

Questions 47-49 refer to the following conversation with three speakers.

W1 What do you think of the International Coffee Expo so far, [47]Jessica?

W2 I'm glad we decided to come, but [47]it's a bit disappointing. I was expecting more samples of coffee for us to try. Anyway, we still need to find some refrigerated cases to display the cakes in our café. This booth looks promising.

M Hello, and welcome to the Norton Supplies booth. Are you familiar with our products?

W1 Yes, we've seen your items in other shops. [48]We're thinking of expanding our café's selection of cakes, so we need new ways to display those.

M [48]We have several sizes available. [49]If you could

please give me your café's address, I can calculate the estimated shipping costs.

여1 [47]제시카, 지금까지 국제 커피 박람회에 대해 어떻게 생각하세요?

여2 우리가 오기로 결정한 것은 기쁘지만, [47]조금 실망스럽네요. 우리가 마셔볼 수 있는 더 많은 커피 샘플을 기대하고 있었거든요. 어쨌든, 우리 카페에 케이크를 진열할 냉장 케이스를 찾아야 해요. 이 부스가 유망해 보이네요.

남 안녕하세요, 노턴 용품점 부스에 오신 걸 환영합니다. 저희 제품을 잘 아시나요?

여1 네, 다른 가게에서 당신의 물건들을 봤어요. [48]저희는 카페의 케이크 선택 폭을 넓히려고 생각 중이라서, 그것들을 진열할 새로운 방법이 필요해요.

남 [48]이용할 수 있는 몇 가지 사이즈가 있습니다. [49]저에게 카페 주소를 알려주시면, 제가 예상되는 배송비를 계산해 드릴 수 있습니다.

어휘 international 국제의 disappointing 실망스러운 refrigerate 냉장하다 promising 유망한 be familiar with ~을 잘 알다 expand 넓히다, 확대하다 selection 선택된 것들, 선택 available 이용할 수 있는 calculate 계산하다 estimated 예상되는

47. 제시카는 무엇에 대해 실망했는가?

(A) 샘플의 부족
(B) 입장료의 가격
(C) 할인의 종료
(D) 군중의 규모

48. 남자의 회사는 무엇을 판매하는가?

(A) 재사용할 수 있는 머그잔
(B) 디지털 저울
(C) 커피 분쇄기
(D) 진열 케이스

49. 남자는 여자들에게 무엇을 해 달라고 요청하는가?

(A) 피드백 설문지 작성하기
(B) 사업체 위치 제공하기
(C) 명함 가져가기
(D) 정보 팸플릿 읽기

패러프레이징 give me your café's address → Provide the location

미남 영녀

Questions 50-52 refer to the following conversation.

M Good morning, Katie. I wanted to tell you that everyone is excited that [50]you've moved to the advertising team. You're doing a great job so far.

W Thanks! Everyone has been really helpful.

M You know, [51]there's an optional training course about the power of social media. I think you should consider taking that to help build your skills.

W That'd be great. How do I sign up?

M I can handle the registration for you, as I have to approve the expense. But [52]I won't have time to do it this afternoon because I'm holding some interviews with job candidates for the content writer position.

남 좋은 아침이에요, 케이티. [50]당신이 광고팀으로 이동한 것에 대해 모두 신나 있다는 걸 이야기해 주고 싶었어요. 당신은 지금까지 잘 하고 있어요.

여 고마워요! 모두가 정말 도움이 되고 있어요.

남 알다시피, [51]소셜 미디어의 힘에 대한 선택 교육 과정이 있어요. 당신의 실력을 쌓는 데 도움이 되도록 그걸 듣는 걸 고려해 보는 게 좋을 것 같아요.

여 그거 좋겠네요. 어떻게 신청하죠?

남 제가 비용을 승인해야 하니 등록을 처리해 드릴 수 있어요. 하지만 [52]제가 콘텐츠 작가 자리에 대한 입사 지원자들과 면접을 치를 거라서 오늘 오후에는 그걸 할 시간이 없을 거예요.

어휘 advertising 광고 optional 선택적인 course 과정, 강좌 consider 고려하다 sign up 신청하다 handle 처리하다 registration 등록 approve 승인하다 expense 비용 job candidate 입사 지원자 position (일)자리, 직위

50. 여자는 최근에 무엇을 했는가?

(A) 그녀는 지점 이동을 요청했다.
(B) 그녀는 책을 출간했다.
(C) 그녀는 새로운 팀으로 이동했다.
(D) 그녀는 출장에서 돌아왔다.

51. 남자는 여자에게 무엇을 고려하도록 권고하는가?

(A) 교육 과정을 수강하는 것
(B) 회식에 참석하는 것
(C) 직원 안내서를 검토하는 것
(D) 소셜 미디어 계정을 개설하는 것

52. 남자는 오늘 오후에 무엇을 할 것인가?

(A) 면접 진행하기
(B) 여행 가기
(C) 주문하기
(D) 발표하기

패러프레이징 holding → Conduct

호남 미녀

Questions 53-55 refer to the following conversation.

M [53]I'd like to start this meeting by checking to see whether or not each department has enough workers. There's some room in the budget for hiring additional employees. Francesca, how about you go first?

W Well... [54]next week, I'm meeting with Kramer Enterprises for the negotiation of their new sales contract. If they increase their monthly order, we may need more help.

M Alright. Please let me know so that I can inform the recruitment agency.

W Actually, [55]about the agency, what do you think about using a different firm? It seems our current one's fees are quite expensive.

M Hmm... [55]let's talk about that at the next meeting.

남 [53]각 부서에 인력이 충분한지 아닌지 확인하는 것으로 이번 회의를 시작하려고 합니다. 예산에 추가 직원을 채용할 여유가 좀 있습니다. 프란체스카, 먼저 말씀해 보시겠어요?

여 음... [54]다음 주에 저는 크레이머 사와 새로운 판매 계약 협상을 위해 만날 겁니다. 만약 그들이 월 주문을 늘린다면, 우리는 도움이 더 필요할지도 모릅니다.

남 알겠어요. 채용 대행사에 알릴 수 있도록 제게 알려 주세요.

여 사실 [55]그 대행사 말인데요, 다른 회사를 이용하는 것에 대해 어떻게 생각하세요? 현재 회사의 수수료가 꽤 비싼 것 같습니다.

남 흠... [55]그건 다음 회의에서 얘기하죠.

어휘 room 여유, 공간 budget 예산 hire 채용하다 additional 추가의 negotiation 협상 contract 계약(서) inform 알리다 recruitment 채용, 모집 agency 대행사, 대리점 firm 회사

53. 화자들은 무엇에 관해 이야기하고 있는가?

(A) 다음 업무
(B) 정책 변경
(C) 생산 목표
(D) 직원 채용 필요성

패러프레이징 hiring additional employees → Staffing

54. 프란체스카는 다음 주에 무엇을 할 것인가?

(A) 계약 협상하기
(B) 문서 보내기
(C) 발표 시청하기
(D) 워크숍 진행하기

55. 다음 회의에서 무엇이 논의될 것인가?

(A) 정보 제공 영상을 제작하는 것
(B) 신규 고객을 모집하는 것
(C) 다른 회사의 서비스를 이용하는 것
(D) 사무실 배치를 변경하는 것

패러프레이징 using a different firm → Using a different company's services

미녀 호남 영녀

Questions 56-58 refer to the following conversation with three speakers.

W1 Hi, Luis. [56]Thanks for visiting us on site to make the repairs. We weren't able to get a tow truck for our broken van. I think you've met Suji, our fleet manager.

M Yes, it's nice to see you again.

W2 You, too. So, the van was running fine yesterday, but it wouldn't start this morning.

W1 [57]It's frustrating because we just bought this van, so it shouldn't be having problems already.

W2 [57]I agree.

M Hmm... you know, it looks like you need a new ignition switch. [58]I brought a spare one, so it won't take me long to replace it.

여1 안녕하세요, 루이스. [56]수리를 위해 현장 방문해 주셔서 감사합니다. 고장 난 밴을 견인할 견인차를 구할 수 없었어요. 당신은 우리 차량 관리자인 수지를 만나 봤을 것 같은데요.

남 네, 다시 뵙게 되어 반갑습니다.

여2 저도요. 자, 밴이 어제는 잘 작동되고 있었는데, 오늘 아침에 시동이 걸리지 않았어요.

여1 [57]저희는 얼마 전에 이 밴을 샀기 때문에 벌써 문제가 생기면 안 되는 거라서 당황스럽네요.

여2 [57]동감이에요.

남 흠... 있잖아요, 새 점화 스위치가 필요해 보여요. [58]제가 여분을 하나 가져왔으니 그걸 교체하는 데 오래 걸리지 않을 거예요.

어휘 on site 현장에 tow truck 견인차 frustrating 실망스럽게 하는 ignition (차량의) 점화 spare 여분의, 예비용의 replace 교체하다

56. 남자는 누구인 것 같은가?

(A) 버스 운전사
(B) 시 공무원
(C) 자동차 정비공
(D) 경비원

57. 여자들은 무엇에 대해 당황스러워 하는가?

(A) 경력 사원을 구하는 것의 어려움

(B) 새로 구입한 물건의 문제

(C) 서비스 요금의 인상

(D) 고객들의 부당한 불평

패러프레이징 just bought → newly purchased

58. 남자에 따르면, 왜 일이 빨리 끝날 것인가?

(A) 그는 최근에 약간의 훈련을 마쳤다.

(B) 그는 필요한 부품을 가져왔다.

(C) 그를 도와줄 조수가 있다.

(D) 그는 전에 비슷한 문제를 해결했다.

영녀 미남

Questions 59-61 refer to the following conversation.

W Hi, Ji-hoon. [59]Have you finished the flyer for our upcoming painting exhibit?

M I've completed the first draft, and I'd like to get your opinion on it. Since [60]we have so many different artists included in the collection, I wanted to make sure they were all listed on the back. Does it look alright?

W Hmm... the list is very long.

M [60]I guess I could just keep the most recognizable names.

W Yes, I think that would be better. And [61]please also add a note about the current hours we're open and our new hours from March 1.

여 안녕하세요, 지훈 씨. [59]곧 있을 우리의 그림 전시회용 전단을 마무리 지었나요?

남 초안을 완성했는데, 그것에 대한 당신의 의견을 듣고 싶어요. [60]컬렉션에 아주 많은 다양한 화가들이 포함되어 있어서, 그들이 뒷면에 다 나와 있는지 확인하고 싶었어요. 괜찮아 보여요?

여 흠... 명단이 아주 기네요.

남 [60]가장 잘 알려진 이름만 남길 수도 있을 것 같아요.

여 네, 그게 나을 것 같아요. 그리고 [61]현재 개장 시간과 3월 1일부터의 새로운 개장 시간에 대한 메모도 추가해 주세요.

어휘 flyer 전단 upcoming 곧 있을, 다가오는 exhibit 전시회 complete 완성하다 draft 초안, 원고 include 포함하다 recognizable 인식 가능한, 잘 알려진

59. 화자들은 어디에서 일하는 것 같은가?

(A) 미술관에서

(B) 신문사에서

(C) 인쇄소에서

(D) 기술 연구소에서

60. 여자는 "명단이 아주 기네요"라고 말할 때 무엇을 암시하는가?

(A) 다른 몇몇 직원들이 도와줘야 한다.

(B) 그녀는 일을 완료하기 위해 더 많은 시간이 필요하다.

(C) 그녀는 남자가 열심히 일했다고 생각한다.

(D) 일부 정보가 제거되어야 한다.

61. 3월에 무엇이 변경될 것인가?

(A) 고용 정책

(B) 현장 관리자

(C) 개장 시간

(D) 로고

미녀 호남

Questions 62-64 refer to the following conversation and advertisement.

W Thank you for calling Rosebud Furniture's customer service line. How may I help you?

M Hi. [62]I was trying to buy an item online from your Classic Styles collection, but when I tried to click on the checkout page, it would not load.

W I'm sorry about that. You can place an order over the phone if you'd prefer.

M In that case, [63]how long would it take for my order to be delivered? I live in Wilmont.

W [63]It would get to you in three days.

M Great! Then [64]I'd like to order the leather armchair.

W Okay. And what are your payment details?

여 로즈버드 가구점의 고객 서비스에 전화해 주셔서 감사합니다. 무엇을 도와드릴까요?

남 안녕하세요. [62]귀사의 클래식 스타일 컬렉션에서 온라인으로 물건을 사려고 했지만, 결제 페이지를 클릭하려고 했을 때 로딩이 되지 않았어요.

여 죄송합니다. 원하신다면 전화로 주문하실 수 있습니다.

남 그렇다면, [63]제 주문품이 배송되는 데 얼마나 걸릴까요? 저는 윌몬트에 삽니다.

여 [63]3일이면 도착할 거예요.

남 좋아요! 그러면 [64]저는 가죽 안락의자를 주문하고 싶습니다.

여 알겠습니다. 귀하의 지불 정보가 어떻게 되시나요?

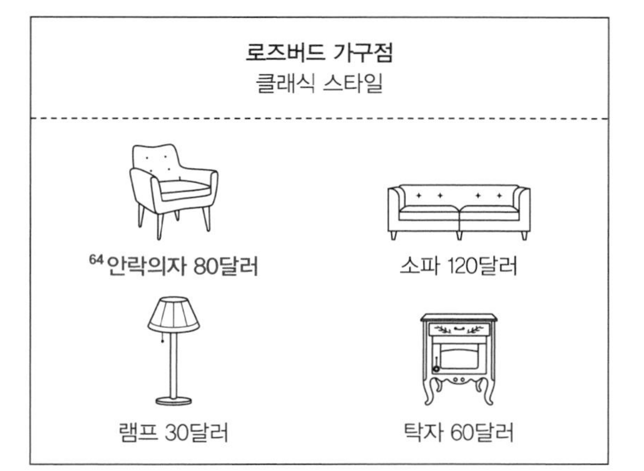

로즈버드 가구점
클래식 스타일
64안락의자 80달러
소파 120달러
램프 30달러
탁자 60달러

어휘 checkout 계산(대) place an order 주문하다 in that case 그렇다면 leather 가죽 payment 지불

62. 남자는 어떤 문제가 있는가?

(A) 신용 카드가 취소되었다.
(B) 웹페이지가 로딩되지 않는다.
(C) 상품이 품절되었다.
(D) 가구가 손상되었다.

63. 여자에 따르면, 3일 후에 무슨 일이 일어날 것인가?

(A) 카탈로그가 발송될 것이다.
(B) 가격이 바뀔 것이다.
(C) 주문품이 도착할 것이다.
(D) 직원이 남자에게 전화할 것이다.

패러프레이징 would get to you → will arrive

64. 시각 자료를 보시오. 남자에게 얼마가 청구될 것인가?

(A) 80달러
(B) 120달러
(C) 30달러
(D) 60달러

호남 영녀

Questions 65-67 refer to the following conversation and schedule.

M Alright, Izumi. Now that [65]you've filled out all of your employment forms for working here at Ellis Financial Consulting, we'll move on to the building tour. We're right on schedule. Do you have any questions before we begin?

W Well, during my final interview, [66]I was told that my supervisor would be Susan McNeil. I'm curious about whether she is part of the orientation day.

M Yes, [66]you'll get a chance to meet her at the lunch we have planned for the entire department. Now [67]let's head to the security office to get your ID badge before completing the rest of the tour.

남 좋습니다, 이즈미. 이제 [65]**이곳 엘리스 금융 컨설팅에서 일하기 위한 귀하의 고용 양식을 모두 작성하셨으니**, 건물 견학으로 넘어가겠습니다. 일정대로 잘 진행되어 가네요. 시작하기 전에 질문 있으신가요?

여 음, 최종 면접에서 [66]**제 상사가 수잔 맥닐 씨일 거라고 들었습니다.** 그녀가 오리엔테이션에 참가하실 건지 궁금합니다.

남 네, 저희가 부서 전체를 위해 계획한 [66]**점심 시간에 그녀를 만날 기회가 있을 거예요.** 이제 나머지 견학을 마치기 전에 [67]**경비실로 가서 신분증 배지를 받아옵시다.**

직원 오리엔테이션
5월 11일

서류 작업:	오전 9시
건물 견학:	오전 11시
66부서 점심:	오후 12시 30분
교육 영상:	오후 2시

어휘 fill out 작성하다 supervisor 감독관, 관리자 entire 전체의 head 가다, 향하다

65. 화자들은 어떤 업계에서 일하는가?

(A) 공학
(B) 금융
(C) 제조
(D) 의료

66. 시각 자료를 보시오. 여자는 언제 수잔 맥닐을 만날 것인가?

(A) 오전 9시에
(B) 오전 11시에
(C) 오후 12시 30분에
(D) 오후 2시에

67. 화자들은 다음에 무엇을 할 것 같은가?

(A) 메뉴 선택하기
(B) 계획 검토하기
(C) 일정표 출력하기
(D) 경비실로 가기

패러프레이징 head → Go

영녀 미남

Questions 68-70 refer to the following conversation and office map.

W Hi, Rishu. This is Loretta from the administration team. [68]Is your first day here at Vega Accountancy going well?

TEST 03

M Yes. All of the accountants have been very welcoming.

W Wonderful. Now, I'm calling because your parking pass is ready to pick up.

M All right. [69]The IT team is visiting me at two o'clock to show me how to sign into the company software and use its features. Could I stop by after that?

W Of course. [70]I'll be in my office all afternoon. It's on the second floor, next to the elevator.

여 안녕하세요, 리슈. 관리팀의 로레타입니다. [68]베가 회계사무소에서의 첫날을 잘 보내고 있나요?

남 네. 모든 회계사들이 매우 환영해 주셨어요.

여 아주 좋아요. 이제, 당신의 주차권이 준비돼서 전화 드렸습니다.

남 알겠습니다. [69]IT팀이 2시에 저를 방문하여 회사 소프트웨어에 로그인하고 기능을 사용하는 방법을 알려 주실 예정입니다. 그 뒤에 들러도 될까요?

여 물론이죠. [70]저는 오후 내내 사무실에 있을 거예요. 사무실은 2층 엘리베이터 옆에 있습니다.

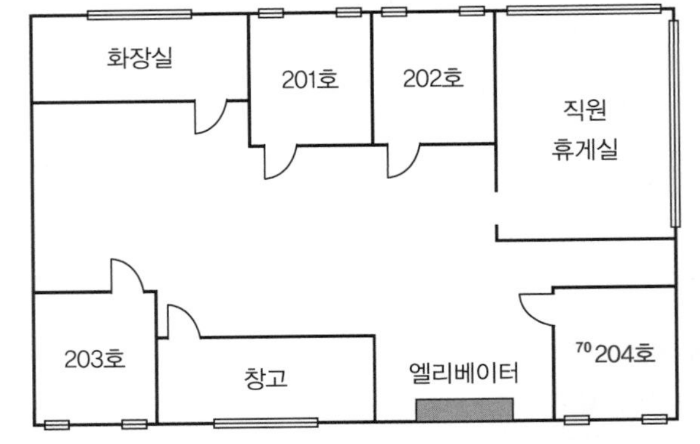

어휘 administration 관리 (업무) accountancy 회계 (업무) accountant 회계사 pick up ~을 찾아가다 sign into 로그인하다 feature 기능, 특징 stop by 잠시 들르다

68. 화자들은 어디에서 일하는가?

(A) 소프트웨어 회사에서
(B) 회계 법인에서
(C) 인터넷 서비스 공급업체에서
(D) 건축 회사에서

69. 남자는 2시에 무엇을 해야 하는가?

(A) 소프트웨어 사용법 배우기
(B) 주차장으로 가기
(C) 서류 찾아가기
(D) 피드백 양식 작성하기

패러프레이징 sign into the company software and use its features → use some software

70. 시각 자료를 보시오. 여자의 사무실은 어디인가?

(A) 201호
(B) 202호
(C) 203호
(D) 204호

PART 4

미남

Questions 71-73 refer to the following talk.

[71]Our next stop on today's tour is the factory floor. There you will see our workers in action, making our ceramics. I've already shown you some of our finished bowls and plates, and now you'll see how we make [72]our vases with handles. As you probably expect, [72]many steps are involved in making these items because multiple pieces are being joined together. You'll see what I mean in a moment, but, first, [73]I'd like you to watch this brief safety video.

[71]오늘 투어의 다음 목적지는 공장 현장입니다. 그곳에서 여러분은 우리 직원들이 도자기 만드는 작업을 보시게 될 겁니다. 제가 이미 완성된 그릇과 접시들을 몇 개 보여 드렸는데, 이제 여러분은 우리가 [72]손잡이가 달린 꽃병을 어떻게 만드는지 보시게 될 겁니다. 여러분이 아마 예상하시듯이, [72]여러 조각들이 접합되어야 하기 때문에 이 물건들을 만드는 데는 많은 단계가 포함됩니다. 잠시 후에 제 말이 무슨 뜻인지 아시게 되겠지만, 먼저, [73]이 짧은 안전 영상을 보시기 바랍니다.

어휘 in action 활동을 하는 ceramics 도자기(류) multiple 여러, 다수의 piece 조각 in a moment 곧 brief 짧은, 간단한

71. 화자는 누구인 것 같은가?

(A) 건물주
(B) 투어 가이드
(C) 판매원
(D) 미술 강사

72. 화자는 손잡이가 달린 꽃병에 대해 무엇이라고 말하는가?

(A) 그것들은 만드는 데 돈이 많이 든다.
(B) 그것들은 점점 더 인기가 많아지고 있다.
(C) 그것들은 최근에 물품 목록에 추가되었다.
(D) 그것들은 복잡한 생산 과정을 가지고 있다.

패러프레이징 many steps are involved in making these items → have a complex production process

73. 화자는 다음에 무엇을 할 것인가?

(A) 영상 보여 주기
(B) 쿠폰 나눠 주기
(C) 질문에 답하기
(D) 다과 준비하기

76. 청자들은 다음에 무엇을 할 것인가?

(A) 유인물 받기
(B) 파일 다운로드하기
(C) 다른 방으로 이동하기
(D) 시연 보기

미녀

Questions 74-76 refer to the following speech.

I'd like to thank the event planners for inviting me to this Technology Expo. My name is Ashley Yates, and my company, Phoenix Tech, is excited about [74]the release of our new product, the Tipani Music Player. This portable device can store thousands of songs, which you can access at the touch of a button. Additionally, it can stream audio files from the Internet. [75]I'm very proud of the final design, as it makes the device so durable that you can be confident that it will withstand the demands of daily life. Now [76]I'll show you how to use the main features. If you have questions, please save them for the end.

이번 기술 박람회에 저를 초대해 주신 행사 기획자분들께 감사드립니다. 제 이름은 애슐리 예이츠이고, 제 회사인 피닉스 테크는 [74]저희 신제품인 티파니 뮤직 플레이어의 출시에 들떠 있습니다. [74]이 휴대용 장치는 수천 곡의 노래를 저장할 수 있는데, 이것은 버튼 한 번만 누르면 이용할 수 있습니다. 또한 인터넷에서 오디오 파일을 스트리밍할 수 있습니다. [75]저는 최종 디자인이 매우 자랑스러운데, 그 덕분에 이 기기는 내구성이 매우 뛰어나 일상의 충격에도 끄떡없을 거라 확신드립니다. 이제 [76]제가 여러분에게 주요 기능을 사용하는 방법을 보여 드리겠습니다. 질문은 발표가 끝난 다음 해 주시면 감사하겠습니다.

어휘 release 출시 portable 휴대용의 device 장치, 기구 store 저장하다 access 이용하다, 접근하다 durable 내구성이 있는 confident 확신하는 withstand 견뎌내다 demand 요구

74. 화자는 어떤 제품을 소개하고 있는가?

(A) 휴대용 음악 장치
(B) 태블릿 컴퓨터
(C) 종이 파쇄기
(D) 디지털 카메라

패러프레이징 Music Player → music device

75. 화자는 제품의 어떤 특징을 강조하는가?

(A) 저렴한 가격
(B) 내구성
(C) 작은 크기
(D) 보증서

호남

Questions 77-79 refer to the following talk.

Good afternoon. I'm Russell Batiste, the instructor for [77]this workshop. Today you're going to learn the best way to photograph various sites. Getting the right angle and framing can make a big difference. [78]This will make the houses and other properties you're selling look more appealing. As a result, you'll get more potential customers. You'll see an overview of each half-hour session on your handout. Some of the activities require discussion, so [79]I'd like you to move your chairs into groups of three to four people.

안녕하세요. 저는 [77]이 워크숍의 강사인 러셀 바티스트입니다. 오늘 [77]여러분은 다양한 장소를 촬영하는 가장 좋은 방법을 배우게 될 겁니다. 올바른 각도와 프레임을 잡는 것이 큰 차이를 만들 수 있습니다. [78]이렇게 하면 여러분이 판매 중인 집과 다른 부동산들이 더 매력적으로 보일 것입니다. 결과적으로, 여러분은 더 많은 잠재 고객을 확보하게 될 것입니다. 여러분의 유인물에 30분 수업 각각의 개요가 보이실 겁니다. 일부 활동은 토론이 필요하므로, [79]여러분이 의자를 옮겨 서너 명의 그룹으로 만들어 주셨으면 합니다.

어휘 instructor 강사 photograph 촬영하다, 사진을 찍다 various 다양한 site 장소, 현장 angle 각도 framing 구성, 틀 잡기 property 부동산, 재산 appealing 매력적인 potential 잠재적인 overview 개요 handout 유인물

77. 워크숍의 주제는 무엇인가?

(A) 다른 사람들을 관리하는 방법
(B) 프레젠테이션을 만드는 방법
(C) 사진을 찍는 방법
(D) 투자를 다루는 방법

패러프레이징 the best way to photograph various sites → How to take pictures

78. 청자들은 어떤 분야에서 일하는 것 같은가?

(A) 법
(B) 교통
(C) 교육
(D) 부동산

79. 화자는 청자들에게 무엇을 해 달라고 요청하는가?

(A) 다른 워크숍에 참석하기
(B) 소그룹 형성하기

(C) 일부 정보를 이메일로 보내기
(D) 자기소개하기

영녀

Questions 80-82 refer to the following telephone message.

Hello, [80]this is Debra Salazar, the manager of the Richmond branch. I'd like to leave a message for the head office. We've been running our currency exchange service for two weeks now. I know that some decision-makers thought that it would be a waste of resources. However, [81]we have a desk set up just for that service, and there's almost always a line. [82]I'd actually like to assign another person to help during busy periods, but we don't have funding for additional workers. I'm not sure how to handle this issue, so any advice would be helpful. If someone could call me back, I would really appreciate it. Thank you.

여보세요, [80]저는 리치몬드 지점 매니저인 데브라 살라자르입니다. 본사에 메시지를 남기고 싶습니다. 우리는 현재 2주째 환전 서비스를 운영하고 있습니다. 저는 몇몇 의사 결정자들이 이게 자원 낭비가 될 거라고 생각했다는 걸 알고 있습니다. 하지만 [81]그 서비스만을 위한 데스크가 설치되어 있고, 거의 항상 줄이 늘어서 있습니다. [82]저는 사실 바쁜 시기 동안 도와줄 다른 사람을 배정하고 싶은데, 저희는 추가 인력을 위한 자금이 없습니다. 저는 이 문제를 어떻게 처리해야 할지 몰라서, 어떤 조언이든 도움이 될 것입니다. 누군가 저에게 다시 전화해 주신다면 정말 감사하겠습니다. 고맙습니다.

어휘 head office 본사 run 운영하다 currency exchange 환전 decision-maker 의사 결정자 waste 낭비 resource 자원 assign 배정하다 period 시기 funding 자금 additional 추가의 handle 처리하다

80. 화자는 누구인가?

(A) 그래픽 디자이너
(B) 지점장
(C) 기자
(D) 공사 감독관

패러프레이징 the manager of the Richmond branch → A branch manager

81. 화자는 "거의 항상 줄이 늘어서 있습니다"라고 말할 때 무엇을 의미하는가?

(A) 서비스가 자주 이용된다.
(B) 환전 과정이 혼란스럽다.
(C) 마감 기한 연장이 필요하다.
(D) 배치가 수정되어야 한다.

82. 화자는 무엇에 관한 조언을 원하는가?

(A) 시장 동향
(B) 이전 정책
(C) 투자 기회
(D) 잠재적 해결책

패러프레이징 how to handle this issue → solutions

미녀

Questions 83-85 refer to the following excerpt from a meeting.

Good afternoon, everyone. I've just reviewed the figures for the previous quarter, and [83]I'm pleased to report that our factory's production levels are twenty percent higher than our goal. Our new equipment, along with increased routine training, seems to be working well. Everything is operating smoothly, and in general, staff members are quite happy. The only problem we need to deal with is [84]the testing room. Since it doesn't have an air conditioner, the temperature in there is too hot for employees. [85]I need a couple of people to write a budget request for installing an air conditioner. Does anyone have time?

안녕하세요, 여러분. 저는 방금 이전 분기의 수치를 검토했고, [83]우리 공장의 생산 수준이 우리 목표보다 20퍼센트 더 높은 걸 전하게 되어 기쁩니다. 늘어난 정기 교육과 더불어, 우리의 새 장비가 효과를 내고 있는 것 같습니다. 모든 것이 원활하게 운영되고 있고, 전반적으로 직원들은 매우 만족하고 있습니다. 우리가 처리해야 할 유일한 문제는 [84]실험실입니다. 에어컨이 없기 때문에, 그곳의 온도는 직원들에게 너무 덥습니다. [85]저는 에어컨 설치를 위한 예산 요청서를 쓸 사람들이 몇 명 필요합니다. 시간 있는 분 계세요?

어휘 review 검토하다 figures 수치 previous 이전의 report 전하다, 알리다 production 생산 along with ~과 더불어, ~에 따라 routine 정기적인 operate 운영되다 smoothly 원활하게, 순조롭게 in general 전반적으로, 대체로 deal with ~을 처리하다 temperature 온도, 기온 install 설치하다

83. 화자는 무엇에 대해 기뻐하는가?

(A) 새로운 규정
(B) 공장 생산량
(C) 예산 흑자
(D) 업계의 상

패러프레이징 factory's production levels → Factory output

84. 화자에 따르면, 실험실의 문제는 무엇인가?

(A) 그곳은 안전하지 않다.
(B) 그곳은 너무 작다.
(C) 그곳은 최근 검사에 불합격했다.
(D) 그곳의 온도가 쾌적하지 않다.

85. 일부 청자들은 다음에 무엇을 할 것 같은가?

(A) 몇몇 직원들 소개하기
(B) 회사 추천하기
(C) 업무에 자원하기
(D) 발표하기

미남

Questions 86-88 refer to the following excerpt from a meeting.

[86] I'd like to talk about the patio area that's being installed at the restaurant. The concrete has been removed, and stone slabs and a railing will be added. We're still on schedule for opening on May 3. [87] Several of you have asked what the work schedule will be after this new area is open. Well, that's about two weeks from now, and the weather will be a factor. You'll likely be assigned extra shifts. So, [88] if you can work longer hours, please complete a new work availability form.

[86] 저는 식당에 설치되고 있는 옥외 테라스 구역에 대해 말씀드리고 싶습니다. 콘크리트는 제거되었고, 석판과 난간이 추가될 것입니다. 우리는 여전히 5월 3일 개방 일정대로 되어가고 있습니다. [87] 여러분 중 몇 분이 이 새로운 구역이 개방된 후의 업무 일정을 물어보셨습니다. 음, 그건 지금부터 2주 후라서, 날씨가 한 요인이 될 겁니다. 여러분은 추가 근무에 할당될 가능성이 있습니다. 따라서, [88] 여러분이 더 많은 시간을 일할 수 있다면, 새로운 근무 가능 양식을 작성해 주세요.

어휘 remove 제거하다 slab 평판, 판 railing 난간 factor 요인 extra 추가의, 여분의 complete 작성하다 availability 이용할 수 있음

86. 청자들은 누구인 것 같은가?

(A) 식당 종업원들
(B) 마케팅 이사들
(C) 무역 박람회 직원들
(D) 인테리어 디자이너들

87. 화자는 "날씨가 한 요인이 될 겁니다"라고 말할 때 무엇을 암시하는가?

(A) 그는 일정을 확정하지 않았다.
(B) 그는 장소를 고르는 데 도움이 필요하다.
(C) 그는 많은 참가자 수를 기대하고 있지 않다.
(D) 그는 유니폼을 바꿀지도 모른다.

88. 화자는 청자들에게 무엇을 하라고 지시하는가?

(A) 물건 정리하기
(B) 일정표 출력하기
(C) 현장에 일찍 도착하기
(D) 근무 가능 여부 업데이트하기

패러프레이징 complete a new work availability form → Update their availability

영녀

Questions 89-91 refer to the following broadcast.

You're listening to the regional news update on Radio KRM. [89] The shuttle company Dempsey Transportation announced this morning that it will begin offering services between Springfield and several new sites, including Roseville and Valleyton. The expansion of the company's network will require new drivers. To help with recruitment efforts, [90] Dempsey Transportation is offering a one-time five-hundred-dollar payment to all new drivers. A company spokesperson said that Springfield's population is growing, creating a need for this service. In addition, it will be helpful to have more transportation options during [91] the upcoming Rock Music Festival in August.

여러분은 KRM 라디오에서 지역 뉴스 업데이트를 듣고 계십니다. [89] 셔틀버스 회사인 뎀프시 교통은 오늘 아침 스프링필드와 로즈빌, 밸리턴을 포함한 몇몇 새로운 장소 간에 서비스 제공을 시작할 거라고 발표했습니다. 이 회사의 네트워크 확장은 새로운 기사들을 필요로 할 것입니다. 채용 노력에 도움이 되도록, [90] 뎀프시 교통은 모든 신규 기사들에게 500달러를 1회 지급합니다. 회사 대변인은 스프링필드의 인구가 증가하고 있어, 이 서비스의 필요성이 야기된다고 말했습니다. 게다가, [91] 다가오는 8월 록 음악 축제 동안 더 많은 교통수단 옵션이 있는 게 도움이 될 것입니다.

어휘 regional 지역의 offer 제공하다 expansion 확장 recruitment 채용, 모집 spokesperson 대변인 population 인구

89. 뎀프시 교통은 오늘 아침에 무엇을 발표했는가?

(A) 그곳은 더 많은 경로를 추가했다.
(B) 그곳은 요금을 인상할 계획이다.
(C) 그곳은 다른 회사와 합병할 것이다.
(D) 그곳은 지도부가 새로 바뀌었다.

90. 화자에 따르면, 신규 기사들은 무엇을 받을 것인가?

(A) 추가 휴가 시간
(B) 무료 연수
(C) 현금 보너스
(D) 초과 근무 수당

91. 8월에 무슨 일이 일어날 것인가?

(A) 제빵 대회
(B) 스포츠 토너먼트
(C) 정치 토론
(D) 음악 축제

미녀

Questions 92-94 refer to the following telephone message.

Hi, Eric. I wanted to let you know [92]how the arrangements are going for the auction we're planning to raise money for the local library. [93]I just checked my e-mail this morning and saw that the city's professional basketball team is donating two season tickets. They're worth over three thousand dollars. I nearly spilled my coffee! [94]I've added the team to the list of donors on our Web site. I'd like your opinion on how I've organized things there. Would you mind taking a look?

안녕하세요, 에릭. [92]우리가 지역 도서관을 위해 모금하고자 계획 중인 경매 준비가 어떻게 되어가고 있는지 알려드리고 싶었습니다. [93]제가 오늘 아침에 막 이메일을 확인했는데 시의 프로 농구팀이 정기 입장권을 두 장 기증한다고 합니다. 그것들은 3천 달러 이상의 가치가 있어요. 하마터면 커피를 쏟을 뻔했다니까요! [94]그 팀을 우리 웹사이트에 있는 기부자 명단에 추가했어요. 제가 웹사이트를 정리해 놓은 방식에 대해 당신의 의견을 듣고 싶어요. 한 번 봐 주시겠어요?

어휘 arrangement 준비 auction 경매 local 지역의 professional 프로의, 전문적인 donate 기부하다 spill 쏟다, 흘리다 donor 기부자 organize 정리하다

92. 화자는 무엇을 계획하고 있는가?

(A) 모금 행사
(B) 시상식
(C) 글짓기 대회
(D) 도서 사인회

패러프레이징 the auction we're planning to raise money → A fund-raiser

93. 화자는 "하마터면 커피를 쏟을 뻔했다니까요"라고 말할 때 무엇을 암시하는가?

(A) 음료가 너무 뜨거웠다.
(B) 제품이 잘 디자인되지 않았다.
(C) 그녀는 아침에 서두르고 있었다.
(D) 그녀는 어떤 소식에 흥분했다.

94. 화자는 청자에게 무엇을 해 달라고 요청하는가?

(A) 초대장 디자인하기
(B) 영수증 보내기
(C) 웹사이트 확인하기
(D) 제조업체에 연락하기

패러프레이징 taking a look → Check

호남

Questions 95-97 refer to the following talk and map.

The Baxter Local Business Expo starts tomorrow. Thank you to everyone who has agreed to work this weekend. This event is the perfect place to promote [95]our low-fat, low-salt snacks. A lot of health-conscious consumers will be there, and we think they'll love our products. Right after the meeting, [96]I'd like you to help put all the boxes onto the truck so it's ready to go in the morning. Fortunately, [97]it'll be fairly easy to set up the booth, as we're right next to the parking lot.

백스터 지역 비즈니스 박람회가 내일 시작됩니다. 이번 주말에 근무하기로 동의해 주신 모든 분께 감사드립니다. 이 행사는 [95]우리의 저지방, 저염 간식을 홍보하기에 최적의 장소입니다. 건강에 신경 쓰는 많은 소비자들이 그곳에 올 것이고, 우리는 그들이 우리 제품을 마음에 쏙 들어 할 것이라고 생각합니다. 회의 바로 후에 [96]저는 여러분이 모든 상자를 트럭에 실어서 아침에 출발할 준비가 되도록 도와주셨으면 합니다. 다행히 [97]우리는 주차장 바로 옆이라서 부스를 설치하는 건 꽤 쉬울 거예요.

어휘 promote 홍보하다 consumer 소비자 fairly 꽤, 상당히

95. 회사는 어떤 종류의 제품을 판매하는가?

(A) 비타민 보충제
(B) 건강 간식
(C) 수제 장신구
(D) 운동 기구

패러프레이징 low-fat, low-salt snacks → Healthy snacks

96. 화자는 청자들에게 무엇을 해 달라고 요청하는가?

(A) 상품에 라벨 붙이기
(B) 출석부에 서명하기
(C) 트럭에 짐 싣기
(D) 고객들에게 전화하기

패러프레이징 put all the boxes onto the truck → Load a truck

97. 시각 자료를 보시오. 회사는 어떤 부스를 사용할 것인가?

(A) 1A 부스

(B) 1B 부스
(C) 2A 부스
(D) 2B 부스

영녀

Questions 98-100 refer to the following talk and schedule.

As I'm sure you've heard, [98]last week we received confirmation of the results of our government inspection. Overall, we did very well. Over the next few months, we'll work on the areas that need improvement. Fortunately, some of our incoming equipment will help. In particular, [99]we've invested in new tractors and field sprayers to replace the outdated ones. We hope this will reduce the number of injuries, as there are more features to protect the operators. All employees on the farm will be trained on how to use the sprayers and tractors. [100]I'll hold a training session on the day the tractors arrive. Please talk to Mario if you can't be there.

여러분도 들으셨으리라 확신하는데요, [98]지난주에 우리는 정부 감사 결과 확인서를 받았습니다. 전반적으로, 우리는 매우 잘 했습니다. 앞으로 몇 개월 동안, 우리는 개선이 필요한 부분들에 대해 노력할 겁니다. 다행히, 들어오는 장비 중 일부가 도움이 될 겁니다. 특히, [99]우리는 구식 트랙터와 농업용 분무기를 교체하는 데 투자했습니다. 기사를 보호할 수 있는 기능들이 더 많기 때문에 우리는 이것이 부상 횟수를 줄여주기를 바랍니다. 농장의 모든 직원은 분무기와 트랙터 사용법에 대한 교육을 받을 것입니다. [100]저는 트랙터가 도착하는 날에 교육 과정을 열겠습니다. 거기에 참석할 수 없다면 마리오에게 이야기하세요.

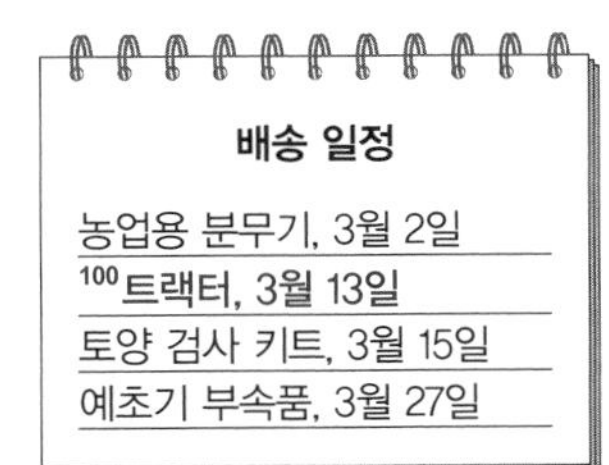

배송 일정
농업용 분무기, 3월 2일
[100]트랙터, 3월 13일
토양 검사 키트, 3월 15일
예초기 부속품, 3월 27일

어휘 confirmation 확인 inspection 감사, 검사 overall 전반적으로 improvement 개선 incoming 들어오는 in particular 특히 invest in ~에 투자하다 replace 대체하다, 교체하다 outdated 구식인 injury 부상 protect 보호하다 operator (기계 · 장치 등의) 기사, 조작자

98. 화자는 지난주에 무슨 일이 있었다고 말하는가?

(A) 일부 감사 결과가 확인되었다.
(B) 업체가 잡지에 실렸다.
(C) 은행 대출이 승인되었다.
(D) 일부 보수 작업이 완료되었다.

99. 일부 장비는 왜 교체될 것인가?

(A) 환경을 돕기 위해
(B) 경쟁업체에 뒤지지 않기 위해
(C) 비용을 절감하기 위해
(D) 안전성 향상을 위해

패러프레이징 reduce the number of injuries → improve safety

100. 시각 자료를 보시오. 화자는 언제 교육 과정을 실시할 것인가?

(A) 3월 2일에
(B) 3월 13일에
(C) 3월 15일에
(D) 3월 27일에

PART 5

101. 소유한정사

Ms. Dalton은 지난 토요일 행사에서 그녀의 책에서 발췌한 부분을 읽었다.

해설 빈칸 앞에 전치사 from이 있고 뒤에는 명사 book이 이어지므로 빈칸은 명사를 수식하는 자리이다. 따라서 소유한정사인 (A) her가 정답이다.

어휘 excerpt 발췌

102. 명사 자리

그 사안에 대한 조사가 문제를 빨리 해결하는 데 도움이 되기를 바랍니다.

해설 빈칸 앞에 소유한정사 your가 있고 뒤에는 전치사구 into the matter가 이어지므로 빈칸은 한정사의 수식을 받는 명사 자리이다. 따라서 (B) investigation이 정답이다.

어휘 investigation 조사 matter 문제, 사안 resolve 해결하다 issue 문제

103. 동사 어휘 wish

연례 마라톤 대회에서 자원봉사를 하고 싶은 사람은 시청에 전화해야 한다.
(A) 원하다, 바라다 (B) 요구하다 (C) 선언하다 (D) 이행하다, 달성하다

해설 wish를 제외한 나머지 선택지들은 to부정사를 목적어로 취하지 못하므로 오답이다.

어휘 volunteer 자원봉사를 하다 annual 연례의 city hall 시청

104. 전치사 어휘 at

Mr. Gardner는 금요일에 있을 저녁 회식 자리에서 자신의 후임자를 소개할 것이다.

해설 빈칸 뒤에 the company dinner가 구체적으로 명시되어 있으므로 (C) at이 정답이다. at은 특정 시각/시점/지점/위치 등을 구체적으로 나타낼 때 쓴다.

어휘 replacement 후임자, 대체

105. 명사 자리+어휘

Ms. Nelson의 주치의는 그녀에게 고단백 음식을 섭취하라고 조언했다.

해설 빈칸 앞에 관사 a가 있으므로 빈칸에는 high-protein과 결합하여 명사구를 이룰 수 있는 말이 들어가야 한다. 따라서 선택지 중 명사인 (A) dieter와 (C) diet가 정답 후보인데, 문맥상 주치의가 '고단백 음식'을 섭취하라고 조언하는 것이 자연스러우므로 (C) diet가 정답이다. dieter는 '다이어트 중인 사람'이므로 의미상 적절하지 않다.

어휘 physician 내과 의사, 주치의 advise 조언하다, 충고하다 high-protein 고단백의 diet 식단, 음식

106. 부사 어휘 strongly

고객들은 새로운 전기차를 시승해 보라는 적극적인 권유를 받았다.
(A) 대략 (B) 고르게, 균등하게 (C) 빠르게 (D) 강력하게, 적극적으로

어휘 encourage 권유하다, 권장하다 electric vehicle 전기차 test drive 시승

107. to부정사 [부사 역할]

우리 회사의 신입 직원들을 환영하기 위해 월요일에 있을 환영회에 참석해 주시기 바랍니다.

해설 빈칸 앞이 완전한 절이므로 빈칸 이하는 부사 역할을 해야 한다. 선택지에서 부사 역할을 할 수 있는 것은 to부정사인 (C) to welcome뿐이다.

어휘 reception 환영회 staff 직원

108. 명사 어휘 set

12개짜리 골프채 세트는 이동하기 쉽도록 바퀴가 달린 가죽 가방과 함께 나옵니다.
(A) 패널, 전문가 집단 (B) 어울림, 조화 (C) 게임, 경기 (D) 세트

어휘 leather 가죽 wheel 바퀴 transportation 운반, 이동

109. 전치사 자리+어휘

Phoenix Inc.는 8월 중에 모든 카펫 청소 서비스를 15% 할인해 드립니다.

해설 빈칸 뒤에 명사 August가 있으므로 빈칸은 전치사 자리이다. (B) during과 (D) than이 정답 후보인데 문맥상 8월 동안에 서비스를 할인해 준다는 내용이 되는 게 자연스러우므로 (B)가 정답이다.

어휘 offer 제공하다

110. 접속사 자리+어휘

비가 내렸지만 기록적인 숫자의 사람들이 퍼레이드에 참여했다.

해설 빈칸 뒤에 주어와 동사를 갖춘 완전한 절이 있고, 콤마로 새로운 절이 연결되어 있으므로 빈칸에는 부사절 접속사가 들어가야 한다. (B) If와 (D) Although가 정답 후보인데 문맥상 비가 내렸지만 행사에 많은 사람이 참여했다는 내용이 되는 게 자연스러우므로 (D) Although가 정답이다. (A) Nevertheless는 '그럼에도 불구하고'를 뜻하는 접속부사이며, 말 그대로 부사이기 때문에 절과 절을 연결하는 역할을 할 수 없다.

어휘 a record number of 기록적인 숫자의 attend 참여하다, 참석하다

111. 재귀대명사 [재귀용법]

새 에어컨은 설정 온도에 도달하면 자동으로 꺼진다.

해설 재귀대명사가 대신하는 대상이 The new air conditioner이므로 (A) itself가 정답이다.

어휘 turn off ~을 끄다 automatically 자동으로 once 일단 ~하면 temperature 온도 reach 도달하다

112. 동사 어휘 discuss

지난주에 경영진은 전면적인 디지털 뉴스 플랫폼으로 전환하는 것에 대해 논의했다.
(A) 위치를 찾아내다 (B) 논의하다 (C) 구독하다 (D) 권리를 주다

어휘 transition 변화, 전환 management 경영(진)

113. 형용사 자리

Kirk's Moving Service는 매우 부서지기 쉬운 물건의 손상을 최소화하여 운반하는 것으로 명성이 높다.

해설 빈칸 앞에 전치사 with가 있고 뒤에는 명사 damage가 있으므로 빈칸은 명사를 수식하는 자리이다. 따라서 형용사인 (D) minimal이 정답이다.

어휘 have a reputation for ~로 유명하다 transport 수송하다, 운반하다 extremely 매우, 극도로 fragile 깨지기 쉬운 minimal 최소의 damage 손상

114. 접속사 자리

Fenway Hair Salon은 가격을 50% 인상했음에도 불구하고 고객의 숫자가 줄어들지 않았다.

해설 빈칸 뒤에 완전한 절이 있으므로 빈칸은 절을 이끌 수 있는 접속사 자리이다. 따라서 (B) even though가 정답이다.

어휘 experience 경험하다 drop 하락 raise 올리다, 인상하다

115. 형용사 어휘 profitable

접객업의 성장 덕분에 새로운 호텔은 수익성이 좋은 사업이 될 것으로 예상된다.
(A) 구조적인 (B) 간편한, 소형의 (C) 수익성이 좋은 (D) 자발적인

어휘 growth 성장 hospitality industry 접객업 expect 예상하다 venture (벤처) 사업, 모험

116. 동사 자리+수 일치

새로운 광고 캠페인은 Mr. Yates가 예상했던 것처럼 매출에 극적인 영향을 미치지는 않았다.

해설 〈명사절 접속사(that)+주어(Mr. Yates)+-------+주어(it)+동사(would)〉 구조이므로 빈칸은 동사 자리이다. (A) assumed와 (D) assume이 정답 후보인데 주어가 단수이므로 (A)가 정답이다.

어휘 advertising campaign 광고 캠페인 dramatic 극적인 effect 효과 assume 예상하다, 추정하다

117. 명사 어휘 summer

VC Roofing의 담당자는 우리가 점검을 예약하려면 여름까지 기다려야 한다고 말했다.
(A) 날, 요일 (B) 여름 (C) 날씨 (D) 달

어휘 representative 담당자, 대표자 book 예약하다 inspection 점검

118. 수량 한정사 each

각 부서의 팀장들은 이 평가 양식들을 작성해야 합니다.

해설 빈칸 뒤의 명사가 단수이므로 단수 명사를 수식하는 (A) each가 정답이다. (D) its는 지칭하는 명사가 불분명하고 문맥상 자연스럽지 않으므로 오답이다.

어휘 department 부서 complete 완료하다, 완성하다 evaluation 평가 form 양식

119. 동사 어휘 mention

많은 청중들은 Dorsey 교수의 강연 도중 언급된 전시회를 이미 방문했다.
(A) 성취하다 (B) 일어나다, 벌어지다 (C) 언급하다 (D) 자격을 주다

어휘 audience 청중 exhibit 전시(회) lecture 강연

120. 명사 자리+어휘

저희 영업 사원들은 아직 마무리되지 않은 어떤 협상도 진전을 시킬 자신이 있습니다.

해설 빈칸 앞에 한정사 any가 있고 뒤에는 주격 관계대명사절이 이어지므로 빈칸은 한정사의 수식을 받는 명사 자리이다. (A) negotiator와 (C) negotiation이 정답 후보인데 문맥상 협상을 진전시킨다는 내용이 되는 게 자연스러우므로 (C)가 정답이다.

어휘 sales staff 영업 사원 make improvements 개선하다 finalize 마무리하다

121. 부사 어휘 also

점심시간에 제공되는 따뜻한 식사 외에도 승객들에게는 비행 내내 간식과 음료가 제공될 것이다.
(A) ~도, 또한 (B) 그럼에도 불구하고 (C) 비록 ~일지라도 (D) 그러므로

해설 문두의 in addition to와 의미가 상통하는 (A) also가 정답이다.

어휘 in addition to ~ 외에도, ~뿐만 아니라 passenger 승객 serve 제공하다 beverage 음료 flight 비행

122. 부사 자리 [수량 표현 수식]

Provost Gallery의 개관식에는 500명 이상이 참석하여 상당한 인파가 있었다.

해설 빈칸 앞에 전치사 with가 있고 뒤에는 수량 표현 500 people이 이어지므로 빈칸은 수량 표현을 수식하는 부사 자리이다. 따라서 (D) over가 정답이다. 그 외에 수량 표현을 수식하는 부사에는 about, almost, nearly, approximately 등이 있다.

어휘 impressive 인상적인 turnout 인파, 참가자의 수 grand opening 개업, 개장 attendance 참여, 참석

123. 형용사 어휘 enthusiastic

Mountainside Resort는 11월에 시즌 개장할 예정이며, 현재 열정적인 스키 강사들을 찾고 있습니다.
(A) 무료의; 칭찬하는 (B) 내구성이 좋은 (C) 정교한 (D) 열정적인

어휘 seek 찾다, 구하다 instructor 강사

124. 부사 자리

새로운 관리자가 채용되었기 때문에 그 팀은 더 엄격하게 규정을 따르기 시작했다.

해설 빈칸은 동사 follow를 수식하는 부사 자리이므로 (C) strictly가 정답이다.

어휘 now that 이제 ~이므로 hire 채용하다 follow 따르다 regulation 규정, 규칙 strictly 엄격하게

125. 전치사 어휘 toward

Daffodil Supermarket은 포장재에서 50%의 플라스틱을 없앤다는 목표를 향해 노력해 왔다.
(A) ~ 사이에 (B) ~을 향해 (C) ~을 가로질러 (D) ~을 제외하고

어휘 eliminate 제거하다 packaging 포장재

126. 형용사 자리

Edelmira Fashion이 재계약 시기에 고객에게 증정하는 사려 깊은 선물은 그 업체를 돋보이게 만들었다.

해설 빈칸 앞에 소유한정사 Edelmira Fashion's가 있고 뒤에는 명사 gifts가 있으므로 빈칸은 명사를 수식하는 형용사 자리이다. 따라서 (A) thoughtful이 정답이다.

어휘 client 고객, 의뢰인 contract 계약 renewal 갱신 stand out 돋보이다, 눈에 띄다

127. 전치사 자리

학교 이사회는 건설 비용 증가에도 불구하고 Merriam Art Building의 증축을 표결로 찬성했다.

해설 빈칸 앞에 완전한 절이 있고 뒤에는 명사구가 있으므로 빈칸은 전치사 자리이다. 따라서 (A) in spite of가 정답이다. (B) on the contrary와 (D) even so는 접속부사이고 (C) so that은 접속사이므로 오답이다.

어휘 vote 투표하다 extension 증축된 건물 increase 증가 construction 공사, 건설 cost 비용

128. 동사 자리 [원형부정사]

Drayson Antiques는 고객들이 가구를 원래의 상태로 복원하는 것을 도울 수 있습니다.

해설 빈칸 앞에 동사 help가 있고 목적어 customers가 이어지므로 빈칸은 목적격 보어 자리이다. help가 목적격 보어를 취할 때는 to부정사나 원형부정사를 쓰므로 동사원형인 (C) restore가 정답이다.

어휘 restore 복원하다, 복구하다 furniture 가구 original 원래의 condition 상태

129. 명사 어휘 material

Ms. Nelson은 수석 사서에게 자료를 청했고, 수석 사서는 기록 보관소에서 오래된 도시 지도들을 복사해 주었다.
(A) 활동 (B) 허가 (C) 자료 (D) 제안, 제의

어휘 seek 찾다, 청하다 librarian 사서 make a copy 복사하다 archive 기록 보관소

130. 부사 자리

정확한 법률 자문을 제공하려면 의뢰인은 자신의 재산 분쟁을 보다 구체적으로 설명해야 한다.

해설 〈주어(the client)+동사(must explain)+목적어(his property dispute)〉 구조의 완전한 절이므로 빈칸은 부사 자리이다. 따라서 (D) more specifically가 정답이다.

어휘 in order to do ~하기 위해 provide 제공하다 accurate 정확한 legal advice 법률 자문 property 재산 dispute 분쟁

PART 6

131-134 안내문

> 특별한 선물을 여러분의 [131]현관 앞까지 배송시킬 수 있는 Gift-Max 온라인 매장에서 쇼핑해 주셔서 감사합니다. 회원들은 할인된 가격의 선물 포장 및 무료 배송을 받으실 수 있다는 점을 알아두시기 바랍니다. 멤버십 프로그램의 [132]혜택을 받기 시작하려면 저희 웹사이트를 방문하시어 '멤버십' 버튼을 클릭하시고 양식을 작성하시면 됩니다. [133]**고작 몇 분밖에 걸리지 않습니다.** 앞으로도 계속해서 Gift-Max를 이용하시고 친구들과 가족에게 특별한 선물을 선사하는 [134]즐거움을 누리시기 바랍니다.

어휘 unique 특별한, 특유의 note 주목하다, 참고하다 discounted 할인된 gift-wrapping 선물 포장 delivery 배송 membership 회원 (자격) simply 그저, 단순히 complete 완료하다, 완성하다 form 양식

131. 명사 어휘 doorstep

(A) 문의 (B) 시장 (C) 현관 (D) 신용 거래; 칭찬, 인정

132. 동명사 자리

해설 빈칸 앞에 동사 start가 있고 뒤에는 전치사구 from the membership program이 이어지므로 빈칸은 동사의 목적어 자리이다. 따라서 동명사인 (D) benefiting이 정답이다.

133. 알맞은 문장 고르기

(A) 연체된 청구서를 정산해 주십시오.
(B) 고작 몇 분밖에 걸리지 않습니다.
(C) 우리 직원들은 매우 해박합니다.
(D) 신제품은 매우 인기가 있습니다.

해설 빈칸 앞에서 멤버십 프로그램의 혜택을 받을 수 있는 방법을 설명했으므로 빈칸에도 그와 관련된 이야기를 이어가는 것이 자연스럽다. 따라서 멤버십 등록은 시간이 오래 걸리지 않는다고 한 (B)가 정답이다.

어휘 settle 정산하다, 해결하다 overdue 연체된, 기간이 지난 bill 청구서 employee 직원 highly 매우 knowledgeable 박식한

134. 명사 자리

해설 빈칸 앞에 관사 the가 있고 뒤에는 전치사 of가 있으므로 빈칸은 관사의 수식을 받는 명사 자리이다. 따라서 (B) enjoyment가 정답이다. 동명사인 (C) enjoying은 관사의 수식을 받을 수 없기 때문에 오답이다.

135-138 이메일

> 수신: Shawn Ayala
> 발신: Varner Communications
> 날짜: 10월 19일
> 제목: 전화 요금 고지서
>
> Mr. Ayala께,
>
> 귀하의 Varner Communications 전화 요금 고지서에 대해 자동 청구 [135]옵션을 신청해 주셔서 감사합니다. 11월 1일을 [136]시작으로, 매월 1일에 79.99달러가 귀하의 은행 계좌에서 인출될 것입니다. 인출 시기에 계좌에 충분한 자금이 없으면 연체료가 [137]부과될 수 있다는 것을 유념해 주시기 바랍니다. [138]**자동 이체는 언제든지 취소하실 수 있습니다.** 그럴 경우 매달 귀하의 주소로 종이 청구서를 다시 보내 드리도록 하겠습니다.
>
> Varner Communications

어휘 sign up for ~을 신청하다 automated 자동화된 billing 청구서 발부 payment 지불(금) deduct 공제하다, 제하다 bank account 은행 계좌 withdrawal 인출 resume 재개하다

135. 명사 어휘 option

(A) 경우, 때 (B) 가치 (C) 옵션, 선택권 (D) 시도

136. 분사 자리

'------- on November 1'가 콤마 뒤의 절을 수식하는 구조이므로 빈칸에는 on November 1와 결합하여 분사구문을 이룰 수 있는 말이 들어가야 한다. 따라서 선택지 중 현재분사인 (A) Beginning이 정답이다. 분사구문은 문장 전체를 수식하는 부사 역할을 하며, beginning은 주로 문장 앞에 위치하며, 어떤 일의 시작 시점을 나타내는 표현으로 항상 현재분사로 사용한다.

137. 동사 자리

해설 빈칸 앞에 조동사 may가 있고 뒤에는 명사 a late fee가 있으므로 빈칸은 동사 자리이다. 따라서 (B) incur가 정답이다.

138. 알맞은 문장 고르기

(A) 계약서 사본을 보내 드리겠습니다.
(B) 자동 이체는 언제든지 취소하실 수 있습니다.
(C) 그 패키지에는 무제한의 문자 메시지와 데이터가 포함되어 있습니다.
(D) 전화기를 껐다 켜는 것이 도움이 될 것입니다.

해설 빈칸 뒤에서 다시 종이 청구서를 보내게 되는 상황에 대해 설명하고 있으므로, 빈칸에는 이와 관련하여 자동 이체 취소를 언급하는 내용이 들어가는 게 적절하다. 따라서 (B)가 정답이다.

어휘 copy 사본 contract 계약서 direct debit 자동 이체, 직불 include 포함하다 unlimited 무제한의 text 문자 메시지 helpful 도움이 되는 restart 다시 시작하다, 재작동하다

139-142 회람

> 수신: Longoria 전 직원
> 발신: Althea Panadio
> 제목: 안전 기록
> 날짜: 7월 3일
> 첨부파일: Q2_Safety_Report
>
> 우리 생산 시설에서 새로운 안전 기록을 달성한 것을 축하합니다! 이번 분기에는 부상 건수가 보고되지 않았습니다. [139]**그럼에도 불구하고** 우리는 계속해서 모든 안전 규칙을 주의 깊게 따를 필요가 있습니다. 이러한 이유로 우리는 월례 [140]**교육** 프로그램을 시작할 것입니다. 이것은 개선 분야를 찾기 위해 우리의 운영을 면밀히 [141]**관찰해** 온 Carmen Riley가 고안했습니다. 업계의 모범 사례에 대한 학습을 통해 여러분은 모든 사람에게 긍정적인 작업 환경을 보장하는 것에 일조할 수 있습니다. [142]**교육 날짜는 다음 주에 발표될 것입니다.** 그동안 계속해서 열심히 해 주시길 바랍니다!

어휘 safety 안전(성) record 기록 production 생산, 제조 facility 시설 injury 부상 quarter 분기 rule 규칙, 규정 launch 시작하다, 출시하다 closely 면밀히, 자세히 operation 운영 area 분야, 영역 improvement 개선 industry 업계 best practice 모범 사례 ensure 보장하다 positive 긍정적인 environment 환경

139. 접속부사 어휘 nevertheless

(A) 차라리 (B) 그렇지 않으면 (C) 비록 ~일지라도 (D) 그럼에도 불구하고

해설 빈칸 뒤에 주어와 동사를 갖춘 완전한 절이 하나만 있는 것으로 보아 빈칸은 접속부사 자리이므로 접속사인 (C) Even if는 오답이다.

140. 명사 어휘 training

(A) 교육, 훈련 (B) 상품권, 할인권 (C) 운동 (D) 치료, 대우

141. 분사 자리+태

해설 빈칸 앞에 조동사 has와 부사 closely가 있고, 뒤에는 명사구 our operations가 있으므로 빈칸은 완료 시제를 만드는 조동사 have와 결합하여 쓰이는 과거분사 자리이다. (C) been observed와 (D) observed가 정답 후보인데 빈칸 뒤에 목적어 역할을 하는 명사가 있으므로 단순 과거분사인 (D)가 정답이다.

142. 알맞은 문장 고르기

(A) 우리 제품에 대한 수요가 증가하고 있습니다.
(B) 우리는 등록 마감일을 연장하기로 결정했습니다.
(C) 교육 날짜는 다음 주에 발표될 것입니다.
(D) 기본적인 응급 처치 키트는 본사에서 구할 수 있습니다.

해설 빈칸 앞에서 Carmen Riley가 기획한 교육에 대해 설명했으므로 빈칸에는 해당 교육에 관한 내용이 이어지는 것이 자연스럽다. 따라서 (C)가 정답이다.

어휘 demand 수요, 요청 grow 자라다, 증가하다 extend 연장하다 registration 등록 deadline 기한, 마감일 session (특정한 활동을 위한) 시간 basic 기본적인 first aid kit 응급 처치 키트

143-146 이메일

> 수신: Thornton 영업 관리 팀
> 발신: Farah Bakir
> 날짜: 9월 22일
> 제목: Natasha Brannon의 은퇴
>
> 영업 관리 팀에게,
>
> 기획 위원회는 [143]곧 있을 Natasha Brannon의 은퇴 파티에서 간단한 연설을 해 줄 몇 명의 사람들을 우리 팀에서 찾고 있습니다. [144]**우리는 이것이 행사를 특별하게 만드는 데 도움이 될 것이라고 생각합니다.**
>
> 연설은 10월 6일 오후 4시에 열리는 파티가 시작할 때 행해질 것입니다. 그녀가 우리 회사에서 보냈던 추억담들을 공유하고자 하는 [145]**사람**은 누구나 위원회 위원에게 연락 주시기 바랍니다. 우리는 또한 Ms. Brannon이 직접 몇 마디 말씀을 하실 수 있도록 충분한 시간을 남겨 두고 싶습니다. [146]**이러한 이유로** 소수의 연설만 듣게 될 것입니다.
>
> Farah Bakir

어휘 retirement 은퇴 planning 기획 committee 위원회 brief 간단한, 짧은 speech 연설 take place 열리다, 일어나다 willing 기꺼이 ~하는 share 공유하다, 나누다 contact 연락하다 leave 남기다; 떠나다

143. 형용사 어휘 upcoming

(A) 곧 있을, 다가오는 (B) 선별된, 다양한 (C) 번창하는 (D) 열정적인

144. 알맞은 문장 고르기

(A) 그러므로 그녀의 후임자를 교육할 누군가가 필요합니다.
(B) 우리는 이것이 행사를 특별하게 만드는 데 도움이 될 것이라고 생각합니다.
(C) 그 대신에 그녀는 파트타임으로 근무하는 상담가가 될 수도 있습니다.
(D) 위원들이 내년도 주제를 논의하고 있습니다.

해설 빈칸 앞에서 은퇴 파티 연설을 언급했으므로 빈칸에는 그 연설과 관련된 내용이 들어가는 게 자연스럽다. 따라서 은퇴 파티에서의 연설을 this로, retirement party를 event로 표현한 (B)가 정답이다.

어휘 train 훈련하다, 교육하다 replacement 대체, 후임자 alternatively 대신에 consultant 상담가

145. 대명사 anyone

해설 빈칸은 현재분사구(willing ~ company)의 수식을 받는 자리이다. 따라서 선택지 중 현재분사구의 수식을 받을 수 있는 (C) Anyone이 정답이다.

146. 접속부사 어휘 for this reason

(A) 예를 들어 (B) 그때 이후로 (C) 반면에 (D) 이러한 이유로

PART 7

147-148 안내문

캠벨 카운티 어류 및 야생 동물과
채용 공고

어류 및 야생 동물과 기사 (#8020C): [147]**캠벨 카운티 전역의 자연 보호 구역과 관광지에서** 수생 서식지의 야생 생물의 건강과 다양성을 유지하는 데 도움을 주면서 웅장한 자연을 즐기세요. 이 직책은 물 표본 데이터를 데이터베이스에 기록하고, [148]**다양한 어종의 숫자를 확인하고 기록하여 시간이 지남에 따라 그 수치가 어떻게 변하는지 확인하고 보고하고,** 새로운 물고기를 특정 지역에 방생하는 것을 포함합니다. 지침을 주의 깊게 따라야 하므로 세심함이 요구됩니다. 경력은 필요 없습니다. www.campbellcounty.gov/jobs/8020C에서 신청하십시오.

어휘 wildlife 야생 생물, 야생 동물 technician 기술자 outdoors 야외, 자연; 야외에서 maintain 유지하다 diversity 다양성 habitat 서식지 nature reserve 자연 보호 구역 tourism site 관광지 include 포함하다 record 기록하다 report 보고하다 various 다양한 species 종 figure 수치 distribute 분포시키다, 분배하다 certain 특정한 attention 주의, 주목 detail 세부 사항 require 요구하다 experience 경험 necessary 필요한, 필수적인 apply 지원하다

147. 직책에 대해 암시된 것은 무엇인가?

(A) 계절적인 업무만을 위한 것이다.
(B) 다수의 장소에서 근무하는 것이 요구된다.
(C) 캠벨 카운티 주민들에게만 문호가 열려 있다.
(D) 숙련된 기술자들을 위한 것이다.

해설 추론/암시
두 번째 줄의 both nature reserves and tourism sites throughout Campbell County는 다수의 자연 보호 구역과 관광지에서 근무하게 된다는 것을 나타내므로 (B)가 정답이다.

어휘 multiple 다수의 location 장소 resident 주민

148. 직무의 한 가지로 언급된 것은 무엇인가?

(A) 공원 입장객 숫자 기록
(B) 보트 수리
(C) 어류 개체군 관찰
(D) 가이드 동반 투어 인솔하기

해설 세부 사항
다양한 어종의 숫자를 확인하고 기록하며 수치 변화를 보고한다고 했으므로 (C)가 정답이다.

어휘 duty 의무 record 기록하다 monitor 관찰하다 population 개체 수 guided tour 가이드 동반 투어

149-150 공지

여러분의 Topeka Carpeting 구매에 감사드립니다!

Topeka Carpeting의 저희들은 저렴한 가격에 고품질 바닥 깔개를 제공하기 위해 노력하고 있습니다. [149]**저희 온라인 상점에 있는 색상은** 여러분의 컴퓨터 화면에서 보이는 색상과 동일하지 않을 수 있으니 제품을 설치하기 전에 주의 깊게 확인하시기 바랍니다. 질문이나 의견이 있으면 고객 상담 전화번호 1-800-555-7826으로 전화하셔서 Topeka Carpeting 담당자와 말씀을 나누실 수 있습니다. 저희가 여러분을 더 잘 도와 드릴 수 있도록 [150]**전화하실 때 제조사의 이름과 제품 번호를 준비해 주시기를 부탁드립니다.**

어휘 carpeting 카펫류 strive 노력하다 floor 마루, 바닥 covering 깔개, 덮개 affordable 저렴한 note 유념하다, 명심하다 install 설치하다 representative 담당자; 대표 helpline 고객 상담 전화 manufacturer 제조사 assist 돕다

149. Topeka Carpeting에 대해 암시된 것은 무엇인가?

(A) 주기적으로 신제품을 추가한다.
(B) 교환을 받지 않는다.
(C) 상품을 웹사이트에서 판매한다.
(D) 설치 비용을 청구한다.

해설 추론/암시
'온라인 상점'이라고 한 것으로 보아 웹사이트에서 상품을 판매한다는 걸 알 수 있으므로 (C)가 정답이다.

어휘 regularly 주기적으로 add 더하다, 추가하다 merchandise 상품, 물품

150. 공지에 따르면, 고객들은 고객 상담 전화번호로 연락하기 전에 무엇을 준비해야 하는가?

(A) 제조사의 주소
(B) 고객의 주문 번호
(C) 제품을 구매한 지점
(D) 제품 식별 번호

해설 세부 사항
전화할 때 제조사의 이름과 제품 번호를 준비하라고 했으므로 (D)가 정답이다.

어휘 location 위치, 장소 identification 식별; 신분 증명(서)

151-152 이메일

수신: Lester Dowell
발신: Clemons Energy
날짜: 6월 3일
제목: 047854번 문의

Mr. Dowell께,

Clemons Energy에 연락해 주셔서 감사합니다. 지연에 대해 사과 드립니다. 보통 저희는 24시간 내내 불편 사항에 답변을 드리지만 [152]**매월 있는 사이트 업그레이드 도중에는 시스템에 로그인할 수 없습니다.**

[151] 귀하의 문제와 관련하여, 5월 청구 금액을 지불하기 위해 신용 카드 정보를 입력하려고 했는데 오류 메시지를 받으신 것으로 알고 있습니다. 이 문제는 [152] 오전 2시에서 4시 사이에 수행된 월례 사이트 업그레이드에서 해결되었습니다. 이제 시스템이 업데이트되었으므로 카드를 다시 시도해 보십시오. 그래도 문제가 있으면 저희 담당자 중 한 명이 귀하에게 전화를 드려 문제를 해결할 수 있습니다. 이렇게 하는 것이 필요한지 알려 주시길 바랍니다.

감사합니다.

[152] Carrie Nugent
고객 서비스 담당자

어휘 contact 연락하다 apologize 사과하다 delay 지연 normally 보통, 일반적으로 respond to ~에 대응하다, 반응하다 complaint 불만, 민원 regarding ~에 관하여 enter 입력하다 bill 고지서, 청구서 matter 문제 resolve 해결하다 take place 발생하다 representative 담당자, 대표

151. Mr. Dowell은 왜 Clemons Energy에 연락했겠는가?

(A) 그는 5월에 새로운 주소지로 이사했다.
(B) 그는 자신의 계정을 갱신하고 싶었다.
(C) 그는 비용 납부에 어려움을 겪었다.
(D) 그는 하나의 서비스가 과다 청구되었다.

해설 추론/암시
두 번째 문단에서 청구서 금액을 지불하기 위해 신용 카드 정보를 입력했지만 오류 메시지를 받았다고 했으므로 (C)가 정답이다.

152. Ms. Nugent에 대해 암시된 것은 무엇인가?

(A) 2시간 동안 시스템에 접속할 수 없었다.
(B) 나중에 Mr. Dowell에게 전화할 계획이다.
(C) 교대 근무가 오전 2시에 끝났다.
(D) 그녀의 첫 번째 메시지에 오류가 있었다.

해설 추론/암시
첫 번째 문단에서 사이트 업그레이드로 인해 시스템에 로그인할 수 없었고, 두 번째 문단에서는 사이트 업그레이드가 오전 2시부터 오전 4시까지 진행되었다고 했으므로 2시간 동안 시스템에 접근할 수 없었다는 것을 추론할 수 있다. 따라서 (A)가 정답이다.

패러프레이징 cannot log into the system → could not access a system
between 2 A.M. and 4 A.M. → for two hours

어휘 access 접근하다, 접속하다 work shift 교대 근무 contain 포함하다

153-155 이메일

수신: Paula Ortiz
발신: Edwin Ramsay
날짜: 7월 25일
제목: 재정 자문가 직위

Ms. Ortiz께,

제 이름은 Edwin Ramsay이고, Cullins Investments의 선임 투자 자산 관리자입니다. [153] 최근 귀사의 재정 자문가 직위에 지원한 제 직원 Rico Alston을 위해 글을 씁니다. 저는 지난 3년 동안 Mr. Alston과 함께 일했고 [153] 그가 귀하의 팀에 훌륭한 자산이 될 것이라고 단언할 수 있습니다. [154] 저는 이 회사에서 10년 동안 일하면서 이토록 업무에 헌신적인 사람은 본 적이 없습니다. 게다가 그는 고객과의 관계를 빠르게 구축할 수 있습니다. Mr. Alston이 저희 회사에 있었던 시간에 대한 [155] 자세한 질문이 있으시면 기꺼이 답변해 드리겠습니다. 제 사무실 번호 746-555-8306으로 언제든지 연락 주십시오.

Edwin Ramsay

어휘 financial 재무의, 금융의 advisor 자문가, 상담역 portfolio 포트폴리오, 유가 증권 보유 일람표 on behalf of ~을 위해, ~ 대신에 recently 최근에 apply 지원하다 confirm 확인해 주다 asset 자산 dedication 헌신 detailed 상세한 feel free to do 마음껏 ~하다

153. 이메일의 목적은 무엇인가?

(A) 회사를 홍보하는 것
(B) 채용 공고를 하는 것
(C) 지원자에게 일자리를 제안하는 것
(D) 동료를 추천하는 것

해설 주제/목적
Mr. Ramsay는 수신인인 Ms. Ortiz의 회사에 재정 자문가로 지원한 자신의 직원을 추천하기 위해 이메일을 썼으므로 (D)가 정답이다.

어휘 promote 홍보하다 announce 발표하다 job opening 일자리, 공석 applicant 지원자 recommend 추천하다 colleague 동료

154. Mr. Ramsay에 대해 시사된 것은 무엇인가?

(A) Ms. Ortiz의 투자 포트폴리오를 관리하고 있다.
(B) 전에 Ms. Ortiz를 직접 만난 적이 있다.
(C) Cullins Investments에서 10년 동안 일했다.
(D) Cullins Investments의 창업자이다.

해설 NOT/True
Cullins Investments에서 10년간 일했다고 했으므로 (C)가 정답이다.

패러프레이징 In my 10 years working for this company → He has worked at Cullins Investments for a decade.

어휘 investment 투자 in person 직접 decade 10년 founder 창업자

155. Mr. Ramsay는 무엇을 하기를 제안하는가?

(A) 전화 통화하기
(B) 몇 가지 갱신된 수치 보내기
(C) Ms. Ortiz의 사무실 방문하기
(D) 자신의 근무 시간 변경하기

해설 세부 사항
Mr. Alston에 대해 궁금한 것이 있으면 자신의 사무실 전화번호로 연락하라고 했으므로 (A)가 정답이다.

어휘 updated 최신의 figure 수치 working hours 근무 시간

156-157 문자 메시지

> **Curtis Burnett** [오후 1:18]
> 안녕하세요, Fiona. 제가 가을 일정을 짜고 있는데요. 원래는 당신이 매달 두 번의 토요일 워크숍을 교육할 수 있다고 했었죠. 아직도 그런가요?
>
> **Fiona Ervin** [오후 1:21]
> 9월은 괜찮지만 다른 달은 어려울 것 같아요. 추가적인 업무가 많이 배정되었거든요.
>
> **Curtis Burnett** [오후 1:22]
> 네, 다들 일이 너무 많아요. [156]**우리는 사람들을 몇 명 더 채용해야 해요.**
>
> **Fiona Ervin** [오후 1:23]
> 그건 확실해요. 그 일을 할 다른 사람을 찾을 수 있다면 작년에 만든 제 슬라이드를 사용해도 돼요. 그 슬라이드에는 [157]**줄거리를 짜고, 캐릭터를 개발하고, 서술적인 언어를 사용하는 것에 관한 좋은 팁이 있어요.**
>
> **Curtis Burnett** [오후 1:24]
> 고마워요! 정말 도움이 될 것 같네요. [157]**일단 9월 첫째 주와 셋째 주 토요일로 당신의 일정을 잡을게요.**
>
> **Fiona Ervin** [오후 1:25]
> 그렇게 할 수 있어요.

어휘 work on ~을 작업하다 schedule 일정; 예정하다, 일정을 잡다 originally 원래, 본래 be the case 사실이 그러하다 assign 배정하다 extra 추가적인 task 업무 overload 너무 많이 부과하다 hire 채용하다 plot 줄거리 descriptive 묘사하는, 서술적인

156. 오후 1시 23분에, Ms. Ervin이 "그건 확실해요"라고 쓸 때 그녀가 의미하는 것은 무엇인가?

(A) 그녀는 과제가 혼란스럽다는 것에 동의한다.
(B) 그녀는 회사가 더 많은 직원을 고용해야 한다고 생각한다.
(C) 그녀는 Mr. Burnett과 함께 초과 근무를 할 계획이다.
(D) 그녀는 9월에 새 직장을 구할 것이다.

해설 의도 파악
Mr. Burnett이 사람을 더 채용해야 한다고 한 말에 동의한 것이므로 (B)가 정답이다.

패러프레이징 hire a few more people → employ more staff members

어휘 confusing 혼란스러운 employ 고용하다 work overtime 초과 근무하다

157. 토요일에는 어떤 종류의 수업이 있겠는가?

(A) 음악
(B) 글쓰기
(C) 미술
(D) 운동

해설 추론/암시
오후 1시 24분에 Mr. Burnett이 9월 첫째 주와 셋째 주 토요일로 Ms. Ervin의 수업 일정을 잡는다고 했다. Ms. Ervin이 맡은 수업의 단서는 오후 1시 23분 대화에 나와 있는데, Ms. Ervin의 슬라이드에 줄거리와 캐릭터 개발, 서술적인 언어 사용에 관한 내용이 있다고 했으므로 글쓰기와 관련된 수업이라는 걸 알 수 있다. 따라서 (B)가 정답이다.

158-160 편지

> Erica Sutton
> 노퍽 타워 304호
> 372 체임벌린 애비뉴
> 애틀랜타, 조지아 30306
>
> Ms. Sutton께,
>
> 저는 휴스턴에 본사를 둔 Waddell Engineering이 주최하는 전국 엔지니어링 콘퍼런스(NEC)의 행사 기획자입니다. [159]**올해 행사는 새크라멘토의 Marietta Center에서 10월 16일과 17일로 예정되어 있습니다.** 주제는 '향상된 웰빙을 위한 반응형 디자인'입니다.
>
> 샬럿 대학교의 Ayaan Vadekar 박사께서 기조 연설자로 나설 예정입니다. 저희는 참석자들에게 자신의 통찰력을 공유해 주실 이 분야의 다른 전문가들도 필요합니다. 따라서 [158]**저는 귀하를 행사의 연사로 초청하고 싶습니다.** 최근에 [160]**Smart Cities Summit에서 있었던 귀하의 강연을 보았습니다.** 관객들의 관심을 사로잡았던 귀하의 방법에 감명을 받았답니다. 저희 행사에서도 그렇게 해 주시면 좋겠습니다.
>
> 저희는 애틀랜타에서 콘퍼런스 장소까지의 항공료를 지불하고, Marietta Center 근처에 있는 무료 숙소를 제공하고, 식권을 제공해 드리려고 합니다. 관심이 있다면 편하실 때 이 사안에 대해 더 논의하고 싶습니다.
>
> Pauline Faber
> Waddell Engineering
> 832-555-4219, 내선 번호 16

어휘 planner 기획자 firm 회사 be scheduled for ~로 예정되어 있다 theme 주제 responsive 즉각 반응하는 keynote speaker 기조 연설자 expert 전문가 field 분야 insight 통찰력 attendee 참석자 invite 초대하다 talk 강연, 연설 flight 비행기, 항공편 accommodation 숙소 meal voucher 식권 at one's convenience 편할 때, 편리한 시기에

158. 편지의 목적은 무엇인가?

(A) 행사의 발표자를 모집하는 것
(B) 콘퍼런스 등록을 확인하는 것
(C) 장소 변경을 알리는 것
(D) 주제 제안을 요청하는 것

해설 주제/목적
편지의 발신인인 Pauline Faber는 편지의 수신인인 Erica Sutton을 콘퍼런스의 연사로 초청하고 싶다고 했으므로 (A)가 정답이다.

어휘 recruit 모집하다, 선발하다 presenter 발표자 confirm 확인하다 registration 등록 announce 발표하다, 알리다 venue 장소 suggestion 제안, 제의

159. 올해 NEC는 어디에서 열릴 예정인가?

(A) 애틀랜타
(B) 샬럿

(C) 휴스턴

(D) 새크라멘토

해설 세부 사항

행사는 새크라멘토의 Marietta Center에서 열릴 것이라고 했으므로 (D)가 정답이다.

160. [1], [2], [3], [4]로 표시된 위치 중 다음 문장이 들어가기에 가장 적절한 곳은?

"관객들의 관심을 사로잡았던 귀하의 방법에 감명을 받았답니다."

해설 문장 삽입

주어진 문장은 편지의 수신인인 Ms. Sutton이 했던 강연에 관한 내용이므로, 해당 내용 뒤에 들어가는 것이 자연스럽다. 따라서 (C)가 정답이다.

161-163 웹페이지

> 여러분의 의견은 중요합니다!
>
> 샌안토니오 소상공 연합회(SASBA)에서 실시하는 연례 설문 조사에 관심을 가져 주셔서 감사합니다. SASBA는 지역 및 주 정치인들에게 영향력을 행사하여 소상공인들을 위한 지원 체계를 제공하는 일에 전념하고 있습니다. [161]이 설문 조사는 샌안토니오의 소상공인들을 대상으로 합니다. [162]귀하의 답변은 저희가 어느 분야에 초점을 맞출지 결정하는 데 도움이 될 것입니다.
>
> 온라인 설문 조사는 완료하는 데 약 10분이 소요됩니다. 귀하의 이름을 답변에 포함시키거나, [163]귀하의 신분이 드러나지 않도록 귀하의 이름을 없앨 수 있습니다. 설문 조사 링크는 11월 7일까지 활성화될 것입니다. 저희는 11월 30일에 조사 결과를 요약하여 웹사이트에 발표할 것입니다. 질문이나 의견은 Molly Steele에게 msteele@sasba.org로 해 주시기 바랍니다.
>
> 참여해 주셔서 감사합니다.
>
> 설문: #07562
> 이름: Audrey Walsh

어휘 survey 설문 조사 annual 연례의 conduct 시행하다 be dedicated to ~에 전념하다 influence 영향을 미치다 local 지역의 politician 정치인 provide 제공하다 supportive 지원하는 framework 체제 intend 의도하다, 작정하다 determine 결정하다 focus on ~에 집중하다 complete 완료하다, 완성하다 include 포함하다 remove 제외하다, 제거하다 identify 식별하다, 찾아내다 publish 출간하다, 발표하다 summary 요약 findings 조사 결과 participation 참여

161. Ms. Walsh에 대해 사실인 것은 무엇인가?

(A) 샌안토니오에서 업체를 운영한다.

(B) SASBA에서 일한다.

(C) 작년 설문 조사를 완료했다.

(D) 첫 번째 링크에서 문제를 겪었다.

해설 NOT/True

설문 조사는 샌안토니오의 소상공인들을 대상으로 한다고 했으므로 Ms. Walsh는 그곳에서 사업체를 운영한다는 걸 알 수 있다. 따라서 (A)가 정답이다.

162. SASBA는 왜 설문 조사를 시행하겠는가?

(A) 회원제 프로그램의 효율성을 평가하기 위해

(B) 어느 업체가 수상해야 하는지 결정하기 위해

(C) 필요한 정책 변화를 알아내기 위해

(D) 사업주들을 위한 교육 프로그램을 개발하기 위해

해설 추론/암시

소상공인들을 위해 어떤 지원 체계에 초점을 맞출 것인지를 파악하기 위해서 설문 조사를 실시한다고 했으므로 (C)가 정답이다.

어휘 evaluate 평가하다 effectiveness 효율성 determine 결정하다 policy 정책

163. 설문 조사에 대해 시사된 것은 무엇인가?

(A) Ms. Steele에 의해 문항이 개발되었다.

(B) 11월 30일까지 설문이 가능하다.

(C) 답변은 제출 이후에 변경 가능하다.

(D) 익명으로 제출할 수 있다.

해설 NOT/True

신분이 드러나지 않도록 이름을 없앨 수 있다고 했으므로 (D)가 정답이다.

패러프레이징 have your name removed so you cannot be identified → be submitted anonymously

어휘 develop 개발하다 available 유효한, 이용할 수 있는 submission 제출 anonymously 익명으로

164-167 공지

> Preston Insurance 전 직원에게 공지함:
>
> 5월 4일
>
> 6월 1일부터 [164]Preston Insurance는 주차장에 있는 모든 차량을 대상으로 주차권을 요구하기 시작할 것입니다. 현재 주차장은 우리 직원들만을 위한 것이지만 외부인들이 허가 없이 사용하는 경우가 많습니다. 따라서 운전해서 출근하는 모든 직원에게 바코드 주차권을 발급할 것입니다. 주차권은 쉽게 스캔할 수 있기 때문에 회사가 주차장을 [165]운영하는 데 있어 많은 시간을 절약하게 해 줄 것입니다.
>
> 주차권에는 스티커 방식 또는 플라스틱 태그의 두 가지 선택권이 있습니다. [166]스티커의 접착제는 잔여물이 남지 않도록 설계되어 쉽게 떼어낼 수 있습니다. 태그는 백미러에 다는 것이기 때문에 주행 중에는 제거해야 합니다. 우리는 스티커를 추천하지만 [167]직원 개개인의 선택에 맡길 테니 어떤 것을 원하시는지 알려 주십시오. 여러분의 차량 번호와 기타 필요한 정보는 이미 기록되어 있습니다. [167]주차권을 받으려면 내선 번호 41로 Reggie Norris에게 연락하십시오.

어휘 require 요구하다, 요청하다 parking pass 주차권 vehicle 차량 lot 주차장 currently 현재, 지금 public 대중, 일반인 authorization 승인, 허가 issue 발급하다, 발행하다 permit 허가(증) scannable 스캔할 수 있는 run 운영하다 stick-on 스티커 방식의 decal 장식 스티커 tag 태그, 꼬리표 adhesive 접착제 residue 잔여물 peel off ~을 떼어 내다, ~을 벗기다 rearview mirror 백미러 recommend 추천하다 license plate number 자동차 등록 번호 necessary 필수적인 extension 내선 번호

164. 공지가 작성된 이유는 무엇인가?

(A) 직원들에게 주차장 폐쇄를 경고하기 위해

(B) 주차비 인상을 설명하기 위해

(C) 주차 시스템의 변화를 알리기 위해

(D) 사람들에게 회사 주차장을 사용하지 말라고 요청하기 위해

해설 주제/목적

목적 문제의 단서는 대개 지문 도입부에 제시된다. 첫 번째 문장에서 Preston Insurance는 차량에 주차권을 요구하기 시작할 것이라는 내용을 언급했으므로 (C)가 정답이다.

어휘 warn 경고하다 closure 폐쇄, 종료 announce 알리다, 발표하다

165. 첫 번째 단락 다섯 번째 줄의 어휘 "running"과 의미상 가장 가까운 것은?

(A) 흐르다

(B) 운영하다

(C) 참여하다

(D) 경쟁하다

해설 동의어 찾기

running이 있는 they will save the company a lot of time on running the parking lot은 회사가 주차장을 운영하는 데 있어 많은 시간을 절약하게 해 줄 것이라는 의미이며, 여기서 running은 '운영하다'라는 뜻으로 쓰였다. 따라서 (B) operating이 정답이다.

166. 스티커의 장점으로 무엇이 언급되었는가?

(A) 제거하기 쉽다.

(B) 크기가 작다.

(C) 저렴하게 인쇄될 수 있다.

(D) 멀리서도 보인다.

해설 세부 사항

두 번째 문단에서 스티커는 잔여물을 남기지 않고 쉽게 떼어 낼 수 있다고 했으므로 (A)가 정답이다.

패러프레이징 be peeled off easily → is easy to remove

어휘 print 인쇄하다 inexpensively 저렴하게 visible 눈에 띄는

167. 사람들은 Mr. Norris에게 어떤 정보를 제공해야 하는가?

(A) 운전면허증 번호

(B) 선호하는 주차권 종류

(C) 차량 등록 번호

(D) 선택된 주차 공간

해설 세부 사항

Mr. Norris가 언급된 지문 후반부를 확인하면, 어떤 주차권을 원하는지 알려 주고 나서 주차권을 받으라고 했으므로 (B)가 정답이다.

패러프레이징 which one you would like → preference

168-171 온라인 채팅

Darlene Gray [오전 10:40] 안녕하세요, Karen, Owen. [168]**Morland Hall이 우리 Falcon Data의 직원들을 위한 4월 4일 워크숍 장소로 확정되었다는 것을 알려 드리려고요.**

Karen Ralston [오전 10:41] 좋네요. [169]**제가 공항에서 Clair Wallace 강사를 만나야 하나요?**

Darlene Gray [오전 10:42] 사실 그분은 공항에서 차를 렌트해서 행사장까지 올 계획이에요. [168]**Morland Hall에는 우리가 사용할 수 있는 테이블과 의자가 있긴 한데 우리가 직접 그것들을 배치해야 해요. 우리는 행사장에서 발표용 장비도 빌릴 수 있어요.**

Karen Ralston [오전 10:44] 알겠어요. [170]**Owen이 모든 것을 준비할 거예요.** 저는 이미 그에게 우리가 논의한 것에 대한 도면을 보냈어요.

[170]**Owen Foley** [오전 10:45] 맞아요. 그리고 출장 뷔페 업체에서 배달이 가능한 것을 확인했는데 비용이 꽤 비싸요. [171]**그냥 도시락이니까 제가 그날 아침에 행사장으로 가는 길에 들러서 가져올게요.**

Darlene Gray [오전 10:47] 완벽하네요, Owen. 고마워요! 비용은 이미 전부 냈으니까 지불해야 할 것은 없을 거예요.

어휘 confirm 확정하다 instructor 강사 actually 사실, 실은 venue 장소 arrange 배열하다, 정리하다 set up ~을 설치하다 drawing 그림, 도면 catering 출장 뷔페 fee 요금, 비용 boxed lunch 도시락 stop by 잠깐 들르다 due 지불해야 하는

168. 온라인 채팅의 목적은 무엇인가?

(A) 몇 가지 작성 업무를 배정하려고

(B) 행사 장소를 예약하려고

(C) 워크숍 계획을 논의하려고

(D) 교육을 진행할 강사를 찾으려고

해설 주제/목적

워크숍이 열릴 장소를 알리고 나서 테이블과 의자 배열, 발표 장비 대여 등으로 대화를 나누고 있으므로 (C)가 정답이다.

어휘 assign 배정하다 task 과제, 업무 book 예약하다

169. Ms. Wallace에 대해 시사된 것은 무엇인가?

(A) Morland Hall의 직원이다.

(B) 전에 Ms. Ralston을 만난 적이 있다.

(C) 작년에 한 행사에 참석했다.

(D) 시외에서 올 것이다.

해설 NOT/True

오전 10시 41분에 Ms. Ralston이 Clair Wallace를 만나러 공항에 나가야 하냐고 물은 것으로 보아 Ms. Wallace는 비행기를 타고 온다는 걸 알 수 있다. 따라서 (D)가 정답이다.

170. 누가 방을 준비할 것인가?

(A) Ms. Ralston

(B) Ms. Gray

(C) Ms. Wallace

(D) Mr. Foley

해설 세부 사항

오전 10시 44분에 Ms. Ralston은 Owen이 모든 걸 준비할 거라고 언급했는데 바로 이어지는 대화에서 Owen의 성이 Foley인 것을 확인할 수 있다. 따라서 (D)가 정답이다.

171. 오전 10시 47분에 Ms. Gray가 "완벽하네요, Owen"이라고 쓸 때 그녀가 의미하는 것은 무엇인가?

(A) 그녀는 행사 때 쓸 도시락을 주문하고 싶다.
(B) 그녀는 Owen이 Ms. Wallace를 일찍 만나야 한다고 생각한다.
(C) 그녀는 Mr. Foley가 음식을 찾아오는 것에 동의한다.
(D) 그녀는 출장 뷔페 회사의 서비스에 만족한다.

해설 의도 파악
바로 앞 대화에서 Mr. Foley가 출장 뷔페 업체에 들러서 도시락을 찾아오겠다고 하자 완벽하다고 응답한 것이다. 따라서 (C)가 정답이다.

어휘 pick up (물건을) 찾아오다 pleased 기쁜

172-175 편지

> 10월 15일
>
> Mr. Craig Jenkins
> 총지배인
> Barrington Hotel
> 4667 워드 스트리트
> 필라델피아, 펜실베이니아 19108
>
> Mr. Jenkins께,
>
> 저는 Modoc Airlines의 숙박 관리자로서 조종사와 승무원들이 업무와 관련된 이유로 도시에 머무를 때 그들이 하룻밤 묵을 숙소를 마련하는 것이 제 책무입니다. 저희 직원 중 많은 사람이 Barrington Hotel의 높은 수준을 칭찬했습니다. 제가 직접 그곳에 묵을 기회는 없었습니다. [175]**하지만 고객 서비스가 훌륭하며 방이 깨끗하고 쾌적하다는 말을 아주 자주 들었습니다.** 또한 [173]**내부 헬스장이 있고** 걸어서 갈 수 있는 거리에 세계적인 수준의 레스토랑이 있다는 것도 편리합니다.
>
> [172]**저는 우리의 사업이 상부상조할 수 있다고 생각합니다. 제가 제안하는 것은 저희가 일단의 객실들을 할인된 가격에 예약하는 것입니다.** 이 객실들은 저희가 객실을 사용하지 않는 날에도 매달 예약 및 결제가 보장될 것입니다. 그렇게 하면 저희는 저렴한 숙소를 얻을 수 있고, 동시에 귀사는 안정적인 수입을 얻을 수 있습니다. Modoc Airlines는 꾸준히 성장하고 있으며, 작년에 직원을 10% 늘렸습니다. 이는 저희가 귀사에 안정성과 오랜 파트너십을 제공할 수 있음을 의미합니다. 또한, 이 방법이 필라델피아에서 효과가 있다면 저희는 귀사의 다른 호텔 체인점에서도 같은 일을 할 수 있을 것입니다. [174]**저희 항공사가 운항하는 노선 목록을 동봉합니다.** 이 문제를 더 상의하려면 327-555-1888로 전화 주십시오.
>
> Raul Flores, 숙박 관리자
> Modoc Airlines

어휘 accommodation 숙박 (시설) procure 확보하다, 구하다 overnight 하룻밤 동안의 flight attendant 승무원 praise 칭찬하다 quality 품질 numerous 수많은 convenient 편리한 on-site 현장의, 현지의 within walking distance 도보 거리에 suggest 제안하다 guarantee 보장하다 affordable 저렴한, 가격이 알맞은 steady 일정한 income 수익 stability 안정성 branch 지점 enclose 동봉하다 further 더 한층

172. Mr. Flores는 왜 편지를 썼는가?

(A) 공석을 알리기 위해
(B) 사업 계약을 제안하기 위해
(C) 호텔 숙박에 대한 후기를 남기기 위해
(D) 호텔을 예약하기 위해

해설 주제/목적
보통 주제나 목적을 찾는 문제의 단서는 도입부에 제시되지만, 이 지문은 첫 번째 문단에서 자신을 소개하고 호텔에 대해 호의적인 평을 하는 등의 인사말을 했기 때문에 두 번째 문단까지 확인해야 한다. 발신인인 Mr. Flores가 수신인인 Mr. Jenkins에게 파트너십을 제안했으므로 (B)가 정답이다.

어휘 job opening 공석 business arrangement 사업 협력, 사업 계약 make a reservation 예약하다

173. Barrington Hotel에 대해 시사된 것은 무엇인가?

(A) 피트니스 시설이 있다.
(B) 투숙객들이 시설 내부에서 식사할 수 있다.
(C) 넓은 객실을 제공한다.
(D) 작년에 직원 수가 10% 증가했다.

해설 NOT/True
호텔 내부에 헬스장이 있어서 편리하다고 했으므로 (A)가 정답이다.

패러프레이징 gym → fitness facility

어휘 facility 시설 spacious 넓은

174. 편지에 무엇이 포함되었는가?

(A) 할인 상품권
(B) 직원 주소록
(C) 견본 계약서
(D) 노선 목록

해설 세부 사항
후반부에 항공사가 운항하는 노선 목록을 동봉했다고 했으므로 (D)가 정답이다.

175. [1], [2], [3], [4]로 표시된 위치 중 다음 문장이 들어가기에 가장 적절한 곳은?

"제가 직접 그곳에 묵을 기회는 없었습니다."

해설 문장 삽입
해당 호텔에 묵을 기회는 없었지만 고객 서비스를 비롯하여 객실이 훌륭하다는 이야기를 자주 들었다는 내용이 이어지는 게 자연스러우므로 주어진 문장은 [1]에 들어가는 것이 가장 적절하다.

176-180 일정 & 이메일

> **Delamore Department Store 요리 시연**
> **9월 일정**
> **주제: 채식주의 음식**
>
> • 9월 4일 토요일 The Wave의 Amber Paschal, 〈Hearty Home Meals〉의 저자
> • [179]9월 11일 토요일 BT Bistro의 Loni McIntyre와 Jerome Kellum

• 9월 19일 일요일 Eagleway Restaurant의 Ralph Scherr
• 9월 23일 목요일 Carmine Café의 Patricia Marquez, 〈Very Veggie〉의 저자

모든 시연은 오후 2시에 주방용품 코너에서 시작됩니다.

여러분이 전문 요리사이고 [176]**10월에 시연을 할 수 있다면** k.briggs@delamore.com으로 Kent Briggs에게 연락하세요. [180]**10월의 주제는 인도 음식입니다.** 시연은 60분에서 90분 정도 소요될 것입니다. [177]**재료뿐만 아니라 필요한 조리 도구도 공급해 드릴 테니 여러분의 요리법에 필요한 것이 무엇인지 알려 주시기 바랍니다.**

어휘 demonstration 시연 vegetarian 채식주의의 author 작가 hearty 영양분이 많은 section 구역, 부문 supply 공급하다 necessary 필요한, 필수적인 equipment 장비 ingredient 재료 recipe 요리법, 레시피

수신: Loni McIntyre
발신: Anthony Ulrich
날짜: 9월 25일
제목: 시연

Ms. McIntyre께,

저는 〈The Colton Times〉에서 음식과 식사 코너에 기사를 쓰고 있습니다. [179]**저는 당신과 당신의 동료인 Jerome Kellum이 Delamore Department Store에서 실시한 시연회에 참석했습니다.** 당신의 기술 수준에 매우 감명을 받았고, 나눠 주신 시식용 음식이 정말 맛있다고 생각했습니다. [178]**당신과 당신의 레스토랑을 다음 기사에 싣고 싶습니다.** 이번 주 중에 전화 통화가 가능하신가요? 저희 독자들은 당신이 어떻게 요리법을 개발하시는지, 처음에 무엇에 영감을 받아서 요리사가 되셨는지에 대해 관심이 많을 거라고 확신합니다. 그것은 제 칼럼에 도움이 될 뿐만 아니라 당신의 레스토랑을 위한 훌륭한 홍보가 될 것입니다. [180]**저는 이미 Mr. Kellum과 약속을 잡았는데 그분은 10월에 백화점에서 다시 시연회를 열겠다고 하십니다.**

관심이 있으시면 제게 알려 주세요. 당신의 일정에 맞출 수 있습니다.

Anthony Ulrich

어휘 article 기사 dining 식사, 정찬 coworker 동료 be impressed with ~에 깊은 인상을 받다 technique 기술 sample 시식용 음식; 견본 simply 정말로, 그야말로 upcoming 다가오는, 곧 있을 develop 개발하다, 발전하다 inspire 고무하다, 영감을 주다 publicity 홍보 make arrangements with ~와 약속이나 일정 등을 잡다

176. 시연 행사들에 대해 시사된 것은 무엇인가?

(A) 10월에도 계속 열릴 것이다.
(B) 발표자는 출간 경험이 있는 작가들뿐이다.
(C) 한 시간보다 길면 안 된다.
(D) 참가자들은 할인을 받을 수 있다.

해설 NOT/True
첫 번째 지문에서 10월에 시연을 할 수 있는 사람을 모집하고 있다고 했으므로 10월에도 같은 행사를 계속 진행한다는 것을 알 수 있다. 따라서 (A)가 정답이다.

어휘 participant 참가자

177. 요리사들은 이메일에 무엇을 포함시켜야 하는가?

(A) 시급 관련 정보
(B) 세부 조리법
(C) 경력 정보가 담긴 이력서
(D) 필요한 재료 목록

해설 세부 사항
첫 번째 지문에서 필요한 재료와 조리 도구가 있다면 알려 달라고 했으므로 (D)가 정답이다.

178. Mr. Ulrich는 왜 이메일을 보냈는가?

(A) 행사용 시식 음식을 요청하기 위해
(B) 간행물에 게재할 인터뷰를 제안하기 위해
(C) 홍보용 서비스를 소개하기 위해
(D) Ms. McIntyre를 개인적인 행사에 고용하기 위해

해설 주제/목적
두 번째 지문에서 Mr. Ulrich는 자신이 기사를 쓰는 〈The Colton Times〉에 Ms. McIntyre와 그녀의 레스토랑에 대한 기사를 쓰고 싶다고 했으므로 (B)가 정답이다.

패러프레이징 feature you and your restaurant in an upcoming article → propose an interview for a publication

어휘 request 요청하다 publication 발행물, 간행물 promotional 홍보의 hire 고용하다

179. Mr. Ulrich는 언제 Ms. McIntyre가 시연하는 것을 보았는가?

(A) 9월 4일
(B) 9월 11일
(C) 9월 19일
(D) 9월 23일

해설 두 지문 연계_세부 사항
먼저 Mr. Ulrich가 발신인인 두 번째 지문에서 단서를 찾아야 한다. Mr. Ulrich는 Ms. McIntyre가 Jerome Kellum과 함께 시연한 것을 봤다고 했는데, 첫 번째 지문에서 일정을 확인해 보면 두 사람은 9월 11일에 시연을 했으므로 (B)가 정답이다.

180. Mr. Kellum에 대해 암시된 것은 무엇인가?

(A) 그는 새로운 식당을 개업하고 싶어 한다.
(B) 그는 인도 음식을 요리할 수 있다.
(C) 그는 요리책을 쓸 예정이다.
(D) 그는 너무 바빠서 Mr. Ulrich를 도울 수 없었다.

해설 두 지문 연계_추론/암시
두 번째 지문에서 Mr. Kellum이 10월에 시연회를 하겠다고 한 것을 알 수 있다. 첫 번째 지문에서는 10월 시연회의 주제가 인도 음식이라고 했으므로 (B)가 정답이다.

181-185 웹페이지 & 이메일

> **Gifts Galore—여러분을 돋보이게 만드는 맞춤형 홍보 물품!**
>
> 고객이나 직원들에게 감사를 표할 방법을 찾고 계신가요? 여러분의 업체를 홍보하고 싶나요? Gifts Galore는 기업 선물, 박람회, 콘테스트, 또는 여러분의 업체를 기억에 남을 만한 것으로 만들고자 하는 순간을 위해 다양한 제품을 보유하고 있습니다. 물병, 토트백, 펜, 달력 등에 여러분의 로고나 다른 이미지를 인쇄하세요. [181]우리는 고객의 구매 습관을 추적하고 그에 따라 재고를 변경합니다. [182D]우리는 귀사의 제품들이 아름답게 보이도록 종이와 리본으로 포장해 드릴 수도 있습니다. 그리고 [182B]최소 5개의 주문도 처리할 수 있으므로 대량 구매하실 필요가 없습니다.
>
> [183]디자인에 대한 조언이 필요한 경우 여러분에게 그래픽 디자이너가 배정되어 모든 것이 좋아 보일 수 있도록 할 것입니다. 저희는 전 세계 어디로든 배송하지만 주문 인쇄 상품이기 때문에 상품을 받는 데 최대 3주가 걸릴 수 있다는 것을 유념해 주십시오. 모든 판매품은 최종 상품입니다. [182C]하지만 고객들이 물품을 되돌려 보낼 수는 없기 때문에 제품 확인을 위해 사전에 견본을 제공해 드릴 수 있습니다.

어휘 custom 주문 제작한 promotional 홍보의 stand out 눈에 띄다, 돋보이다 a wide range of 다양한, 광범위한 corporate 기업의 trade fair 무역 박람회 memorable 기억에 남는 purchasing habit 구매 습관 inventory 재고 accordingly 그에 따라 wrap 포장하다 ensure 보장하다 bulk purchase 대량 구매 process 처리하다 minimum 최소, 최저 assign 배정하다 note 유념하다, 주의하다 in advance 사전에

> 수신: Courtney Fitch
> 발신: Warren Evans
> 날짜: 1월 9일
> 제목: 감사합니다!
>
> 제가 귀사에 첫 주문을 했는데 매우 긍정적인 경험을 했다는 것을 알려 드리고 싶습니다. [183]Howard Lopez가 일대일 디자인 조언을 해 주신 것은 정말 도움이 되었습니다. [185]저는 Gifts Galore에 다양한 물품을 선택할 수 있는 많은 옵션이 있다는 데 깊은 인상을 받았고, 그래서 귀사를 한번 이용해 보기로 했습니다. 제가 그렇게 했다는 사실에 기쁩니다! Gifts Galore의 대량 주문 할인가는 귀사가 저희 회사에 적절한 선택권이 되는 데 확실한 [184]고려 사항이기 때문에 곧 대량 주문을 하기를 희망합니다.
>
> Warren Evans
>
> 고객 관계 관리자

어휘 positive 긍정적인 place an order 주문하다 on an individual level 개별적인 차원에서 impress 깊은 인상을 주다 give it a chance 시도를 해 보다 pricing 가격 책정 definitely 분명히, 확실히

181. Gifts Galore에 대해 사실인 것은 무엇인가?

(A) 제품이 높은 품질 관리 기준을 충족한다.
(B) 다양한 무역 박람회를 후원한다.
(C) 유행에 따라 재고를 조정한다.
(D) 국내에서 생산된 물품을 전문으로 한다.

해설 NOT/True
첫 번째 지문에서 고객의 구매 습관에 따라 재고를 변경한다고 했으므로 (C)가 정답이다.

패러프레이징 customers' purchasing habits → trends
change our inventory → adjusts its stock

어휘 quality control 품질 관리 standard 기준 sponsor 후원하다 adjust 조정하다 stock 재고 specialize in ~을 전문으로 하다 domestically 국내에서

182. Gifts Galore의 제품에 대해 시사되지 않은 것은 무엇인가?

(A) Gifts Galore의 로고가 있다.
(B) 소량 주문이 가능하다.
(C) 반품이 불가능하다.
(D) 선물 포장이 가능하다.

해설 NOT/True
물품에 Gifts Galore의 로고가 있다는 내용은 없으므로 (A)가 정답이다.

패러프레이징 (B) process orders with a minimum of just 5 items → be made in small orders
(D) wrap your items in paper and ribbons → be gift-wrapped

어휘 be eligible for ~할 자격이 있다 gift-wrap 선물용으로 포장하다

183. Howard Lopez는 누구이겠는가?

(A) 회사 소유주
(B) 그래픽 디자이너
(C) 재무 관리자
(D) 배달 기사

해설 두 지문 연계_추론/암시
두 번째 지문에서 Howard Lopez가 Mr. Evans에게 디자인 조언을 해 줬다는 내용이 있다. 첫 번째 지문에서는 디자인에 대한 조언이 필요하면 그래픽 디자이너가 배정된다고 했으므로 Howard Lopez는 Mr. Evans에게 배정된 디자이너라는 걸 알 수 있다. 따라서 (B)가 정답이다.

184. 이메일에서 첫 번째 단락 다섯 번째 줄의 어휘 "consideration"과 의미상 가장 가까운 것은?

(A) 보증금
(B) 요인
(C) 결과
(D) 친절

해설 동의어 찾기
consideration이 있는 your bulk discount pricing is definitely a consideration in making Gifts Galore the right choice는 Gifts Galore의 대량 주문 할인가가 적절한 선택권이 되는 데 확실한 고려 사항이라는 의미이며, 여기서 consideration은 '고려 사항, 요소'라는 뜻으로 쓰였다. 따라서 (B) factor가 정답이다.

185. Mr. Evans에 대해 암시된 것은 무엇인가?

(A) 그는 Gifts Galore가 다양성이 많다고 생각한다.
(B) 그는 빠른 서비스에 놀랐다.

(C) 그는 서로 다른 크기의 물품들을 주문했다.
(D) 그는 아직 그의 첫 번째 주문품을 기다리고 있다.

해설 추론/암시
두 번째 지문에서 Mr. Evans는 Gifts Galore가 보유한 다양한 물품에 깊은 인상을 받았다는 내용을 확인할 수 있으므로 (A)가 정답이다.

패러프레이징 Gifts Galore had so many options for different items → Gifts Galore has a good variety

어휘 variety 다양성

186-190 표지판 & 영수증 & 이메일

> Cicero Auction House
> 경매 낙찰자를 위한 정보
>
> 1. [186]**대금은 영업일 기준 3일 이내에 지불되어야 합니다. 그렇지 않으면 물품은 다음 경매로 넘어갈 것입니다.**
> 2. 대금이 지불된 물품은 1주일 이내에 배송됩니다. 지역 내 배송은 무료입니다. 다른 지역에 관해서는 직원과 상의하십시오.
> 3. [188]**특대 물품(어떤 방향으로든 3피트 초과)**은 1층 보관실이 아닌 저희의 안전한 지하실에 보관됩니다.
> 4. 모든 구매에는 해당 물품에 대한 보험이 포함됩니다.
> 5. 반품은 접수하지 않습니다.
>
> [187] ***영업 시간: 화요일 - 금요일 오전 8시~오후 6시***
> ***토요일 - 일요일 오전 10시~오후 4시***

어휘 auction 경매 make payment 대금을 지불하다 business day 영업일 dispatch 발송하다 regarding ~에 관하여 oversized 특대의, 크기가 큰 exceed 초과하다 direction 방향 store 보관하다 secure 안전한 storage room 보관실 insurance 보험

> Cicero Auction House 고객 영수증
>
> [189]**품목 번호: 06251**
> 예술가 이름: Antone Vinson
> 총 금액: 385달러
> 이전 소유주: Daniel Bartholomew
> [188]**크기: 3.5피트 × 4피트**
> [189]**고객 이름: Beatrice Mueller**
> 경매일: 1월 9일
> 픽업/배송: 1월 14일 배송 예정

어휘 receipt 영수증 previous 이전의 owner 소유주 dimension 치수, 크기

> 수신: Cicero Auction House
> 발신: Beatrice Mueller
> 날짜: 1월 12일
> 제목: 경매 물품 문의
>
> 안녕하세요.
>
> 저는 최근에 귀사에서 경매에 낙찰되어 같은 날 물품 대금을 지불했습니다. 원래는 [189]**그 그림**이 제가 가지고 있는 골동품 꽃병 및 양탄자와 어울려서 [190]**제 사무실로 보내려고 계획했습니다. 하지만 지금은 그 대신에 그것을 저의 집이 있는 324 오즈번 스트리트에 두기로 결정했습니다.** 그것을 거실에 있는 조각품 위에 걸어 두고 싶기 때문입니다. 이것이 가능하면 좋겠습니다. 알려 주시기 바랍니다.
>
> Beatrice Mueller

어휘 win an auction 경매에서 낙찰을 받다 originally 원래 antique 골동품의 rug 깔개 instead 대신에 sculpture 조각상

186. 표지판은 제시간에 결제되지 않은 물품에 관해 무엇을 시사하는가?
(A) 추가 요금을 발생시킬 것이다.
(B) 앞으로 열릴 행사에 추가될 것이다.
(C) 자선 단체에 기부될 것이다.
(D) 두 번째로 높은 입찰가를 부른 입찰자에게 팔릴 것이다.

해설 세부 사항
3일 이내에 결제되지 않은 물품은 다음 경매로 넘어간다고 했으므로 (B)가 정답이다.

패러프레이징 be put up for the next auction → be added to a future event

어휘 incur 발생시키다 additional 추가의 donate 기부하다 charity 자선 단체 bidder 입찰자

187. Cicero Auction House에 대해 사실인 것은 무엇인가?
(A) 월요일은 문을 닫는다.
(B) 지점이 2개 이상이다.
(C) 지역 내에서만 배송한다.
(D) 가족이 운영하는 업체이다.

해설 NOT/True
Cicero Auction House의 운영 시간은 첫 번째 지문의 하단에 나오는데, 월요일은 운영 시간에 포함되어 있지 않으므로 (A)가 정답이다.

어휘 family-owned business 가족이 운영하는 사업체

188. Ms. Mueller의 물품에 대해 시사된 것은 무엇인가?
(A) 1월 14일에 구매되었다.
(B) 500달러 이상의 가격에 팔렸다.
(C) 특대로 분류되었다.
(D) Daniel Bartholomew가 제작했다.

해설 두 지문 연계_NOT/True
두 번째 지문에 물품의 크기가 '3.5피트 x 4피트'라고 나와 있는데 첫 번째 지문에서 물품의 크기가 어느 방향으로든 3피트 이상이면 특대라고 했다. 따라서 Ms. Mueller의 물품은 특대로 분류된다는 것을 알 수 있으므로 (C)가 정답이다.

어휘 classify 분류하다

189. 06251은 어떤 종류의 물품이겠는가?
(A) 조각상
(B) 꽃병
(C) 그림

(D) 깔개

해설 두 지문 연계_추론/암시
두 번째 지문에서 해당 물품을 Beatrice Mueller가 낙찰받았다는 것을 알 수 있는데 세 번째 지문에서 Beatrice Mueller가 경매에서 낙찰받은 그림의 배송과 관련하여 문의를 하고 있으므로 (C)가 정답이다.

190. Ms. Mueller는 왜 이메일을 썼는가?

(A) 배송지 변경을 요청하기 위해
(B) 결제 문제를 알리기 위해
(C) 구매 물품 수령을 연기하기 위해
(D) 물품 세척에 대한 조언을 구하기 위해

해설 주제/목적
세 번째 지문에서 Ms. Mueller는 낙찰받은 그림을 원래 배송지인 사무실 대신 집으로 보내고 싶다고 했으므로 (A)가 정답이다.

어휘 postpone 미루다, 지연하다

191-195 웹페이지 & 광고 & 이메일

> 여러분의 사업을 지원할 상업 트럭 기사를 찾고 계신가요? [191]**지난 몇 년 동안 늘어난 수요로 인해 숙련된 트럭 기사를 구하기가 어려워졌습니다.** Nolen Recruitment가 여러분을 돕겠습니다!
>
> 우리는 지난 10년간 트럭 운송 및 건설을 위한 상업 트럭 기사 모집에 있어 선두 주자였습니다. 우리는 모든 취업 지원자를 주의 깊게 심사하여 자격증을 검증하고 [193]**우리가 요구하는 전문 추천서를 확인합니다.** 또한 우리 팀은 귀사에 추천하는 모든 운전자가 무사고 운전 기록을 보유하고 있다는 것을 확인하여 귀사의 보험율을 낮게 유지할 수 있도록 돕습니다.
>
> 우리가 귀사를 도울 방법을 알아보려면 오늘 우리 고객 서비스 팀에 이메일을 보내세요!

어휘 commercial 상업의 experienced 숙련된 demand 수요 recruitment 채용 construction 건설 decade 10년 screen 심사하다 verify 검증하다 license 자격증 reference 추천서 insurance rate 보험율

> **상업 트럭 기사 모집**
>
> [192]**Lakeland Trucking은 CW Industries에 인수된 후 직원을 늘리고 있습니다.**
>
> **직무 설명**: 소매 물품을 운송할 장거리 트럭 기사 필요. 납품일을 준수하고, 상근직으로 근무하고, 모든 도로 안전 규정을 준수할 수 있어야 함.
>
> **자격 요건**: 유효한 상업용 운전 면허증을 소지하고 현재 또는 이전 고용주로부터의 [193]**추천서를 2장 제출해야 함.** 최소 2년 이상의 경력. [195]**첫 번째 업무 전에 2주간의 오리엔테이션에 참여해야 함.**
>
> **급여**: 경력에 따라 45,000달러 – 55,000달러의 초봉 지급. 분기별 성과급.
>
> **지원 절차**: 10월 3일 오전 8시부터 오후 8시까지 Fulton Convention Center에서 열리는 우리의 채용 행사에 이력서를 가지고 오십시오.

어휘 expand 확장하다, 확대하다 transportation 운송, 교통 retail goods 소매품 meet a deadline 마감 기한을 맞추다 adhere to ~을 준수하다 valid 유효한 driver's license 운전면허증 submit 제출하다 letter of recommendation 추천서 previous 예전의 quarterly 분기의 performance 성과, 실적 résumé 이력서

> 수신: contact@nolenrecruitment.com
> 발신: d_williford@lakelandtrucking.com
> 날짜: 10월 13일
> 제목: 채용 요청
>
> 관계자 귀하:
>
> 저는 귀사의 서비스를 이용하여 5 – 10명의 경력직 상업용 트럭 기사를 채용하는 데 관심이 있습니다. 우리 회사는 이달 초에 채용 행사를 열었습니다. 하지만 [194]**예상했던 것만큼 많은 사람이 오지 않아서 충분한 숫자의 적합한 후보자를 찾는 데 어려움을 겪었습니다.** 우리는 최소 2년 경력의 운전자를 받고 있으며, 가능한 한 빨리 일을 시작할 수 있어야 합니다. [195]**우리는 신입 사원 전원에게 일주일의 오리엔테이션을 참석하도록 할 것입니다.** 귀사의 수수료와 우리에게 후보자 명단을 얼마나 빨리 줄 수 있는지 알려 주십시오.
>
> Diana Williford

어휘 show up 나타나다, 등장하다 suitable 적합한 candidate 후보 recruit 신입 사원 commission rate 수수료율

191. 웹페이지에 따르면 무엇이 변했는가?

(A) 연료비
(B) 트럭 운전사 수요
(C) 교통 법규
(D) 차량 가격

해설 세부 사항
늘어난 수요로 인해 숙련된 트럭 운전사를 구하기가 어려워졌다고 했으므로 (B)가 정답이다.

192. 광고에서 Lakeland Trucking에 대해 암시된 것은 무엇인가?

(A) 새로운 서비스를 제공하기 시작했다.
(B) 비정규직 공석이 있다.
(C) 새로운 업주가 왔다.
(D) 도로 안전 과정을 운영한다.

해설 추론/암시
Lakeland Trucking이 CW Industries에 인수되었다고 했으므로 (C)가 정답이다.

패러프레이징 being purchased by CW Industries → under new ownership

어휘 ownership 소유권 safety 안전(성)

193. Nolen Recruitment와 Lakeland Trucking의 공통점은 무엇인가?

(A) 운전자들을 위한 보험을 제공한다.
(B) 모두 운전 시험을 개발했다.

(C) 직원들에게 상여금을 준다.

(D) 전문 추천서를 요구한다.

해설 두 지문 연계_세부 사항

첫 번째 지문에 Nolen Recruitment가 전문 추천서를 요구한다는 내용이 있고, 두 번째 지문에는 Lakeland Trucking이 트럭 기사 지원자들에게 2장의 추천서를 제출할 것을 요구한다는 내용이 있으므로 (D)가 정답이다.

어휘 insurance 보험 develop 개발하다 reference 추천서

194. Ms. Williford는 채용 행사에 대해 무엇을 언급하는가?

(A) 갑작스럽게 취소되었다.

(B) 새로운 행사 기획자가 필요하다.

(C) 참석률이 낮았다.

(D) 매년 개최된다.

해설 세부 사항

세 번째 지문을 보면 Ms. Williford가 발신인인데, 채용 행사에 예상보다 적은 사람이 참석했다고 했으므로 (C)가 정답이다.

패러프레이징 not as many people showed up as we expected → had a low turnout

어휘 unexpectedly 갑작스럽게 turnout 참가자의 수

195. Lakeland Trucking의 공석 정보에서 무엇이 수정되었는가?

(A) 오리엔테이션 기간

(B) 필요한 경력

(C) 연봉

(D) 근무 시간

해설 두 지문 연계_세부 사항

두 번째 지문에서는 오리엔테이션이 2주라고 했는데, 세 번째 지문에서는 신입 사원에게 일주일의 오리엔테이션에 참여하도록 할 거라고 했으므로 (A)가 정답이다.

196-200 기사 & 일정 & 이메일

Brenton Industries가 새로운 보조금을 지원하다

(4월 9일)—어제 열린 기자 회견에서 스타트업 기술 회사인 Brenton Industries는 다양한 산업과 분야에서 일하는 개인에게 5개의 민간 보조금을 제공할 것이라고 발표했다. [196]보조금은 개별적인 연구를 통해 혁신을 장려하는 것을 목적으로 한다. 보조금을 받은 사람들은 Bright Future Conference에도 무료로 초대될 것이다.

"미래는 근로자들의 창의성에 달려 있고, 우리는 주요한 돌파구를 마련할 수 있는 잠재력을 가진 사람들에게 보상하고 싶습니다."라고 Brenton Industries의 부사장인 Ruth Gillis가 말했다. "이러한 자금을 통해 우리는 노동 인구 내에서 영감을 촉진하고 싶습니다."

[197]지원자들은 현재 석사 또는 박사 수준의 강의를 수강하고 있어야 한다. [199]지원자들은 그들의 아이디어를 입증하는 예전 프로젝트들의 사례를 제공해야 한다. 자세한 내용은 www.brentonind.com/grant에서 확인할 수 있다.

어휘 grant 보조금, 지원금 press conference 기자 회견 a variety of 다양한 field 분야 aim 목표로 하다 innovation 혁신 award 수여하다 creativity 창의력 potential 잠재력 achieve 얻다 breakthrough 돌파구 facilitate 촉진하다 inspiration 영감 workforce 노동 인구, 인력 applicant 지원자 demonstrate 보여 주다, 발휘하다

Bright Future Conference

Concord Convention Center

아래는 올해 콘퍼런스 행사 일정입니다. **[198]연사의 최종 명단이 확정되면 늦어도 7월 3일까지 참가자들에게 발송될 예정입니다.**

오전 8시	리셉션 및 친목 도모 조식 — 로비
오전 9시	환영사와 Brenton Industries 사명 선언문
오전 9:30 - 오전 10:30	패널 토론 — 주 강당
오전 10:30 - 오후 12:30	발표 — 다수의 강의실
오후 12:30 - 오후 1:30	중식 — 103호에서 뷔페식 중식. 참석자들은 입장하려면 콘퍼런스 출입증을 제시해야 합니다.
오후 1:30 - 오후 4:30	워크숍 — 다수의 강의실
[200]오후 4:30 - 오후 5:00	의견 청취 시간

어휘 activity 활동 finalize 마무리하다, 완성하다 reception 환영회, 리셉션 networking 인맥 형성 mission statement 사명 선언문 panel 패널, 토론 참가자 pass 출입증 admission 입장 feedback 의견, 피드백

발신: Brigida Marino
수신: Michael Tran
날짜: 7월 6일
주제: Bright Future Conference

Mr. Tran께,

[199]귀사에서 제게 지급한 보조금에 깊은 감사를 드리고 싶습니다. 이번 지원금을 통해 로봇 공학 분야에서 저의 연구 아이디어를 추구할 수 있게 되어 이 기회를 감사하게 생각합니다. 저는 또한 Bright Future Conference에 참석하여 저와 같은 관심사를 가진 사람들을 만나기를 고대하고 있습니다.

귀사의 게스트로 행사에 참석하는 것이니 **[200]제가 변경할 수 없는 출장으로 인해 행사 당일 4시 30분까지는 행사장을 떠나야 한다는 사실이 문제가 되지 않았으면 좋겠습니다.** 행사에서 직접 만나 뵙길 바랍니다.

Brigida Marino

어휘 express 표현하다 appreciation 감사 issue 주다, 발급하다 pursue 추구하다 robotics 로봇 공학 opportunity 기회 look forward to ~을 기대하다 share 공유하다 interest 관심(사)

196. Brenton Industries는 보조금으로 무엇을 돕고 싶어 하는가?

(A) 일자리 창출

(B) 창의적인 아이디어

(C) 문화적 다양성

(D) 환경 보호

해설 세부 사항
Brenton Industries의 보조금이 언급되는 첫 번째 지문에서 보조금은 혁신을 장려하는 것을 목표로 한다고 했으므로 이를 바꿔 표현한 (B)가 정답이다.

패러프레이징 innovation → Creative ideas

197. 기사에 따르면, Brenton Industries가 지원자에게 요구하는 것은 무엇인가?

(A) 고등 교육 과정 등록
(B) 온라인 설문 조사 참여
(C) 특정 산업에서의 전문성
(D) 대중 연설 경험

해설 세부 사항
첫 번째 지문에서 지원자는 석사 또는 박사 수준의 강의를 수강하고 있어야 한다고 했으므로 (A)가 정답이다.

패러프레이징 be currently taking classes at the master's or Ph.D. level → Enrollment in higher education courses

어휘 enrollment 등록, 입학 participation 참여, 참가 questionnaire 설문 조사 specialization 전문성

198. 일정에서 콘퍼런스에 대해 암시된 것은 무엇인가?

(A) 대부분의 행사는 주 강당에서 열릴 것이다.
(B) 패널 토론은 촬영될 것이다.
(C) 참가자들은 사전에 점심을 주문해야 한다.
(D) 몇몇 발표자가 확정되지 않았다.

해설 추론/암시
일정 도입부에서 최종 발표자 명단이 아직 확정되지 않은 것을 알 수 있으므로 (D)가 정답이다.

어휘 take place 열리다, 일어나다 film 촬영하다 in advance 사전에 confirm 확인하다, 확정하다

199. Ms. Marino에 대해 암시된 것은 무엇인가?

(A) 해외에서 행사장으로 이동할 것이다.
(B) 자신의 연구 샘플을 제출했다.
(C) 콘퍼런스에서 연설을 할 것이다.
(D) Brenton Industries의 직원이다.

해설 두 지문 연계_추론/암시
세 번째 지문을 보면 Ms. Marino가 발신인인데, 그녀가 Brenton Industries의 보조금을 받았다는 것을 알 수 있다. 첫 번째 지문 후반부에서는 보조금을 받으려면 자신의 아이디어를 입증하는 예전 프로젝트의 사례를 제출해야 한다고 했으므로 (B)가 정답이다.

패러프레이징 provide examples of previous projects → submitted samples of her work

어휘 overseas 해외에 submit 제출하다 give a talk 연설하다

200. Ms. Marino는 콘퍼런스의 어느 부분에 참석할 수 없는가?

(A) 발표 중 하나
(B) 친목 도모 조식
(C) 워크숍 중 하나
(D) 의견 청취 시간

해설 두 지문 연계_세부 사항
세 번째 지문에서 Ms. Marino는 출장으로 인해 4시 30분까지는 콘퍼런스 행사장을 떠나야 한다고 했다. 두 번째 지문을 보면 4시 30분부터 의견 청취 시간이 시작되므로 (D)가 정답이다.

TEST 04

LISTENING TEST

1. (D)	**2.** (B)	**3.** (C)	**4.** (A)	**5.** (D)
6. (A)	**7.** (A)	**8.** (C)	**9.** (A)	**10.** (A)
11. (B)	**12.** (A)	**13.** (B)	**14.** (C)	**15.** (B)
16. (A)	**17.** (C)	**18.** (B)	**19.** (C)	**20.** (A)
21. (B)	**22.** (B)	**23.** (C)	**24.** (B)	**25.** (B)
26. (A)	**27.** (A)	**28.** (B)	**29.** (B)	**30.** (C)
31. (B)	**32.** (C)	**33.** (B)	**34.** (D)	**35.** (C)
36. (B)	**37.** (D)	**38.** (B)	**39.** (C)	**40.** (D)
41. (C)	**42.** (B)	**43.** (A)	**44.** (A)	**45.** (B)
46. (D)	**47.** (C)	**48.** (A)	**49.** (A)	**50.** (C)
51. (B)	**52.** (B)	**53.** (C)	**54.** (B)	**55.** (A)
56. (B)	**57.** (B)	**58.** (D)	**59.** (C)	**60.** (C)
61. (D)	**62.** (B)	**63.** (B)	**64.** (C)	**65.** (C)
66. (B)	**67.** (B)	**68.** (C)	**69.** (C)	**70.** (D)
71. (C)	**72.** (B)	**73.** (A)	**74.** (B)	**75.** (C)
76. (B)	**77.** (D)	**78.** (C)	**79.** (B)	**80.** (C)
81. (A)	**82.** (C)	**83.** (C)	**84.** (B)	**85.** (B)
86. (B)	**87.** (A)	**88.** (D)	**89.** (B)	**90.** (A)
91. (D)	**92.** (C)	**93.** (D)	**94.** (A)	**95.** (B)
96. (D)	**97.** (A)	**98.** (B)	**99.** (C)	**100.** (A)

READING TEST

101. (C)	**102.** (D)	**103.** (B)	**104.** (B)	**105.** (D)
106. (C)	**107.** (D)	**108.** (A)	**109.** (C)	**110.** (C)
111. (B)	**112.** (A)	**113.** (B)	**114.** (B)	**115.** (C)
116. (D)	**117.** (D)	**118.** (A)	**119.** (B)	**120.** (D)
121. (B)	**122.** (D)	**123.** (C)	**124.** (B)	**125.** (D)
126. (B)	**127.** (C)	**128.** (B)	**129.** (A)	**130.** (A)
131. (C)	**132.** (D)	**133.** (C)	**134.** (C)	**135.** (B)
136. (C)	**137.** (C)	**138.** (D)	**139.** (D)	**140.** (C)
141. (B)	**142.** (A)	**143.** (C)	**144.** (D)	**145.** (D)
146. (C)	**147.** (A)	**148.** (B)	**149.** (B)	**150.** (A)
151. (C)	**152.** (B)	**153.** (D)	**154.** (B)	**155.** (B)
156. (B)	**157.** (D)	**158.** (C)	**159.** (D)	**160.** (B)
161. (C)	**162.** (C)	**163.** (B)	**164.** (C)	**165.** (B)
166. (D)	**167.** (C)	**168.** (D)	**169.** (B)	**170.** (A)
171. (C)	**172.** (D)	**173.** (A)	**174.** (B)	**175.** (B)
176. (C)	**177.** (D)	**178.** (B)	**179.** (A)	**180.** (D)
181. (B)	**182.** (A)	**183.** (C)	**184.** (A)	**185.** (D)
186. (B)	**187.** (D)	**188.** (B)	**189.** (A)	**190.** (C)
191. (C)	**192.** (B)	**193.** (A)	**194.** (C)	**195.** (D)
196. (A)	**197.** (B)	**198.** (C)	**199.** (B)	**200.** (A)

PART 1

1. 호남

(A) A woman is piling up some platters.
(B) A woman is putting away some dishes.
(C) A woman is serving a meal to customers.
(D) A woman is getting some food from a buffet.

(A) 여자가 서빙 접시를 쌓고 있다.
(B) 여자가 접시를 치우고 있다.
(C) 여자가 손님들에게 음식을 내오고 있다.
(D) 여자가 뷔페에서 음식을 가져가고 있다.

어휘 pile up 쌓다 platter (음식을 차려 내는 데 쓰는 큰 서빙용) 접시 put away 치우다 buffet 뷔페

2. 영녀

(A) The man is drawing on some paper.
(B) The man is pointing at a location on a map.
(C) The woman is resting her hand on a chair.
(D) The woman is handing him a pen.

(A) 남자가 종이에 그림을 그리고 있다.
(B) 남자가 지도 위의 한 장소를 가리키고 있다.
(C) 여자가 의자 위에 손을 얹고 있다.
(D) 여자가 남자에게 펜을 건네주고 있다.

어휘 point at 가리키다 rest 받치다 hand 건네다

3. 미남

(A) She's walking toward a tree.
(B) She's standing in a doorway.
(C) She has a rolled mat under her arm.
(D) She's unpacking her bag on the grass.

(A) 그녀가 나무 쪽으로 걸어가고 있다.
(B) 그녀가 출입구에 서 있다.
(C) 그녀가 말아진 매트를 팔 아래에 끼고 있다.
(D) 그녀가 풀밭에서 가방을 풀고 있다.

어휘 doorway 출입구 roll 말다 unpack 짐을 풀다

4. 호남

(A) A woman is reaching into her bag.
(B) A man is wiping down a countertop.
(C) They are removing boxes from a desk.
(D) They are wrapping some merchandise.

(A) 여자가 봉지 안으로 손을 집어넣고 있다.
(B) 남자가 조리대를 닦고 있다.
(C) 그들은 책상에서 상자들을 치우고 있다.
(D) 그들은 상품을 포장하고 있다.

어휘 reach into ~ 안으로 손을 뻗다 wipe down (젖은 걸레나 행주로) 말끔히 닦다 (wipe up 물기를 닦아내다) countertop 주방의 조리대 remove 제거하다 wrap 포장하다

5. 미녀

(A) There is a stack of plates on a tray.
(B) Containers have been placed on the ground.
(C) Some tables are covered with tablecloths.
(D) Sets of utensils have been arranged on tables.

(A) 쟁반 위에 접시들이 쌓여 있다.
(B) 용기들이 바닥에 놓여 있다.
(C) 몇몇 테이블에 식탁보가 씌워 있다.
(D) 식사 도구 세트들이 테이블 위에 정돈되어 있다.

어휘 container 용기 cover 덮다 tablecloth 식탁보 utensil (가정에서 사용하는) 기구[도구] (cooking/kitchen utensils 요리 도구/주방 용품)

6. 영녀

(A) One of the workers is carrying a box.
(B) Some people are assembling some shelves.
(C) The contents of a box are being examined.
(D) A box is being loaded onto a truck.

(A) 일꾼들 중 한 명이 상자를 나르고 있다.
(B) 몇몇 사람들이 선반을 조립하고 있다.
(C) 상자 안의 내용물을 조사하고 있다.
(D) 상자를 트럭에 싣고 있다.

어휘 carry 나르다, (이동 중에) 들고 있다 assemble 조립하다 (↔ disassemble) examine 조사하다 load 싣다, 적재하다 (↔ unload)

PART 2

7. 미남 영녀

Where's the vice president's office?
(A) At the end of the hall.
(B) My office is spacious.
(C) When is he retiring?

부사장 사무실은 어디에 있나요?
(A) 복도 끝에 있습니다.
(B) 제 사무실은 공간이 넓습니다.
(C) 그는 언제 퇴직하나요?

어휘 spacious 널찍한

8. 영녀 미남

> What time does the train to Boston depart?
> (A) In first class.
> (B) That's my hometown.
> **(C) At eleven forty-five.**

몇 시에 보스턴 행 열차가 출발하나요?
(A) 일등석에요.
(B) 그곳이 제 고향입니다.
(C) 11시 45분에요.

9. 미녀 호남

> Who will attend the press conference?
> **(A) Our lead journalist.**
> (B) Sure, I had a lot of fun.
> (C) Tomorrow morning.

누가 기자회견에 참석하나요?
(A) 우리의 메인 기자요.
(B) 물론이죠, 저는 재미있었어요.
(C) 내일 아침이요.

어휘 attend ~에 참석하다 press conference 기자회견

10. 호남 영녀

> How much is the entry fee?
> **(A) I think it's fifteen dollars.**
> (B) Enter through the main doors.
> (C) The museum exhibit was interesting.

참가비는 얼마예요?
(A) 제 생각에 15달러인 것 같습니다.
(B) 정문으로 들어가세요.
(C) 박물관 전시가 흥미로웠습니다.

어휘 entry 입장, 출입, 가입, 응모 exhibit 전시품, 전시회(= exhibition); 전시하다

11. 미남 미녀

> Would you like a ride to the trade fair?
> (A) He set up the booth.
> **(B) Thanks, but I'm not going.**
> (C) They tried a few times.

무역 박람회까지 태워 드릴까요?
(A) 그가 부스를 설치했어요.
(B) 고마워요, 근데 저는 안 가요.
(C) 그들이 몇 번 시도했어요.

어휘 set up 설치하다

12. 미남 영녀

> Should we go over these evaluations now or tomorrow?
> **(A) Let's do it now.**
> (B) Sometime last month.
> (C) She has enough experience.

여기 평가서들을 지금 검토해야 할까요, 내일 할까요?
(A) 지금 합시다.
(B) 지난달쯤에요.
(C) 그녀는 충분한 경험을 가지고 있어요.

어휘 go over 검토하다 evaluation 평가

13. 미녀 호남

> Why did you work from home yesterday?
> (A) I was just about to head home.
> **(B) My car broke down.**
> (C) Please update my address.

어제는 왜 재택 근무를 하셨나요?
(A) 막 집에 가려던 참이었어요.
(B) 제 차가 고장나서요.
(C) 제 주소를 갱신해 주세요.

어휘 work from home 재택 근무하다 be about to do 막 ~하려 하다 break down 망가지다

14. 영녀 호남

> Isn't the concert hall reopening this weekend?
> (A) I don't have weekend plans.
> (B) Some popular musicians.
> **(C) No, there were some delays.**

이번 주말에 콘서트홀이 다시 열리지 않나요?
(A) 주말 계획이 없습니다.
(B) 몇몇 유명 음악가들이요.
(C) 아니요, 조금 지연되었습니다.

어휘 musician 음악가 delay 지연

15. 미녀 미남

> When was Alberto promoted to manager?
> (A) We were able to resolve it.
> **(B) I believe it was in January.**
> (C) The sales promotion went well.

알베르토는 언제 지배인으로 승진했나요?
(A) 우리가 해결할 수 있었어요.
(B) 1월이었을 거예요.
(C) 판촉이 성공적이었어요.

어휘 go well 잘되다

16. 호남 영녀

We sell accessories for the Myra brand laptops, right?
(A) Yes, they're in the display case.
(B) Try restarting it.
(C) I prefer to use a tablet computer.

우리는 미라 노트북 주변 기기도 판매하죠?
(A) 네, 진열장 안에 있습니다.
(B) 다시 시작해보세요.
(C) 저는 태블릿 컴퓨터를 쓰는 걸 선호합니다.

어휘 prefer to do ~하는 것을 선호하다

17. 미녀 미남

Haven't you proofread the article yet?
(A) Probably a daily newspaper.
(B) Thanks, I'd like that.
(C) I've been in meetings all day.

아직 그 기사 교정을 안 하셨나요?
(A) 아마 일간지일 거예요.
(B) 감사합니다, 좋을 것 같아요.
(C) 저는 하루 종일 회의가 있었어요.

어휘 proofread 교정을 보다

18. 영녀 미남

Do you want to have dinner before the movie?
(A) Because she's a vegetarian.
(B) When does it start?
(C) The moving company said so.

영화 보기 전에 저녁 드실래요?
(A) 그녀가 채식주의자라서요.
(B) 그건(영화는) 언제 시작하나요?
(C) 이사 업체에서 그렇게 말했어요.

19. 미녀 호남

Who's designing the posters for the summer marathon?
(A) About forty-two kilometers.
(B) Usually at Meadowcrest Park.
(C) Liam's in charge of that team.

누가 여름 마라톤 포스터들을 디자인하고 있나요?
(A) 42킬로미터 정도요.
(B) 보통 메도우크레스트 파크에서요.
(C) 리암이 그 팀을 맡고 있어요.

어휘 be in charge of ~을 맡다/책임지다

20. 미남 호남

Why don't I take new photos for the product catalog?
(A) Sure, if you have time.
(B) You can take a brochure.
(C) To sell our new footwear.

제가 제품 목록용 사진을 새로 찍으면 어떨까요?
(A) 물론이죠, 시간 있으시다면요.
(B) 책자를 가져가셔도 돼요.
(C) 우리의 새로운 신발을 팔려고요.

어휘 footwear 신발

21. 호남 영녀

There is no charge for delivery, is there?
(A) My business address is better.
(B) As long as you're a premium member.
(C) I'm charging my device now.

배달료는 없는 거죠, 그렇죠?
(A) 제 회사 주소가 나을 거예요.
(B) 당신이 프리미엄 회원이라면요.
(C) 제 기기를 충전하고 있어요.

어휘 charge 요금; 충전하다 as long as ~하는 한, ~인 한

22. 호남 미녀

When will the new smartphone be available?
(A) Sure, I'm free anytime.
(B) It has already sold out.
(C) At local electronics stores.

언제 새로운 스마트폰이 들어오죠?
(A) 물론이죠, 저는 언제든 시간 있어요.
(B) 그건 벌써 다 팔렸어요.
(C) 지역 전자 기기 매장에서요.

어휘 available 이용[구매] 가능한 sell out 다 팔다, 매진되다

23. 미녀 미남

Have any of the staff members been assigned to lead the tour?
(A) You can learn a great deal.
(B) Sorry, I forgot to sign it.
(C) I'm afraid it's been postponed.

견학 안내할 직원이 배정되었나요?
(A) 당신은 많은 것을 배울 수 있습니다.

(B) 죄송합니다, 서명하는 것을 깜빡했어요.
(C) 안타깝게도 그것은 연기되었어요.

어휘 assign 배정하다 postpone 연기하다

24. 호남 영녀

How do I set the security alarm?
(A) Yes, before you leave.
(B) A few employees are still here.
(C) It comes in a complete set.

어떻게 보안 경보기를 설정하나요?
(A) 네, 당신이 떠나기 전에요
(B) 아직 직원 몇 명이 남아 있어요.
(C) 그것은 한 세트로 되어 있어요.

어휘 set 설정하다 come in (제품이 특정 색상/사이즈/형태 등으로) 팔리다/생산되다

25. 영녀 호남

I'd like to book an appointment for a haircut with Tina.
(A) A more modern style for summer.
(B) Alright, she has an opening on Friday morning.
(C) Yes, I enjoyed reading it.

티나에게 커트 예약을 하고 싶은데요.
(A) 여름을 위한 더 현대적인 스타일입니다.
(B) 네, 그녀는 금요일 아침에 빈 시간이 있어요.
(C) 네, 재미있게 읽었어요.

어휘 book an appointment 예약하다 have an opening 빈 자리가 있다

26. 미남 영녀

The hallway light still isn't fixed yet, is it?
(A) I'll contact the landlord right away.
(B) A three-bedroom apartment.
(C) There's a lighter version available.

아직 복도 조명이 수리되지 않았죠, 그렇죠?
(A) 바로 집주인에게 연락하겠습니다.
(B) 방 세 개짜리 아파트예요.
(C) 더 가벼운 버전을 이용하실 수 있습니다.

어휘 hallway 복도 contact ~에게 연락하다 landlord 집주인

27. 영녀 호남

Did you finish the testing of the prototype?
(A) The lab has been busier than usual.
(B) A team of scientists.
(C) Yes, I type very quickly.

시제품 시험을 마치셨나요?
(A) 실험실이 평소보다 붐비더라고요.
(B) 한 팀의 과학자들이에요.
(C) 네, 전 타이핑이 매우 빨라요.

어휘 prototype 원형, 시제품

28. 호남 미녀

What's the fastest way to drive to the post office?
(A) My car is fairly new.
(B) It's closed on national holidays.
(C) Overnight or express mail.

우체국으로 가는 가장 빠른 길이 어디죠?
(A) 제 차는 꽤 새것입니다.
(B) 우체국은 국경일에는 문을 닫아요.
(C) 익일 우편 또는 속달 우편입니다.

어휘 overnight 밤사이에, 하룻밤 동안(의)

29. 미남 영녀

Could you attend the quarterly meeting at the headquarters on my behalf?
(A) Brian commutes from far away.
(B) I do like visiting the head office.
(C) Ten more would be enough.

저 대신 본사에서 열리는 분기 회의에 참석해 주실 수 있나요?
(A) 브라이언은 멀리서 통근해요.
(B) 제가 본사에 가는 걸 좋아하긴 하죠.
(C) 10개 더하면 충분할 거예요.

어휘 headquarters 본사 on one's behalf ~를 대신하여 (= on behalf of)

30. 호남 영녀

The air conditioner has been blowing out hot air all morning.
(A) No, I think it'll be cool weather today.
(B) Let's move these papers out of the way.
(C) We'd better call a repair technician.

에어컨이 오전 내내 더운 바람을 내보내고 있어요.
(A) 아니요, 오늘은 시원한 날씨일 것 같아요.
(B) 이 서류들을 좀 치워 놓죠.
(C) 수리 기사를 부르는 게 좋겠네요.

어휘 blow out 내보내다 move ~ out of the way ~을 치우다 repair technician 수리 기사

31. 미남 미녀

Where can I purchase a leather briefcase like yours? (A) The meeting will probably be brief. **(B) I'll send you a link to the brand Web site.** (C) Yes, I do a lot of traveling.

어디서 그런 가죽 서류 가방을 살 수 있나요?
(A) 아마 회의는 짧을 거예요.
(B) 그 브랜드의 웹 사이트 링크를 보내줄게요.
(C) 네, 저는 여행을 많이 합니다.

어휘 briefcase 서류 가방 brief 간단한

PART 3

미남 미녀

Questions 32-34 refer to the following conversation.

M Maria, I heard [32]you're going to London to represent our company at the annual awards show.

W That's right. I'm looking forward to it.

M The theater district there is famous. Are you going to catch any shows while you're there?

W I haven't had time to look into that. [33]I've been so busy planning the employee quarterly banquet.

M Well, you can sometimes get good deals on tickets at the last minute.

W Oh, really?

M Yeah. [34]There's a smartphone app that can alert you to deals. You should download it. Let me show you.

남 마리아, 연례 시상식에 회사 대표로 [32]**당신이 런던에 간다는 것을** 들었어요.

여 맞아요. 무척 기대돼요.

남 거기 극장가가 유명해요. 거기 있는 동안 공연을 관람하실 건가요?

여 찾아볼 시간이 없었어요. [33]**분기별로 열리는 직원 연회를 계획하느라 너무 바빴거든요.**

남 음, 가끔씩 막바지에 표를 싸게 구할 수 있어요.

여 아, 진짜요?

남 네. [34]**가격에 대해 알림을 보내 주는 스마트폰 앱이 있어요. 다운로드해 보세요.** 제가 보여 드릴게요.

어휘 represent 대표하다 look forward to ~을 고대하다 district (특정한 특징이 있는) 지구[지역] catch a show 쇼를 보다/보러 가다 (catch a movie 영화를 보러 가다) look into 조사하다, 들여다보다 get a good deal on ~을 저렴한[좋은/적절한] 가격에 사다 at the last minute 막판에 alert A[사람] to B[사물] B에 대해 A에게 알리다

32. 화자들은 주로 무엇에 관해 논의하고 있는가?
(A) 마케팅 계획들
(B) 회사 투자자들
(C) 다가오는 여행
(D) 수상 후보 지명

33. 여자는 왜 바빴는가?
(A) 그녀는 휴가에서 돌아왔다.
(B) 그녀는 행사를 계획하고 있었다.
(C) 그녀는 공연을 준비하고 있었다.
(D) 그녀는 분기 보고서를 작성했다.

패러프레이징 the employee quarterly banquet → an event

34. 남자는 무엇을 할 것을 제안하는가?
(A) 관리자에게 말하는 것
(B) 정책을 주의 깊게 확인하는 것
(C) 예약을 하는 것
(D) 모바일 앱을 다운로드하는 것

미녀 호남

Questions 35-37 refer to the following conversation.

W Good morning, and welcome to Galvan Automotive. How may I help you?

M Hi. My friend David works here, and he said that [35]you were looking for new car salespeople.

W Oh, I know David. That's right. We're looking to hire three people.

M [36]What is the application process?

W We're accepting résumés until May 2 and then conducting interviews the following week. [37]Our Web site has the full job description plus a link to submit your application and documents. I'll write down the address for you.

M Sounds great. Thanks for the information!

여 좋은 아침입니다. 갤번 자동차에 오신 것을 환영합니다. 어떻게 도와 드릴까요?

남 안녕하세요. 제 친구 데이비드가 여기서 일하는데, [35]**새로운 자동차 판매원들을 찾고 있다고** 들었습니다.

여 아, 데이비드 알아요. 맞습니다. 저희는 세 명을 채용할 계획이에요.

남 [36]**지원 절차가 어떻게 되죠?**

TEST 04

여 5월 2일까지 지원서를 받고, 그 다음주에 면접을 볼 거예요. [37]저희 웹 사이트에 직무 소개가 올라가 있어요. 그리고 지원서랑 서류들을 제출할 링크도 걸려 있어요. 웹 사이트 주소 적어드릴게요.

남 네, 정보 알려 주셔서 감사합니다!

어휘 look for 찾다 be looking to do ~할 계획이다 (= be planning to do, be expecting to do) application 지원(서) conduct an interview 면접을 시행하다 the following week 그 다음주 job description (채용중인) 일자리에 대한 설명 submit 제출하다

35. 여자는 어디에서 일하는 것 같은가?

(A) 신문사에서
(B) 여행사에서
(C) 자동차 대리점에서
(D) 직업소개소에서

36. 남자는 무엇에 관해 질문하는가?

(A) 환불 정책
(B) 취업 기회
(C) 할인 판매
(D) 신제품

37. 여자는 남자에게 무엇을 하도록 권하는가?

(A) 행사에 참여하는 것
(B) 책자를 가져가는 것
(C) 계정을 만드는 것
(D) 웹 사이트에 방문하는 것

미녀 호남 미남

Questions 38-40 refer to the following conversation with three speakers.

W Well, Mr. Berg and Mr. Soto, before I begin any consulting for [38]your accounting firm, I'd like to get an idea of why you hired me.

M1 We have a solid customer base, and there is enough demand to expand further. [39]But there's one issue.

M2 That's right. [39]We're having problems with finding employees who have enough experience.

W I see. So, you've already tried to do some hiring?

M1 Yes, but without much luck.

W [40]Have you considered changing the benefits you offer to employees? For example, better bonuses and more vacation time will attract high-quality candidates.

여 음, 버그 씨와 소토 씨, [38]당신들의 회계 법인 상담을 진행하기에 앞서, 저를 채용하신 이유를 들어보고 싶습니다.

남1 저희는 견고한 고객층을 보유하고 있고, 확장하기에 충분한 수요가 있습니다. [39]하지만 한 가지 문제점이 있어요.

남2 맞습니다. [39]저희는 충분한 경력이 있는 직원들을 찾는 데 문제가 있어요.

여 알겠습니다. 그래서, 이미 채용 시도는 해보셨나요?

남1 네, 하지만 별 성과가 없었어요.

여 [40]직원들에게 주는 혜택을 바꾸는 것을 고려해 보셨나요? 예를 들어, 더 많은 상여금과 더 긴 휴가 기간을 준다면 능력 있는 후보들을 끌어들일 수 있을 거예요.

어휘 accounting firm 회계 사무소 get an idea of ~을 이해하다 customer base 고객 기반 demand 수요 expand 확장하다 high-quality 질 높은, 고급의

38. 남자들은 어디에서 일하는가?

(A) 그래픽 디자인 회사에서
(B) 회계 법인에서
(C) 병원에서
(D) 법률 사무소에서

39. 남자들은 어떤 문제를 가지고 있는가?

(A) 새로운 기술을 구현하는 것
(B) 기존 고객들을 유지하는 것
(C) 경력 있는 직원을 찾는 것
(D) 믿을 수 있는 공급처를 파악하는 것

패러프레이징 employees who have enough experience → experienced staff

40. 여자는 무엇을 할 것을 제안하는가?

(A) 영업시간을 늘리는 것
(B) 더 많은 교육을 제공하는 것
(C) 광고를 온라인에 게시하는 것
(D) 복리후생 제도를 조정하는 것

패러프레이징 changing the benefits → adjusting a benefits package

미녀 미남

Questions 41-43 refer to the following conversation.

W Hi, Ross. A delivery of [41]watercolor paints and paintbrushes has just arrived. [42]The delivery person is at the entrance. Can you help with that?

M I'm in the middle of assembling these shelves, so I can deal with that later.

W I think he needs a signature.

M Oh, alright. In that case, can you make sure no one

comes into this area? The shelves are loose, and I don't want any customers to get hurt. [43]I put up a sign, but they often forget to read those.

W No problem.

여 안녕하세요, 로스. [41]**수채화 물감과 붓이 방금 도착했어요.** [42]**배달원이 입구에 있어요. 도와주실 수 있나요?**

남 이 선반들을 조립하는 중이라서, 나중에 처리할 수 있어요.

여 그가 서명이 필요한 것 같아요.

남 아, 알았어요. 그렇다면, 이쪽에 아무도 안 오도록 확인해 주실 수 있나요? 선반들이 헐렁거리고, 손님들이 다치는 것은 싫어요. [43]**표지판을 세워 놓긴 했는데, 사람들이 읽는 것을 자주 까먹어요.**

여 문제없어요.

어휘 watercolor paint 수채 물감 paintbrush 붓 assemble 조립하다 signature 서명 loose 느슨한 get hurt 다치다

41. 화자들의 업체는 무엇을 판매하는가?

(A) 촬영 장비들
(B) 청소 용품들
(C) 미술 용품들
(D) 컴퓨터 주변 기기들

42. 여자는 "그가 서명이 필요한 것 같아요"라고 말할 때 무엇을 의미하는가?

(A) 계약서의 효력이 곧 발생한다.
(B) 배송이 완료되지 않았다.
(C) 수표가 아직 유효하지 않다.
(D) 일정 변경이 승인되지 않았다.

43. 남자에 따르면, 손님들은 무엇 하는 것을 잊어버리는가?

(A) 표지판 읽는 것
(B) 신분증 제시하는 것
(C) 영수증 보관하는 것
(D) 쿠폰 쓰는 것

미녀 미남 호남

Questions 44-46 refer to the following conversation with three speakers.

W Kevin and Mark, I see you've already unpacked [44]the pipes and other plumbing supplies for the work here at the Vista Building.

M1 Yes, we can begin soon. Is something wrong?

W Actually, the client has decided to use plastic pipes instead of copper, as originally planned.

M2 [45]How frustrating! The work order form still says copper. No one updated it.

M1 Yeah, and we didn't bring any plastic piping to the job site.

W I understand, and I'm sorry. I'll ask someone from the warehouse to bring what you need. In the meantime, [46]I have a drawing of what the system layout is supposed to look like when it's all done. I'd like you to take a look at it and let me know if you have any questions.

여 케빈과 마크, 벌써 비스타 건물을 위한 작업을 하려고 [44]**배관과 배관 용품들을 꺼내셨네요.**

남1 네, 곧 시작할 거예요. 무슨 문제라도 있나요?

여 사실, 고객이 구리 대신 플라스틱 배관을 사용하기로 결정했어요. 원래 계획대로 말이죠.

남2 [45]**당황스럽네요! 작업 주문서엔 아직도 구리라고 써 있는데요. 아무도 수정해 놓지를 않았어요.**

남1 맞아요, 그리고 우리는 작업 현장에 플라스틱 배관을 하나도 가져오지 않았어요.

여 이해해요, 그리고 미안해요. 창고에 있는 사람에게 당신들이 필요한 것을 가져오도록 요청할게요. 그러는 동안, [46]**작업이 모두 끝났을 때 시스템 배치가 어떻게 되어야 하는지에 대한 도면을 제가 가져왔으니까,** 살펴보시고 질문 있으면 말씀해 주세요.

어휘 unpack 짐을 풀다/꺼내다 supplies 용품 (medical/cleaning/camping/school supplies 의료 용품/청소 용품/캠핑 용품/학용품) as originally planned 원래 계획대로 frustrating 불만스러운 job site 작업 현장 warehouse 창고 in the meantime 그 와중에, 도중에

44. 남자들은 누구일 것 같은가?

(A) 배관공들
(B) 운동 강사들
(C) 내과 의사들
(D) 여행사 직원들

45. 남자들은 무엇에 관해 당황하였는가?

(A) 빌딩이 잠겨 있었다.
(B) 서류가 갱신되지 않았다.
(C) 동료가 결근하였다.
(D) 택배에 라벨이 붙어 있지 않았다.

46. 여자는 남자들에게 무엇을 보여줄 것인가?

(A) 추가 견적
(B) 수정된 계약서
(C) 제품 목록
(D) 시스템 배치도

영녀 미남

Questions 47-49 refer to the following conversation.

W Good morning, Mr. Garcia. Since you're the Parks and Recreation Director, I wanted to suggest [47]adding a tennis court to Overland Park. I think a lot of people would use it. And there's an open field near the West Parking Lot.

M Hmm... that'd be a good spot. But the budget is very tight this year. [48]It would be hard to get the funding we need for a project like this.

W What if that could be raised privately?

M In that case, I think it would be approved. [49]You should get in touch with local businesses to see if they are willing to donate to the project.

여 좋은 아침입니다, 가르시아 씨. 당신이 공원 및 위락 시설 관리국의 책임자이시니 오버랜드 공원에 [47]**테니스장을 추가하는 것**을 제안드리고 싶었습니다. 제 생각에 많은 사람들이 이용할 것 같아요. 그리고 웨스트 주차장 쪽에 빈터가 있고요.

남 흠… 좋은 자리일 것 같네요. 그런데 금년 예산이 빠듯해요. [48]**이런 프로젝트를 위한 자금을 얻기는 어려울 거예요.**

여 민간 자금을 모을 수 있다면요?

남 그런 경우라면, 승인될 수 있을 것 같아요. [49]**지역 업체들에 연락해서 프로젝트에 기부할 뜻이 있는지 확인해 보는 게 좋을 것 같군요.**

어휘 spot 장소 budget 예산 get the funding 자금을 얻다 what if...? ~라면 어떻게 될까? raise 모금하다 approve 승인하다 get in touch with ~에게 연락하다 donate ~ to ~ ~을 ~에 기부하다

47. 여자는 어떤 프로젝트를 제안하는가?

(A) 들판에 꽃 심기
(B) 시 건물 보수하기
(C) 테니스장 추가하기
(D) 주차장 확장하기

48. 남자는 무엇이 어려울 것이라고 말하는가?

(A) 충분한 자금을 확보하는 것
(B) 주차 요금을 인상하는 것
(C) 건축 허가증을 받는 것
(D) 적합한 공간을 찾는 것

패러프레이징 get the funding → secure enough funds

49. 남자는 여자에게 무엇을 하도록 조언하는가?

(A) 지역 업체들에 연락하는 것
(B) 회의에 참석하는 것
(C) 시 웹 사이트에 방문하는 것
(D) 자원 봉사자 교육을 받는 것

패러프레이징 get in touch with → contact

영녀 호남

Questions 50-52 refer to the following conversation.

W That's nearly all the time we have for today's program. Thank you so much for sharing the insights you've gained from [50]your career in the food service industry.

M It's my pleasure. [51]As I said in the keynote speech I gave at a conference last month, catering is so rewarding because I get to be a part of the special events in people's lives.

W That's wonderful. Now, we have time for just one more question from our Web site. Let's see... Bradley says he's just starting out in the industry and [52]he's wondering how to get new customers to try his business.

여 오늘 프로그램을 위한 시간은 대략 여기까지입니다. [50]**당신의 요식업계 경력**을 통해 얻은 통찰을 공유해 주신 것에 대해 정말 감사드립니다.

남 저도 기쁩니다. [51]**지난달 콘퍼런스에서 했던 기조 연설에서 말했듯**, 음식을 공급하는 것은 매우 보람 있습니다. 왜냐하면 사람들의 삶에서 중요한 행사들의 일부분이 될 수 있거든요.

여 그거 멋지네요. 이제, 우리 웹 사이트에서 가져온 질문 하나 정도 할 시간이 남았네요. 어디 보자… 브래들리라는 분이 그가 업계에 이제 막 진출하려 하는데, [52]**어떻게 새로운 고객들이 그의 업체를 이용해 보도록 유치할지 고민 중이라고 하네요.**

어휘 insight 통찰 keynote speech 기조 연설 cater 음식을 공급하다 rewarding 보람 있는 start out 시작하다

50. 남자는 어떤 업계에서 일하는 것 같은가?

(A) 수송
(B) 농업
(C) 식품
(D) 의료

51. 남자는 지난달에 무엇을 하였는가?

(A) 그는 책을 출판하였다.
(B) 그는 연설을 하였다.
(C) 그는 상을 받았다.
(D) 그는 사업을 시작하였다.

52. 남자가 다음에 무엇에 대해 말할 것 같은가?

(A) 직원의 불평 해결
(B) 새로운 고객 유치
(C) 알맞은 도구 선택
(D) 사업 대출 신청

패러프레이징 get new customers → attract new customers

영녀 미남

Questions 53-55 refer to the following conversation.

W Adam, I'm so pleased with [53]our real estate agency's performance this past quarter.

M Me too. I was looking at the balance sheet and noticed we still have some funds at our disposal.

W Exactly. And since our computers were recently upgraded, [54]how about using the funds to buy another sofa and table for the waiting room?

M That sounds great.

W All right. I'll place an order today with Mesa Co. since everything they have is so stylish. [55]How soon do you think we could get it?

M Last time, it took two weeks.

W Okay. I'll look through the catalog now.

여 아담, [53]**우리 부동산 사무소**의 지난 분기 실적에 대해 저는 아주 기뻐요.

남 저도요. 대차대조표를 보고 있었는데, 여전히 잉여 자금이 있어요.

여 그러니까요. 그리고 우리 컴퓨터들은 최근에 업그레이드되었으니, [54]**그 자금으로 대기실의 소파와 테이블을 더 구매하는 것이 어떨까요?**

남 그거 좋은데요.

여 좋습니다. 메사 사에 오늘 주문 넣을게요. 거기 상품들은 다 스타일이 세련되거든요. [55]**얼마나 빨리 받을 수 있을 것 같나요?**

남 저번엔, 2주가 걸렸어요.

여 알겠어요. 지금 품목들을 살펴볼게요.

어휘 real estate agency 부동산 중개업소 performance 실적 balance sheet 대차대조표 at one's disposal 마음대로 쓸 수 있는 place an order 주문하다 look through 살펴보다

53. 화자들은 어디서 일하는가?

(A) 주택 개량 용품점에서
(B) 광고 대행사에서
(C) 부동산 중개업체에서
(D) 투자은행에서

54. 여자는 무엇을 사는 걸 제안하는가?

(A) 컴퓨터 용품
(B) 가구
(C) 회사 차량
(D) 카펫

패러프레이징 sofa and table → furniture

55. 남자는 왜 "저번엔, 2주가 걸렸어요"라고 말하는가?

(A) 추측하기 위해
(B) 불만을 표명하기 위해
(C) 변명을 하기 위해
(D) 제안을 거절하기 위해

호남 영녀

Questions 56-58 refer to the following conversation.

M Hi, Ms. Ellerman. It's Adam Mendoza.

W Oh, hi, Adam. It's been a while. I've been wondering how you've been since [56]you did the renovations on my house last year.

M Things are going great. [57]In fact, in just a few weeks, I'm planning to bid on the renovation project at the public library.

W That sounds like a great opportunity. Good luck!

M Thanks! Actually, as part of my proposal, [58]I need a reference letter from a previous client. Would you be willing to write one?

W Of course! What does it need to include?

M In the letter, just share your opinions about my work, and then e-mail it to the library. I'll send you the contact details.

W Okay. I'll do it this week.

남 안녕하세요, 엘러먼 씨. 아담 멘도자입니다.

여 오, 안녕하세요, 아담. 뵌 지 오래되었네요. [56]**작년에 저희 집 개조를 마친** 이후로 어떻게 지내시는지 궁금했어요.

남 잘 지내고 있습니다. [57]**사실, 몇 주 후에, 공공 도서관 개조 프로젝트에 응찰할 계획이에요.**

여 아주 좋은 기회인 것 같은데요. 행운을 빌어요!

남 고마워요! 사실, 제 제안서의 일부로, [58]**이전 고객의 추천서가 필요해요.** 당신이 하나 써 주실 수 있나요?

여 당연하죠! 어떤 내용을 포함해야 하나요?

남 편지에 저에 대한 당신의 의견을 공유해 주시면 돼요. 그런 다음 편지를 이메일로 도서관에 보내주시면 돼요. 연락처를 보내드릴게요.

여 알겠어요. 이번 주에 할게요.

어휘 It's been a while 오래간만이다 be planning to do ~하려고 계획중이다 bid on/for ~에 응찰하다 renovation 개조 reference letter 추천서 previous 이전의 be willing to do 기꺼이 ~하다

56. 여자는 누구일 것 같은가?

(A) 남자의 동창
(B) 남자의 전 고객
(C) 남자의 상사
(D) 남자의 동료

57. 남자는 몇 주 뒤 무엇을 하려고 하는가?

(A) 시 의원에 출마하기
(B) 프로젝트에 응찰하기
(C) 도서관 워크숍에서 교육하기
(D) 여자의 집 방문하기

패러프레이징 bid on the renovation project → submit a bid for a project

58. 남자는 무엇이 필요한가?

(A) 기업 명부
(B) 예산 요약표
(C) 안전 증서
(D) 추천서

호남 미녀

Questions 59-61 refer to the following conversation.

M [59]Thanks for tuning in. Now it's time for our traffic update with Angela Fleming. Angela, how are things looking this morning?

W Traffic is flowing much better than usual. [60]That's because Warner Road is finally open again after two months of closure. However, there will soon be traffic problems again once construction on the new stadium begins in the Montague neighborhood.

M And how long will that take?

W It's happening in several phases. [61]To learn more, download the brochure about the stadium project from the city's Web site at www.fairfield.gov.

남 [59]청취해 주셔서 감사합니다. 이제 앤젤라 플레밍과 함께하는 교통 속보 시간입니다. 앤젤라, 오늘 아침 상황은 어때 보이나요?

여 평소보다 교통이 순조롭습니다. [60]이건 워너 도로가 두 달간의 폐쇄 이후 다시 열렸기 때문입니다. 하지만, 몬태규 인근 지역의 새로운 경기장 건축이 시작되면 다시 곧 교통 문제가 생길 겁니다.

남 그럼 그 건축이 얼마나 걸릴 예정이죠?

여 건축은 여러 단계로 진행됩니다. [61]더 알아보시려면, 시 웹 사이트 www.fairfield.gov에서 경기장 계획에 대한 안내 책자를 다운로드 하실 수 있습니다.

어휘 tune in (라디오 · TV의) 주파수/채널에 맞춰 듣다 flow (차량이나 사람 등이) 흘러가다, 이동하다 closure 폐쇄 phase 단계

59. 화자들은 어디서 일하는 것 같은가?

(A) 건축 회사에서
(B) 자동차 공장에서
(C) 라디오 방송국에서
(D) 연락선 터미널에서

60. 여자는 워너 도로에 대해 무엇을 말하는가?

(A) 그것은 경기장 옆을 지난다.
(B) 그것은 대대적인 보수가 필요하다.
(C) 그것은 다시 개통되었다.
(D) 그것은 오늘 통행이 혼잡하다.

패러프레이징 is finally open again → has reopened

61. 청자들은 어떻게 새로운 프로젝트에 대해 더 알아볼 수 있는가?

(A) 우편물 수신자 명단에 등록함으로써
(B) 회의에 참가함으로써
(C) 업체에 연락함으로써
(D) 안내 책자를 다운로드함으로써

미남 미녀

Questions 62-64 refer to the following conversation and schedule.

M Sonora Community Center. How can I help you?

W Hi. [63]I'd like to sign up for the class starting next Tuesday, [62]but I couldn't find any information online about paying the course fee.

M We only accept cash or credit card here at the front desk.

W Alright. I know I have to pay for all the sessions, but I have to miss the second one since [64]I'm going to a concert in Atlanta on April 16.

M No problem. Ask the instructor about make-up classes.

남 소노라 지역 문화 센터입니다. 어떻게 도와드릴까요?

여 안녕하세요. [63]다음주 화요일부터 시작하는 수업에 등록하고 싶은데요, [62]온라인에서 수업료 지불에 대한 정보를 찾을 수가 없었어요.

남 여기 안내 데스크에서 현금이나 신용카드만을 받고 있습니다.

여 알겠습니다. 모든 차시에 대한 수업료를 지불해야 하는 건 알고 있는데, [64]4월 16일에 애틀랜타에서 열리는 콘서트에 갈 거라서 두 번째 시간은 참석을 못 해요.

남 문제없습니다. 강사님께 보강 수업에 대해 여쭤 보세요.

소노라 지역 문화센터 봄 스케줄				
월	63화	수	목	금
제빵	바느질	도자기	그림	스페인어

어휘 sign up for 등록하다 course fee 수업료 miss 놓치다, (수업을) 빼먹다

62. 여자는 왜 전화하고 있는가?

(A) 운전 경로를 물어보기 위해
(B) 지불에 관해 문의하기 위해
(C) 수업을 가르치는 것에 자원하기 위해
(D) 현장 주차가 가능한지 확인하기 위해

패러프레이징 pay the course fee → make a payment

63. 시각 자료를 보시오. 여자는 어떤 수업에 참가하고 싶어 하는가?

(A) 제빵
(B) 바느질
(C) 도자기
(D) 그림

64. 여자는 애틀랜타에서 무엇을 할 것인가?

(A) 연설하기
(B) 인터뷰 참석하기
(C) 음악 공연 보기
(D) 은퇴 파티 가기

패러프레이징 a concert → a musical performance

미녀 호남

Questions 65-67 refer to the following conversation and chart.

W Thanks for being here for this meeting, everyone. Our company is expanding rapidly, but as I explained in my e-mail, we're having a problem hiring more people to help design 65our refrigerators, ovens, and dishwashers. Does anyone have any ideas for this?

M I've been doing some research on this. I've prepared a graph to show the most common ways that people in our industry find jobs.

W Well, we already advertise on job Web sites, which eighty-two percent of people look at. 66But we haven't done anything with the next-highest category. If sixty-seven percent of people are using it, we'd better spend some money in that area, too.

M I completely agree. 67How about I find out what events are coming up in our area?

여 회의에 참석해 주셔서 감사합니다, 여러분. 우리 회사는 빠르게 확장하고 있지만 메일로 설명드린 것처럼 **65우리의 냉장고, 오븐, 식기 세척기를 설계해 줄 사람들을 더 채용하는 데 문제를 겪고 있습니다.** 혹시 이에 대해 좋은 아이디어 있으신가요?

남 이와 관련하여 조사를 좀 하고 있었습니다. 우리 업계 사람들이 직장을 찾는 가장 흔한 방법들을 보여주기 위해 그래프를 준비했습니다.

여 음, 우리는 이미 구직 웹 사이트들에 홍보하고 있네요. 82%의 사람들이 보고 있군요. **66하지만 그 다음으로 높은 부문에서 아무것도 하지 않았네요.** 만약 67%의 사람들이 이걸 이용하고 있다면, 우리는 그곳에도 돈을 좀 쓰는 것이 좋겠군요.

남 전적으로 동의해요. **67우리 지역에서 어떤 행사들이 열릴 예정인지 제가 알아보는 게 어떨까요?**

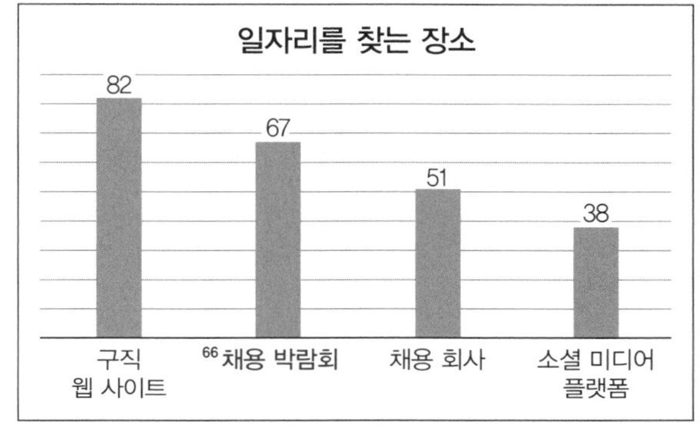

어휘 expand 확대하다 rapidly 빠르게 do some research on ~에 대해 조사하다 advertise 광고하다 find out 알아보다

65. 화자들은 어디서 일할 것 같은가?

(A) 그래픽 디자인 회사에서
(B) 청소 서비스 업체에서
(C) 가전 기기 제조사에서
(D) 부동산 관리 회사에서

66. 시각 자료를 보시오. 회사는 어떤 부문에 돈을 쓸 것인가?

(A) 구직 웹 사이트
(B) 채용 박람회
(C) 채용 회사
(D) 소셜 미디어 플랫폼

67. 남자는 무엇을 하기로 제안하는가?

(A) 직무 설명 작성하기
(B) 다가오는 행사 찾아보기
(C) 예산 변경 승인하기
(D) 이력서 검토하기

패러프레이징 find out what events are coming up → look for upcoming events

영녀 호남

Questions 68-70 refer to the following conversation and product design.

W Do you have a minute to discuss our new running shoes, Eddie?

M Of course. What's going on?

W Well, we've confirmed that we'll have nylon for the outer fabric. [68]However, I can't decide what colors to use.

M Can't you use the combinations we used last year?

W No, [69]we need to change the design because it looked too much like the one made by Felosa Shoes. We need to make our product more distinct.

M Hmm... Maybe you could make a few samples and get opinions from people at our next meeting. And are you planning to put our logo on the side again?

W No. [70]This time, it's going at the top of the back heel.

여 우리의 새로운 운동화에 대해 논의할 시간 있나요, 에디?

남 물론이죠. 무슨 일인가요?

여 음, 겉을 감싸는 소재로 나일론을 쓰기로 확정했어요. [68]**그런데, 어떤 색깔을 사용할지 결정할 수 없네요.**

남 우리가 작년에 사용했던 조합은 안 되나요?

여 안 돼요, [69]**디자인을 바꿔야 해요. 왜냐면 펠로사 신발에서 만든 것과 너무 닮았거든요.** 우리의 제품을 더 구별되게 만들어야 해요.

남 흠… 견본을 좀 만들고 다음 회의에서 사람들에게 의견을 구할 수도 있겠네요. 그리고 전처럼 옆에 우리의 로고를 박을 계획인가요?

여 아니요. [70]**이번엔 뒤꿈치 윗부분에 넣을 거예요.**

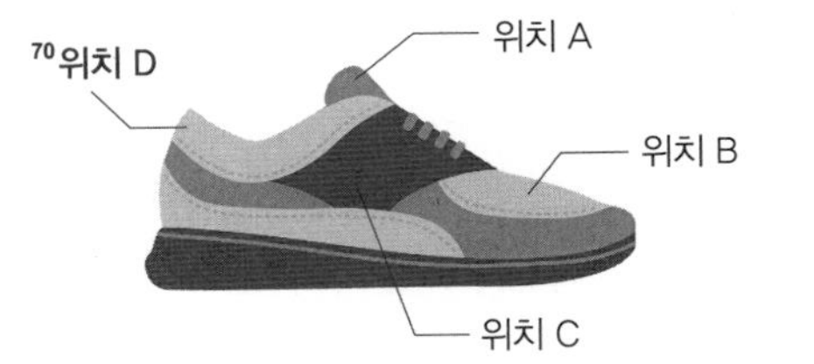

어휘 confirm 확정하다 outer 외부의, 바깥 표면의 distinct 뚜렷이 다른 at the top of ~의 꼭대기에

68. 여자는 신발에 대해 어떤 것을 결정하는 데 어려움을 겪는가?

(A) 직물 종류
(B) 출시 날짜
(C) 색깔
(D) 가격

69. 여자에 따르면, 디자인은 왜 바뀌어야 하는가?

(A) 제조 비용을 줄이기 위해
(B) 젊은 고객들을 사로잡기 위해
(C) 경쟁사와 비슷하게 보이지 않기 위해
(D) 고객 피드백에 답하기 위해

70. 시각 자료를 보시오. 로고는 어디에 위치할 것인가?

(A) 위치 A
(B) 위치 B
(C) 위치 C
(D) 위치 D

PART 4

미녀

Questions 71-73 refer to the following telephone message.

Hi. My name is Patricia Simms. [71]I ordered a suitcase from your Web site, and it just arrived today. When I opened the package, [72]I noticed that the top handle was cracked. I've sent the item back according to the instructions on your Web site. [73]I would like a refund, and I'm wondering how long it takes to process that. I paid with a credit card, if that makes any difference. Please call me back at 555-4978. Thank you.

안녕하세요. 제 이름은 패트리샤 심스입니다. 귀사의 웹 사이트에서 [71]**여행 가방을 주문하였고,** 오늘 막 도착했습니다. 택배를 열어보니, [72]**윗부분 손잡이에 금이 가있는 걸 알게 되었습니다.** 귀사의 웹 사이트에 올라와 있는 지시에 따라 물품을 반송하였습니다. [73]**환불받고 싶은데, 얼마나 걸리는지 궁금합니다.** 참고로, 저는 신용카드로 결제하였습니다. 555-4978로 전화해 주시기 바랍니다. 감사합니다.

어휘 suitcase 여행 가방 crack 갈라지다, 금이 가다, 깨지다 instructions 지시, 안내 refund 환불 process 처리하다

71. 화자는 회사에서 무엇을 주문하였는가?

(A) 골프채 세트
(B) 접시 세트
(C) 짐 가방
(D) 안경

패러프레이징 a suitcase → a piece of luggage

72. 화자는 청자에게 어떠한 문제에 대해 말하는가?

(A) 크기가 부정확했다.
(B) 일부분이 망가졌다.
(C) 웹 사이트가 로딩되지 않는다.
(D) 청구서가 너무 높게 쓰였다.

패러프레이징 was cracked → was damaged

73. 화자는 무엇에 관해 질문하는가?

(A) 처리 시간
(B) 이메일 주소
(C) 배달 경로
(D) 상점 위치

패러프레이징 how long it takes to process that → a processing time

미남

Questions 74-76 refer to the following announcement.

Now I'd like to [74]announce the award for best graphic design at our company. I'm pleased to say that the winner is Sheila Eldridge. Her work on the book cover for Arthur Brown's latest novel was amazing, and everyone on the judging panel was very impressed with it. [75]For winning this award, Ms. Eldridge will be given one additional day of paid leave. She's earned it! [76]And if you want to see what the finished book looks like before it hits stores, we'll have a copy to show you next week.

이제 우리 회사의 [74]**최우수 그래픽 디자인 상을 발표하겠습니다.** 기쁜 마음으로 쉴라 엘드리지가 수상자임을 알립니다. 아서 브라운의 새로운 소설을 위한 그녀의 책 표지 작업물은 놀라웠고, 모든 심사위원들은 이를 매우 인상 깊게 보았습니다. [75]**이 상과 함께 엘드리지 씨는 하루의 유급 휴가를 추가적으로 받게 됩니다.** 그녀는 그럴 만한 자격이 있습니다! [76]**그리고 책이 서점에 배포되기 전에 최종본을 보고 싶으시다면, 다음주에 견본이 준비되어 있을 것입니다.**

어휘 announce 발표하다 book cover 책 표지 judging panel 심사 위원단 be impressed with ~에 감명받다 paid leave 유급 휴가 earn (그럴 만한 자격이 되어서 무엇을) 얻다[받다] hit stores 구매할 수 있게 서점에 유통되다 (hit the market/shops/shelves/streets 등으로도 쓰인다)

74. 화자는 어떤 종류의 상을 발표하는가?

(A) 공로상
(B) 최우수 그래픽 디자인
(C) 올해의 직원
(D) 우수 영업 사원

75. 수상자에게 무엇이 주어질 것인가?

(A) 사무실 파티
(B) 현금 보너스
(C) 추가 휴일
(D) 트로피

패러프레이징 one additional day of paid leave → an extra day off

76. 화자에 따르면, 청자들은 다음주에 무엇을 볼 수 있는가?

(A) 새로운 웹 사이트
(B) 완성된 책
(C) 단체 사진
(D) 후보 추천 양식

패러프레이징 the finished book → a completed book

영녀

Questions 77-79 refer to the following information.

I hope you are all enjoying the training so far. We're excited about having you work at our shop. As you know, one of your main responsibilities will be [77]helping customers choose the power tools they need. So, you'll sometimes be asked to give demonstrations of our products. Now that you've all watched the safety video, [78]I'll be giving you a test to prove your knowledge. [79]Some of you indicated that you were worried about failing the test. So far, no one has done so, and I've been doing this training for more than five years.

여러분 모두가 지금까지의 교육 과정을 즐기셨기를 바랍니다. 저희는 여러분이 우리 상점에서 일할 수 있게 되어 기쁩니다. 아시다시피, 여러분의 책무들 중 하나는 [77]**고객들이 전동 공구를 고를 수 있게 도와주는 것입니다.** 그러므로, 여러분은 종종 우리의 제품들에 대한 시연 요청을 받게 될 것입니다. 이제 여러분 모두 안전 영상을 시청하였으니, 여러분의 이해도를 입증할 [78]**시험을 실시할 것입니다.** [79]**여러분 중 몇 분은 이 시험에 통과하지 못할까 봐 우려하였습니다.** 지금까지 그런 사람은 아무도 없었습니다. 그리고 저는 이 교육을 5년 넘게 해 왔습니다.

어휘 so far 지금껏 main responsibility 주요 책임/책무 be asked to do ~하도록 요청받다 give a demonstration 시연하다 now that 이제 ~이므로 prove 입증하다 indicate (간접적으로) 내비치다[시사하다] fail a test 시험에서 떨어지다

77. 화자의 회사는 무엇을 파는가?

(A) 사무용 소프트웨어
(B) 휴대 전화
(C) 조명 기구
(D) 전동 공구

78. 청자들은 다음에 무엇을 할 것인가?

(A) 현장 견학하기
(B) 동영상 시청하기
(C) 시험 보기
(D) 계약서 서명하기

79. 화자는 왜 "지금까지 그런 사람은 아무도 없었습니다"라고 말하는가?

(A) 일을 배정하기 위해
(B) 청자들을 안심시키기 위해

TEST 04

(C) 불평을 하기 위해
(D) 일정을 조정하기 위해

미녀

Questions 80-82 refer to the following excerpt from a meeting.

The expenses for transporting our goods have been increasing steadily. [80]Now we're looking for ways to reduce the cost of operating our fleet of trucks. A recent report showed that routine inspections of a truck's engine and tires can save a lot of money in the long run. Therefore, [81]we want to expand our team of mechanics next month so they can handle more frequent inspections. [82]If you would like to recommend someone for one of these roles, please talk to Ricky in the human resources department by Friday.

우리의 제품들을 수송하기 위한 비용이 꾸준히 증가하고 있습니다. **[80]이제 우리는 트럭들의 운용비를 낮추기 위한 방안을 모색하고 있습니다.** 최근의 보고를 보면 트럭 엔진과 타이어에 대한 규칙적인 점검이 장기적으로 많은 돈을 절약할 수 있다는 것을 알 수 있습니다. 그래서 정비공들이 더욱 자주 점검할 수 있도록 **[81]다음달에 정비팀을 확대하고 싶습니다.** **[82]만약 여러분이 이 역할에 누군가를 추천하고 싶다면, 금요일까지 인사과의 리키에게 말해 주시기 바랍니다.**

어휘 expense 비용 transport 수송하다 look for 찾다 operate 운용하다, 운영하다 fleet (한 기관이 소유한 전체 비행기·버스·택시 등의) 무리

80. 회의의 주제는 무엇인가?

(A) 상품 포장 개선
(B) 새로운 규정 준수
(C) 수송 비용 감소
(D) 교육 과정 간소화

81. 회사는 다음달에 무엇을 할 것인가?

(A) 수리공을 더 채용하는 것
(B) 다른 회사와 제휴하는 것
(C) 기업 대출을 신청하는 것
(D) 포장 형태를 바꾸는 것

패러프레이징 expand our team of mechanics → hire more mechanics

82. 청자들은 추천하기 위해 무엇을 해야 하는가?

(A) 나중에 화자에게 전화하는 것
(B) 온라인 양식을 작성하는 것
(C) 인사과 직원에게 연락하는 것
(D) 추천서 제출하기

패러프레이징 talk to Ricky in the human resources department → contact an HR employee

영녀

Questions 83-85 refer to the following speech.

Welcome to the fifth annual [83]Nursing Association Convention. There are a wide variety of lectures and workshops for you this year. Although this event is open to members and non-members alike, we encourage everyone to register because there are benefits throughout the year. You can sign up at the registration desk. [84]If you would like to learn more about the program, volunteers will be there until 3 P.M. And don't forget that your ticket gives you entry to [85]the banquet in the main hall this evening. I'm really looking forward to that.

다섯 번째를 맞이하는 연례 **[83]간호 협회** 컨벤션에 오신 것을 환영합니다. 금년엔 여러 다양한 강의와 워크숍이 준비되어 있습니다. 이 행사는 회원과 비회원, 모두에게 열려 있지만, 회원에게는 연중 많은 혜택이 부여되기에 여러분 모두 회원에 가입하실 것을 권유드립니다. 회원 가입은 등록 창구에서 하실 수 있습니다. **[84]만약 프로그램에 대해 더 알고 싶으시다면, 자원 봉사자들이 오후 3시까지 거기에 있을 겁니다.** 그리고 소지하신 표로 오늘 밤 대강당에서 열리는 **[85]만찬**에 입장하실 수 있다는 것을 잊지 마세요. 저는 그것을 정말 고대하고 있습니다.

어휘 association 협회 alike 똑같이 encourage 고무/장려/독려하다 throughout the year 일년 내내 sign up 등록하다 entry 입장/출입(할 수 있는 권리·기회) banquet 연회

83. 청자들은 누구일 것 같은가?

(A) 교사들
(B) 기자들
(C) 간호사들
(D) 변호사들

84. 화자는 "자원 봉사자들이 오후 3시까지 거기에 있을 겁니다"라고 말할 때 무엇을 의미하는가?

(A) 예기치 못한 일정 변경이 있었다.
(B) 사람들 몇 명이 질문에 답할 수 있을 것이다.
(C) 참가자들은 오후에 선물을 수령할 수 있다.
(D) 새로운 회원들에게 둘러볼 기회가 주어질 것이다.

85. 화자는 무엇을 고대한다 말하는가?

(A) 발표를 보는 것
(B) 식사를 즐기는 것
(C) 표를 업그레이드 하는 것
(D) 수상자를 발표하는 것

호남

Questions 86-88 refer to the following broadcast.

You're listening to [86] *Medicine Today*, the show that keeps you informed on the top topics in the medical field. Today we're welcoming Asano Tanaka to the studio. For the past six years, she's been studying how stress affects the body. [87] The data from this work is used by professionals and policymakers to try to get people to make healthy choices in their lives. Ms. Tanaka recently wrote a book called *In Control*, which gives you practical tips on this matter. [88] For today only, you can get a copy of this book at no charge by visiting our Web site at www.radiokttr.com.

여러분은 의료계에서 가장 떠오르는 주제들을 알려드리는 [86]〈의학 오늘〉을 청취하고 계십니다. 오늘은 아사노 다나카 씨를 스튜디오에 모십니다. 지난 6년 동안, **그녀는 스트레스가 어떻게 인체에 영향을 끼치는지에 관해 연구해 오셨습니다.** [87]**이 연구의 자료는 사람들이 인생에서 건강한 선택을 하는 것을 돕기 위해 전문가들과 정책 담당자들에 의해 사용되고 있습니다.** 다나카 씨는 최근에 「In Control」이라는 책을 쓰셨는데, 이는 이 주제에 관한 현실적인 팁들을 줍니다. [88]**오늘에 한해서, 저희 웹 사이트 www.radiokttr.com에 방문하시면, 여러분은 무료로 이 책을 받으실 수 있습니다.**

어휘 keep 사람 informed on ~에 대해 지속적으로 정보를 알려주다 affect 영향을 미치다 policymaker 정책 입안자 at no charge 아무 요금 없이, 무료로

86. 아사노 다나카는 누구인가?

(A) 대학 교수
(B) 의학 연구원
(C) 사업주
(D) 잡지 편집자

87. 다나카 씨의 작업은 무엇에 사용될 것 같은가?

(A) 건강한 생활 방식 격려
(B) 업계 동향 평가
(C) 새로운 제품 개발
(D) 환경 보호

패러프레이징 try to get people to make healthy choices → encourage healthy lifestyles

88. 화자에 따르면, 웹 사이트에서 오늘 무엇을 할 수 있는가?

(A) 행사에 등록하기
(B) 다나카 씨에게 질문하기
(C) 자금 제공 지원하기
(D) 무료 도서 신청하기

패러프레이징 get a copy of this book at no charge → request a free book

영녀

Questions 89-91 refer to the following excerpt from a meeting.

Let's get this management meeting started. [89] While customers love our high-quality clothes, that is not enough to keep our sales strong. As I'm sure you're aware, [90] a lot of similar businesses have opened in the area. That makes it more difficult for us to stand out. So, we've decided to invest some money in TV advertising. [91] A crew will visit our store next week to shoot a commercial that will be aired on local channels. Please cooperate with them if they need assistance with anything. Thanks.

이번 경영 회의를 시작하겠습니다. [89]**고객들은 우리의 고품질 의류를 애호하지만,** 이는 우리의 판매를 굳건히 유지하는 데 부족합니다. 여러분도 아시다시피, [90]**비슷한 업체들이 지역에 많이 들어섰습니다.** 이는 우리가 돋보이는 것을 더 어렵게 만듭니다. 그래서, 우리는 텔레비전 광고에 돈을 좀 투자하기로 하였습니다. [91]**다음주에 촬영팀이 우리 상점에 와서 지역 채널에서 방영될 광고를 촬영할 예정입니다.** 그들이 도움을 필요로 한다면 협조해 주시기를 부탁드립니다. 감사합니다.

어휘 get ~ started ~을 시작하다 high-quality 고품질의 stand out 눈에 띄다, 빼어나다 invest ~ in ~을 ~에 투자하다 shoot a commercial 광고를 찍다 air 방영하다 cooperate with ~와 협조하다

89. 화자들은 어디서 일할 것 같은가?

(A) 영화관에서
(B) 의류 가게에서
(C) 가구 제조업체에서
(D) 광고 대행사에서

90. 화자는 어떠한 문제를 언급하는가?

(A) 경쟁이 심해졌다.
(B) 업체가 형편없는 평가를 받았다.
(C) 임대차 계약이 곧 만료된다.
(D) 몇몇 직원들이 퇴사했다.

91. 다음주에 어떤 일이 일어날 것인가?

(A) 투자자들이 업체를 방문할 것이다.
(B) 화자가 교육을 진행할 것이다.
(C) 신제품이 출시될 것이다.
(D) 광고가 촬영될 것이다.

패러프레이징 shoot a commercial → an advertisement will be filmed

미남

Questions 92-94 refer to the following talk.

Good morning, everyone, and [92] thanks for joining me for this press conference. I wanted to give an update on the repairs to Collins Road. This is an extensive project, as new water pipes need to be placed underground and a new road surface will be constructed. [93]I know that many residents have complained about noisy equipment working overnight. I'm very sorry for any inconvenience this has caused. [94]Unfortunately, Collins Road is a major roadway for commuters. It has to be open during the day. The good news is that the work is on schedule and should be completed in less than a week. In the meantime, please continue sharing your feedback, as it is very helpful to our team.

좋은 아침입니다, 여러분, 그리고 [92]**이번 기자회견에 함께해 주셔서 감사드립니다.** 콜린스 도로 수리에 관한 최신 정보를 알려 드리고 싶었습니다. 새로운 배수관이 지하에 매장되고 노면 공사가 새로 이뤄질 것이므로 이는 광범위한 프로젝트가 될 것입니다. [93]**많은 주민들께서 밤새 작업하는 시끄러운 장비들 때문에 불만을 표하신 걸로 알고 있습니다.** 이로 인해 불편을 끼쳐드려 매우 죄송합니다. [94]**불행하게도, 콜린스 도로는 통근자들의 주요 차도입니다.** 낮에는 열려 있어야 합니다. 좋은 소식은, 작업이 일정대로 진행되고 있고 일주일 안에 완료될 예정이란 것입니다. 그동안에, 의견을 계속해서 나눠 주십시오. 이는 저희 팀에 아주 유용하기 때문입니다.

어휘 press conference 기자 회견 extensive 광범위한 construct 건설하다 inconvenience 불편 commuter 통근자 during the day 낮 동안 on schedule 예정대로 (= on time) *ahead of/behind schedule 예정보다 일찍/늦게 *according to schedule = as planned 계획한 대로

92. 청자들은 어떤 행사에 참석하고 있는가?

(A) 지역 모금 행사
(B) 시상식
(C) 기자회견
(D) 극장 공연

93. 화자는 무엇에 대해 사과하는가?

(A) 자리가 부족한 것
(B) 장소를 변경한 것
(C) 예기치 않게 지연된 것
(D) 소음 공해를 일으킨 것

94. 화자는 "낮에는 열려 있어야 합니다"라고 말할 때 무엇을 암시하는가?

(A) 그녀는 문제를 해결할 수 없다.
(B) 그녀는 변화를 요구했다.
(C) 일정에 오류가 있었다.
(D) 더 많은 일꾼들이 필요하다.

호남

Questions 95-97 refer to the following telephone message and seating arrangement.

Hi, I'm Peter from Casper Incorporated. [95]I'm calling in reference to our company's annual fund-raising dinner scheduled for this Saturday at 7 P.M. We need to set up a podium for our event host. I reviewed the venue's layout, and [96]I think it's probably best to set it up next to the table closest to the auction items and near a window. [97]Also, I had our company's branded coffee mugs sent to the hotel. I made sure there are enough for us to hand out to each guest after the event. Thank you.

안녕하세요, 캐스퍼 주식회사의 피터입니다. [95]**이번 주 토요일 오후 7시에 열리는 저희 회사의 연례 모금 행사에 관하여 연락드립니다.** 저희의 행사 진행자를 위해 강단을 설치해야 합니다. 제가 행사 장소의 배치도를 검토해 보았는데, [96]**제 생각엔 강단을 경매 물품들과 가장 가까운 곳에 있는 탁자 옆 창가에 설치하는 것이 최선일 것 같습니다.** [97]**그리고, 저희 회사의 로고가 새겨진 머그 컵들을 호텔에 보냈습니다.** 행사가 끝난 후에 각 손님에게 나눠드릴 만큼 충분한 양인 것을 확인하였습니다. 감사합니다.

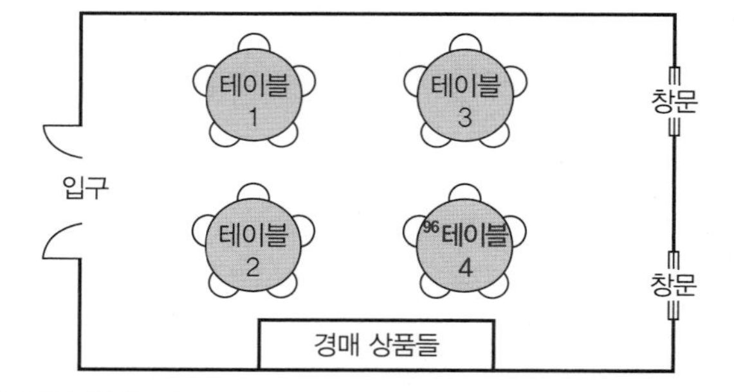

어휘 in reference to ~에 관련하여 annual 연례의 fund-raising 모금 활동(의), 자금 조달(의), 모금(의) scheduled for ~ (언제로) 예정된 podium (연설자 · 지휘자 등이 올라서는) 단 host (행사의) 주최국[측] venue (행사를 위한) 장소 our company's branded 우리 회사의 브랜드가 새겨진 hand out 나눠주다

95. 금주 토요일에 무엇이 일어날 것인가?

(A) 생일 파티
(B) 모금 행사
(C) 예비 교육 행사
(D) 은퇴 기념 파티

96. 시각 자료를 보시오. 화자는 어디에 강단이 설치되길 원하는가?

(A) 테이블 1 옆에
(B) 테이블 2 옆에
(C) 테이블 3 옆에
(D) 테이블 4 옆에

97. 화자는 호텔에 무엇을 보냈는가?

(A) 컵
(B) 장식
(C) 팸플릿
(D) 앞치마

패러프레이징 coffee mugs → some cups

미녀

Questions 98-100 refer to the following excerpt from a meeting and chart.

Today I'd like to talk about our expansion into printing 3D models for board game companies. [98]Last month, we hired a consultant in the field to get advice on finding new clients. As we work with a wider variety of companies, it's still important that we meet our deadlines. So, I've run an analysis on all the machines. This chart here shows that most of our machines are exceeding our estimated output of thirty models per 24-hour period. [99]However, this one here is doing just twenty-eight, so our technician, Joseph, is going to examine it to identify the problem. [100]I'd like us to start producing even more items per hour, so I'm also thinking about purchasing another machine.

오늘 저는 3D 모형 프린트 사업을 보드 게임 회사를 대상으로 확대하는 것에 대해 얘기하고 싶습니다. [98]**지난달, 저희는 새로운 고객 유치에 대한 자문을 얻기 위해 업계 전문가를 고용하였습니다.** 우리는 더 다양한 회사들과 일하게 될 것이고, 마감 일자를 지키는 것은 여전히 중요합니다. 그래서, 저는 모든 기계를 분석해 보았습니다. 여기 표는 대부분의 기계가 24시간 동안의 추정 생산량인 30개를 넘어서고 있다는 것을 보여줍니다. [99]**하지만, 여기 이것은 28개 생산에 그치고 있기에, 우리의 기술자인 조셉이 문제를 찾기 위해 이를 조사할 것입니다.** [100]**저는 우리가 시간당 더 많은 제품을 생산하기를 원하고,** 그래서 또한 기계의 추가 구매를 고려하고 있습니다.

3D 프린트 모형	
기계 번호	24시간당 생산량
1	33
2	32
[99]3	28
4	35

어휘 expansion 확장 (expand 확장하다) expert 전문가 consultant 상담가, 자문 위원, 컨설턴트 (consult ~에게 상의하다, ~와 상담하다) a wider variety of 더 다양한 meet the deadline 마감일을 지키다 run/do/carry out/perform/conduct/make an analysis 분석하다 exceed 초과하다 estimated output 추정[예상] 생산량 identify the problem 문제를 파악하다

98. 화자에 의하면, 회사는 지난달에 무엇을 하였는가?

(A) 다른 공급 업체로 전환하였다.
(B) 자문가를 고용하였다.
(C) 새로운 장비를 구매하였다.
(D) 소프트웨어를 업데이트하였다.

99. 시각 자료를 보시오. 조셉은 어떤 기계를 점검할 것인가?

(A) 기계 1
(B) 기계 2
(C) 기계 3
(D) 기계 4

100. 화자는 무엇 하기를 원한다고 말하는가?

(A) 생산력을 증대하는 것
(B) 다른 소재로 실험해 보는 것
(C) 제조 업체에 불만을 표하는 것
(D) 보드 게임 컨벤션에 참석하는 것

패러프레이징 start producing even more items per hour → increase the production capacity

PART 5

101. 동사 자리+수 일치

항공기 탑승에 추가로 시간이 필요하신 분들을 위해 지금 탑승 수속을 시작하겠습니다.

해설 빈칸 앞에 anyone을 선행사로 하는 주격 관계대명사가 있으므로 빈칸은 관계사절의 동사 자리이다. 따라서 (A) need와 (C) needs가 정답 후보인데, anyone은 단수 취급하므로 단수 동사인 (C)가 정답이다.

어휘 board 탑승하다 procedure 절차 additional 추가의 get on a plane 비행기를 타다

102. 전치사 어휘 with

Banyan의 선글라스는 휴대용 보호 케이스와 함께 제공된다.
(A) ~ 전에 (B) ~을 따라 (C) ~에 (D) ~와 함께

해설 빈칸 앞의 comes와 함께 쓰여 선글라스가 보호 케이스와 함께 제공된다는 내용이 되는 게 자연스러우므로 (D) with가 정답이다.

어휘 protective 보호용의

103. 형용사 어휘 routine

북쪽으로 향하는 13번 고속도로의 차선은 정기 유지 보수로 인해 내일 폐쇄될 것이다.
(A) 책임에 태만한 (B) 정기적인 (C) 변함없는 (D) 법적인

어휘 northbound 북쪽으로 가는 lane 차선 maintenance 유지, 보수

104. 소유한정사

기술 문제에 대한 지원을 받으려면 1-800-555-9733으로 그 회사의 지원팀에 전화하실 수 있습니다.

해설 빈칸 앞에 동사 call이 있고 뒤에는 명사 support team이 이어지므로 빈칸은 명사를 수식하는 자리이다. 따라서 소유한정사인 (B) their가 정답이다.

어휘 assistance 도움 technical 기술의 issue 문제

105. 부사 자리

그 댄스 교습소는 지역 언론 매체에 공격적으로 광고함으로써 성공을 거두었다.

해설 빈칸 앞에 전치사가 있고 뒤에는 동명사가 이어지므로 빈칸은 동명사를 수식하는 부사 자리이다. 따라서 (D) aggressively가 정답이다.

어휘 aggressively 공격적으로

106. 수동태

철물점의 35주년 기념행사는 고객들을 위한 파티와 함께 지난달에 거행되었다.

해설 빈칸 뒤에 목적어가 없고 주어 The hardware store's 35th anniversary는 행위를 받는 대상이므로 빈칸에는 〈be+과거분사〉 형태의 수동태가 적절하다. 따라서 (C) was celebrated가 정답이다.

어휘 hardware store 철물점 anniversary 기념일 celebrate 축하하다, 기념하다

107. 명사 어휘 requirement

부기 직무에 필요한 주요 자격 요건은 회계 소프트웨어를 가지고 일할 수 있는 능력이다.

(A) 수익자, 수취인 (B) 충고 (C) 조수, 비서 (D) 요건, 필요 조건

어휘 main 주된, 주요한 bookkeeping 부기, 회계 장부 정리 accounting 회계

108. 명사 자리+어휘

입주자들은 토요일 오후 4시에 건물 안전 훈련에 참여하여 대피 절차를 익힐 것이다.

해설 빈칸 뒤에 동사가 있으므로 빈칸은 주어 자리이다. 문맥상 건물 안전 훈련에 참여하는 주체는 사람이어야 하므로 '입주자'를 뜻하는 (A) Occupants가 정답이다.

어휘 occupant 입주자, 점유자 participate in ~에 참여하다 drill 훈련 evacuation 대피 procedure 절차 occupancy 사용, 점유

109. 전치사 어휘 under

그 식당에 새 경영진이 들어왔기 때문에 인테리어에 변화를 꾀할 것이다.

(A) ~에 관해 (B) ~을 향해 (C) ~의 아래에 (D) ~을 가로질러

해설 빈칸 뒤의 new management와 함께 쓰여 새로운 경영진의 운영하에 인테리어 변화를 줄 거라는 내용이 되는 게 자연스러우므로 (C) under가 정답이다.

어휘 management 경영(진)

110. 한정사 all

Avery Bay Tour의 모든 참가자는 보트에 탑승하는 동안 구명조끼를 착용해야 한다.

해설 빈칸 뒤에 복수 명사가 있으므로 (C) All이 정답이다. 나머지 선택지들은 단수 명사를 수식하기 때문에 답이 될 수 없다. 또한 (B) Entire는 형용사이므로 명사를 수식할 때 반드시 앞에 관사나 소유한정사가 있어야 한다.

어휘 life vest 구명조끼 while ~하는 동안 on board 탑승한, 승선한

111. 명사 어휘 satisfaction

정기적으로 피드백을 수집하는 것은 Wesley Shoes가 고객 만족도를 향상시키는 데 도움이 된다.

(A) 플랫폼, 기반 (B) 만족 (C) 생산 (D) 결과

어휘 regularly 주기적으로, 정기적으로 collect 수집하다, 모으다 feedback 의견, 피드백 improve 향상시키다

112. 관계대명사 [주격]

공휴일에 근무하기로 되어 있는 버스 기사들은 더 높은 시급을 받게 될 것이다.

해설 The bus drivers가 주어이고 will receive가 동사이므로 '------- ~ holiday'는 The bus drivers를 수식하는 관계사절이다. 또한 수식 대상이 사람이고 빈칸 뒤에 동사가 바로 이어지는 것으로 보아 빈칸은 주격 관계대명사 자리이므로 (A) who가 정답이다.

어휘 be scheduled to do ~하기로 예정되어 있다 national holiday 공휴일, 국경일 wage 임금, 급여

113. 형용사 어휘 available

호텔 레스토랑으로부터 하루 24시간 룸서비스를 이용할 수 있다.

(A) 그 후의 (B) 이용 가능한 (C) 긴급한 (D) 실용적인

114. 명사 자리+수 일치

다른 요인들 중에서도 그 부동산의 인근 지역이 그곳의 시장 가치에 크게 영향을 미칠 수 있다.

해설 빈칸 앞에 전치사 Among이 있으므로 빈칸은 명사 자리이다. (A) factor와 (B) factors가 정답 후보인데, 한정사 other 뒤에는 가산명사 복수형이나 불가산명사가 이어지므로 (B)가 정답이다.

어휘 factor 요인, 원인 property 부동산 neighborhood 인근, 근처 affect 영향을 미치다 value 가치

115. 동명사 자리

새 관리자를 고용하기 위한 첫 번째 단계는 온라인에 직무 기술서를 게시하는 것이다.

해설 빈칸 앞에 is가 있고 뒤에는 명사 a job description이 있으므로 빈칸에는 be동사의 보어 역할을 하는 동시에 a job description을 목적어로 취할 수 있는 말이 들어가야 한다. 따라서 동명사인 (C) posting이 정답이다.

어휘 hire 고용하다 job description 직무 기술서 online 온라인에

116. 동사 어휘 make

Reyna 전기 자동차는 지난봄에 Vehicle Trade Show가 끝난 후 처음으로 시장에 모습을 드러냈다.

(A) ~처럼 보이다 (B) 끌어내다 (C) 느끼다 (D) 만들다

어휘 electric 전기의 make one's appearance 모습을 드러내다 vehicle 차량 trade show 무역 박람회

117. 등위 접속사

업주들은 Office-Tech의 최신 급여 및 세금 소프트웨어의 30일 무료 체험판을 받을 수 있다.

해설 빈칸을 기준으로 명사 payroll과 tax가 대등하게 연결되어 있으므로 '그리고'를 뜻하는 (D) and가 정답이다.

어휘 business owner 업주 free 무료의 trial 시용, 시험 payroll 임금 대장 tax 세금

118. 부사 자리

제품 안내 책자의 최종 디자인은 고객이 요청한 것과는 눈에 띄게 달랐다.

해설 빈칸은 형용사 different를 수식하는 자리이므로 선택지 중 부사인 (A) noticeably가 정답이다.

어휘 brochure 브로슈어, 안내 책자 noticeably 눈에 띄게 client 고객

119. 부사 어휘 enough

Rigsby Resort의 골프 카트에 달린 모터는 최대 6인과 그들의 장비를 운반할 수 있을 정도로 충분히 튼튼하다.

(A) 꽤, 상당히 (B) 충분히 (C) 아직, 여전히 (D) 매우, 많이

해설 선택지 중 (A) quite와 (B) enough가 문맥에 가장 어울리는데 형용사를 뒤에서 수식해야 하므로 (B)가 정답이다.

어휘 motor 모터, 전동기 up to ~까지 equipment 장비

120. 형용사 자리

항공사 체크인 직원들 간의 의사소통이 원활하지 않으면 여행객들에게 실망스러운 경험을 안길 수 있다.

해설 빈칸 앞에 동사 cause가 있고 뒤에는 명사 experiences가 있으므로 빈칸은 명사를 수식하는 형용사 자리이다. (A) frustrated와 (D) frustrating이 정답 후보인데, 수식 대상인 experiences는 실망스러운 감정을 느끼는 대상이 아니라 실망감을 주는 주체이므로 -ing 형용사인 (D)가 정답이다.

어휘 communication 의사소통 check-in (공항의) 탑승 수속 frustrating 불만스러운, 좌절감을 주는

121. 소유한정사

쇼핑객들은 판매 담당자와 이야기함으로써 우리의 보디로션에 대해 더 많은 것을 알아낼 수 있다.

해설 빈칸 앞에 전치사 about이 있고 뒤에는 명사 body lotions가 이어지므로 빈칸은 명사를 수식하는 자리이다. 따라서 소유한정사인 (B) our가 정답이다. (A) each는 뒤에 단수 명사가 이어져야 하므로 오답이다.

어휘 sales representative 판매 담당자

122. 형용사 자리

Sea Shanty 음악단은 여름 내내 다양한 장소에서 대중 공연을 한다.

해설 빈칸 앞에 동사 gives가 있고 뒤에는 명사 performances가 이어지므로 빈칸은 명사를 수식하는 형용사 자리이다. 따라서 (D) public이 정답이다.

어휘 give a performance 공연하다 throughout ~ 내내 site 위치, 장소

123. 부사 어휘 reasonably

BC Transportation은 Arbor Hotel에서 공항까지 왕복 교통편을 제공하는데, 그것은 18달러의 합리적인 가격으로 책정되어 있다.

(A) 열성적으로 (B) 부분적으로 (C) 합리적으로 (D) 즉시, 즉각

어휘 offer 제공하다 shuttle 왕복 교통편 price 값을 매기다

124. 부사+한정사

현재 집을 구하는 세입자들이 너무 많기 때문에 월세 가격이 상당히 올랐다.

해설 빈칸은 복수 명사 renters를 수식하는 자리이다. 따라서 〈부사+한정사〉로 구성된 (B) so many가 정답이다.

어휘 renter 임차인 housing 주택 at the moment 바로 지금 rate 요금 significantly 상당히, 크게

125. 최상급

Blaze Marketing에는 귀하의 사업을 홍보하기 위한 가장 성공적인 캠페인을 만들 수 있는 전문가들이 있습니다.

해설 빈칸 앞에 정관사 the가 있고 뒤에는 명사 campaign이 있으므로 빈칸은 명사를 수식하는 형용사 자리이다. 따라서 (D) most successful이 정답이다.

어휘 expert 전문가 promote 홍보하다

126. 동사 어휘 appeal

Vincent Art Museum의 이사회는 젊은 방문객들의 관심을 끌 만한 활동들을 찾고 있다.

(A) 달라지다 (B) 관심을 끌다 (C) (결과로) 발생하다, 생기다 (D) 감독하다

어휘 board of directors 이사회 activity 활동

127. 명사 자리+어휘

그 식당이 냉장 시설들을 개선할 필요가 있다는 보건부의 평가는 공정한 것으로 여겨졌다.

해설 빈칸 뒤에 본동사 was considered가 있으므로 'that ~ facilities'는 'The Health Department -------'을 수식하는 동격의 접속사절임을 알 수 있다. 따라서 빈칸에는 The Health Department와 결합하여 주어 역할을 할 수 있는 명사가 들어가야 하므로 (C) assessment와 (D) assessor가 정답 후보인데, 문맥상 보건부의 평가가 공정한 것으로 여겨졌다는 내용이 되는 게 자연스러우므로 '평가'를 뜻하는 (C)가 정답이다.

어휘 upgrade 업그레이드하다, 상향 조정하다 refrigeration facility 냉장 시설 consider 여기다, 간주하다 fair 공정한, 공평한 assessor 감정인

128. 전치사 자리

지난주의 거센 폭풍우로 인한 피해 때문에 Rainbow Coffee Shop은 앞으로 2주간 문을 닫을 예정입니다.

해설 빈칸 뒤에 〈명사(damage)+전치사구(from ~ storm)〉가 있고, 콤마로 절이 이어져 있으므로 빈칸은 전치사 자리이다. 따라서 (B) Due to가 정답이다.

어휘 damage 피해 severe 심한 storm 폭풍우

129. 명사 자리

Fullerton Insurance는 열심히 일한 직원들에게 승진과 연간 보너스로 보상한다.

해설 빈칸 앞에 전치사 with가 있고 뒤에는 등위 접속사 and로 이어진 명사 annual bonuses가 있으므로 빈칸은 명사 자리이다. 따라서 (A) promotions가 정답이다.

어휘 reward 보상하다 hard-working 열심히 일하는 annual 연간의, 연례의

130. 명사 어휘 agent

프로 스포츠 팀의 선수들을 모집하는 에이전트들은 전국에서 재능 있는 사람들을 찾는다.
(A) (스포츠) 에이전트 (B) 예술가 (C) 판매상 (D) 아나운서

어휘 recruit 모집하다 athlete 운동선수 talented 재능 있는 individual 사람, 개인

PART 6

131-134 공지

위원회 회의 공지

케너윅 퍼레이드 기획 위원회는 4월 3일 오후 7시 30분에 케너윅 주민 센터에서 회의를 개최할 예정입니다. 모든 구성원은 [131]**참석해** 주시기 바랍니다. 지역 업체들의 퍼레이드용 장식 차량에 맞춰 우리는 올해의 테마[132]**인** "By the Seaside"를 바탕으로 우리만의 장식 차량을 디자인할 것입니다. 회의에서는 Rhonda Delgado가 작년 행사에서 찍은 사진 몇 장을 보여 줄 것입니다. [133]**또한** 그녀는 장식 차량을 만드는 데 사용되는 가장 일반적인 재료에 대해서 이야기할 것입니다.

회의가 끝나고 나서 회원 여러분은 다음 회의 날짜인 4월 17일 전에 Rhonda에게 이메일로 아이디어를 공유해 주세요. [134]**그날 우리는 가장 좋은 아이디어를 투표로 정할 것입니다.**

어휘 committee 위원회 planning 기획 be expected to do 마땅히 ~을 해야만 하다; ~할 것으로 예상되다 accompany 동반하다, 동행하다 float (퍼레이드의) 장식 차량 theme 테마, 주제 common 일반적인, 흔한 material 재료, 자재

131. 동사 어휘 attend

(A) 확보하다 (B) 유지하다 (C) 참석하다 (D) 기부하다

132. 관계대명사 [주격]

해설 빈칸 앞에 완전한 절이 있고 뒤에는 따옴표로 묶여 명사 역할을 하는 By the Seaside가 있으므로 빈칸에는 접속사 역할을 하는 동시에 빈칸이 포함된 절에서 주어와 동사 역할을 할 수 있는 말이 들어가야 한다. 따라서 선택지 중 주격 관계대명사와 be동사가 결합된 (D) which is가 정답이다. (C) what must be는 빈칸 앞에 선행사 this year's theme이 있기 때문에 답이 될 수 없다.

133. 접속부사 어휘 in addition

(A) 그럼에도 불구하고 (B) 그 대신에 (C) 또한 (D) 만약 ~라면

해설 빈칸 뒤에 주어와 동사를 갖춘 완전한 절이 하나만 있는 것으로 보아 빈칸은 접속부사 자리이므로 접속사인 (D) Provided that은 오답이다.

134. 알맞은 문장 고르기

(A) 참가자의 질문에 신속하게 답변할 것입니다.
(B) 신입 회원들은 이 서류를 작성해야 합니다.
(C) 그날 우리는 가장 좋은 아이디어를 투표로 정할 것입니다.
(D) 행사는 지역 주민들과 관광객 모두에게 인기가 있습니다.

해설 빈칸 앞에서 4월 17일 전에 이메일로 아이디어를 공유하라고 했으므로 빈칸에는 그날 무엇을 할 것인지 설명하는 내용이 이어지는 게 자연스럽다. 따라서 (C)가 정답이다.

135-138 이메일

수신: 모든 판매원
발신: Elaine Spangler
날짜: 3월 10일
제목: 제품

우리 고객들에게 최상의 서비스를 제공하기 위해서는 모든 직원이 제품에 대한 충분한 지식을 갖추는 것이 가장 중요합니다. [135]**그러한 이유로** 우리는 직원들이 우리 상품에 대한 세부 정보를 복습하는 걸 도울 재미있는 방법을 고안했습니다. 이번 주 후반에 여러분 모두는 여러분이 외워야 할 모든 정보가 들어 있는 카탈로그를 [136]**지급받게 될 것입니다.**

그러고 나서 3월 22일에 우리는 퀴즈의 밤을 진행할 수 있는 [137]**장소를** 예약할 것입니다. 직원들은 4명까지 팀을 이루어 경쟁할 수 있습니다. 여러분은 우리 제품에 대한 질문에 정확하게 답을 하면 점수를 얻게 됩니다. 우리는 가장 높은 점수를 얻는 팀들을 위해 상품을 준비했습니다. 모두가 즐거운 시간을 보내길 바랍니다. [138]**행사가 성공적이라면 우리는 앞으로도 비슷한 행사를 할 계획입니다.**

Elaine Spangler
Nature Health Foods

어휘 in order to do ~하기 위하여 serve (서비스 등을) 제공하다 essential 필수적인, 매우 중요한 sufficient 충분한 review 복습하다, 검토하다 details 세부 사항 merchandise 상품, 물품 contain 포함하다, 들어 있다 memorize 외우다 reserve 예약하다 venue 장소 compete 경쟁하다 up to ~까지 earn 얻다, 벌다 correctly 정확히

135. 접속부사 어휘 for that reason

(A) 불행히도 (B) 그러한 이유로 (C) 그렇기는 하지만 (D) 예를 들어

136. 수동태+미래 시제

해설 빈칸 뒤에 목적어가 없으므로 빈칸에는 수동태가 들어가야 한다. (B) was provided와 (C) will be provided가 정답 후보인데, 빈칸 앞에 미래를 나타내는 표현인 Later this week가 있으므로 미래 시제인 (C)가 정답이다.

137. 관계부사 where

해설 빈칸 앞뒤에 완전한 절이 있으므로 빈칸에는 부사와 접속사 역할을 겸하는 관계부사가 들어가야 한다. 선행사가 장소를 나타내는 a venue이므로 (C) where가 정답이다.

138. 알맞은 문장 고르기

(A) 카탈로그는 여러분의 집으로 가져갈 수 있습니다.
(B) 우리는 내일 수상자들을 발표할 계획입니다.
(C) 고객들은 개선 사항을 바로 알아차렸습니다.
(D) 행사가 성공적이라면 우리는 앞으로도 비슷한 행사를 할 계획입니다.

해설 빈칸 앞에서 퀴즈의 밤에 대해 설명하고 있으므로 빈칸에도 그에 관한 내용이 이어지는 게 자연스럽다. 따라서 퀴즈의 밤이 좋은 성과를 거둘 경우 앞으로도 비슷한 행사를 하겠다고 한 (D)가 정답이다.

어휘 notice 알아차리다 similar 비슷한

139-142 이메일

> 수신: Stephen Gilden
> 발신: Cory Dixon
> 날짜: 11월 3일
> 제목: 인터넷 서비스
>
> Mr. Gilden께,
>
> 요청하신 대로 11월 12일에 귀하의 사무실에 저희 기사 중 한 명이 초고속 인터넷 회선을 [139]**설치할** 수 있다는 것을 확인해 드리고자 합니다. 기사는 귀하의 필요와 사무실 구조에 따라 라우터를 설치하기에 가장 좋은 위치를 [140]**찾아볼 것입니다.** 오전 9시 30분에 방문할 예정이며, 늦어도 오전 11시 30분에는 작업이 완료될 것으로 예상됩니다. [141]**그 이후에는 언제든지 인터넷에 접속하실 수 있습니다.** 만약 어떤 이유로든 [142]**예약**을 취소하거나 연기해야 한다면 저희에게 알려 주십시오.
>
> Cory Dixon
> Ward Communications

어휘 confirm 확인하다, 확정하다 technician 기술자, 기사 request 요청하다 router 라우터, 데이터 중계 장치 depending on ~에 따라 need 요구, 필요(성) be scheduled to do ~하기로 예정되다 take place 일어나다, 열리다 complete 완료하다 no later than 늦어도 ~까지 cancel 취소하다 postpone 연기하다 for any reason 어떤 이유로든

139. 동사 어휘 install

(A) 강조하다 (B) 점검하다 (C) (법 등을) 집행하다 (D) 설치하다

140. 미래 시제

해설 메일을 보낸 날짜는 11월 3일이고, 빈칸이 포함된 문장에서는 11월 12일에 기사가 방문하면 하게 될 일을 언급하고 있으므로 빈칸에는 미래 시제가 들어가는 게 자연스럽다. 따라서 (C) will identify가 정답이다.

141. 알맞은 문장 고르기

(A) 이 서비스는 점점 더 인기를 얻고 있습니다.
(B) 그 이후에는 언제든지 인터넷에 접속하실 수 있습니다.
(C) 저희 직원들은 다양한 지역에서 근무합니다.
(D) 저희에게 희망 날짜를 알려 주시기 바랍니다.

해설 빈칸 앞에서 인터넷 설치 기사의 방문일과 시간, 그리고 예상 작업 시간 등을 알렸으므로 빈칸에는 그로 인한 결과나 효과를 언급하는 게 자연스럽다. 따라서 그 이후에는 인터넷을 마음껏 쓸 수 있다고 한 (B)가 정답이다.

어휘 go online 온라인에 접속하다 a variety of 다양한 neighborhood 지역; 인근, 근처 prefer 선호하다

142. 명사 어휘 appointment

(A) 약속, 예약 (B) 지시, 설명 (C) 회원 (자격) (D) 해결책

143-146 이메일

> 수신: Vega Supermarket 직원들
> 발신: Charles Siems
> 날짜: 8월 6일
> 제목: 환경
>
> 직원 여러분,
>
> 캐나다 최대의 식료품 체인점 중 하나로서, 우리는 환경에 미치는 부정적인 영향을 최소화하기 위해 [143]**노력하고 있습니다.** 우리는 최근에 Vega Supermarket 상표를 단 제품의 포장을 다른 디자인으로 변경했습니다. [144]**이렇게 해서 우리는 그러한 제품들의 플라스틱 쓰레기 양을 15퍼센트까지 줄였습니다.**
>
> 다음 달부터 우리는 더 이상 농산물을 담을 비닐봉지를 제공하지 않을 것입니다. 고객들은 물품들을 비닐봉지 없이 구매하거나 집에서 봉지를 가져올 수 있습니다. 이것은 고객들이 자신들의 습관을 바꾸기 위한 [145]**단호한** 노력을 하는 데 도움이 될 것입니다. [146]**게다가** 우리는 우리의 공급자들에게 그들의 제품에 환경 친화적인 포장재만을 사용할 것을 장려하고 있습니다.
>
> Charles Siems
> Vega Supermarket 공급 담당자

어휘 environment 환경 grocery store 식료품점 chain 체인점 minimize 최소화하다 negative 부정적인 effect 영향 packaging 포장(재) no longer 더 이상 ~않는 plastic bag 비닐봉지 produce 농산물 purchase 구입하다 item 품목 habit 습관 encourage 장려하다 supplier 공급사

143. 동사 어휘 strive

(A) 상담하다 (B) 기억하다 (C) 노력하다 (D) 달성하다

144. 알맞은 문장 고르기

(A) 매장 자체 제품은 일반적으로 국내 브랜드보다 저렴합니다.
(B) 그 도시는 다양한 재활용품들을 수집합니다.
(C) 고객들은 자신의 기준에 맞지 않는 물건들을 반품하고 있습니다.
(D) 이렇게 해서 우리는 그러한 제품들의 플라스틱 쓰레기 양을 15퍼센트까지 줄였습니다.

해설 빈칸 앞에서 Vega Supermarket은 환경에 미치는 영향을 최소화하기 위해 노력하고 있다고 했으므로 빈칸에는 그로 인한 결과에 대한 내용이 이어지는 게 자연스럽다. 따라서 (D)가 정답이다.

어휘 meet a standard 기준을 충족시키다 thus 이렇게 하여, 따라서

145. 형용사 자리+어휘

해설 빈칸 앞에 관사 a가 있고 뒤에는 명사 effort가 있으므로 빈칸은 명사를 수식하는 형용사 자리이다. (C) determining과 (D) determined가 정답 후보인데, 문맥상 엄격하고 철저한 노력을 한다는 뜻이 되는 게 자연스러우므로 '단호한'을 뜻하는 (D)가 정답이다. (C) determining은 '결정하는'을 뜻하여 문맥상 적절하지 않으므로 답이 될 수 없다.

146. 접속부사 어휘 additionally

(A) 예를 들어 (B) 대신에 (C) 또한, 게다가 (D) 그러므로

PART 7

147-148 광고

> **상업용 공간 임대**
>
> 예전에 미용실로 사용되었던 Coleman Building의 109호실을 9월 1일부터 임차할 수 있게 됩니다. 그 장소는 1,500평방피트이고 2년 임대 방식으로 매월 1,800달러의 임대료에 제공됩니다. 건물의 대형 진열창은 여러분의 업체를 선보이기에 완벽하며, [147]**냉난방 비용을 줄이기 위해 단열이 잘 되어 있습니다.** [148A]**건물에서 도보로 이동 가능한 거리에 해변과 몇몇 유명 레스토랑이 있습니다.** [148C]**임차인들은 차량 보호를 위해 천장이 있는 개인 주차 공간을 받게 됩니다.** [148D]**하루 24시간 운영되는 보안 팀도 있습니다.** 매물을 보시려면 555-7820으로 전화 주세요.

어휘 commercial 상업의 space 공간 rent 임대(료) previously 전에 unit (건물의) 한 공간 site 부지, 위치 comprise 차지하다, 구성되다 square feet 평방피트 lease 임대차 계약 rate 요금 showcase 선보이다 insulated 단열 처리가 된 within walking distance 걸어서 갈 수 있는 거리 내에 waterfront 해안가, 물가 tenant 임차인, 세입자 security 보안 viewing 보기, 조망

147. Coleman Building에 대해 암시된 것은 무엇인가?

(A) 에너지 효율에 좋은 창문이 있다.
(B) 2년 전에 완공되었다.
(C) 건물 안에 여러 개의 미용실이 있다.
(D) 대중교통 근처에 있다.

해설 추론/암시
냉난방 비용을 줄이기 위해 진열창은 단열이 잘 되어 있다고 했으므로 (A)가 정답이다.

패러프레이징 well insulated → energy-efficient

어휘 energy-efficient 에너지 효율이 좋은 house 수용하다, 거처를 제공하다 public transportation 대중교통

148. 편의시설로 시사되지 않은 것은 무엇인가?

(A) 식사 시설과의 근접성
(B) 물가가 보이는 전망
(C) 천장이 있는 주차 구역
(D) 24시간 보안

해설 NOT/True
해변에서 도보로 이동 가능한 거리에 있다고 했을 뿐 해변 풍경에 대한 언급은 없으므로 (B)가 정답이다.

패러프레이징 (A) within walking distance of several popular restaurants → Proximity to dining facilities
(D) a security team on site 24 hours a day → Round-the-clock security

어휘 proximity to ~에의 근접성 dining facilities 식당 시설 round-the-clock 24시간 계속되는

149-150 공지

> 미라마 베이의 Tirado Whale-Watching Tours에 관심을 가져 주셔서 감사합니다! [149]**티켓 소지자인 여러분은** 이제 곧 일생일대의 모험을 경험하게 될 것입니다. 경험이 풍부한 저희 선장들이 여러분을 고래를 발견할 수 있는 최고의 지역으로 모실 것이며, 여러분은 이 놀라운 동물들을 가까이에서 볼 수 있을 것입니다. 투어 예정일로부터 7일 이내에 취소하게 될 경우 환불이 불가하다는 것에 주의해 주시기 바랍니다.
>
> 승객들의 안전을 위해 악천후에는 투어를 취소해야 하는 경우도 있습니다. 이 경우에는 전액 환불됩니다. 가끔은 취소 안내가 투어 예정일에 임박해서 올 수도 있으므로 [150]**저희에게 올바른 전화번호와 이메일 주소를 제공하셨는지 다시 한번 확인해 주십시오.**

어휘 holder 소지자 be about to do 막 ~하려고 하다 adventure 모험 lifetime 일생 experienced 숙련된, 경험이 있는 captain 선장 up-close 바로 가까이에 note 주목하다, 주의하다 issue 발급하다, 지급하다 make a cancellation 취소하다 safety 안전 passenger 승객 inclement weather 악천후 announcement 발표, 안내 at the last minute 막바지에, 임박해서 double-check 다시 확인하다 provide 제공하다

149. 공지가 의도하는 대상은 누구이겠는가?

(A) 선장 직업을 위해 교육을 받는 사람들
(B) 표를 구매한 사람들
(C) Tirado Whale-Watching Tours에서 일하는 사람들
(D) 미라마 베이로 향하는 교통편을 제공하는 사람들

해설 추론/암시
글의 대상은 지문의 초반부에 나온다. As a ticket holder에서 공지의 대상

은 표를 구매하여 소지하고 있는 사람들이라는 것을 알 수 있으므로 (B)가 정답이다.

패러프레이징 a ticket holder → People who have purchased tickets

어휘 train 훈련하다, 교육하다 transportation 교통(편); 이동, 운송

150. 공지에서 권장되는 것은 무엇인가?

(A) 연락처 정보가 올바른지 확인하기
(B) 악천후를 대비해 특수한 옷을 가져오기
(C) 취소 확인을 위해 업체에 전화하기
(D) 이메일로 소식지 받아 보기

해설 세부 사항
요청 사항은 〈(please)+동사원형〉의 형태로 많이 나온다. 두 번째 문단의 마지막 문장에서 'please double-check ~'로 다시 한번 연락처를 확인하라고 요청했으므로 (A)가 정답이다.

패러프레이징 the right phone number and e-mail address → contact information is correct

어휘 ensure 확인하다 contact 연락처

151-152 문자 메시지

> Sheila Engel (오후 12:51) [151]일이 어떻게 되고 있나요? 어디 계세요?
>
> Frederick Kocher (오후 12:53) [151]저희는 6층 객실 청소를 거의 끝냈습니다. 오늘 아침에 카트에 물품을 채울 때, 얼룩 제거제의 재고가 떨어지고 있다는 것을 알아차렸어요. 좀 더 주문해 주시겠어요?
>
> Sheila Engel (오후 12:55) 물론이죠. [151]제가 오늘 우리 부서 물품의 재고를 파악해서 주문할 거예요.
>
> Frederick Kocher (오후 12:56) 좋아요. Dana와 저는 다음에 7층으로 이동할 예정인데, 모든 일은 늦어도 1시 50분까지는 끝날 거예요.
>
> Sheila Engel (오후 12:58) [152]그러면 시간이 얼마 남지 않았네요. 2시에 그 층 객실에 입실하는 손님들이 있거든요.
>
> Frederick Kocher (오후 1:00) 그건 이해하는데, [152]Beth가 오늘 아침에 병가를 냈기 때문에 인력이 부족합니다.
>
> Sheila Engel (오후 1:01) 그럴 수 있겠네요. 다른 팀이 일찍 끝나면 7층으로 보낼게요.

어휘 floor 층 stock (재고를) 채우다 notice 알아차리다 stain 얼룩 run low 모자라게 되다 take inventory 재고를 조사하다 supplies 공급품 place an order 주문하다 at the latest 늦어도 check into ~에 입실하다 call in sick 병가를 내다 short-staffed 인력이 부족한

151. Ms. Engel의 직업은 무엇이겠는가?

(A) 여행사 직원
(B) 행사 기획자
(C) 시설 관리자
(D) 배달원

해설 추론/암시
Ms. Engel은 객실을 청소하는 Mr. Kocher의 관리자로 보이므로 (C)가 정답이다.

어휘 housekeeping (호텔의) 시설 관리

152. 오후 1시 01분에 Ms. Engel이 "그럴 수 있겠네요"라고 쓸 때 그녀가 의미하는 것은 무엇이겠는가?

(A) 더 많은 근로자들을 채용해야 한다는 것에 동의한다.
(B) 왜 업무가 완료되지 않는지 이해한다.
(C) Mr. Kocher가 몸이 좋지 않다는 것을 안다.
(D) 왜 물품의 수량이 적은지 기억한다.

해설 의도 파악
'fair enough'는 약한 수준의 동의를 나타내는 표현이다. 2시에 입실하는 손님이 있다는 Ms. Engel의 말에 Mr. Kocher가 병가를 낸 직원 때문에 인력이 부족하다고 말함으로써 1시 50분보다는 일을 일찍 끝낼 수 없음을 우회적으로 표현했다. 이에 대해 Ms. Engel이 그럴 수 있겠다고 한 것으로 보아 Mr. Kocher의 말에 어느 정도 동의했음을 알 수 있으므로 (B)가 정답이다.

어휘 task 업무, 과제 complete 끝내다, 완료하다

153-154 광고

> **Valley Lighting 재고 정리 세일!**
> 282 시글리 로드
>
> Valley Lighting은 6월 1일부터 6월 8일까지 재고 정리 세일을 하고 있습니다. 저희는 수백 개의 조명과 부속품들을 판매하고 있습니다. 최대 80%나 되는 엄청난 할인을 받을 수 있습니다! 일부 제품은 예전 전시품들이며, 원래의 포장이 없습니다. 하지만 [153]저희가 판매하는 모든 것은 정상적으로 작동합니다.
>
> [154]Valley Lighting은 다음 달에 Baldwin Mall로 이전할 예정이기 때문에 새로운 지점의 줄어든 보관 공간과 전시 공간에 맞추기 위해 저희 재고를 줄여야만 합니다. 저렴하게 구매할 수 있는 기회를 놓치지 마세요!

어휘 lighting 조명 clearance sale 재고 정리 세일 fixture 고정 세간 (light fixture 천장이나 벽 등에 고정된 조명) fitting 부속품 up to ~까지 former 이전의 display 전시 original 원래의 packaging 포장(재) in working order 정상적으로 작동하는 inventory 재고, 물품 목록 accommodate 공간을 제공하다, 수용하다 storage 보관, 저장 miss 놓치다 deal 할인품

153. 재고 정리 제품에 대해 시사된 것은 무엇인가?

(A) 원래 포장과 함께 판매된다.
(B) 단종된 브랜드의 것이다.
(C) 반품이 허용되지 않는다.
(D) 모두 제대로 작동한다.

해설 NOT/True
모두 정상적으로 작동한다고 했으므로 (D)가 정답이다. 원래의 포장은 없다고 했으므로 (A)는 오답이다.

패러프레이징 in working order → functioning properly

어휘 discontinued 단종된 function 기능하다, 작동하다 properly 제대로

154. Valley Lighting의 새로운 매장에 대해 암시된 것은 무엇인가?

(A) 운영 시간이 더 길 것이다.

(B) 현재의 장소보다 더 작을 것이다.

(C) 새로운 소유주가 올 것이다.

(D) 재고 정리 세일을 계속할 것이다.

해설 추론/암시

새로운 매장인 Baldwin Mall에서는 보관 공간과 전시 공간이 줄어든다고 했으므로 (B)가 정답이다.

어휘 operating hours 영업 시간 current 현재의 site 장소, 부지 ownership 소유권

155-157 소식지

Arroyo Theater 보존 협회 (ATPS)

분기별 소식지

ATPS 회원들은 지난 분기를 바쁘게 보냈습니다! 우리는 아름답고 역사적인 Arroyo Theater를 보존하기 위해 계속 헌신하고 있습니다. 우리의 주요 성과들은 아래에 나열되어 있습니다.

- 4월에 우리는 극장의 옛날 사진들을 로비에 전시하여 극장이 오랜 세월 동안 어떻게 변해 왔는지를 보여 주었습니다.
- [155]**5월에 우리는 지역 내 음악가들과 댄서들의 특별 공연으로 극장의 125주년 기념일을 경축했습니다.**
- 6월에 [156]**우리는 동료 회원인 Thomas Lewis가 제출하신 검사 요약본을 바탕으로 가장 필요한 개선 사항 목록을 작성했습니다.** 우리는 7월부터 이것에 대한 작업을 시작할 것입니다.

향후 몇 개월 동안 우리는 다음과 같은 것을 계획하고 있습니다:

- 필요한 수리를 위한 모금 활동 시작
- 전국의 유사한 보존 단체들과 화상 회의 진행
- 어린이 극장 프로그램 개시
- 극장에서 공연할 더 많은 연극 단체 모집

신입 회원은 언제든지 환영입니다. ATPS에 가입하고 싶으시면 Shirley Deleon에게 sdeleon@trmail.com으로 이메일을 보내 주십시오. 우리의 다음 회의는 7월 11일 화요일 정오입니다. 우리는 지역 사회의 재정적 지원도 감사히 받습니다. [157]**www.atps.org에서 기부를 하세요.** 몇 분 밖에 걸리지 않습니다!

어휘 theater 극장 preservation 보존 society 협회 quarterly 분기의 newsletter 소식지, 뉴스레터 be dedicated to ~에 헌신하다 historic 역사적인 accomplishment 업적 list 나열하다 display 전시 anniversary 기념일 performance 공연 improvement 개선 inspection 검사, 점검 summary 요약, 개요 submit 제출하다 fellow 동료 upcoming 다가오는, 곧 있을 fundraising 모금 teleconference 화상 회의 appreciate 감사하다 make a donation 기부하다

155. ATPS는 언제 기념일 축하 행사를 열었는가?

(A) 4월

(B) 5월

(C) 6월

(D) 7월

해설 세부 사항

5월에 극장의 125주년을 기념했다고 했으므로 (B)가 정답이다.

156. ATPS는 개선되어야 할 사항에 대한 정보를 어디서 얻었는가?

(A) 인터뷰에서

(B) 보고서에서

(C) 웹사이트에서

(D) 뉴스 기사에서

해설 세부 사항

Thomas Lewis라는 회원이 제출한 검사 요약본을 바탕으로 개선 사항 목록을 작성했다고 했으므로 (B)가 정답이다.

157. ATPS에 기부할 수 있는 방법은 무엇인가?

(A) 7월 11일 회의에 참석함으로써

(B) 극장에 들름으로써

(C) Ms. Deleon에게 이메일을 보냄으로써

(D) 웹사이트를 방문함으로써

해설 세부 사항

특정 웹사이트 주소를 언급하며 기부하라고 했으므로 (D)가 정답이다.

어휘 stop by 잠시 들르다

158-160 광고

Lunsford Properties에서 선임 부동산 관리자를 찾고 있습니다!

Lunsford Properties는 필라델피아에서 영업을 하는 평판이 좋은 부동산 관리 회사입니다. 우리는 빠르게 성장하고 있으며 우리 팀에 두 명의 선임 부동산 관리자를 충원하려고 합니다.

직무

이상적인 후보자는 부동산 분야와 현재의 규정을 [158]**완전히** 이해해야 합니다. 직무에는 세입자와 집주인 사이의 주요한 연락처 역할을 하고, 유지 관리 문제를 신속히 처리하고, 부동산의 입주와 퇴거 날짜를 조율하는 업무가 포함됩니다. 또한 부동산의 손상 정도와 건물의 개선 필요성을 평가하기 위해 검사를 수행해야 합니다.

우리 직원들의 말

"이토록 친근한 팀원들과 함께 일하고, 웹사이트를 운영하고 최신 부동산 사진을 업로드하는 것은 멋진 일입니다. [160]**며칠 동안 재택근무를 한 후에는,** 사무실로 돌아와 제 동료들을 만나는 것을 항상 즐깁니다." – Maria Carter

"저는 부동산 관련 업무를 직접 하지는 않지만 Lunsford Properties의 사명과 연결되어 있다고 느끼며, [159]**저의 회계 업무를 통해 기여할 수 있다고 생각합니다.** [160]**한 주에 이틀간 재택근무를 할 수 있어서 좋고,** 작은 팀을 운영하며 리더십 경험을 쌓을 수 있어서 기뻤습니다. 이 회사를 누구에게나 강력 추천합니다." – [159]Felix Diaz

어휘 ideal 이상적인 candidate 후보자 sector 부문, 분야 current 현재의 regulation 규정 tenant 세입자 landlord 집주인, 임대인 address 해결하다, 다루다 maintenance 유지 관리 issue 문제 promptly 신속히 coordinate 조정하다 carry out ~을 수행하다 inspection 점검 damage 손상, 피해 work from home 재택근무를 하다 coworker 동료 directly 직접적으로

mission 사명 contribute 기여하다 accounting 회계 telecommuting 재택근무

158. 두 번째 단락 첫 번째 줄의 어휘 "complete"와 의미상 가장 가까운 것은?

(A) 성취된
(B) 끝낸
(C) 철저한
(D) 순수한

해설 동의어 찾기
have a complete understanding of는 '~을 완전히 이해하고 있다'라는 의미이므로, complete는 '완전한'을 뜻한다. 따라서 이와 유사한 의미를 가진 (C)가 정답이다.

159. Mr. Diaz의 직업은 무엇이겠는가?

(A) 사무장
(B) 사진작가
(C) 웹 개발자
(D) 회계원

해설 추론/암시
마지막 문단을 보면 Felix Diaz는 '직원들의 말'을 작성한 사람이라는 걸 알 수 있는데, 회계 업무를 통해 회사에 기여하고 있다고 했으므로 (D)가 정답이다.

160. Ms. Carter와 Mr. Diaz의 공통점은 무엇인가?

(A) 둘 다 다른 직원들을 관리한다.
(B) 둘 다 때로는 원격으로 근무한다.
(C) 둘 다 부동산과 직접적으로 관련되어 일한다.
(D) 둘 다 장기 근무 직원들이다.

해설 세부 사항
두 사람 모두 재택근무를 한다는 내용을 찾을 수 있으므로 (B)가 정답이다. Mr. Diaz는 부동산과 직접 관련된 업무를 하고 있지 않다고 했으므로 (C)는 오답이다.

패러프레이징 have been working from home, have a telecommuting option → work remotely

어휘 manage 관리하다 long-term 장기간의

161-163 편지

9월 3일

[161] Nellie Tomberlin
City Dental Clinic
854 세네카 애비뉴
포틀랜드, 오리건 97204

Ms. Tomberlin께,

[161] **저는 City Dental Clinic의 치위생사 지원자 중 한 명인 Victoria Lowell을 위해 편지를 쓰고 있습니다.** 저는 지난 4년 동안 Hermes Dental에서 Ms. Lowell과 함께 즐겁게 일했고, 그녀가 귀 병원의 훌륭한 자산이 될 것이라고 생각합니다. 저희와 함께 일하는 동안 그녀는 항상 높은 수준의 전문성을 보여 주었습니다. [163] **그녀는 신중하게, 그리고 비밀을 유지하며 환자들의 기록을 다루는 훈련을 받았습니다.** 따라서 저는 민감한 정보를 다루는 Ms. Lowell의 능력에 믿음을 가지고 있습니다.

Ms. Lowell은 프로젝트를 어려움 없이 독자적으로 처리할 수 있기 때문에 저는 항상 그녀에게 업무를 믿고 맡겼습니다. 예를 들어, [162] **저는 보험 회사에 정기적으로 청구서를 제출해야 합니다.** 제가 이 일이 밀려 있을 때마다 Ms. Lowell은 필요한 서류를 제가 제때에 작성하는 데 도움을 줄 수 있었습니다.

Ms. Lowell의 경력에 대해 더 자세히 논의할 수 있다면 좋겠습니다.

Maxine Blake
Hermes Dental, 관리자
(479) 555-0863

어휘 dental clinic 치과 on behalf of ~을 위해, ~을 대신하여 applicant 지원자 dental assistant 치위생사 asset 자산 demonstrate 증명하다, 보여주다 professionalism 전문성 at all times 항상 handle 다루다 discretion 신중함 confidentiality 기밀, 비밀성 delegate 위임하다 independently 독립적으로 submit 제출하다 bill 청구서, 고지서 insurance 보험 regularly 주기적으로 get behind 밀리다, 뒤지다 in a timely manner 시기적절하게 further 더

161. Ms. Tomberlin은 누구이겠는가?

(A) Hermes Dental의 대표자
(B) 입사 지원자
(C) City Dental Clinic 직원
(D) 교육 담당자

해설 추론/암시
Ms. Tomberlin은 편지의 수신인으로 치위생사를 구하고 있는 City Dental Clinic의 관계자이다. 따라서 (C)가 정답이다.

어휘 representative 대표(자)

162. Ms. Blake에 대해 사실인 것은 무엇인가?

(A) 직원 채용을 책임지고 있다.
(B) 전에 보험 회사에서 일했었다.
(C) 다른 업체에 서류를 제출해야 한다.
(D) 4년 전에 치과를 개원했다.

해설 NOT/True
Ms. Blake는 자신이 보험 회사에 정기적으로 청구서를 제출한다고 했으므로 (C)가 정답이다.

패러프레이징 submit bills to insurance companies → supply forms to other businesses

어휘 supply 공급하다 form 양식 found 설립하다

163. [1], [2], [3], [4]로 표시된 위치 중 다음 문장이 들어가기에 가장 적절한 곳은?

"따라서 저는 민감한 정보를 다루는 Ms. Lowell의 능력에 믿음을 가지고 있습니다."

해설 문장 삽입
주어진 문장은 민감한 정보를 다루는 Ms. Lowell의 능력에 믿음이 있다는 내용이므로, 그렇게 생각하게 된 계기나 원인이 되는 내용의 뒤에 위치하는 것이 적절하다. 따라서 Ms. Lowell이 비밀을 유지하며 환자들의 기록을 다루는 훈련을 받았다는 문장 다음인 [2]가 정답이다.

164-167 문서

> Morrison Research
>
> [164]**모든 안전 절차를 따르는 것은 우리 실험실 작업자들의 부상 위험을 제한하는 데 있어 [165]중요한 부분입니다. 실험을 수행하는 동안 아래에 나오는 지침을 명심하세요.**
>
> 적절한 실험 복장 착용
> - 실험실 가운, 장갑 및 보안경은 항상 착용해야 합니다.
> - 사용한 가운은 문 옆에 있는 바구니에 넣어야 합니다.
>
> 작업 구역 관리
> - [166]**교차 오염을 방지하기 위해 실험대를 정기적으로 닦으세요.**
> - [166]**나가기 전에 바닥이나 모든 테이블 위에 잔여물이 남아 있지 않은지 확인하세요.**
> - [167A]**모든 용기에는 정확한 내용물, 날짜 및 알려진 위험 요소가 라벨로 표시되어야 합니다.**
>
> 금지 품목
> - [167B]**실험실에 음식이나 음료를 반입하지 마시고 구내에서 어떤 것도 섭취하지 마세요.**
> - 라이터 및 기타 불과 관련된 물품은 실험실에 반입할 수 없습니다.
>
> 청결한 위생 상태
> - [167D]**도착했을 때, 재료를 다룬 후, 그리고 실험실을 나가기 전에 손을 씻으세요.**
> - 매번 사용할 때마다 장비를 살균하세요.

어휘 procedure 절차 limit 제한하다 risk 위험성 injury 부상 lab 실험실 keep ~ in mind ~을 명심하다 carry out ~을 수행하다 experiment 실험 proper 적절한 attire 복장 at all times 항상 maintain 유지하다 counter 작업대; 조리대 avoid 피하다 cross-contamination 교차 오염 residue 잔여물 container 용기 label 라벨을 붙이다 precise 정확한 contents (용기의) 내용물 hazard 위험 (요인) prohibit 금지하다 item 물품, 품목 beverage 음료 premises 부지, 구내 hygiene 위생 sterilize 살균하다 equipment 장비

164. 문서는 누구를 위해 작성되었겠는가?
(A) 안전 점검원
(B) 배달원
(C) 실험실 기사
(D) 기업 투자자

해설 추론/암시
글의 대상을 묻는 문제의 단서는 보통은 문두에 나온다. 첫 번째 문단에 실험실 작업자들의 부상을 막기 위한 지침이라는 내용이 나오므로 (C)가 정답이다.

165. 첫 번째 단락 첫 번째 줄의 어휘 "critical"과 의미상 가장 가까운 것은?
(A) 미심쩍은
(B) 필수적인
(C) 급박한
(D) 위험한

해설 동의어 찾기
critical이 있는 Following all safety procedures is a critical part of limiting the risk of injury는 모든 안전 절차를 따르는 것은 부상 위험을 제한하는 데 있어 중요한 부분이라는 의미이며, 여기서 critical은 '중요한'이라는 뜻으로 쓰였다. 따라서 (B) essential이 정답이다.

166. 문서에서 암시된 것은 무엇인가?
(A) 몇 가지 안전 규칙은 곧 바뀔 수도 있다.
(B) 장비를 소독하는 데 시간이 오래 걸린다.
(C) 실험용 가운은 직원이 집으로 가져갈 수 있다.
(D) 표면을 깨끗하게 유지하는 것이 중요하다.

해설 추론/암시
실험대를 정기적으로 닦아서 교차 오염을 막고, 테이블 위에 잔여물이 남아 있지 않도록 하라는 내용이 있으므로 실험대의 표면을 깨끗이 닦는 게 중요하다는 것을 알 수 있다. 그러므로 (D)가 정답이다.

167. 문서에서 언급된 안전 조치가 아닌 것은 무엇인가?
(A) 용기에 정확한 라벨을 붙이는 것
(B) 먹고 마시는 것을 피하는 것
(C) 부지 밖에 물품을 보관하는 것
(D) 정기적으로 손을 씻는 것

해설 NOT/True
부지 밖에 물품을 보관하라는 언급은 없으므로 (C)가 정답이다.

어휘 accurately 정확히 off site 부지 밖에

168-171 기사

> **Collins Park의 쟁점**
>
> 뉴턴 (8월 2일)—Collins Park에 장식용 분수를 추가하는 것은 처음 제안되었을 때는 좋은 아이디어인 것 같았으며, [169]**뉴턴 시 의회는 작년에 그것을 현실화하는 데 필요한 28만 달러의 예산을 빠르게 승인했다.** 안타깝게도 그 이후로 많은 문제들이 그 프로젝트를 에워쌌다.
>
> 분수는 건축 회사인 Luu Designs에 의해 설계되었다. 대부분의 주민은 시의 웹사이트에 게시된 초기 도면의 모양에 호의적인 반응을 보였다. [168]**하지만 그들은 분수의 규모를 고려하지 않았고, 완공된 분수가 얼마나 큰지를 본 후 많은 사람이 프로젝트에 대해 반대 의견을 냈다.**
>
> Collins Park는 시에서 가장 작은 공원이며, 축구장보다도 크기가 작기 때문에 [171]**사람들은 분수를 위한 공간을 만들기 위해 공원에 있는 기존의 벤치들을 들어내야 하지 않는지 염려했다.** <u>바로 그러한 일이 일어난 것이다.</u>
>
> "저는 공원 바로 옆에 살고 있는데, 사람들은 끊임없이 제 정원 담장에 앉아 있습니다. 실제 공원에는 앉을 곳이 없기 때문이죠."라고 오랜 주민인 Iris Bailey가 말했다.

공원 레크리에이션과의 과장인 Warren Pursell은 애초의 작업은 제때에 완료되었으며, [169]프로젝트에 지출된 32만 달러는 그만한 가치가 있었다고 말했다. 하지만 [170]그는 프로젝트의 단점을 인식하고 있으며, 분수 주위에 의자를 둥글게 설치하기 위해 이미 Luu Designs를 고용했는데, 그 의자들은 설계에 통합될 것이다.

어휘 issue 문제, 이슈 decorative 장식의 fountain 분수 propose 제안하다 city council 시 의회 approve 승인하다 budget 예산 reality 현실 numerous 수많은 architectural 건설의 favorably 호의적으로 initial 초기의, 최초의 drawing 도면 post 게시하다 take into account 고려하다 scale 규모 express 표현하다 opposition 반대 existing 기존의 space 공간 next to ~의 옆에 constantly 끊임없이, 계속 on time 제시간에 worthwhile 가치 있는 shortcoming 단점 incorporate 결합하다, 포함하다

168. 기사에 따르면, 주민들은 분수에 대해 어떤 점을 싫어하는가?

(A) 소음
(B) 자재
(C) 비용
(D) 크기

해설 세부 사항
두 번째 문단에서 주민들은 완공된 분수의 크기를 본 후 반대 의견을 냈다고 했으므로 (D)가 정답이다.

169. 뉴턴 시에 대해 암시된 것은 무엇인가?

(A) 다른 분수에 대한 계획을 취소했다.
(B) 프로젝트 예산을 초과했다.
(C) 주민들은 새로운 농구장을 원한다.
(D) 다른 도시들과 비교했을 때 공원이 작다.

해설 추론/암시
첫 번째 문단에는 분수 설치 예산이 28만 달러로 나오는데, 마지막 문단에서 32만 달러가 지출되었다고 했으므로 예산이 초과되었다는 걸 알 수 있다. 따라서 (B)가 정답이다.

어휘 cancel 취소하다 exceed 초과하다 budget 예산

170. Collins Park의 문제는 어떻게 해결될 것인가?

(A) 좌석 공간을 추가함으로써
(B) 다른 디자인 회사를 고용함으로써
(C) 더 많은 표지판을 설치함으로써
(D) 지역 법률을 시행함으로써

해설 세부 사항
마지막 문단에서 사람들이 앉을 공간이 부족한 문제점을 해결하기 위해 디자인 업체를 고용해서 분수 주위에 둥글게 의자를 설치한다고 했으므로 (A)가 정답이다.

패러프레이징 a chairs → a seating area

어휘 add 더하다, 추가하다 put up ~을 세우다, ~을 설치하다 sign 표지판 enforce 시행하다

171. [1], [2], [3], [4]로 표시된 위치 중 다음 문장이 들어가기에 가장 적절한 곳은?

"바로 그러한 일이 일어난 것이다."

해설 문장 삽입
주어진 문장의 That은 분수의 크기가 커서 공원 내에 벤치를 놓을 공간이 없어지는 걸 걱정한 것을 지칭하는 게 적절하고, 바로 그런 일이 생겨서 공원을 찾은 사람들이 다른 사람의 정원 담장에 앉는 일이 발생했다는 내용과도 자연스럽게 연결되므로 (C)가 정답이다.

172-175 온라인 채팅

Levi Avila [오전 10:09] Scenic Shuttles 고객 서비스에 연락 주셔서 감사합니다. 무엇을 도와 드릴까요?

Eleanor Worley [오전 10:11] [172]제 회사인 Landeros가 새크라멘토에서 열리는 전국 공학 학회에 우리 직원들을 태우고 가기 위해 귀사의 셔틀버스 한 대를 예약했거든요. 예약 번호는 T7893입니다. 차에 미니 냉장고 한 대를 가지고 탈 예정이라 콘센트가 있는지 확인하고 싶어서요.

Levi Avila [오전 10:12] 예약에 따르면 고객님은 21인승 셔틀버스를 예약하셨네요. [173]그 셔틀버스에는 콘센트가 없습니다.

Eleanor Worley [오전 10:14] 그럴 리가요! 저는 그게 그 정도 크기의 셔틀버스의 표준이라고 생각했는데요. 우리는 모든 사람들에게 줄 음료수와 도시락을 가져가야 하는데, 얼음을 넣은 아이스박스는 사용하고 싶지 않아요. 너무 지저분할 테니까요. [174]제가 당신의 상사와 이 문제에 대해 이야기할 수 있을까요?

[174]Rafael Duke [오전 10:18] 안녕하세요, Ms. Worley. 곧 있을 여행을 위한 21인승 셔틀버스에서 제공되는 기능에 실망하셨다고 하니 죄송합니다. 빌트인 냉장고뿐만 아니라 콘센트도 있는 37인승으로 상향 조정하실 수 있습니다. 하루에 85달러가 추가되지만 제가 할인을 해 드려서 하루에 60달러만 추가 요금이 부과되도록 할 수 있습니다.

Eleanor Worley [오전 10:19] 그게 더 나을 것 같네요. 감사합니다. [175]하지만 제가 추가 비용에 대한 결재를 받아야 할 것 같아서요. 그 점 확인해 보고 다시 연락 드리겠습니다.

어휘 contact 연락하다 book 예약하다 engineering 공학 conference 학회, 콘퍼런스 refrigerator 냉장고 on board 차내의, 탑승한 make sure 확인하다, 확실히 하다 outlet (전기) 콘센트 reservation 예약 -seater ~인승의 자동차 packed lunch 도시락 cooler 아이스박스 messy 지저분한 supervisor 관리자, 감독관 feature 특징, 특성 upcoming 다가오는, 곧 있을 upgrade 업그레이드하다, 상향 조정하다 built-in 내장의 charge 부과하다 extra 추가의 approve 승인하다

172. Ms. Worley의 회사는 왜 Scenic Shuttles의 서비스를 이용할 것인가?

(A) 지역의 관광지를 즐기기 위해
(B) 새 사무실로 이전하기 위해
(C) 다른 회사 지점을 방문하기 위해
(D) 전문 학회에 참석하기 위해

해설 세부 사항
오전 10시 11분에 전국 공학 학회로 직원들을 데리고 가기 위해 셔틀버스를 예약했다고 했으므로 (D)가 정답이다.

어휘 tourist attraction 관광지 relocate 이전하다 branch 지점, 지사 professional 전문적인, 전문가의

173. 오전 10시 14분에 Ms. Worley가 "그럴 리가요"라고 쓸 때 그녀가 암시하는 것은 무엇인가?

(A) 그녀는 어떤 기능이 포함되지 않은 것에 놀랐다.
(B) 그녀는 셔틀버스가 더 많은 사람들을 태울 것이라고 생각했다.
(C) 그녀는 제안된 가격에 동의하지 않는다.
(D) 그녀는 예약 접수가 분실되어 불만이다.

해설 의도 파악
의도 파악 문제는 바로 앞의 내용을 확인해야 한다. 오전 10시 12분에 셔틀버스에 콘센트가 없다고 한 말에 실망과 놀라움을 나타냈으므로 (A)가 정답이다.

패러프레이징 It doesn't have any outlets. → a feature is not included

어휘 include 포함하다 seat 앉히다, 앉다 frustrated 좌절한

174. Mr. Duke는 누구이겠는가?

(A) Mr. Avila의 비서
(B) Mr. Avila의 관리자
(C) 셔틀버스 기사
(D) 여행 가이드

해설 추론/암시
오전 10시 14분에 Ms. Worley가 Mr. Avila의 상사와 이야기하겠다고 요구하자 오전 10시 18분에 Mr. Duke가 답변한 것으로 보아 Mr. Duke는 Mr. Avila의 관리자라는 걸 추론할 수 있다. 따라서 (B)가 정답이다.

175. Ms. Worley는 무엇을 할 계획인가?

(A) 용역 계약을 취소하기
(B) 예산 증액을 요청하기
(C) 인원수를 확인하기
(D) 은행 송금을 하기

해설 세부 사항
향후 계획에 대한 단서는 주로 지문의 마지막 부분에 나온다. 추가 비용에 대한 결재를 받은 후 다시 연락하겠다고 했으므로 (B)가 정답이다.

패러프레이징 get the extra cost approved → Request a budget increase

어휘 contract 계약 confirm 확인하다, 확정하다 head count 인원수 (조사) bank transfer 계좌 이체

176-180 이메일 & 기사

수신: Laura Navarre
발신: Max Stallworth
날짜: 2월 17일
제목: 운동 코스

Ms. Navarre께,

저의 지난 이메일에서도 확인했듯이 Cole 시장님은 3월 3일에 [179]Primrose Construction이 건설한 시의 신설 다용도 운동 코스의 개장을 축하하기 위해 곧 있을 행사에 참석할 예정이십니다. [176]**하지만 시장님은 가능하다면 Sandra Krone도 대동하고 싶어 하세요. 행사장의 VIP석에 이 추가 참석자를 위한 자리를 마련해 주실 것을 요청드립니다.**

아시다시피 [177 180]**Ms. Krone은 환경 단체가 계획에 반대 입장을 나타냈을 때 이 프로젝트의 수석 디자이너인 Gregory Burkett와 환경 단체 Eco-Friends의 회장인 Marian Conroy 사이에서 합의안을 협상하는 것을 도왔습니다.**

Max Stallworth
Roger Cole 시장 비서
커빌 시청

어휘 trail 코스, 루트 mayor 시장 celebrate 축하하다 grand opening 개장 multi-use 다용도의 accompany 대동하다 make room for ~을 위해 자리를 만들다 additional 추가적인 attendee 참석자 section 부분, 구획 negotiate 협상하다 agreement 합의 environmental 환경의 opposition 반대 proposal 계획, 제안 assistant 비서

지역 주민들을 위한 운동 선택권이 늘어나다

커빌([180]3월 4일)—[178 180]**어제 열린 기념식에서 시 공무원들은 커빌의 다용도 운동 코스 개장을 축하했다.** 10마일 이상 뻗어 있으며, 자전거 타기, 조깅, 걷기에 적합한 그 코스는 예산 범위 내에서 일정에 맞게 완공되었다. 코스의 일부 구간은 코스를 내기 위한 공간을 만들기 위해 나무를 베기보다는 기존의 나무들을 그대로 유지하기 위해 방향을 틀었다. [180]**기념식에서는 시의 공원 및 여가 부서 책임자뿐만 아니라 코스의 디자이너가 연설을 했다.**

[179]**프로젝트 기획자들은 작업을 맡은 건설사에 매우 만족했기 때문에 그들은 이미 이 회사를 고용하여 Spencer Park에 테니스장을 짓기로 했다.** 이러한 계획들의 최신 소식은 시의 웹사이트에서 찾을 수 있다. 웹사이트에서는 새로운 코스의 지도도 볼 수 있다.

어휘 official 공무원 stretch 뻗어 있다 suitable for ~에 적합한 on time 제시간에 estimated 견적의; 추측의 budget 예산 redirect 경로를 재설정하다 existing 기존의 carry out ~을 수행하다 update 최신 정보

176. 이메일의 목적은 무엇인가?

(A) 활동을 제안하기 위해
(B) 수신인을 축하하기 위해
(C) 손님 명단을 조정하기 위해
(D) 일부 숙박 시설을 변경하기 위해

해설 주제/목적
행사장에 Sandra Krone을 위한 자리를 마련해 달라고 요청하는 이메일이므로 (C)가 정답이다.

어휘 activity 활동 recipient 수신인, 수취인 adjust 조정하다 modify 변경하다 overnight 하룻밤 동안의 accommodations 숙박 시설

177. Ms. Krone은 프로젝트를 어떻게 지원했는가?

(A) 행사에 자금을 제공함으로써
(B) 환경 단체를 설립함으로써

(C) 건설 회사를 추천함으로써
(D) 불만을 해결하는 것을 도움으로써

해설 세부 사항
Ms. Krone이 프로젝트 디자이너와 환경 단체의 회장 사이에서 협상을 도왔다고 했으므로 (D)가 정답이다.

어휘 fund 자금 found 설립하다 resolve 해결하다 complaint 불만, 민원

178. 기사는 왜 작성되었는가?
(A) 몇몇 수상자를 축하하기 위해
(B) 프로젝트의 완료를 알리기 위해
(C) 투표 결과를 확인하기 위해
(D) 시 인원의 변경을 보고하기 위해

해설 주제/목적
다용도 운동 코스의 개장을 알리는 기사이므로 (B)가 정답이다.

어휘 recognize 인정하다, 표창하다 award winner 수상자 completion 완료 personnel 인원

179. Primrose Construction에 대해 암시된 것은 무엇인가?
(A) Spencer Park에서 프로젝트를 진행할 것이다.
(B) 어떤 지역에서 나무 몇 그루를 제거했다.
(C) Mr. Stallworth의 소유이다.
(D) 계약 세부 사항은 시의 웹사이트에 있다.

해설 두 지문 연계_추론/암시
첫 번째 지문에서 Primrose Construction이 다용도 운동 코스를 건설했다고 했고, 두 번째 지문에서는 다용도 운동 코스를 건설한 회사를 다시 고용해서 Spencer Park에 테니스장을 짓는다고 했다. 따라서 Primrose Construction이 Spencer Park에 테니스장을 짓는다는 걸 추론할 수 있으므로 (A)가 정답이다.

어휘 remove 제거하다 own 소유하다 contract 계약(서) details 세부 사항

180. 3월 3일 행사에서 누가 연설을 했는가?
(A) Ms. Conroy
(B) Mr. Cole
(C) Ms. Krone
(D) Mr. Burkett

해설 두 지문 연계_세부 사항
두 번째 지문은 작성일이 3월 4일인데, 3월 3일 있었던 기념식에서 운동 코스의 디자이너가 연설을 했다는 내용이 나온다. 첫 번째 지문에서 프로젝트 수석 디자이너 이름이 Gregory Burkett라고 했으므로 (D)가 정답이다.

181-185 편지 & 영수증

7월 27일

[183 184]Lisa Alford, 컴퓨터 부장
Hickory Electronics
3179 테렐 스트리트
휴스턴, 텍사스 77056

Ms. Alford께,

[182]저는 이번 주 초에 새 데스크톱 컴퓨터를 구입하기 위해 귀사의 상점을 방문했습니다. Mr. Bradshaw가 저를 도와주셨는데, 제가 얼마나 많은 메모리가 필요한지 알아내는 것을 도와주셨습니다. 그분은 또한 안티바이러스 프로그램을 추천해 주셨습니다. 하지만 저는 귀사의 상점에서 판매되는 제한된 종류의 그래픽 카드에 실망했는데요, 저는 온라인 게임용으로 매우 강력한 그래픽 카드가 필요하기 때문입니다.

저는 제 필요에 딱 맞는 것으로 보이는 그래픽 카드를 온라인에서 찾았습니다. [181 183]**제가 그래픽 카드를 제삼자로부터 구매하더라도 귀사의 직원께서 그것을 설치해 주실 수 있는지 궁금합니다.** 저에게 가부를 알려 주십시오. 832-555-6541로 연락하시면 됩니다. 저는 귀사의 총괄 관리자인 Steven Noguera에게 물품 목록을 확대해 달라고 편지를 쓸 계획도 가지고 있습니다.

Evan Irving

어휘 figure out 알아내다 limited 제한된 selection 선발, 선택(된 것들) suitable for ~에 적합한 need 필요(성) install 설치하다 third party 제삼자 reach 연락하다 expand 확대하다, 확장하다 inventory 재고, 물품 목록

CYBER PARTS INC.
www.cyberpartsinc.com

주문 날짜: 7월 29일
주문 번호: 0456218
주문 처리자: Sarah Lombardo
[183]**고객**: Evan Irving, 966 하이랜드뷰, 휴스턴, 텍사스 77102
[183]**설명**: 12GB Loomis RX 그래픽 카드 (품목 번호 G97002)
[185]**가격**: 525달러, Maxxo 신용 카드 XXXX XXXX XXXX 9032로 결제됨
[183 184]**배달지**: 컴퓨터 부장, Hickory Electronics, 3179 테렐 스트리트, 휴스턴, 텍사스 77056
배달 종류: 일반
예상 배송일: 8월 3일
비고: 물품 수령 시 서명 필요.

어휘 process 처리하다 description 설명, 묘사 charge 부과하다 type 종류, 유형 estimated 추측의; 견적의 signature 서명 receipt 수령

181. 편지의 목적 중 하나는 무엇인가?
(A) 공석에 대해 문의하려고
(B) 특별 서비스를 요청하려고
(C) 파손된 물품에 대해 항의하려고
(D) 신제품을 소개하려고

해설 주제/목적
다른 곳을 통해 구입한 그래픽 카드를 설치해 줄 수 있는지 궁금하다고 했으므로 (B)가 정답이다.

어휘 job opening 공석 complain 불평하다, 민원을 제기하다 damaged 파손된, 손상된

182. Mr. Bradshaw는 어디서 근무하겠는가?
(A) 전자 제품 매장
(B) 온라인 소매점

TEST 04

(C) 비디오 게임 개발사
(D) 택배 회사

해설 추론/암시
Mr. Irving이 컴퓨터를 구입하기 위해 방문한 매장에서 Mr. Bradshaw가 도움을 줬다고 했으므로 (A)가 정답이다.

183. Hickory Electronics에 대해 암시된 것은 무엇인가?
(A) 곧 새로운 품목을 재고 목록에 추가할 것이다.
(B) 일부 제품을 온라인에서 판매한다.
(C) 자사의 매장에서 판매되지 않는 부품을 설치할 것이다.
(D) 다양한 종류의 그래픽 카드를 제공한다.

해설 두 지문 연계_추론/암시
첫 번째 지문에서 Mr. Irving은 Hickory Electronics의 컴퓨터 부장에게 다른 곳을 통해 구입한 그래픽 카드를 설치해 줄 수 있는지 문의했는데, 두 번째 지문에서 Mr. Irving이 구입한 그래픽 카드의 배송지가 Hickory Electronics의 컴퓨터 부장인 것으로 보아 그 요청을 수락했다고 추론할 수 있다. 따라서 (C)가 정답이다.

어휘 component 부품 a wide range of 다양한

184. 누가 Cyber Parts Inc.로부터 소포를 받게 되는가?
(A) Ms. Alford
(B) Mr. Noguera
(C) Mr. Irving
(D) Ms. Lombardo

해설 두 지문 연계_세부 사항
두 번째 지문에서 물품 배송지가 Hickory Electronics의 컴퓨터 부장으로 되어 있는데, 첫 번째 지문을 보면 Hickory Electronics의 컴퓨터 부장은 Lisa Alford라고 되어 있으므로 (A)가 정답이다.

185. 주문품에 대해 사실인 것은 무엇인가?
(A) 휴스턴에서 발송될 것이다.
(B) 7월 29일에 배달될 것으로 예상된다.
(C) 할인된 품목이 포함되어 있었다.
(D) 물품 비용을 지불하는 데 신용 카드가 사용되었다.

해설 NOT/True
두 번째 지문에서 신용 카드로 비용이 지불되었다는 정보를 찾을 수 있으므로 (D)가 정답이다. 예상 배송일은 8월 3일이므로 (B)는 오답이다.

어휘 ship 배송하다 discounted 할인된

186-190 웹페이지 & 일정표 & 이메일

Senoia Moving Services
1161 크렌쇼 애비뉴, 애크런, 오하이오주 44310

[186]여러분이 애크런 내에서 이사를 하건 다른 도시로 이사를 하건 Senoia Moving Services가 여러분을 도울 수 있습니다. 우리의 숙련된 이사 직원들이 여러분의 물품을 조심스럽게 다룰 것입니다. 우리는 개인과 기업 모두에 서비스를 제공하며, 필요한 경우 안전 보관 서비스를 제공할 수 있습니다. 우리의 서비스를 예약하는 것은 쉽습니다!

1. 이사 일정을 잡으려면 330-555-8522로 연락하세요.
2. 우리 직원 중 한 명이 여러분의 물품을 파악해서 비용 견적을 제공할 것입니다.
3. [189]이사 날짜를 확정하고 나면 보증금을 지불하셔야 합니다. 그런 다음 여러분에게 필요한 모든 박스와 포장 용품을 제공하겠습니다.
4. 우리 작업반이 합의된 날짜와 시간에 이사를 수행할 것입니다.

어휘 move 이사하다 mover 이사업체 직원 treat 다루다, 취급하다 belongings 재산, 소유물 with care 주의 깊게, 신중히 serve (서비스를) 제공하다 individual 개인 business 업체 secure 안전한 storage 보관 book 예약하다 contact 연락하다 assess 평가하다, 가늠하다 estimate 견적 confirm 확정하다 deposit 보증금 packaging 포장 crew 작업반 carry out ~을 수행하다

Senoia Moving Services
[187 188]3월 22일 작업반 이삿짐 상차 배정

작업반/작업 인원	차량 크기	상차 장소	시간
Robin 작업반/2명	승합차	247 올버니 레인	오전 9:00
[188]Dove 작업반/5명	26피트 트럭	[188]432 자바 스트리트	오전 9:00
Canary 작업반/2명	12피트 트럭	950 Columbia Building 309호, 2746 로셀 스트리트	오전 10:30
[190]Sparrow 작업반/3명	[190]16피트 트럭	1614 캑슨 스트리트	오전 10:00
Robin 작업반/2명	승합차	30 휘트먼 애비뉴	오후 1:00

보다 자세한 내용은 여러분의 작업반장으로부터 확인할 수 있습니다. [190]4월 1일부터 Sparrow 작업반(16피트 트럭)에 한 명이 추가된다는 것을 알아 두시기 바랍니다.

어휘 assignment 배정 vehicle 차량 further 더 이상의, 추가의 details 세부 사항 available 구할 수 있는 note 유념하다, 알고 있다

수신: Joseph Ayers
발신: Christina Walden
날짜: 4월 4일
제목: 회신: 919 블룸필드 로드

Mr. Ayers께,

[189 190]제 이사 날짜를 4월 13일로 확정해 주셔서 감사합니다. 귀하의 빠른 답장에 깊은 인상을 받았습니다. [190]16피트 트럭을 이용하라는 귀하의 권고를 따르겠습니다. [189]방금 귀사의 업체 계좌로 보증금을 보냈습니다. 저에게서 더 필요한 것이 있으면 알려 주세요.

Christina Walden

어휘 response 답장, 답변 recommendation 추천, 권고

186. Senoia Moving Services에 대해 사실인 것은 무엇인가?
(A) 기업 고객들을 위해서만 일한다.

(B) 애크런 외곽 지역에 서비스를 제공한다.
(C) 최근에 경쟁사에 매각되었다.
(D) 현재 경력 있는 이사 직원을 찾아서 고용하려고 한다.

해설 NOT/True
다른 도시로 이사를 해도 도울 수 있다고 했으므로 (B)가 정답이다. 개인 고객과 기업 고객 모두에게 서비스를 제공한다고 했으므로 (A)는 오답이다.

어휘 commercial 상업의 competitor 경쟁자, 경쟁사 seek 찾다 experienced 노련한, 경력 있는

187. 일정표는 누구를 위해 작성되었는가?
(A) Senoia Moving Services의 투자자
(B) Senoia Moving Services의 고객
(C) Senoia Moving Services 입사 지원자
(D) Senoia Moving Services 직원

해설 대상
이사 직원들의 작업반과 차량 배정, 장소, 그리고 시간이 일정표의 전반적인 내용을 이루므로 (D)가 정답이다.

어휘 investor 투자자 client 고객 job applicant 입사 지원자

188. Dove 작업반은 3월 22일에 어디로 가야 하는가?
(A) 올버니 레인
(B) 자바 스트리트
(C) 캑슨 스트리트
(D) 휘트먼 애비뉴

해설 세부 사항
두 번째 지문에서 Dove 작업반의 상차 장소가 자바 스트리트임을 확인할 수 있으므로 (B)가 정답이다.

189. Senoia Moving Services 직원들은 이메일에 대응하여 무엇을 하겠는가?
(A) 몇 가지 포장 재료를 가져다 놓기
(B) 몇 가지 개인 소지품을 측정하기
(C) 청구서의 한 가지 오류를 수정하기
(D) 비어 있는 시간대가 있는지 일정표를 확인하기

해설 두 지문 연계_추론/암시
세 번째 지문에서 발신인이자 고객인 Christina Walden이 자신의 이사 일정이 확정되었으며, 그에 따라 보증금을 지불했다고 밝혔다. 첫 번째 지문에서는 보증금을 지불하면 박스와 포장 용품을 제공한다고 했으므로 Senoia Moving Services는 Christina Walden에게 박스와 포장 용품 등의 이사 용품을 제공할 것임을 알 수 있다. 따라서 (A)가 정답이다.

패러프레이징 give you all the boxes and packaging supplies → Drop off some packing materials

어휘 drop off ~을 내려놓다 packing 포장 measure 재다, 측정하다 personal belongings 개인 소지품 correct 수정하다, 바로잡다 invoice 청구서, 송장

190. 얼마나 많은 사람들이 Ms. Walden의 이사를 돕겠는가?
(A) 2
(B) 3
(C) 4
(D) 5

해설 두 지문 연계_추론/암시
세 번째 지문에서 Ms. Walden은 16피트 트럭을 이용하겠다고 했는데, 두 번째 지문에서 16피트 트럭은 Sparrow 작업반에 배정된 걸 확인할 수 있다. 원래 해당 작업반의 인원은 3명이지만 하단 정보를 보면 4월 1일부터 Sparrow 작업반에 1명이 추가된다는 내용이 있으므로 Ms. Walden의 이사 날짜인 4월 13일에는 4명이 올 것임을 추론할 수 있다. 따라서 (C)가 정답이다.

191-195 메뉴 & 청구서 & 이메일

Nicolette Italian Catering

[191]파스타 뷔페: 1인당 20달러
다음과 같은 조합으로 5가지 요리로 구성된 사용자 지정 메뉴를 만드세요.
파스타 종류: 스파게티, 페투치네, 펜네
고기/채식주의자: 닭고기, 쇠고기, 새우, 두부, 콩
소스: 토마토, 갈릭과 오일, 크림
[191]**뷔페 요금에는 은 포크와 스푼, 나이프뿐만 아니라 커피, 차, 탄산음료, 유리잔, 도자기 접시도 포함되어 있습니다.**

추가 요리: 1인당 가격이며, 각 카테고리의 옵션은 저희 웹사이트를 참조하세요.
[193]**수프: 2달러**
애피타이저: 2.25달러
샐러드: 1.50달러
치즈 접시: 2.50달러

디저트 뷔페: 1인당 가격
커피, 차와 함께 제공됩니다. 이탈리아 아이스크림, 티라미수 (커피에 적신 케이크), 신선한 과일 샐러드, 레몬 치즈 케이크, 초콜릿 케이크 중에서 고르세요.
3가지 선택: 8달러
4가지 선택: 10.50달러
5가지 선택: 12달러

[194]**주문을 하시려면 저희의 행사 담당자인 Camelia Rossi에게 555-7019로 연락하십시오.** [191]**의자, 식탁보, 식탁 장식물 등의 대여 옵션에 대해서도 문의하실 수 있습니다.**

어휘 catering 출장 뷔페 custom 맞춤 주문한 combination 조합 vegetarian 채식주의자; 채식의 fee 요금 ceramic 도자기 plate 접시 extra 추가의 serve 제공하다 coordinator 코디네이터, 조정자 place an order 주문하다 inquire about ~에 대해 문의하다 rental 임대 centerpiece 테이블 중앙의 장식물

Nicolette Italian Catering 청구서
고객: Aaron Kendall

품목 설명	단가	수량	소계
파스타 뷔페	20.00달러	35	700.00달러
[193]추가 음식	2.00달러	35	70.00달러

[192]배송 [792 오크 레인, 오후 5시 30분, 4월 19일]		15.00달러
디저트 뷔페	10.50달러 20	210.00달러
[192]배송 [1960 스트랫퍼드 애비뉴, 오후 8시, 4월 19일]		15.00달러
소계		1,010.00달러
세금 (7.25%)		73.23달러
전체 지불 예정 금액 (4월 12일까지)		**1,083.23달러**

어휘 description 설명, 묘사 per ~당 unit 개, 단위 quantity 수량 subtotal 소계 due 지불해야 하는 금액

수신: Francesco Marcelo
발신: Aaron Kendall
날짜: 4월 10일
제목: 청구서

Mr. Marcelo께,

[194]Ms. Rossi가 휴가 중일 때 임시로 그분의 직무를 인수하신다는 것을 제게 알려 주셔서 감사합니다. 청구서를 받았는데, 오류를 발견했습니다. 저는 주문을 할 때 100달러의 보증금을 지불했는데, 이 금액이 전체 지불 예정 금액에서 공제되지 않았습니다. **[195]보증금 액수가 나오는 새로운 청구서를 만들어 주실 수 있나요?** 그러면 그것을 받는 즉시 결제를 할 수 있습니다.

감사합니다.

Aaron Kendall

어휘 temporarily 임시로 take over ~을 넘겨받다 on leave 휴가 중인 notice 알아차리다 deposit 보증금 deduct 공제하다 make a payment 지불하다

191. 파스타 뷔페 패키지의 일부로 표시되지 않은 것은 무엇인가?

(A) 식기류
(B) 유리 제품
(C) 식탁보
(D) 접시

해설 **NOT/True**
첫 번째 지문에 나열된 내용에 해당하지 않는 것은 (C)이다. 마지막 문단에서 식탁보는 대여 옵션에 속해 있음을 알 수 있다.

패러프레이징 silver forks, spoons, and knives → Utensils

192. 청구서에는 배송에 대해 어떻게 명시되어 있는가?

(A) 배송 시간은 1시간이다.
(B) 두 개의 분리된 장소로 배송될 것이다.
(C) 수수료가 인하되었다.
(D) 두 개의 다른 날짜로 예정되어 있다.

해설 세부 사항
두 번째 지문을 보면 두 곳으로 배송된다는 것을 알 수 있으므로 (B)가 정답이다. 배송일은 4월 19일로 동일하므로 (D)는 오답이다.

어휘 delivery window 배달 시간대 separate 별도의, 분리된 location 장소, 지점 be scheduled for ~로 예정되어 있다

193. Mr. Kendall은 어떤 추가 요리를 주문했는가?

(A) 수프
(B) 애피타이저
(C) 샐러드
(D) 치즈 접시

해설 두 지문 연계_세부 사항
두 번째 지문을 보면 Mr. Kendall은 추가 음식에 1인당 2달러를 지불했는데, 첫 번째 지문에서 추가 음식 중 1인당 2달러에 해당하는 메뉴는 수프임을 확인할 수 있다. 따라서 (A)가 정답이다.

194. Mr. Marcelo는 누구의 업무를 대신하고 있는가?

(A) 업주
(B) 주방장
(C) 행사 담당자
(D) 회계원

해설 두 지문 연계_세부 사항
세 번째 지문에서 Mr. Marcelo가 휴가 중인 Ms. Rossi의 업무를 인수했다는 정보를 찾을 수 있다. Ms. Rossi는 첫 번째 지문의 마지막 문단에서 행사 담당자라고 언급되어 있으므로 (C)가 정답이다.

195. Mr. Kendall은 Mr. Marcelo가 무엇을 하기를 가장 기대하겠는가?

(A) 손님 인원 조정하기
(B) 환불하기
(C) 새 메뉴 제공하기
(D) 갱신된 청구서 발송하기

해설 추론/암시
다중 지문의 마지막 문제는 일반적으로 마지막 지문에서 단서를 찾을 수 있다. 세 번째 지문에서 Mr. Kendall은 Mr. Marcelo에게 보증금 액수가 나오는 새로운 청구서를 만들어 달라고 요청했으므로 (D)가 정답이다.

패러프레이징 create a new invoice → Send an updated invoice

어휘 adjust 조정하다 issue 발급하다, 지급하다 refund 환불 update 갱신하다, 업데이트하다

196-200 기사 & 보도 자료 & 이메일

피터즈버그 기업 주요 소식

4월 9일—화장품 업계의 치열한 경쟁으로 인해 기업주들은 항상 그들의 브랜드에 성장과 안정성을 제공할 수 있는 방법들을 찾고 있다. **[196]점점 더 인기를 끌고 있는 전략은 고급 호텔 체인의 투숙객들을 위해 호텔에 샘플 크기의 작은 제품들을 판매하는 것이다. 이것은 그 제품들이 더 넓은 범위의 잠재 고객들에 의해 사용된다는 것을 의미한다.**

마케팅 컨설턴트 Eric Weiss는 이 접근 방식이 왜 효과적일 수 있는지를 설명한다. "고객들은 편안한 환경에서 제품을 사용하기 때문에 구매 결정을 내려야 한다는 부담을 느끼지 않습니다. 효과는 동일하지만 광고처럼 느껴지지 않는 것이죠."

[198]Farland Cosmetics와 Arrowood 같은 회사들은 이미 Grant Hotel

및 Terra Hotel과 각각 이러한 제휴 관계를 맺었다. 더 많은 최고급 브랜드들이 이 같은 선례를 따를 것으로 예상된다.

어휘 highlight 하이라이트, 가장 흥미로운 부분 fierce 치열한 competition 경쟁 cosmetics 화장품 business leader 기업주 stability 안정 increasingly 점점 더 strategy 전략 luxury 고급스러운 sample 샘플; 시용하다, 시식하다 potential 잠재적인 approach 접근 effective 효과적인 relaxed 편안한, 느긋한 pressured 압박을 받는 make a decision 결정하다 form 형성하다 partnership 파트너십, 제휴 respectively 각각 high-end 최고급의 follow suit 선례를 따르다

즉시 배포 요망

[197]8월 2일

연락처: Sarah Calderon, scalderon@farlandcosmetics.com

(피터즈버그)— [198]**Farland Cosmetics는 8월 15일부터 Jia Zheng이 최고 경영자의 자리를 이어받게 된다고 발표했다.** 3월에 시작된 수개월간의 협상 끝에 [197]**회사는 마침내 지난달에 Fieldcrest Group에 의해 인수되었다.** 현 최고 경영자인 Duane Baur는 인수 과정을 돕기 위해 일시적으로 자리에 남았다. [198]**Ms. Zheng은 다른 확장 기회를 모색할 뿐만 아니라 현재의 모든 제휴 관계를 계속할 계획이다.**

Fieldcrest Group의 투자자들은 Ms. Zheng의 사업 경험에 확신을 가지고 있다. [199]**Ms. Zheng은 대학 친구인 Marilyn Burks와 대학에서 경영학을 공부한 후, 빠르게 성장한 비타민 보충제 회사를 설립했다.** 업체는 3년 후에 상당한 이익을 남기고 매각되었다. [200]**Ms. Zheng은 또한 Valentine Inc.의 최고 재무 책임자와 Womack International의 최고 경영자로도 일했다.**

어휘 immediate 즉각적인, 즉시의 release 발표, 공개 negotiation 협상 current 현재의 temporarily 임시로, 일시적으로 transition 전환, 이행 as well as ~뿐만 아니라 explore 탐구하다, 개척하다 expansion 확장 investor 투자자 confident 자신하는, 확신하는 launch 시작하다, 개시하다 supplement 보충제, 보조 식품 substantial 상당한 profit 이익, 수익 CFO 최고 재무 책임자

수신: Jia Zheng
발신: Fabian Cattaneo
날짜: 10월 11일
제목: 축하합니다!

Ms. Zheng께,

최근에 Farland Cosmetics에서 당신이 맡은 새로운 직책에 대한 글을 읽었고, 축하를 드리고 싶었어요. [200]**몇 년 전에 당신의 휘하에서 근무했을 때 저는 당신을 훌륭한 최고 경영자라고 생각했는데,** 그렇기 때문에 새로운 직책에서도 잘 해내실 거라고 확신합니다.

Fabian Cattaneo

어휘 recently 최근에 congratulate 축하하다

196. 기업들이 기사에 설명된 전략으로부터 이익을 얻을 수 있는 방법은 무엇인가?

(A) 더 많은 사람들이 그들의 제품을 사용하도록 함으로써
(B) 수입에 대한 규제를 피함으로써
(C) 숙련된 직원들을 보유함으로써
(D) 일부 배송 비용을 줄임으로써

해설 세부 사항
첫 번째 지문에 잠재 고객들에게 제품을 사용하도록 하는 전략이 소개되었으므로 (A)가 정답이다.

패러프레이징 the products are sampled by a wider range of potential customers → By getting more people to try their products

어휘 try 사용해 보다 avoid 피하다 regulation 규제 import 수입품 retain 유지하다, 보유하다

197. Farland Cosmetics는 언제 소유권이 바뀌었는가?

(A) 3월
(B) 7월
(C) 8월
(D) 10월

해설 세부 사항
두 번째 지문에 Farland Cosmetics가 지난달에 Fieldcrest Group에 의해 인수되었다는 내용이 나오는데, 작성일이 8월이므로 지난달은 7월이라는 것을 알 수 있다. 따라서 (B)가 정답이다.

198. Ms. Zheng에 대해 암시된 것은 무엇인가?

(A) 그녀는 근무를 하기 위해 새로운 도시로 이사할 계획이다.
(B) 그녀는 회사의 협상 팀을 이끌었다.
(C) 그녀는 Grant Hotel과 사업 관계를 유지할 것이다.
(D) 그녀는 Terra Hotel의 전 직원이다.

해설 두 지문 연계_추론/암시
두 번째 지문에 Ms. Zheng은 Farland Cosmetics의 신임 최고 경영자이며, 현재의 모든 제휴 관계를 유지할 것이라는 내용이 있다. 또한 첫 번째 지문에서 Farland Cosmetics는 Grant Hotel과 제휴 관계를 맺고 있다는 정보를 찾을 수 있으므로 Ms. Zheng은 Grant Hotel과의 제휴 관계를 유지할 것임을 유추할 수 있다. 따라서 (C)가 정답이다.

패러프레이징 continue all current partnerships → maintain a business relationship

어휘 take on (일을) 맡다 former 예전의

199. 보도 자료에 따르면 Ms. Burks는 무엇을 했는가?

(A) Ms. Zheng을 Farland Cosmetics에 영입했다.
(B) 성공적인 회사를 공동으로 설립했다.
(C) 새로운 종류의 비타민을 발명했다.
(D) Valentine Inc.에 업체를 매각했다.

해설 세부 사항
두 번째 지문에서 Ms. Burks가 Ms. Zheng과 함께 비타민 보충제 회사를 설립했다고 했으므로 (B)가 정답이다.

어휘 recruit 채용하다, 영입하다 co-found 공동으로 창업하다

TEST 04

200. Mr. Cattaneo에 대해 암시된 것은 무엇인가?

(A) 전에 Womack International에서 근무했다.

(B) 현재 화장품 업계에 종사하고 있다.

(C) Ms. Zheng에 대한 기사를 쓰고 싶어 한다.

(D) Ms. Zheng의 팀에서 할 수 있는 역할을 찾고 있다.

해설 두 지문 연계_추론/암시

세 번째 지문에 Mr. Cattaneo가 Ms. Zheng이 최고 경영자였을 때 그녀의 휘하에서 근무했다는 내용이 있다. 또한 두 번째 지문의 마지막 문단에서 Ms. Zheng이 Womack International에서 최고 경영자를 역임했다고 했으므로, Mr. Cattaneo는 Womack International에서 근무했었다는 것을 추론할 수 있다. 따라서 (A)가 정답이다.

어휘 previously 전에 article 기사 seek 찾다, 모색하다 role 역할, 임무

TEST 05

LISTENING TEST

1. (C)	**2.** (B)	**3.** (B)	**4.** (C)	**5.** (B)
6. (B)	**7.** (B)	**8.** (A)	**9.** (A)	**10.** (B)
11. (A)	**12.** (C)	**13.** (B)	**14.** (A)	**15.** (A)
16. (B)	**17.** (A)	**18.** (A)	**19.** (C)	**20.** (C)
21. (B)	**22.** (B)	**23.** (A)	**24.** (A)	**25.** (B)
26. (A)	**27.** (C)	**28.** (C)	**29.** (B)	**30.** (B)
31. (A)	**32.** (C)	**33.** (B)	**34.** (A)	**35.** (B)
36. (C)	**37.** (A)	**38.** (D)	**39.** (B)	**40.** (A)
41. (D)	**42.** (C)	**43.** (A)	**44.** (C)	**45.** (A)
46. (C)	**47.** (C)	**48.** (B)	**49.** (C)	**50.** (A)
51. (D)	**52.** (C)	**53.** (C)	**54.** (C)	**55.** (B)
56. (D)	**57.** (B)	**58.** (A)	**59.** (C)	**60.** (A)
61. (B)	**62.** (C)	**63.** (D)	**64.** (B)	**65.** (C)
66. (A)	**67.** (B)	**68.** (A)	**69.** (B)	**70.** (C)
71. (C)	**72.** (A)	**73.** (B)	**74.** (A)	**75.** (D)
76. (D)	**77.** (C)	**78.** (B)	**79.** (D)	**80.** (D)
81. (A)	**82.** (C)	**83.** (B)	**84.** (B)	**85.** (A)
86. (A)	**87.** (D)	**88.** (B)	**89.** (C)	**90.** (A)
91. (D)	**92.** (D)	**93.** (B)	**94.** (C)	**95.** (A)
96. (C)	**97.** (B)	**98.** (D)	**99.** (C)	**100.** (D)

READING TEST

101. (D)	**102.** (B)	**103.** (B)	**104.** (A)	**105.** (C)
106. (D)	**107.** (A)	**108.** (D)	**109.** (C)	**110.** (B)
111. (A)	**112.** (D)	**113.** (C)	**114.** (A)	**115.** (A)
116. (C)	**117.** (A)	**118.** (B)	**119.** (B)	**120.** (B)
121. (D)	**122.** (D)	**123.** (C)	**124.** (B)	**125.** (D)
126. (D)	**127.** (B)	**128.** (D)	**129.** (B)	**130.** (A)
131. (C)	**132.** (B)	**133.** (C)	**134.** (D)	**135.** (A)
136. (B)	**137.** (C)	**138.** (D)	**139.** (B)	**140.** (A)
141. (A)	**142.** (D)	**143.** (C)	**144.** (A)	**145.** (D)
146. (B)	**147.** (C)	**148.** (C)	**149.** (B)	**150.** (A)
151. (B)	**152.** (D)	**153.** (C)	**154.** (C)	**155.** (B)
156. (A)	**157.** (B)	**158.** (B)	**159.** (C)	**160.** (A)
161. (B)	**162.** (A)	**163.** (C)	**164.** (D)	**165.** (D)
166. (C)	**167.** (B)	**168.** (B)	**169.** (C)	**170.** (D)
171. (C)	**172.** (B)	**173.** (B)	**174.** (D)	**175.** (B)
176. (D)	**177.** (C)	**178.** (B)	**179.** (B)	**180.** (D)
181. (A)	**182.** (B)	**183.** (C)	**184.** (A)	**185.** (B)
186. (C)	**187.** (A)	**188.** (A)	**189.** (B)	**190.** (D)
191. (B)	**192.** (D)	**193.** (B)	**194.** (A)	**195.** (C)
196. (B)	**197.** (A)	**198.** (D)	**199.** (A)	**200.** (D)

PART 1

1. 미녀

(A) They're adjusting their helmets.
(B) One of the men is sharpening a pencil.
(C) One of the men is marking a drawing.
(D) They're folding some paper.

(A) 그들은 헬멧을 고쳐 쓰고 있다.
(B) 남자들 중 한 명이 연필을 깎고 있다.
(C) 남자들 중 한 명이 도면에 표시하고 있다.
(D) 그들은 종이를 접고 있다.

어휘 adjust (약간) 조정[조절]하다, (매무새 등을) 바로잡다 sharpen (날카롭게) 갈다[깎다] mark 표시하다 drawing (연필이나 펜 등으로 그린) 그림, 도면 fold 접다

2. 미남

(A) Some binders have been stacked on a desk.
(B) A woman is reaching for a box on a shelf.
(C) Some packages are being delivered.
(D) A woman is removing some labels.

(A) 바인더들이 책상 위에 쌓여 있다.
(B) 여자가 선반에 놓인 상자를 향해 손을 뻗고 있다.
(C) 소포가 배달되고 있다.
(D) 여자가 라벨을 제거하고 있다.

어휘 stack 쌓다 reach for ~을 향해 손을 뻗다 remove 제거하다

3. 영녀

(A) A customer is trying on some sneakers.
(B) A customer is holding an item.
(C) A customer is approaching a counter.
(D) A customer is taking out his wallet.

(A) 손님이 운동화를 착용해 보고 있다.
(B) 손님이 물건을 들고 있다.
(C) 손님이 카운터에 다가가고 있다.
(D) 손님이 지갑을 꺼내고 있다.

어휘 try on 입어보다/착용해보다 hold 들다 approach ~에 다가가다 take out 꺼내다

4. 호남

(A) He's turning on a bedside lamp.
(B) He's organizing some bookshelves.
(C) He's wiping down a desk.
(D) He's putting on a pair of gloves.

(A) 남자가 침대 옆 램프를 켜고 있다.
(B) 남자가 책장을 정리하고 있다.
(C) 남자가 책상을 닦고 있다.
(D) 남자가 장갑을 끼는 중이다.

어휘 turn on 켜다 organize 정리하다 wide down 닦다 put on ~을 입다 (is putting on은 입고 있는 동작, is wearing은 입고 있는 상태를 나타낸다.)

5. 미녀

(A) Some flowerpots have been arranged on a porch.
(B) A lawn mower has been placed on the grass.
(C) A wood fence lines an athletic field.
(D) Some leaves have been raked into a pile.

(A) 화분 몇 개가 현관에 놓여 있다.
(B) 잔디 깎는 기계가 잔디에 놓여 있다.
(C) 나무 울타리가 운동장을 둘러싸고 있다.
(D) 긁어모은 나뭇잎이 쌓여 있다.

어휘 flowerpot 화분(a potted plant 화분에 심겨진 식물) arrange 정리하다, 배열하다 porch 현관 line ~을 따라 늘어서다 athletic field 운동장 rake 갈퀴로 모으다

6. 호남

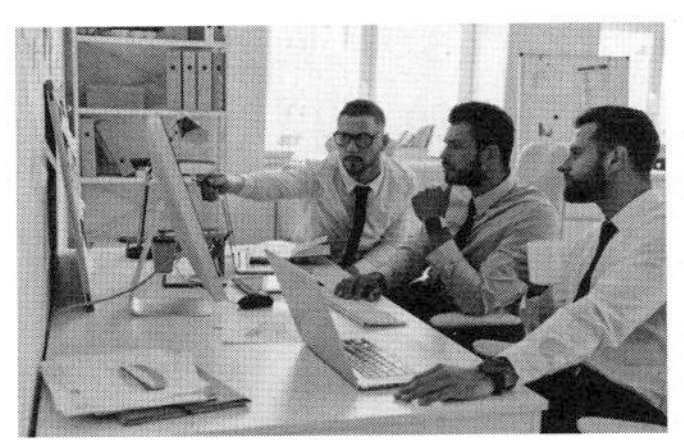

(A) One of the men is checking his watch.
(B) The men are wearing ties.
(C) One of the men is writing notes.
(D) The men are looking at each other.

(A) 남자들 중 한 명이 손목시계를 확인하고 있다.
(B) 남자들이 넥타이를 하고 있다.
(C) 남자들 중 한 명이 메모를 하고 있다.
(D) 남자들이 서로를 바라보고 있다.

어휘 wear 입고 있다(상태) write notes 메모하다

PART 2

7. 미남 영녀

Who's writing the press statement?
(A) Press the red button.
(B) Karen is doing it.
(C) At the newsstand down the street.

누가 언론 발표문을 쓰고 있나요?
(A) 빨간 버튼을 누르세요.
(B) 캐런이 하고 있어요.
(C) 거리 아래쪽의 가판대에서요.

어휘 press statement 언론 성명 newsstand (거리 · 역 구내 등의) 신문[잡지] 판매점, 가판대

8. 호남 미녀

Where is the next business conference?
(A) In Kyoto, Japan.
(B) I have some work to do now.
(C) The second week in July, I think.

다음 업무 콘퍼런스는 어디에서 열리나요?
(A) 일본 교토에서요.
(B) 지금 할 일이 좀 있어요.
(C) 7월 둘째 주일 것 같아요.

9. 영녀 미남

Why are you going to the airport next week?
(A) To pick up my clients.
(B) Around three o'clock.
(C) Let's meet at Terminal B.

다음주에 왜 공항으로 가시나요?
(A) 고객들을 데리러 가요.
(B) 3시쯤에요.
(C) B 터미널에서 만나도록 해요.

10. 미녀 미남

Does Ms. Denver work at the law firm or does she have a private practice?
(A) We should practice for our demonstration.
(B) At the law firm, I think.
(C) I'll meet the client in person.

덴버 씨는 로펌에서 일하시나요, 아니면 개인 사무실이 있으신가요?
(A) 우리의 시연을 위해 연습해야 해요.
(B) 로펌에서 일하는 것 같아요.
(C) 제가 고객을 직접 만날게요.

어휘 law firm 법률 사무소, 로펌 private practice (의사나 변호사 등의) 개인 영업 meet ~ in person ~를 직접 만나다

11. 호남 미녀

What's the best way for us to get to the client's office?
(A) A taxi is probably best.
(B) I was out of the office.
(C) They are in a meeting now.

우리가 고객의 사무실로 갈 수 있는 가장 좋은 방법은 무엇인가요?
(A) 아마 택시가 최선일 거예요.
(B) 저는 사무실에 없었어요.
(C) 그들은 지금 회의 중이에요.

12. 영녀 미남

When will the new forklift arrive?
(A) I also need a knife and spoon.
(B) At least 20.
(C) Sometime tomorrow.

새로운 지게차는 언제 도착하나요?
(A) 나이프와 수저도 필요해요.
(B) 적어도 20이요.
(C) 내일쯤요.

어휘 forklift 지게차

13. 호남 미남

Would you like me to show them the new rental property?
(A) The sound system isn't working properly.
(B) Yes, I'd appreciate that.
(C) I would like to borrow it.

제가 그들에게 새로운 임대 건물을 보여드릴까요?
(A) 사운드 시스템이 제대로 작동하지를 않아요.
(B) 네, 그러면 감사하죠.
(C) 그것을 빌리고 싶어요.

어휘 property 재산, 부동산, 건물

14. 영녀 호남

Did you remember to hire security guards for tonight's movie premiere?
(A) They should be arriving soon.
(B) Please lift it up a little higher.
(C) Did you secure a ticket?

오늘 밤 영화 시사회에 경비원 고용하는 거 잊지 않으셨죠?
(A) 그들은 곧 도착할 거예요.
(B) 그걸 좀 더 높이 올려주세요.
(C) 입장권을 확보하셨나요?

어휘 premiere (영화의) 개봉, (연극의) 초연 secure (특히 힘들게) 얻어 내다, 획득[확보]하다

15. 미남 영녀

Why was your flight delayed?
(A) Because there was bad weather.
(B) Let's review the itinerary for our trip.
(C) We should get something to eat while we wait.

비행기가 왜 연착되었죠?
(A) 날씨가 안 좋아서요.
(B) 여행 일정을 검토해 보죠.

(C) 기다리는 동안 뭘 좀 먹어야겠어요.

어휘 itinerary 여행 일정표

16. 영녀 미녀

Who's going to stock the store shelves?
(A) Only if you have time.
(B) Yasmin said she would do it.
(C) During his commute to work.

누가 가게 선반들을 채워 놓을 건가요?
(A) 당신이 시간이 있으시다면요.
(B) 야스민이 자기가 할 거라고 했어요.
(C) 그가 출근하는 동안요.

어휘 stock 채우다

17. 미남 영녀

How many paper cups can these machines produce each hour?
(A) I just started working here.
(B) Mainly coffee shops and bakeries.
(C) Did anyone fix the fax machine?

이 기계들은 시간당 얼마나 많은 종이컵을 생산할 수 있나요?
(A) 저는 이곳에서 갓 일을 시작했어요.
(B) 주로 커피숍과 빵집이요.
(C) 팩스기를 누군가 고쳤나요?

어휘 produce 생산하다 fix 고치다

18. 미녀 호남

Aren't these necklaces supposed to be on sale?
(A) No, only the bracelets are.
(B) Unfortunately, we couldn't complete the merger.
(C) Here are the sales figures.

이 목걸이들은 할인되는 거 아닌가요?
(A) 아니에요, 팔찌만 할인돼요.
(B) 안타깝게도, 저희는 합병을 끝마칠 수 없었습니다.
(C) 매출액 여기 있습니다.

어휘 be supposed to do ~하기로 되어 있다 on sale 할인중인, 판매되는 sales figures 매출액

19. 영녀 호남

Do we have enough time for all of the presentations?
(A) Yes, I really enjoyed the show.
(B) It left on time from Orlando.
(C) I think we'll have to finish tomorrow.

모든 발표를 할 충분한 시간이 있나요?
(A) 네, 정말 즐거운 쇼였어요.
(B) 그건 올란도에서 정시에 떠났어요.
(C) 내일 끝내야 할 것 같아요.

20. 미남 영녀

When do you leave for your trip?
(A) Two round-trip tickets.
(B) The package arrived this morning.
(C) Tomorrow evening.

언제 여행을 떠나시나요?
(A) 왕복 표 두 장이요.
(B) 소포가 오늘 아침에 도착했어요.
(C) 내일 밤에요.

21. 미녀 영녀

I'm going to go out for lunch today.
(A) Several new menu items.
(B) I'll join you.
(C) I want to go to Paris.

오늘 저는 밖에서 점심을 먹을 거예요.
(A) 몇 가지 새로운 메뉴 아이템이요.
(B) 저도 같이 갈게요.
(C) 파리에 가고 싶어요.

22. 미녀 호남

Can you make sure all the guests sign in, please?
(A) I need your signature here.
(B) Sure, no problem.
(C) We are happy to welcome you to our hotel.

모든 손님들이 기록부에 서명하고 들어오게 해 주실래요?
(A) 여기에 서명해 주세요.
(B) 물론이죠, 문제없습니다.
(C) 귀하를 저희 호텔에서 맞이할 수 있어 기쁩니다.

어휘 sign in (회사 · 클럽 등의 기록부에) 서명하고 들어가다

23. 미남 미녀

The marketing team is going to show us the ad before it's released, isn't it?
(A) I should ask about that.
(B) He was promoted to manager!
(C) Yes, I added your name to the list.

광고가 나오기 전에 마케팅 팀이 우리에게 먼저 보여줄 거죠, 아닌가요?

(A) 그것에 대해 물어봐야겠네요.
(B) 그가 과장으로 승진했어요!
(C) 네, 당신 이름을 명단에 올렸어요.

어휘 release (대중들에게) 공개[발표]하다

24. 호남 미녀

What do most people do for work in this area?
(A) They're employed by the car manufacturing plant.
(B) There's a workshop scheduled for tomorrow.
(C) About 20 minutes from here.

이 지역 사람들은 주로 어떤 일에 종사하나요?
(A) 그들은 자동차 제조 공장에 고용되어 일합니다.
(B) 내일 워크숍이 예정되어 있습니다.
(C) 여기서 20분 정도예요.

어휘 employ 고용하다

25. 영녀 미남

How can I add ink to the printer?
(A) Because the copier is out of toner.
(B) Let's check the instructions.
(C) I like that idea.

프린터에 어떻게 잉크를 넣나요?
(A) 복사기에 토너가 다 떨어졌거든요.
(B) 설명서를 확인해 봅시다.
(C) 그거 괜찮은 생각인데요.

어휘 be out of ~이 떨어지다(바닥나다) instructions 설명서

26. 미녀 호남

Can you e-mail me a copy of the press release?
(A) Can I send it to you after lunch?
(B) Sure, I'll sign for the delivery.
(C) There are no pressing issues at the moment.

공식 발표문의 사본을 저에게 이메일로 보내주실 수 있나요?
(A) 점심 이후에 보내도 될까요?
(B) 물론이죠. 제가 택배에 서명할게요.
(C) 지금은 긴급한 문제가 없습니다.

어휘 press release 대언론 공식 발표[성명] pressing 긴급한

27. 호남 영녀

Isn't the heater supposed to be turned off at 6?
(A) Let's switch on the radio.
(B) These lights are too bright.
(C) Maybe the janitor forgot to do it.

난방기가 6시에 꺼져야 하지 않나요?
(A) 라디오를 켭시다.
(B) 이 조명들은 너무 밝아요.
(C) 아마도 관리원이 깜박한 것 같네요.

어휘 turn off 끄다 switch on ~을 켜다 janitor (건물 등의) 관리인

28. 미녀 미남

Oh, I can't see the clock.
(A) About three weeks from now.
(B) I drove them to the job site.
(C) It's 4 P.M. now.

어, 시계가 없네요.
(A) 지금으로부터 3주 정도 후에요.
(B) 제가 그들을 작업 현장까지 태워다 줬어요.
(C) 지금 오후 4시입니다.

29. 영녀 호남

Where can I go to have our company vehicle inspected?
(A) In December of every year.
(B) There's a mechanic around the corner.
(C) I have to put some air in my tires.

우리 회사 차량을 점검받으려면 어디로 가야 하죠?
(A) 매년 12월이요.
(B) 근처에 정비소가 있어요.
(C) 타이어에 바람을 좀 넣어야겠네요.

어휘 inspect 점검하다 mechanic 정비사 around the corner 근처에

30. 호남 미녀

Do I have to use a passcode or ID badge to get in the room?
(A) Down the hall to the right.
(B) The door should be unlocked.
(C) I left my ID card at home.

그 방에 들어가려면 비밀번호를 사용해야 하나요, 아니면 신분증을 사용해야 하나요?
(A) 복도를 따라 오른쪽이요.
(B) 아마 문이 잠겨 있지 않을 거예요.

(C) 신분증을 집에 두고 왔는데요.

어휘 unlock 문의 자물쇠를 열다

31. 영녀 미녀

I can still change my order, right?
(A) I'll ask the chef.
(B) Clyde will go first.
(C) Yes, she does.

아직 제 주문을 바꿀 수 있죠, 그렇죠?
(A) 주방장에게 물어보겠습니다.
(B) 클라이드가 먼저 할 거예요.
(C) 네, 그녀가 합니다.

PART 3

호남 영녀

Questions 32-34 refer to the following conversation.

M Hi, Rebecca. Later today I'm going to meet Ms. Gupta, our former marketing director. [32]She just got promoted to board executive, so I wanted to give her a nice present. Do you know of any florists around here?

W [33]Alice's Flower Shop is great. It's inside the Austins Department Store, next to the west entrance.

M Thanks. [34]After I send out a few e-mails, I'll make my way to the shop.

남 안녕하세요, 레베카. 오늘 이따가 우리의 전 마케팅 부장인 굽타 씨를 만날 거예요. [32]**그녀가 막 임원으로 승진하여서, 그녀에게 좋은 선물을 해주고 싶었어요.** 여기 주변에 아는 플로리스트 있나요?

여 [33]**앨리스 꽃집이 좋아요. 오스틴즈 백화점 안에 들어가면 서쪽 입구 옆에 있어요.**

남 감사합니다. [34]**이메일을 좀 보낸 후에 그 가게에 가 봐야겠네요.**

어휘 former 전직 get promoted to ~으로 승진하다
board executive 이사회 임원 make my way to ~쪽으로 가다

32. 남자는 왜 굽타 씨에게 꽃을 사주고 싶어 하는가?
(A) 그녀가 은퇴한다.
(B) 그녀가 이직한다.
(C) 그녀가 승진했다.
(D) 그녀가 상을 받았다.

패러프레이징 got promoted → got a promotion

33. 여자에 따르면, 앨리스 꽃집은 어디에 있는가?
(A) 기차역 옆에
(B) 백화점 안에
(C) 학교 건너편에
(D) 도서관 근처에

34. 남자는 사무실을 떠나기 전에 무엇을 할 것이라 말하는가?
(A) 이메일 보내기
(B) 전화하기
(C) 회의 참석하기
(D) 프로젝트 확정하기

패러프레이징 send out a few e-mails → send some e-mails

호남 미녀

Questions 35-37 refer to the following conversation.

M Ms. Rocha, I booked a hotel for your trip to Barcelona next month. [35]Luckily, I found a hotel within 10 minutes of the conference center.

W Wonderful! Thank you so much.

M No problem at all. [36]And remember to get to the event early, since there will be a lot of people in attendance this year.

W I'll do that. [37]Oh, and does the hotel have a computer room with Internet access? I have some work to do on the computer while I'm away, but I don't want to bring my laptop with me.

남 로카 씨, 다음 달에 있을 당신의 바르셀로나 출장을 위해 호텔을 예약하였습니다. [35]**운좋게도, 회의장에서 10분 거리인 호텔을 발견했어요.**

여 잘됐네요! 정말 감사합니다.

남 천만에요. [36]**그리고 행사에 일찍 가는 것을 잊지 마세요, 금년엔 참석하는 사람들이 많을 테니까요.**

여 그렇게 할게요. [37]**아, 혹시 호텔에 인터넷 되는 컴퓨터실 있나요?** 출장 가 있는 동안 컴퓨터로 할 일이 좀 있는데, 제 노트북을 들고 가기는 싫어서요.

어휘 within 10 minutes of ~에서 10분 거리에 있는 in attendance 참석한
while I'm away 출장 가 있는 동안

35. 남자는 여자를 위해 무엇을 하였는가?
(A) 그는 그녀의 항공편을 마련해 주었다.
(B) 그는 그녀의 숙소를 찾아 주었다.
(C) 그는 여자의 콘퍼런스 입장권을 샀다.
(D) 그는 그녀에게 기사를 구해줬다.

패러프레이징 found a hotel → found her accomodations

36. 남자는 여자에게 무엇을 하도록 상기시켜 주는가?

(A) 그녀의 발표 자료를 가져오도록
(B) 그녀의 영수증을 보관하도록
(C) 콘퍼런스에 일찍 도착하도록
(D) 신중하게 짐을 싸도록

패러프레이징 get to the event early → arrive at the conference early

37. 여자는 남자에게 무엇에 대해 묻는가?

(A) 컴퓨터실
(B) 호텔 헬스장
(C) 회의장
(D) 식당

영녀 미남

Questions 38-40 refer to the following conversation.

W Jerome, do you have any ideas on how we can make [38]our new formal wear collection more unique?

M [39]I was thinking about using cashmere instead of cotton for our fabric. Most other brands just use cheaper materials, but we can stand out if we have higher quality clothing.

W [40]That's a good idea, but I worry that would greatly raise production costs. We can't make such a major change so suddenly. Let's try using cashmere for one of our men's sweaters and see how the sales go. If it makes a lot of money, we can make more of the sweaters out of cashmere next season.

여 제롬, [38]우리의 새로운 정장 컬렉션을 더욱 특별하게 만들 수 있는 좋은 방안 있나요?

남 [39]면 대신 캐시미어를 쓰는 건 어떨까 생각하는 중이었어요. 대부분의 다른 브랜드에서는 싼 가격의 재료를 사용하지만, 우리가 고품질의 옷을 만든다면 눈에 띄게 될 거예요.

여 [40]좋은 생각이에요. 하지만 그러면 생산 비용이 크게 증가할 것 같아 걱정돼요. 갑자기 그렇게 큰 변화를 줄 수는 없어요. 남자 스웨터들 중 하나에 캐시미어를 사용해 본 뒤 판매가 어떤지 지켜보죠. 만약 이게 수익이 괜찮다면, 다음 시즌에 더 많은 스웨터를 캐시미어로 만들 수 있을 거예요.

어휘 fabric 직물, 천 stand out 빼어나다, 눈에 띄다 raise 올리다 production cost 생산 비용

38. 화자들은 어떤 업계에서 일할 것 같은가?

(A) 원예
(B) 금융
(C) 광고
(D) 패션

39. 남자는 무엇을 제안하는가?

(A) 현 품목들을 늘리는 것
(B) 천의 종류를 바꾸는 것
(C) 새로운 가게를 여는 것
(D) 공식적인 행사에 참여하는 것

40. 여자는 무엇에 관해 걱정하는가?

(A) 계획에 너무 많은 비용이 든다.
(B) 무늬가 너무 산만하다.
(C) 손님들이 불평할 수 있다.
(D) 몇몇 품목들이 잘 팔리고 있지 않다.

영녀 호남 미녀

Questions 41-43 refer to the following conversation with three speakers.

W1 Hi, Mark. Do you have some time to spare? Bianca and I need your help with the company's intranet.

M Sure. What's the problem?

W1 No matter how many times we try, [41]we can't log into the system. We've been trying to access the Web site for at least 30 minutes, right, Bianca?

W2 That's right. We need to access some sales figures for the annual sales report by tomorrow, so can you help us right away?

M [42]Actually, a number of people have called the IT department and reported similar issues. It's our top priority right now.

W2 Thank you. [43]We have to have a meeting in the conference room right now, but could you let us know when the problem is fixed?

여1 안녕하세요, 마크. 시간 좀 내 주실 수 있나요? 비앙카와 제가 사내 전산망 관련해서 당신의 도움이 필요해요.

남 물론이죠. 어떤 문제인가요?

여1 몇 번을 시도해 보아도 [41]시스템에 접속할 수가 없어요. 적어도 30분 동안 계속 웹 사이트에 접속 시도를 해 보고 있었어요, 맞죠, 비앙카?

여2 맞아요. 내일까지 연간 매출 보고서를 위한 매출 수치를 파악해야 하는데, 지금 바로 도와주실 수 있나요?

남 [42]실은, 여러 사람들이 IT부서에 전화해서 비슷한 문제를 보고했어요. 그게 지금 우리의 최우선 사항이에요.

여2 감사합니다. [43]저희는 지금 회의실에서 회의를 해야 하는데, 문제가 해결되면 알려주실 수 있나요?

어휘 intranet 인트라넷, 내부 전산망 access 접속하다 sales figures 매출

액 a number of 여러 (= several) top priority 최고 우선순위

41. 어떤 문제가 논의되고 있는가?

(A) 복사기가 제대로 작동하지 않는다.

(B) 회의실이 이미 사용되고 있다.

(C) 배송이 제시간에 이뤄지지 않았다.

(D) 몇몇 직원들이 본인의 계정에 접속할 수 없다.

패러프레이징 can't log into the system → cannot access their accounts

42. 남자는 누구일 것 같은가?

(A) 회사 임원

(B) 광고 부장

(C) 컴퓨터 전문가

(D) 신입 인턴

43. 여자들은 다음에 무엇을 할 계획인가?

(A) 회의하기

(B) 고객 만나기

(C) 공항에 가기

(D) 계약서에 서명하기

영녀 미남

Questions 44-46 refer to the following conversation.

W Anthony's [44]Italian Bistro. How can I help you?

M I'm from Colonel and Company, and I'd like to book a table for six for my colleagues and me. If possible, we'd like to go for dinner next Wednesday around 7 P.M.

W I apologize, but we'll be closed next Wednesday. [45]We will be having a deep, professional cleaning on that day.

M I see. Then, can I make a reservation for the following day—May fifth?

W Of course. 7 P.M., right?

M Yes, and I have a rewards card with you already, so I believe my information should already be on file.

W Great. [46]Just tell me your name, and I'll make the reservation right away.

여 안토니즈 [44]이탈리안 비스트로입니다. 어떻게 도와드릴까요?

남 여긴 컬러널 앤 컴퍼니인데요, 저와 제 동료들을 위해 6인 테이블을 예약하고 싶습니다. 가능하다면, 다음주 수요일 오후 7시쯤에 저녁 식사를 하러 가려고요.

여 죄송합니다만, 저희는 다음주 수요일에 휴업합니다. [45]그날 대대적으로 전문적인 청소를 할 거라서요.

남 알겠습니다. 그럼, 그 다음날인 5월 5일로 예약할 수 있을까요?

여 물론이죠. 오후 7시 맞죠?

남 네, 그리고 저는 이미 식당 적립 카드가 있으니, 제 정보가 등록되어 있을 거예요.

여 네, [46]**그럼 성함만 얘기해 주시면, 바로 예약해 드리겠습니다.**

어휘 bistro (편안한 분위기의) 작은 식당 book a table 식사할 좌석을 예약하다 go for dinner 저녁 식사하러 가다 make a reservation 예약하다

44. 여자는 어디에서 일하는가?

(A) 미용실에서

(B) 여행사에서

(C) 식당에서

(D) 자동차 대리점에서

45. 남자는 왜 다음주 수요일로 예약을 잡을 수 없는가?

(A) 시설들이 청소될 것이다.

(B) 모든 직원이 휴가를 떠날 것이다.

(C) 일정표에 예약이 다 찼다.

(D) 장비가 교체되고 있다.

패러프레이징 will be having a deep, professional cleaning → will be cleaned

46. 남자는 다음에 무엇을 할 것 같은가?

(A) 다시 전화하기

(B) 다른 장소 찾아보기

(C) 자신의 이름 알려주기

(D) 온라인에 후기 쓰기

미남 미녀

Questions 47-49 refer to the following conversation.

M [47]Ms. Ridley, this is Kenneth Belton, one of the freelance writers for your magazine. I'm calling about the April issue.

W Hi, Kenneth. I know we're using your article on the best ways to recycle for our "Protecting the Earth" series.

M Right. But I just discovered a few more recycling tips online recently. [48]Would you allow me to edit the article to include them?

W The issue has already gone to the printer.

M Oh, I see. Sorry to bother you.

W I'm actually glad you called. [49]We're looking to hire a new associate editor, so I was wondering if you could come in for a job interview. I think you'd be a great fit for the position.

남 [47]리들리 씨, 케네스 벨턴이에요. 귀사 잡지의 프리랜스 작가들 중 한 명입니다. 4월 호에 관해 연락드립니다.

여 안녕하세요, 케네스. 당신이 재활용을 하는 최선의 방법에 대해 쓴 글이 우리의 〈지구 지키기〉 시리즈에 실린다고 알고 있어요.

남 맞아요. 그런데 제가 최근에 온라인에서 재활용 팁을 몇 개 더 알게 되었어요. [48]그것들을 포함해서 기사를 수정할 수 있을까요?

여 이미 해당 호를 인쇄소로 보냈어요.

남 아, 알겠습니다. 괜히 성가시게 해 드렸네요.

여 사실 전화 주시길 잘 하셨어요. [49]저희가 새로 부편집자를 채용하려 하는데, 면접을 보러 와 주실 수 있는지 궁금했거든요. 당신이 이 자리의 적임자일 것 같아요.

어휘 printer 인쇄업자, 인쇄소 be looking to do ~하려고 계획 중이다 (= be planning to do) associate (흔히 직함에 쓰여) 준/부/조

47. 남자는 누구인가?

(A) 통역사
(B) 편집장
(C) 작가
(D) 판매원

48. 여자는 왜 "이미 해당 호를 인쇄소로 보냈어요"라고 말하는가?

(A) 불만을 제기하려고
(B) 제안을 거절하기 위해
(C) 실수에 대해 사과하기 위해
(D) 약속을 다시 잡으려고

49. 여자는 남자에게 무엇을 청하는가?

(A) 새로운 원고를 쓰는 것
(B) 작가들을 더 모집하는 것
(C) 면접을 보러 오는 것
(D) 잡지 표지에 출연하는 것

호남 미녀 영녀

Questions 50-52 refer to the following conversation with three speakers.

M Harriet and Paige — could you give me updates on the projects you're planning?

W1 [50]Government officials expressed interest in using our company to build the new highway, but I haven't heard back from them since I sent them a quote.

W2 I've been working with the city government to make a plan to repave some old roads, [51]and I have the same problem. They haven't replied back yet, either.

M [52]Hmm, how about we offer them both a 10% discount? That should get them to make a decision more quickly.

남 해리엇, 그리고 페이지 — 계획하고 있는 프로젝트는 어떻게 돼 가죠?

여1 [50]새로운 고속도로를 짓기 위해 우리 회사를 이용하는 데 정부 관계자들이 관심을 보였어요. 하지만 제가 견적서를 보내 준 이후로 다시 연락을 받지 못했어요.

여2 오래된 도로의 재포장 계획을 세우기 위해 시청과 일하고 있는데, [51]저도 같은 문제를 겪고 있어요. 저 역시 아직 답변을 못 받았어요.

남 [52]흠, 두 곳 모두에 10% 할인을 제안하면 어떨까요? 그러면 더 빨리 결정할 수 있게 만들 수 있을 거예요.

어휘 quote 견적서 (= estimate) make a plan 계획을 세우다 repave 다시 포장하다 (pave 포장하다) make a decision 결정하다

50. 화자들은 어떤 업체에서 일할 것 같은가?

(A) 건설 회사
(B) 의원
(C) 장난감 회사
(D) 정부 기관

51. 여자들은 어떤 문제를 말하는가?

(A) 대금이 지불되지 않았다.
(B) 몇몇 시설들이 수리되어야 한다.
(C) 공급 업체가 올바른 제품을 배달하지 않았다.
(D) 예비 고객들이 답하지 않고 있다.

패러프레이징 haven't replied back → have not answered back

52. 남자는 어떤 것을 추천하는가?

(A) 새로운 지점을 여는 것
(B) 다른 고객들을 찾아보는 것
(C) 할인된 가격을 제안하는 것
(D) 새로운 공급 업체를 찾는 것

미남 미녀

Questions 53-55 refer to the following conversation.

M [53]Ms. Moore, thank you for agreeing to participate in our product-testing session.

W No problem. So I'll be testing out some new designs for ergonomic keyboards?

M That's right. We want to see if our keyboards are more comfortable than traditional keyboards. [54]Before we start, do you mind providing me with your ID? We need your information for tax purposes.

TEST 05

W Sure. But I actually have a question. I have some joint problems in my wrist. Will that get in the way of the testing?

M Oh, not at all. In fact, we need to test the keyboards out on people with different ability levels. I'll bring you to the other participants now. [55]Please follow me to Room 212.

남 [53]무어 씨, 저희 제품 시험 참가에 동의해 주셔서 감사합니다.

여 천만에요. 그러니까 제가 인체공학적 키보드의 새로운 디자인들을 시험해보면 되는 거죠?

남 그렇습니다. 저희는 기존의 키보드보다 우리의 키보드가 더 편한지 확인해 보고 싶어요. **[54]시작하기 전에, 당신의 신분증을 제시해 주실 수 있을까요?** 세금 때문에 당신의 정보가 필요하거든요.

여 물론이죠. 그런데 실은 질문이 하나 있어요. 제 손목 관절에 문제가 좀 있는데, 시험해 볼 때 문제가 될까요?

남 아, 전혀요. 사실, 저희는 각기 다른 수행 능력을 가진 사람들에게 시험해 봐야 하거든요. 이제 당신을 다른 참가자들 쪽으로 모시겠습니다. **[55]저를 따라 212호로 가실까요.**

어휘 test out ~를 시험해 보다 ergonomic 인체공학적 for ~ purposes ~ 목적으로 (for medical/cosmetic/leisure purposes 의료/미용/여가 목적으로) joint 관절 get in the way of ~을 방해하다

53. 여자는 무엇을 하기로 동의하였는가?
(A) 키보드 구매하기
(B) 회의 이끌기
(C) 제품 시험해 보기
(D) 새로운 광고 기획하기

54. 남자는 여자에게 무엇을 원하는가?
(A) 동의서
(B) 그녀의 성명
(C) 그녀의 신분증
(D) 그녀의 이력서 사본

55. 여자는 다음에 무엇을 할 것 같은가?
(A) 그녀의 집으로 돌아가기
(B) 남자 따라가기
(C) 일자리 제의 받아들이기
(D) 전화 걸기

미남 영녀

Questions 56-58 refer to the following conversation.

M Hey, Nadia. Did you finish setting up everything for tonight's dinner service?

W Almost. [56]I'm waiting for the kitchen staff to finish cleaning the silverware so I can set all the tables.

M Great. I wanted to talk to you about something... It seems we're all using too much water every month. We should each think of ways to reduce our water consumption.

W Really? I didn't know that was an issue.

M [57]Well, similar businesses I own spend about half of what this location does in a month.

W Hmm. They seem to have fewer customers, though.

M That's true, but we all need to make changes regardless. [58]Let's discuss it further at the staff meeting later today.

남 안녕, 나디아. 오늘 밤 저녁 서비스를 위한 준비는 다 끝마쳤나요?

여 거의 다요. **[56]주방 직원이 은식기류를 닦는 것을 기다리고 있어요.** 그래야 테이블들을 세팅할 수 있거든요.

남 고생했어요. 당신에게 말하고 싶었던 게 있는데... 우리가 매달 너무 많은 물을 사용하는 것 같아 보여요. 물 소비량을 줄이는 방법을 우리 모두 각자 생각해 보는 것이 좋겠어요.

여 그래요? 저는 그게 문제가 될지 몰랐어요.

남 **[57]음, 제가 소유하고 있는 비슷한 사업장들에서는 이 사업장이 한 달에 쓰는 양의 반밖에 사용하지 않아요.**

여 흠. 근데, 그곳들은 손님이 더 적은 것 같은데요.

남 맞아요, 하지만 그래도 우리 모두 변화할 필요가 있어요. **[58]오늘 오후에 직원 회의에서 이것에 대해 더 논의해 봅시다.**

어휘 set up 준비하다 set the table 테이블을 세팅하다 consumption 소비 location 지점 regardless 그럼에도 불구하고

56. 여자는 무엇을 기다리고 있는가?
(A) 매니저가 질문에 답하는 것
(B) 손님이 주문을 하는 것
(C) 직원들이 출근하는 것
(D) 식기가 세척되는 것

패러프레이징 silverware → untensils

57. 여자는 왜 "근데, 그곳들은 손님이 더 적은 것 같은데요"라고 말하는가?
(A) 이 지점의 성공을 강조하기 위해
(B) 높은 비용을 정당화하기 위해
(C) 전략을 바꿀 것을 제안하기 위해
(D) 이전의 주장을 부인하기 위해

58. 오늘 오후 무슨 일이 일어날 것인가?
(A) 직원 회의가 열릴 것이다.
(B) 홍보가 시작될 것이다.
(C) 새로운 제품이 출시될 것이다.

(D) 청소 업체 직원들이 방문할 것이다.

미녀 미남

Questions 59-61 refer to the following conversation.

W Thanks for meeting with me today, Angelo. M&N Investment [59]contacted us about designing a solar-powered office building. They want to reduce their carbon emissions and run their office on clean energy.

M I see. A solar-powered building needs lots of sunlight. [60]I'm concerned about whether the solar panels can produce enough for an entire office building.

W That's a good point. [60]We don't get a lot of sun here in Seattle.

M Then maybe we should make a hybrid system that runs on both solar energy and natural gas.

W That might work. [61]Can you do some research on that right away? Since M&N is a major client, we need to reply quickly.

M No problem.

여 오늘 저를 만나줘서 고마워요, 앤젤로. M&N 투자가 [59]태양열 발전으로 운용되는 사무실 건물을 설계하는 것에 대해 저희에게 연락했어요. 그들은 탄소 배출량을 줄이고 사무실을 청정에너지로 운용하는 것을 원하고 있어요.

남 그렇군요. 태양열 건물은 많은 태양광이 필요해요. [60]태양 전지판이 건물 전체를 위해 충분한 전력을 생산할 수 있을지 걱정이네요.

여 좋은 지적이에요. [60]여기 시애틀에서는 햇빛을 많이 못 받죠.

남 그렇다면 태양열과 천연가스를 함께 운용할 수 있는 혼합 시스템을 만드는 것이 어떨까요?

여 가능할 수도 있겠네요. [61]그 방법에 대해 바로 조사 좀 해 주시겠어요? M&N은 주요 고객이기 때문에, 빨리 회신해 줘야 해요.

남 문제없어요.

어휘 solar-powered 태양열 동력의 carbon emission 탄소 배출 run 작동하다, 운행하다 major 주요한 reply 응답하다

59. 화자들은 어떤 업계에서 일할 것 같은가?

(A) 금융
(B) 패션
(C) 엔지니어링
(D) 관광

60. 남자는 무엇이 걱정된다고 말하는가?

(A) 햇빛의 지속 시간
(B) 초기 비용
(C) 환경 오염
(D) 안전 절차

61. 남자는 무엇을 하는 것에 동의하는가?

(A) 고객에게 전화하기
(B) 조사하기
(C) 콘퍼런스 계획하기
(D) 예산 삭감하기

패러프레이징 do some research → carry out some research

호남 미녀

Questions 62-64 refer to the following conversation and traffic sign.

M Joanne, thanks again for offering to drive me to the digital marketing seminar. I'm not too familiar with the city of Calton.

W My pleasure. [62]I grew up in downtown Calton, remember? My parents still live there.

M Oh — that's right. Will it take long to get to the conference center from here? I know it's on Rosebud Street.

W It usually doesn't, but the traffic report earlier said that the exit to Rosebud Street is under repair. [63]I guess we'll have to take exit 24 instead. It'll take about 40 minutes to get there.

M Well, we might miss the first session, [64]so I should call our colleagues and ask them to record it.

W Good idea.

남 조앤, 저를 디지털 마케팅 세미나까지 태워 주신다 해서 다시 한번 고마워요. 저는 캘톤 시에 그리 익숙하지가 않아요.

여 천만에요. 그거 기억해요? [62]저는 캘톤 시내에서 자랐잖아요. 제 부모님은 아직 거기에서 살고 계세요.

남 아—그랬었죠. 여기서 회의장까지 가는 데 오래 걸릴까요? 로즈버드 가에 있는 건 알고 있어요.

여 보통은 오래 걸리지 않는데 아까 교통 정보에서 로즈버드 가로 나가는 출구가 보수 중이라고 했어요. [63]대신 24번 출구로 나가야 할 것 같네요. 거기까지 가는 데 한 40분 정도 걸릴 거예요.

남 흠, 첫 번째 세션을 놓칠 수도 있으니, [64]동료들에게 전화해서 녹화해 놓으라고 부탁해야겠어요.

여 좋은 생각이에요.

캘톤 출구 ↱	
굿먼 도로	출구 21
킹슬리 길	출구 22
로즈버드 가	출구 23
[63]마커스 도로	출구 24

어휘 be familiar with ~에 익숙하다 grow up 자라다 under repair 보수중

62. 여자는 남자에게 무엇을 상기시키는가?

(A) 그녀는 세미나를 이끌 것이다.
(B) 그녀는 숙련된 운전자다.
(C) 그녀는 그 지역에서 살았었다.
(D) 그녀는 지갑을 가지러 다시 집으로 돌아가야 한다.

63. 시각 자료를 보시오. 화자들은 어떤 출구로 나갈 것인가?

(A) 굿먼 도로
(B) 킹슬리 길
(C) 로즈버드 가
(D) 마커스 도로

64. 남자는 동료들에게 무엇을 해 달라고 요청할 것인가?

(A) 여분의 좌석을 맡아 달라고
(B) 세미나를 녹화해 달라고
(C) 사무실로 복귀하라고
(D) 발표 준비를 해 달라고

영녀 호남

Questions 65-67 refer to the following conversation and layout.

W [65]Thanks for helping our hospital go paperless, Travis. You scanned and shredded all the documents containing patient records, right?

M Yes, and these documents can be recycled. The recycling bins are near the back entrance, right?

W That entrance is closed for repairs. [66]You can just put them by the office next to the main entrance. You'll see some boxes in the corner of the waiting room. I'll help you move those documents.

M Thanks, but these boxes are way too heavy to carry. [67]I'd better bring a cart. I was on my way to the maintenance closet to get more work gloves for other colleagues.

여 [65]종이 문서 없는 병원으로 전환하는 것을 도와줘서 고마워요, 트래비스. 환자 기록이 담긴 모든 문서를 스캔하고 파기하셨죠, 그렇죠?

남 네, 그리고 이 서류들은 재활용할 수 있어요. 재활용 쓰레기통이 뒷문 쪽에 있죠, 그렇죠?

여 그 출입문은 수리하느라 막아놨어요. [66]정문 바로 옆 진료실 옆에 놓아두시면 돼요. 대기실 모퉁이에 상자들이 보일 거예요. 제가 서류 옮기는 걸 도와드릴게요.

남 고마워요. 그런데 이 상자들은 너무 무거워요. [67]제가 카트를 가져오는 게 낫겠어요. 그렇지 않아도 다른 직원들이 쓸 작업용 장갑을 더 가지러 정비 용품 창고에 가는 길이었어요.

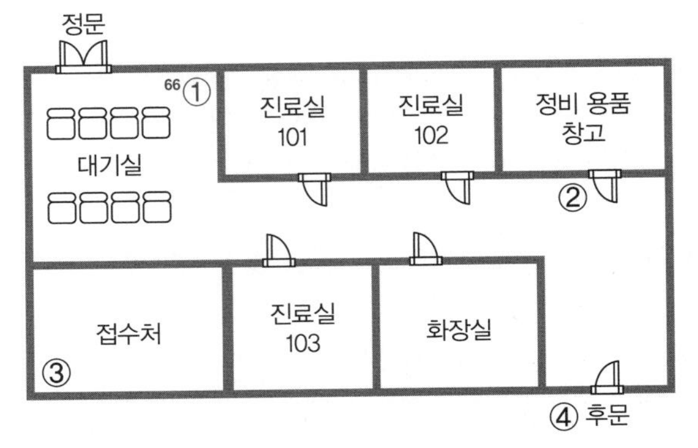

어휘 go paperless (기업이나 기관에서) 종이를 쓰지 않다 shred 분쇄하다 maintenance closet 정비 용품 창고[벽장, 보관실] (= maintenance room, storage room)

65. 대화는 어디에서 일어나는 것 같은가?

(A) 대학교에서
(B) 로펌에서
(C) 의료기관에서
(D) 출판사에서

패러프레이징 our hospital → healthcare organization

66. 시각 자료를 보시오. 남자는 문서들을 어디에 둘 것인가?

(A) 1번 장소
(B) 2번 장소
(C) 3번 장소
(D) 4번 장소

67. 남자는 다음에 무엇을 할 것인가?

(A) 서류 출력하기
(B) 장비 가져오기
(C) 선반 주문하기
(D) 온라인 양식 작성하기

패러프레이징 a cart, work gloves → equipment

미남 미녀

Questions 68-70 refer to the following conversation and inbox.

M Hi, Kimberly. You asked me to add a video to the slide show presentation I made, [68]but the link to the video file isn't working. I keep getting the same error message.

W Oh, [69]you mean the company introduction video? That's strange — I had no problem opening it earlier. I forwarded the e-mail to you just after I checked that it's working. I'll ask him to send a copy of the file directly to you.

M I appreciate that. [70]The investor meeting is Wednesday morning, so I'll finish this slide show by tomorrow and send it to you so that you can take a look at it before the meeting.

남 안녕하세요, 킴벌리. 제가 만든 슬라이드 쇼 발표 자료에 영상을 넣으라고 하셨는데, [68]영상에 연결된 링크가 작동을 안 합니다. 계속 동일한 오류 메시지만 떠요.

여 아, [69]회사 소개 영상 말씀하시는 거죠? 이상하네요. 좀 전에 열었을 때 문제가 없었는데. 제가 제대로 되는지 확인하고 바로 그 이메일을 전달해 드린 거였어요. 제가 그에게 당신에게 직접 영상 파일을 보내라고 요청할게요.

남 고마워요. [70]투자자 회의가 수요일 오전이니까 제가 내일까지 이 슬라이드 쇼를 끝내고 당신이 회의 전에 검토해 볼 수 있게 보내드릴게요.

받은 메일함

발신	제목	받은 시각
타일러 어반	매출 보고서	11:46 A.M.
[69]칼 주엣	회사 소개 영상	11:16 A.M.
벤 훌리	소비자 설문	10:45 A.M.
톰 더럼	면접 일정	09:31 A.M.

어휘 work 작동하다 have no problem -ing ~하는 데 문제가 없다 forward 전달하다 [행동] so that [목적] ~할 수 있게 ~하다

68. 화자들은 무슨 문제를 논의하고 있나?

(A) 영상 파일이 작동하지 않는다.
(B) 제품 출시가 지연되었다.
(C) 행사 장소를 이용할 수 없다.
(D) 프로젝트 마감일이 지났다.

69. 시각 자료를 보시오. 여자는 누구의 이메일을 언급하고 있는가?

(A) 타일러 어반의 이메일
(B) 칼 주엣의 이메일
(C) 벤 훌리의 이메일
(D) 톰 더럼의 이메일

70. 수요일에 어떤 행사가 열릴 것인가?

(A) 제품 시연
(B) 기금 모금 행사
(C) 투자자 미팅
(D) 극장 공연

PART 4

미남

Questions 71-73 refer to the following announcement.

You're listening to radio station WBJH. Turning to local business updates, [71]Friday marked the grand opening of Brittany's Corner's first location in Greenville. [72]Brittany's Corner is a renowned beauty supply company that has finally made its way to our beloved town. It is world-famous for its collection of lipsticks, eyeshadows, and make-up brushes. So far, the new shop has employed over a dozen residents and is looking to expand in the future. [73]To learn more about job opportunities, please visit our Web site, which will redirect you to the Brittany's Corner online recruitment portal.

여러분은 지금 WBJH 라디오 방송을 청취하고 계십니다. 지역 업체 뉴스로 넘어가겠습니다. [71]금요일은 브리트니즈 코너의 그린빌 첫 지점이 개업하는 날이었는데요. [72]브리트니즈 코너는 사랑하는 우리 도시에 드디어 입점한 유명 미용 용품 회사입니다. 이 회사는 립스틱, 아이섀도우, 그리고 메이크업 브러쉬 컬렉션으로 세계적으로 유명합니다. 지금까지 새로 개점한 매장은 12명이 넘는 주민들을 고용하였고, 앞으로 더욱 확장할 계획을 가지고 있습니다. [73]채용 기회에 대해 더 알아보고 싶으시다면, 저희 웹 사이트를 방문해 주세요. 그곳에서 브리트니즈 코너의 온라인 채용 포털로 연결될 것입니다.

어휘 turn to (특정 화제로) 넘어가다 mark (특정 연도, 월, 날짜 등이 주어로 쓰여) ~이 되는 해/월/날이다 renowned 유명한, 명성 있는 supply 공급 make its way to ~로 향하다 employ 고용하다 redirect (다른 주소나 방향으로) 다시 보내다

71. 브리트니즈 코너는 최근에 무엇을 하였는가?

(A) 새로운 제품 라인을 출시하였다.
(B) 유명 인사를 스폰서로 고용하였다.
(C) 새로운 매장을 열었다.
(D) 회계 감사를 실시하였다.

72. 브리트니즈 코너는 어떤 종류의 제품을 만드는가?

(A) 화장품
(B) 전자기기

TEST 05

(C) 의류
(D) 가구

패러프레이징 beauty supply company → cosmetics

73. 웹 사이트에서 무엇이 이용 가능할 것인가?

(A) 업데이트된 일정표
(B) 입사 지원서
(C) 독점 인터뷰
(D) 청취자 설문조사

영녀

Questions 74-76 refer to the following speech.

Thank you all for coming to this celebration. I know I speak for everyone here when I say that [74]I am happy to welcome our new recruits [75]for the magazine. Our new employees are some of the best young writers New York has to offer. We look forward to the insightful film articles they will write for us. [76]As a way to welcome our new hires, I am offering each of them a tablet computer with the company logo. If you are a recent hire, please come to the stage now to receive your welcome gift.

이번 축하 행사에 와 주신 모든 분들께 감사드립니다. [75]**저희 잡지사에** [74]**새로 입사하신 분들을 진심으로 환영하며**, 모두들 한마음으로 축하해 주시리라 생각합니다. 우리의 신입 사원들은 뉴욕이 배출해 낸 최고의 젊은 작가 반열에 오른 이들입니다. 저희는 그들이 써 줄 통찰력 있는 영화 기사들을 고대하고 있습니다. [76]**새로운 직원들에게 환영의 뜻을 전하고자 각각에게 회사 로고가 새겨진 태블릿 컴퓨터를 제공할 것입니다.** 만약 당신이 최근에 채용되셨다면, 지금 무대 위로 올라오셔서 환영 선물을 받아주세요.

어휘 I know I speak for everyone here when I say that... 모두를 대표하여 말하다, ...라는 점에서 모두가 한마음일 것이다 new recruit 신입사원 (= new hire)

74. 어떤 종류의 행사가 열리고 있는가?

(A) 환영식
(B) 영화 시상식
(C) 은퇴 기념 파티
(D) 잡지 출간

75. 청자들은 어떤 종류의 업체에서 일하는가?

(A) 신문사
(B) 영화 제작사
(C) 미술관
(D) 잡지사

76. 신입사원들은 무엇을 받을 것인가?

(A) 단체복
(B) 교육 안내서
(C) 사원증
(D) 전자기기

패러프레이징 tablet computer → electronic device

호남

Questions 77-79 refer to the following excerpt from a meeting.

The last thing I'd like to talk about is maintaining safety protocols [77]while making electric cars here at Armin Automatics. [78]If you're working on the assembly line, please make sure you wear your rubber gloves and the rest of your safety equipment. It's especially important to remember your gloves because they do not conduct electricity and can greatly reduce your chances of electric shock. We'd like to maintain our stellar safety record, so we thank you in advance. If you need more information, [79]you can download the safety manual from our internal company Web site.

제가 마지막으로 얘기하고 싶은 것은 [77]**여기 아르민 오토매틱스에서 전기 자동차를 만들 때** 안전 수칙을 지키는 것입니다. [78]**만약 조립 라인에서 일하신다면, 반드시 고무장갑과 기타 안전 장비를 착용해 주세요.** 고무장갑은 전기를 전도하지 않고 감전될 확률을 현저히 떨어뜨려 주기 때문에 장갑 착용은 특히나 중요한 사항입니다. 저희는 저희의 뛰어난 안전 기록을 유지하고 싶습니다. 그러니 협조에 미리 감사드리겠습니다. 더 많은 정보를 원하신다면, [79]**회사 내부 웹 사이트에서 안전 수칙 매뉴얼을 다운로드 받으실 수 있습니다.**

어휘 safety protocol 안전 규정[수칙] conduct electricity 전기를 전도하다 chances of ~의 가능성 electric shock 감전 stellar 뛰어난 (= excellent) manual 설명서, 편람

77. 화자의 회사는 무엇을 생산하는가?

(A) 어린이용 장난감
(B) 약
(C) 전기 자동차
(D) 스포츠 용품

78. 청자들은 무엇을 하도록 상기되는가?

(A) 설명서 읽기
(B) 특정 장비 착용하기
(C) 근무 시간 기록하기
(D) 교육 과정 참석하기

79. 온라인에서 무엇을 구할 수 있나?

(A) 소프트웨어 업데이트
(B) 상품 목록
(C) 평면도
(D) 안내서

패러프레이징 the safety manual → a handbook

영녀

Questions 80-82 refer to the following telephone message.

Hi, Anna. [80]I'm setting up at the park for the craft market. I just set out our handmade plates and cups that I'll be selling today. Everything should be fine, but the sky looks a little cloudy. [81]The weather forecast calls for rain later today, but I didn't bring an umbrella. So I might have to pack up and head back to the office earlier than planned. Anyways, the real reason I called was to [82]remind you to register our company for the city's Local Business Award. I think we have a pretty good chance of winning for our handmade ceramics collection.

안녕하세요, 안나. [80]수공예품 장터에 참여하기 위해 공원에서 준비하고 있어요. 오늘 판매할 우리의 수공예 접시와 컵들을 지금 막 진열했어요. 다 괜찮은데, 하늘이 좀 흐려 보여요. [81]일기예보에서 오늘 오후에 비가 온다고 했는데 파라솔을 안 가져 왔어요. 그래서 짐을 챙겨서 예정보다 일찍 사무실로 복귀해야 할지도 모르겠어요. [82]어쨌든, 제가 전화한 진짜 이유는 우리 회사를 '지역 기업상' 후보에 등록하라고 다시 한번 알려드리기 위해서입니다. 우리가 수공예 도자기 컬렉션으로 우승할 수 있는 가능성이 상당히 높다고 생각해요.

어휘 craft (수)공예 set out ~을 정리[진열]하다 call for 예보하다 pack up (떠나기 위해) 짐을 싸다[챙기다] earlier than planned 계획보다 일찍 anyways 어쨌든 (= anyway) have a chance of[at] winning 우승할 가능성이 있다

80. 화자는 공원에서 무엇을 할 것 같은가?

(A) 운동하기
(B) 캠핑장 예약하기
(C) 사진 찍기
(D) 도자기 판매하기

패러프레이징 handmade plates and cups → pottery

81. 화자는 왜 "하늘이 좀 흐려 보여요"라고 말하는가?

(A) 우려를 표하기 위해
(B) 경고를 주기 위해
(C) 안심시키기 위해
(D) 불만을 나타내기 위해

82. 화자는 청자에게 무엇을 하도록 상기시키는가?

(A) 장비 가져오기
(B) 재료 구입하기
(C) 대회에 등록하기
(D) 이메일 보내기

호남

Questions 83-85 refer to the following announcement.

[83]Attention, Justine's Department Store employees. The software program we use for scanning coupons isn't working. This means you cannot scan customer coupons at the register. Instead, please manually enter the coupon code into the register and collect the coupons from customers. [84]At the end of your shift, bring all the coupons to Customer Service. Entering the codes manually will most likely increase wait times, so please ensure customers that this is only temporary. [85]The coupon scanning software should be fixed by tomorrow.

[83]저스틴 백화점 직원들은 경청해 주시기 바랍니다. 우리가 쿠폰을 스캔할 때 사용하는 소프트웨어 프로그램이 작동하지 않고 있습니다. 이건 계산대에서 손님의 쿠폰을 스캔할 수 없다는 뜻입니다. 그 대신, 쿠폰 번호를 등록기에 직접 입력하고 쿠폰을 손님들로부터 걷어 주시기 바랍니다. [84]근무 시간이 끝날 때, 모든 쿠폰을 고객 서비스 창구로 가져와 주세요. 번호를 일일이 입력하면 대기 시간이 늘어날 수 있으므로, 손님들에게 이것이 일시적인 것임을 주지해 주시기 바랍니다. [85]쿠폰 스캔 소프트웨어는 내일까지 수리될 것입니다.

어휘 manually 수동으로 enter ~을 입력하다 collect 수거하다, 모으다 shift 교대 근무 (시간) temporary 일시적인 fix ~을 고치다

83. 공지는 어디에서 이루어지고 있는가?

(A) 의류 공장에서
(B) 백화점에서
(C) 광고 대행사에서
(D) 소프트웨어 회사에서

84. 청자들은 근무 시간이 끝난 후에 어디로 가야 하는가?

(A) 직원 휴게실로
(B) 고객 서비스 창구로
(C) 관리자 사무실로
(D) 주차장으로

85. 내일 어떤 일이 일어날 것 같은가?

(A) 컴퓨터 프로그램이 고쳐질 것이다.
(B) 매장 전품목 할인이 시작될 것이다.
(C) 새로운 물품들이 배송될 것이다.
(D) 사무 용품들이 주문될 것이다.

패러프레이징 software → a computer program

미녀

Questions 86-88 refer to the following excerpt from a meeting.

The first point on our agenda is the annual community

job fair. Like previous years, we will set up a booth at the fair, [86]where one of our lawyers will be available to answer questions and hopefully bring some new members to our team. In the past, Martha Stewart has always managed our booth, but she will be away on business during that time. You should know that working at the fair is a great experience, so feel free to get in touch with me if you're interested. [88]Now, let's talk about the Stanley case.

저희 안건의 첫 번째 사항은 연례 지역 사회 취업 박람회입니다. 예년과 같이 저희는 박람회에서 부스를 설치할 것이고, [86]**그곳에서 저희 변호사들 중 한 명이 질의응답 시간을 가질 것입니다.** 이를 통해 새로운 직원들을 저희 팀에 데려올 수 있길 바랍니다. 과거엔 마사 스튜어트가 항상 저희 부스를 관리했지만, 이번 기간에는 그녀가 출장 중일 것입니다. 박람회에서 일하는 것은 큰 경험이니, 관심 있으시다면 자유롭게 저에게 연락해 주시기 바랍니다. [88]**이제, 스탠리 사건에 대해 얘기해 봅시다.**

어휘 previous 이전의 set up ~을 설치하다 be away on business 출장 중이다 feel free to do 부담 갖지 말고[언제든] ~하세요 get in touch with ~에게 연락하다

86. 청자들은 어디서 일하는가?

(A) 변호사 사무실에서
(B) 채용 대행 업체에서
(C) 주민회관에서
(D) 수리점에서

87. 화자는 "그녀가 출장 중일 것입니다"라고 말할 때 무엇을 암시하는가?

(A) 몇몇 행사가 취소될 것이다.
(B) 화상 회의가 열려야 한다.
(C) 몇몇 계획이 재검토되어야 한다.
(D) 대신할 사람을 찾아야 한다.

88. 청자들은 다음에 무엇을 할 것 같은가?

(A) 취업 박람회 가기
(B) 논의하기
(C) 양식 작성하기
(D) 고객에게 전화하기

호남

Questions 89-91 refer to the following telephone message.

Good afternoon, Susan. I wanted to talk to you about our potential client HJC Corporation. [89]But first, thank you for sending me the slides for the presentation you'll be giving to them at the meeting on Wednesday. I know you were a bit worried about your design choices... you're concerned that your slides might be a bit too bold. Well, always remember that the consulting business is very competitive. It's good to stand out. [91]Second, Kento said that he wanted to speak with you about finding new hires. Make sure you see him before you leave.

좋은 오후입니다, 수잔. 우리의 잠재 고객 HJC 기업에 대해 얘기하고 싶었어요. [89]**하지만 먼저, 그들과의 수요일 회의에서 사용할 발표 슬라이드들을 보내 주셔서 감사합니다.** 당신의 디자인 선택에 대해 걱정하는 거 알고 있어요... 당신이 만든 슬라이드들이 너무 대담한 게 아닐까 염려하는 것일 텐데. 흠, 이 자문 업계는 경쟁이 매우 심하다는 것을 항상 기억하세요. 눈에 띄는 것은 좋은 거예요. [91]**두 번째로, 켄토가 새로운 직원들을 찾는 것에 대해 당신과 얘기하고 싶다고 말했어요.** 떠나기 전에 그를 만나보는 것을 잊지 말아주세요.

어휘 potential client 잠재 고객, 잠정 고객 be concerned that ~할까 봐 걱정하다 bold 대담한 competitive 경쟁을 벌이는 stand out 눈에 띄다 new hire 새 직원 make sure 반드시 ~하도록 하세요

89. 수요일에 무엇이 계획되어 있는가?

(A) 지역 사회 보건 박람회
(B) 은퇴 기념 파티
(C) 고객 회의
(D) 환영 조찬

90. 화자는 왜 "이 자문 업계는 경쟁이 매우 심하다"라고 말하는가?

(A) 동료를 안심시키기 위해
(B) 새로운 직원을 구하는 것을 정당화하기 위해
(C) 청자에게 일을 다시 할 것을 제안하기 위해
(D) 청자에게 가격을 내릴 것을 요청하기 위해

91. 화자는 켄토에 대해 무엇을 말하는가?

(A) 그는 여자의 발표를 도울 것이다.
(B) 그는 여자의 항공편을 마련할 것이다.
(C) 그는 HJC 산업과 친숙하다.
(D) 그는 청자와 얘기하기를 원한다.

미남

Questions 92-94 refer to the following excerpt from a meeting.

I'd like to thank you all for coming to today's optional professional development meeting. Our presenter is Samuel McNeil, and he is an expert in writing grant proposals. His skills are unparalleled, and [92]he's here to share some of his insights on how to secure funding for a business. [93]It seems like we're having some issues with the projector, however, so the IT department needs a moment to set everything up. In the meantime, [94]I hope everyone will take part in the feedback session after the meeting. By filling out the survey and answering questions, you'll be able to help us improve future professional development sessions. Thank you!

오늘 선택적 직무 역량 개발 회의에 참여해 주셔서 감사합니다. 오늘 발표해 주실 분은 사무엘 맥닐 씨이며, 보조금 신청 제안서 작성 전문가이십니다. 그의 노하우는 타의 추종을 불허하며, [92]사업 자금을 확보하는 방법에 대한 통찰력을 공유하기 위해 이 자리에 모셨습니다. [93]그런데 프로젝터에 문제가 있는 것 같으므로 IT 부서에서 다시 설정할 시간이 필요합니다. 그사이 한 가지 말씀드리자면, [94]맥닐 씨의 강연이 끝난 후 피드백 세션에 모두 참여해 주시길 바랍니다. 설문조사를 작성하고 질문에 답변함으로써 향후 직무 역량 개발 회의를 개선하는 데 도움이 될 수 있습니다. 감사합니다!

어휘 unparalleled 비할 데 없는 (parallel 평행한) secure 확보하다 set up 설치하다 in the meantime 그동안, 그사이에 take part in ~에 참여하다 fill out a survey 설문조사를 작성하다

92. 회의의 목적은 무엇인가?

(A) 새로운 직원을 소개하기 위해
(B) 관리자의 퇴임을 축하하기 위해
(C) 새로운 마케팅 전략을 짜기 위해
(D) 전문 기술을 가르치기 위해

93. 무엇이 지연을 일으키고 있는가?

(A) 화자가 노트를 잘못 두었다.
(B) 프로젝터에 문제가 있다.
(C) 마이크가 고장났다.
(D) 정전이 있었다.

94. 화자들은 무엇을 하도록 권고되는가?

(A) 보조금 제안서 작성하기
(B) 국제회의에 참석하기
(C) 피드백 세션에 참석하기
(D) 자금 조달 전략 수립하기

패러프레이징 take part in → participate in

미녀

Questions 95-97 refer to the following telephone message and table.

Hello, Ms. Mower. This is Debra calling. [95]I've been getting the paperwork ready for the vehicle you're renting from us for your upcoming trip. When you come to the rental shop to pick up your car, you'll have to pay some taxes and fees. [96]Please remember that the fifteen-dollar charge must be paid in cash. You can pay the other fees with your credit card. [97]And the shop is a bit far from the airport, so we offer a free shuttle service. It leaves from Terminal A every 30 minutes.

안녕하세요, 모워 씨. 데브라입니다. [95]다가오는 여행을 위해 고객님께서 대여하실 차량을 위한 서류를 준비하고 있습니다. 차를 가지러 대여점에 오실 때, 소정의 세금과 수수료를 지불하셔야 합니다. [96]15달러의 요금은 현금으로 계산하셔야 한다는 점 기억해 주시기 바랍니다. 다른 요금들은 신용카드로 결제하실 수 있습니다. [97]그리고 대여점이 공항에서 다소 멀리 떨어진 관계로, 무료 셔틀 서비스를 제공하고 있습니다. 셔틀은 터미널 A에서 30분 간격으로 출발합니다.

수수료 & 세금		지불	미지불
보증금	$25.00	✓	
기본 대여 요금 ($24 × 5일)	$120.00		✓
[96]시설비	$15.00		✓
주세	$6.90		✓

어휘 paperwork 서류 작업 get ~ ready ~을 준비하다 upcoming 다가오는 fee 수수료 charge 요금

95. 화자는 누구일 것 같은가?

(A) 자동차 대여점 직원
(B) 자동차 기술자
(C) 세무사
(D) 항공사 직원

96. 시각 자료를 보시오. 어떤 요금이 현금으로 지불되어야 하는가?

(A) 보증금
(B) 기본 대여 요금
(C) 시설비
(D) 주세

97. 화자는 청자에게 어떤 서비스에 대해 상기시키는가?

(A) 무이자 할부
(B) 셔틀 서비스
(C) 주유 쿠폰
(D) 정비 알림

미남

Questions 98-100 refer to the following excerpt from a meeting and pie chart.

During this staff meeting, I want to talk about some changes we'll be implementing [98]here at Betty's Books. First, to increase sales and attract new clientele, [99]we will be having poetry readings every other Saturday. A few local poets already agreed to regularly participate. Second, have a look at this chart from our annual sales report. I'm not too worried about the travel category. [100]But look at this section—they only constitute 4% of our sales. That's not a lot, and those books take up a lot of space in our inventory. So, after careful consideration, I've decided to stop selling books in that category.

TEST 05

이번 직원 회의에서, [98]저희 베티스 북스에서 시행할 몇몇 변화들에 대해 이야기하고 싶습니다. 첫 번째로, 판매를 늘리고 새로운 고객들을 유치하기 위해 [99]격주 토요일마다 시 낭송회를 가질 것입니다. 몇몇 지역 시인들이 이미 정기적으로 참여하는 것에 동의하였습니다. 두 번째로, 우리 연간 매출 보고서에서 따온 이 도표를 봐 주시기 바랍니다. 여행 부문에 대해서는 별로 걱정하지 않습니다. [100]하지만 이 부문을 봐 주십시오 – 이것은 우리 매출의 4%밖에 차지하지 않습니다. 이것은 그리 많지 않고, 그 책들은 우리 서고의 상당한 공간을 차지합니다. 그래서, 많은 고민 끝에, 이 부문의 책 판매를 중단하기로 결정하였습니다.

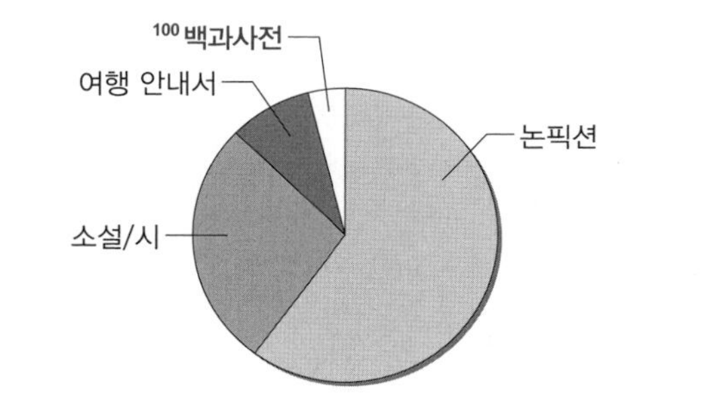

어휘 implement 시행하다 clientele (어떤 기관 · 상점 등의) 모든 의뢰인들[고객들] */클라이언텔/로 발음되며 /텔/에 강세가 놓인다. every other Saturday 격주 토요일마다 constitute 구성하다 take up (시간/공간을) 차지하다

98. 화자는 누구일 것 같은가?

(A) 여행 안내원
(B) 지역 시인
(C) 책 저자
(D) 점장

99. 격주 토요일마다 어떤 행사가 열릴 것인가?

(A) 장기 자랑
(B) 음악 공연
(C) 시 낭송회
(D) 자선 행사

100. 시각 자료를 보시오. 화자는 어떤 종류의 책에 주목하는가?

(A) 논픽션
(B) 소설 및 시
(C) 여행 안내서
(D) 백과사전

PART 5

101. 형용사 자리

계약서에 서명하기 전에 계약 조건에 대한 세심한 검토가 필요하다.

해설 빈칸 앞에 관사가 있고 뒤에는 명사가 있으므로 빈칸은 명사를 수식하는 형용사 자리이다. 따라서 (D) careful이 정답이다.

어휘 examination 검사, 조사 contract 계약(서) term 조항

102. 부사 어휘 regularly

화가 Wayne Frazer는 주민 센터에서 정기적으로 무료 미술 수업을 한다.

(A) 함께 (B) 정기적으로 (C) 더 빨리 (D) 극도로

어휘 community 지역 사회

103. 명사 어휘 attendance

행사 기획자들은 행사가 점점 인기를 얻고 있는지 알아보기 위해 매년 행사 참석률을 추적 조사하고 있다.

(A) 참석자 (B) 참석 (C) 안내원 (D) 참석하는 것

해설 (A) attendee는 가산명사이므로 관사 없이 쓰려면 복수형으로 써야 하기 때문에 오답이다.

어휘 planner 기획자 track 추적하다 rate 비율

104. 명사 어휘 appointment

예약을 취소하려면 Watson Dental Clinic의 환자들은 가능한 한 빨리 접수처에 전화해야 한다.

(A) 예약 (B) 예, 사례 (C) 기원 (D) 문제

어휘 cancel 취소하다 patient 환자 front desk 접수처, 프런트

105. 한정사 자리

Benson Automotive는 매월 말에 최고의 영업 사원에게 보너스를 제공한다.

해설 빈칸 앞에 전치사가 있고 뒤에는 명사가 있으므로 빈칸은 명사를 수식하는 한정사 자리이다. 따라서 (C) each가 정답이다.

106. 접속사 어휘 because

이 서류는 사업 계약서이기 때문에 매우 노련한 번역가가 필요하다.

(A) 그렇지 않으면 (B) ~한 반면에 (C) 만약 ~가 아니라면 (D) ~하기 때문에

해설 빈칸 뒤에 주어와 동사를 갖춘 완전한 절이 이어진 것으로 보아 빈칸은 접속사 자리이므로 부사인 (A) otherwise는 오답이다.

어휘 highly 매우 experienced 노련한, 경험이 많은 translator 번역가 contract 계약(서)

107. 형용사 자리

NC Enterprises의 사무실에서는 평상복을 입고 출근하는 것이 전적으로 허용된다.

해설 문장의 주어는 동명사구인 wearing casual clothing to work이고 동사는 is이므로 빈칸은 부사의 수식을 받는 보어 자리이다. 따라서 형용사인 (A) acceptable이 정답이다.

어휘 casual clothing 평상복

108. 전치사 어휘 in

고객 서비스 담당자들은 원래의 포장 상태인 경우에만 상품이 반품될 수 있다는 점을 기억해야 합니다.

(A) ~로, ~의 위로 (B) ~을 제외하고 (C) ~할 때; 언제 (D) ~에

해설 빈칸 뒤에 명사구 its original packaging이 있는 것으로 보아 빈칸은 전치사 자리이므로 부사 또는 접속사인 (C) when은 오답이다.

어휘 customer service representative 고객 서비스 담당자 remind 상기시키다, 기억나게 하다 merchandise 상품, 물품 packaging 포장(재)

109. 전치사 자리

성수기 이후에는 Herron Golf Resort의 직원 수가 크게 줄어들 것이다.

해설 빈칸 뒤에 명사 the peak season이 있으므로 빈칸은 전치사 자리이다. (B) Such as와 (C) After가 정답 후보인데, 문맥상 성수기가 지나고 나서 직원 수가 줄어들 거라는 내용이 되는 게 자연스러우므로 (C)가 정답이다.

어휘 peak season 성수기 significantly 상당히

110. 동사 자리+수 일치

자연 하이킹 참가자들은 등산로의 어려운 구간 전에 휴식을 취한다.

해설 빈칸 앞에 주어 역할을 하는 명사구가 있고 뒤에는 전치사구가 이어지므로 빈칸은 동사 자리이다. (B) rest와 (C) rests가 정답 후보인데, 주어가 복수 명사(Participants)이므로 (B)가 정답이다.

어휘 participant 참가자 hike 하이킹, 도보 여행 trail 등산로, 오솔길

111. 형용사 어휘 mindful

근처에 주거용 아파트들이 있기 때문에 손님들은 식당을 나설 때 그들의 소음 수준을 신경 써야 한다.

(A) 염두에 두는, 신경 쓰는 (B) 배타적인 (C) 특정한 (D) 책임 있는

해설 주격 보어로서 주어(customers)를 의미상 알맞게 수식하는 동시에 빈칸 뒤에 있는 전치사 of와 함께 쓰일 수 있는 것은 (A) mindful이다.

어휘 residential 주거의, 주택지의 nearby 근처의

112. 부사 자리

제빵사들은 빵을 비닐봉지에 넣기 전에 완전히 식혀야 한다.

해설 〈주어(Bakers)+동사(should allow)+목적어(the bread)+목적격 보어(to cool)〉 구조의 완전한 절이므로 빈칸은 부사 자리이다. 따라서 (D) completely가 정답이다.

어휘 baker 제빵사 allow A to do A가 ~하게 하다 cool 식히다 prior to ~ 전에 plastic bag 비닐봉지

113. 동사 어휘 consider

다음에 대출을 받을 생각이 있을 때는 Laurel Bank를 고려해 주세요.

(A) 인식하다 (B) 균형을 이루다 (C) 고려하다 (D) 보험에 들다

어휘 loan 대출(금)

114. 대명사 [목적격]

9월은 우리가 호텔에서 몇 가지 보수를 하기에 좋은 달이 될 것이다.

해설 빈칸 앞에 전치사 for가 있고 뒤에는 to부정사구가 이어지므로 빈칸에는 전치사의 목적어 역할을 할 수 있는 말이 들어가야 한다. 따라서 (A) us가 정답이다.

어휘 carry out ~을 실행하다, ~을 수행하다 renovation 수리, 보수

115. 형용사 어휘 eager

동틀 무렵 폭포의 아름다움을 매우 포착하고 싶어 하는 사진작가들은 항상 아침 일찍 그 장소에 도착한다.

(A) 간절히 바라는 (B) 다정한 (C) 자발적인 (D) 안심하는

어휘 photographer 사진작가 capture 포착하다 waterfall 폭포 site 장소, 현장

116. 동사 자리

Ainsley Construction은 최초 12개월의 기간이 끝나면 계약 조건을 조정할 것이다.

해설 빈칸은 Ainsley Construction을 주어로 하는 동사 자리이다. 따라서 (C) will modify가 정답이다.

어휘 contract 계약(서) terms 조건, 조항 initial 최초의, 초기의 period 기간

117. 부사 어휘 primarily

식사 손님들은 주로 그들의 주요리를 받기까지 걸리는 긴 대기 시간에 대해 불평했다.

(A) 주로 (B) 융통성 있게 (C) 이상적으로 (D) 믿을 수 없을 정도로

어휘 diner 식사 손님 complain 항의하다, 불평하다

118. 접속사 자리

은행 계좌 이체 요청이 오후 3시 이전에 이루어진다면 자금은 그날 송금될 것이다.

(A) ~에도 불구하고 (B) ~하는 한 (C) ~보다는 (D) ~ 이후로 줄곧

해설 빈칸 뒤에 절이 이어지므로 빈칸은 접속사 자리이다. (B) As long as와 (D) Ever since가 정답 후보인데, 문맥상 오후 3시 전에 계좌 이체를 요청한다는 조건이 맞으면 그날 돈이 송금된다는 내용이 되는 게 자연스러우므로 (B)가 정답이다.

어휘 bank transfer 은행 계좌 이체 make a request 요청하다 fund 자금

119. 동사 어휘 hold

인사 팀은 금요일 오후에 팀 단합 활동 시간을 가질 예정이다.

(A) 만나다 (B) 열다, 개최하다 (C) 동기를 부여하다 (D) 떠나다

어휘 HR 인사(= human resources) team building 팀 단합 활동 session (특정) 시간

120. 형용사 자리

협력적인 근무 환경 덕분에 직무 만족 평가를 높게 주는 직원들이 생겨난다.

해설 빈칸은 명사 working environments를 수식하는 자리이므로 형용사인 (B) Cooperative가 정답이다.

어휘 cooperative 협력하는 environment 환경 result in 결과적으로 ~가 되다 rating 순위, 평가

121. 전치사 어휘 without

그 회사가 사용하는 화상 회의 소프트웨어 덕분에 팀원들은 집을 나서지 않고도 쉽게 협업할 수 있다.

(A) 비록 ~일지라도 (B) ~까지 (C) ~ 중에 (D) ~하지 않고

해설 빈칸 뒤에 동명사 leaving이 있는 것으로 보아 빈칸은 전치사 자리이므로 접속사인 (A) although는 오답이다.

어휘 thanks to ~ 덕분에 teleconferencing 화상 회의 collaborate 협력하다

122. 분사 자리

저작권이 있는 자료를 복제하는 사람들은 그렇게 하라는 허가를 받지 못했다면 벌금을 물게 될 수도 있다.

해설 빈칸 앞에 주어 People이 있고 뒤에는 본동사 could face가 있으므로 '------- ~ copyright'는 주어를 수식하는 수식어구이다. 빈칸 뒤의 명사 materials를 목적어로 취하면서 앞에 있는 명사 People을 수식할 수 있는 것은 현재분사이므로 (D) duplicating이 정답이다. 참고로 that are under copyright는 materials를 선행사로 하는 주격 관계대명사절이다.

어휘 duplicate 복제하다, 복사하다 material 자료 copyright 저작권 face 직면하다 fine 벌금 permission 허가

123. 접속사 자리

Midland Communications는 관리자로 하여금 가능할 때마다 고객 불만 사항을 처리하게 한다.

해설 빈칸 앞에 〈주어(Midland Communications)+동사(has)+목적어(a manager)+목적격 보어(handle ~ complaints)〉 구조의 완전한 절이 있고 뒤에는 형용사 possible이 있으므로 빈칸은 접속사 자리이다. 따라서 (C) whenever가 정답이다. whenever possible은 '가능할 때마다'라는 의미이며, whenever와 같이 일부 부사절 접속사는 뒤에 〈주어+be동사〉가 생략되어 형용사나 분사구만 남은 형태로 쓰이기도 한다.

어휘 handle 처리하다, 다루다 complaint 불만, 민원

124. 명사 어휘 limit

Rockford Building의 주차장이 작기 때문에 건물주는 방문객 주차를 3시간으로 제한하기로 결정했다.

(A) 발언, 논평 (B) 제한 (C) 절차 (D) 개념

어휘 place a limit 제한을 두다

125. 소유한정사

계약직 직원의 경우에는 계약 기간이 만료될 때 신분증이 비활성화될 것이다.

해설 빈칸 앞에 접속사 when이 있고 뒤에는 명사 contract가 이어지므로 빈칸은 명사를 수식하는 자리이다. 따라서 소유한정사인 (D) their가 정답이다.

어휘 in the case of ~의 경우에는 temporary 임시의 employee 직원 disable 비활성화하다

126. 동사 어휘 expect

기술 회사인 Vidalia의 최고경영자인 Robert Holley는 기자회견에서 자신의 사임을 발표할 것으로 예상된다.

(A) 문의하다 (B) 분석하다 (C) 빈틈없이 계획하다 (D) 예상하다

어휘 technology 기술 announce 발표하다 resignation 사임, 퇴임 press conference 기자회견

127. 부사 자리

Phoenix Electronics의 신형 노트북 컴퓨터는 화면이 크지만 놀라울 정도로 가볍다.

해설 빈칸 앞에 동사 is가 있고 뒤에는 형용사 lightweight가 있으므로 빈칸은 형용사를 수식하는 부사 자리이다. 따라서 (B) surprisingly가 정답이다.

어휘 laptop 노트북 컴퓨터 lightweight 경량의

128. 형용사 어휘 amateur

머피빌에 있는 새로운 스포츠 경기장은 아마추어 운동선수들이 이용하도록 설계되었다.

(A) 남는, 여분의 (B) 실재하는, 유형의 (C) 눈에 보이는 (D) 아마추어의

어휘 arena 경기장 athlete 운동선수

129. 명사 자리

정부가 통과시킨 새로운 조치들은 경제 안정에 기여하도록 의도된 것이다.

해설 빈칸 앞에 관사가 있고 뒤에는 전치사가 있으므로 빈칸은 명사 자리이다. 따라서 (B) stability가 정답이다.

어휘 measure 조치, 방안 pass 통과시키다 intend 의도하다 contribute to ~에 기여하다 stability 안정

130. 부사 어휘 periodically

혈액 순환을 위해 교대 근무 동안 주기적으로 일어서서 다리를 스트레칭하세요.

(A) 주기적으로 (B) 분명히, 눈에 띄게 (C) 상호 간에 (D) 마지못해

어휘 work shift 교대 근무 improve 향상시키다 flow 흐름

PART 6

131-134 공지

> Palm Tree Amusement Park가 여름 시즌[131]을 위해 직원들을 채용하고 있습니다. [132]주요 업무는 고객들에게 티켓을 판매하는 것을 포함합니다. 또한 직원들은 놀이공원에 재입장하는 고객들의 입장권을 확인하고, 놀이공원의 활동에 관한 질문에 답해야 할 수도 있습니다. 경력은 필요하지 않지만 우리는 예의 바르고 [133]사려 깊은 사람들을 찾고 있습니다. 지원하는 데 관심이 있다면 www.palmtreepark.com을 방문하시기 바랍니다. [134]마감일은 3월 22일입니다.

어휘 amusement park 놀이공원 hire 고용하다, 채용하다 in addition 또한, 게다가 check 검사하다, 확인하다 pass 출입증 regarding ~에 관해 previous 이전의, 예전의 polite 예의 바른 apply 지원하다

131. 전치사 어휘 for

(A) ~에도 불구하고 (B) ~로서 (C) ~을 위해 (D) ~에 대하여

132. 알맞은 문장 고르기

(A) 정문 근처의 주차 구역은 매우 넓습니다.

(B) 주요 업무는 고객들에게 티켓을 판매하는 것을 포함합니다.

(C) 우리는 가족들에게 인기 있는 관광지입니다.

(D) 우리 놀이공원에서는 악단의 라이브 공연도 합니다.

해설 빈칸 뒤에서 놀이공원 직원이 하는 일을 추가적으로 언급하고 있으므로 빈칸에는 직무와 관련된 내용이 들어가는 게 적절하다. 따라서 (B)가 정답이다.

133. 형용사 자리

해설 빈칸 앞에 접속사가 있고 뒤에는 명사가 있으므로 빈칸은 명사를 수식하는 형용사 자리이다. 따라서 (C) considerate가 정답이다.

134. 명사 어휘 deadline

(A) 설치 (B) 벤처 기업 (C) 축하 (D) 마감일

135-138 기사

> **호반의 도시가 기술의 중심지가 되다**
>
> 브룩필드—브룩필드의 작은 도시가 기술 산업의 주요 부지가 될 예정이다. 시에 많은 [135]**투자**를 한 덕분에 더 많은 기술 회사들이 그 지역에 관심을 보이고 있다. 시 공무원들은 디지털 인프라에 수백만 달러를 쓰고 있다. 이 돈은 현대적인 기업들의 운영을 지원하기 [136]**위한 목적이다**. 예를 들어 초고속 인터넷망이 추가되었다. [137]**이 프로젝트는 기업체에 필수적인 도구를 제공한다.**
>
> 일부 주민들은 신규 업체의 유입이 문제가 될 수도 있다고 우려한다. [138]**그럼에도 불구하고** 그 지역의 대다수 사람들은 이 같은 운영에 수반될 가능성이 높은 경제 성장을 환영한다.

어휘 lakeside 호숫가, 호반 tech 기술 hub 중심지, 중추 be positioned to do ~하는 상황에 놓이다 industry 산업 thanks to ~ 덕분에 official 공무원 infrastructure 사회 기반 시설, 인프라 fund 자금, 돈 support 지원하다 add 추가하다 concerned 걱정하는, 염려하는 influx 유입 problematic 문제가 있는 the majority of 다수의 accompany 동반하다, 수반하다

135. 명사 어휘 investment

(A) 투자 (B) 합병 (C) 관광업 (D) 처리

136. 수동태+to부정사

해설 빈칸 뒤에 목적어가 없고 주어 These funds는 행위를 받는 대상이므로 빈칸에는 〈be+과거분사〉 형태의 수동태가 적절하다. (A) are meant for와 (B) are meant to가 정답 후보인데, 빈칸 뒤에 동사원형이 있으므로 (B)가 정답이다. be meant to do(~하기로 되어 있다)는 토익에 자주 출제되는 표현이니 통으로 외워 두자.

137. 알맞은 문장 고르기

(A) 브룩필드의 공무원들은 4년마다 재선된다.
(B) 다른 사람들은 도시의 웹사이트가 기능적이라고 생각한다.
(C) 이 프로젝트는 기업체에 필수적인 도구를 제공한다.
(D) 프로그래머들이 소프트웨어를 조정하고 있다.

해설 빈칸 앞 문장에 언급된 '초고속 인터넷망을 추가하는 것'을 This project로 표현한 (C)가 정답이다.

138. 접속부사 어휘 nonetheless

(A) 그렇지 않으면 (B) ~한 경우에 대비하여 (C) 결과적으로 (D) 그럼에도 불구하고

해설 빈칸 뒤에 주어와 동사를 갖춘 완전한 절이 하나만 있는 것으로 보아 빈칸은 접속부사 자리이므로 접속사인 (B) In case는 오답이다.

139-142 광고

> Abia Aquarium에서 수중 세계를 탐험해 보세요! 1605 셔먼 애비뉴에 위치해 있는 우리는 국경일을 제외하고 연중무휴 운영합니다. Abia Aquarium에서 여러분은 아주 다양하고 놀라운 바다 생물들에 대해 배울 수 있을 뿐만 아니라 수중 터널에서 해양 생물에 몰입[139]**할 수도** 있습니다. 또한 우리의 최신 [140]**볼거리도** 마음에 드실 겁니다. Abia Touch Pool은 개방형 수조로 가오리, 뱀장어 등을 만질 수 있고 먹이도 줄 수 있습니다.
>
> 우리는 학교 단체들을 위한 다양한 교육 기회를 제공하는 것에 자부심을 가지고 있습니다. [141]**선생님이라면 우리의 웹사이트를 확인하여 더 많은 정보를 얻으세요.** 특별한 경험을 드리기 위해 우리는 지역 단체에 영업시간이 끝난 후 투어를 [142]**제공합니다.** 저희 수족관에서 개인 파티도 하실 수 있습니다. 독특한 경험을 찾고 있다면 Abia Aquarium 방문을 놓치지 마세요.

어휘 explore 탐험하다 underwater 수중의 aquarium 수족관 all year round 일 년 내내 excluding ~을 제외하고 a wide variety of 아주 다양한 amazing 놀라운 creature 생물, 생명체 immerse oneself in ~에 몰두하다 stingray 가오리 eel 뱀장어 unique 특별한, 독특한 after-hours 영업시간 후의 community 지역 사회 miss 놓치다

139. 상관 접속사

해설 빈칸은 앞에 있는 not only와 짝을 이루는 말이 들어갈 자리이므로 (B) but also가 정답이다.

어휘 in addition to ~ 외에도, ~ 뿐만 아니라 while ~하는 동안; ~한 반면에

140. 명사 어휘 attraction

(A) 볼거리, 명소; 매력 (B) 거래 (C) 회원 (D) 발표; 진술

141. 알맞은 문장 고르기

(A) 선생님이라면 우리의 웹사이트를 확인하여 더 많은 정보를 얻으세요.
(B) 이 종들 중 일부는 멸종 위기에 처해 있습니다.
(C) 공석에 대해 문의하려면 저희 사이트 관리자에게 연락하세요.
(D) 우리는 몇 년간 입장료를 올리지 않았습니다.

해설 빈칸 앞에서 '학교 단체들을 위한 다양한 교육 기회'를 언급했으므로 빈칸에는 그와 관련된 내용이 들어가는 게 자연스럽다. 따라서 (A)가 정답이다.

어휘 species (생물의) 종 be in danger of ~할 위험에 처하다 extinct 멸종한 job opening 공석 admission fee 입장료

142. 능동태+현재 시제

해설 빈칸 뒤에 목적어(after-hours tours)가 있으므로 빈칸에는 능동태

가 들어가야 한다. (A) were providing과 (D) provide가 정답 후보인데, 문맥상 현재 시점에 투어 서비스를 제공하고 있는 것이므로 현재 시제인 (D)가 정답이다.

143-146 편지

Winfrey Snow Removal
602 버논 스트리트
어빙턴, 뉴저지 07111

2월 13일

Daniel Roldan
9141 빙어몬 로드
어빙턴, 뉴저지 07111

Mr. Roldan께,

아시다시피 우리는 지난 8년간 매년 겨울에 제설 사업을 [143]운영해 왔습니다. [144]하지만 당신과 같은 직원들은 1년의 나머지 기간 동안 일거리를 구하기가 어렵다는 것을 알고 있습니다. 우리는 최근에 Garner Construction으로부터 봄과 여름에 우리 장비를 사용하는 것과 관련하여 연락을 받았습니다. [145]그 회사의 도로 보수 작업에 필요하다고 합니다. 우리는 이미 자재 운반 트럭과 같은 이런 장비를 운용한 경험이 있는 직원들이 있기 때문에 그 회사는 우리의 추천에 따라 사람을 고용할 것입니다. 관심이 있으면 당신의 연락처 세부 정보를 전달할 테니 우리에게 알려 주시기 바랍니다. [146]이 기회를 놓치지 않으려면 서두르셔야 합니다.

Jeremy Winfrey

어휘 removal 제거 contact 연락하다; 연락처 equipment 장비 operate 운전하다, 작동하다 haul 운반하다, 끌다 material 자재, 재료 based on ~에 근거하여 recommendation 추천 details 세부 정보

143. 현재완료 시제

해설 빈칸 뒤에 현재완료 시제와 어울려 쓰이는 표현(for the past 8 years)이 있으므로 (C) have operated가 정답이다.

144. 접속부사 어휘 however

(A) 하지만 (B) 그 당시에 (C) 예를 들어 (D) 오히려

145. 한정사

해설 work on repairing roads는 앞에 언급된 Garner Construction에서 진행할 작업이므로 (D) its가 정답이다.

146. 알맞은 문장 고르기

(A) 고객들은 진입로가 신속하게 치워지기만 기다리고 있습니다.
(B) 이 기회를 놓치지 않으려면 서두르셔야 합니다.
(C) 어떤 폭풍들은 다른 폭풍들보다 더 많은 눈을 초래합니다.
(D) 우리는 당신이 은퇴 기념 파티에서 우리와 함께 축하하기를 바랍니다.

해설 앞 문장에서 의향이 있다면 다른 업체에 연락처 정보를 전달하겠다고 했으므로 빈칸에는 그와 관련된 내용이 들어가는 게 자연스럽다. 따라서 (B)가 정답이다.

어휘 rely on ~에 의존하다 prompt 신속한 clearance 제거, 없애기 driveway 진입로 miss 놓치다 result in 결과적으로 ~가 되다 retirement 은퇴, 퇴직

PART 7

147-148 문자 메시지

Janet Woodall [오전 11:43]
안녕하세요, Patrick. 방금 Mr. Howard에게 보낼 쿠키와 컵케이크를 상자에 넣었어요. 다른 할 일이 있나요?

Patrick Ladner [오전 11:45]
고마워요. [147]오늘 오후 4시에 Reno Accounting의 사람이 케이크를 찾으러 올 거니까 시간 내에 일을 끝내야 해요. 그리고 [148]여름 음식 축제의 날짜가 7월 22일로 확정되었어요.

Janet Woodall [오전 11:46]
아, 어쩌죠. 저는 그건 안 되겠네요.

Patrick Ladner [오전 11:47]
[148]아, 정말이요? 작년에 그랬던 것처럼 당신이 부스를 운영할 수 있기를 바랐는데요.

Janet Woodall [오전 11:49]
저는 그 주에 로스앤젤레스로 휴가를 가잖아요, 기억하시죠? 하지만 Nora가 작년에 저를 도왔으니 그녀가 그 일을 처리할 수 있다고 확신해요. [147]아무튼 저는 지금 Reno Accounting의 주문 건에 대한 일을 시작할게요. 완료하는 데 시간이 좀 걸려서요.

Patrick Ladner [오전 11:50]
알았어요.

어휘 box up ~을 상자에 넣다 on time 제때에 confirm 확정하다 shame 유감스러운 일 work 유효하게 작용하다 run 운영하다 be on vacation 휴가 중이다 handle 다루다, 처리하다

147. Ms. Woodall은 다음에 무엇을 작업하겠는가?

(A) 쿠키
(B) 컵케이크
(C) 케이크
(D) 빵 한 덩어리

해설 추론/암시
오전 11시 49분에 Ms. Woodall이 Reno Accounting의 주문 건에 대한 일을 시작한다고 했는데, 오전 11시 45분에 Mr. Ladner가 Reno Accounting에서 오후 4시에 케이크를 찾으러 온다고 한 것으로 보아 해당 주문 건은 케이크와 관련된 것임을 알 수 있다. 따라서 (C)가 정답이다.

148. 오전 11시 46분에 Ms. Woodall이 "저는 그건 안 되겠네요"라고 쓸 때 그녀가 의미하는 것은 무엇인가?

(A) 그녀는 Mr. Ladner에게 조언해 줄 수 없다.

(B) 그녀는 몇 대의 기계 때문에 애를 먹고 있다.
(C) 그녀는 행사에 참여할 수 없다.
(D) 그녀는 Nora를 만날 시간이 없다.

해설 의도 파악
오전 11시 45분에 Mr. Ladner가 여름 음식 축제 날짜가 확정되었다고 한 말에 대한 답변이며, 이를 보고 Mr. Ladner가 Ms. Woodall에게 부스를 운영하기를 바랐다며 아쉬움을 드러낸 것으로 보아 Ms. Woodall이 축제에 참석하지 못한다고 표현한 것임을 알 수 있다. 따라서 (C)가 정답이다.

어휘 give ~ advice ~에게 충고를 하다 have trouble with ~에 문제를 겪다 machinery 기계류

149-150 공지

Yogtastic 스마트폰 애플리케이션을 이용해 주셔서 감사합니다! 귀하는 현재 베이직 회원으로 가입되어 있습니다. 이것으로 귀하는 하루에 최대 2개의 요가 동영상을 스트리밍하고, 50개가 넘는 요가 자세에 대한 우리의 안내를 이용할 수 있습니다. [149]귀하의 피트니스 목표를 달성하는 데 도움이 되도록 플래티넘 회원으로 상향 조정해 보는 것은 어떠세요? 결제하지 않고 30일 동안 이 회원 자격을 이용해 보실 수 있습니다. 플래티넘 회원 자격이 있으면 동영상을 무제한 다운로드하고, 진도를 확인하고, 전문가의 조언을 얻는 등의 혜택을 받을 수 있습니다. [150]플래티넘 회원 페이지에서 새로운 회원에게 제공되는 모든 것들을 보실 수 있습니다.

어휘 application 앱, 애플리케이션 currently 현재, 지금 sign in 서명하여 ~에 입회시키다 allow 허용하다 stream 스트리밍하다 up to ~까지 access 접근하다, 이용하다 pose 자세, 포즈 upgrade 상향 조정하다 membership 회원 자격 make a payment 결제하다, 대금을 지불하다 track 추적하다 progress 진척, 진행 expert 전문가

149. 공지의 독자들은 무엇을 할 것을 권장받는가?
(A) 스트리밍 문제 알리기
(B) 무료 체험 신청하기
(C) 자신의 요가 동영상을 업로드하기
(D) 매일 새로운 포즈를 시도하기

해설 세부 사항
결제 없이 요가 관련 애플리케이션의 플래티넘 회원 자격을 이용해 볼 것을 권하고 있으므로 (B)가 정답이다.

패러프레이징 without making a payment → free

어휘 report 보고하다, 알리다 sign up for ~을 신청[가입]하다 trial 시용

150. 공지에 따르면, 웹페이지에서 이용할 수 있는 것은 무엇인가?
(A) 기능의 목록
(B) 추적 조회 번호
(C) 대금 지불 정보
(D) 제품 후기

해설 세부 사항
플래티넘 회원 페이지에서 새로운 회원에게 제공되는 모든 것들을 볼 수 있다고 했으므로 (A)가 정답이다.

어휘 list 목록 feature 특징, 기능 review 후기

151-152 이메일

수신: Audrey Swenson
발신: Herman Bray
날짜: 3월 25일
제목: 468 트루히요 스트리트에서의 서비스

Ms. Swenson께,

귀하의 부지에 잔디 관리 서비스를 3개월 계약해 주셔서 감사합니다. 합의한 대로 저희 팀은 한 달에 두 번 귀하의 잔디를 깎고, 한 달에 한 번 덤불을 다듬을 것입니다. 저희의 첫 방문은 4월 3일이며, 저희는 모든 장비를 가지고 갈 것입니다. [151]귀하의 부지에 정원 쓰레기 수거함이 있는지 아니면 저희가 잔디와 덤불 쓰레기를 버리길 원하는지 알려 주시겠습니까? 이것은 저희가 사전에 계획하는 데 도움이 될 것입니다. 또한 저희의 첫 번째 방문 후에는 [152]서비스에 대한 간단한 설문 조사를 이메일로 받게 되실 것입니다. 그것을 완료하시면 다음 서비스 방문 시 15% 할인을 받게 되십니다.

Herman Bray
BC Landscaping

어휘 contract 계약 lawn care 잔디 관리 property 부동산, 토지 mow (잔디를) 깎다 trim (가지를) 다듬다 bush 덤불 equipment 장비 collection 수거 bin 쓰레기통 trimmings 깎아 낸 것 ahead 미리, 사전에 brief 간단한, 짧은 questionnaire 설문 조사 complete 완료하다, 끝내다 discount 할인 landscaping 조경

151. Ms. Swenson은 무엇을 확정하라는 요청을 받는가?
(A) 몇몇 장비를 어디에 보관해야 하는지
(B) 일부 쓰레기를 어떻게 처리해야 하는지
(C) 얼마나 자주 잔디를 깎아야 하는지
(D) 어떤 종류의 덤불을 심어야 하는지

해설 세부 사항
잔디와 덤불 쓰레기를 버릴 수 있는 쓰레기통이 있는지 아니면 업체에서 쓰레기를 버려 주기를 원하는지를 묻고 있으므로 (B)가 정답이다.

패러프레이징 the grass and bush trimmings → some waste

어휘 store 보관하다, 저장하다 waste 쓰레기 plant 심다

152. Ms. Swenson은 어떻게 서비스에 대한 할인을 받을 수 있는가?
(A) 업체를 다른 사람들에게 추천함으로써
(B) 선불로 작업 비용을 지불함으로써
(C) 3개월짜리 계약을 체결함으로써
(D) 의견을 제공함으로써

해설 세부 사항
설문 조사를 완료하면 15% 할인을 받을 수 있다고 했으므로 (D)가 정답이다.

어휘 recommend 추천하다 business 업체 up front 선불로 feedback 의견, 피드백

153-154 이메일

수신: Kevin Moore
발신: Mona Russell
날짜: 10월 14일
제목: 회의

안녕하세요, Kevin.

안타깝게도 내일 11시 30분에 우리 사무실에서 하기로 했던 회의에 문제가 생겼어요. [153] **대신 당신이 모스케라 인근에 있는 Galindo Restaurant에 올 수 있는지 알고 싶어요.** 제가 그 근처에 있는 Rowe Manufacturing과 오전 회의가 있는데, 1시에 역시 그 근처에 있는 Eugene Conner를 만나야 하거든요. [153] **우리 회의를 위해 사무실에 돌아갔다가 1시까지 Mr. Conner의 사무실로 다시 갈 수는 없을 것 같아요.**

Galindo Restaurant은 칸막이가 있는 별도의 공간이 있고 주차장도 넓으니까 [154] **우리는 점심 식사를 하면서 입사 지원서를 검토해서 누구를 면접에 불러야 할지 정할 수 있을 것 같아요.** 이 일정이 괜찮으시다면 저에게 알려 주세요.

고마워요!

Mona

어휘 run into (어려움, 곤란, 문제 등을) 겪다 issue 문제 neighborhood 인근, 이웃 instead 그 대신에 all the way 줄곧, 처음부터 끝까지 booth 부스, 칸막이로 된 공간 go through ~을 검토하다 job application 입사 지원서

153. Ms. Russell은 왜 회의 장소를 바꾸기를 원하는가?

(A) 그녀는 그 지역의 주차장 부족에 대해 걱정하고 있다.
(B) 그녀는 원래 장소의 예약이 꽉 찼다는 것을 알았다.
(C) 그녀는 아주 멀리 이동할 시간이 없을 것이다.
(D) 그녀는 고객이 참석하기를 원한다.

해설 세부 사항
Ms. Russell이 외부 일정 때문에 사무실로 복귀할 시간이 없다고 말하며 Mr. Moore에게 사무실 대신 Galindo Restaurant으로 나와 줄 것을 요청하고 있다. 따라서 (C)가 정답이다.

패러프레이징 get all the way back → travel very far

어휘 concerned 걱정하는, 염려하는 lack 부족 original 원래의 fully booked 예약이 꽉 찬 travel 이동하다 client 고객

154. Mr. Moore와의 회의에서 무엇이 논의되겠는가?

(A) 발표 준비
(B) 제조 공정 개선
(C) 입사 지원자 선정
(D) 직원 생산성 향상

해설 추론/암시
입사 지원서를 검토해서 면접자를 선정한다고 했으므로 (C)가 정답이다.

어휘 presentation 발표 improve 개선하다, 향상시키다 manufacturing 제조 process 과정 select 선정하다 boost 신장시키다 productivity 생산성

155-157 의견 카드

Gateway Housewares 고객 의견 카드

[155] **최근에 회사가 제삼자에 의해 인수되었고,** 그에 따라 우리는 모든 고객님의 쇼핑 경험을 개선할 방법을 찾고 있습니다. 귀하의 솔직한 의견에 매우 감사드리며, 귀하의 의견을 [156] **다루는** 변화를 시행하기 위해 최선을 다하겠습니다. 저희의 월별 경품 추첨에 참여하시려면 아래에 귀하의 연락처 정보를 포함시켜 주십시오.

이름 (선택 사항): Alanna Bianco
이메일 주소 (선택 사항): abianco@perineenterprises.com
방문 일자: 2월 8일

의견: [157] **저는 친척에게 줄 선물을 구매하기 위해 귀사의 매장을 방문했습니다.** 귀사의 판매원 중 한 명인 Elizabeth가 제품에 대한 질문에 답해 주었습니다. 그녀는 제 쿠폰이 만료되었다고 설명했지만 그래도 제 가격대 안에 있는 물품을 찾는 것을 도와주었습니다. 그것은 고급 양초였는데 품질이 좋아 보였습니다. 사실 [157] **저는 그 양초가 너무 좋아서 제가 쓸 것도 하나 샀습니다.** 전반적으로 저는 귀사의 상점을 다른 사람들에게 추천하겠습니다.

어휘 comment 의견 opinion 의견 greatly 매우 appreciate 감사하다 implement 시행하다 prize drawing 경품 추첨 contact 연락처 details 세부 정보 optional 선택적인 relative 친척 expire 만료되다 price range 가격대 luxury 호화로운 overall 전반적으로 recommend 추천하다

155. Gateway Housewares에 대해 시사된 것은 무엇인가?

(A) 최근에 이전했다.
(B) 소유권이 바뀌었다.
(C) 매월 물품 목록을 변경한다.
(D) 직원들을 교육하고 있다.

해설 NOT/True
첫 번째 문단에서 제삼자에 의해 인수되었다고 했으므로 (B)가 정답이다.

패러프레이징 has recently been purchased by a third party → had a change of ownership

어휘 recently 최근에 relocate 이전하다 ownership 소유권 inventory 물품 목록, 재고

156. 첫 번째 단락 네 번째 줄의 어휘 "address"와 의미상 가장 가까운 것은?

(A) 다루다
(B) 말을 걸다
(C) 보내다
(D) 라벨을 붙이다

해설 동의어 찾기
address가 있는 we will do our best to implement changes that address your feedback은 고객의 의견을 다루어[반영하여] 변화를 시행하기 위해 애쓰겠다는 의미이며, 여기서 address는 '다루다'라는 뜻으로 쓰였다. 따라서 (A) deal with가 정답이다.

157. Ms. Bianco는 자신의 쇼핑 경험에 대해 무엇을 암시하는가?

(A) 그녀는 추천을 받고 매장을 방문했다.

(B) 그녀는 원래 의도했던 것보다 더 많은 물품을 샀다.
(C) 그녀는 구매 시 쿠폰을 사용했다.
(D) 그녀는 상품의 가격에 놀랐다.

해설 추론/암시
친척에게 줄 선물을 사기 위해 매장을 방문했다가 자신이 쓸 것도 추가로 샀다고 했으므로 (B)가 정답이다. 쿠폰은 만료되었다고 했으므로 (C)는 오답이다.

어휘 based on ~에 근거하여 recommendation 추천 originally 원래 intend 의도하다 merchandise 상품, 물품

158-160 이메일

수신: staff@vasquezpharma.com
발신: tphillips@vasquezpharma.com
날짜: 8월 15일
제목: 공지

[158]우리 연구 데이터베이스에 쓰이는 소프트웨어 프로그램이 이번 주 금요일인 8월 19일에 업데이트된다는 것을 주지해 주시기 바랍니다. [160]금요일에 여러분이 퇴근한 후에 IT 팀원들이 필요한 업무를 수행할 것입니다. 작업 속도를 높이기 위해 컴퓨터를 켠 상태 그대로 두십시오.

업데이트 후에도 여러분의 로그인 세부 정보는 동일하게 유지됩니다. 그러나 일부 기밀 파일은 적절한 인증이 없으면 접근할 수 없을 겁니다. 또한 [159]전보다 더 많은 검색 기능이 있을 것입니다. 이것은 여러분이 보다 빨리 검색 결과 범위를 좁히는 데 도움이 될 겁니다.

월요일에 컴퓨터를 시작하는 데 평소보다 시간이 더 걸릴 수 있지만 이것은 정상적인 과정이며, 이런 일은 한 번만 있을 것입니다. 질문이나 의견이 있으면 내선 번호 30으로 직접 IT 팀에 연락하세요. 이 사안에 인내하고 협조해 주셔서 감사드립니다.

Thomas Phillips

어휘 note 주목하다, 주의하다 carry out ~을 수행하다 leave for the day 퇴근하다 log-in 로그인, 접속 confidential 기밀의 access 접근하다, 접속하다 proper 적절한 authorization 인증, 승인 in addition 또한, 게다가 function 기능 narrow down ~을 좁히다 directly 직접, 곧장 extension 내선 번호 cooperation 협조

158. 이메일의 목적은 무엇인가?
(A) 데이터베이스 업그레이드 요청 방법을 설명하려고
(B) 직원들에게 일부 소프트웨어 변경 사항을 알리려고
(C) 기밀 기록 유지에 관한 지시를 하려고
(D) 직원들에게 로그인 세부 정보를 업데이트할 것을 상기시키려고

해설 주제/목적
직원들에게 소프트웨어 업데이트를 알리고 있으므로 (B)가 정답이다.

어휘 request 요청하다 inform 알리다 give instructions 지시하다 maintain 유지하다 remind 상기시키다

159. Mr. Phillips에 따르면, 이용자들은 8월 19일 이후에 어떤 경험을 할 것인가?

(A) 결과는 알파벳순으로 표시될 것이다.
(B) 승인 코드가 조정될 것이다.
(C) 더 많은 검색 옵션이 사용 가능할 것이다.
(D) 홈페이지가 더 빨리 로딩될 것이다.

해설 세부 사항
두 번째 문단에서 전보다 더 많은 검색 기능이 있을 것이라고 했으므로 (C)가 정답이다.

어휘 display 보여 주다, 전시하다 alphabetically 알파벳순으로 adjust 조정하다 load 로딩되다

160. [1], [2], [3], [4]로 표시된 위치 중 다음 문장이 들어가기에 가장 적절한 곳은?

"작업 속도를 높이기 위해 컴퓨터를 켠 상태 그대로 두십시오."

해설 문장 삽입
주어진 문장의 the process가 무엇인지 앞 또는 뒤 문장에 관련 내용이 언급되어야 한다. [1] 앞에서 IT 팀이 소프트웨어 프로그램 업데이트를 진행한다고 했으므로 the process는 업데이트하는 작업 과정을 가리킨다는 걸 알 수 있다. 따라서 (A)가 정답이다.

161-163 웹페이지

Salvo Electronics의 Delima-XR 스마트폰 리콜

[161]Salvo Electronics는 설계 결함으로 인해 특정 Delima-XR 스마트폰의 자진 리콜을 진행하고 있습니다. 우리 품질 관리 팀은 배터리가 과열될 수 있다고 판단했습니다. [161]만약 1월 1일부터 3월 31일 사이에 이 스마트폰 모델을 구입하셨다면 일련번호를 확인해 주십시오. 숫자가 56이나 57로 시작하는 경우 그 기기는 리콜 대상입니다. 모든 Salvo Electronics 매장에서 전화기를 반납하시면 전액 환불을 받으실 수 있습니다. [162]그렇게 하기 위해 원래의 포장이나 영수증을 요구하지 않습니다. 아니면 저희 고객 상담 전화인 1-800-555-7932로 전화하셔서 반품용 상자를 요청하셔도 됩니다. 반품용 상자가 여러분에게 발송될 것이며, 우편 요금은 선납될 것입니다. [163]상자는 "지상 운송 전용"으로 지정되어 있다는 것을 알아 두시기 바랍니다.

어휘 recall 리콜, 회수 issue 발표하다 voluntary 자발적인 certain 특정한 due to ~ 때문에 flaw 결함 overheat 과열되다 serial number 일련번호 device 기기 be eligible for ~의 자격이 있다 full refund 전액 환불 packaging 포장 receipt 영수증 alternatively 그렇지 않으면, 그 대신에 helpline 상담 전화 postage 우편 요금, 우송료 prepaid 선불된 designate 지정하다 transport 수송; 수송하다

161. 웹페이지는 누구를 의도한 것이겠는가?
(A) Salvo Electronics 영업 사원
(B) Salvo Electronics 고객
(C) 제품 디자이너
(D) 품질 관리 검사원

해설 추론/암시
스마트폰의 리콜 사실을 알린 후 제품을 구입한 사람들에게 리콜 방법을 설명하고 있으므로 (B)가 정답이다.

TEST 05

162. Delima-XR 스마트폰에 대해 암시된 것은 무엇인가?

(A) 영수증 없이 반품 가능하다.
(B) 3월 31일 이후에 단종되었다.
(C) 배터리는 교체될 수 있다.
(D) 잘 팔리지 않는다.

해설 추론/암시
원래의 포장이나 영수증이 없어도 반품할 수 있다고 했으므로 (A)가 정답이다.

어휘 discontinue 단종하다 replace 교체하다, 대체하다

163. 반품용 상자에 대해 시사된 것은 무엇인가?

(A) 여러 가지 다른 크기로 구입 가능하다.
(B) 수령하는 즉시 우편 요금을 지불해야 한다.
(C) 항공편으로 운송되어서는 안 된다.
(D) 이틀 내에 도착할 것이다.

해설 NOT/True
반품용 상자는 지상 운송 전용으로 지정되어 있다고 했으므로 항공편이나 선박으로는 운송될 수 없다는 것을 알 수 있다. 따라서 (C)가 정답이다.

어휘 several 여러 개의 upon receipt 수령 즉시

164-167 온라인 채팅

Teresa Juarez (오후 12:32)
안녕하세요, Chen, Bonnie. 두 사람 중 점심 식사를 마치고 돌아온 분이 있나요? Strauss Logistics의 담당자들과 회의를 하러 지금 사무실로 돌아가는 길인데, 버스가 막혀서요. [164]회의가 오후 1시부터라서 준비할 시간이 별로 없을 것 같아요.

Chen Xuan (오후 12:33)
저는 점심을 먹으러 나가지 않았어요. 뭘 도와드리면 될까요, Teresa?

Bonnie Eley (오후 12:34)
저도 여기 있어요. 회의를 위해 Juniper Room을 준비해야 하나요? 영사 스크린은 이미 그 안에 있고, 앞쪽에는 연단이 있습니다.

Teresa Juarez (오후 12:36)
사실 [165]Juniper Room은 12명을 위한 공간만 있기 때문에 안 될 거예요. 제 책상 위에 방문객들을 Spruce Room으로 안내하는 표지판이 있어요. [166]그분들이 도착하면 어디로 가야 할지 알 수 있도록 표지판을 입구에 걸어 줄 사람이 필요해요.

Bonnie Eley (오후 12:37)
네. 그 일은 오래 걸리지 않을 거예요.

Chen Xuan (오후 12:39)
그 층에 있는 커피 머신은 잘 작동하는데, 다른 제공할 것이 있나요? 제가 길 건너편 [167]식료품점에서 모둠 과일과 페이스트리를 살 수 있어요.

Teresa Juarez (오후 12:41)
그게 좋겠네요, Chen. 감사해요! 법인 카드를 사용해도 돼요. 그리고 당신도 고마워요, Bonnie. 최대한 빨리 갈게요. 지금 교통이 좀 정리되고 있는 것 같아요.

어휘 representative 대표자, 담당자 be stuck in traffic 교통체증에 걸리다 projection screen 영사막, 영사 스크린 podium 연단 space 공간 sign 표지판 direct 길을 안내하다 hang up ~을 걸다 entrance 입구 serve 제공하다 grocery store 식료품점 clear up 정리하다, 치우다

164. Ms. Juarez는 왜 Mr. Xuan과 Ms. Eley에게 연락했는가?

(A) 점심 식사 주문을 받기 위해
(B) 오류에 대해 사과하기 위해
(C) 회의에 그들을 초대하기 위해
(D) 도움을 요청하기 위해

해설 주제/목적
Ms. Juarez는 1시에 있을 회의를 준비할 시간이 없어서 Mr. Xuan과 Ms. Eley에게 연락했으므로 (D)가 정답이다.

어휘 take an order 주문을 받다 apologize 사과하다 assistance 도움, 지원

165. Strauss Logistics 담당자들과의 회의에 대해 암시된 것은 무엇인가?

(A) Ms. Eley가 주관할 것이다.
(B) Juniper Room에서 열릴 것이다.
(C) 제품 시연을 포함할 것이다.
(D) 12명 이상의 참석자가 있을 것이다.

해설 추론/암시
오후 12시 36분에 Ms. Juarez가 Juniper Room은 12명밖에 수용하지 못하기 때문에 Spruce Room으로 안내하라고 한 것으로 보아 회의에는 그 이상의 인원이 참석한다는 것을 추론할 수 있으므로 (D)가 정답이다.

어휘 demonstration 시연 participant 참가자, 참석자

166. 오후 12시 37분에 Ms. Eley가 "네"라고 쓸 때 그녀가 의미하는 것은 무엇이겠는가?

(A) 그녀는 몇몇 방문객들을 맞이할 것이다.
(B) 그녀는 안내문을 온라인에 게시할 것이다.
(C) 그녀는 표지판을 설치할 것이다.
(D) 그녀는 입구를 개방할 것이다.

해설 의도 파악
Ms. Juarez가 표지판을 입구에 걸 사람이 필요하다고 한 말에 대한 대답이므로 (C)가 정답이다.

패러프레이징 hang it up → put up a sign

어휘 post 게시하다 put up ~을 설치하다

167. Mr. Xuan은 무엇을 하겠다고 제안하는가?

(A) 영사 스크린을 옮기는 것
(B) 다과를 구매하는 것
(C) 서류를 인쇄하는 것
(D) 더 많은 의자를 가지고 오는 것

해설 세부 사항
오후 12시 39분에 Mr. Xuan이 식료품점에 가서 모둠 과일과 페이스트리를 살 수 있다고 했으므로 (B)가 정답이다.

패러프레이징 buy a fruit plate and some pastries → Purchasing some refreshments

168-171 이메일

수신: staff@elswicksoftware.com
발신: gferraz@elswicksoftware.com
날짜: 10월 6일
제목: 참고하세요

Elswick Software 직원 여러분께

[168]**우리 회사가 계속해서 번창함에 따라 여러분은 사무실 주변에서 새로운 얼굴들을 볼 수 있을 것입니다.** Lara Yi는 10월 12일부터 베리니 지점의 마케팅 책임자로 취임할 것입니다. 그녀는 Brasilia Tech에서 이직하여 우리와 합류하게 되었습니다.

Nicole Rocha 또한 베리니에서 증원되는 직원 중 한 명입니다. 그녀는 행정 업무를 하게 되며 Diego Barbosa의 지원을 받게 되는데, [169]**그는 현재 월요일, 수요일, 금요일에는 베리니에서, 그리고 화요일과 목요일에는 이비라푸에라에서 근무하고 있습니다.**

이비라푸에라에서는 [170]Julio Azevedo가 새로운 사무실 관리자로 채용되었습니다. [170B]**그는 소프트웨어 업계에서 20년 넘게 일해 왔습니다.** [170C]**모에마 지점의 Luisa Sousa가 그를 채용할 것을 제안했고,** 그는 면접 위원단의 모든 사람들에게 깊은 인상을 주었습니다. [170A]**그는 직원들이 그를 알 수 있는 기회를 가질 수 있도록 출근 첫날인 10월 19일에 질의응답 시간을 가질 것입니다.**

다른 인사 이동에 대해서도 여러분에게 계속해서 새 소식을 알려 드리겠습니다. [171]**모에마 지점이 운영을 중단하게 되면 많은 인력 이동이 있을 것으로 예상합니다.** 우리는 아직 그곳의 직원들에게 일어날 일을 마무리하는 중입니다.

Gustavo Ferraz

어휘 thrive 성장하다, 번창하다 branch 지점, 지사 director 책임자, 이사 expansion 확장 perform 수행하다 administrative 행정의 support 지원하다 currently 현재, 지금 assign 배정하다 impress 깊은 인상을 주다 panel 위원단 session (특정) 시간 keep ~ updated ~에게 계속해서 새로운 소식을 전하다 personnel 인력, 인원 transfer 이동 in operation 운영 중인 finalize 마무리하다

168. Mr. Ferraz가 이메일을 보낸 이유는 무엇인가?

(A) 직원들의 노고에 감사하기 위해
(B) 새로운 직원 몇 명을 소개하기 위해
(C) 얼마 후 찾아오는 방문자들에 대해 논의하기 위해
(D) 지점의 성과를 요약하기 위해

해설 주제/목적
첫 번째 문장에서 신규 직원 충원 사실을 알린 후 여러 명의 이름을 언급하고 있으므로 (B)가 정답이다.

어휘 upcoming 다가오는, 곧 있을 summarize 요약하다 achievement 성과

169. 둘 이상의 지점에서 일하는 사람은 누구인가?

(A) Ms. Yi
(B) Ms. Rocha
(C) Mr. Barbosa
(D) Mr. Ferraz

해설 세부 사항
Diego Barbosa는 월요일, 수요일, 금요일에는 베리니에서, 화요일과 목요일에는 이비라푸에라에서 근무한다고 했으므로 (C)가 정답이다.

170. Mr. Azevedo에 대해 언급되지 않은 것은 무엇인가?

(A) 그는 직원들의 질문에 답할 것이다.
(B) 그는 20년의 경력을 가지고 있다.
(C) 그는 회사 직원의 추천을 받았다.
(D) 그는 10월 19일에 계약서에 서명할 것이다.

해설 NOT/True
10월 19일은 Mr. Azevedo의 출근 첫날인데, 계약서 서명과 관련된 내용은 나오지 않았으므로 (D)가 정답이다.

패러프레이징 (A) hold a question-and-answer session → respond to questions
(B) has worked in the software industry for over 20 years → has two decades of experience
(C) Luisa Sousa at the Moema branch suggested hiring him → He was recommended by a company employee.

어휘 respond to ~에 답하다 decade 10년 contract 계약서

171. Mr. Ferraz가 모에마 지점에 대해 암시하는 것은 무엇인가?

(A) 다른 건물로 이전될 것이다.
(B) 직원 수가 가장 많다.
(C) 영구적으로 폐쇄될 것이다.
(D) 그의 새로운 사무실이 있는 곳이다.

해설 추론/암시
운영을 중단한다고 했으므로 (C)가 정답이다.

패러프레이징 is no longer in operation → is scheduled to permanently close

어휘 relocate 이전하다 be scheduled to do ~하기로 예정되어 있다 permanently 영구적으로 site 현장, 부지

172-175 웹페이지

홈	**박물관 소개**	사진 갤러리	연락처

[172]질레트 카운티 역사 박물관

[172]**질레트 카운티 역사 박물관은 1963년 클루슨 시내에 있는 작은 건물에서 비영리 기관으로 설립되었습니다.** [173]**25년 후, 박물관은 그린우드에 있는 현재의 상설 전시관으로 이전했습니다.** 이곳은 대중을 위한 교육 프로그램을 제공할 뿐만 아니라 질레트 카운티의 역사와 관련된 역사적 가치가 있는 유물들을 보존하는 데 전념하고 있습니다.

요즘 사람들이 현대적인 기술과 경험을 중시하는 것은 놀라운 일이 아닙니다. [175]**박물관은 시의성을 유지하고, 사람들이 과거와 연결되는 것의 중요성을 이해하도록 돕기 위해 노력하고 있습니다.** 잘 정리된 문서, 사진, 수제품 등의 제공을 통해 박물관의 직원과 자원봉사자들은

TEST 05

질레트 카운티가 과거에 어떠했는지 보여 주는 그림을 만들어 내길 희망합니다. 우리가 어디에 있었는지를 이해함으로써 우리는 우리가 어디로 가고 있는지 이해할 수 있습니다.

박물관은 멀게는 알래스카 케치칸으로부터 강사를 불러 강연을 개최하고, 관련 다큐멘터리를 상영하고, 역사적 발견에 대한 토론회를 주최했습니다. [174]**모든 특별 행사는 Leonard Bryant의 가족이 기증한 예술품으로 장식된 Bryant Room에서 열립니다. 최근 몇 년 동안 박물관에서 가장 인기 있었던 특별 행사는 연례 질레트 패션 워크숍이었습니다.** 참가자들은 박물관의 기록 보관소에 있는 사진들을 바탕으로 전통 의복을 재현하는 걸 배웠습니다.

로건에 있는 군사 기지의 역사, 법 집행 방식의 변화, 농업 방법 등, 무엇을 배우고 싶던지 간에 박물관은 흥미로운 무언가를 가지고 있을 것입니다. 박물관이 개장하는 화요일에서 토요일, 오전 10시부터 오후 4시까지 무료로 박물관을 탐험해 보세요.

어휘 found 설립하다 non-profit organization 비영리 단체 current 현재의 permanent 상설의, 영구적인 be dedicated to ~에 전념하다 preserve 보존하다 artifact 유물 relevant 적절한, 관련 있는 presentation 제시, 제공 handmade 수제의 host 주최하다 screening 상영 debate 토론 take place 일어나다, 열리다 donate 기증하다 recreate 재현하다 archive 기록 보관소 base 기지 enforcement 집행 agriculture 농업

172. 웹페이지의 목적은 무엇인가?

(A) 박물관 전시회를 홍보하려고
(B) 지역 박물관을 부각시키려고
(C) 박물관의 개관을 발표하려고
(D) 자원봉사자 모집 프로젝트를 소개하려고

해설 주제/목적
웹페이지 제목이 '질레트 카운티 역사 박물관'이며, 이어지는 내용에서 박물관에 대한 전반적인 정보를 알리고 있으므로 (B)가 정답이다.

어휘 promote 홍보하다 exhibit 전시(회) highlight 강조하다, 부각시키다 recruitment 모집

173. 질레트 카운티 역사 박물관은 어디에 있는가?

(A) 클루슨
(B) 그린우드
(C) 케치칸
(D) 로건

해설 세부 사항
현재 그린우드에 있다고 했으므로 (B)가 정답이다. 클루슨은 박물관이 25년 전에 있었던 곳이므로 오답이다.

174. Bryant Room에 대해 시사된 것은 무엇인가?

(A) 최근에 재단장되었다.
(B) 전시품은 정기적으로 바뀐다.
(C) 희귀한 문서들이 보관되는 곳이다.
(D) 워크숍이 열리는 장소이다.

해설 NOT/True
Bryant Room에서 연례 워크숍이 열린다고 했으므로 (D)가 정답이다.

어휘 display 전시 regularly 주기적으로, 정기적으로 rare 희귀한 store 보관하다

175. [1], [2], [3], [4]로 표시된 위치 중 다음 문장이 들어가기에 가장 적절한 곳은?

"요즘 사람들이 현대적인 기술과 경험을 중시하는 것은 놀라운 일이 아닙니다."

해설 문장 삽입
주어진 문장과 관련된 내용이 나오는 곳을 찾아야 한다. [2] 뒤에서 박물관이 시의성을 유지하고 과거와의 연결성이 중요하다는 걸 이해시키기 위해 노력한다는 것은 현대적인 것을 중시하는 요즘 사람들에게 호소하려 한다는 의미이므로 (B)가 정답이다.

176-180 안내 책자 & 이메일

Carolina Solar에서는 지속 가능한 에너지원으로의 전환을 통해 에너지 효율을 달성할 수 있다고 생각합니다. [176]**여러분이 현재 어떤 공공기업을 이용하셔도 여러분은 가정에 태양 전지판을 설치함으로써 환경을 돕는 데 일조할 수 있고, 장기적으로는 비용을 절약할 수 있습니다.** [177]**여러분의 주거지 유형과 지역에 따라 허가가 필요할 수도 있고 아닐 수도 있으므로 더 자세히 알아보려면 www.carolinasolar.net을 방문하십시오.**

신규 고객을 위한 우리의 절차에는 네 가지 단계가 있습니다.

1단계: (919) 555-5228로 전화를 주시면 기사가 여러분의 자택을 방문하여 치수를 재고 여러분의 에너지 필요성에 대해 논의할 것입니다.

[179]**2단계: 기사가 여러분의 옥상에 설치할 태양 전지판 권장 배열의 가상 3D 디자인을 보내 드립니다. 여기에는 예상되는 에너지 절약 보고서가 함께 제공됩니다.**

3단계: 계약이 체결되면 [178]**우리의 숙련된 작업반원 중 한 명이 정해진 비용을 받고** 댁에 전지판을 설치할 것입니다. 6월에서 8월은 저희가 바쁜 시즌이라는 것을 유념해 두세요.

4단계: 설치 2주 후에 회사 담당자가 여러분의 집을 방문하여 모든 것이 제대로 작동하는지 확인하고 여러분의 후속 질문에 답할 것입니다.

어휘 efficiency 효율성 achieve 성취하다, 달성하다 transition 이전하다, 이행하다 sustainable 지속 가능한 utility company (가스, 전기, 수도 등을 공급하는) 공공 기업 in the long run 결국에는 solar panel 태양 전지판 install 설치하다 permit 허가, 허락 depending on ~에 따라 property 부동산 neighborhood 인근, 이웃 technician 기사, 기술자 take a measurement 치수를 재다 virtual 가상의 array 배열 rooftop 지붕 accompany 동반하다 projected 예상되는 contract 계약서 experienced 노련한, 경험 많은 crew 작업반 fixed 고정된, 일정한 representative 담당자 ensure 확실히 하다 adequately 적절히 follow-up 후속의

수신: Theresa Ruiz
발신: Alan Knox
날짜: 8월 8일
제목: 192 홀랜드 스트리트 프로젝트
첨부 파일: Ruiz1.doc, Ruiz2.doc

Ms. Ruiz께,

[179]첨부된 태양 전지판의 설계 도면과 귀하의 사용량을 바탕으로 에너지 절약 효과를 요약한 내용을 확인해 주십시오. 저는 귀하께서 전지판 시스템에 Nuzum 배터리를 사용하고 싶어 했다는 것을 압니다. 하지만 저는 그 대신에 Girard Co.의 배터리를 추천합니다. [180]이 제품은 선납 비용은 다소 비싸지만 확장성이 있는데, 그 말은 향후 몇 년 동안 장치를 교체하지 않고 배터리를 추가할 수 있는 선택권이 있다는 것입니다. 그것은 Nuzum 배터리와 보증 기간이 동일합니다.

귀하께서 이 계획을 승인하시는지 그리고 질문이 있는지를 알려 주십시오. 답장 기다리겠습니다!

Alan Knox

어휘 attach 첨부하다 drawing 도면, 그림 summary 요약, 개요 save 절약하다 usage 사용(량) recommend 추천하다 instead 대신에 a bit 약간 up front 선불로 scalable 확장할 수 있는 replace 교체하다, 대체하다 unit (작은) 기구, 장치 warranty 보증 period 기간 approve 승인하다

176. 안내 책자는 회사의 태양 전지판에 대해 무엇을 암시하는가?

(A) 공장에서 결함 여부를 주의 깊게 검사받는다.
(B) 환경 친화적인 재료로 만들어진다.
(C) 집주인이 쉽게 관리할 수 있다.
(D) 에너지 공급업체와 함께 사용될 수 있다.

해설 추론/암시
기존의 공공 기업을 이용하면서도 태양 전지판을 설치할 수 있다고 했으므로 (D)가 정답이다.

패러프레이징 utility company → energy supplier

어휘 defect 결함 environmentally friendly 환경 친화적인 material 재료 maintain 유지하다

177. 안내 책자에 따르면, 독자들이 회사의 웹사이트를 방문해야 하는 이유는 무엇인가?

(A) 자신의 지붕 사진을 업로드하기 위해
(B) 현재 고객들의 의견을 읽기 위해
(C) 허가 조건에 대한 정보를 얻기 위해
(D) 필요한 시스템의 크기를 추정하기 위해

해설 세부 사항
허가가 필요한지 아닌지 여부를 확인하기 위해 웹사이트를 방문하라고 했으므로 (C)가 정답이다.

어휘 comment 의견 current 현재의 requirement 필요조건, 요건 estimate 추산하다, 추정하다

178. Carolina Solar에 대한 사실은 무엇인가?

(A) 8월 이후에는 예약이 불가능하다.
(B) 한 명 이상의 설치 작업반원을 보유하고 있다.
(C) 설치 시간을 바탕으로 요금을 계산한다.
(D) 국내 공급사만 이용하는 것을 목표로 한다.

해설 NOT/True
첫 번째 지문에서 숙련된 작업반원 중 한 명이 태양 전지판을 설치할 거라고 했으므로 작업반원이 여러 명이라는 걸 알 수 있다. 따라서 (B)가 정답이다.

어휘 appointment 예약 calculate 계산하다 aim 목표로 하다 domestic 국내의

179. Ms. Ruiz는 어느 단계에 있는가?

(A) 1단계
(B) 2단계
(C) 3단계
(D) 4단계

해설 두 지문 연계_세부 사항
두 번째 지문에서 Mr. Knox가 Ms. Ruiz에게 태양 전지판의 설계 도면과 에너지 절약 효과를 요약한 내용을 보냈다고 했다. 첫 번째 지문에서 이러한 과정은 2단계에서 시행된다고 했으므로 (B)가 정답이다.

180. Mr. Knox는 왜 배터리를 바꿀 것을 제안하는가?

(A) 보다 신뢰할 수 있는 제품을 사용하기 위해
(B) 연장된 보증을 이용하기 위해
(C) 프로젝트 비용을 절감하기 위해
(D) 향후에 보다 많은 유연성을 제공하기 위해

해설 세부 사항
두 번째 지문에서 향후 몇 년 동안 장치를 교체하지 않고 배터리를 추가할 수 있기 때문에 Nuzum 배터리 대신 Girard Co.의 배터리를 추천하고 있으므로 (D)가 정답이다.

패러프레이징 have the option of adding more battery power → provide more flexibility
in the coming years → in the future

어휘 reliable 신뢰할 수 있는 take advantage of ~을 이용하다 extended 연장된 provide 제공하다 flexibility 유연성

181-185 공지 & 이메일

글로버스빌 농민 협회
공지

판매자와 일반인 모두를 대상으로 한 광범위한 의견 조사에 따라 [181]**글로버스빌 농민 협회는 지역 농산물 직매장에 다음과 같은 변화를 즉시 시행할 것입니다.**

꽃시장: 더 많은 노점을 위한 공간을 만들고 야외에서 전기를 이용할 수 있도록 꽃시장을 Lance Park에서 Grove Plaza로 이전할 것입니다. 꽃시장은 원래와 같이 화요일과 토요일에 문을 열 것입니다.

[182]**종합 시장**: 판매자들은 여전히 Renner Park에 있는 이 시장에서 잼, 과일, 야채, 그리고 허브들을 팔 수 있으며, 이제 화분에 심은 식물도 허용합니다. 전과 같이 [182]**수요일과 토요일에 문을 열고 월요일도 개장일로 추가했습니다.**

[183]**육류 및 기타 시장: 지역에서 생산된 육류, 생선, 유제품을 파는 이 시장은 토요일과 일요일에 Sunset Hall에서 계속 운영될 것입니다.** 하지만 전보다 한 시간 이른 오전 7시에 문을 열 것입니다.

농산물 시장: 우리는 신선한 과일과 채소를 구매하러 이 시장에 오는

TEST 05

사람들에게 무료 쇼핑백을 나눠 줄 예정인데, 이곳은 목요일, 금요일, 그리고 토요일에 Crosswind Field에서 운영됩니다.

어휘 association 협회 extensive 광범위한 survey 설문 조사 vendor 판매자 farmers market 농산물 직매장 effective 시행되는, 발효되는 immediately 즉시 space 공간 stall 가판대, 좌판 gain 얻다 outdoor 야외의 access 접근권 electricity 전기 as usual 늘 그렇듯이 potted 화분에 심은 in addition to ~ 외에도, ~ 뿐만 아니라 dairy product 유제품 in operation 운영 중인 distribute 나누어 주다, 배포하다

수신: Lisa Jordan
[183]발신: Joe Cawthorn
날짜: 7월 14일
제목: 농산물 직매장

안녕하세요, Lisa.

제 스케줄을 확인했는데 [183]이번 주 토요일에 시장에서 Olivia의 교대 근무를 제가 맡아도 문제없습니다. 우리가 판매하는 다양한 생선 종류를 이미 잘 알고 있기 때문에 고객들에게 도움을 드릴 수 있을 것 같네요. [185]저를 위해 주차권을 확보해 주겠다고 하시니 고마워요. 하지만 지금 제 차가 정비소에 들어가 있기 때문에 그건 필요하지 않아요. 제가 정확히 몇 시에 [184]가야 하는지 알려 주세요.

Joe

어휘 cover 대신하다 shift 교대 근무 familiar 익숙한 variety 종류, 품종 secure 확보하다 parking pass 주차권 shop 수리소 exactly 정확히

181. 공지는 왜 작성되었는가?

(A) 지역 시장의 개선 사항을 발표하기 위해
(B) 판매자들에게 몇몇 행사에 참석할 것을 요청하기 위해
(C) 쇼핑객들의 필요성에 대한 의견을 수집하기 위해
(D) 글로버스빌 농민 협회 가입을 장려하기 위해

해설 주제/목적
첫 번째 지문에서 다양한 개선 사항을 언급하고 있으므로 (A)가 정답이다.

어휘 improvement 개선, 향상 gather 모으다, 수집하다 promote membership 회원 가입을 장려하다

182. 종합 시장에 대해 암시된 것은 무엇인가?

(A) 주말 이틀간 모두 문을 연다.
(B) 전에는 일주일에 두 번만 운영했다.
(C) 가장 방문객이 많은 시장이다.
(D) 더 이상 식물 판매를 허용하지 않는다.

해설 추론/암시
첫 번째 지문에서 종합 시장은 수요일과 토요일에 문을 열었는데 월요일을 개장일로 추가했다고 했으므로 원래는 이틀만 문을 열었다는 것을 추론할 수 있다. 따라서 (B)가 정답이다.

어휘 operate 운영하다 twice 두 번 no longer 더 이상 ~ 않는

183. Mr. Cawthorn은 이번 주 토요일에 어디서 근무하겠는가?

(A) Grove Plaza
(B) Renner Park
(C) Sunset Hall
(D) Crosswind Field

해설 두 지문 연계_추론/암시
두 번째 지문을 보면 Mr. Cawthorn은 이메일 발신자인데, 토요일에 Olivia 대신 근무를 해도 괜찮다고 했고 판매하는 생선 종류를 잘 알고 있다고 했다. 첫 번째 지문에서 토요일에 운영되면서 생선을 판매하는 시장은 육류 및 기타 시장으로 나와 있는데, 해당 시장은 Sunset Hall에서 운영된다고 했으므로 (C)가 정답이다.

184. 이메일에서, 첫 번째 단락 네 번째 줄의 어휘 "turn up"과 의미상 가장 가까운 것은?

(A) 도착하다
(B) 발견하다
(C) 늘리다
(D) 적응하다; 각색하다

해설 동의어 찾기
turn up이 있는 what time you need me to turn up은 내가 몇 시에 가야 하는지 묻는 의미이며, 여기서 turn up은 '가다, 나타나다'라는 뜻으로 쓰였다. 따라서 (A) arrive가 정답이다.

185. Mr. Cawthorn은 자신의 이메일에서 무엇을 암시하는가?

(A) 그는 주차권이 만료되지 않았다고 생각한다.
(B) 그는 행사에 차를 운전해서 갈 계획이 없다.
(C) 그는 교대 근무 후에 쇼핑을 하고 싶어 한다.
(D) 그는 Olivia로부터 제품 정보를 얻을 것이다.

해설 추론/암시
Mr. Cawthorn은 자신의 차량이 정비소에 있기 때문에 주차권이 필요하지 않다고 했으므로 시장에는 차를 가져가지 않을 것이다. 따라서 (B)가 정답이다.

어휘 expire 만료되다

186-190 전단지 & 안내 책자 & 이메일

Community Plus Workshop Series

웨이크필드 주민들은 3월 28일에 열리는 Community Plus Workshop Series에 참여하여 다양한 분야에서 여러분의 실력을 향상시키세요. 작문으로 창의력의 빗장을 푸는 것과 같은 새로운 것을 시도해 보는 건 어떨까요? [186]아니면 빗물을 모아서 정원에서 물을 적게 사용하는 방법을 배우는 것과 같은 좀 더 실용적인 것을 노려 보세요. [187]우리는 여러분이 Erica Cantrell과 같은 강사들에게 깊은 인상을 받으실 거라고 확신하는데, 그녀는 중고 재료로 흥미로운 공예품을 만드는 법을 보여 줄 것입니다.

워크숍 참가비는 무료이며, 사전 등록은 필요하지 않습니다. 좌석은 선착순으로 이용 가능하므로, 좋은 자리를 얻고 싶다면 일찍 도착하는 것을 추천합니다. 문의 사항이 있으면 Ralph Quinn에게 quinnr@wakefieldcomm.org로 직접 문의하세요.

어휘 community 지역 사회 resident 주민 improve 향상시키다 a variety

of 다양한 take part in ~에 참여하다 unlock (열쇠로) 열다 creativity 창의성 practical 실용적인 rainwater 빗물 be impressed with ~에 깊은 인상을 받다 instructor 강사 craft 공예 material 재료 fee 요금 advance 사전의 registration 등록 seating 좌석, 자리 on a first-come, first-served basis 선착순으로 direct 향하다 inquiry 문의

Community Plus Workshop Series – **최종 일정**
3월 28일

[188]오전 9시	[188]Kitchen Cuts – 한정된 예산으로 요리를 한다고 해서 반드시 맛을 희생해야 하는 것은 아닙니다! 저렴한 재료들로 맛있는 저녁을 만들어 보세요. Insects That Help – 벌과 기타 정원 친화적인 곤충들을 여러분의 정원으로 끌어들일 식물을 기르세요. 여러분 가정의 그늘에 맞는 품종을 고르세요.
오전 11시	Nature Made – 지붕에 빗물 수집 시설을 설치하는 방법과 모은 빗물을 유지하는 방법에 대한 조언을 얻으세요.
오후 2시	Perfect Plots – 줄거리 전개를 연습하고 독자들을 몰입시키기 위한 조언을 얻음으로써 창의적인 글쓰기 기술을 연마하세요. [190]Turning Inward – 여러분을 언제든지 차분하고 편안한 상태로 만들 수 있는 간단한 요가 자세와 호흡 운동법을 배우세요.
오후 3시 30분	[187]Trash to Treasure – 보통은 내다 버리는 일반적인 재료를 재사용하여 아름다운 선물과 장식으로 바꾸세요. 이 주제에 대해 수상 경력이 있는 예술가가 가르칩니다.

어휘 on a budget 한정된 예산으로 sacrifice 희생하다 affordable 저렴한 ingredient (식)재료 insect 곤충 attract 유인하다 variety 품종, 종류 shade 그늘 set up ~을 설치하다 supply 공급(품) plot 줄거리, 플롯 hone 연마하다 engaged 몰두한 inward 안쪽으로 calm 차분한 relaxed 긴장이 풀린, 편안한 state 상태 reuse 재사용하다 ordinary 평범한 normally 보통은 throw away ~을 버리다 convert 변환하다, 바꾸다 decoration 장식

수신: Ralph Quinn
[189]발신: Monique Evans
날짜: 3월 24일
제목: 워크숍

Mr. Quinn께,

저는 최근에 새로운 일을 맡기 위해 웨이크필드로 이사했습니다. 제가 예상했던 것보다 훨씬 힘든 일이라서 [190]스트레스를 줄이기 위한 기술을 배우는 데 도움이 될 만한 이번 워크숍에 대해 제 동료를 통해 알게 되어 기뻤습니다. [189]워크숍에 갈 때 특별히 챙겨야 할 것이 있는지 궁금합니다. 저는 시작 시간보다 훨씬 일찍 도착할 계획을 벌써부터 세우고 있습니다.

감사합니다!

Monique Evans

어휘 take on a job 일을 맡다 demanding 힘든, 부담이 큰 coworker 동료 technique 기술, 기법 in particular 특히 ahead of time 예정보다 빨리

186. 전단지에 따르면, 워크숍에서 다룰 주제 중 하나는 무엇인가?

(A) 주택 보수하기
(B) 창업하기
(C) 물 절약하기
(D) 듣기 능력 향상시키기

해설 주제/목적
빗물을 모아서 정원에서 물을 적게 사용하는 방법을 배워 보라는 내용이 있으므로 (C)가 정답이다.

패러프레이징 use less water → Saving water

어휘 renovate 보수하다, 수선하다

187. Ms. Cantrell에 대해 사실인 것은 무엇이겠는가?

(A) 자신의 작품으로 상을 받았다.
(B) 하나 이상의 워크숍을 가르칠 것이다.
(C) Community Plus Workshop Series를 마련했다.
(D) 웨이크필드의 오랜 주민이다.

해설 두 지문 연계_추론/암시
첫 번째 지문에 Ms. Cantrell이 중고 재료로 공예품 만드는 방법을 보여 줄 것이라는 내용이 있다. 두 번째 지문에서 언급된 Trash to Treasure가 이에 해당하며, 수상 경력이 있는 예술가가 가르친다고 했으므로 Ms. Cantrell이 상을 받은 적이 있다는 걸 추론할 수 있다. 따라서 (A)가 정답이다.

어휘 found 설립하다

188. 참가자들은 언제 식비를 절약하는 것에 대해 배울 수 있는가?

(A) 오전 9시
(B) 오전 11시
(C) 오후 2시
(D) 오후 3시 30분

해설 세부 사항
두 번째 지문에 있는 Kitchen Cuts의 설명 중 저렴한 재료로 맛있는 저녁을 만들어 보라는 내용이 있는 것으로 보아 이 워크숍에서 식비 절약 방법을 배울 수 있다. 따라서 (A)가 정답이다.

189. Ms. Evans는 워크숍에 대해 무엇을 알고 싶어 하는가?

(A) 어디로 가야 하는지
(B) 무엇을 가져가야 하는지
(C) 어떻게 등록해야 하는지
(D) 언제 도착해야 하는지

해설 세부 사항
세 번째 지문을 보면 Ms. Evans가 이메일 발신자인데, 워크숍을 갈 때 특별히 챙길 것이 있는지 문의하고 있으므로 (B)가 정답이다.

190. Ms. Evans는 어떤 워크숍에 참석하겠는가?

(A) Insects That Help
(B) Nature Made

(C) Perfect Plots

(D) Turning Inward

해설 두 지문 연계_추론/암시

세 번째 지문에서 Ms. Evans는 스트레스를 줄이기 위한 기술을 배우는 데 도움이 될 만한 워크숍을 알게 되어 기쁘다고 했다. 두 번째 지문의 워크숍 목록 중에서 스트레스를 줄이는 것과 관련된 것은 Turning Inward이므로 (D)가 정답이다.

191-195 이메일 & 차트 & 온라인 후기

수신: Dawson Horse-Riding Center 전 직원
발신: Suzan Salazar
날짜: 2월 6일
제목: 메모

오늘 아침 여러분의 적극적인 참여에 감사드립니다. [191]**우리는 3월 첫째 주 월요일에 열리는 연례 말 산업 박람회로 바쁠 것이기 때문에 4월 첫째 주 월요일이 되어야 전 직원 회의를 하게 될 것 같습니다.**

그사이에 우리는 사람들이 말을 탈 차례를 기다리는 동안 점심이나 간식을 즐길 수 있도록 우리 정원에 피크닉 쉼터를 추가하는 계획을 추진할 것입니다. [192]**Alfonso Miller의 조경 회사가 공간을 만들기 위해 그 구역에서 두 개의 화단을 제거할 것입니다.** [193]**Esther Francis는 쉼터 제작 비용을 조사할 것입니다.** 그리고 Glenn Lopez는 주차장을 재포장하고 그곳에 다른 개선 작업을 수행할 사람을 고용할 것입니다.

Dawson Horse-Riding Center에서 앞으로 있을 변화가 무척 기대됩니다!

감사합니다.

Suzan Salazar
Dawson Horse-Riding Center

어휘 active 적극적인 participation 참여 annual 연례의 in the meantime 그사이에, 그동안 go forward 진척시키다 shelter 쉼터, 대피소 turn 차례 landscaping 조경 firm 회사 section 부분, 구획 in addition 또한, 게다가 repave 다시 포장하다 carry out ~을 수행하다 improvement 개선

[193]피크닉 쉼터 건설 비용

회사	비용	예상 완료 날짜
Dillon Construction	8,550달러	6월 27일
Edgewood	7,800달러	7월 11일
[195]Hale Construction	8,200달러	[195]6월 4일
Outdoor Shelters Inc.	7,995달러	7월 31일

의견: Dillon Construction과 Hale Construction은 고객들로부터 지속적으로 최고의 평점을 받았습니다.

어휘 estimated 견적의, 추측의 consistently 지속적으로 rating 평가, 등급

★★★★★

저는 어제 가족과 함께 Dawson Horse-Riding Center를 방문했습니다. 제 아이들은 말을 타며 즐거운 시간을 보냈습니다. 센터는 각기 다른 연령과 경험 수준을 가진 승마 참가자들에게 적합한 다양한 종류의 말을 마구간에 보유하고 있습니다. [194]**비용이 아주 적긴 하지만 주차 요금을 청구하기 시작했다는 사실에 놀랐습니다.** [195]**정원에 새로 생긴 피크닉 쉼터가 인상적이어서** 다음 방문 시 도시락을 챙겨 갈 계획입니다. 이 시설은 여가 시간을 보내기에 아주 좋은 장소입니다!

후기 작성: Clara Hamilton, [195]**6월 15일**

어휘 a wide range of 아주 다양한 stable 마구간 suitable for ~에 적합한 charge 비용을 부과하다 site 부지, 장소 minimal 아주 적은 packed lunch 도시락 facility 시설

191. 이메일에 따르면, Dawson Horse-Riding Center는 얼마나 자주 전 직원 회의를 하겠는가?

(A) 일주일에 한 번
(B) 한 달에 한 번
(C) 한 달에 두 번
(D) 1분기에 한 번

해설 추론/암시

첫 번째 지문에서 3월 첫째 주 월요일은 바쁘기 때문에 4월 첫째 주 월요일에나 전 직원 회의를 할 수 있을 거라고 했으므로 (B)가 정답이다.

192. Ms. Salazar는 업체의 정원에 대해 무엇을 시사하는가?

(A) 방문객들에게 인기 있는 장소이다.
(B) 꽃들 중 일부는 판매될 것이다.
(C) 조경 회사에 의해 식수될 것이다.
(D) 몇 개의 화단이 제거될 것이다.

해설 NOT/True

첫 번째 지문을 보면 Ms. Salazar는 이메일 발신자인데, Alfonso Miller의 조경 회사가 피크닉 쉼터 공간을 만들기 위해 두 개의 화단을 제거할 거라고 했으므로 (D)가 정답이다.

193. 누가 차트를 준비했겠는가?

(A) Mr. Miller
(B) Ms. Francis
(C) Mr. Lopez
(D) Ms. Salazar

해설 두 지문 연계_추론/암시

차트는 피크닉 쉼터 건설 비용에 관한 것이다. 첫 번째 지문에 Esther Francis가 쉼터 제작 비용을 조사할 것이라는 내용이 있으므로 (B)가 정답이다.

194. Ms. Hamilton은 자신의 후기에서 Dawson Horse-Riding Center에 대해 무엇을 암시하는가?

(A) 전에는 무료 주차를 제공했었다.
(B) 현장에서 음식을 판매한다.

(C) 마구간 무료 견학을 제공한다.
(D) 어린이들을 위한 특별 활동을 진행한다.

해설 추론/암시
세 번째 지문을 보면 Ms. Hamilton이 후기 작성자인데, Dawson Horse-Riding Center에서 주차 요금을 받기 시작했다고 언급했으므로 전에는 요금을 받지 않았다는 것을 알 수 있다. 따라서 (A)가 정답이다.

어휘 previously 전에 on site 현장에 activity 활동

195. Dawson Horse-Riding Center가 피크닉 구역을 짓기 위해 고용했을 회사는 어느 곳이겠는가?

(A) Dillon Construction
(B) Edgewood
(C) Hale Construction
(D) Outdoor Shelters Inc.

해설 두 지문 연계_추론/암시
후기 작성일이 6월 15일인데, 정원에 새로 생긴 피크닉 쉼터가 인상적이었다고 한 것으로 보아 이미 쉼터가 지어졌다는 것을 알 수 있다. 차트에서 각 회사별 쉼터 예상 완공 일자를 확인하면 6월 15일 이전에 쉼터를 완성할 수 있는 곳은 Hale Construction뿐이므로 (C)가 정답이다.

196-200 안내 책자 & 차트 & 이메일

Grand Canyon Adventures (GCA)
그랜드 캐니언 국립 공원 주간 투어!

경험이 풍부한 가이드가 인솔하고 관광 해설이 동반되는 투어를 즐기세요. [196]**Carabello Hotel에서 무료로 데려오고 데려다주는 서비스를 제공합니다.** 더 자세한 정보를 원하시면 (928) 555-4983으로 연락하세요.

Explorer Tour — 2시간, 1인당 450달러
이 잊을 수 없는 투어로 헬리콥터 위에서 내려다보이는 협곡의 숨 막히는 경치를 보세요! 긴 바지와 앞이 막힌 신발을 신으세요. 점심 포함.

West Rim Tour — 4시간, 1인당 150달러
버스를 타고 공원의 West Rim 지역을 통과하면 독수리처럼 생겼다고 하는 바위 형상인 Eagle Point와 같은 유명한 곳을 볼 수 있습니다. 아침과 점심 포함.

[198]South Rim Tour — 3시간, 1인당 110달러
특히 사진작가들이 South Rim의 놀랍도록 아름다운 경치를 좋아할 것입니다. [198]**버스는 Mather Point를 비롯한 경치가 좋은 여러 지점에 정차할 것입니다.** 점심 포함.

[200]Valley Tour — 3시간, 1인당 175달러
[200]**이 특별한 보트 여행을 통해 협곡의 중심부로 들어가 보세요.** 버스를 타고 거의 4천 피트나 되는 협곡 바닥까지 내려가서 Colorado River를 따라 보트를 탑니다. 점심 포함.

어휘 guided 가이드가 안내하는 narrate 이야기를 하다, 내레이션을 하다 experienced 능숙한, 경험이 풍부한 contact 연락하다 explorer 탐험가 breathtaking 숨이 막히는 view 경치, 풍경 unforgettable 잊을 수 없는 closed-toed 신발의 앞이 막힌 rim 가장자리 formation 형성 stunning 굉장히 아름다운, 깜짝 놀랄 make a stop 멈추다 multiple 많은 scenic 경치가 좋은 spot 장소, 곳 unique 특별한, 고유의 descend 내려가다, 하강하다 all the way 내내

GCA 6월 투어 요약

투어 종류	주당 투어	투어당 평균 수익	주당 평균 수익	평균 평점
[197]Explorer Tour	7	217달러	1,519달러	[197]4.9
[197]West Rim Tour	12	725달러	8,700달러	[197]3.7
[198]South Rim Tour	[198]14	454달러	6,356달러	4.2
Valley Tour	9	83달러	747달러	4.0

수신: Jodi Luther
발신: Anne Vaughn
날짜: 9월 15일
제목: 투어

Ms. Luther께,

[199]**우리가 투어 일정 변경을 논의하기 위해 9월 18일에 만나기로 한 것으로 알고 있습니다.** 미안하지만 제가 그날 몇 명의 잠재 투자자들을 만나기로 되어 있습니다. [199]**그 대신 9월 22일 월요일에 시간이 되시나요? 아니면 그 주 언제라도 가능하신가요?** [200]**우리가 보트 탑승 옵션이 있는 투어를 취소하기로 결정했기 때문에 그 투어의 가이드인 Marvin Faulkner가 다른 일을 할 수 있습니다.** 그래서 지금은 다른 가이드를 고용할 필요가 없을 것 같아요. 이 문제는 직접 만나서 더 논의하죠.

Anne Vaughn

어휘 be supposed to do ~하기로 되어 있다 potential 잠재적인 investor 투자자 instead 대신에 cancel 취소하다 hire 고용하다 at this time 지금 further 더 in person 직접

196. 안내 책자에서 모든 투어에 대해 동일하게 제시하는 것은 무엇인가?

(A) 참가자당 비용
(B) 호텔로부터의 이동
(C) 투어 시간
(D) 포함된 식사 횟수

해설 세부 사항
Carabello Hotel에서 무료로 데려오고 데려다주는 서비스를 제공한다고 했으므로 (B)가 정답이다.

어휘 transportation 이동 (방법) duration 지속 기간

197. 차트에 따르면, West Rim Tour에 대해 사실인 것은 무엇인가?

(A) Explorer Tour보다 낮은 평점을 받았다.
(B) 가장 자주 제공되는 투어이다.

TEST 05

(C) South Rim Tour보다 투어당 수익이 적다.
(D) 주당 두 번째로 수익성이 높은 투어이다.

해설 **NOT/True**
West Rim Tour의 평균 평점은 3.7이고 Explorer Tour는 4.9이므로 (A)가 정답이다.

어휘 frequently 자주, 빈번히 profitable 수익성이 좋은

198. GCA는 일주일에 몇 번이나 Mather Point로 가는 투어를 제공하는가?

(A) 7
(B) 9
(C) 12
(D) 14

해설 두 지문 연계_세부 사항
첫 번째 지문의 South Rim Tour 설명에 Mather Point를 비롯한 여러 경치 좋은 지점을 다닌다고 되어 있다. 또한 세 번째 지문에서 South Rim Tour의 주당 투어 횟수가 14라고 나와 있으므로 (D)가 정답이다.

199. Ms. Vaughn은 왜 이메일을 썼는가?

(A) 회의 일정을 다시 잡으려고
(B) 투어 일정의 오류에 대해 사과하려고
(C) 채용을 위해 새 여행 가이드를 추천하려고
(D) 몇 명의 투자자를 소개하려고

해설 주제/목적
투자자를 만나기로 했기 때문에 9월 18일로 예정되었던 회의 일정을 다른 날짜로 변경하려 한다는 것을 알 수 있으므로 (A)가 정답이다.

200. Mr. Faulkner가 인솔하는 투어는 무엇인가?

(A) The Explorer Tour
(B) The West Rim Tour
(C) The South Rim Tour
(D) The Valley Tour

해설 두 지문 연계_세부 사항
세 번째 지문에서 Marvin Faulkner가 보트 타기 옵션이 있는 투어의 가이드라는 단서를 찾을 수 있다. 첫 번째 지문에서 보트 여행이 포함된 투어는 Valley Tour라는 것을 확인할 수 있으므로 (D)가 정답이다.

테스트별
핵심 어휘

자르는 선

TEST 01

PART 1

☐ **photocopy** 복사하다

She's photocopying a document.
그녀는 문서를 복사하고 있다.

☐ **plug in** ~의 플러그를 꽂다, 전원을 연결하다

☐ **doorway** 현관

☐ **wait in line** 줄을 서서 기다리다

☐ **walkway** 산책로, 보도

☐ **mount** 올라타다

☐ **protective gear** 보호 장비

☐ **stroll** 거닐다

☐ **dock** 선착장, 부두

PART 2

☐ **parking fee** 주차 요금

☐ **transfer** 전근 가다, 이동하다

☐ **replace** 교체하다

☐ **handle** 처리하다

☐ **issue** 발급하다

☐ **access** 출입, 접근

☐ **restricted** 출입이 제한되는

☐ **send in** 제출하다

☐ **form** 양식, 서식

☐ **insurance** 보험

☐ **protection** (보험) 보장

☐ **property** 재산, 부동산

☐ **sign up for** ~을 신청하다

☐ **be out of town** 출장 가다

☐ **take down** (구조물을 해체하여) 치우다

Why was the fence taken down?
왜 울타리가 철거되었나요?

☐ **boundary** 경계

☐ **cancellation fee** 취소 수수료

PART 3

☐ **participant** 참가자

☐ **convenience store** 편의점

☐ **place an order** ~을 주문하다

☐ **spare part** 예비 부품

☐ **organic** 유기농의

☐ **produce** 생산물, 농작물

☐ **low-fat** 저지방의

☐ **wellness** 건강

☐ **give a talk** 강연하다

☐ **make adjustments to** ~을 조정하다

☐ **in transit** 운송 중에

They must have been damaged in transit.
운송 중에 손상된 게 틀림없어요.

☐ **front yard** 앞마당

☐ **attention** 주의

☐ **invest in** ~에 투자하다

☐ **flower bed** 화단

☐ **first impression** 첫인상

☐ **buyer** 구매자

☐ **inexpensive** 값싼, 비용이 많이 들지 않는

☐ **have ~ in mind** ~에 관해 생각하고 있다

☐ **hang up** 걸다

☐ **on short notice** 촉박하게

We've got to rent a van on short notice.
우리는 급하게 승합차를 빌려야 해요.

☐ **forward** 전달하다

☐ **renovation** 수리, 수선

☐ **notice** 알다, 알아차리다

☐ **block** 막다

☐ **temporary** 일시적인, 임시의

☐ **unload** (짐을) 내리다

☐ **add up to** 합계 ~이 되다

☐ **a range of** 다양한

☐ **suitable** 적합한

☐ **electrician** 전기 기술자

I've called an electrician, but I don't think they'll be fixed by then.
전기 기술자를 불렀는데, 그때까지는 수리되지 않을 것 같아요.

☐ **charity** 자선 단체

☐ **environmental** 환경의

☐ **conservation** 보전, 보존

PART 4

☐ **right-hand side** 오른쪽

☐ **take a seat** 자리에 앉다

☐ **board** 탑승하다

☐ **architect** 건축가

☐ **be familiar with** 잘 알다, ~에 익숙하다

☐ **structure** 구조

☐ **discuss** 논의하다

☐ **inspire** 영감을 주다

☐ **dive into** ~으로 뛰어 들다

☐ **headquarters** 본사

☐ **transportation** 운송

☐ **assign** 배정하다, 맡기다

☐ **itemize** 항목별로 적다

I've assigned Melissa Collins the task of creating an itemized list of all of our equipment on site.
멜리사 콜린스에게 현장에 있는 우리 장비를 모두 항목별 표로 작성하는 일을 배정했습니다.

- ☐ **on site** 현장에 있는, 현지의
- ☐ **keep in mind** 명심하다
- ☐ **turnout** 참가자의 수
- ☐ **batch** 한 묶음, 1회분
- ☐ **contaminate** 오염시키다
- ☐ **specialist** 전문가
- ☐ **restoration** 복구
- ☐ **essential** 필수적인
- ☐ **historically** 역사적으로
- ☐ **accurate** 정확한
- ☐ **deposit** 계약금, 보증금
- ☐ **take on** (일 등을) 맡다

> We don't usually take on projects with such difficult requirements.
> 우리는 보통은 그렇게 어려운 요구 사항이 있는 프로젝트는 맡지 않습니다.

- ☐ **requirement** 요구되는 것
- ☐ **regular client** 고정 거래처, 단골 고객
- ☐ **have the day off** 쉬다
- ☐ **complete** 완료하다, 끝마치다
- ☐ **make a delivery** 배달하다
- ☐ **exhibition** 전시회
- ☐ **profit** 이익, 이윤
- ☐ **make up for** ~을 만회하다
- ☐ **sluggish** 부진한, 느릿느릿 움직이는
- ☐ **as a token of** ~의 표시로

> As a token of my appreciation, I'll buy you all lunch from Connie's Pizza around the corner at noon.
> 감사의 표시로 정오에 모퉁이에 있는 코니스 피자에서 여러분 모두에게 점심을 사겠습니다.

- ☐ **appreciation** 감사
- ☐ **nominate** (후보로) 지명하다
- ☐ **award** 상
- ☐ **prestigious** 명망 있는, 일류의
- ☐ **literary** 문학의
- ☐ **make public** 일반에게 알리다, 공표하다
- ☐ **ceremony** 의식, 식
- ☐ **in attendance** 참석한
- ☐ **connecting flight** 연결 항공편
- ☐ **creation** 창작
- ☐ **address** 다루다

PART 5

- ☐ **committee** 위원회
- ☐ **take a tour** 견학하다, 둘러보다
- ☐ **secure** 얻어 내다, 확보하다; 안전한
- ☐ **merger** 합병
- ☐ **deal** 거래
- ☐ **rate** 평가하다
- ☐ **efficient** 효율적인
- ☐ **leading** 선두의, 주요한, 가장 중요한
- ☐ **corporate** 회사의, 기업의
- ☐ **suggest** 제안하다
- ☐ **draft** 원고, 초안
- ☐ **contain** 포함하다
- ☐ **vague** 모호한, 애매한
- ☐ **major** 주요한
- ☐ **supporter** 지지자, 후원자
- ☐ **make a donation** 기부하다
- ☐ **behavior** 행동
- ☐ **damaged** 손상된, 파손된
- ☐ **quality** 품질
- ☐ **promote** 승진하다; 홍보하다
- ☐ **voter** 투표자, 유권자
- ☐ **public facilities** 공공시설
- ☐ **trend** 추세, 동향
- ☐ **depend on** ~에 의존하다, ~에 따라 결정되다
- ☐ **durable** 내구성이 있는, 오래가는
- ☐ **conference** 학회, 회의
- ☐ **region** 지역
- ☐ **be likely to do** ~할 것 같다

> The royal couple's visit is likely to dramatically affect traffic in the area.
> 왕족 부부의 방문은 그 지역의 교통에 큰 영향을 미칠 것으로 보인다.

PART 6

- ☐ **spokesperson** 대변인
- ☐ **commitment** 헌신, 전념
- ☐ **keep up with** ~에 뒤지지 않다
- ☐ **demand** 수요
- ☐ **engaging** 남을 매혹하는
- ☐ **gear** 장비
- ☐ **counterpart** (동일한 지위의) 상대편, 대응물
- ☐ **admission** 입장료
- ☐ **experienced** 경험 많은, 노련한
- ☐ **dedicated** 헌신적인

PART 7

- ☐ **reschedule** 일정을 다시 잡다
- ☐ **obligation** 의무, 책무
- ☐ **trade fair** 무역 박람회
- ☐ **be devoted to** ~에 전념하다
- ☐ **complement** 보완하다
- ☐ **inconvenience** 불편
- ☐ **adopt** 채택하다
- ☐ **be set to do** ~하도록 예정되어 있다

> Please note that your membership is set to expire on December 31.
> 귀하의 회원 자격이 12월 31일에 만료된다는 것을 양지하시기 바랍니다.

- ☐ **irregular** 불규칙한
- ☐ **unexpectedly** 뜻밖에, 갑자기
- ☐ **around the clock** 24시간 내내
- ☐ **security** 보안
- ☐ **shelf** 선반
- ☐ **stock** 상품을 채우다
- ☐ **location** 지점; 위치, 장소
- ☐ **limit** (장소 등의) 경계; 한계
- ☐ **promotion** 승진
- ☐ **utility** 공공요금
- ☐ **otherwise** 그렇지 않으면
- ☐ **layout** 배치
- ☐ **fundraiser** 모금 행사
- ☐ **pick up** ~을 찾아오다, ~을 수령하다

☐ **sponsorship** 후원

☐ **publicize** 알리다, 공표하다

☐ **electronics** 전자 제품

☐ **last** 지속되다

☐ **deadline** 기한

☐ **work on** ~을 작업하다

☐ **analyze** 분석하다

☐ **recall** 리콜, 회수

☐ **present** (문제 등을) 야기하다

☐ **faulty** 결함이 있는

☐ **replacement** 교체, 교환; 후임자

☐ **complex** (건물) 단지

☐ **approximate** 대략의

☐ **ongoing** 진행 중인

☐ **capacity** 용량

☐ **dimension** 크기, 치수

☐ **on one's own** 자기 스스로, 혼자서

☐ **in light of** ~에 비추어, ~을 고려하여

☐ **article** 글, 기사

☐ **destination** 목적지

☐ **package** 패키지 상품

☐ **be encouraged to do** ~하도록 장려되다

> Local residents are encouraged to volunteer at the community center.
> 지역 주민들은 지역 문화 센터에서 자원 봉사를 하는 것이 장려된다.

☐ **contribute** 기고하다, 기여하다

☐ **edit** 편집하다

☐ **steady** 꾸준한

☐ **reasonable** 합리적인

☐ **disrupt** 방해하다, 지장을 주다

☐ **apprentice** 견습생

☐ **networking** 인맥 형성

☐ **potential** 잠재적인; 잠재력

☐ **graduate** 졸업생

☐ **exclusive** 독점적인

☐ **lump sum** 일시불

☐ **emergency** 비상 (사태), 긴급

☐ **register for** ~에 등록하다

☐ **prior** 이전의

☐ **mailing list** 우편물 수신자 명단

☐ **reserve** 예약하다

☐ **moderate** 적당한, 보통의

☐ **public transportation** 대중교통

☐ **accessible** 접근할 수 있는

☐ **proceed** 진행하다, 나아가다

☐ **aim** 목표로 하다

☐ **recent** 최근의

☐ **shipment** 출하, 선적

☐ **stick to** ~을 고수하다

☐ **inform A of B** A에게 B를 알리다

> The travel agent informed Ms. Bryant of the change in her flight time.
> 여행사 직원은 Bryant 씨에게 그녀의 비행 시간 변경 사실을 알려 주었다.

☐ **terms** (계약의) 조건

☐ **subscriber** 구독자

☐ **issue** (정기 간행물의) 호

☐ **refer** 언급하다, 인용하다

☐ **participate in** ~에 참여하다

☐ **referral** 소개, 추천

☐ **quote** 인용하다, 전하다

☐ **subscription** 구독

☐ **status** 상태

☐ **account** 계정

☐ **process** 처리하다

☐ **expire** 만료되다

☐ **renew** 갱신하다

☐ **reminder** 상기시키는 것, 독촉장

☐ **give a demonstration** 시연하다

☐ **industry** 산업, 업계

☐ **review** 검토하다; 복습하다

☐ **fulfill** 이행하다, 만족시키다

☐ **engage** 관여하다

☐ **hands-on** 직접 해 보는

> During the course, 70 percent of the course time is dedicated to hands-on learning.
> 과정에서는 수업 시간의 70%가 실습 학습에 할애됩니다.

☐ **unsuitable** 부적당한

☐ **lack** 없다, 부족하다

☐ **custom** 맞춤의

☐ **reflect** 반영하다

☐ **fabric** 직물, 천

☐ **notification** 알림

☐ **testimonial** 추천의 글

☐ **representative** 대표자, 담당 직원

☐ **exact** 정확한

☐ **performance** 성능

☐ **eventually** 결국, 궁극적으로

☐ **as well** 또한, 역시

☐ **make a purchase** 구매하다

☐ **drawing** 추첨

☐ **be in attendance** 참석하다

☐ **outstanding** 뛰어난

☐ **feature** 특징, 기능; 특징으로 하다, 특별히 선보이다

☐ **hand in** ~을 제출하다

☐ **application** 지원서, 신청서

☐ **endorse** (유명인이 특정 상품을) 홍보하다

☐ **compliance** 준수

☐ **reach out to** ~에게 접근하다

☐ **contact** 연줄, 인맥

☐ **qualification** 자격

☐ **be concerned about** ~에 대해 걱정하다

> Experts are increasingly concerned about the high prices of imports.
> 전문가들은 수입품의 높은 가격에 대해 점점 더 우려하고 있다.

☐ **time-consuming** 시간이 많이 걸리는

☐ **urgent** 긴급한

☐ **approval** 승인

☐ **founder** 설립자, 창립자

☐ **additional** 추가의

TEST 02

PART 1

- ☐ **face** ~을 마주 보다, 향하다
- ☐ **water** 물을 주다
- ☐ **lean against** ~에 기대다
- ☐ **place** 놓다, 두다
- ☐ **sweep** 쓸다
- ☐ **in a circle** 원형을 이루어
- ☐ **stairway** 계단
- ☐ **portion** 일부, 부분
- ☐ **unfinished** 완성되지 않은
- ☐ **be propped against** ~에 기대어 있다

Tools are propped against a wall.
도구들이 벽에 기대어 있다.

- ☐ **shovel** 삽
- ☐ **rack** 선반
- ☐ **railing** 난간
- ☐ **repair** 수리하다

PART 2

- ☐ **flyer** 전단
- ☐ **promote** 홍보하다
- ☐ **sign up** 등록하다
- ☐ **be in good shape** (몸의) 상태가 좋다
- ☐ **process** 과정
- ☐ **charger** 충전기
- ☐ **be supposed to do** ~하기로 되어 있다

Priya's supposed to handle it.
프리야가 처리하기로 되어 있어요.

- ☐ **handle** 처리하다, 다루다
- ☐ **paycheck** 봉급, 급료
- ☐ **generous** 후한, 관대한
- ☐ **fund-raising** 모금의; 모금
- ☐ **banquet** 연회

Who has the guest list for the fund-raising banquet?
누가 모금 연회의 손님 명단을 갖고 있나요?

- ☐ **briefcase** 서류 가방
- ☐ **inspection** 검사
- ☐ **supply chain** 공급망
- ☐ **issue** 문제, 사안
- ☐ **absent** 결석한, 없는

Why is Peter absent today?
피터는 오늘 왜 결석했나요?

- ☐ **replace** 대신하다, 교체하다
- ☐ **afford** ~할 여유가 되다
- ☐ **basement** 지하실
- ☐ **plenty of** 많은
- ☐ **room** 공간, 자리
- ☐ **relaxing** 편안한
- ☐ **depend on** ~에 달려 있다, 의존하다

It depends on the weather.
그건 날씨에 달려 있어요.

- ☐ **be on the market** (물건이) 시장에 나와 있다

When will the updated software be on the market?
업데이트된 소프트웨어는 언제 시장에 출시될까요?

- ☐ **purpose** 용도, 목적
- ☐ **talented** 재능이 있는

PART 3

- ☐ **reserve** 예약하다
- ☐ **over the phone** 전화로
- ☐ **loyalty program** 고객 보상 프로그램
- ☐ **sign up** 가입하다
- ☐ **benefit** 혜택, 이득
- ☐ **on-site** 현장의, 건물 내의
- ☐ **for free** 무료로

We've just opened an on-site gym that all guests can use for free.
저희는 모든 손님이 무료로 이용하실 수 있는 호텔 내 헬스장을 열었습니다.

- ☐ **rail line** 철도
- ☐ **construction** 건설, 공사
- ☐ **waste** 폐기물, 쓰레기
- ☐ **specific** 특정한
- ☐ **piece** 조각
- ☐ **matter** 중요하다
- ☐ **own** 소유하다
- ☐ **construct** 건설하다
- ☐ **environmentally friendly** 환경 친화적인
- ☐ **transfer** 넘겨주다, 옮기다
- ☐ **overall** 전반적으로
- ☐ **meet one's target** 목표를 달성하다

Overall, we're meeting or exceeding our targets, with one exception.
전반적으로, 우리는 한 가지를 제외하고는 우리 목표액을 달성하거나 초과하고 있습니다.

- ☐ **exceed** 초과하다
- ☐ **branch** 지점, 지사
- ☐ **in person** 직접
- ☐ **monitor** 감시하다, 조사하다
- ☐ **procedure** 절차, 과정
- ☐ **go over** 검토하다
- ☐ **consult** 상담하다
- ☐ **via** 통하여, 경유하여
- ☐ **video conference** 화상 회의
- ☐ **restrict** 제한하다
- ☐ **involve** 수반하다, 포함하다
- ☐ **purchase** 구입하다
- ☐ **attract** 끌어들이다
- ☐ **worth** ~의 가치가 있는
- ☐ **financial** 재무의, 재정의
- ☐ **contain** 포함하다
- ☐ **projection** 추정, 예상
- ☐ **release** 출시하다
- ☐ **noticeable** 눈에 띄는, 현저한

- ☐ **texture** 감촉, 질감
- ☐ **have ~ in stock** ~의 재고가 있다
- ☐ **give it a try** 한번 해 보다
- ☐ **knowledgeably** 박식하게
- ☐ **area** 분야, 지역
- ☐ **perform** 행하다
- ☐ **get crushed** 찌부러지다
- ☐ **contents** 내용물
- ☐ **dent** 움푹 들어가게 만들다
- ☐ **replacement** 대체물
- ☐ **to-go** 포장의

> A lot of our customers are having their drinks on site these days anyway, so we don't need a lot of cups for to-go coffee.
> 어차피 요즘 많은 손님들이 매장에서 음료를 마시기 때문에, 저희는 포장 커피 컵이 많이 필요하지는 않아요.

- ☐ **sturdy** 견고한
- ☐ **promotion** 판촉 (활동)
- ☐ **prize drawing** 경품 추첨
- ☐ **recognition** 인지, 알아봄
- ☐ **give away** 나눠 주다
- ☐ **promote** 홍보하다
- ☐ **figures** 수치
- ☐ **findings** 조사 결과
- ☐ **city council** 시 의회
- ☐ **preliminary** 예비의
- ☐ **approval** 승인
- ☐ **take effort** 노력을 필요로 하다
- ☐ **evaluate** 평가하다
- ☐ **utilities** 공공요금

PART 4

- ☐ **a wide range of** 다양한, 광범위한
- ☐ **spokesperson** 대변인
- ☐ **nonprofit organization** 비영리 단체
- ☐ **be dedicated to** ~에 전념하다

> Our nonprofit organization is dedicated to funding projects that help the environment.
> 우리 비영리 단체는 환경을 돕는 프로젝트에 자금을 제공하는 데 전념하고 있습니다.

- ☐ **fund** ~에 자금을 제공하다
- ☐ **contribute to** ~에 기여하다
- ☐ **wind farm** 풍력 발전 시설
- ☐ **household** 가구, 가정
- ☐ **turnout** 참가자 수
- ☐ **closure** 폐쇄
- ☐ **remove** 치우다, 제거하다
- ☐ **extensive** (수량 · 규모 · 정도 따위가) 큰, 엄청난
- ☐ **litter** 쓰레기
- ☐ **shoreline** 물가, 해안가
- ☐ **upset** 속상한
- ☐ **recreational** 휴양의, 오락의
- ☐ **highlight** 강조하다
- ☐ **take time off** 휴가를 내다
- ☐ **return ticket** 왕복표
- ☐ **outfit** 의상
- ☐ **district** 지구, 구역
- ☐ **architecture** 건축
- ☐ **first-hand** 직접
- ☐ **world-renowned** 세계적으로 유명한
- ☐ **architect** 건축가
- ☐ **fascinating** 대단히 흥미로운, 매력적인
- ☐ **occasion** (특별한) 행사, 경우
- ☐ **wrap** 포장하다, 싸다; 포장지
- ☐ **package** 포장하다
- ☐ **plant-based** 식물성의
- ☐ **compost** 퇴비가 되다
- ☐ **waste** 폐기물
- ☐ **heavy-duty** 튼튼한
- ☐ **cotton thread** 면사
- ☐ **at the same time** 동시에
- ☐ **tight** 빠듯한, 단단한
- ☐ **finished product** 완제품
- ☐ **unexpected** 예상 밖의
- ☐ **do volunteer work** 자원봉사를 하다

> I was doing volunteer work for a nonprofit organization that supports schools overseas.
> 저는 해외 학교를 후원하는 비영리 단체에서 자원봉사를 하고 있었습니다.

PART 5

- ☐ **observation** (관찰에 따른) 논평, 의견
- ☐ **facility** 시설
- ☐ **due to** ~ 때문에
- ☐ **mechanical** 기계적인
- ☐ **fault** 결함, 잘못
- ☐ **human resources** 인적 자원, 인사부
- ☐ **paperwork** 서류 작업
- ☐ **presumably** 아마
- ☐ **reliability** 신뢰도
- ☐ **fleet** (기관이나 회사 등이 소유한) 모든 차량
- ☐ **apply for** ~에 지원하다
- ☐ **selective** 선별적인, 까다로운
- ☐ **position** (일)자리, 직위
- ☐ **inform** 알리다, 통지하다
- ☐ **cashier** 계산원
- ☐ **retail** 소매
- ☐ **clearance** 재고 정리 세일
- ☐ **inspect** 면밀히 살피다, 검사하다
- ☐ **make a contribution** 기여하다, 기부하다

> Ms. Jennings makes a monthly contribution to a charity for the homeless.
> Jennings 씨는 노숙자들을 위한 자선단체에 매달 기부하고 있다.

- ☐ **acknowledge** (사실임을) 인정하다, 받아들이다
- ☐ **meet the deadline** 마감일을 맞추다
- ☐ **locate** 위치시키다, (특정 위치에) 두다
- ☐ **report** 보고하다, 알리다
- ☐ **subscriber** 구독자
- ☐ **explicit** 명시적인

- ☐ **permission** 허가
- ☐ **connect** 연결하다
- ☐ **language** 언어, 표현
- ☐ **thoroughly** 철저히
- ☐ **preparation** 준비
- ☐ **hygienic** 위생의
- ☐ **practice** 실행; 관행
- ☐ **overlook** 간과하다
- ☐ **acclaimed** 호평을 받은
- ☐ **financial** 금융의

PART 6

- ☐ **ingredient** 재료, 성분
- ☐ **effective** 효과적인
- ☐ **cause** 일으키다, 야기하다
- ☐ **on the contrary** 그와는 반대로
- ☐ **significant** 중요한, 상당한
- ☐ **investor** 투자자
- ☐ **reject** 거부하다
- ☐ **sector** 부문
- ☐ **thrive** 번창하다
- ☐ **lead to** ~로 이어지다

Ms. Park accepted the internship because it had the potential to lead to a permanent position.
Park 씨는 인턴직이 정규직으로 이어질 가능성이 있기 때문에 인턴직을 수락했다.

- ☐ **diversify** 다양화하다
- ☐ **consumer** 소비자
- ☐ **inspector** 검사자, 조사관
- ☐ **consistency** 일관성
- ☐ **stand out** 눈에 띄다, 두드러지다
- ☐ **reach** 이르다, 도달하다
- ☐ **material** 재료, 직물
- ☐ **expand** 넓히다, 확장하다
- ☐ **board** 이사회
- ☐ **consider** 고려하다

PART 7

- ☐ **convenience** 편리, 편의
- ☐ **be equipped with** ~을 갖추고 있다

All of the guest rooms are equipped with a microwave and a refrigerator.
모든 객실에 전자레인지와 냉장고가 구비되어 있다.

- ☐ **container** 용기, 컨테이너
- ☐ **depart** 출발하다
- ☐ **fee** 수수료, 요금
- ☐ **valuable** 귀중한
- ☐ **cancel** 취소하다
- ☐ **extra** 추가의, 여분의
- ☐ **aisle** 통로, 복도
- ☐ **meet a goal** 목표를 달성하다
- ☐ **accompany** 동반하다, 동행하다
- ☐ **flexible** 유연한
- ☐ **video conferencing** 화상 회의
- ☐ **commute** 통근하다
- ☐ **property** 건물; 부동산, 재산
- ☐ **foundation** 재단
- ☐ **undertake** 맡다, 착수하다
- ☐ **external** 외부의
- ☐ **degree** 학위
- ☐ **equivalent** 동등한
- ☐ **considerable** 상당한
- ☐ **extensively** 광범위하게, 폭넓게
- ☐ **usage** 사용(량)
- ☐ **expertise** 전문 지식

Mr. Nelson gave a speech on automobile design, his area of expertise.
Nelson 씨는 자신의 전문 분야인 자동차 디자인에 대한 연설을 했다.

- ☐ **expectation** 기대
- ☐ **form** 서식, 양식
- ☐ **specialist** 전문가
- ☐ **appliance** 가전제품, 기기
- ☐ **application** 애플리케이션, 앱
- ☐ **a range of** 다양한
- ☐ **via** ~을 통하여
- ☐ **transport** 수송, 운송
- ☐ **fragile** 깨지기 쉬운
- ☐ **exterior** 외부, 겉면
- ☐ **bottom** 바닥
- ☐ **make a recommendation** 추천하다
- ☐ **assignment** 과제, 임무
- ☐ **multiple** 다수의, 복수의
- ☐ **rate** 요금, 요율
- ☐ **helpline** 고객 상담 전화
- ☐ **efficiently** 효율적으로
- ☐ **notify** 알리다, 통지하다
- ☐ **personnel** 인원, 직원
- ☐ **release** 출시하다, 공개하다; 발표, 공개
- ☐ **value** 가치
- ☐ **risky** 위험한
- ☐ **post** 올리다, 게시하다
- ☐ **exclusively** 배타적으로, 독점적으로
- ☐ **publicity** 홍보, (매스컴의) 관심
- ☐ **investment** 투자
- ☐ **previous** 이전의, 예전의
- ☐ **revise** 변경하다, 수정하다
- ☐ **set up** (일정 등을) 수립하다

Mr. Wakefield set up a training session for employees in the accounting department.
Wakefield 씨는 경리과의 직원들을 위한 교육 시간을 마련했다.

- ☐ **move forward** 전진하다, 추진하다
- ☐ **gain** 얻다
- ☐ **mainstream** 주류의
- ☐ **adapt** 각색하다
- ☐ **remarkable** 놀라운
- ☐ **engaged** 몰두하는
- ☐ **give a speech** 연설하다
- ☐ **productive** 생산적인
- ☐ **wing** 부속 건물
- ☐ **enhance** 강화하다, 향상시키다
- ☐ **license** 출판을 허가하다, 면허를 주다
- ☐ **commercial** 광고 (방송); 상업적인
- ☐ **format** 형식, 형태
- ☐ **on the market** 시중에 나온
- ☐ **upon receipt of** ~을 받는 즉시

A full refund will be given upon receipt of the defective product.
불량품을 수령하는 즉시 전액 환불해 드릴 것입니다.

- ☐ **lack** 결핍, 부족
- ☐ **restriction** 제한
- ☐ **give notice of** ~을 통지하다
- ☐ **confidential** 기밀의
- ☐ **installation** 설치
- ☐ **disrupt** 방해하다
- ☐ **consultation** 상담
- ☐ **opening** 빈자리
- ☐ **issue** 문제, 사안
- ☐ **schedule** 일정을 잡다
- ☐ **measure** 대책, 조치
- ☐ **with the exception of** ~을 제외하고
- ☐ **summary** 요약
- ☐ **range** 범위
- ☐ **describe** 설명하다, 묘사하다
- ☐ **relieved** 안심한
- ☐ **ahead of schedule** 예정보다 일찍

As a result of considerable effort, the project was completed ahead of schedule.
상당한 노력의 결과로 프로젝트가 예정보다 빨리 완료되었다.

- ☐ **ample** 충분한
- ☐ **seat** (특정 수의) 좌석이 있다
- ☐ **preference** 선호(도)
- ☐ **executive** 임원
- ☐ **recognize** (공로를) 인정하다, 표창하다
- ☐ **dedicate** 헌신하다
- ☐ **attendance** 참석
- ☐ **headquarters** 본사
- ☐ **completion** 완성, 완공
- ☐ **relax** 휴식을 취하다
- ☐ **equipment** 장비, 기기
- ☐ **storage** 보관, 저장
- ☐ **spacious** 넓은

TEST 03

PART 1

☐ **hallway** 복도

☐ **polish** 닦다, 광을 내다

☐ **window shade** 블라인드, 차양

☐ **turn on** (전기 · 가스 · 수도 등을) 켜다
(↔ turn off)

☐ **dine** 식사를 하다

One of the people is dining alone.
사람들 중 한 명이 혼자 식사하고 있다.

☐ **sidewalk** 보도, 인도

☐ **ladder** 사다리

☐ **debris** 잔해, 파편

☐ **broom** 빗자루

☐ **outdoors** 야외에서

☐ **be seated** 앉아 있다

PART 2

☐ **drop off** 갖다 주다, 내려 주다

☐ **rental** 대여, 임대

☐ **drop** 떨어뜨리다

☐ **by accident** 잘못해서, 우연히

☐ **raise** (자금을) 모으다, 들어올리다

☐ **downtown** 시내에

☐ **company retreat** 회사 야유회

☐ **confidential** 기밀의, 비밀의

☐ **submit** 제출하다

☐ **loan** 대출

☐ **application** 신청(서), 지원(서)

☐ **fill out** 작성하다, 기입하다

I'm almost done filling it out.
거의 다 작성했어요.

☐ **medium** 중간의

☐ **install** 설치하다

☐ **go downstairs** 아래층으로 내려가다

☐ **line up** 줄을 서다

☐ **temporary** 임시의, 일시적인

☐ **expire** 만료되다

☐ **business hours** 영업시간

☐ **assign** 배정하다, 부과하다

☐ **assignment** 과제, 임무

☐ **put up** 내붙이다, 게시하다

☐ **flyer** 전단

☐ **take down** 치우다, 내리다

☐ **inventory** 재고(품)

I've checked the inventory.
제가 재고를 확인했어요.

☐ **energy-efficient** 에너지 효율이 좋은

☐ **appliance** 가전제품

☐ **all the way** 줄곧, 내내

☐ **handle** 처리하다, 다루다

☐ **hand in** 제출하다

Where can I hand in this comment card?
이 의견 카드를 어디에 제출하면 되나요?

☐ **comment** 의견, 논평

☐ **applicant** 지원자

☐ **be headed** ~로 향하여 가다

☐ **awards ceremony** 시상식

☐ **beforehand** 사전에, 앞서

There's time for networking beforehand.
앞서 인맥을 쌓기 위한 시간이 있어요.

PART 3

☐ **book an appointment** 예약하다

☐ **dental** 치과의

☐ **record** 기록

☐ **missing** 빠진, 없어진

☐ **previous** 이전의

☐ **pace** 속도

☐ **section** 부분, 구역

☐ **insurance** 보험

☐ **deal** 거래

☐ **as far as** ~하는 한

☐ **policy** 보험 증권

☐ **serve** 취급하다, 다루다

☐ **residential** 주거의

☐ **in the meantime** 그 동안에

☐ **ship** ~을 보내다, 부치다

☐ **warehouse** 창고

☐ **make adjustments to** ~을 조정하다

☐ **disappointing** 실망스러운

☐ **refrigerate** 냉장하다

☐ **selection** 선택된 것들, 선택

☐ **estimated** 예상되는

☐ **optional** 선택적인

☐ **room** 여유, 공간

☐ **budget** 예산

☐ **hire** 채용하다

☐ **additional** 추가의

☐ **negotiation** 협상

☐ **inform** 알리다

☐ **recruitment** 채용, 모집

☐ **agency** 대행사, 대리점

☐ **tow truck** 견인차

☐ **draft** 초안, 원고

☐ **checkout** 계산(대)

☐ **supervisor** 감독관, 관리자

During my final interview, I was told that my supervisor would be Susan McNeil.
최종 면접에서 제 상사가 수잔 맥닐 씨일 거라고 들었습니다.

☐ **entire** 전체의

☐ **head** 가다, 향하다

☐ **administration** 관리 (업무)

☐ **accountancy** 회계 (업무)

☐ **accountant** 회계사

☐ **pick up** ~을 찾아가다

☐ **sign into** 로그인하다

☐ **stop by** 잠시 들르다

PART 4

- ☐ **in action** 활동을 하는
- ☐ **ceramics** 도자기(류)
- ☐ **multiple** 여러, 다수의
- ☐ **in a moment** 곧

> You'll see what I mean in a moment.
> 곧 제 말이 무슨 뜻인지 알게 될 거예요.

- ☐ **portable** 휴대용의
- ☐ **confident** 확신하는
- ☐ **withstand** 견뎌내다
- ☐ **instructor** 강사
- ☐ **photograph** 촬영하다, 사진을 찍다
- ☐ **angle** 각도
- ☐ **framing** 구성, 틀 잡기
- ☐ **appealing** 매력적인
- ☐ **overview** 개요
- ☐ **handout** 유인물
- ☐ **head office** 본사
- ☐ **currency exchange** 환전
- ☐ **decision-maker** 의사 결정자
- ☐ **along with** ~과 더불어, ~에 따라

> Our new equipment, along with increased routine training, seems to be working well.
> 늘어난 정기 교육과 더불어, 우리의 새 장비가 효과를 내고 있는 것 같습니다.

- ☐ **routine** 정기적인
- ☐ **operate** 운영되다
- ☐ **smoothly** 원활하게, 순조롭게
- ☐ **in general** 전반적으로, 대체로
- ☐ **slab** 평판, 판
- ☐ **railing** 난간
- ☐ **factor** 요인
- ☐ **regional** 지역의
- ☐ **population** 인구
- ☐ **auction** 경매
- ☐ **spill** 쏟다, 흘리다
- ☐ **donor** 기부자
- ☐ **organize** 정리하다
- ☐ **incoming** 들어오는
- ☐ **in particular** 특히

> In particular, we've invested in new tractors and field sprayers to replace the outdated ones.
> 특히, 우리는 구식의 것들을 대체할 새로운 트랙터와 농업용 분무기에 투자했습니다.

- ☐ **invest in** ~에 투자하다
- ☐ **outdated** 구식인
- ☐ **injury** 부상
- ☐ **protect** 보호하다
- ☐ **operator** (기계 · 장치 등의) 기사, 조작자

PART 5

- ☐ **excerpt** 발췌
- ☐ **investigation** 조사
- ☐ **matter** 문제, 사안
- ☐ **volunteer** 자원봉사를 하다
- ☐ **annual** 연례의
- ☐ **encourage** 권유하다, 권장하다
- ☐ **staff** 직원
- ☐ **transportation** 운반, 이동
- ☐ **offer** 제공하다
- ☐ **attend** 참여하다, 참석하다
- ☐ **once** 일단 ~하면
- ☐ **temperature** 온도
- ☐ **management** 경영(진)
- ☐ **extremely** 매우, 극도로
- ☐ **minimal** 최소의
- ☐ **damage** 손상
- ☐ **venture** (벤처) 사업, 모험
- ☐ **dramatic** 극적인
- ☐ **assume** 예상하다, 추정하다
- ☐ **audience** 청중
- ☐ **exhibit** 전시(회)
- ☐ **lecture** 강연
- ☐ **sales staff** 영업 사원
- ☐ **finalize** 마무리하다
- ☐ **in addition to** ~ 외에도, ~ 뿐만 아니라

> Mr. Gilbert believes that in addition to arriving early, employees must be prepared for all staff meetings.
> Gilbert 씨는 직원들이 일찍 도착하는 것뿐만 아니라 모든 직원 회의에도 준비가 되어 있어야 한다고 생각한다.

- ☐ **passenger** 승객
- ☐ **impressive** 인상적인
- ☐ **turnout** 인파, 참가자의 수
- ☐ **grand opening** 개업, 개장
- ☐ **now that** 이제 ~이므로

> The house looks remarkable now that the renovations on it are complete.
> 그 집은 보수 공사가 다 끝나니 눈에 확 띈다.

- ☐ **regulation** 규정, 규칙
- ☐ **eliminate** 제거하다
- ☐ **client** 고객, 의뢰인
- ☐ **renewal** 갱신
- ☐ **restore** 복원하다, 복구하다
- ☐ **make a copy** 복사하다
- ☐ **archive** 기록 보관소
- ☐ **accurate** 정확한
- ☐ **dispute** 분쟁

PART 6

- ☐ **unique** 특별한, 특유의
- ☐ **note** 주목하다, 참고하다
- ☐ **delivery** 배송
- ☐ **complete** 완료하다, 완성하다
- ☐ **settle** 정산하다, 해결하다
- ☐ **overdue** 연체된, 기간이 지난
- ☐ **bill** 청구서
- ☐ **employee** 직원
- ☐ **knowledgeable** 박식한
- ☐ **sign up for** ~을 신청하다

> Employees can sign up for the workshop by e-mailing the instructor.
> 직원들은 강사에게 이메일을 보냄으로써 워크숍을 신청할 수 있다.

- ☐ **payment** 지불(금)
- ☐ **deduct** 공제하다, 제하다

- [ ] **withdrawal** 인출
- [ ] **resume** 재개하다
- [ ] **copy** 사본
- [ ] **include** 포함하다
- [ ] **unlimited** 무제한의
- [ ] **quarter** 분기
- [ ] **operation** 운영
- [ ] **area** 분야, 영역
- [ ] **demand** 수요, 요청
- [ ] **extend** 연장하다
- [ ] **session** (특정한 활동을 위한) 시간
- [ ] **retirement** 은퇴
- [ ] **planning** 기획

PART 7

- [ ] **maintain** 유지하다
- [ ] **diversity** 다양성
- [ ] **distribute** 분포시키다, 분배하다
- [ ] **strive** 노력하다
- [ ] **representative** 담당자; 대표
- [ ] **add** 더하다, 추가하다
- [ ] **identification** 식별; 신분 증명(서)
- [ ] **normally** 보통, 일반적으로
- [ ] **respond to** ~에 대응하다, 반응하다
- [ ] **resolve** 해결하다
- [ ] **work shift** 교대 근무
- [ ] **on behalf of** ~을 위해, ~ 대신에
- [ ] **asset** 자산
- [ ] **dedication** 헌신
- [ ] **detailed** 상세한
- [ ] **colleague** 동료
- [ ] **in person** 직접
- [ ] **updated** 최신의
- [ ] **figure** 수치
- [ ] **descriptive** 묘사하는, 서술적인
- [ ] **be scheduled for** ~로 예정되어 있다
- [ ] **keynote speaker** 기조 연설자
- [ ] **field** 분야
- [ ] **at one's convenience** 편할 때, 편리한 시기에

Please reply to this letter at your earliest convenience.
가급적 빨리 이 편지에 회신해 주세요.

- [ ] **recruit** 모집하다, 선발하다
- [ ] **conduct** 시행하다
- [ ] **be dedicated to** ~에 전념하다
- [ ] **supportive** 지원하는
- [ ] **intend** 의도하다, 작정하다
- [ ] **focus on** ~에 집중하다
- [ ] **remove** 제외하다, 제거하다
- [ ] **identify** 식별하다, 찾아내다
- [ ] **findings** 조사 결과
- [ ] **evaluate** 평가하다
- [ ] **extension** 내선 번호; 증축된 건물
- [ ] **visible** 눈에 띄는
- [ ] **catering** 출장 뷔페
- [ ] **due** 지불해야 하는

Payment is due upon completion of the work.
일이 끝나는 즉시 비용 지불을 하기로 되어 있다.

- [ ] **task** 과제, 업무
- [ ] **within walking distance** 도보 거리에
- [ ] **guarantee** 보장하다
- [ ] **affordable** 저렴한, 가격이 알맞은
- [ ] **stability** 안정성
- [ ] **enclose** 동봉하다
- [ ] **further** 더 한층
- [ ] **make a reservation** 예약하다
- [ ] **demonstration** 시연
- [ ] **recipe** 요리법, 레시피
- [ ] **sample** 시식용 음식; 견본
- [ ] **upcoming** 다가오는, 곧 있을
- [ ] **inspire** 고무하다, 영감을 주다
- [ ] **publication** 발행물, 간행물
- [ ] **promotional** 홍보의
- [ ] **corporate** 기업의
- [ ] **minimum** 최소, 최저
- [ ] **give it a chance** 시도를 해 보다
- [ ] **definitely** 분명히, 확실히
- [ ] **sponsor** 후원하다
- [ ] **adjust** 조정하다
- [ ] **stock** 재고
- [ ] **specialize in** ~을 전문으로 하다
- [ ] **be eligible for** ~할 자격이 있다

If you have your student ID, you're eligible for a 10% discount.
학생증이 있으면 10% 할인을 받을 수 있습니다.

- [ ] **receipt** 영수증
- [ ] **incur** 발생시키다
- [ ] **charity** 자선 단체
- [ ] **classify** 분류하다
- [ ] **postpone** 미루다, 지연하다
- [ ] **decade** 10년
- [ ] **screen** 심사하다
- [ ] **verify** 검증하다
- [ ] **license** 자격증
- [ ] **reference** 추천서
- [ ] **meet a deadline** 마감 기한을 맞추다
- [ ] **adhere to** ~을 준수하다
- [ ] **valid** 유효한
- [ ] **performance** 성과, 실적
- [ ] **résumé** 이력서
- [ ] **grant** 보조금, 지원금
- [ ] **facilitate** 촉진하다
- [ ] **reception** 환영회, 리셉션
- [ ] **pursue** 추구하다
- [ ] **look forward to** ~을 기대하다
- [ ] **enrollment** 등록, 입학
- [ ] **questionnaire** 설문 조사
- [ ] **take place** 열리다, 일어나다

The spring festival will take place for six days starting this Tuesday.
봄 축제는 이번 주 화요일부터 6일간 열린다.

- [ ] **in advance** 사전에

TEST 04

PART 1

- ☐ **platter** (큰 서빙용) 접시
- ☐ **doorway** 출입구
- ☐ **countertop** 주방의 조리대
- ☐ **container** 용기
- ☐ **tablecloth** 식탁보
- ☐ **utensil** (가정에서 사용하는) 기구, 도구

Sets of utensils have been arranged on tables.
식사 도구 세트들이 테이블 위에 정돈되어 있다.

PART 2

- ☐ **press conference** 기자회견
- ☐ **entry** 입장, 출입, 가입, 응모
- ☐ **exhibit** 전시품, 전시회(= exhibition); 전시하다
- ☐ **break down** 망가지다

My car broke down.
제 차가 고장났어요.

- ☐ **go well** 잘되다

The sales promotion went well.
판촉이 성공적이었어요.

- ☐ **sell out** 다 팔다, 매진되다

It has already sold out.
그건 벌써 다 팔렸어요.

- ☐ **postpone** 연기하다
- ☐ **on one's behalf** ~를 대신하여 (= on behalf of)

Could you attend the quarterly meeting at the headquarters on my behalf?
저 대신 본사에서 열리는 분기 회의에 참석해 주실 수 있나요?

- ☐ **repair technician** 수리 기사

PART 3

- ☐ **catch a show** 쇼를 보다/보러 가다
- ☐ **look into** 조사하다, 들여다보다
- ☐ **get a good deal on** ~을 저렴한 [좋은/적절한] 가격에 사다
- ☐ **at the last minute** 막판에
- ☐ **alert A[사람] to B[사물]** B에 대해 A에게 알리다
- ☐ **look for** 찾다
- ☐ **be looking to do** ~할 계획이다 (= be planning to do, be expecting to do)
- ☐ **application** 지원(서)
- ☐ **conduct an interview** 면접을 시행하다
- ☐ **the following week** 그 다음 주
- ☐ **job description** (채용 중인) 일자리에 대한 설명
- ☐ **submit** 제출하다
- ☐ **accounting firm** 회계 사무소
- ☐ **get an idea of** ~을 이해하다
- ☐ **customer base** 고객 기반
- ☐ **demand** 수요
- ☐ **expand** 확장하다

There is enough demand to expand further.
더 확장하기에 충분한 수요가 있습니다.

- ☐ **high-quality** 질 높은, 고급의
- ☐ **watercolor paint** 수채 물감
- ☐ **paintbrush** 붓
- ☐ **assemble** 조립하다
- ☐ **loose** 느슨한
- ☐ **get hurt** 다치다
- ☐ **unpack** 짐을 풀다/꺼내다
- ☐ **as originally planned** 원래 계획대로
- ☐ **job site** 작업 현장
- ☐ **warehouse** 창고
- ☐ **in the meantime** 그 와중에, 도중에
- ☐ **spot** 장소
- ☐ **budget** 예산
- ☐ **get the funding** 자금을 얻다
- ☐ **what if ...?** ~라면 어떻게 될까?
- ☐ **raise** 모금하다
- ☐ **approve** 승인하다
- ☐ **get in touch with** ~에게 연락하다

You should get in touch with local businesses to see if they are willing to donate to the project.
지역 업체들에 연락해서 프로젝트에 기부할 뜻이 있는지 확인해 보는 게 좋을 것 같군요.

- ☐ **donate ~ to ~** ~을 ~에 기부하다
- ☐ **insight** 통찰
- ☐ **keynote speech** 기조연설
- ☐ **cater** 음식을 공급하다
- ☐ **rewarding** 보람 있는
- ☐ **start out** 시작하다
- ☐ **real estate agency** 부동산 중개업소
- ☐ **performance** 실적
- ☐ **balance sheet** 대차대조표
- ☐ **at one's disposal** 마음대로 쓸 수 있는

We still have some funds at our disposal.
아직 잉여 자금이 남아 있어요.

- ☐ **place an order** 주문하다
- ☐ **look through** 살펴보다
- ☐ **It's been a while** 오래간만이다
- ☐ **bid on/for** ~에 응찰하다

I'm planning to bid on the renovation project at the public library.
공공 도서관 개조 프로젝트에 응찰할 계획이에요.

- ☐ **renovation** 개조
- ☐ **reference letter** 추천서
- ☐ **previous** 이전의
- ☐ **tune in** (라디오 · TV의) 주파수/채널에

맞춰 듣다

- ☐ **flow** (차량이나 사람 등이) 흘러가다, 이동하다
- ☐ **closure** 폐쇄
- ☐ **phase** 단계
- ☐ **sign up for** ~에 등록하다
- ☐ **course fee** 수업료
- ☐ **miss** 놓치다, (수업을) 빼먹다
- ☐ **do some research on** ~에 대해 조사하다
- ☐ **advertise** 광고하다
- ☐ **find out** 알아보다
- ☐ **confirm** 확정하다
- ☐ **outer** 외부의, 바깥 표면의
- ☐ **distinct** 뚜렷이 다른
- ☐ **at the top of** ~의 꼭대기에

PART 4

- ☐ **suitcase** 여행 가방
- ☐ **crack** 갈라지다, 금이 가다, 깨지다
- ☐ **instructions** 지시, 안내
- ☐ **refund** 환불
- ☐ **process** 처리하다

> I would like a refund, and I'm wondering how long it takes to process that.
> 환불받고 싶은데, 얼마나 걸리는지 궁금합니다.

- ☐ **judging panel** 심사 위원단
- ☐ **be impressed with** ~에 감명받다
- ☐ **paid leave** 유급 휴가

> For winning this award, Ms. Eldridge will be given one additional day of paid leave.
> 이 상과 함께 엘드리지 씨는 하루의 유급 휴가를 추가적으로 받게 됩니다.

- ☐ **earn** (그럴 만한 자격이 되어서 무엇을) 얻다[받다]
- ☐ **hit stores** 구매할 수 있게 서점에 유통되다 (= hit the market/shops/shelves/streets)
- ☐ **so far** 지금껏
- ☐ **main responsibility** 주요 책임/책무
- ☐ **be asked to do** ~하도록 요청받다
- ☐ **give a demonstration** 시연하다
- ☐ **now that** 이제 ~이므로
- ☐ **prove** 입증하다
- ☐ **indicate** (간접적으로) 내비치다
- ☐ **fail a test** 시험에서 떨어지다
- ☐ **expense** 비용
- ☐ **transport** 수송하다
- ☐ **operate** 운용하다, 운영하다
- ☐ **fleet** (한 기관이 소유한 전체 비행기 · 버스 · 택시 등의) 무리
- ☐ **association** 협회
- ☐ **alike** 똑같이

> This event is open to members and non-members alike.
> 이 행사는 회원과 비회원, 모두에게 똑같이 열려 있습니다.

- ☐ **encourage** 고무/장려/독려하다
- ☐ **throughout the year** 일 년 내내
- ☐ **banquet** 연회
- ☐ **keep 사람 informed on** ~에 대해 지속적으로 정보를 알려주다
- ☐ **policymaker** 정책 입안자
- ☐ **at no charge** 아무 요금 없이, 무료로

> For today only, you can get a copy of this book at no charge.
> 오늘에 한해서, 이 책을 무료로 받으실 수 있습니다.

- ☐ **get ~ started** ~을 시작하다
- ☐ **high-quality** 고품질의
- ☐ **stand out** 눈에 띄다, 빼어나다
- ☐ **invest ~ in** ~을 ~에 투자하다
- ☐ **shoot a commercial** 광고를 찍다
- ☐ **air** 방영하다
- ☐ **cooperate with** ~와 협조하다
- ☐ **extensive** 광범위한
- ☐ **construct** 건설하다
- ☐ **inconvenience** 불편
- ☐ **commuter** 통근자
- ☐ **during the day** 낮 동안
- ☐ **on schedule** 예정대로 (= on time)
- ☐ **ahead of/behind schedule** 예정보다 일찍/늦게
- ☐ **according to schedule** 계획한 대로(= as planned)
- ☐ **in reference to** ~에 관련하여
- ☐ **annual** 연례의
- ☐ **fund-raising** 모금 활동(의), 자금 조달(의), 모금(의)
- ☐ **scheduled for** (언제로) 예정된
- ☐ **podium** (연설자 · 지휘자 등이 올라서는) 단
- ☐ **host** (행사의) 주최국[측]
- ☐ **venue** (행사를 위한) 장소
- ☐ **our company's branded coffee mugs** 우리 회사의 브랜드가 새겨진 커피 머그컵
- ☐ **hand out** 나눠주다
- ☐ **expert** 전문가
- ☐ **consultant** 상담가, 자문 위원, 컨설턴트 (consult ~에게 상의하다, ~와 상담하다)
- ☐ **a wider variety of** 더 다양한
- ☐ **meet the deadline** 마감일을 지키다
- ☐ **estimated output** 추정[예상] 생산량
- ☐ **identify the problem** 문제를 파악하다

> Our technician, Joseph, is going to examine it to identify the problem.
> 우리의 기술자인 조셉이 문제를 찾기 위해 이를 조사할 것입니다.

PART 5

- ☐ **board** 탑승하다
- ☐ **protective** 보호용의
- ☐ **maintenance** 유지, 보수
- ☐ **technical** 기술의
- ☐ **celebrate** 축하하다, 기념하다
- ☐ **main** 주된, 주요한
- ☐ **accounting** 회계

- ☐ **occupant** 입주자, 점유자
- ☐ **on board** 탑승한, 승선한
- ☐ **wage** 임금, 급여
- ☐ **factor** 요인, 원인
- ☐ **neighborhood** 인근, 근처

No other bakery existed in this neighborhood until we opened our business.
우리가 가게를 열기 전까지 이 동네에는 다른 제과점이 존재하지 않았다.

- ☐ **affect** 영향을 미치다
- ☐ **make one's appearance** 모습을 드러내다
- ☐ **vehicle** 차량
- ☐ **trial** 시용, 시험
- ☐ **noticeably** 눈에 띄게
- ☐ **frustrating** 불만스러운, 좌절감을 주는
- ☐ **sales representative** 판매 담당자
- ☐ **throughout** ~ 내내
- ☐ **shuttle** 왕복 교통편
- ☐ **at the moment** 바로 지금
- ☐ **significantly** 상당히, 크게
- ☐ **board of directors** 이사회
- ☐ **activity** 활동
- ☐ **consider** 여기다, 간주하다
- ☐ **severe** 심한
- ☐ **reward** 보상하다
- ☐ **talented** 재능 있는
- ☐ **individual** 사람, 개인

PART 6

- ☐ **common** 일반적인, 흔한
- ☐ **serve** (서비스 등을) 제공하다
- ☐ **essential** 필수적인, 매우 중요한
- ☐ **sufficient** 충분한
- ☐ **merchandise** 상품, 물품
- ☐ **no later than** 늦어도 ~까지
- ☐ **go online** 온라인에 접속하다

Customers can go online and view all the items.
고객들은 온라인으로 모든 제품을 볼 수 있습니다.

- ☐ **prefer** 선호하다
- ☐ **minimize** 최소화하다
- ☐ **effect** 영향
- ☐ **no longer** 더 이상 ~않는
- ☐ **produce** 농산물
- ☐ **supplier** 공급사
- ☐ **thus** 이렇게 하여, 따라서

PART 7

- ☐ **rent** 임대(료)
- ☐ **unit** (건물의) 한 공간

More than half of the units in the apartment complex require renovations.
아파트 단지 가구의 절반 이상이 보수공사를 필요로 한다.

- ☐ **comprise** 차지하다, 구성되다
- ☐ **lease** 임대차 계약
- ☐ **showcase** 선보이다
- ☐ **tenant** 임차인, 세입자
- ☐ **proximity to** ~에의 근접성
- ☐ **be about to do** 막 ~하려고 하다
- ☐ **issue** 발급하다, 지급하다
- ☐ **make a cancellation** 취소하다
- ☐ **ensure** 확인하다
- ☐ **take inventory** 재고를 조사하다
- ☐ **supplies** 공급품
- ☐ **at the latest** 늦어도
- ☐ **call in sick** 병가를 내다
- ☐ **clearance sale** 재고 정리 세일
- ☐ **former** 이전의
- ☐ **inventory** 재고, 물품 목록
- ☐ **accommodate** 공간을 제공하다, 수용하다
- ☐ **function** 기능하다, 작동하다
- ☐ **current** 현재의
- ☐ **ownership** 소유권
- ☐ **society** 협회
- ☐ **quarterly** 분기의
- ☐ **accomplishment** 업적
- ☐ **anniversary** 기념일

- ☐ **inspection** 검사, 점검
- ☐ **appreciate** 감사하다
- ☐ **candidate** 후보자
- ☐ **landlord** 집주인, 임대인
- ☐ **address** 해결하다, 다루다
- ☐ **coordinate** 조정하다
- ☐ **work from home** 재택근무를 하다

Working from home without a supervisor's approval is strictly prohibited.
관리자의 승인 없이 재택근무를 하는 것은 엄격히 금지되어 있다.

- ☐ **coworker** 동료
- ☐ **manage** 관리하다
- ☐ **applicant** 지원자
- ☐ **demonstrate** 증명하다, 보여 주다
- ☐ **at all times** 항상
- ☐ **confidentiality** 기밀, 비밀성
- ☐ **delegate** 위임하다
- ☐ **in a timely manner** 시기적절하게

New deliveries should be unloaded in the warehouse in a timely manner.
새 배송품들은 적시에 창고에 하역되어야 한다.

- ☐ **found** 설립하다
- ☐ **procedure** 절차
- ☐ **keep ~ in mind** ~을 명심하다
- ☐ **precise** 정확한
- ☐ **prohibit** 금지하다
- ☐ **premises** 부지, 구내
- ☐ **propose** 제안하다
- ☐ **initial** 초기의, 최초의
- ☐ **take into account** 고려하다

Mr. Wright always takes the budget into account when making purchasing decisions.
Wright 씨는 구매 결정을 내릴 때 항상 예산을 고려한다.

- ☐ **existing** 기존의
- ☐ **next to** ~의 옆에
- ☐ **on time** 제시간에
- ☐ **worthwhile** 가치 있는
- ☐ **shortcoming** 단점

- [ ] **exceed** 초과하다
- [ ] **sign** 표지판
- [ ] **enforce** 시행하다
- [ ] **make sure** 확인하다, 확실히 하다
- [ ] **reservation** 예약
- [ ] **charge** 부과하다
- [ ] **branch** 지점, 지사
- [ ] **frustrated** 좌절한
- [ ] **confirm** 확인하다, 확정하다
- [ ] **attendee** 참석자
- [ ] **section** 부분, 구획
- [ ] **negotiate** 협상하다
- [ ] **agreement** 합의
- [ ] **proposal** 계획, 제안
- [ ] **update** 최신 정보
- [ ] **modify** 변경하다
- [ ] **accommodations** 숙박 시설
- [ ] **fund** 자금
- [ ] **complaint** 불만, 민원
- [ ] **personnel** 인원
- [ ] **figure out** 알아내다
- [ ] **suitable for** ~에 적합한

Our furniture is suitable for both homes and businesses.
저희 가구는 가정용이나 업무용으로 모두 적합합니다.

- [ ] **description** 설명, 묘사
- [ ] **signature** 서명
- [ ] **receipt** 수령
- [ ] **ship** 배송하다
- [ ] **belongings** 재산, 소유물
- [ ] **assess** 평가하다, 가늠하다
- [ ] **estimate** 견적
- [ ] **crew** 작업반
- [ ] **available** 구할 수 있는
- [ ] **recommendation** 추천, 권고
- [ ] **competitor** 경쟁자, 경쟁사
- [ ] **measure** 재다, 측정하다
- [ ] **correct** 수정하다, 바로잡다
- [ ] **invoice** 청구서, 송장
- [ ] **quantity** 수량
- [ ] **notice** 알아차리다
- [ ] **deposit** 보증금
- [ ] **deduct** 공제하다
- [ ] **make a payment** 지불하다

If you fail to make the payment on time, your account will be temporarily suspended.
제때 비용을 지불하지 못한다면, 당신의 계정은 일시적으로 정지될 것입니다.

- [ ] **fierce** 치열한
- [ ] **stability** 안정
- [ ] **increasingly** 점점 더
- [ ] **strategy** 전략
- [ ] **respectively** 각각
- [ ] **immediate** 즉각적인, 즉시의
- [ ] **temporarily** 임시로, 일시적으로
- [ ] **transition** 전환, 이행
- [ ] **expansion** 확장
- [ ] **confident** 자신하는, 확신하는
- [ ] **launch** 시작하다, 개시하다
- [ ] **substantial** 상당한
- [ ] **avoid** 피하다
- [ ] **regulation** 규제
- [ ] **retain** 유지하다, 보유하다
- [ ] **previously** 전에

TEST 05

PART 1

- ☐ **mark** 표시하다
- ☐ **drawing** (연필이나 펜 등으로 그린) 그림, 도면
- ☐ **take out** 꺼내다
- ☐ **wide down** 닦다

He's wiping down a desk.
남자가 책상을 닦고 있다.

- ☐ **flowerpot** 화분
- ☐ **porch** 현관
- ☐ **lawn mower** 잔디 깎는 기계
- ☐ **write notes** 메모하다

PART 2

- ☐ **press statement** 언론 성명
- ☐ **newsstand** (거리 · 역 구내 등의) 신문[잡지] 판매점, 가판대
- ☐ **private practice** (의사나 변호사 등의) 개인 영업
- ☐ **meet ~ in person** ~를 직접 만나다

I'll meet the client in person.
제가 고객을 직접 만날게요.

- ☐ **forklift** 지게차
- ☐ **property** 재산, 부동산, 건물
- ☐ **premiere** (영화의) 개봉, (연극의) 초연
- ☐ **secure** (특히 힘들게) 얻어 내다, 획득[확보]하다
- ☐ **stock** 채우다

Who's going to stock the store shelves?
누가 가게 선반들을 채워 놓을 건가요?

- ☐ **on sale** 할인 중인, 판매되는
- ☐ **sales figures** 매출액
- ☐ **sign in** (회사 · 클럽 등의 기록부에) 서명하고 들어가다

Can you make sure all the guests sign in, please?
모든 손님들이 기록부에 서명하고 들어오게 해 주실래요?

- ☐ **release** (대중들에게) 공개[발표]하다
- ☐ **employ** 고용하다
- ☐ **instructions** 설명서
- ☐ **press release** 대언론 공식 발표[성명]
- ☐ **pressing** 긴급한

There are no pressing issues at the moment.
지금은 긴급한 문제가 없습니다.

- ☐ **janitor** (건물 등의) 관리인
- ☐ **inspect** 점검하다
- ☐ **mechanic** 정비사
- ☐ **around the corner** 근처에

PART 3

- ☐ **former** 예전의
- ☐ **get promoted to** ~으로 승진하다
- ☐ **board executive** 이사회 임원
- ☐ **make one's way to** ~쪽으로 가다
- ☐ **within 10 minutes of** ~에서 10분 거리에 있는
- ☐ **in attendance** 참석한
- ☐ **while I'm away** 출장 가 있는 동안
- ☐ **stand out** 빼어나다, 눈에 띄다
- ☐ **raise** 올리다
- ☐ **production cost** 생산 비용
- ☐ **intranet** 인트라넷, 내부 전산망
- ☐ **access** 접속하다
- ☐ **bistro** (편안한 분위기의) 작은 식당
- ☐ **book a table** 식사할 좌석을 예약하다

I'd like to book a table for six for my colleagues and me.
저와 제 동료들을 위해 6인 테이블을 예약하고 싶습니다.

- ☐ **go for dinner** 저녁 식사하러 가다
- ☐ **make a reservation** 예약하다
- ☐ **printer** 인쇄업자, 인쇄소
- ☐ **associate** (흔히 직함에 쓰여) 준/부/조
- ☐ **quote** 견적서 (= estimate)
- ☐ **make a plan** 계획을 세우다
- ☐ **repave** 다시 포장하다
- ☐ **make a decision** 결정하다
- ☐ **test out** ~를 시험해 보다
- ☐ **ergonomic keyboard** 인체공학적 키보드
- ☐ **for ~ purposes** ~ 목적으로 (for medical/cosmetic/leisure purposes 의료/미용/여가 목적으로)

We need your information for tax purposes.
세금 때문에 귀하의 정보가 필요합니다.

- ☐ **joint** 관절
- ☐ **get in the way of** ~을 방해하다
- ☐ **set up** 준비하다
- ☐ **set the table** 테이블을 세팅하다
- ☐ **consumption** 소비
- ☐ **location** 지점
- ☐ **regardless** 그럼에도 불구하고
- ☐ **solar-powered** 태양열 동력의
- ☐ **carbon emission** 탄소 배출
- ☐ **run** 작동하다, 운행하다
- ☐ **major client** 주요 고객
- ☐ **reply** 응답하다
- ☐ **under repair** 보수 중인

The exit to Rosebud Street is under repair.
로즈버드 가로 나가는 출구가 보수 중입니다.

- ☐ **go paperless** (기업이나 기관에서) 종이를 쓰지 않다
- ☐ **shred** 분쇄하다
- ☐ **maintenance closet** 정비 용품 창고[벽장, 보관실]
- ☐ **have no problem -ing** ~하는 데 문제가 없다

I had no problem opening it earlier.
저는 그것(파일)을 여는 데 아무런 문제가 없었어요.

PART 4

- ☐ **turn to** (특정 화제로) 넘어가다
- ☐ **mark** (특정 연도, 월, 날짜 등이 주어로 쓰여) ~이 되는 해/월/날이다

Friday marked the grand opening of Brittany's Corner's first location in Greenville.
금요일은 브리트니즈 코너의 그린빌 첫 지점이 개업하는 날이었습니다.

- ☐ **renowned** 유명한, 명성 있는
- ☐ **make its way to** ~로 향하다
- ☐ **redirect** (다른 주소나 방향으로) 다시 보내다
- ☐ **safety protocol** 안전 규정[수칙]
- ☐ **conduct electricity** 전기를 전도하다
- ☐ **chances of** ~의 가능성
- ☐ **electric shock** 감전

Rubber gloves do not conduct electricity and can greatly reduce your chances of electric shock.
고무장갑은 전기를 전도하지 않아서 감전 확률을 현저히 떨어뜨릴 수 있습니다.

- ☐ **stellar** 뛰어난 (= excellent)
- ☐ **craft** (수)공예
- ☐ **set out** ~을 정리[진열]하다
- ☐ **call for** 예보하다
- ☐ **pack up** (떠나기 위해) 짐을 싸다[챙기다]
- ☐ **earlier than planned** 계획보다 일찍
- ☐ **anyways** 어쨌든 (= anyway)
- ☐ **have a chance of winning** 우승할 가능성이 있다
- ☐ **manually** 수동으로
- ☐ **enter** ~을 입력하다
- ☐ **collect** 수거하다, 모으다
- ☐ **be away on business** 출장 중이다
- ☐ **get in touch with** ~에게 연락하다

Feel free to get in touch with me if you're interested.
관심 있으시면 편하게 연락주세요.

- ☐ **potential client** 잠재 고객, 잠정 고객
- ☐ **be concerned that** ~할까 봐 걱정하다
- ☐ **competitive** 경쟁을 벌이는
- ☐ **stand out** 눈에 띄다
- ☐ **new hire** 새 직원
- ☐ **unparalleled** 비할 데 없는 (parallel 평행한)
- ☐ **fill out a survey** 설문조사를 작성하다
- ☐ **paperwork** 서류 작업
- ☐ **get ~ ready** ~을 준비하다
- ☐ **upcoming** 다가오는
- ☐ **implement** 시행하다
- ☐ **clientele** (어떤 기관 · 상점 등의) 모든 의뢰인들[고객들]
- ☐ **every other Saturday** 격주 토요일마다
- ☐ **constitute** 구성하다
- ☐ **take up** (시간/공간을) 차지하다

PART 5

- ☐ **contract** 계약(서)
- ☐ **term** 조항
- ☐ **track** 추적하다
- ☐ **remind** 상기시키다, 기억나게 하다
- ☐ **peak season** 성수기
- ☐ **residential** 주거의, 주택지의
- ☐ **nearby** 근처의
- ☐ **prior to** ~ 전에
- ☐ **loan** 대출(금)
- ☐ **carry out** ~을 실행하다, ~을 수행하다

The board of directors asked Mr. Pennington to carry out the plan.
이사회는 Pennington 씨에게 계획을 수행할 것을 요청했다.

- ☐ **renovation** 수리, 보수
- ☐ **capture** 포착하다
- ☐ **period** 기간
- ☐ **cooperative** 협력하는
- ☐ **collaborate** 협력하다
- ☐ **face** 직면하다
- ☐ **handle** 처리하다, 다루다
- ☐ **in the case of** ~의 경우에는
- ☐ **temporary** 임시의
- ☐ **resignation** 사임, 퇴임
- ☐ **press conference** 기자회견
- ☐ **athlete** 운동선수
- ☐ **measure** 조치, 방안

PART 6

- ☐ **regarding** ~에 관해
- ☐ **thanks to** ~ 덕분에
- ☐ **official** 공무원
- ☐ **the majority of** 다수의
- ☐ **excluding** ~을 제외하고
- ☐ **after-hours** 영업시간 후의
- ☐ **miss** 놓치다
- ☐ **be in danger of** ~할 위험에 처하다
- ☐ **removal** 제거
- ☐ **operate** 운전하다, 작동하다; 운영하다
- ☐ **rely on** ~에 의존하다
- ☐ **prompt** 신속한
- ☐ **result in** 결과적으로 ~가 되다

Hiring a logistics consultant has resulted in the faster distribution of goods. 물류 컨설턴트의 고용은 보다 빨라진 상품 유통이라는 결과를 가져왔다.

PART 7

- ☐ **machinery** 기계류
- ☐ **allow** 허용하다
- ☐ **up to** ~까지
- ☐ **access** 접근하다, 이용하다; 접근권
- ☐ **membership** 회원 자격
- ☐ **progress** 진척, 진행
- ☐ **review** 후기
- ☐ **equipment** 장비
- ☐ **brief** 간단한, 짧은

☐ **run into** (어려움, 곤란, 문제 등을) 겪다
☐ **all the way** 줄곧, 처음부터 끝까지
☐ **go through** ~을 검토하다
☐ **concerned** 걱정하는, 염려하는

Experts are increasingly concerned about the high prices of imports.
전문가들은 수입품의 높은 가격에 대해 점점 더 우려하고 있다.

☐ **presentation** 발표
☐ **improve** 개선하다, 향상시키다
☐ **manufacture** 제조하다
☐ **select** 선정하다
☐ **boost** 신장시키다
☐ **productivity** 생산성
☐ **comment** 의견
☐ **implement** 시행하다
☐ **details** 세부 정보
☐ **optional** 선택적인
☐ **overall** 전반적으로
☐ **recommend** 추천하다
☐ **relocate** 이전하다
☐ **based on** ~에 근거하여

The fee varies based on the total weight of the items ordered.
요금은 주문한 물품의 전체 무게에 따라 달라집니다.

☐ **originally** 원래
☐ **proper** 적절한
☐ **authorization** 인증, 승인
☐ **function** 기능
☐ **directly** 직접, 곧장
☐ **cooperation** 협조
☐ **display** 보여 주다, 전시하다
☐ **voluntary** 자발적인
☐ **device** 기기
☐ **designate** 지정하다
☐ **transport** 수송; 수송하다
☐ **discontinue** 단종하다
☐ **upon receipt** 수령 즉시
☐ **direct** 길을 안내하다, 향하다
☐ **take an order** 주문을 받다

☐ **apologize** 사과하다
☐ **assistance** 도움, 지원
☐ **participant** 참가자, 참석자
☐ **policy** 정책, 방침
☐ **director** 책임자, 이사
☐ **perform** 수행하다
☐ **administrative** 행정의
☐ **assign** 배정하다

As part of her duties, she assigned work to freelance authors.
그녀는 직무의 일환으로 프리랜서 작가들에게 업무를 할당했다.

☐ **impress** 깊은 인상을 주다
☐ **keep ~ updated** ~에게 계속해서 새로운 소식을 전하다
☐ **personnel** 인력, 인원
☐ **transfer** 이동
☐ **in operation** 운영 중인
☐ **summarize** 요약하다
☐ **site** 현장, 부지
☐ **non-profit organization** 비영리 단체
☐ **permanent** 상설의, 영구적인
☐ **preserve** 보존하다
☐ **relevant** 적절한, 관련 있는
☐ **host** 주최하다
☐ **donate** 기증하다
☐ **highlight** 강조하다, 부각시키다
☐ **achieve** 성취하다, 달성하다
☐ **sustainable** 지속 가능한

The fabric is soft, durable, and also environmentally sustainable.
그 직물은 부드럽고 내구성이 있으며 환경 친화적이기까지 합니다.

☐ **in the long run** 결국에는
☐ **permit** 허가, 허락
☐ **technician** 기사, 기술자
☐ **take a measurement** 치수를 재다
☐ **virtual** 가상의
☐ **follow-up** 후속의
☐ **attach** 첨부하다

☐ **replace** 교체하다, 대체하다
☐ **warranty** 보증
☐ **defect** 결함
☐ **requirement** 필요조건, 요건
☐ **estimate** 추산하다, 추정하다
☐ **appointment** 예약
☐ **calculate** 계산하다
☐ **domestic** 국내의
☐ **reliable** 신뢰할 수 있는
☐ **take advantage of** ~을 이용하다
☐ **provide** 제공하다
☐ **association** 협회
☐ **extensive** 광범위한
☐ **survey** 설문 조사
☐ **vendor** 판매자
☐ **effective** 시행되는, 발효되는
☐ **outdoor** 야외의
☐ **electricity** 전기
☐ **variety** 종류, 품종
☐ **secure** 확보하다
☐ **exactly** 정확히
☐ **gather** 모으다, 수집하다
☐ **community** 지역 사회
☐ **resident** 주민
☐ **take part in** ~에 참여하다
☐ **practical** 실용적인
☐ **be impressed with** ~에 깊은 인상을 받다

I was very impressed with the customer service I received from the company.
저는 그 회사로부터 받은 고객 서비스에 깊은 인상을 받았습니다.

☐ **advance** 사전의
☐ **registration** 등록
☐ **attract** 유인하다
☐ **supply** 공급(품)
☐ **relaxed** 긴장이 풀린, 편안한
☐ **state** 상태
☐ **ordinary** 평범한
☐ **convert** 변환하다, 바꾸다
☐ **demanding** 힘든, 부담이 큰

- ☐ **technique** 기술, 기법
- ☐ **in particular** 특히
- ☐ **renovate** 보수하다, 수선하다
- ☐ **in the meantime** 그사이에, 그동안
- ☐ **in addition** 또한, 게다가
- ☐ **on site** 현장에
- ☐ **contact** 연락하다
- ☐ **formation** 형성
- ☐ **spot** 장소, 곳
- ☐ **be supposed to do** ~하기로 되어 있다
- ☐ **hire** 고용하다
- ☐ **at this time** 지금
- ☐ **duration** 지속 기간

할 수 없는 이유는 수없이 많지만
할 수 있는 이유는 단 한 가지입니다.
당신이 하기로 결정했기 때문입니다.

당신이 결정하면 온 세상이
그 결정을 따라 움직입니다.

– 조정민, 『사람이 선물이다』, 두란노

정답 및 해설

에듀윌 토익 실전 LC+RC Vol.2

정답 및 해설

고객의 꿈, 직원의 꿈, 지역사회의 꿈을 실현한다

펴낸곳 (주)에듀윌 **펴낸이** 권대호, 김재환 **출판총괄** 김형석
개발책임 이순옥 **개발** 김기상, 김상미, 박은석, 천주영, Julie Tofflemire
주소 서울시 구로구 디지털로34길 55 코오롱싸이언스밸리 2차 3층
대표번호 1600-6700 **등록번호** 제25100-2002-000052호

에듀윌 도서몰 book.eduwill.net
- 부가학습자료 및 정오표: 에듀윌 도서몰 → 도서자료실
- 교재 문의: 에듀윌 도서몰 → 문의하기 → 교재(내용, 출간) / 주문 및 배송

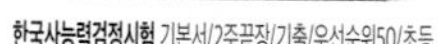
한국사능력검정시험 기본서/2주끝장/기출/우선순위50/초등

조리기능사 필기/실기

제과제빵기능사 필기/실기

SMAT 모듈A/B/C

ERP정보관리사 회계/인사/물류/생산(1, 2급)

전산세무회계 기초서/기본서/기출문제집

무역영어 1급 | 국제무역사 1급

KBS한국어능력시험 | ToKL

한국실용글쓰기

매경TEST 기본서/문제집/2주끝장

TESAT 기본서/문제집/기출문제집

운전면허 1종·2종

스포츠지도사 필기/실기구술 한권끝장

산업안전기사 | 산업안전산업기사

위험물산업기사 | 위험물기능사

토익 입문서 | 실전서 | 종합서

컴퓨터활용능력 | 워드프로세서

정보처리기사

월간시사상식 | 일반상식

월간NCS | 매1N

NCS 통합 | 모듈형 | 피듈형

PSAT형 NCS 수문끝

PSAT 기출완성 | 6대 출제사 | 10개 영역 찐기출

한국철도공사 | 서울교통공사 | 부산교통공사

국민건강보험공단 | 한국전력공사

한수원 | 수자원 | 토지주택공사

행과연형 | 휴노형 | 기업은행 | 인국공

대기업 인적성 통합 | GSAT

LG | SKCT | CJ | L-TAB

ROTC·학사장교 | 부사관

※ YES24 수험서 자격증 주택관리사 베스트셀러 1위 (2010년 12월, 2011년 3월, 9월, 12월, 2012년 1월, 3월~12월, 2013년 1월~5월, 8월~11월, 2014년 2월~8월, 10월~12월, 2015년 1월~5월, 7월~12월, 2016년 1월~12월, 2017년 1월~12월, 2018년 1월~12월, 2019년 1월~12월, 2020년 1월~7월, 9월~12월, 2021년 1월~12월, 2022년 1월~11월 월별 베스트, 매월 1위 교재는 다름)

※ YES24, 알라딘 국내도서 해당분야 월별, 주별 베스트 기준

업계 최초 대통령상 3관왕, 정부기관상 18관왕 달성!

2010 대통령상 · 2019 대통령상 · 2019 대통령상

대한민국 브랜드대상 국무총리상 · 서울특별시장상 · 과학기술부장관상 · 정보통신부장관상 · 산업자원부장관상

고용노동부장관상 · 미래창조과학부장관상 · 법무부장관상 · 여성가족부장관상 · 과학기술정보통신부 장관상 · 문화체육관광부 장관상 · 농림축산식품부 장관상

- 2004
  서울특별시장상 우수벤처기업 대상
- 2006
  산업자원부장관상 대한민국 e비즈니스대상
- 2007
  정보통신부장관상 디지털콘텐츠 대상
  산업자원부장관 표창 대한민국 e비즈니스대상
- 2010
  대통령 표창 대한민국 IT 이노베이션 대상
- 2013
  고용노동부장관 표창 일자리 창출 공로
- 2014
  미래창조과학부장관 표창 ICT Innovation 대상
- 2015
  법무부장관 표창 사회공헌 유공
- 2017
  여성가족부장관상 사회공헌 유공
  2016 합격자 수 최고 기록 KRI 한국기록원 공식 인증
- 2018
  2017 합격자 수 최고 기록 KRI 한국기록원 공식 인증
- 2019
  대통령 표창 범죄예방대상
  대통령 표창 일자리 창출 유공
  과학기술정보통신부장관상 대한민국 ICT 대상
- 2020
  국무총리상 대한민국 브랜드대상
  2019 합격자 수 최고 기록 KRI 한국기록원 공식 인증
- 2021
  고용노동부장관상 일·생활 균형 우수 기업 공모전 대상
  문화체육관광부장관 표창 근로자휴가지원사업 우수 참여 기업
  농림축산식품부장관상 대한민국 사회공헌 대상
  문화체육관광부장관 표창 여가친화기업 인증 우수 기업
- 2022
  농림축산식품부장관상 대한민국 ESG 대상